Dirk Ifenthaler • Deniz Eseryel • Xun Ge
Editors

Assessment in Game-Based Learning

Foundations, Innovations, and Perspectives

 Springer

D0124856

Editors
Dirk Ifenthaler
Department of Educational Science
University of Mannheim
Mannheim, BW
Germany

Deniz Eseryel
Department of Educational Psychology
University of Oklahoma
Norman, OK
USA

Xun Ge
Department of Educational Psychology
University of Oklahoma
Norman, OK
USA

ISBN 978-1-4899-9601-5   ISBN 978-1-4614-3546-4 (eBook)
DOI 10.1007/978-1-4614-3546-4
Springer New York Heidelberg Dordrecht London

© Springer Science+Business Media New York 2012
Softcover reprint of the hardcover 1st edition 2012
This work is subject to copyright. All rights are reserved by the Publisher, whether the whole or part of the material is concerned, specifically the rights of translation, reprinting, reuse of illustrations, recitation, broadcasting, reproduction on microfilms or in any other physical way, and transmission or information storage and retrieval, electronic adaptation, computer software, or by similar or dissimilar methodology now known or hereafter developed. Exempted from this legal reservation are brief excerpts in connection with reviews or scholarly analysis or material supplied specifically for the purpose of being entered and executed on a computer system, for exclusive use by the purchaser of the work. Duplication of this publication or parts thereof is permitted only under the provisions of the Copyright Law of the Publisher's location, in its current version, and permission for use must always be obtained from Springer. Permissions for use may be obtained through RightsLink at the Copyright Clearance Center. Violations are liable to prosecution under the respective Copyright Law.
The use of general descriptive names, registered names, trademarks, service marks, etc. in this publication does not imply, even in the absence of a specific statement, that such names are exempt from the relevant protective laws and regulations and therefore free for general use.
While the advice and information in this book are believed to be true and accurate at the date of publication, neither the authors nor the editors nor the publisher can accept any legal responsibility for any errors or omissions that may be made. The publisher makes no warranty, express or implied, with respect to the material contained herein.

Springer is part of Springer Science+Business Media (www.springer.com)

Preface

The capabilities and possibilities of emerging game-based learning technologies bring about a new perspective of learning and instruction. This, in turn, necessitates alternative ways to assess the kinds of learning that are taking place in the virtual worlds or informal settings. Accordingly, aligning learning and assessment is the core for creating a favorable and effective learning environment. A favorable learning environment is one that is learner-centered, knowledge-centered, and assessment-centered. However, how do we know if students have learned in games? What do we assess, and how do we assess students' learning outcomes in a game-based learning environment? After a critical literature review, we discovered that there was a missing link between game-based learning and game-based assessment, particularly in assessing complex problem-solving processes and outcomes in a digital game-based learning environment.

This edited volume covers the current state of research, methodology, assessment, and technology of game-based learning. The contributions from international distinguished researchers present innovative work in the areas of educational psychology, educational diagnostics, educational technology, and learning sciences. We organized the chapters included in this edited volume into three major parts: (1) Foundations of game-based assessment, (2) technological and methodological innovations for assessing game-based learning, and (3) realizing assessment in game-based learning.

The *first part* of the book provides the reader the background of learning and assessment in game-based environments. First, the question is raised concerning if all games are the same? As the characteristics of games vary widely, the authors examine three frameworks for assessing learning from, with, and in games (Schrader and McCreery, Chap. 2). The third chapter focuses on the role of formative assessment in game-based learning. The underlying process of theory specification, construct generation, test item development, and construct refinement is discussed by considering construct validity in assessment development (Belland, Chap. 3). Furthermore, the authors address the question of how to embed assessments within games to provide a way to monitor a player's current level on valued competencies, and then use that information as the basis for support (Shute and Ke, Chap. 4). The first section concludes by defining three things game designers need to know about assessment (Mislevy, Behrens, Dicerbo, Frezzo, and West, Chap. 5).

The *second part* presents innovative ways for assessing learning in game-based environments. New technological and methodological developments help to design a new generation of game-based learning environments including automated, fast, and individualized assessment as well as feedback for learners. It is shown how patterns of game playing behavior can function as indicators of mastery (Jantke, Chap. 6). The authors identify a set of design decisions as the result of building an automated assessment prototype within an open-ended 3D environment (Shelton and Parlin, Chap. 7). The information-trails approach represents a next step for in-process assessment of game-based learning (Loh, Chap. 8). The Timed Report tool represents another sensitive measure of learning within games (Reese, Seward, Tabachnick, Hitt, Harrison, and McFarland, Chap. 9). Furthermore, using computer-adaptive testing and hidden Markov modeling is a promising methodology for driving assessment of students' explanations in game dialog (Clark, Martinez-Garza, Biswas, Luecht, and Sengupta, Chap. 10). The TPACK-PCARD framework and methodology is successfully used for assessing learning games for school content (Foster, Chap. 11). A guide to learner-centered design and assessment for implementing game-based learning is provided by the MAPLET (Gosper and McNeill, Chap. 12). Finally, innovative assessment technologies in educational games designed for young students are discussed (Csapó, Lőrincz, and Molnár, Chap. 13).

The *third part* provides an insight into the latest empirical research findings and best practice examples of game-based assessment. Remarkable examples help readers to orchestrate both findings reported in this book and their own projects within their individual task domain. The authors highlight the interactivity[3] design and assessment framework for educational games to promote motivation and complex problem-solving skills (Eseryel, Guo, and Law, Chap. 14). The rapidly emerging field of computer-based assessment for gaming from the perspective of sound measurement principles is highly important for future principles of game-based assessment (Scalise and Wilson, Chap. 15). Challenges and recommendations for using institutional data to evaluate game-based instructional designs are highlighted next (Warren and Bigenho, Chap. 16). The seemingly incongruous use of 2D media-avatar drawings- and 3D media-math-based digital gameplay is reported in the following chapter (Katz-Buonincontro and Foster, Chap. 17). Furthermore, the authors show current trends in the assessment of learner motivation (Ghergulescu and Muntean, Chap. 18) and emotion assessment methods (Novak and Johnson, Chap. 19). A design model for obtaining diverse learning outcomes in innovative learning environments is exemplified in the following contribution (Hickey and Jameson, Chap. 20). Finally, computer games are questioned as preparation for future learning (Frey, Chap. 21).

Without the assistance of experts in the field of game-based learning and assessment, the editors would have been unable to prepare this volume for publication. We wish to thank our board of reviewers for their tremendous help with both reviewing the chapters and linguistic editing. Our thanks also go to Marco Brenneisen for preparing the chapters to meet the guidelines for editorial style.

Mannheim, Germany   Dirk Ifenthaler
Norman, OK, USA   Deniz Eseryel
                                                                                                                          Xun Ge

Contents

About the Authors

John T. Behrens is Director of Networking Academy Learning Systems Development at Cisco. He is responsible for the design and development of the Networking Academy's global online instructional offerings that integrate interactive curricular and assessment technologies with hands on activities. These curriculum, assessment, and gaming tools serve more than 1,000,000 students per year in 165 countries. Dr. Behrens' team integrates advanced work in assessment, simulation, and curriculum. His research interests focus on the intersection of cognitive, statistical, and computing issues in instruction, assessment, and online learning. Dr. Behrens has published chapters in a number of widely used psychology reference books along with articles in a range of educational, psychological, and statistical journals. In addition to his work at Cisco, Dr. Behrens is an Adjunct Assistant Research Professor in the Department of Psychology at the University of Notre Dame (Indiana, USA). Dr. Behrens received his Master's Degree in Special Education and Ph.D. in Educational Psychology from Arizona State University. He received his B.A. in Psychology and Philosophy from the University of Notre Dame. Prior to joining Cisco, he was a tenured Associate Professor of Psychology in Education at Arizona State University.

Brian R. Belland is Assistant Professor of Instructional Technology and Learning Science at Utah State University. His primary research interest centers on the use of technology to support middle school students' argumentation during problem-based learning. He is a recipient of a 2010 National Science Foundation CAREER award, in which he researches middle school students' use of scaffolds to support argumentation during problem-based science units. He has also won research awards such as the 2007 Educational Technology Research and Development Young Scholar Award and the 2009 AERA SIG-IT Best Paper Award, and has published in such journals as *Educational Technology Research and Development, Computers & Education, and Instructional Science*. He is also interested in mental measurement, specifically the measurement of higher-order learning outcomes.

Chris Bigenho works as the Director of Educational Technology at Greenhill School in Dallas, Texas and is a doctoral candidate in Educational Computing and Cognitive Systems in the Department of Learning Technologies and Educational Computing at the University of North Texas in Denton, Texas. Chris' research interests include

xiv   About the Authors

emerging technologies in learning environments, cognitive aspects of technology in learning environments, and narrative-based alternate reality games for learning. Additionally, he is working in the areas of self-regulated learning and the development of synergistic knowledge. Chris received his M.A. in Educational Technology from Pepperdine University in California.

Gautam Biswas is a Professor of Computer Science, Computer Engineering, and Engineering Management in the EECS Department and a Senior Research Scientist at the Institute for Software Integrated Systems (ISIS) at Vanderbilt University. Prof. Biswas conducts research in Intelligent Systems with primary interests in hybrid modeling and simulation, diagnosis and prognosis of complex systems, and intelligent learning environments. He is involved in developing open-ended learning environments for learning and instruction, such as the Teachable Agents project. He has also developed innovative educational data mining techniques for studying students' learning behaviors and linking them to metacognitive strategies. He has published extensively, and has over 300 refereed publications. Dr. Biswas is an associate editor of the *IEEE Transactions on Systems, Man, and Cybernetics, Prognostics and Health Management*, and *Educational Technology and Society* journals. He has served on the Program Committee of a number of conferences, and most recently was Program cochair for the 15th International Conference on Artificial Intelligence in Education. He is currently serving on the Executive committee of the Asia Pacific Society for Computers in Education and is the IEEE Computer Society representative to the Transactions on Learning Technologies steering committee. He is also serving as the Secretary/Treasurer for ACM Sigart.

Douglas B. Clark is an Associate Professor of Science Education at Vanderbilt University. Clark completed his doctoral and postdoctoral work at UC Berkeley and his master's at Stanford. His research analyzes students' science learning processes in technology-enhanced environments and digital games with a particular focus on conceptual change, representations, and argumentation in these environments. Much of this research focuses on public middle school and high school students in classroom settings. Clark's work has been funded by the National Science Foundation, Department of Education, and the National Academy of Education/ Spencer Foundation. Clark's current game-focused grants include SURGE and EGAME from the National Science Foundation and EPIGAME from the Department of Education.

Benö Csapó is a Professor of Education (1997–) at the University of Szeged, the head of the Graduate School of Educational Sciences (2003–), the Research Group on the Development of Competencies, Hungarian Academy of Sciences (2002–), and the Center for Research on Learning and Instruction he founded in 2003. He was a Humboldt research fellow at the University of Bremen (1989) and at the Center for Advanced Study in the Behavioral Sciences, Stanford, CA (1994–1995). He has been participating in several international research projects. He was a member of the Functional Expert Group that devised the framework for the assessment of Problem Solving within the 2003 OECD PISA survey, and he was the leader of the

Technological Issues Working Group in the Assessment and Teaching of twenty-first century Skills initiative (2009–2010). At present, he is an external expert of the Kompetenzmodelle zur Erfassung individueller Lernergebnisse und zur Bilanzierung von Bildungsprozessen program (Germany, 2007–). He is a member of the PISA Governing Board (2005–, vice chair: 2008–). His research areas include cognition, cognitive development, structure and organization of knowledge, longitudinal studies, educational evaluation, and technology-based assessment.

Kristen E. Dicerbo is an Educational Psychologist who provides methodological consultation to the Cisco Networking Academy. Her research interests center on the use of interactive technologies to promote student learning and the use of assessment data to inform instruction. Her recent research has focused on qualitative and quantitative investigation of games in classrooms, as well as the identification and accumulation of evidence that comes from the use of digital technologies in the classroom. She works closely with technology development teams, conducting formative research to inform the design of classroom tools.

Deniz Eseryel is an Assistant Professor in the Instructional Psychology & Technology Program at the University of Oklahoma. Her research focuses on issues related to learning, problem-solving, and expertise development in complex, ill-structured knowledge domains such as STEM. She is concerned with developing and evaluating new instructional approaches for advanced computer-based learning environments to facilitate development of complex learning and problem-solving outcomes. Towards this direction, she applies cognitive theories to educational practice, and uses evaluations of instructional processes and outcomes to illuminate further development of cognitive and instructional theories. Dr. Eseryel's recent work included development of a methodology for assessing complex learning outcomes and benchmarking levels of expertise in complex knowledge domains. In addition, she developed a framework for designing and implementing advanced learning environments, such as dynamic system modeling, simulations, virtual worlds, and digital games to facilitate complex learning, ill-structured problem-solving skills. Dr. Eseryel's research is recognized by four awards: *2010 Young Researcher Award* by AERA Instructional Technology SIG; 2009 *Design & Development Showcase Award* by AECT; *2006 Outstanding Dissertation Research Award* by Syracuse University and *2000 International Scholar Honor* by Phi Beta Delta. Dr. Eseryel serves on the editorial boards of the *International Journal of Mobile Learning & Organization* and the *International Journal of Knowledge & Learning*; and as the President of the AECT Design and Development Division.

Aroutis Foster teaches, publishes, and conducts research on the design, integration, and implementation of immersive digital environments for learning. Dr. Foster's research interests focus on model testing and development to address the design, pedagogic, assessment, and motivational affordances of games for learning. His research aims to help learners construct knowledge, value school content, and explore selves that they may or may not want to be. He also examines innovative ways to design technologies for learning seamlessly considering the interplay of technology, content, and pedagogy. Dr. Foster's background is in educational psychology, educational technology, digital media, and communications. His professional agenda has emerged from both his research and life experiences growing up in the Caribbean, and studying and living in New York City and East Lansing, MI. He serves on several editorial review boards and has published book chapters and articles about games and learning. He has won awards for his work on digital games and learning. He is a Phi Beta Kappa Member, a Mellon Mays Fellow, and the recipient of a Spencer Research Training Grant. He is the founder of the Drexel Learning Games Network.

Rick Chan Frey is a Doctoral Candidate in Education at UC Berkeley focusing on early literacy development and educational technology. He has worked for the last 25 years as a computer programmer, game designer, computer teacher, reading specialist, and avid gamer.

Dennis C. Frezzo joined Cisco in 1998 and today manages an instructional research team that creates learning products for the Cisco Networking Academy, a key component of Cisco's Corporate Social Responsibility efforts. He is responsible for providing innovation, strategy, and development of high-impact instructional technologies to advance the Cisco Networking Academies' global online instructional systems. He helped invent Packet Tracer: simulation, visualization, collaboration, and performance assessment software, whose free distribution to approximately one million students helps address the digital divide in networking education. Dr. Frezzo's research interests include interaction design ($I \times D$) of useful and usable educational software, computer-supported collaborative learning (CSCL), teaching issues associated with green initiatives, and educational games, particularly a strategic simulation game for teaching networking and entrepreneurial skills called Aspire. Dr. Frezzo received his Ph.D. in Educational Psychology from the University of Hawai'i in May 2009. He received his Master's Degree in Education and teaching credential from Stanford in 1994, his Master's Degree in Electrical Engineering from UC Berkeley in 1988, and his Bachelor's Degree in Electrical Engineering from Brown in 1986. Prior to joining Cisco, he was a community college instructor, high school teacher, and fiber optic development engineer.

Xun Ge is an Associate Professor with the Program of Instructional Psychology and Technology, Department of Educational Psychology, at the University of Oklahoma. She holds a Ph.D. in Instructional Systems from the Pennsylvania State University. Dr. Ge's primary research interest involves scaffolding student complex and ill-structured problem-solving and self-regulated learning through designing and developing instructional scaffolds, learning technologies, and open learning environments. Recently, she has been studying the impact and assessment of game-based learning in supporting complex, ill-structured problem-solving. Dr. Ge has published multiple book chapters and numerous articles in leading journals of the field, and she is recognized for the two awards—*2003 Young Scholar* by *Educational Technology Research & Development* and *2004 Outstanding Journal Article* by American Educational Communications and Technology.

Ioana Ghergulescu received her BSc in Software Engineering at "Politehnica" University of Timisoara, Timisoara, Romania in 2009. She is a Ph.D. Researcher with National College of Ireland, Dublin, Ireland under IRCSET "Embark Initiative" Postgraduate Scholarship Scheme. Her research areas of interest include gaming based e-learning, motivation assessment and adaptation, and adaptive and personalized e-learning.

Maree Gosper is an Associate Professor in Academic Development (e-Learning) and Director of Technologies in Learning and Teaching at the Learning and Teaching Centre, Macquarie University. As a teacher and active researcher, Maree has extensive experience in the development, implementation, and evaluation of teaching programs designed to make effective use of information and communication technologies. She has been involved in a number of university and sector-wide projects to promote the effective use of learning technologies. A current focus is on the development of policy, planning, and quality enhancement frameworks for technologies in learning and teaching. Her research focus is on integrating technologies into the curriculum, matching cognitive processes underpinning learning with cognitive enabling features of technologies, and the development of effective and sustainable learning communities and e-learning environments. Current research projects include the MAPLET framework, the student experience of technologies, and how students learn in technology-rich environments.

Yu Guo is an Instructional Designer with Faculty Development of the Institute for Teaching and Learning Excellence at Oklahoma State University. He holds a Master in Education degree in Instructional Psychology and Technology from the University of Oklahoma with a focus on Design and Development of Instructional Software. He also earned dual Bachelor's degrees in Computer Science and English Language and Literature from Beijing Normal University. He has extensive teaching experience in both secondary education and higher education in China and in the United States. Currently, his major job responsibility is to improve faculty's instructional effectiveness and students' engagement at Oklahoma State University by teaching face-to-face and online courses, observing faculty's teaching practice, and providing constructive feedback. He also explores emerging Internet technologies and uncovers their learning affordance. By helping faculty adopt pedagogically sound course designs and innovative ways of implementing new technologies, he strives to do his part in improving OSU's teaching and learning excellence.

Andrew Harrison is a Web Application Developer at Wheeling Jesuit University's Center for Educational Technologies. He focuses on data-driven web applications. He is fluent in C, C++, C#, Objective-C, ASP.NET, PHP, and SQL (My, MS, Oracle).

Daniel T. Hickey is an Associate Professor in the Learning Sciences program at Indiana University in Bloomington, and a Research Professor with the Indiana University Center for Research on Learning and Technology. He completed his Ph.D. in Psychology at Vanderbilt University, where he studied with James Pellegrino and the other member of the Cognition and Technology Group at

Vanderbilt. He also completed postdoctoral training at the Center for Performance Assessment at Educational Testing Service. He studies participatory approaches to assessment, feedback, evaluation, and motivation. He primarily works with technology-supported learning environments including videogames, digital networks, and e-learning. He has directed projects in these areas funded by the National Science Foundation, NASA, and the MacArthur Foundation, and has published both practical and theoretical papers in leading journals.

Ben A. Hitt has served as Chief Scientist/CTO and cofounder of Correlogic Systems Inc. in Bethesda, M.D. At Correlogic, he coinvented the pattern recognition approach to disease detection, as well as the company's proprietary Proteome Quest™ software, which is designed to analyze patterns in human blood proteins to detect disease. His works also include inventions for analyzing disparate data streams, near real-time analysis of audio and text information streams, applications for the detection of credit card fraud, and optimization solutions for direct marketing problems. He is currently senior partner and founder of Serenity Hill Informatics.

Dirk Ifenthaler's research interests focus on the learning-dependent progression of mental models, complex problem-solving, decision-making, situational awareness, and emotions. He developed automated and computer-based methodologies for the assessment and analysis of graphical and natural language representations (SMD Technology, HIMATT, AKOVA). Additionally, he developed components of course management software and an educational simulation games (DIVOSA, SEsim). He is also interested in the development of educational software and learning management systems (LMS) as well as technology integration into the classroom. Dr. Ifenthaler has published multiple books and book chapters as well as numerous articles in leading journals of the field.

Ellen Jameson is a Visiting Scholar in the School of Education at Indiana University in Bloomington. She completed her MSES in Applied Ecology at the School for Public and Environmental Affairs at Indiana University in Bloomington, and worked as a research associate in the Indiana University Center for Research on Learning and Technology. She is currently working as a curriculum and game designer for One Planet Education Network under a US Department of Education SBIR grant. Her past work as a content specialist for Quest Atlantis included designing, building, and implementing educational game narratives centered around social-ecological systems. In her research, she looks at how the design of narrative games can affect the way people think about, and act on, social-ecological systems in the real world.

Klaus P. Jantke born in Berlin, Germany, studied Mathematics at Humboldt University of Berlin. He graduated with an honors degree in Theoretical Computer Science and received both his doctorate and his habilitation at Humboldt. Jantke won the Weierstrass Award for his diploma thesis and the Humboldt Prize for his Ph.D. Klaus Jantke started his academic career as a full professor at Kuwait University and simultaneously at Leipzig University of Technology, aged 35. Since then he has been teaching at several German Universities such as Chemnitz, Cottbus, Darmstadt, Ilmenau, Leipzig, and Saarbrücken. Klaus Jantke has been working at the International Computer Science Institute, Berkeley, at the Fujitsu Research Labs, Numazu, and at the Meme Media Lab, Sapporo. He sees himself as a logician in the school of Heinrich Scholz and Karl Schröter. Jantke's scientific interest ranges from algorithmic learning theory through digital games to qualitative and quantitative research into the impact of media. Fraunhofer Society, Germany's largest research institution with currently 18,000 scientists and 60 institutes in operation, decided to establish its own children's media research center. In January 2008, Klaus Jantke was put in charge of developing this research center in Erfurt, Germany. Jantke's contributions include the design of digital games. Since its establishment, he is a member of the jury for the German Computer Games Award.

Tristan E. Johnson is on the faculty with both the Learning Systems Institute and the Instructional Systems program in the Department of Educational Psychology and Learning Systems at Florida State University. Dr. Johnson has several years of experience studying team cognition, team-based learning, measuring shared mental models, team assessment and diagnostics, and team interventions. He is also involved in the development of agent-based modeling and the creation of data-driven algorithms for modeling training and instructional effects within performance models.

Jen Katz-Buonincontro is an Assistant Professor of Educational Leadership in the School of Education at Drexel University, Philadelphia, PA. She holds a Ph.D. in Educational Leadership with a specialization in Policy, Management and Organization from the University of Oregon and an M.F.A. in Visual Arts from the Mason Gross School of the Arts at Rutgers, The State University of New Jersey. Research expertise includes qualitative methodologies and quantitative methodologies. In addition, she has a background in evaluation, policy development, and program management and accreditation. Dr. Katz-Buonincontro's publications focus on creative thinking and problem-solving in leaders, leadership development through the arts, e.g., role-playing in improvisational theater, and applications of aesthetic theory to leadership and teaching. Research areas include educational leaders' approaches to creative thinking and problem-solving, adolescent identity exploration through drawing in game-based learning environments, and the assessment of student creativity in the arts and other academic subjects. Current funded research projects include the use of handheld mobile devices to document educational leaders' mood states during creative problem-solving tasks. She teaches graduate-level leadership development and research methodology courses and has prior experience teaching art.

Fengfeng Ke is an Assistant Professor in Educational Psychology and Learning Systems at the Florida State University. Her research has focused on digital game-based learning, computer-supported collaborative learning, and instructional multimedia. Particularly, her research attempts to design and examine comprehensive game-based learning systems, which integrate not only learning game design but also game-oriented content authoring, game-based pedagogy, and game-based learning evaluation.

Victor Law is a Ph.D. candidate with the Department of Educational Psychology at the University of Oklahoma. His primary research interests include game-based and simulation-based learning, scaffolding, self-regulation, ill-structured problem-solving, and computer-supported collaborative learning. He has been conducting studies examining the effect of different scaffolding approaches, including massively multiplayer online games, computer-based simulation, and dynamic modeling, on students' complex problem-solving learning outcomes; the research results have been presented at prestigious national and international conferences, such as Annual Meeting of the American Educational Research Association, Association for Educational Communications and Technology, and International Conference of Learning Sciences. Mr. Law has published several empirical studies in national and international refereed journals.

Christian S. Loh is an Associate Professor of Learning Systems Design and Technology, and the Director of the Virtual Environment Lab (V-Lab) of the Department of Curriculum and Instruction, at the Southern Illinois University Carbondale. Dr. Loh's research interests include assessment of learning within multiuser virtual environments and digital games with Information Trails©—an assessment framework he pioneered for game-based learning. He serves as associate editor for two international journals: the *International Journal for Games and Computer Mediated Simulations (IJGCMS)* and the *International Journal for Game-Based Learning (IJGBL)*. He is a past President of the Multimedia Production Division (MPD) of the Association for Educational Communications and Technology (AECT) and a regular judge (academic) for the annual Serious Games Showcase & Challenge (SGS&C) competition hosted by the Interservice/Industry Training, Simulation and Education Conference (I/ITSEC).

András Lőrincz is Head Senior Researcher at the Neural Information Processing Group, Eötvös Loránd University, Budapest, Hungary. He graduated in physics at the Eötvös Loránd University in 1975 where he earned his Ph.D. in 1978. He conducted research on quantum control and artificial intelligence at the University of Chicago, Brown University, Princeton University, the Illinois Institute of Technology, and ETH Zürich. He authored about 200 peer-reviewed scientific publications. In 1997–1998 he was the scientific director of the Hungarian subsidiary of US-based Associative Computing Ltd. His research focuses on distributed intelligent systems and their applications in neurobiological and cognitive modeling. He founded the Neural Information Processing Group and he directs a team of mathematicians, programmers, computer scientists, and physicists. He has been the PI of several international projects in collaboration with Panasonic, Honda Future Technology Research, and the Information Directorate of the US Air Force in image processing and human–computer collaboration. He has received the Széchenyi Professor Award (2000), the Széchenyi István Award (2004), and the Kalmár Prize of the John von Neumann Computer Society of Hungary (2004). He became an elected Fellow of the European Coordinating Committee for Artificial Intelligence in 2006.

Richard M. Luecht is a Professor of Educational Research Methodology at the University of North Carolina at Greensboro where he teaches graduate courses in applied statistics and advanced measurement. He is also a technical consultant for many US testing organizations and government agencies. His research interests involve applying engineering design principles to testing, computer-based and adaptive testing, automated test assembly algorithms, psychometric modeling, and diagnostic/formative assessment. Ric has published numerous articles and book chapters on technical measurement issues. His recent work involves the development of a comprehensive methodological framework for large-scale formative assessment design and implementation called assessment engineering.

Mario M. Martinez-Garza is a Doctoral Student of Math, Science and Engineering Education at Vanderbilt University. A life-long gamer and student of games, his main areas of interest are investigating the potential of play as a method of learning and applications of theory-based design principles to support learning through game environments of all kinds. He has alternated careers between technology and education, serving as a middle-school math and science teacher, a competition math coach, and also cofounder and lead game designer of Kognitia Games, a start-up devoted to delivering fun, competitive games to support school mathematics.

Michael McCreery is an Assistant Professor of Educational Foundations at the University of Arkansas at Little Rock. Dr. McCreery earned his Ph.D. from the Learning and Technology program, housed within the Educational Psychology department at the University of Nevada, Las Vegas. His dissertation focused on human behavior and personality within the World of Warcraft. Currently, he is exploring how human behavior is influenced through interaction with virtual spaces. His background includes over a dozen years of technology experience including 4 years as a programmer for the Intel Corporation.

Lisa Mcfarland became Research Assistant for the Wheeling Jesuit University Center for Educational Technologies CyGaMEs Selene project team soon after its inception in 2006. She assisted Reese and game development personnel as needed while also having a key role in the registration and training of adults as recruiters of youth players for the Selene game. McFarland assisted in the processing of game data for statistical analysis as well as the development of the player/recruiter website interface, online assessments, and reporting tools. She continued to work as the Selene game recruitment coordinator and project assistant through April 2011. Currently, McFarland is project associate for the Emergency Preparedness project, also at the Center for Educational Technologies.

Margot McNeill is a Lecturer in Higher Education Development at Macquarie University's Learning and Teaching Centre. Her primary research interest is educational technologies, in particular academic practice in using appropriate technologies in curriculum design. Informed by this research, Margot teaches on the University's Higher Education Post-graduate Program and conducts a range of professional development workshops to equip academics on the selection and use of technologies within an aligned curriculum. Having been involved in a range of educational technology projects in the University, technical college, and private sectors, Margot currently manages the Change Management Stream of the Learning Management System Implementation project at Macquarie. This project provides an opportunity to lead a large-scale program of curriculum enhancement in the use of technologies across the whole university.

Robert J. Mislevy is the Frederic M. Lord Chair in Measurement and Statistics at ETS. He was previously Professor of Measurement and Statistics at the University of Maryland, and Affiliate Professor of Survey Methods and of Second Language Acquisition. Dr. Mislevy's research applies developments in technology, statistical methods, and cognitive science to practical problems in assessment. He developed the "plausible values" methodology for analyzing data from the National Assessment of Educational Progress. His publications include *Automated Scoring of Complex Tasks in Computer-Based Testing* (with Williamson and Bejar), the BILOG computer program (with R. Darrell Bock), and the chapter on Cognitive Psychology in Educational Measurement (4th Ed.). His current projects include the NSF-supported PADI project, which is developing an assessment design system with a focus on science inquiry, and work with CRESST and Cisco on simulation- and game-based assessments. He received AERA's Lindquist award for career contributions, TOEFL's Samuel J. Messick Memorial Lecture Award, and NCME's Career Contributions Award and Award for Technical Contributions. He is a past-president of the Psychometric Society and a member of the National Academy of Education.

Gyöngyvér Molnár is an Associate Professor of Education at the University of Szeged. She was a fellow of the Hungarian Republic (1997–1999), and was a DAAD fellow at the Ruprecht-Karls-Universität in Heidelberg (1996), and at the Westfälische Wilhelms-Universität in Münster (1997–1998). She was a recipient of János Bolyai Research Fellowship of Hungarian Academy of Sciences (2005–2008, 2009–2012). She received the Award of Young Researchers 2006 of Hungarian Academy of Sciences (2007). At present, she is a member (2005–) and the program director (2007–) of Information and Communication Technologies in Education of the Graduate School of Educational Sciences at the University of Szeged. She is the president of the Educational Committee of the Hungarian Academy of Sciences in Szeged (2006–) and she is an External reviewer of RGC (Research Grants Council, 2007–). Her main research areas are measuring and developing of problem solving, application of information-communication technologies in education, and technology-based assessment.

Cristina Hava Muntean is a Lecturer with School of Computing, National College of Ireland. She received her Ph.D. from Dublin City University, Ireland in 2005 for research on end-user quality of experience-aware adaptive hypermedia systems. She was awarded a BEng Degree from the Computer Science Department, "Politehnica" University of Timisoara, Romania in 2000. Currently she coordinates the NCI Research Laboratory and supervises MSc and Ph.D. students. She is actively involved in research in the areas of user-centered m/e-learning environments, personalized educational multimedia content, and gaming based e-learning systems.

She published a book, three book chapters, and over 50 peer-reviewed publications in prestigious journals and international conferences. Dr. Muntean is reviewer for important international journals and conferences. She was awarded three best paper awards at international conferences.

Elena Novak is an Instructor and Research Assistant at Florida State University. Elena Novak is also a Ph.D. candidate in Instructional Systems, at the Department of Educational Psychology and Learning Systems, Florida State University. Her research interests include instructional games and simulations, gaming characteristics, storyline, active learning, and human performance improvement.

Mary Ann Parlin is Project Manager in the IDIAS Institute at Utah State University. Her research interests include interactive learning environments and instructional games and simulations. She has participated in the design and development of many instructional products including emergency first responder firefighter training, teaching math to children who are deaf or hard-of-hearing, and patient education for postsurgical patients.

Debbie Denise Reese invented the CyGaMEs formula for game-based learning and assessment as senior educational researcher at Wheeling Jesuit University's Center for Educational Technologies and NASA-sponsored Classroom of the Future, CyGaMEs readies learners for academic success by translating challenging science concepts (what scientists think) into gameplay (what learners do). CyGaMEs' award-winning Selene: A Lunar Construction GaME (http://selene.cet.edu) tracks gameplay to assess learning and flow. Reese applies cognitive science theory to design learning environments and educational technologies. She is principal investigator for CyGaMEs, an NSF-funded REESE project. Reese has led design and research teams in development and study of technology tools for enhancing self-efficacy, identity, and argumentation. She also conducts evaluations and needs assessments and is part of the Classroom of the Future team producing and conducting research using MoonWorld, a virtual world in which educators and/or students conduct lunar science fieldwork.

Kathleen Scalise is an Associate Professor at the University of Oregon, in the Department of Educational Methodology, Policy and Leadership. Her main research areas are dynamically delivered content in e-learning, computer-adaptive testing, item response models with innovative item types, and applications to equity studies. She recently served as a core member of the methodological group for the Assessment and Teaching of twenty-first century Skills project created by Cisco, Intel, and Microsoft; for the Oregon state task force writing legislation for virtual public schools; and as codirector of the UC Berkeley Evaluation and Assessment Research Center (BEAR). She also served with the Curriculum Frameworks and Instructional Resources Division of the California Department of Education, and holds teaching credentials for K-12 physical and life sciences. Her primary areas of work are in science and mathematics education. She received her Ph.D. in quantitative measurement at the University of California, Berkeley, in 2004.

P.G. Schrader is an Associate Professor of Educational Technology in the Department of Teaching and Learning at the University of Nevada, Las Vegas. Dr. Schrader's recent work involves understanding learning in complex nonlinear digital environments like Massively Multiplayer Online Games and Hypertext. In these contexts, he has examined aspects of expertise, literacy, and the dynamic exchange of information. His work has appeared in a number of journals, books, and national and international conferences.

Pratim Sengupta is an Assistant Professor of Science Education at Vanderbilt University who is interested in several issues central to the design of learning technologies for science education: (a) design and classroom implementation of agent-based modeling platforms and programming languages environments in physics and biology across multiple grades, (b) developing generalizable principles that can guide the design of agent-based models and modeling platforms as instructional units in science, and (c) investigating several issues pertaining to student cognition (knowledge representation, conceptual change, visuospatial thinking) as they interact with these learning environments. Along with Doug Clark, he also cowrote the introductory topic paper for the National Academies Board on Science Education workshop in 2009 on Computer Games, Simulations, and Education.

Ralph J. Seward is the CyGaMEs project data analyst and web applications programmer for the Center for Educational Technologies at Wheeling Jesuit University. Seward's preferred programming language is Python, although he also works with PHP, Flash, and Action Script 3. Steward is a strong advocate of open source platforms such as Linux, Apache, and Drupal.

Brett E. Shelton uses a variety of mixed-method research approaches to study vision, perception, cognition, and the design and assessment of innovative technologies for learning. Other interests include immersive and interactive learning environments, data visualizations, open education, instructional simulations, and educational gaming. He is the former director of the Center for Open and Sustainable Learning whose mission involves extending educational opportunity to all those who desire it, including the building of hybrid open coursework to maximize accessibility of educational resources. He now directs the IDIAS Institute which has projects based on the development of handheld application development for learning, as well as virtual world training applications that use unique design attributes to facilitate after-action review and assessments. The IDIAS Institute offers a multidisciplinary media design and development program by supporting undergraduate and graduate students from the Departments of Art, Computer Science, and Instructional Technology and Learning Sciences.

Valerie J. Shute is a Professor at Florida State University. Before coming to FSU in 2007, she was a principal research scientist at Educational Testing Service (2001–2007) where she was involved with basic and applied research projects related to assessment, cognitive diagnosis, and learning from advanced instructional systems and where she generally honed her psychometric skills. Her general research interests hover around the design, development, and evaluation of advanced systems to support learning—particularly related to twenty-first century competencies. Towards this end, she's been involved in (a) exploratory and confirmatory tests of aptitude–treatment interactions using the controlled environments offered by intelligent tutoring systems, (b) student modeling research using evidence-centered design, and (c) developing automated knowledge elicitation and organization tools. An example of current research involves using immersive games with stealth assessment to support learning—of cognitive and noncognitive knowledge and skills.

Barbara G. Tabachnick is Professor emerita of Psychology at California State University, Northridge, and coauthor of Using Multivariate Statistics and Experimental Designs Using ANOVA. She has published more than 60 articles and technical reports and participated in more than 50 professional presentations, many invited. She currently presents workshops in computer applications in univariate and multivariate data analysis and consults in a variety of research areas, including professional ethics in and beyond academia, effects of such factors as age and substances on driving and performance, educational computer games, effects of noise on annoyance and sleep, and fetal alcohol syndrome. She is the recipient of the 2012 Western Psychological Association Lifetime Achievement Award.

Scott J. Warren works as an Associate Professor of Learning Technologies at the University of North Texas. His current research examines the use of emerging online technologies such as immersive digital learning environments, educational games and simulations, and open source course management tools in complex systems in K-20 settings. Prior to working in higher education as a professor, researcher, and designer, he taught both social studies and English in public schools for nearly a decade. He has also worked on the Quest Atlantis National Science Foundation project, creating the Anytown world to support writing, reading, and problem-solving. His current work with The Door, Broken Window, and The 2015 Project alternate reality courses is partly funded with grants from the University of North Texas. Further, he works with Created Realities on the development and research of the online literacy game Chalk House. He completed his Ph.D. in Instructional Systems Technology at Indiana University-Bloomington.

Patti West is a Cisco Networking Academy instructor and former Cisco employee. She was responsible for the design and development of the Cisco CCNA Discovery curriculum and provided significant contribution to the Aspire educational game. Her current interests include the development of intelligent assessment, tutoring, and feedback systems. Recent projects focus on the use of problem-solving and simulation technologies in the classroom.

Mark Wilson's interests focus on measurement and applied statistics. His work spans a range of issues in measurement and assessment: the development of new statistical models for analyzing measurement data; the development of new assessments in areas such as science education, patient-reported outcomes, and child development; and policy issues in the use of assessment data in accountability systems. He has recently published three books: the first, *Constructing Measures: An item Response Modeling Approach* (Erlbaum), is an introduction to modern measurement; the second (with Paul De Boeck of the University of Leuven in Belgium), *Explanatory Item Response Models: A Generalized Linear and Nonlinear Approach* (Springer-Verlag), introduces an overarching framework for the statistical modeling of measurements that makes available new tools for understanding the meaning and nature of measurement; the third, *Towards Coherence Between Classroom Assessment and Accountability* (University of Chicago Press—National Society for the Study of Education), is an edited volume that explores the issues relating to the relationships between large-scale assessment and classroom-level assessment. He currently chairs a National Research Council committee on assessment of science achievement. He is founding editor of the new journal *Measurement: Interdisciplinary Research and Perspectives.*

Reviewers

Names	Institution	Email
Yu-Hui Ching	Boise State University, USA	yuhuiching@boisestate.edu
Benjamin Erlandson	California State University, Monterey Bay, USA	berlandson@csumb.edu
Eva Grundl	Department of Educational Science, University of Mannheim, Germany	egrundl@rumms.uni-mannheim.de
Yu Guo	Oklahoma State University, USA	bryan.guo@okstate.edu
Jason P. Herron	University of Oklahoma, USA	sooner1906@ou.edu
Yu-Chang Hsu	Boise State University BOISE, ID, USA	hsu@boisestate.edu
Sheng-Hui Hsu	National Cheng Kung University, Taiwan	obs945@gmail.com
Kun Huang	University of North Texas Health Science Center, USA	kun.huang@unthsc.edu
Woei Hung	University of North Dakota, USA	woei.hung@und.edu
Dirk Ifenthaler	University of Mannheim, Germany	ifenthaler@uni-mannheim.de
Fengfeng Ke	Florida State University, USA	fke@fsu.edu
Victor Law	University of Oklahoma, USA	vlaw@ou.edu
Thomas Lehmann	University of Freiburg, Germany	thomas.lehmann@ezw.uni-freiburg.de
Tamera L. McCuen	University of Oklahoma, USA	tammymccuen@ou.edu
Jonathan McKeown	University of Tampa, USA	jmckeown@ut.edu
Michael Thomas	University of Wisconsin-Madison, USA	mthomas@education.wisc.edu
Hakan Tuzun	Hacettepe University, Turkey	htuzun@hacettepe.edu.tr
Feng Wang	Mount Saint Mary College, USA	feng.wang@msmc.edu
Ke Zhang	Wayne State University, USA	ke.zhang@wayne.edu

Chapter 1
Assessment for Game-Based Learning

Dirk Ifenthaler, Deniz Eseryel, and Xun Ge

1.1 Games: A Historical Synopsis

What is a game? Why do we play games? When do we play games? Who plays games? Games are a universal part of human experience and present in all cultures. Characteristics of a game include goals, rules, competition, and interaction. However, a historical synopsis of games shows that the conception of *game* and *play* changed during the centuries.

As games are associated with enjoyment, they are distinct from work (Ganguin, 2010). Looking at the ancient world (800 BC–400 AD), Platon describes a close connection between *play* (paidiá) and *education* (paideia). Games during childhood shape the future adult. On the other hand, Aristotle conceived the game as an opposite of learning. Therefore, learning is endeavor while games are recreation (Ganguin). Later, the Romans introduced the importance of games for the society by the phrase *panis et circenses* (bread and circuses, i.e., games). This phrase summarizes life in the Roman society. *Panis* reflects the free distribution of crop to the Roman citizens and *circenses* refers to the preferred entertainment, such as circus, chariot racing, stage plays (Bernstein, 1998). Apparently, games were utilized to distract the Roman people from politics. Moreover, Cicero suggested that games might cause buzz or exhilaration, and therefore games need to be controlled (Ganguin, 2010).

During the Middle Ages and the Early Modern Age, games were considered as a waste of time or even as evil as well as an expression of harmful nature

D. Ifenthaler (✉)
Department of Educational Science, University of Mannheim, A5, 6,
Mannheim 68131, Germany
e-mail: ifenthaler@uni-mannheim.de

D. Eseryel • X. Ge
University of Oklahoma, 820 Van Vleet Oval Room 323B, Norman,
OK 73019-2041, USA
e-mail: eseryel@ou.edu; xge@uo.edu

D. Ifenthaler et al. (eds.), *Assessment in Game-Based Learning: Foundations,*
Innovations, and Perspectives, DOI 10.1007/978-1-4614-3546-4_1,
© Springer Science+Business Media New York 2012

(Parmentier, 2004). Accordingly, the notion of games lost more and more its positive meaning and the notion of work gained a much more positive meaning. During the thirteenth century, traveling artists were disenfranchised and minstrels were attributed as sinful people (Dirx, 1981). As a consequence, games were made illegal through local policy, because it stopped people from working. Later, Kant declared games as an enjoyable activity. Work and game were clearly delimitated. Following the argument of Aristotle, Kant attributed games being as relaxation; and disconnected it from work. Thus, Kant clearly stated that games did not have a positive effect on formal education (Kant, 1803).

The nineteenth century showed a recovery of the negative allocation of games. Fröbel (the founder of kindergartens) identified games as valuable for education and developed special games for children. Accordingly, the focus of Fröbel's educational theory was on games (Ganguin, 2010). During the twentieth century, the scientific controversy on games emerged. Freud used games to overcome psychological problems (Freud, 1920). *Homo Ludens* (first published in 1938) was regarded as a major work in game theory (Huizinga, 1955). Five characteristics of games were identified: (1) Playing a game is freedom, (2) playing a game is not *real* life, (3) locality and duration of games are distinct from *ordinary* life, (4) playing a game demands order absolute and supreme, and (5) playing a game is not connected with material interest or profit. Caillois (2001) criticized and extended the above-mentioned characteristics of games because gambling, despite its focus on profit, was regarded as a game. Piaget (1975) considered play and imitation as two crucial functions in a child's intellectual development process: play as an assimilation strategy and imitation as an accommodation strategy. Further, he showed how variations of games are connected to the cognitive development. The *sensorimotor stage* is linked to *practice match*, the *preoperational stage* is linked to *symbol games*, the concrete operational stage is linked to rule-based games, and the concrete operational stage is linked to construction games (Piaget). Further, Dörner, Kreuzig, Reither, and Stäudel (1983) used games in their experimental studies to investigate the processes of complex problem solving. With the beginning of the twenty-first century, publications in social science focusing on games increased tremendously to approximately 20,000 in the last 10 years.

Looking at the historical synopsis of games, an antagonism between games (recreation, easy, fun, leisure, enjoyment) and work (effort, difficult, serious, profession, strain) is noticeable. However, another important question is present: How can a game be beneficial for life? In the foreground of this question are learning processes which may result from games—a game's hidden expedience (Scheuerl, 1988).

1.2   Games and Learning

A close examination of the history of the field of instructional design and technology (IDT) reveals an eclectic field with three main influences: instructional theories, learning theories, and instructional technologies (Fig. 1.1). At times, the developments in

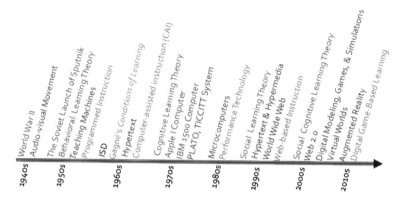

Fig. 1.1 Brief history of the field of instructional design and technology

instructional theories led the changes in the field driving the research and practice; other times it was the developments in learning theories. However, more often than not, biggest driving force in the field has been the developments in instructional technologies. More than we, the scholars and the researchers would like to admit it has been the developments in the technologies that has excited the field the most forcing paradigm shifts in the learning theories as well as in the instructional theories. It was the developments in the instructional technologies that have forced us to define and redefine what was meant by *learning* and *instruction*. It was the developments in the capabilities of instructional technologies that have enabled us to put into the practice these emerging conceptions of learning and instruction.

Recent years have witnessed yet another leap in technology, which many have argued are ushering in a new media paradigm (Galarneau & Zibit, 2007). Digital game-based technologies are nudging the field to redefine what is meant by learning and instruction. Proponents of game-based learning argue that we should prepare the students to meet the demands of the twenty-first century by teaching them to be innovative, creative, and adaptable so that they can deal with the demands of learning in domains that are complex and ill-structured (Federation of American Scientists, 2005; Gee, 2003; Prensky, 2001; Shaffer, 2006). Furthermore, proponents argue that games provide many of the essential affordances that are needed for learning in these contexts (Foreman, 2004) and that games are different from any other media because "one literally learns by playing" and usually does not sit down to read a manual first (Sandford & Williamson, 2005). Hence, it is argued that games could change education because it makes it possible to learn on a massive scale by doing things that people do in the world outside of school: "They make it possible for students to learn to think in innovative and creative ways just as innovators in the real world learn to think creatively…but they can do this only of we first understand how computers change what it means to be educated in the first place" (Shaffer, 2006, p. 23).

On the other hand, opponents of games argue that games are just another technological fad, which emphasize superficial learning. In addition, opponents argue that

Table 1.1 Emergent themes from the claims of games (adapted from Mishra & Foster, 2007)

Cognitive skills	Practical skills	Motivation	Social skills	Physiological
Innovative/critical thinking	Digital/technological literacy	Self-esteem/ confidence	Communications	Aggressiveness
Systemic thinking	Multi-representational understanding	Immersion (fantasy/ curiosity)	Interpersonal skills	Antisocial behavior
Inquiry skills	Expertise development	Immediate feedback/ scaffolds	Competitive behavior	Coordination
Deductive/ inductive reasoning	Innovative/creative design skills	Control, choice autonomy/ clear goals	Communities/ emergent culture	Motor skills
Metaphoric to model-based reasoning	Data handling	Discovery/ exploration	Civic roles/ duties/ informed citizenry	Violence
Causal/complex/ iterative relations	Multimodal literacy	Valuing	Collaboration	Obesity
Memorizing	Time management		Identity formation	

games cause increased violence, aggression, inactivity, and obesity while decreasing prosocial behaviors (Walsh, 2002). A comprehensive survey conducted by Mishra and Foster (2007) further identifies 250 distinct claims about games for learning. Using grounded theory analysis, these claims were categorized under five themes (Mishra & Foster): cognitive skills, practical skills, motivation, social skills, and physiological. Table 1.1 summarizes their findings. Careful examination of their findings reveals that, irrespective of which camp one may belong, there is a general consensus: Games can lead to changes in attitudes, behavior, and skills—isn't that how *learning* is defined?

As the border between *game, play, learning,* and *instruction* is getting blurry we are once again faced with paradigm shifts in epistemology, learning theory, and instructional theory. However, before we get excited like Edison did over educational movies and claim that digital games will change education we need to study what it means for instruction. A mature theory of game-based learning should take into account the underlying principles by which they work as learning environments. Despite the arguments for the potential of digital game-based learning, the empirical evidence for their effectiveness is scant (Eseryel, Ifenthaler, & Ge, 2011). Therefore, we argue for the need to systematically study, which instructional design strategies work in game-based learning environments to take full advantage of what these emerging technologies can offer for education and training. Towards this goal, a scientific attitude with regard to the design of educational games requires validated measures of learning outcomes and the associated assessment methods in order to determine which design elements work best, when, and why.

1.3 Implementation of Assessment into Games

The implementation of assessment features into game-based learning environments is only in its early stages because it adds a very time-consuming step to the design process (Chin, Dukes, & Gamson, 2009). Additionally, the impact on learning and quality criteria (e.g., reliability and validity) of technology-based assessment systems are still being questioned (Pellegrino, Chudowsky, & Glaser, 2003). Closely related to psychological and educational assessment of games is the requirement for adequate and immediate feedback while playing a game. It is considered to be any type of information provided to learners (Wagner & Wagner, 1985). Feedback plays a particularly important role in highly self-regulated game-based learning environments because it facilitates the development of mental models and schemata, thus improving expertise and expert performance (Ifenthaler, 2010; Johnson-Laird, 1989). Not only do new developments in computer technology enable us to dynamically generate simple conceptual models and expert representations, but also direct responses to the learner's interaction with the learning environment (Ifenthaler, 2009a, 2011). Nevertheless, dynamic feedback within a game-based learning environment presupposes a reliable and valid educational assessment (Eseryel et al., 2011).

Basically, we distinguish between (1) game scoring, (2) external, and (3) embedded assessment of game-based learning (see Fig. 1.2). First, game scoring focuses on targets achieved or obstacles overcome while playing the game (Chung & Baker, 2003). Another indicator for game scoring is the time needed for completing a specific task (Reese & Tabachnick, 2010). Second, external assessment is not part of the game-based environment. It is realized through (de-)briefing interviews (Chin et al., 2009; Ifenthaler, 2009b), knowledge maps (O'Neil, Chuang, & Chung, 2003) or causal diagrams (Spector & Koszalka, 2004), and test scores based on multiple-choice questions or essays (Schrader & McCreery, 2008). Third, embedded or internal assessment is part of the gameplay and does not interrupt the game. Rich data about the learner's behavior while playing the game are provided by clickstreams or log-files (Chung & Baker, 2003; Dummer & Ifenthaler, 2005). Another promising embedded assessment technique is information trails (Loh, 2006), which is a series of event markers deposited within any game at certain intervals over a period of time.

While assessment after learning in a game-based environment often focuses on the outcome, it may neglect important changes during the learning process (see Fig. 1.3). Accordingly, instructors and teachers can only compare the individual outcome with previous outcomes, check against other learners or experts. Still, this assessment method does not allow conclusions on the cause of a possible incorrect result. Did the learner not understand the task? Was the task too difficult? Was he or she too excited? Was it a matter of motivation? In addition, an educational assessment after playing the game cannot involve instant feedback while playing the game (Eseryel et al., 2011).

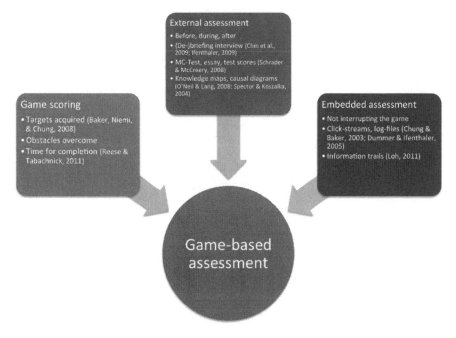

Fig. 1.2 Types of game-based assessment

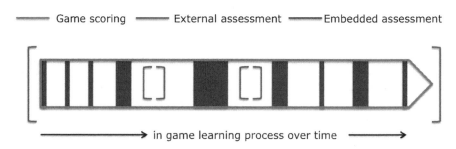

Fig. 1.3 Learning process and assessment

In contrast, assessment while learning in a game-based environment mostly focuses on the process. The benefits of this assessment method are manifold. Firstly, assessing learners while playing a game will provide detailed insights into underlying learning processes. Secondly, tracking motivational, emotional, and metacognitive characteristics while playing a game will help us to better understand specific behavior and the final outcomes. Thirdly, immediate feedback based on the embedded or stealth assessment can point to specific areas of difficulties learners are having while playing the game (Shute & Spector, 2010). Finally, assessment of *clickstreams* (Chung & Baker, 2003; Dummer & Ifenthaler, 2005) could point out strengths and weaknesses of the game design. Hence, an embedded and process-oriented assessment must always include multiple measurement procedures which raises the question of reliable and valid ways of analyzing such longitudinal data (Ifenthaler, 2008; Willett, 1988) and provide instant feedback based on the individual assessment (Ifenthaler, 2009a). Such an intelligent assessment and feedback would result in an adaptive game environment, which changes in response to the learner's activity.

Intelligent assessment of game-based learning will be the challenges for the twenty-first century instructional designers and serious games developers. This edited volume will provide a first insight into the future developments of game-based assessment.

References

Bernstein, F. (1998). *Ludi publici. Untersuchungen zur Entstehung und Entwicklung der öffentlichen Spiele im republikanischen Rom.* Stuttgart: Franz Steiner.

Caillois, R. (2001). *Man, play and games.* Champaign, IL: University of Illinois Press.

Chin, J., Dukes, R., & Gamson, W. (2009). Assessment in simulation and gaming: A review of the last 40 years. *Simulation and Gaming, 40*(4), 553–568.

Chung, G. K. W. K., & Baker, E. L. (2003). An exploratory study to examine the feasibility of measuring problem-solving processes using a click-through interface. *Journal of Technology, Learning and Assessment, 2*(2), Retrieved November 27, 2011, from http://www.jtla.org.

Dirx, R. (1981). *Das Buch vom Spiel. Das Spiel einst und jetzt.* Gelnhausen: Burckhardthaus.

Dörner, D., Kreuzig, H. W., Reither, F., & Stäudel, T. (1983). *Lohhausen. Vom Umgang mit Unbestimmtheit und Komplexität. [Lohhausen. On dealing with uncertainity and complexity].* Bern: Huber.

Dummer, P., & Ifenthaler, D. (2005). Planning and assessing navigation in model-centered learning environments. Why learners often do not follow the path laid out for them. In G. Chiazzese, M. Allegra, A. Chifari, & S. Ottaviano (Eds.), *Methods and technologies for learning* (pp. 327–334). Southhampton, UK: WIT Press.

Eseryel, D., Ifenthaler, D., & Ge, X. (2011). Alternative assessment strategies for complex problem solving in game-based learning environments. In D. Ifenthaler, P. Kinshuk, D. Isaias, G. Sampson, & J. M. Spector (Eds.), *Multiple perspectives on problem solving and learning in the digital age* (pp. 159–178). New York: Springer.

Federation of American Scientists. (2005). *Summit of educational games: Harnessing the power of video games for learning.* Washington, DC: Federation of American Scientists

Foreman, J. (2004). Game-based learning: How to delight and instruct in the 21st century. *Educause Review, 39*(5), 50–66.

Freud, S. (1920). *Gesammelte Werke* (Vol. 20). Frankfurt am Main: Fischer.

Galarneau, L., & Zibit, M. (2007). Online games for 21st century skills. In D. Gibson, C. Aldrich, & M. Prensky (Eds.), *Games and simulations in online learning: Research and development frameworks* (pp. 59–88). Hershey, PA: Information Science Publishing, Inc.

Ganguin, S. (2010). *Computerspiele und lebenslanges Lernen. Eine Synthese von Gegensätzen.* Wiesbaden: VS Verlag für Sozialwissenschaften.

Gee, J. P. (2003). *What video games have to teach us about learning and literacy.* New York: Palgrave-Macmillan.

Huizinga, J. (1955). *Homo ludens: A study of the play-element in culture.* Boston, MA: Beacon.

Ifenthaler, D. (2008). Practical solutions for the diagnosis of progressing mental models. In D. Ifenthaler, P. Pirnay-Dummer, & J. M. Spector (Eds.), *Understanding models for learning and instruction. Essays in honor of Norbert M. Seel* (pp. 43–61). New York: Springer.

8   D. Ifenthaler et al.

Ifenthaler, D. (2009a). Model-based feedback for improving expertise and expert performance. *Technology, Instruction, Cognition and Learning, 7*(2), 83–101.
Ifenthaler, D. (2009b). Using a causal model for the design and development of a simulation game for teacher education. *Technology, Instruction, Cognition and Learning, 6*(3), 193–212.
Ifenthaler, D. (2010). Bridging the gap between expert-novice differences: The model-based feedback approach. *Journal of Research on Technology in Education, 43*(2), 103–117.
Ifenthaler, D. (2011). Intelligent model-based feedback. Helping students to monitor their individual learning progress. In S. Graf, F. Lin, Kinshuk, & R. McGreal (Eds.), *Intelligent and adaptive systems: Technology enhanced support for learners and teachers* (pp. 88–100). Hershey, PA: IGI Global.
Johnson-Laird, P. N. (1989). Mental models. In M. I. Posner (Ed.), *Foundations of cognitive science* (pp. 469–499). Cambridge, MA: MIT Press.
Kant, I. (1803). *Über Pädagogik*. Königsberg: Friedrich Theodor Rink.
Loh, D. C. (2006). Designing online games assessment as "Information Trails". In D. Gibson, C. Aldrich, & M. Prensky (Eds.), *Games and simulation in online learning: Research and development frameworks* (pp. 323–348). Hershey, PA: Idea Group, Inc.
Mishra, P., & Foster, A. (2007). The claims of games: A comprehensive review and directions for future research. In R. Carlsen, K. McFerrin, J. Price, R. Weber, & D. A. Willis (Eds.), *Proceedings of the 18th International Conference of the Society for Information Technology & Teacher Education*. San Antonio, TX: Association for the Advancement of Computing in Education (AACE).
O'Neil, H. F., Chuang, S.-H., & Chung, G. (2003). Issues in the computer-based assessment of collaborative problem solving. *Assessment in Education: Principles, Policy & Practice, 10*(3), 361–373.
Parmentier, M. (2004). Spiel. In D. Benner & J. Oelkers (Eds.), *Historisches Wörterbuch der Pädagogik* (pp. 929–945). Weinheim: Beltz.
Pellegrino, J. W., Chudowsky, N., & Glaser, R. (Eds.). (2003). *Knowing what students know. The secience and design of educational assessment*. Washington, DC: National Academy Press.
Piaget, J. (1975). *Nachahmung, Spiel und Traum. Die Entwicklung der Symbolfunktion beim Kinde*. Stuttgart: Klett-Cotta.
Prensky, M. (2001). *Digital game-based learning*. New York: McGraw-Hill.
Reese, D. D., & Tabachnick, B. G. (2010). The moment of learning: Quantitative analysis of exemplar gameplay supports CyGaMEs approach to embedded assessment. Paper presented at the Society for Research on Educational Effectiveness, Washington, DC
Sandford, R., & Williamson, B. (2005). *Games and learning: A handbook from futurelab*. Bristol, UK: Futurelab.
Scheuerl, H. (1988). Zwanglose Selbstbildung im Spiel. Entwicklungsförderung im Spiel? *Spielmittel, 2*(88), 8–12.
Schrader, P. G., & McCreery, M. (2008). The acquisition of skill and expertise in massively multiplayer online games. *Educational Technology Research and Development, 56*, 557–574.
Shaffer, D. W. (2006). *How computer games help children learn?* New York: Palgrave Macmillan.
Shute, V. J., & Spector, J. M. (2010). Stealth assessment in virtual worlds. Retrieved November 27, 2011, from http://www.adlnet.gov/Technologies/Evaluation/Library/AdditionalResources/LETSI White Papers/Shute-Stealth Assessment in Virtual Worlds.pdf.
Spector, J. M., & Koszalka, T. A. (2004). The DEEP methodology for assessing learning in complex domains (final report to the National Science Foundation Evaluative Research and Evaluation Capacity Building). Syracuse, NY: Syracuse University
Wagner, W., & Wagner, S. U. (1985). Presenting questions, processing responses, and providing feedback in CAI. *Journal of Instructional Development, 8*(4), 2–8.
Walsh, D. (2002). *Video game violence and public policy*. Retrieved October 27, 2011, from http://www.soc.iastate.edu/sapp/videogames2.pdf.
Willett, J. B. (1988). Questions and answers in the measurement of change. *Review of Research in Education, 15*, 345–422.

Part I
Foundations of Game-Based Assessment

Chapter 2
Are All Games the Same?

P.G. Schrader and Michael McCreery

2.1 Introduction

Unlike historical views of learning that are biased toward knowledge transmission, memorization, and acquisition of procedural skill, contemporary research has established the importance of conceptual understanding of complex systems and concepts, the ability to transfer skills to new contexts, and the critical thinking required to judiciously apply those skills (Bransford, Brown, & Cocking, 2000). Twenty-first-century skills, like problem solving, communication, and collaboration, are among several activities that have been shown to enhance meaningful learning (Jonassen & Strobel, 2006; Sawyer, 2006; Spiro, Feltovich, Jacobson, & Coulson, 1991). More importantly, these skills are crucial for students' future success in a knowledge-based economy and globalizing world.

The study and assessment of learning in authentic environments provides unique insights into those contexts and a necessary step to understanding contemporary learning (Lave, 1988; Lave & Wenger, 1991; Sawyer, 2006; Spiro et al., 1991). Over the last several years, video games have gained considerable attention because they provide a pervasive, authentic context to study learning interactions (Gee, 2003, Squire, 2006). Accordingly, researchers have lauded games for their ability to promote situated activity, problem solving, and collaboration (Gee, 2003; Squire, 2006; Steinkuehler, 2007; Young, Schrader, & Zheng, 2006).

P.G. Schrader (✉)
Department of Teaching and Learning, University of Nevada,
4505 Maryland Parkway, Las Vegas, NV 89154-3005, USA
e-mail: pg.schrader@unlv.edu

M. McCreery
Department of Educational Leadership, University of Arkansas,
Little Rock, 2801 S. University Avenue, Little Rock, AR 72204, USA
e-mail: mpmccreery@ualr.edu

D. Ifenthaler et al. (eds.), *Assessment in Game-Based Learning: Foundations,*
Innovations, and Perspectives, DOI 10.1007/978-1-4614-3546-4_2,
© Springer Science+Business Media New York 2012

Unfortunately, the characteristics of games vary widely (e.g., content, graphics, technological affordances). Some games constrain player's experience to a left to right narrative experience (e.g., Mario Brothers) while others immerse the user in a 3D environment with thousands of peers (e.g., EverQuest). Although the field is fraught with complexity, the community appears eager to implement games in education. We are reminded that research into games as a context for communication, complex problem solving, and other twenty-first-century skills inform decisions associated with instructional strategies and the design of educational contexts (Barab, Squire, & Dueber, 2000; Barab, Thomas, Dodge, Carteaux, & Tuzun, 2005; Squire, 2006).

While the merits of games appear valid in principle, there pragmatic integration of games in teaching and learning is complicated. Decades of research has documented that learning benefits are best achieved when we design technology to be closely integrated with objectives for learning and student and teacher interactions (Sawyer, 2006; Schrader, 2008). It follows that effective assessment practices must take pedagogical objectives, environment characteristics, and learning affordances into account.

Further, there are numerous challenges associated with assessing learning and games. Games vary in terms of what they communicate (i.e., content), how they communicate (i.e., design), and the manner in which users interact with them (i.e., technological tools). Similarly, developers approach the creation of games from different paradigms, assumptions, and leverage rules differently in the core system (e.g., physics, movement, economics).

Ultimately, these nuances and distinctions lead to a range of pedagogical decisions (O'Brien, Lawless, & Schrader, 2010). To name a few, practitioners choose to integrate games as a delivery medium and source for content (e.g., drill and practice), as a partner in cognition and tool to achieve complex learning (e.g., simulation or model), or as a context for interaction (e.g., virtual space) (Jonassen, 2000; Jonassen, Campbell, & Davidson, 1994; Schrader, 2008; Solomon, Perkins, & Globerson, 1991). Although this variety of pedagogical options allows for a degree of instructional control, the choice is not without cost.

The type of game, its affordances, and the manner in which it is used as an educational tool determine the frame for the assessment questions, the nature of those questions, and the sources of data to address those questions. Without some context to examine video games and learning, assessment can be overwhelming. As a result, this chapter frames assessment and games as a direct consequence of instructional objectives and game-based learning.

We address the following questions to help frame this discussion: (1) how have games been implemented in educational contexts, (2) how does the nature of a game (i.e., its affordances) influence assessment of learning with that game, and (3) what are the implications for learning, assessment, and instruction overall? To exemplify the points, we provide three examples (i.e., *BrainAge²*, *SPORE*, and the *World of Warcraft*) and identify the games' affordances, pedagogical implications for learning, and implied assessment philosophies and practices. Throughout, we thread the concept of learning *from*, *with*, and *in* games as it relates to instruction and assessment.

2.2   Paradigms of Serious Games Research

Researchers have considered the educational implications of digital video games since their inception (Bowman, 1982) and interest in them has grown significantly in the past decade (Gee, 2007; Squire, 2006). Games are more popular than ever, they allow players to interact with one another regardless of geopolitical boundaries, and they are fun. These facts are rarely questioned. Video games have enabled people to collaborate online in sophisticated, enduring environments like the *World of Warcraft*, but have also gained criticism and notoriety as a result of alleged links between violent actions and games (e.g., Columbine High School shootings) or their perceived frivolity. However, even with the abundant media, scholarship, and research associated with electronic video games, there remain numerous questions about serious games.

Overall, video games have been linked to a variety of positive and negative consequences ranging from simple behaviors (e.g., eye poking; Kennedy & Souza, 1995) to complex cognitive dynamics (Barab et al., 2005). Game studies cover a wide range of outcomes, behaviors, and variables partly because scientists adopt different paradigms concerning the role of games in research, which has an impact on everything from the hypotheses and design to the inferences drawn from the results.

2.2.1   Games as Interventions

For some researchers, digital games provide the source of an intervention and the means to achieve a change in learning or some cognitive variable. This paradigm is most closely related to learning *from* technology and positions the game as a delivery mechanism, from which a result occurs (Barnett & Archambault, 2010; Schrader, 2008; Solomon et al., 1991). Metrics include a variety of standard approaches to assessment, including psychometrically valid instruments, multiple-choice tests, rubrics, and essays. An underlying hypothesis here is one of causation; change occurs as a direct result experience *from* a game.

Adopting this view, researchers have examined outcomes, cognitive residue, or changes in behavior as a result of play, both positive and negative. Findings associated with negative aspects of games include gender bias, addiction, and aggression (Anderson & Bushman, 2001; Gentile, Lynch, Linder, & Walsh, 2004; Kafai, 1996; Salguero & Moran, 2002; Sherry, 2001; Webber, Ritterfeld, & Mathiak, 2006). Positive results consist of an increase in motivation, spatial ability, and development of complex motor skills (Bowman, 1982; Day, Arthur, & Gettman, 2001; Greenfield, Brannon, & Lohr, 1994; Malouf, 1987; Mane, Adams, & Donchin, 1989; Millar & Navarick, 1984; Subrahmanyam & Greenfield, 1994).

2.2.2 Games as Interactive Tools

A second paradigm involves the view that games are tools *with* which users interact (Jonassen, 2000, 2005). For some, they are simulations and models that provide meaningful experiences and allow users to accomplish tasks (Turkle, 2009). In this way, games serve as a "partner in cognition" (Solomon et al., 1991). Researchers espouse this view because the partnership between technology and learner enables goals that go beyond those attainable by one or the other alone, and it promotes meaningful learning (Jonassen, 2005; Sawyer, 2006). Because this paradigm assumes that users meaningfully interact with the game, assessment approaches typically involve process variables (e.g., log files, think aloud strategies, etc.) coupled with appropriate learning measures (e.g., concept maps, performance tasks, etc.).

More recently, researchers have adopted a view that games are environments that afford many useful and educationally relevant actions. In contrast to studies exploring outcomes, research of this ilk is often conducted from within the game, involving complex data collection approaches like cognitive ethnographies or direct observation protocols (McCreery, Schrader, & Krach, 2011; Steinkuehler, 2006, 2007; Thomas, Ge, & Greene, 2011). These methodologies address alternate hypotheses, many of which pertain to the breadth of knowledge, meaningful learning, or other cognitive tasks.

From this paradigm, games have served as platform to discuss issues of twenty-first century skills, literacy, communication, collaboration, and complex problem solving (Hayes, 2007; Schrader & Lawless, 2010). As a broad context, video games are also characterized as social phenomena that provide a space for mentoring, leadership practices, and training (Schrader & McCreery, 2007; Steinkuehler, 2007). Researchers have prompted educators, instructional designers, and game developers to adopt the view that video games are designed experiences, suitable for situating, scaffolding, and constraining goal-driven action (Squire, 2006; Young et al., 2006).

In this paradigm, learning is associated with the activities that occur within the system. As a result, players may learn *from* the system or *with* elements of the game as they interact within it. The exact nature of each depends upon how the game is designed and the objectives involved in the experience. As a result, research from this paradigm must consider the game's technological affordances, goals inherent to the activity, the role the game plays in the intervention, and interaction among the three.

While the findings support continued exploration of serious gaming, the divergent roles of games in research are analogous for educators, who must first determine the learning objectives and select a technology suitable to those goals.

Teachers often find games powerful because of their ludic properties and potential connections between technological affordances and learning goals (e.g., multi-player interaction and collaboration). However, educators must ultimately balance relevant classroom objectives, the game's natural set of technological affordances, and the way those two elements support one another. More importantly, they must understand what it means to evaluate performance and learning when leveraging these technologies.

2.2.3   Immersive Games

Schrader (2008) described the manner in which these four separate roles influenced evaluation and assessment strategies. For example, assessing learning *from* technology implies a reliance on outcome measures. Typically, practitioners employ content tests in the form of rubrics, multiple-choice tests, essays, etc.... to determine the quantity and nature of content learned. However, the nature of learning *with* technology implies an interaction in addition to knowledge gains. More importantly, learning *with* technology suggests very different types of learning. Jonassen (2000, 2005) described meaningful, critical analysis, breadth of understanding, and elaboration on existing schemas. In this case, the role of the technology in instruction has significant bearing on the assessment practices.

Learning *in* technology is somewhat unique from the other types. Learning *in* technology presupposes a level of immersion and presence. As noted, numerous learning goals are possible in this case. However, the technological environment in which the interactions take place always mediates them. As a result, evaluators consider the interactions within the space as well as the cognitive outcomes of those interactions. Given the range of possible environments, from engaging, content-based websites to immersive, 3D virtual worlds, the number and type of interactions are overwhelming. Further, the most complex environments have been purposed to deliver information (*from*) and to provide simulacra and models *with* which users interact and learn (Jonassen, 2000; Solomon et al., 1991).

Although these distinctions are far from absolute, they help frame instruction and guide assessment practices. In general, they prompt the educator to consider their objectives, the role of the technology, and how the technological affordances serve both. In particular, assessment strategies follow from the nature of the objectives, the type of questions involved, and the sources of data (Schrader & Lawless, 2004, 2007). Ultimately, the ways in which game technology serves the pedagogy relate to what is assessed (e.g., knowledge, skills, attitudes, beliefs), how it is assessed (e.g., formative, objective, formal, informal), and the context in which it is assessed (i.e., individual, class, school, or system overall).

This important role of technology in objective-driven instruction and assessment is exemplified in three specific examples: *BrainAge²*, *SPORE*, and the *World of Warcraft*. With *BrainAge²*, players learn valuable content by playing the game. In this case, knowledge and skill are evaluated. In *SPORE*, players interact with the game as a simulation and challenge scientific assumptions. *SPORE* provides an opportunity for a performance assessment and meaningful learning. Finally, the *World of Warcraft* provides a rich, immersive example of the many ways users interact within a 3D environment. Players' behaviors and experiences are recorded, analyzed, and interpreted within the context of their goals.

2.3   Assessing Learning from Brainage[2]

Gee (2003, 2007) presented arguments that reinvigorated scholarly discourse associated with serious games. Although digital games and their potential link to education date as far back as the late 1970s and early 1980s, technological advancements in recent years have elevated games from cultural and fiscal phenomena to one that elicits governmental funding on federal and global levels. Improved graphics capabilities, networking technologies, sound replication, and computing power are only a few of the properties designers, researchers, and educators have sought to leverage. Even artists have used games as a medium; the National Endowment for the Arts recently offered funding for innovative video game designs (McElroy, 2011).

Although the gaming technology, types of interactions available, plots, genres, cultures, and their implications for education have evolved, the core integration paradigms remain. As noted previously, learning *from* technology is typically associated with the presentation of content and the repetition of tasks. From this perspective, suitable objectives include those associated with knowledge gains and skill improvements. Historically, there have been numerous games both designed with these outcomes in mind as well as implemented in classrooms in this way. Classical examples include *Math Blaster* or *Reader Rabbit*, both classified as drill-and-practice games, *from* which students were to glean mathematics and literacy knowledge, respectively.

Although these examples tend to follow a stimulus–response approach reminiscent of behaviorist ideals, developers have improved designs of these games to align more closely with our current understand of the learning. For example, *BrainAge²* is a game that is portable (i.e., played on a handheld system) and based on the notion of mental fitness, allowing players the opportunity to practice in a variety of locations and situations (Kawashima, 2005; Nintendo, 2007). In *BrainAge²*, players engage in activities including problem solving, counting, drawing pictures, playing music, or memory drills. There are numerous types of puzzles to work through, all of which take a relatively short amount of time to complete when compared to other games (a few minutes vs. hours or days).

The educational and pedagogical implications associated with *BrainAge²* follow from its natural set of technological affordances. *BrainAge²* was designed to improve learning characteristics like memory, numeracy, math speed and skill, and word fluency. The game randomizes these challenges and invites the player to practice them repeatedly without inducing a testing effect. In a typical classroom, *BrainAge²* could serve as a daily warm-up activity or as a skill builder. *BrainAge²* could also serve some stand-alone function as a math and literacy center. Both examples leverage *BrainAge²* as an intervention to improve knowledge and skill.

Assessing learning as a result of playing *BrainAge²* when it is used as an intervention follows a fairly common approach. At its core, *BrainAge²* is designed to improve skills in math, literacy, and overall brain function. As a result, traditional metrics that target these areas easily inform performance. The pedagogical approach mirrors pre-post studies in which gains are examined. Educators are adept with cloze deletion tests, multiple-choice content measures, and arithmetic quizzes. Further, essays and simple performance measures that are directly aligned with the core educational objectives and design parameters can be easily repurposed to evaluate learning *from BrainAge²*.

As an intervention, standard assessment practices apply to learning from these types of games, and this chapter has little to add here. However, designers have expanded this genre by infusing games like *BrainAge²*, with modern technologies (e.g., multiplayer capabilities, recording, portability, etc.). One distinguishing affordance associated with *BrainAge²* is that it provides immediate feedback regarding performance and growth. This feedback comes in the form of scores shown on the screen, successes, rewards, and sound. Each provides a response to user input and offers meaningful cues to the player about how they are performing. Individual performance based on speed and accuracy is recorded and plotted over time. Some form of embedded assessment system is available in many contemporary games, which may take the form of achievements, levels, activity logs, or measurable rewards. Whatever the form, this feedback allows teachers and students the opportunity to review progress and adjust instruction accordingly.

Another common attribute used in games is the ability to work with or compete against other players. In *BrainAge²*, players can compare their scores and performance statistics to others in the class to gain a relative ranking. Further, as many as 16 players may connect their devices with the expressed intent of competing for the fastest and most accurate puzzle completion. Alternatively, growth metrics for each individual (i.e., personal improvement) rather than raw scores can be used to provide feedback. This may be an advantageous assessment strategy due to the fact that boys and girls differ in their desire to compete with games (Kafai, 1996). In either case, the system is designed with assessment in mind, and the measurement of growth is one tool to determine performance.

Although some may criticize learning from games, objectives associated with knowledge and skill are both legitimate and required by nearly all curriculum standards. Further, teachers regularly address these types of objectives. As a result, it is instrumental to account for the manner in which students may learn from games as well as the ways to assess performance. With *BrainAge²*, educators are presented with the option of assessing learning as a result of interacting with the game or evaluating performance using the embedded technologies. In either case, the instructional paradigm and technological affordances bear significantly on the assessment practices.

2.4   Assessing Learning with Spore

When *SPORE* was released in 2008, it was preceded by an aggressive marketing campaign that promised "experiences in evolution." Documentaries, promotional videos, and discussions with the game's creator Will Wright were released to promote the scientific basis for *SPORE*. After release, the game was generally decried as falling short of promises and rhetoric (Bohannon 2008a; Schrader, Lawless, & Deniz, 2010). The scientists who were featured in the documentaries criticized the developer for misrepresenting them and the game as a model of evolution (Bohannon 2008b). The main issue stems from the obvious disconnect between the game's purported scientific foundations and accurate scientific understanding (Bean, Sinatra, & Schrader, 2010; Bohannon 2008a). More specifically, *SPORE* misrepresents crucial concepts that are difficult for young learners and has the potential to reinforce, or even instantiate, common misconceptions and biases.

Organisms in *SPORE* do not evolve over time; rather, they change dramatically in one generation. Students who play SPORE may interpret this as an immutable essence (i.e., the two organisms are distinct rather than evolved) and establish or reinforce an essentialist bias. Alternatively, players may view the inherent progression in the game as evidence of a teleological. In this case, the games creatures evolve toward sentience and students may misinterpret "purpose" as a mechanism of evolution. Lastly, players control the actions and direction of their species. While this may be a necessary game mechanic, the top-down control coincides with the belief that an intelligent agent directs the course of evolution (i.e., the intentionality bias).

Although many games lack obvious ties to curricula, an issue that Gee (2003) termed the problem of content, few exhibit such an obvious disconnect between game models and contemporary understanding. This introduces difficulties for educators who may be eager to leverage serious games, whether this is due to the scholarly endorsement of games or advertising campaigns that misrepresent them. Admittedly, few science teachers would expend the considerable effort required to plan any technology lesson without becoming somewhat familiar with the educational implications of that tool. While *SPORE* falls short in this respect, it provides an interesting case to examine learning *with* a game.

Although the algorithms and assumptions upon which *SPORE* are based may support misconceptions, the game is not without merit. Jonassen (2005) indicated that meaningful learning could also be achieved by evaluating, understanding, and criticizing the algorithms and models used by simulations. When used as a simulation, *SPORE* also provides opportunities to experience events, models, and other phenomena (Jonassen, 2000, 2005; Turkle, 2009). As a result, players may be able to draw connections across play events (i.e., trials), discern patterns, generate hypotheses, or expand the breadth of their knowledge and understanding. In this way, misconceptions become the target of instruction and the purpose of play. Students could reflect and argue what is inherently wrong with the evolution models in the game. As we have suggested previously, this subtle shift requires that teachers are aware of both their objectives and the affordances of *SPORE*.

In this example, *SPORE* serves as a tool with which students learn about evolution, albeit indirectly. Educators could invite students to examine the mechanics of the game and discuss how the models used do not align with modern science. Specifically, students could engage in scientific inquiry and collect evidence through repeated trials (i.e., play episodes from "saved game" spots; Squire & Durga, 2008). These data may come in the form of field notes, screen shots, game videos, or creature models that can be shared with the rest of the class. Further, these data could provide the basis for comparison to other simulation environments (Bean et al., 2010). These experiences provide a foundation for scientific argumentation for or against relevant hypotheses. Applied this way, students learn with *SPORE* by using it as a common experience, digital petri dish, and source of data. In this way, they use the game to accomplish something that neither the student nor the game could accomplish independently, creating a form of cognitive partnership (Solomon et al., 1991).

When used in this way, *SPORE* is inseparable from the lesson. As a result, assessment must draw on students' experiences with the game as well on their overall learning. In particular, the objectives in this case focus on inquiry. Therefore, teachers could evaluate students' interaction with information throughout the inquiry process. Digital artifacts, including communications, presentations, and game logs, could be used to document students' knowledge and growth. Artifacts like these are sometimes evaluated holistically or using objective-linked rubrics. Students could also document change in their overall schemas through the use of concepts maps. Although more difficult to evaluate, evaluators could examine the quantity of nodes, the level of nodes, accuracy of the links, and overall complexity of the concept map to provide some indication of breadth of knowledge and change.

SPORE is an interesting example of learning *with* a game because of its limitations with respect to content and scientific understanding. Informed teachers are able to exploit these shortcomings to the advantage of their students. Coincidentally, these deficiencies also make it possible to employ *SPORE* as an authentic assessment. Rather than examining assessment from the paradigm of learning with the technology, this approach employs the technology as the assessment itself. Students could play *SPORE* and then criticize the embedded scientific models based on their understanding of Darwinian evolution as a summative activity. Specifically, students could be prompted to devise an argument that identifies the critical flaws in *SPORE's* models (or argues in favor of them). This argument would be used to document students' applied understanding of Darwinian evolution.

For many educators, *SPORE* represents a failure to build serious games. In terms of educational content and the models upon which the game is built, *SPORE* exhibits many faults. As such, it does not provide appropriate structure *from* which students could learn content. However, *SPORE* provides an opportunity to consider learning *with* a game in conjunction with authentic assessment practices. The resultant pedagogical opportunities provide a valid and precise way to evaluate learning as well as the documentation of misconceptions and biases. *SPORE* could serve as a learning context *with* which students explore content or an analogous, authentic task toward which students must apply their understanding. In either case, teachers promote a deep and broad understanding of how models succeed and fail.

2.5   Assessing Learning in the World of Warcraft

The advancements that allowed *BrainAge²* to evolve beyond a simple drill-and-practice have also been applied to other games. As long as there is a pedagogical niche for these types of games, developers continue to produce them. Developments in technology as well as learning theory have allowed educators and researchers to examine interactions with games like SPORE. Ultimately, games could take the form of designed, pedagogical experiences that provide participants several paths to choose from and require some level of discernment among available skills in order to problem solve and complete performance tasks (Squire, 2006).

In recent years, a new game genre has also evolved, which is notable in the way it exploits networking technologies. Specifically, Massively Multiplayer Online Games (MMOG) like *Ultima Online*, *EverQuest*, or *Eve Online* allow thousands of players to interact simultaneously in a persistent environment. Although the setting may vary from a medieval kingdom with dragons and orcs to an interplanetary space adventure, each game in the genre has the ability to immerse players within a virtual environment, which is often a 3D representation of physical reality.

MMOGs have emerged as a significant source of interest for practitioners, researchers, and other educational constituents for many reasons. This genre afforded its participants the opportunity to pursue shared goals and objectives, socially construct knowledge, and engage in both cognitive apprenticeship as well as expert to novice mentoring (Churchill & Snowdon, 1998; McCreery et al., in press; Schrader & McCreery, 2007; Squire, 2006; Young et al., 2006). As immersive environments, MMOGs situate learning in ways that are distinct from other experiences. Although players may interact *with* games like SPORE, they interact with*in* games like the World of Warcraft (WoW).

Fundamental to learning *in* MMOGs like World of Warcraft (Squire, 2006) is the design of the environment (McCreery, 2011, pp. 36–37):

1. MMOGs are a mixed goal orientation; they have no beginning or end, no score; instead, these environments have merged sociocultural components… with the momentary excitement found within first-person shooters. Inhabitants can socialize, build relationships, and develop cultural artifacts central to the play space or take part in a token economy, which reward accomplishments upon the completion of tasks or perhaps overcoming an opponent in battle.
2. MMOGs are pseudo-extensible; a user… can instantiate a room, or object (e.g., sword or armor), from predefined list of content.

3. MMOGs are multiplayer; all participants must connect to the same remote computer that houses the virtual environment in order to interact within the play space.
4. MMOGs are persistent; the virtual environment continues to exist and narratives evolve regardless of whether participants are connected.

This design provides participants a semi-structured, open-ended environment in which to develop twenty-first-century skills (McCreery et al., 2011). The mixed goal orientation affords participants a space to pool resources, socially construct knowledge (Salt, Atkins, & Blackall, 2008), and collaboratively solve problems (Childress & Braswell, 2006; Esteves, Antunes, Fonseca, Morgado, & Martins, 2008). The design allows participants access to a broad range of affordances as a means to complete increasingly complex, performance-based activities (Barab et al., 2005). Developers have created many systems that scaffolding knowledge and skill acquisition, from trial and error to the application of elaborate strategies.

The multiplayer component of MMOGs is a defining element that underscores all activity within the game. Interaction among participants results in the development of social agency (Steinkuehler & Williams, 2006), cognitive apprenticeship, and expert to novice mentoring (Schrader & McCreery, 2007). Finally, the persistent nature of such environments leads to ongoing changes and the introduction of new problem sets that provide participants an authentic environment in which to learn (Squire, 2006).

Although learning in MMOGs have been documented for over a decade, the development and usage of data driven assessment practices have been slow to follow. This issue stems from pedagogical challenges (i.e., defining appropriate goals and technological role) but is exacerbated by the inability to capture meaningful data and inability to link those measures to learning. For example, MMOGs can be contexts for complex interaction, opportunities to experience scientific models (e.g., embedding a physics engine in Second Life), or they can simply deliver information (e.g., use a mail system to communicate). The various opportunities may cause indecision or confusion over the most appropriate role for the technology.

Learning *in* games also shifts the role of the teacher and the educational context well outside the normal range. In terms of context, MMOGs have the ability to transport students from the classroom context to a virtual one. This may be difficult for a teacher to conceptualize especially because a MMOG could be used to achieve a variety of objectives. The teacher may frame the instruction as an experience within a game, or they may frame the game as an activity within the context of the class. These decisions bear heavily on the types of assessment and evaluation that is necessary to document learning.

In the broadest frame, an MMOG may serve as an activity that contextualizes some other, more comprehensive, project. Thomas et al. (2011) described a programming course that used Quest Atlantis as their programming context. In this course, a technological ethnography was used to capture all digital materials and document growth. In other circumstances, assessment practices such as think aloud strategies, journals, and self-observation have been used to examine various cognitive constructs. However, many of these have been argued to increase the cognitive load of the learner (Schrader & Lawless, 2007) and interfere with the learning tasks (Mills, 2004).

Alternatively, learning within a game presents unique challenges that have not been completely resolved in the literature. Ultimately, the mediated nature of the environment, (i.e., choices made in the physical world manifest within a virtual) has led to difficulties in data capture. However, in recent years, researchers have begun to turn to new measures, including log or dribble files (Schrader & Lawless, 2007), virtual artifacts (Schrader, 2008), and direct observation (McCreery, 2011; McCreery et al., 2011), to assess activities within the game space (i.e., learning).

Server log files (a.k.a., audit trails or dribble files) refer to time stamped data that contain information about participant movements, clicks, actions, or other ways they interact with the environment. Although much of the work on dribble files has been done in hypertext environments (Lawless & Kulikowich, 1996, 1998; Mills, 2001, 2004), traditional audit trails have also been applied to MMOGs (Rankin, Gold, & Gooch, 2006). Further, researchers have also turned to automated mini-programs, or bots, as a new means for capturing these files (Ducheneaut, Yee, Nickell, & Moore, 2006; Young et al., 2006). For example, Schrader, Lawless, and Mayall (2008) defined duration of visit, frequency of visits, and the deviations from a predefined path to inform the nature of navigation. Regardless of the source, the key issue is applying a method to infer meaning from the difficult data sets.

Virtual and digital artifacts also provide another source of data for assessment. Within a MMOG, participants engage in a variety of activities including in-game talk (i.e., linguistic practices used to communicate), in-game letters (i.e., asynchronous communication), and metagaming practices (e.g., strategy development, problem-solving game mechanics) (Steinkuehler, 2007). In each case, these virtual artifacts provide educators an opportunity to assess the processes, language, and interaction that result in work products, rather than the work product alone. Further, this form of assessment affords educators the opportunity to examine whether scaffolded activities produce the knowledge and skill sets that are needed and expected across a variety of authenticity, performance, and collaborative tasks.

Finally, systematic direct observation (SDO) holds substantial promise as an assessment tool, particularly when assessing behavioral constructs related to acclimation, social agency, and a broad range of knowledge acquisition and skills development (McCreery, 2011; McCreery et al., 2011). SDO is a behavioral observation technique that uses video to record participants' activities within the game. The recordings are divided into time segments and coded based on the behaviors observed, using a checklist similar to those employed by school psychologists during classroom visits (Goodenough, 1928). In its most formal state, this technique is somewhat laborious. However, teachers could develop similar checklists as they roam a room and observe student behavior "over-their-shoulders" or while they are in the game with them.

For many, immersive environments represent untapped potential for education and serious gaming. However, these games are less well known when compared to other genres and more difficult to use in classrooms. Assuming teachers are knowledgeable in the development of instruction, they must also be versed in technology as well as the paradigms of integration. Their use in classrooms their role in assessing learning ultimately depends on the fit among objectives, affordances, and students abilities.

2.6   Discussion and Conclusion

We have long sought to identify what it means for a "thing" to be considered a "game." Probably the most encapsulating definition comes from a game developer and researcher. McGonigal (2011) described four essential traits of a game: a goal, rules, a feedback system, and voluntary participation. Each trait is essential, but each trait may be actualized in radically distinct ways. As a result, designers and developers imbue tremendous variety across the games they create. Said another way, *no two games are the same*. Every game presents unique capabilities for learners and, as a result, challenges for educators. The games discussed in this chapter, their breadth in affordances and pedagogical implications, should exemplify this.

For many, the apparent variety suggests unbounded opportunities for authentic practice and situated learning. At most, serious games are considered to be an untapped frontier for informal learning. At least, games are a useful supplement to existing practice. Regardless of their potential, we need to tread carefully and thoughtfully when examining learning in these environments. It seems evident that the assessment methods applied to games require clear and precise definitions of how the games are used as educational tools as well as the educational objectives involved.

Philosophically, any approach to assessment should begin with a clear description of what will be learned, how it will be learned, and under what conditions (i.e., context). Assessment is subsequently based on the response to these questions and outlines what will be measured (e.g., learning, skill, knowledge), how it will be measured (e.g., rubrics, essays, multiple-choice, observation), and under what conditions (e.g., classroom context, virtual context, dynamic interactions). Broadly speaking, games address one or many of these questions, depending on the affordances involved and the capabilities of the students.

In this chapter, we have addressed several questions about assessment and games. As shown in Fig. 2.1, the response to these questions depends upon the ways that educators approach assessment as it pertains to their objectives, pedagogies, and integration of games. For example, a teacher who is interested in knowledge gains may decide that the features of *BrainAge^2* are best used to capture data about student performance. Given the capabilities of *BrainAge^2*, the decision seems both efficient and appropriate. By contrast, the *World of Warcraft* is neither efficient nor effective when used to document growth. MMOGs play sessions last 30 or more minutes and in general lack a mechanism to store data. More importantly, any documented growth in MMOGs (e.g., performance, character development) is linked to content that is not necessarily relevant to classroom curricula.

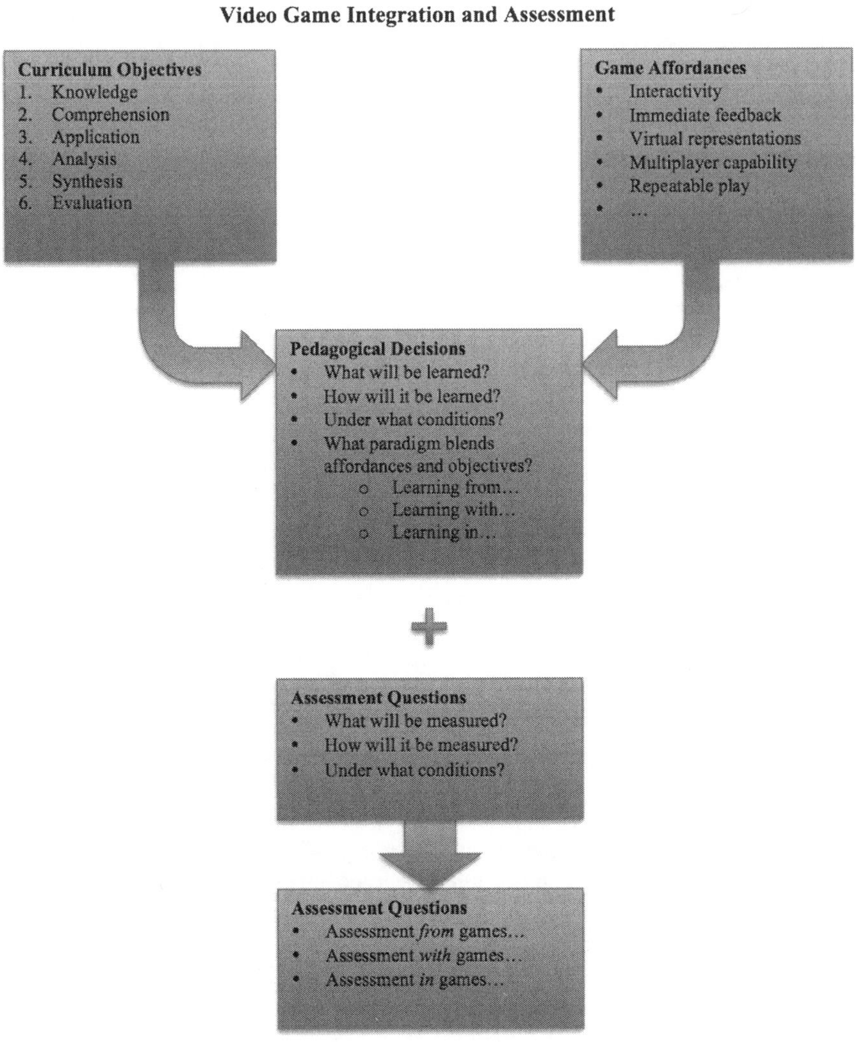

Video Game Integration and Assessment

Fig. 2.1 The decisions involved in integrating educational games in education as they lead and inform assessment

Ultimately, judicious assessment decisions results from the broad perspective described in this chapter. Overall, assessment practices can be derived from the process of (a) evaluating curricular objectives, (b) identifying the affordances of games, and (c) drawing pedagogical connections among them. Unfortunately, this process is laborious and involves an overwhelming number of decisions. Further, the decisions rely on a detailed understanding of content, teaching, and the games involved. It is very probable that many educators may decide that the potential gains are not worth the cost. However, other educators may be interested in documenting the effectiveness of games or leveraging their potential in education. In this case, the perspective and process described in this chapter may align assessment *of*, *with*, and *in* games to practice.

References

Anderson, C. A., & Bushman, B. J. (2001). Effects of violent video games on aggressive behavior, aggressive cognition, aggressive affect, physiological arousal, and prosocial behavior: A meta-analytic review of the scientific literature. *Psychological Science, 12*(5), 353–359.

Barab, S., Squire, K., & Dueber, W. (2000). A co-evolutionary model for supporting the emergence of authenticity. *Educational Technology Research and Development, 48*(2), 37–62.

Barab, S., Thomas, M., Dodge, T., Carteaux, R., & Tuzun, H. (2005). Making learning fun: Quest Atlantis, a game without guns. *Educational Technology Research and Development, 53*(1), 86–107.

Barnett, J. H., & Archambault, L. M. (2010). The game massive multiplayer online games incorporate principles of economics. *TechTrends, 54*(6), 29–35.

Bean, T. E., Sinatra, G. M., & Schrader, P. G. (2010). Spore: Spawning evolutionary misconceptions? *Journal of Science Education and Technology, 19*(5), 409–414.

Bohannon, J. (2008a). The gonzo scientist: Flunking SPORE. *Science, 322*(5901), 531. Retrieved June 9, 2011, from http://www.sciencemag.org/content/322/5901/531.3.full.

Bohannon, J. (2008b). 'Spore' documentary spawns protest by scientists who starred in it. *Science, 322*(5901), 517.

Bowman, R. (1982). A "Pac-Man" theory of motivation: Tactical implications for classroom instruction. *Educational Technology, 22*(9), 14–16.

Bransford, J. D., Brown, A. L., & Cocking, R. R. (2000). *How people learn: Brain, mind, experience, and school*. Washington, DC: National Academies Press.

Childress, M. D., & Braswell, R. (2006). Using massively multiplayer online role-playing games for online learning. *Distance Education, 27*(2), 187–196.

Churchill, E. F., & Snowdon, D. (1998). Collaborative virtual environments: An introductory review of issues and systems. *Virtual Reality, 3*, 3–15.

Day, E. A., Arthur, W., & Gettman, D. (2001). Knowledge structures and the acquisition of complex skill. *Journal of Applied Psychology, 85*(5), 1022–1033.

Ducheneaut, N., Yee, N., Nickell, E., & Moore, R. J. (2006). Building an MMO with mass appeal: A look at gameplay in World of Warcraft. *Games and Culture, 1*(4), 281–317.

Esteves, M., Antunes, R., Fonseca, B., Morgado, L., & Martins, P. (2008). Using second life in programming communities of practice. In R. O. Briggs, P. Antunes, G. de Vreede, & A. S. Read (Eds.), *Groupware: Design, implementation, and use* (pp. 99–106). New York: Springer.

Gee, J. P. (2003). *What video games have to teach us about learning and literacy*. New York: Palgrave Macmillan.

Gee, J. P. (2007). *What video games have to teach us about learning and literacy: Revise and updated edition*. New York: Palgrave Macmillan.

Gentile, D. A., Lynch, P. J., Linder, J. R., & Walsh, D. A. (2004). The effects of violent video game habits on adolescent hostility, aggressive behaviors, and school performance. *Journal of Adolescence, 27*, 5–22.

Goodenough, F. (1928). Measuring behavior traits by means of repeated short samples. *Journal of Juvenile Research, 12*, 230–235.

Greenfield, P. M., Brannon, C., & Lohr, D. (1994). Two-dimensional representation of movement through three-dimensional space: The role of video game expertise. *Journal of Applied Developmental Psychology, 15*, 87–103.

Hayes, E. (2007). *Computer and video gaming and IT proficiency: An exploratory study*. In Paper presented at the Annual Meeting of the American Educational Research Association, Chicago, IL.

Jonassen, D. H. (2000). *Computers as mindtools for schools: Engaging critical thinking* (2nd ed.). Upper Saddle River, NJ: Merrill.

Jonassen, D. H. (2005). *Modeling with technology: Mindtools for conceptual change* (3rd ed.). New York, NY: Prentice Hall.

Jonassen, D. H., Campbell, J. P., & Davidson, M. E. (1994). Learning with media: Restructuring the debate. *Educational Technology Research and Development, 42*(2), 31–39.

Jonassen, D. H., & Strobel, J. (2006). Modeling for meaningful learning. In D. Hung & M. S. Khine (Eds.), *Engaged learning with emerging technologies* (pp. 1–27). The Netherlands: Springer.

Kafai, Y. B. (1996). Electronic play worlds: Gender differences in children's construction of video games. In Y. Kafai & M. Resnick (Eds.), *Constructivism in practice: Designing, thinking, and learning in a digital world* (pp. 97–123). Mahwah, NJ: Erlbaum.

Kawashima, R. (2005). *Train your brain: 60 days to a better brain*. Teaneck, NJ: Kumon Publishing North America.

Kennedy, C. H., & Souza, G. (1995). Functional analysis and treatment of eye poking. *Journal of Applied Behavior Analysis, 28*(1), 27–37.

Lave, J. (1988). *Cognition in practice*. New York, NY: Cambridge University Press.

Lave, J., & Wenger, E. (1991). *Situated learning: Legitimate peripheral participation*. New York: Cambridge University Press.

Lawless, K. A., & Kulikowich, J. M. (1996). Understanding hypertext navigation through cluster analysis. *Journal of Educational Computing Research, 14*(4), 385–399.

Lawless, K. A., & Kulikowich, J. M. (1998). Domain knowledge, interest, and hypertext navigation: A study of individual differences. *Journal of Educational Multimedia and Hypermedia, 7*(1), 51–70.

Malouf, D. B. (1987). The effect of instructional computer games on continuing student motivation. *The Journal of Special Education, 21*(4), 27–38.

Mane, A. M., Adams, J. A., & Donchin, E. (1989). Adaptive and part: Whole training in the acquisition of a complex perceptual-motor skill. *Acta Psychologica, 71*, 179–196.

McCreery, M. P. (2011). *Personality, presence, and the virtual self: A five-factor model approach to behavioral analysis within a virtual environment*. Doctoral dissertation, ProQuest.

McCreery, M. P., Schrader, P. G., & Krach, S. K. (2011). Navigating massively multiplayer online games (MMOGs): Evaluating 21st century skills for learning in virtual environments. *Journal of Educational Computing Research, 44*(4), 473–493.

McElroy, G. (2011). National endowment for the arts grants now available for games. *joysiq*. Retrieved June 1, 2011, from http://www.joystiq.com/2011/05/08/national-endowment-for-the-arts-grants-now-available-for-games/.

McGonigal, J. (2011). *Reality is broken: Why games make us better and how they can change the world*. New York, NY: The Penguin Press.

Millar, A., & Navarick, D. J. (1984). Self-control and choice in humans: Effects of video game playing as a positive reinforcer. *Learning and Motivation, 15*, 203–218.

Mills, R. J. (2001). Analyzing instructional software using a computer-tracking system. *Information Technology, Learning, and Performance Journal, 19*(1), 21–30.

Mills, R. J. (2004). Using a computer-tracking system as an unobtrusive software data collection technique. *International Journal of Instructional Media, 1*(3), 273–282.

Nintendo (2007). *Brain age2: More training in minutes a day!* Nintendo of America. Retrieved June 1, 2011, from http://brainage.com/launch/what.jsp.

O'Brien, D. A., Lawless, K. A., & Schrader, P. G. (2010). A taxonomy of educational games: Genres and applications. In Y. K. Baek (Ed.), *Gaming for classroom-based learning: Digital role playing as a motivator of study* (pp. 1–23). Hershey, PA: Information Science Reference.

Rankin, Y., Gold, R., & Gooch, B. (2006). Evaluating interactive gaming as a language learning tool. In *Conference proceedings of SIGGRAPH 2006*, Boston, MA.

Salguero, R. A., & Moran, R. M. (2002). Measuring problem video game playing in adolescents. *Addiction, 97,* 1601–1606.

Salt, B., Atkins, C., & Blackall, L. (2008). Engaging with second life: Real education in a virtual world. The SLENZ Project for the New Zealand Tertiary Education Commission. Retrieved from Virtual Life Education New Zealand website: January 23rd, 2012. http://slenz.files.wordpress.com/2008/12/slliteraturereview1.pdf.

Sawyer, R. K. (2006). Introduction: The new science of learning. In R. K. Sawyer (Ed.), *Cambridge handbook of the learning sciences* (pp. 1–16). New York, NY: Cambridge University Press.

Schrader, P. G. (2008). Learning in technology: Reconceptualizing immersive environments. *AACE Journal, 16*(4), 457–475.

Schrader, P. G., & Lawless, K. A. (2004). The knowledge, attitudes, and behaviors (KAB) approach: How to evaluate performance and learning in complex environments. *Performance Improvement, 43*(9), 8–15.

Schrader, P. G., & Lawless, K. A. (2007). Dribble files: Methodologies to evaluate learning and performance in complex environments. *Performance Improvement, 46*(1), 40–48.

Schrader, P. G., & Lawless, K. A. (2010). The hidden literacies of massively multiplayer online games. In D. L. Pullen, C. Gitsaki, & M. Baguley (Eds.), *Technoliteracy, discourse, and social practice: Frameworks and applications in the digital age* (pp. 200–219). Hershey, PA: Information Science Reference.

Schrader, P. G., Lawless, K. A., & Deniz, H. (2010). Videogames in education: Opportunities for learning beyond the rhetoric and hype. In P. Zemliansky & D. Wilcox (Eds.), *Design and implementation of educational games: Theoretical and practical perspectives* (pp. 293–314). Hershey, PA: Information Science Reference.

Schrader, P. G., Lawless, K. A., & Mayall, H. J. (2008). The model of domain learning as a framework for understanding Internet navigation. *Journal of Educational Multimedia and Hypermedia, 17*(2), 235–258.

Schrader, P. G., & McCreery, M. (2007). The acquisition of skill and expertise in massively multiplayer online games. *Educational Technology Research & Development*. Retrieved October 10, 2007, from http://www.springerlink.com/content/n2496u376825u512/.

Sherry, J. (2001). The effects of violent video games on aggression: A meta-analysis. *Human Communication Research, 27*(3), 409–431.

Solomon, G., Perkins, D. N., & Globerson, T. (1991). Partners in cognition: Extending human intelligence with intelligent technologies. *Educational Researcher, 20*(3), 2–9.

Spiro, R. J., Feltovich, P. J., Jacobson, M. J., & Coulson, R. L. (1991). Cognitive flexibility, constructivism, and hypertext: Random access instruction for advanced knowledge acquisition in ill-structured domains. *Educational Technology, 31*(5), 24–33.

Squire, K. D. (2006). From content to context: Videogames as designed experience. *Educational Researcher, 35*(8), 19–29.

Squire, K., & Durga, S. (2008). Productive gaming: The case for historiographic game play. In R. E. Ferdig (Ed.), *Handbook of research on effective electronic gaming in education* (Vol. I). Hershey, PA: Information Science Reference.

Steinkuehler, C. (2006). Massively multiplayer online video gaming as participation in a discourse. *Mind, Culture, & Activity, 13*(1), 38–52.

Steinkuehler, C. (2007). Massively multiplayer online gaming as a constellation of literacy practices. *eLearning, 4*(3), 297–318.

Steinkuehler, C. A., & Williams, D. (2006). Where everybody knows your (screen) name: Online games as "third places". *Journal of Computer-Mediated Communications, 11,* 885–909.

Subrahmanyam, K., & Greenfield, P. M. (1994). Effect of video game practice on spatial skills in girls and boys. *Journal of Applied Developmental Psychology, 15,* 13–32.

Thomas, M., Ge, X., & Greene, B. A. (2011). Fostering 21st century skill development by engaging students in authentic game design projects in a high school computer programming class. *Journal of Educational Computing Research, 45*(1), 391–408.

Turkle, S. (2009). *Simulation and its discontents.* Cambridge, MA: MIT Press.

Webber, R., Ritterfeld, U., & Mathiak, K. (2006). Does playing violent video games induce aggression? Empirical evidence of a functional magnetic resonance imaging study. *Media Psychology, 8*, 39–60.

Young, M. F., Schrader, P. G., & Zheng, D. P. (2006). MMOGs as learning environments: An ecological journey into Quest Atlantis and the Sims Online. *Innovate, 2*(4). Retrieved June 7, 2011, from http://innovateonline.info/pdf/vol2_issue4/MMOGs_as_Learning_Environments-__An_ Ecological_Journey_into__Quest_Atlantis__and__The_Sims_Online_.pdf.

Chapter 3
The Role of Construct Definition in the Creation of Formative Assessments in Game-Based Learning

Brian R. Belland

3.1 Introduction

Games, especially highly realistic ones, are very expensive to develop. But if they can produce higher learning gains with fewer teacher hours, then their development may well be worth it (Fletcher, 2011). Almost half of the educational games either still in use or just developed by 2005 cost at least $100,000 to produce, and the creation of advanced simulations costs considerably more (Torrente, Moreno-Ger, Fernandez-Manjon, & Sierra, 2008). Systems and strategies to make it easier (and hopefully cheaper) to develop educational games are in development (Shelton et al., 2010; Torrente et al., 2008). However, game development is still likely to require substantial funding.

In an era of tight federal budgets, it is crucial for the game development community to collect better data on student learning from games. While useful, data on affective outcomes from games is not enough. Without better data on learning from games, funding for game development is likely to diminish. Simply put, designing appropriate assessments is central to designing games (Rupp, Gushta, Mislevy, & Shaffer, 2010). But it is not enough to simply measure student learning after students have used games; rather, it is important to measure learning during game play. Formative assessments can indicate if students are on track to meet learning objectives, and if not, what needs to be done to get them back on track (Wiliam, 2010a).

It has long been held that assessments need to be aligned with learning objectives; indeed, instructional designers are usually advised to develop test items before designing instruction (Gagné, Briggs, & Wager, 1988; Smith & Ragan, 1999). This chapter aims to address the following research question: How can formative assessments be designed that allow students' progress to be measured when using games?

B.R. Belland (✉)
Department of Instructional Technology and Learning Sciences, Utah State University,
2830 Old Main Hill, Logan, UT 84322, USA
e-mail: brian.belland@usu.edu

D. Ifenthaler et al. (eds.), *Assessment in Game-Based Learning: Foundations,*
Innovations, and Perspectives, DOI 10.1007/978-1-4614-3546-4_3,
© Springer Science+Business Media New York 2012

It describes a crucial step in the designing of assessments: the specification of learning goals and associated constructs. The specification of learning goals and associated constructs is central to the creation of assessments that provide meaningful feedback on student learning. In the next section, formative assessments are described. Then, existing work on formative assessment in games is discussed. Subsequently, the role of learning objectives and constructs in the formation of assessments in games is described. Next, the process of specifying constructs to be assessed during games is described. Finally, recommendations for future research are presented.

3.2 Formative Assessment

Assessments can be used for either formative or summative purposes (Wiliam & Black, 1996). When used for summative purposes, assessments provide information for such activities as grading or certification (Wiliam & Black). When used for formative purposes, assessments provide information directly to students to inform them of the adequacy of their learning and performance, and to provide direction for improvement (Wiliam & Black).

Formative assessment consists of learning activities in which students perform actions (e.g., respond to questions) and receive feedback regarding the quality of their actions (Shute, 2008). Whether an assessment is formative or summative has to do with its purpose. Formative assessment is designed to inform students of the adequacy of their learning process and what can be done to improve learning (Shute).

Wiliam and Black (1996) distinguished between two types of evidence that can be collected during formative assessment: purposive and incidental evidence. Purposive refers to evidence collected through the deliberate provision of assessments to students. For example, a teacher in a face-to-face class may ask students questions to ascertain whether they understand a concept just covered in class. Incidental refers to evidence that is "spontaneously and continuously generated" (Wiliam & Black, p. 541).

Formative assessment can be either administered by a teacher or embedded within a game. A formative assessment strategy often administered by teachers employs debriefing sessions (Delacruz, 2010). After using the game for a day, students need to respond to the questions either orally or in writing to their teacher, and are given feedback accordingly. Teachers often use rubrics to guide their assessment in such debriefing sessions. Providing rubrics directly to students is another way to provide formative assessment for students (Delacruz). With such rubrics, students can either self-assess or assess the performance of peers. If scoring rules for the game are tied to learning goals, then tying the rubric to scoring rules can make assessment transparent (Delacruz).

By carefully designing a game with structured learning activities and embedded formative assessment, designers risk creating a game that does not interest students (Walker & Shelton, 2008). But requiring a teacher to dynamically administer formative assessment to students as they work during games may not be realistic, especially in games students can explore in a non-linear path (Walker & Shelton). In short, designing formative feedback that is effective in guiding students' learning, while still creating an engaging game, is difficult. To help guide that process, the role of feedback and student mindfulness is explored in the next sections.

3.2.1   The Role of Feedback in Formative Assessment

In formative assessment, feedback is designed to inform students if they are learning what they should be learning and can be used by students to indicate what they need to do differently to learn optimally (Shute, 2008). Feedback has two functions: verification (i.e., informing students if the response was correct or incorrect) and elaboration (i.e., telling students how to improve performance; Shute). Feedback that only performs the verification function is unlikely to help students improve, and in fact may decrease student motivation (Shepard, 2009; Shute, 2008). In a meta-analysis of research on feedback, Bangert-Drowns, Kulik, Kulik, and Morgan (1991) found that providing verification feedback alone actually led to a negative effect size (−0.08) on average. The more detailed the feedback, the more it can potentially help students improve (Shute, 2008). Feedback that gave the correct answer led to an average effect size of 0.22, while feedback that (a) forced students to repeat until correct or (b) explained why answers were correct or incorrect led to an average effect size of 0.53 (Bangert-Drowns et al., 1991).

Hattie and Timperley (2007) described four types of feedback: "feedback about the task (FT), about the processing of the task (FP), about self-regulation (FR), and about the self as a person (FS)" (p. 90). Feedback about the self is rarely useful, as it has no connection to the learning task (Hattie & Timperley). Feedback about the task informs students about the quality of their completion of a learning task (Hattie & Timperley). Feedback about the processing of the task provides students with an evaluation of the processes they use (e.g., error correction strategies) to accomplish the tasks (Hattie & Timperley). Feedback about self-regulation informs students about the extent to which they monitor and direct their own learning (Hattie & Timperley).

3.2.2   The Role of Student Mindfulness

For educational games it is especially important to consider how students use the feedback they receive through formative assessment practices (Delacruz, 2010). That is, just because students receive specific feedback does not mean that they will use the feedback as intended by instructors. Students need to receive and mindfully engage with the feedback (Shepard, 2009). Engaging mindfully with feedback means carefully considering from multiple perspectives how such feedback can inform performance improvement (Langer, 1993, Langer 1989). In contract, mindless engagement with feedback can be defined as considering that feedback is context-free and can be implemented in an algorithmic manner (Langer, 1993, Langer 1989). Unfortunately, students with poor self-regulation skills often ignore feedback (Hattie & Timperley, 2007). Feedback is most likely to be well received when students fail using a strategy that they thought would work (Hattie & Timperley).

3.3   Existing Work on Formative Assessment in Games

Much existing research on formative assessment in games either embeds questions to which students respond while participating in games (e.g., Clarke & Dede, 2009) or examines what students do during games to make inferences about what they have learned (Moreno-Ger, Burgos, & Torrente, 2009; Nelson, Erlandson, & Denham, 2011; Shute, Ventura, Bauer, & Zapata-Rivera, 2009). A classic game with embedded questions is *Math Blasters*, an arcade-style game in which students answer mathematics questions to destroy space garbage, earn points and move to new levels (DeVoss, 1997). Games such as *Math Blasters* are firmly rooted in the tradition of drill and practice, which was informed by the operant conditioning of Skinner (1966). According to operant conditioning, it was deemed to be crucial to learning to have students perform tasks (e.g., answer questions) and either provide or withhold reinforcement. Delacruz (2010) noted that the drill and practice tradition continues to be carried on in many current games.

Many newer games are rooted in the social cognitive theories of scholars like Vygotsky (1962), according to which learning results from solving problems in collaboration with others. According to some authors, the approach to formative assessment also needs to be changed to reflect the change in emphasis on student activity in games (e.g., Nelson et al., 2011; Shute et al., 2009). Games can log what tools students use and for how long, as well as where they go. This information can then be used to make inferences about what students learned (Moreno-Ger et al., 2009; Nelson et al., 2011). An example of a game in which what students do can be examined to see what they learned is *Simlandia* (Nelson et al.). In *Simlandia*, students need to investigate the spread of disease. Nelson et al. argued that if students go to locations in the town where there are many people, then this may suggest that the latter understand the nature of the disease transmission. In a game for Navy personnel, students need to simulate putting out a fire on a ship (Koenig, Lee, Iseli, & Wainess, 2010). If they use the wrong tool to put out the fire given the conditions, they are given feedback explaining why their choice was incorrect (Koenig et al.). Statistical models embedded in the software can dynamically provide feedback based on trace data (e.g., how long students spent in a particular area) received (Rupp et al., 2010). However, it is much easier to collect trace data of student actions than it is to know what trace data can validly indicate (Rupp et al.).

Other authors have described methods to embed assessment of student engagement and emotion. For example, Conati (2002) described a method to embed a dynamic assessment of students' emotions while engaging in games. The information gleaned from the assessments could then be used to adjust levels of emotional support for students.

3.4 Specification of Learning Goals

It is important that game developers not lose track of learning goals in the development of formative assessment. Indeed, consideration of learning goals should drive the development of instructional games. Learning objectives are traditionally thought of as observable behaviors; instructional designers need to ensure that any statement of learning objectives include only words that reflect observable behaviors (Smith & Ragan, 1999). For example, *students will understand problem-solving* is insufficient as a learning objective, for it is unclear how one can observe the understanding of problem-solving, or what understanding problem-solving even means. *Students will exhibit problem-solving ability* is similarly flawed as a learning objective, for it is not clear what exhibiting problem-solving ability really means. A learning objective of the form *given a tub of water and a leaky tire tube, learners will be able to determine the source of the air leak* is closer to what is needed as a learning objective, as that can be clearly observed. In the simplest of cases, one can observe the learner performing the task specified in the learning objective, and know that the instruction led to the intended learning outcome. This is often, but not always, useful as a summative measure (Messick, 1994). Performance assessments are not unproblematic in that rubrics are needed to assess the performance, and the validity of both the rubric and its use must be determined (Messick). If the objective is broad enough in scope—e.g., *given access to records of expenses, liabilities, and income, the learner will be able to audit a company's annual report*—it may not be reasonable to expect that a performance test be used as a summative assessment due to time and funding constraints (Messick). Audits of large companies can cost millions of dollars and take a substantial amount of time. Furthermore, such a performance assessment is not useful as a formative assessment (Messick).

Assessments based on learning objectives are task-driven assessments (Messick, 1994). But simply assessing students' ability to perform tasks may not fully measure the intended impact of an instructional intervention (Messick). In the example objective above—given a tub of water and a leaky tire, learners will be able to determine the source of the air leak—instructional designers may want students to be able to do more in the future than just diagnose leaky bicycle tire tubes. It may be desired that students be able to engage in case-based reasoning, defined as the ability to solve problems by referring to previously encountered problems, selecting the problem solution principle, adapting it for present needs, and applying it to the new problem (Jonassen & Hernandez-Serrano, 2002; Kolodner, 1993). Unfortunately, constructing an appropriately formulated learning objective to express this desire is difficult. This is because case-based reasoning ability is an unobservable trait. One way to counteract this problem is to base assessments around constructs rather than objectives.

3.4.1 The Role of Constructs

A construct can be defined as an (usually) unobservable trait (e.g., problem-solving ability) of an individual about which researchers or instructors want to know (Kerlinger & Lee, 2000). Constructs do not "correspond to any single empirical measure" (Anastasi, 1986, p. 5). Constructs can be defined either constitutively (i.e., using other constructs) or operationally (i.e., such that it "can be observed and measured" (Kerlinger & Lee, 2000, p. 40)). On a certain level, all learning objectives can be associated with constructs. For example, a learning objective may be *Given access to sulfate testing kits, the learner will be able to determine where excess sulfates enter a river.* An associated construct may be problem-solving ability. Problem-solving ability can be defined constitutively as the ability to develop and support a feasible solution to the problem. Problem-solving ability can be defined operationally as the ability to (a) define the problem, (b) activate relevant problem schema, (c) retrieve and optimize problem solution principle, and (d) apply optimized problem solution principle (Jonassen & Hernandez-Serrano, 2002). However, it is not clear if it is justifiable to simply assess that learners can perform each of the four hypothesized steps in problem-solving (Belland, French, & Ertmer, 2009). Can a learner who can perform each of those four steps separately, effectively solve problems? Or is problem-solving more than just the sum of several steps? It is important to consider constructs because the appropriateness of a measure for a particular purpose can be assessed by its construct validity.

3.4.2 Construct Validity

Many educational researchers see tests as endowed with validity or reliability, or ignore validity and reliability altogether (Belland et al., 2009; Zientek, Capraro, & Capraro, 2008). Evidence of poor understanding of construct validity abounds: of 33 studies reviewed by Belland et al. (2009), only three gave a theoretical rationale for the use of particular assessments, and only six gave sufficient reliability evidence. Of 174 studies reviewed by Zientek et al., only 13 reported validity evidence and only 22 reported reliability for their data. The editor of *Psychological Assessment* recently highlighted the problem of receiving many submissions in which authors demonstrated poor understanding of core measurement concepts and proper test construction techniques (Reynolds, 2010).

Tests cannot be endowed with validity or reliability (Messick, 1989; Wiliam, 2010a). Rather, specific interpretations of specific test scores can be valid or invalid (Messick; Wiliam). Central to the definition of validity is the idea of construct. Validity is a summative judgment about the extent to which test scores indicate the amount of a particular construct the test taker has (Anastasi & Urbina, 1997; Messick, 1989). Test scores can be considered to have good construct validity for particular purposes, but poor construct validity for other purposes (Messick). For example, the SAT has been found to be an effective predictor of college grade-point average (GPA) in many circumstances (Linn, 2009). However, different components of SAT scores (e.g., SAT verbal or SAT math) do a better or worse job predicting the GPA of students of different ethnicities (Culpepper & Davenport, 2009). Furthermore, the predictive power of SAT scores can vary by college characteristics (Culpepper & Davenport). As another example, scores on a computer-self efficacy test may exhibit good construct validity for predicting student performance in an online course, but they would have poor construct validity for predicting a student's 40-yard dash time.

3.4.2.1   Threats to Construct Validity

Threats to construct validity include construct underrepresentation and construct irrelevant variance (Messick, 1995). Construct underrepresentation happens when the assessment does not cover all dimensions of the construct. Construct irrelevant variance happens when the assessment is too broad, and thus some variance in the scores is attributable to variance in other constructs. These threats are important to keep in mind because often the goal of a computer game is to enable learners to solve problems as an expert does. Just as it is hard to represent expert processes adequately with a single learning objective, it is also hard to adequately represent all dimensions of expert processes in a construct definition.

3.4.2.2   Sources of Evidence for Construct Validity

Sources of evidence for construct validity include (a) content representativeness, (b) criterion-relatedness, and (c) social consequences (Messick, 1995). Content representativeness can be determined by having a panel of experts rate the extent to which test items cover the content inherent in a construct. Criterion-relatedness refers to the extent to which individuals' scores on the new measure correlate with scores on measures that purportedly measure the same construct. Social consequences refer to the appropriateness of decisions made on the basis of the interpretation of scores. For example, if student A scores high on a problem-solving measure and student B scores low, what will be done with that information?

3.4.3   Reliability

Reliability indicates how much score variance is attributable to variance in the construct measured (Kerlinger & Lee, 2000). There are two approaches to assessing reliability: (a) test the same people with the same assessment (or parallel assessments) multiple times, and (b) examine the consistency of scoring on similar test items (Kerlinger & Lee). Reliability contributes to the evidence of construct validity. Though many scholars suggest that there is a minimally acceptable reliability coefficient, the minimal reliability coefficients that can be accepted vary depending on the specific purposes for which test scores are used (Cronbach & Gleser, 1959). If no other suitable measure is available and the consequences of the test are not severe, then it makes sense to use tests with less than ideal reliability. The magnitudes of effects of interest are underestimated when test scores exhibit low reliability (Nunnally & Bernstein, 1994). Educational research reports have long failed to include sufficient information about the reliability and validity of test scores (Belland et al., 2009; Randel, Morris, Wetzel, & Whitehill, 1992; Zientek et al., 2008).

3.5 The Process of Construct Definition

The first step of construct measurement is construct definition (Anastasi & Urbina, 1997). Indeed, paying insufficient attention to construct development precludes meaningful validation (Stone, Koskey, & Sondergeld, 2011; Strauss & Smith, 2009). As noted by Strauss and Smith, "In the absence of a commitment to precise construct definitions and specific theories, validation research can have an ad hoc, opportunistic quality (Kane, 2001), the results of which tend not to be very informative" (p. 9). Constructs can be defined differently by diverse test developers, and as such need to be defined precisely (Blanton & Jaccard, 2006). Construct definition proceeds according to the following process: (1) theory specification, (2) construct generation, (3) develop test items, and (4) construct refinement (see Fig. 3.1).

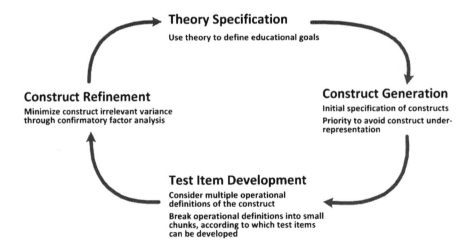

Fig. 3.1 The process of construct definition

3.5.1   Theory Specification

At the beginning of the construct definition process, researchers need to consider the educational goals addressed by a game in development (Anastasi, 1986). It is crucial that the educational goals be considered broadly, and not in terms of very specific observable behaviors so as to ensure adequate construct coverage in the corresponding assessment. Focusing solely on very specific observable behaviors, results in low reliability and inadequate construct representation (Anastasi).

Constructs can be considered broadly by allowing theory to play a central role in construct development (Anastasi, 1986). Privileging theory in the development of constructs does not diminish the importance of empirical results, as good theory should be associated with a strong base of empirical results, and empirical techniques (e.g., factor analysis) should also play a role in construct validation (Anastasi). Theory both informs the development of construct definitions and is referenced in construct definitions. For example, designers of a game intended to facilitate the development of problem-solving ability among learners need to ask a few questions (Rupp et al., 2010). First, what kind of problem-solving skill is the game supposed to develop? What are the characteristics of "expert" problem solvers in the domain? There are many definitions of problem-solving ability, and each of these definitions is driven by particular theories. One theory of problem-solving holds that experts solve problems by forming a hypothesis about the problem solution and then engaging in deductive reasoning to ascertain the tenability of the hypothesis (Coderre, Mandin, Harasym, & Fick, 2003; Kagan, 1988). Yet another theory holds that experts define the problem and then search through their memory for similar problems encountered in the past, recall the solution principle, and then adapt the principle to fit the new problem (Gick, 1986; Jonassen & Hernandez-Serrano, 2002; Kolodner, 1993; Weisburg, 1993). Depending on the theory one espouses, the definition of problem-solving ability will vary. The measure of quality of a construct definition as pertains to test construction is not absolute; rather, a construct definition is of high quality to the extent that it is very specific and informative (Strauss & Smith, 2009).

3.5.2   Construct Generation

Once the underlying theory is specified, the central constructs can begin to be specified. It is crucial that all possible dimensions of the construct be explored because one of the potential problems that can reduce construct validity of test scores is construct under-representation. Construct under-representation happens when a measure does not assess all aspects of the construct. This is especially important in the case of formative assessment, because students who receive formative feedback (a) that they are on track and should carry on as they have been doing or (b) that to get back on track they need to do x, y, z, should not find out during the summative assessment that they really also should have done several other things.

In short, it is crucial that formative assessment developers prevent construct under-representation (Wiliam, 2010b). Construct under-representation can be avoided at the theoretical level by ensuring that the construct reflects all relevant theory.

3.5.3 Develop Test Items

Once defined, constructs can form the basis of test specifications, which can in turn be used to formulate test questions. To move from a construct definition to test specifications, it is first helpful to think of constructs in terms of smaller chunks. For example, to measure problem-solving ability, researchers often break problem-solving into smaller parts, such as problem definition, and attempt to construct a test around these smaller parts (Belland et al., 2009). However, it is important to not be limited to one operational definition of the construct. If constructs represent unobservable traits, then it follows that representing a construct by just one operational definition is akin to transforming the construct into a learning objective.

Test specifications should include the number of test items needed and possible factors. In general, as the number of test items increases, the reliability will also increase provided that each items measure the different aspects of the construct (Anastasi & Urbina, 1997). Then, test items should be written. Note that test items need not be multiple-choice questions—they could include essay questions or tasks for students to perform in the game.

3.5.4 Construct Refinement

Just as construct under-representation can impact construct validity, so can construct-irrelevant variance, which can be defined as variance in test scores not due to variance in the level of the construct (Messick, 1989). Construct-irrelevant variance happens when some test items do not align with the construct in question. Detecting construct-irrelevant variance is largely an empirical question and can be accomplished by having target students complete the draft test and then performing a confirmatory factor analysis on the resulting data.

3.6 The Role of Norming in the Avoidance of Arbitrariness of Scale

Of crucial importance to the use of tests in formative assessment is the issue of arbitrariness of scale. Arbitrary scales are of little use in formative assessment because they do not allow for detailed guidance of student remediation. As noted earlier, feedback that simply provides verification is of no benefit to achievement (Bangert-Drowns et al., 1991). Assessment scales are ordinarily arbitrary in that a given score on a scale is meant to reference a certain "amount" of an unobservable construct (Blanton & Jaccard, 2006). But without further information, a raw score cannot indicate how much of the construct a student has. Being able to match test scores with students' amounts of a given construct is clearly important for assessment purposes, especially formative assessment. Given sufficient validity and reliability evidence for the given test score use, one strategy to get a sense for how much more or less of a construct a given student has than another student is to calculate a standardized mean effect size by dividing the mean difference by the pooled standard deviation. However, this strategy still requires interpretation in terms of the underlying construct to be meaningful (Blanton & Jaccard, 2006). To accomplish such a meaningful interpretation, a sense of the alignment of the scale with the unobservable construct is needed (Blanton & Jaccard, 2006). One way this can be done is through norming, a process in which a group of test-takers are categorized on the basis of a related measure. For example, examinees may be subjected to an alternative test of problem-solving ability and categorized as high-ability, average ability, or low-ability, and then cutoff scores for the new measure can be established for high-achievers, average-achievers, and low-achievers.

3.7   Conclusion and Future Directions

This chapter explored the issue of formative assessment in instructional games. Game developers should be careful to (a) specify constructs they wish to address through the games before development, and (b) develop formative assessments that provide feedback to students on their progress towards attaining the specified construct(s). With greater attention paid to construct validity in assessments embedded in games, game developers can collect the data they need to optimize games and provide evidence of learning that can be used to persuade funding agencies to fund further game development. However, important questions remain regarding the format of formative assessments and how students respond to feedback.

3.7.1   Format of Formative Assessments

One open question concerns the format of formative assessments. Simply put, once one develops test specifications and then works to develop test items, what form should those test items take? Test items do not have to be multiple choice. The items are adequate if, taken together; they provide evidence of a student's level of the underlying construct. So items could relate to how long students remain in a particular area of the game space, or what tools they use, as long as the relationship of such data and the underlying construct clearly constitutes construct validity evidence. With the continual advance in computer technology, perhaps in the future open response questions can be embedded into games. Currently, computers cannot dynamically rate and provide feedback to answers to open response questions written in natural language.

Some authors caution that formative assessment should be undertaken in games so as to minimize interference with student engagement (e.g., Shute et al., 2009). So a natural question is: Is the use of trace data (e.g., how long students spend in a particular area) the only way to avoid interference with student engagement? And is interference with student engagement really a problem? This appears to be an empirical question, but one that is fraught with logistical issues. One can certainly engage in close studies of student engagement during games with and without embedded questions, or with embedded questions and formative assessment that relies on trace data. But studying engagement is not a simple endeavor. Self-report measures are often used to collect data on engagement with games; rarely are any objective measures used (Garris, Ahlers, & Driskell, 2002). The extensive use of self-report data and corresponding lack of objective data, in motivational research has been heavily criticized (Senko, Hulleman, & Harackiewicz, 2011). Measuring engagement objectively can be difficult, but may be accomplished by observing students as they play games using a structured observation protocol.

3.7.2   Student Response to Feedback

It is also important to consider how to ensure that students use the feedback that they receive from formative assessment in an appropriate manner. Half the battle is in simply getting students to receive, and not ignore, the feedback. But even if they receive the feedback, they need to mindfully engage with it. Central to mindful engagement are the ideas of reflection on feedback and the avoidance of algorithmic processes (Krause, Stark, & Mandl, 2009; Quintana, Zhang, & Krajcik, 2005). But it is unclear for example how students could be encouraged to reflect on feedback. Should they be required to write reflections based on the feedback upon receipt of the feedback? If so, would this interrupt the game flow? Also, it is unclear if feedback formulated such that it does not present information as certain would be effective in guiding students to modifying their learning process. And avoiding the promotion of algorithmic processes in feedback makes sense especially in the case of realistic simulations in which students learn how to act like an expert. But it is unclear if this principle would hold across subject matters and grade levels. Judging the usefulness of these principles appears to be an empirical question.

References

Anastasi, A. (1986). Evolving concepts of test validation. *Annual Review of Psychology, 37*, 1–15.
Anastasi, A., & Urbina, S. (1997). *Psychological testing* (7th ed.). Upper Saddle River, NJ: Prentice Hall.
Bangert-Drowns, R. L., Kulik, C. C., Kulik, J. A., & Morgan, M. (1991). The instructional effect of feedback in test-like events. *Review of Educational Research, 61*(2), 213–238.

Belland, B. R., French, B. F., & Ertmer, P. A. (2009). Validity and problem-based learning research: A review of instruments used to assess intended learning outcomes. *The Interdisciplinary Journal of Problem-Based Learning, 3*(1), 59–89.

Blanton, H., & Jaccard, J. (2006). Arbitrary metrics in psychology. *American Psychologist, 61*(1), 27–41.

Clarke, J., & Dede, C. (2009). Design for scalability: A case study of the river city curriculum. *Journal of Science Education and Technology, 18*, 353–365.

Coderre, S., Mandin, H., Harasym, P. H., & Fick, G. H. (2003). Diagnostic reasoning strategies and diagnostic success. *Medical Education, 37*, 695–703.

Conati, C. (2002). Probabilistic assessment of user's emotions in educational games. *Applied Artificial Intelligence, 16*(7&8), 555–575.

Cronbach, L. J., & Gleser, G. C. (1959). Interpretation of reliability and validity coefficients: Remarks on a paper by Lord. *Journal of Educational Psychology, 50*(5), 230–237.

Culpepper, S. A., & Davenport, E. C. (2009). Assessing differential prediction of college grades by race/ethnicity with a multilevel model. *Journal of Educational Measurement, 46*(2), 220–242.

Delacruz, G. C. (2010). *Games as formative assessment environments: Examining the impact of explanations of scoring and incentives on math learning, game performance, and help seeking.* Doctoral dissertation, University of California, Los Angeles. UMI number 3446784.

DeVoss, V. (1997). Mega math blaster. *Teaching Children Mathematics, 4*, 120–121.

Fletcher, J. D. (2011). Cost analysis in assessing games for learning. In S. Tobias & J. D. Fletcher (Eds.), *Computer games and instruction* (pp. 417–434). Charlotte, NC: Information Age Publishing.

Gagné, R. M., Briggs, L. J., & Wager, W. W. (1988). *Principles of instructional design* (3rd ed.). New York: Holt, Rinehart, and Winston.

Garris, R., Ahlers, R., & Driskell, J. E. (2002). Games, motivation and learning: A research and practice model. *Simulation & Gaming, 33*, 441–467.

Gick, M. L. (1986). Problem solving strategies. *Educational Psychologist, 21*(1&2), 99–120.

Hattie, J., & Timperley, H. (2007). The power of feedback. *Review of Educational Research, 77*(1), 81–112.

Jonassen, D. H., & Hernandez-Serrano, J. (2002). Case-based reasoning and instructional design: Using stories to support problem-solving. *Educational Technology Research and Development, 50*(2), 65–77.

Kagan, D. M. (1988). Teaching as clinical problem solving: A critical examination of the analogy and its implications. *Review of Educational Research, 58*(4), 482–505.

Kane, M. T. (2001). Current concerns in validity theory. *Journal of Educational Measurement, 38*(4), 319–342.

Kerlinger, F. N., & Lee, H. B. (2000). *Foundations of behavioral research* (4th ed.). South Melbourne, Australia: Wadsworth.

Koenig, A. D., Lee, J. J., Iseli, M., & Wainess, R. (2010). *A conceptual framework for assessing performance in games and simulations.* CRESST Report 771. Los Angeles: Center for Research on Evaluation, Standards, and Student Testing.

Kolodner, J. L. (1993). *Case-based reasoning.* San Mateo, CA: Morgan Kaufmann.

Krause, U., Stark, R., & Mandl, H. (2009). The effects of cooperative learning and feedback on e-learning in statistics. *Learning and Instruction, 19*, 158–170.

Langer, E. J. (1989). *Mindfulness.* Reading, MA: Addison-Wesley.

Langer, E. J. (1993). A mindful education. *Educational Psychologist, 28*(1), 43–50.

Linn, R. L. (2009). Comments on Atkinson and Geiser: Considerations for college admissions testing. *Educational Researcher, 38*, 677–679.

Messick, S. (1989). Validity. In R. L. Linn (Ed.), *Educational measurement* (3rd ed., pp. 13–103). New York: American Council on Education.

Messick, S. (1994). The interplay of evidence and consequences in the validation of performance assessments. *Educational Researcher, 23*(2), 13–23.

Messick, S. (1995). Validity of psychological assessment: Validation of inferences from persons' responses and performances as scientific inquiry into score meaning. *American Psychologist, 50*(9), 741–749.

Moreno-Ger, P., Burgos, D., & Torrente, J. (2009). Digital games in eLearning environments: Current uses and emerging trends. *Simulation & Gaming, 40*, 669–687.

Nelson, B. C., Erlandson, B., & Denham, A. (2011). Global channels of evidence for learning and assessment in complex game environments. *British Journal of Educational Technology, 42*(1), 88–100.

Nunnally, I. H., & Bernstein, I. H. (1994). *Psychometric theory*. New York: McGraw-Hill.

Quintana, C., Zhang, M., & Krajcik, J. (2005). A framework for supporting metacognitive aspects of online inquiry through software scaffolding. *Educational Psychologist, 40*(4), 235–244.

Randel, J. M., Morris, B. A., Wetzel, C. D., & Whitehill, B. V. (1992). The effectiveness of games for educational purposes: A review of recent research. *Simulation & Gaming, 23*(3), 261–276.

Reynolds, C. R. (2010). Measurement and assessment: An editorial view. *Psychological Assessment, 22*(1), 1–4.

Rupp, A. A., Gushta, M., Mislevy, R. J., & Shaffer, D. W. (2010). Evidence-centered design of epistemic games: Measurement principles for complex learning environments. *Journal of Technology, Learning, and Assessment, 8*(4), 4–47.

Senko, C., Hulleman, C. S., & Harackiewicz, J. M. (2011). Achievement goal theory at the crossroads: Old controversies, current challenges, and new directions. *Educational Psychologist, 46*(1), 26–47.

Shelton, B. E., Scoresby, J., Stowell, T., Capell, M. R., Alverez, M. A., & Coats, K. C. (2010). A Frankenstein approach to open source: The construction of a 3D game engine as meaningful educational process. *IEEE Transactions on Learning Technologies, 3*(2), 85–90.

Shepard, L. A. (2009). Commentary: Evaluating the validity of formative and interim assessment. *Educational Measurement: Issues and Practice, 28*(3), 32–37.

Shute, V. J. (2008). Focus on formative feedback. *Review of Educational Research, 78*, 153–189.

Shute, V., Ventura, M., Bauer, M., & Zapata-Rivera, D. (2009). Melding the power of serious games and embedded assessment to monitor and foster learning: Flow and grow. In U. Ritterfield, M. Cody, & P. Vorderer (Eds.), *Serious games: Mechanisms and effects* (pp. 295–321). New York: Routledge.

Skinner, B. F. (1966). The phylogeny and ontogeny of behavior. *Science, 153*(3741), 1205–1213.

Smith, P., & Ragan, T. (1999). *Instructional design*. Hoboken, NJ: Wiley.

Stone, G. E., Koskey, K. L. K., & Sondergeld, T. A. (2011). Comparing construct definition in the Angoff and Objective Standard Setting models: Playing in a house of cards without a full deck. *Educational and Psychological Measurement, 71*(6), 942–962.

Strauss, M. E., & Smith, G. T. (2009). Construct validity: Advances in theory and methodology. *Annual Review of Clinical Psychology, 5*, 1–25.

Torrente, J., Moreno-Ger, P., Fernandez-Manjon, B., & Sierra, J. (2008). Instructor-oriented authoring tools for educational videogames. In *Proceedings of the eighth IEEE international conference on advanced learning technologies* (pp. 516–518), Santander, Spain.

Vygotsky, L. S. (1962). *Thought and language* (E. Hanfmann & G. Vakar, Trans.). Cambridge, MA: MIT Press.

Walker, A., & Shelton, B. E. (2008). Problem-based educational games: Connections, prescriptions, and assessment. *Journal of Interactive Learning Research, 19*(4), 663–684.

Weisburg, R. W. (1993). *Creativity: Beyond the myth of genius*. New York: W. H. Freeman.

Wiliam, D. (2010a). What counts as evidence in educational achievement? The role of constructs in the pursuit of equity in assessment. *Review of Research in Education, 34*, 254–284.

Wiliam, D. (2010b). Standardized testing and school accountability. *Educational Psychologist, 45*(2), 107–122.

Wiliam, D., & Black, P. (1996). Meanings and consequences: A basis for distinguishing formative and summative functions of assessment? *British Educational Research Journal, 22*(5), 537–548.

Zientek, L. R., Capraro, M. M., & Capraro, R. M. (2008). Reporting practices in quantitative teacher education research: One look at the evidence cited in the AERA panel report. *Educational Researcher, 37*, 208–216.

Chapter 4
Games, Learning, and Assessment

Valerie J. Shute and Fengfeng Ke

4.1 Introduction

Scholars from various disciplines have recently shown increasing interest in using well-designed digital games to support learning (e.g., Gee, 2003; Prensky, 2006; Shaffer, Squire, Halverson, & Gee, 2005; Shute, Rieber, & Van Eck, 2011). A common motivation for studying games as vehicles to support learning is frustration with the current education system and a desire for alternative ways of teaching—ways that increase student engagement and yield a rich, authentic picture of the learner(s).

Frustration stems from the fact that most schools in the U.S. are not adequately preparing kids for success in the twenty-first century (e.g., Partnership for 21st Century Skills, 2006). Learning in school is still heavily geared toward the acquisition of content within a teacher-centered model, with instruction too often abstract and decontextualized and thus not suitable for this age of complexity and interconnectedness (Shute, 2007). One downside of this outdated pedagogy is that other developed countries of the world are surpassing the U.S. on measures of important competencies (e.g., mathematics problem solving) as assessed by international tests such as the PISA and TIMSS (Gonzales et al., 2008; Howard, Paul, Marisa, & Brooke, 2010).

To make the problem with today's schools clearer, consider the following scenario involving a prototypical student. Maya (13 years old) is sitting in her bedroom with two of her friends. They are playing *Little Big Planet*—a digital game involving sack-person characters, clever and complex problems to solve, and compelling music and graphics. The game can not only be played (for countless hours), but it also provides tools to develop one's own levels and worlds which can then be shared

V.J. Shute (✉) • F. Ke
Florida State University, 3205C Stone Building, 1114 West Call Street,
Tallahassee, FL 32306-4453, USA
e-mail: vshute@fsu.edu; fke@fsu.edu

D. Ifenthaler et al. (eds.), *Assessment in Game-Based Learning: Foundations,
Innovations, and Perspectives*, DOI 10.1007/978-1-4614-3546-4_4,
© Springer Science+Business Media New York 2012

and played with the rest of the Internet community. Fully engaging in the game requires problem solving skills, persistence, and creativity—i.e., competencies which are increasingly critical to success in the twenty-first century but are not supported by our current educational system.

Like so many young people today, Maya and her friends are bored with school, and their mediocre grades reflect that attitude. But if Maya's teachers could see what she was doing in Little Big Planet, their views of her as a "slacker" would be quite different. For instance, Maya created and uploaded a new level in the game and is showing it to her friends—both in her bedroom and all over the world via the Internet. Several weeks ago, she began by writing a creative storyline, and used the in-game toolbox to create a visually-stunning environment complete with actions and reactions in the environment that reflect highly sophisticated physics understanding (as well as a good command of AI programming skills that goes beyond what most of her teachers are capable of doing). She regularly contributes detailed descriptions of how she solved her various coding problems to the Little Big Planet discussion forum, crafting her messages so they communicate clearly to all of the Little Big Planet players. Is Maya completely wasting her time with this game when she could be studying for her science test (e.g., memorizing the parts of a cell) or writing an expository essay for English class (e.g., on "why someone you care about is important to you")?

To answer the question above and to be able to make the claim that Maya is indeed developing valuable skills like problem solving, creativity, and writing, we need to employ some type of valid assessment to understand what Maya is learning from playing the game, to what degree, and in which contexts. The main challenges involved with creating such an assessment is that it must be suitable for the dynamic nature of digital games, unobtrusive to the player, while not sacrificing reliability and validity in the process.

The purpose of this chapter is to take a closer look at issues relating to game-based assessment and learning. What are the core elements of a good game? Can good games be used to support learning, based on the cumulative findings of the literature? How can game-based learning be assessed without interrupting the engagement? To address these questions, we begin by defining games and learning, provide some examples of learning from games, and then present a new approach to dynamically and validly assess learning within game environments (i.e., evidence-based stealth assessment).

4.2   Games

According to Klopfer, Osterweil, and Salen (2009), games refer to structured or organized play. Play is voluntary, intrinsically motivating, and involves active cognitive and/or physical engagement that allows for the freedom to fail (and recover), to experiment, to fashion identities, and freedom of effort and interpretation (Klopfer et al., 2009; Pellegrini, 1995; Rieber, 1996). Different from "free play," a game is usually a contest of physical or mental skills and strengths, requiring the player to follow a specific set of rules to attain a goal (Hogle, 1996).

A more succinct definition of "games" comes from Suits (1978), who describes games as, "unnecessary obstacles we volunteer to tackle." To illustrate this idea, he used the game of golf where the objective is to get the ball into the hole. The most obvious (and easiest) way to accomplish that goal is to just pick up the ball and put it in the hole. But when you include the rules of the game (e.g., you must hit the ball with a stick that has a small piece of metal on the end, while standing 200 yards or so away from the hole) and other challenges (e.g., sand traps), this makes the game much more difficult and thus all the more compelling. In games, these unnecessary obstacles become something that we want to overcome because reaching for goals and ultimately succeeding is highly rewarding. Games and their associated obstacles also create a positive kind of stress, called eustress, which is actually good for us, providing us with a sense of motivation and desire to succeed (McGonigal, 2011).

Taking a more componential tack, Prensky (2001) has argued that a game consists of a number of key elements: rules, goals and objectives, outcomes and feedback, conflict (or competition, challenge, opposition), interaction, and representation or story. Using Prensky's definition, a game differs from a simulation in that a game is intrinsically motivating and involves competition. A competitive format does not, however, require two or more participants (Dempsey, Haynes, Lucassen, & Casey, 2002). That is, if a simulation enables a learner to compete against him/herself by comparing scores over successive attempts at the simulation, or has a game structure imposed on the system, it is regarded as a type of game. If the focus of a simulation involves the completion of an event only, the simulation is not a game. In addition, a simulation generally requires representing certain key characteristics or behaviors of a selected real-world phenomenon or system. But not all games are created to simulate dynamic systems in reality. For instance, fantasy may be part of the game design.

4.2.1 Core Elements of Good Games

Diverse perspectives exist in the literature on what a good game should be. Gee (2009) recently defined six key properties for good digital games to promote deep learning: (a) an underlying rule system and game goal to which the player is emotionally attached; (b) micro-control that creates a sense of intimacy or a feeling of power; (c) experiences that offer good learning opportunities; (d) a match between affordance (allowing for a certain action to occur) and effectivity (the ability of a player to carry out such an action), (e) modeling to make learning from experience more general and abstract, and (f) encouragement to players to enact their own unique trajectory through the game (p. 78).

Other gaming scholars have focused on the playability of the game and player motivation in describing a good game (e.g., Fabricatore, Nussbaum, & Rosas, 2002;

Kirkpatrick, 2007; Yee, 2006). For example, Sweetser and Wyeth (2005) developed and validated an analytic model of game engagement called the *GameFlow model*. This model captures and evaluates a game's enjoyment or engagement quality through eight game flow elements, including concentration, challenge, player skills, control, clear goals, feedback, immersion, and social interaction. Each element encompasses a list of design criteria.

Concentration prescribes that games should provide stimuli from different sources to grab and maintain players' attention, but not burden players with trivial tasks or overload them beyond their cognitive, perceptual, and memory limits. Challenge in a game should match the player's skill level, be increased as the player progresses through the game, and allow for player-centered pacing. The element of player skills suggests that games should have an easy and user-friendly interface, provide a tutorial or online help that enables players' skill development as they progress through the game, and reward players for skill development. The element of control indicates that players should have a sense of control over the characters and movements in the game world, the game interface, and gameplay (i.e., actions and strategies players take or use when playing the game). Games should also present clear overall and intermediate goals, as well as provide immediate feedback and score status during the gaming process. As a result, games should support players becoming fully immersed in the game, losing a sense of time and environment in the process. Finally, games should support social interactions (including competition and cooperation) between players, and support social communities inside and outside the game.

By synthesizing the aforementioned findings from the literature and other discussions on good games, we have derived seven core elements of well-designed games that are presented below.

- *Interactive problem solving*: Games require ongoing interaction between the player and the game, which usually involves the requirement to solve a series of problems or quests.
- *Specific goals/rules*: Games have rules to follow and goals to attain which help the player focus on what to do and when. Goals in games may be implicit or explicit.
- *Adaptive challenges*: Good games balance difficulty levels to match players' abilities. The best games and instruction hover at the boundary of a student's ability.
- *Control*: A good game should allow or encourage a player's influence over gameplay, the game environment, and the learning experience.
- *Ongoing feedback*: Good games should provide timely information to players about their performance. Feedback can be explicit or implicit, and as research has indicated, has positive effects on learning.
- *Uncertainty* evokes suspense and player engagement. If a game "telegraphs" its outcome, or can be seen as predictable, it will lose its appeal.
- *Sensory stimuli* refer to the combination of graphics, sounds, and/or storyline used to excite the senses, which do not require "professional" graphics or sound to be compelling.

4.2.2 Good Games as Transformative Learning Tools

As many researchers have argued, good games can act as transformative digital learning tools to support deep and meaningful learning. Based on the situated learning theory (Brown, Collins, & Duguid, 1989), learning in a mindful way results in knowledge that is considered meaningful and useful, as compared to the inert knowledge that results from decontextualized learning strategies.

Learning is at its best when it is active, goal-oriented, contextualized, and interesting (e.g., Bransford, Brown, & Cocking, 2000; Bruner, 1961; Quinn, 2005; Vygotsky, 1978). Instructional environments should thus be interactive, provide ongoing feedback, grab and sustain attention, and have appropriate and adaptive levels of challenge—i.e., the features of good games. With simulated visualization and authentic problem solving with instant feedback, computer games can afford a realistic framework for experimentation and situated understanding, hence can act as rich primers for active learning (Gee, 2003; Laurel, 1991).

In this chapter, learning is defined as a lifelong process of accessing, interpreting, and evaluating information and experiences, then translating the information/experiences into knowledge, skills, values, and dispositions. It also involves change—from one point in time to another—in terms of knowing, doing, believing, and feeling. Prior research on games for learning usually focused on *content* learning in schools, such as learning the subjects of reading, writing, and mathematics. For example, major literature reviews on educational gaming research (Dempsey, Rasmussen, & Lucassen, 1996; Emes, 1997; Hays, 2005; Ke, 2008; Randel, Morris, Wetzel, & Whitehill, 1992; Vogel et al., 2006; Wolfe, 1997) have indicated that the majority of gaming studies have focused on content-specific learning. Learning in game studies encompasses the following subject areas: science education, mathematics, language arts, reading, physics, and health, among others (Ke, 2008). Substantially fewer studies to date have examined the development of cognitive processes in games (e.g., Alkan & Cagiltay, 2007; Pillay, 2002; Pillay, Brownlee, & Wilss, 1999).

While games can support content learning, we believe that games are actually better suited to support more complex competencies. As many researchers have pointed out (e.g., Gee, 2003; Malone & Lepper, 1987; Rieber, 1996), games, as a vehicle for play, can be viewed as a natural cognitive tool or toy for both children and adults (Hogel, 1996). And rather than being used as a means to achieve an external goal (e.g., learning mathematics), games are often made to align with players' intrinsic interests and challenge learners to use skills they would not otherwise tend to use (Malone & Lepper, 1987), thus enabling the design of intrinsically motivating environments, with knowledge and skill acquisition as a positive by-product of gameplay.

Besides providing opportunities for play, games enable extensive and multiple types of cognitive learning strategies. For example, games can be used as an anchor for learning-by-design to reinforce creativity of learners (Kafai, 2005). Games can involve players in forming, experimenting with, interpreting, and adapting playing strategy in order to solve problems, thus enabling players to practice persistent problem solving (Kiili, 2007). Games can also be developed as dynamic systems with which players can observe and play out key principles inherent in the systems, and hence develop organizational and systemic thinking skills (Klopfer et al., 2009). Finally, games can express and inspire certain underlying epistemic frames, values, beliefs, and identities (Shaffer, 2005).

There is a convergence between the core elements of a good game and the characteristics of productive learning. The constructivist problem-based and inquiry learning methods indicated the success of learning in the context of challenging, open-ended problems (Hmelo-Silver, 2004). Goal-based scenarios have long been viewed as an active primer for situated learning (Bransford et al., 2000). Correspondingly, in a good game a player is involved in an iterative cycle of goal-based, interactive problem solving. Psychologists (e.g., Falmagne, Cosyn, Doignon, & Thiery, 2003; Vygotsky, 1987) have long argued that the best instruction hovers at the boundary of a student's competence. Along the same line, Gee (2003) has argued that the secret of a good game is not its 3D graphics and other bells and whistles, but its underlying architecture where each level dances around the outer limits of the player's abilities, seeking at every point to be hard enough to be just doable. Moreover, a good game reinforces a sense of control—a critical metacognitive component for self-regulated learning (Zimmerman & Schunk, 2001). Similarly, both well-designed games and productive learning processes employ ongoing feedback as a major mechanism of play/learning support. Finally, the literature on the contribution of curiosity for learning motivation (Krapp, 1999) and the critical role of sensory memory in information processing (Anderson, 1995) is closely connected with the discussion of uncertainty and sensory stimuli in good games.

The problem with offering a game as a transformative learning tool to support complex competencies is that its effectiveness often cannot be directly or easily measured by traditional assessment instruments (e.g., multiple-choice tests). Implicit learning occurs when players are not consciously intending to learn some content. Therefore, focusing solely on knowledge-test-scores as outcomes is too limited since the games' strength lies in supporting emergent complex skills.

4.3   Evidence of Learning from Games

Following are four examples of learning from digital games that represent commercial as well as educational games. Preliminary evidence suggests that students can learn deeply from such games, and acquire important twenty-first century competencies.

4.3.1   Deep Learning in Civilization

Our first example illustrates how a commercial digital game can be used to support deep learning of history. Kurt Squire, at the University of Wisconsin, used a strategy game called Civilization in a high school world history class (Squire, 2004). The goal of this game is to build, advance, and protect a civilization. This game starts with kids picking a civilization that they want to build (e.g., ancient Mesopotamia). Kids make many decisions about how to build and grow their civilization. Sometimes their decisions can be as simple as deciding where to put a new bridge, but they can be as complex as deciding whether to start a nuclear war. To make successful decisions, a player needs to consider important elements of human history, including economy, geography, culture, technology advancement, and war.

So what do kids learn from playing this game? Squire reported that players mastered many historical facts (e.g., where Rome was located), but more importantly, at the end of the game, they took away a deep understanding about the intricate relationships involving geographical, historical, and economic systems within and across civilizations.

4.3.2 Gamestar Mechanic and Systems Thinking

Our next example illustrates how digital games can be used to support systems thinking skill. Systems thinking skill refers to a particular way of looking at the world which involves seeing the "big picture" and the underlying interrelationships among the constituent elements rather than just as isolated bits. Gamestar Mechanic is an online game that is intended to teach kids basic game design skills and also allows them to actually build their own games for themselves, friends, and family to play. To design a functioning and challenging game in Gamestar Mechanic, players need to think hard about various game elements, parameters, and their interrelationships. If they think too simply, and just change a few elements of the game without considering the whole system, the game will not work.

For example, consider a player who included too many enemies in her game (each one with full strength). The consequence of this decision would be that other players would not be able to beat the game, so it would not be any fun. With a little reflection, she would realize the impact that the number/strength of enemies feature of the game would have on other elements of the game, and revise accordingly. Torres (2009) recently reported on his research using Gamestar Mechanic. He found that kids who played the game did, in fact, develop systems thinking skills along with other important skills such as innovative design.

4.3.3 Epistemic Games

Another example of a type of digital game that supports learning is the epistemic game. An epistemic game is a unique game genre where players virtually experience the same things that professional practitioners do (e.g., urban planner, journalist, and engineer). Epistemic games are being developed by Shaffer and his research team at the University of Wisconsin-Madison (Shaffer, 2007). These games are based on the idea that learning means acquiring and adopting knowledge, skills, values, and identities that are embedded within a particular discipline or professional community. For example, to really learn engineering means being able to think, talk, and act like an engineer.

One example of an epistemic game is Urban Science. In Urban Science, players work as interns for an urban and regional planning center. Players as a group develop landscape planning proposals for the mayor of the city where they live. As part of the game play process, they first conduct a site visit interviewing virtual stakeholders in the area to identify different interests. For instance, some stakeholders may want a parking garage while others want affordable housing. Players need to consider various social and economic impacts of their decisions. They also use a special mapping tool called iplan (which is a tool similar to an actual Geographic Information System) to come up with their final planning. Towards the end of the game, they write their final proposal to the mayor discussing strengths and weaknesses of their final planning ideas.

4.3.4   Taiga Park and Science Content Learning

Our last example illustrates how kids learn science content and inquiry skills within an online game called Quest Atlantis: Taiga Park. Taiga Park is an immersive digital game developed by Barab et al. at Indiana University (Barab, Gresalfi, & Ingram-Goble, 2010; Barab et al., 2007). Taiga Park is a beautiful national park where many groups co-exist, such as the fly-fishing company, the Mulu farmers, the lumber company, and park visitors. In this game, Ranger Bartle calls on the player to investigate why the fish are dying in the Taiga River. To solve this problem, players are engaged in scientific inquiry activities. They interview virtual characters to gather information, and collect water samples at several locations along the river to measure water quality. Based on the collected information, players make a hypothesis and suggest a solution to the park ranger.

To move successfully through the game, players need to understand how certain science concepts are related to each other (e.g., sediment in the water from the loggers' activities causes an increase to the water temperature, which decreases the amount of dissolved oxygen in the water, which causes the fish to die). Also, players need to think systemically about how different social, ecological, and economical interests are intertwined in this park. In a controlled experiment, Barab et al. (2010) found that the middle school students learning with Taiga Park scored significantly higher on the posttest (assessing knowledge of core concepts such as erosion and eutrophication) compared to the classroom condition. The same teacher taught both treatment and control conditions. The Taiga Park group also scored significantly higher than the control condition on a delayed posttest, thus demonstrating retention of the content relating to water quality.

As these examples show, digital games appear to support learning. But how can we more accurately measure learning, especially as it happens (rather than after the fact)? The answer is not likely to be via multiple choice tests or self-report surveys as those kinds of assessments cannot capture and analyze the dynamic and complex performances that inform twenty-first century competencies. A new approach to assessment is needed.

4.4 Assessment in Games

In a typical digital game, as players interact with the environment, the values of different game-specific variables change. For instance, getting injured in a battle reduces health and finding a treasure or another object increases your inventory of goods. In addition, solving major problems in games permits players to gain rank or "level up." One could argue that these are all "assessments" in games—of health, personal goods, and rank. But now consider monitoring educationally-relevant variables at different levels of granularity in games. In addition to checking health status, players could check their current levels of systems thinking skill, creativity, and teamwork, where each of these competencies is further broken down into constituent knowledge and skill elements (e.g., teamwork may be broken down into cooperating, negotiating, and influencing skills). If the estimated values of those competencies got too low, the player would likely feel compelled to take action to boost them.

4.4.1 Evidence-Centered Design

One main challenge for educators who want to employ or design games to support learning involves making valid inferences—about what the student knows, believes, and can do—at any point in time, at various levels, and without disrupting the flow of the game (and hence engagement and learning). One way to increase the quality and utility of an assessment is to use evidence-centered design (ECD), which informs the design of valid assessments and can yield real-time estimates of students' competency levels across a range of knowledge and skills (Mislevy, Steinberg, & Almond, 2003).

ECD is a conceptual framework that can be used to develop assessment models, which in turn support the design of valid assessments. The goal is to help assessment designers coherently align (a) the claims that they want to make about learners, and (b) the things that learners say or do in relation to the contexts and tasks of interest (for an overview, see Mislevy & Haertel, 2006; Mislevy et al., 2003). There are three main theoretical models in the ECD framework: competency, evidence, and task models.

The competency model consists of student-related variables (e.g., knowledge, skills, and other attributes) on which we want to make claims. For example, suppose that you wanted to make claims about a student's ability to "design excellent presentation slides" using MS PowerPoint. The competency model variables (or nodes) would include technical as well as visual design skills. The evidence model would show how, and to what degree, specific observations and artifacts can be used as evidence to inform inferences about the levels or states of competency model variables. For instance, if you observed that a learner demonstrated a high level of technical skill but a low level of visual design skill, you may estimate her overall ability to design excellent slides to be approximately "medium"—if both the technical and aesthetic skills were weighted equally.

The task model in the ECD framework specifies the activities or conditions under which data are collected. In our current PowerPoint example, the task model would define the actions and products (and their associated indicators) that the student would generate comprising evidence for the various competencies.

There are two main reasons why we believe that the ECD framework fits well with the assessment of learning in digital games. First, in digital games, people learn in action (Gee, 2003; Salen & Zimmerman, 2005). That is, learning involves continuous interactions between the learner and the game, so learning is inherently situated in context. Therefore, the interpretation of knowledge and skills as the products of learning cannot be isolated from the context, and neither should assessment. The ECD framework helps us to link what we want to assess and what learners do in complex contexts. Consequently, an assessment can be clearly tied to learners' actions within digital games, and can operate without interrupting what learners are doing or thinking (Shute, 2011).

The second reason that ECD is believed to work well with digital games is because the ECD framework is based on the assumption that assessment is, at its core, an evidentiary argument. Its strength resides in the development of performance-based assessments where what is being assessed is latent or not apparent (Rupp, Gushta, Mislevy, & Shaffer, 2010). In many cases, it is not clear what people learn in digital games. However in ECD, assessment begins by figuring out just what we want to assess (i.e., the claims we want to make about learners), and clarifying the intended goals, processes, and outcomes of learning.

Accurate information about the student can be used as the basis for (a) delivering timely and targeted feedback, as well as (b) presenting a new task or quest that is right at the cusp of the student's skill level, in line with flow theory (e.g., Csikszentmihalyi, 1900) and Vygotsky's zone of proximal development (Vygotsky, 1978).

4.4.2 Stealth Assessment

Given the goal of using educational games to support learning in school settings (and elsewhere), we need to ensure that the assessments are valid, reliable, and also pretty much invisible (to keep engagement intact). That is where "stealth assessment" comes in (Shute, 2011; Shute, Ventura, Bauer, & Zapata-Rivera, 2009). Very simply, stealth assessment refers to ECD-based assessments that are woven directly and invisibly into the fabric of the learning environment. During game play, students naturally produce rich sequences of actions while performing complex tasks, drawing on the very skills or competencies that we want to assess (e.g., scientific inquiry skills, creative problem solving). Evidence needed to assess the skills is thus provided by the players' interactions with the game itself (i.e., the processes of play), which can be contrasted with the product(s) of an activity—the norm in educational environments.

Making use of this stream of evidence to assess students' knowledge, skills, and understanding (as well as beliefs, feelings, and other learner states and traits) presents problems for traditional measurement models used in assessment. First, in traditional tests the answer to each question is seen as an independent data point. In contrast, the individual actions within a sequence of interactions in a game are often highly dependent on one another. For example, what one does in a particular game at one point in time affects the subsequent actions later on. Second, in traditional tests, questions are often designed to measure particular, individual pieces of knowledge or skill. Answering the question correctly is evidence that one may know a certain fact: one question—one fact. But by analyzing a sequence of actions within a quest (where each response or action provides incremental evidence about the current mastery of a specific fact, concept, or skill), stealth assessments within game environments can infer what learners know and do not know at any point in time. Now, because we typically want to assess a whole cluster of skills and abilities from evidence coming from learners' interactions within a game, methods for analyzing the sequence of behaviors to infer these abilities are not as obvious. As suggested above, evidence-based stealth assessments can address these problems.

As a brief example of stealth assessment, Shute et al. (2009) used a commercial video game called Oblivion (i.e., *The Elder Scrolls® IV: Oblivion©*, 2006, by Bethesda Softworks) and demonstrated how assessment can be situated within a game environment and the dynamic student data can be used as the basis for diagnosis and formative feedback. A competency model for creative problem solving was created, which was divided into two parts—creativity and problem solving. These, in turn, were divided into novelty and efficiency indicators which were tied to particular actions one could take in the game. Different actions would have different impacts on relevant variables in the competency model. For instance, if a player came to a river in the game and dove in to swim across it, the system would recognize this as a common (not novel) action and automatically score it accordingly (e.g., low on novelty). Another person who came to the same river but chose to use a spell to freeze the river and slide across would be evidencing more novel (and efficient) actions, and the score for the creative variable in the competency model would be updated accordingly.

The models are updated via Bayesian inference networks (or Bayes nets). That is, the model of a student's game-play performance (i.e., the "student model") accumulates and represents probabilistic belief about the targeted aspects of skill, expressed as probability distributions for competency-model variables (Almond & Mislevy, 1999). Evidence models identify what the student says or does that can provide evidence about those skills (Steinberg & Gitomer, 1996) and express in a psychometric model how the evidence depends on the competency-model variables (Mislevy, 1994). Task models express situations that can evoke required evidence.

One upside of the evidence-based stealth assessment approach relates to its ability to assess general and content-specific learning in games. That is, stealth assessment is able to assess a range of attributes—from general abilities or dispositions (e.g., problem solving, creativity, and persistence) to content-specific learning (e.g., water quality, physics concepts), or even current beliefs.

4.5 Conclusion

At the beginning of this chapter we listed several questions and attempted to answer them throughout. That is, we (a) described a set of core elements of a well-designed game distilled from the literature, (b) presented examples of research studies where games were shown to support learning, and (c) discussed an approach to game-based learning using stealth assessment techniques. Our stealth assessment approach involves the use of ECD which enables the estimation of students' competency levels and further provides the evidence supporting claims about competencies. Consequently, ECD has built-in diagnostic capabilities that permits a stakeholder (i.e., the teacher, student, parent, and others) to examine the evidence and view the current estimated competency levels. This in turn can inform instructional support or provide valuable feedback to the learner.

While there seems to be a lot of promise in relation to the evidence-based stealth assessment idea, what are some of the downsides or possible limitations of this approach? First, Rupp et al. (2010) noted that when developing games that employ ECD for assessment design, the competency model must be developed at an appropriate level of granularity to be implemented in the assessment. Too large a grain size means less specific evidence is available to determine student competency, while too fine a grain size means a high level of complexity and increased resources to be devoted to the assessment. Second, the development costs of ECD-based assessments can be relatively high for complex competencies. To counter this obstacle, we are currently exploring ways to create stealth assessment models that can be used in related but different games (i.e., in a plug-and-play manner). Creating such cross-platform models for digital games would be useful and cost effective for educators interested in using games for assessment and support of learning. Finally, some people may not be "into games" thus there may be individual (or cultural) differences relating to prior game experience or differential interests that affect learning. That is, certain personal or cultural variables may be identified that interact, mediate, or moderate the effects of gameplay on learning. This is all valuable future research to pursue.

In conclusion, the world is changing rapidly but education is not. Preparing our kids to succeed in the twenty-first century requires fresh thinking on how to foster new competencies. There's an associated need to design and develop valid and reliable assessments of these new skills. We have suggested that ECD should be used as the framework for developing new assessments that can yield valid measures; provide accurate estimates of complex competencies embedded in dynamic performances; and aggregate information from a variety of sources. We also believe that well-designed games can serve as one excellent type of learning environment because games are intrinsically motivating and can facilitate learning of academic content and twenty-first century competencies within complex and meaningful environments. Such games can also promote social skills (like communication, collaboration, negotiation, and perspective taking), higher-order thinking skills (like problem solving and critical reasoning), and ownership of learning.

Designing evidence-based stealth assessments and weaving them directly within digital games will allow all kids to become fully engaged, to the point where they want (perhaps even demand) to play/learn, even outside of school. That is a lovely vision, especially in contrast with often frequent struggles to get kids to do their homework.

Acknowledgments   We'd like to offer special thanks to Matthew Ventura and Yoon Jeon Kim for their help on conceptualizing various parts of this paper, regarding the categorization of the seven core elements of games and game-based assessment issues.

References

Alkan, S., & Cagiltay, K. (2007). Studying computer game learning experience through eye tracking. *British Journal of Educational Technology, 38*(3), 538–542.
Almond, R. G., & Mislevy, R. J. (1999). Graphical models and computerized adaptive testing. *Applied Psychological Measurement, 23*(3), 223–237.
Anderson, J. R. (1995). *Learning and memory: An integrated approach.* New York: Wiley.
Barab, S. A., Gresalfi, M., & Ingram-Goble, A. (2010). Transformational play. *Educational Researcher, 39*(7), 525–536.
Barab, S. A., Zuiker, S., Warren, S., Hickey, D., Ingram-Goble, A., Kwon, E.-J., et al. (2007). Situationally embodied curriculum: Relating formalisms and contexts. *Science Education, 91*(5), 750–782.
Bethesda Softworks (2006). *Elder schools VI: Oblivion.* Retrieved April 9, 2012, from http://www.bethsoft.com/games/games_oblivion.html.
Bransford, J., Brown, A., & Cocking, R. (2000). *How People Learn: Brain, Mind, and Experience & School.* Washington, DC: National Academy Press.
Brown, J. S., Collins, A., & Duguid, P. (1989). Situated cognition and the culture of learning. *Educational Researcher, 18*(1), 32–42.
Bruner, J. S. (1961). The act of discovery. *Harvard Educational Review, 31*(1), 21–32.
Csikszentmihalyi, M. (1990). Flow: *The psychology of optical experience.* New York: Harper Perrennial.
Dempsey, J. V., Haynes, L. L., Lucassen, B. A., & Casey, M. S. (2002). Forty simple computer games and what they could mean to educators. *Simulation & Gaming, 33*(2), 157–168.
Dempsey, J. V., Rasmussen, K., & Lucassen, B. (1996). *Instructional gaming: Implications for instructional technology.* Paper presented at the annual meeting of the Association for Educational Communications and Technology, Nashville, TN.
Emes, C. E. (1997). Is Mr Pac Man eating our children? A review of the effect of digital games on children. *Canadian Journal of Psychiatry, 42*(4), 409–414.

Fabricatore, C., Nussbaum, M., & Rosas, R. (2002). Playability in action videogames: A qualitative design model. *Human Computer Interaction, 17*(4), 311–368.

Falmagne, J.-C., Cosyn, E., Doignon, J.-P., & Thiery, N. (2003). The assessment of knowledge, in theory and in practice. In R. Missaoui & J. Schmidt (Eds.), *Fourth international conference on formal concept analysis* (Lecture notes in computer science, Vol. 3874, pp. 61–79). New York: Springer.

Gee, J. P. (2003). *What digital games have to teach us about learning and literacy.* New York: Palgrave Macmillan.

Gee, J. P. (2009). Deep learning properties of good digital games: How far can they go? In U. Ritterfeld, M. Cody, & P. Vorderer (Eds.), *Serious games: Mechanisms and effects* (pp. 65–80). New York: Routledge.

Gonzales, P., Williams, T., Jocelyn, L., Roey, S., Kastberg, D., & Brenwald, S. (2008). *Highlights from TIMSS 2007: Mathematics and science achievement of U.S. fourth- and eighth-grade students in an international context (NCES 2009–001).* Washington, DC: National Center for Education Statistics, Institute of Education Sciences, U.S. Department of Education.

Hays, R. T. (2005). *The effectiveness of instructional games: A literature review and discussion.* Retrieved May 10, 2006, from http://adlcommunity.net/file.php/23/GrooveFiles/Instr_Game_Review_Tr_2005.pdf.

Hmelo-Silver, C. E. (2004). Problem-based learning: What and how do students learn? *Educational Psychology Review, 16*(3), 235–266.

Hogle, J. G. (1996). *Considering games as cognitive tools: In search of effective "Edutainment".* Retrieved January 12, 2005, from ERIC, ED 425737.

Howard, L. F., Paul, J. H., Marisa, P. P., & Brooke, E. S. (2010). *Highlights from PISA 2009: Performance of U.S. 15-year-old students in reading, mathematics, and science literacy in an international context (NCES 2011–004).* Washington, DC: National Center for Education Statistics, Institute of Education Sciences, U.S. Department of Education.

Kafai, Y. B. (2005). The classroom as "living laboratory": Design-based research for understanding, comparing, and evaluating learning science through design. *Educational Technology, 65*(1), 28–34.

Ke, F. (2008). A qualitative meta-analysis of computer games as learning tools. In R. E. Ferdig (Ed.), *Handbook of research on effective electronic gaming in education* (pp. 1–32). New York: IGI Global.

Kiili, K. (2007). Foundation for problem-based gaming. *British Journal of Educational Technology, 38*(3), 394–404.

Kirkpatrick, G. (2007). Between art and gameness: Critical theory and computer game aesthetics. *Thesis Eleven, 89,* 74–93.

Klopfer, E., Osterweil, S., & Salen, K. (2009). *Moving learning games forward: Obstacles, opportunities & openness.* Cambridge, MA: The Education Arcade.

Krapp, A. (1999). Interest, motivation and learning: An educational-psychological perspective. *European Journal of Psychology of Education, 14*(1), 23–40.

Laurel, B. (1991). *Computers as theatre.* Reading, MA: Addison-Wesley.

Malone, T. W., & Lepper, M. R. (1987). Making learning fun: A taxonomy of intrinsic motivations for learning. In R. E. Snow & M. J. Farr (Eds.), *Aptitude, learning and instruction: III. Cognitive and affective process analyses* (pp. 223–253). Hilsdale, NJ: Erlbaum.

McGonigal, J. (2011). *Reality is broken: Why games make us better and how they can change the world.* New York: Penguin Press.

Mislevy, R. J. (1994). Evidence and inference in educational assessment. *Psychometrika, 59,* 439–483.

Mislevy, R. J., & Haertel, G. D. (2006). Implications of evidence-centered design for educational testing. *Educational Measurement: Issues and Practice, 25*(4), 6–20.

Mislevy, R. J., Steinberg, L. S., & Almond, R. G. (2003). On the structure of educational assessments. *Measurement: Interdisciplinary Research and Perspectives, 1,* 3–62.

Partnership for 21st Century Skills. (2006). *Results that matter: 21st century skills and high school reform.* Retrieved from April 28, 2012. http://www.p21.org/documents/RTM2006.pdf.

Pellegrini, A. D. (1995). *The future of play theory: A multidisciplinary inquiry into the contributions of Brian Sutton-Smith*. Albany, NY: State University of New York Press.

Pillay, H. (2002). An investigation of cognitive processes engaged in by recreational computer game players: Implications for skills of the future. *Journal of Research on Technology in Education, 34*(3), 336–350.

Pillay, H., Brownlee, J., & Wilss, L. (1999). Cognition and recreational computer games: Implications for educational technology. *Journal of Research on Computing in Education, 32*(1), 203.

Prensky, M. (2001). *Digital game-based learning*. New York: McGraw-Hill.

Prensky, M. (2006). *Don't bother me mom, I'm learning!: How computer and digital games are preparing your kids for 21st century success and how you can help!* St. Paul, MN: Paragon House.

Quinn, C. (2005). *Engaging learning: Designing e-learning simulation games*. San Francisco: Pfeiffer.

Randel, J. M., Morris, B. A., Wetzel, C. D., & Whitehil, B. V. (1992). The effectiveness of games for educational purposes: A review of recent research. *Simulation & Gaming, 23*(3), 261–276.

Rieber, L. P. (1996). Seriously considering play: Designing interactive learning environments based on the blending of microworlds, simulations, and games. *Educational Technology Research and Development, 44*(1), 43–58.

Rupp, A. A., Gushta, M., Mislevy, R. J., & Shaffer, D. W. (2010). Evidence-centered design of epistemic games: Measurement principles for complex learning environments. *The Journal of Technology, Learning, and Assessment, 8*(4). Retrieved April 9, 2012, from http://escholarship. bc.edu/jtla/vol8/4.

Salen, K., & Zimmerman, E. (2005). Game design and meaningful play. In J. Raessens & J. Goldstein (Eds.), *Handbook of computer game studies* (pp. 59–80). Cambridge, MA: MIT Press.

Shaffer, D. W. (2005). *Studio mathematics: The epistemology and practice of design pedagogy as a model for mathematics learning*. Wisconsin Center for Education Research Working paper, No. 2005-3.

Shaffer, D. W. (2007). *How computer games help children learn*. New York: Palgrave.

Shaffer, D. W., Squire, K. A., Halverson, R., & Gee, J. P. (2005). Digital games and the future of learning. *Phi Delta Kappan, 87*(2), 104–111.

Shute, V. J. (2007). Tensions, trends, tools, and technologies: Time for an educational sea change. In C. A. Dwyer (Ed.), *The future of assessment: Shaping teaching and learning* (pp. 139–187). New York: Lawrence Erlbaum/Taylor & Francis.

Shute, V. J. (2011). Stealth assessment in computer-based games to support learning. In S. Tobias & J. D. Fletcher (Eds.), *Computer games and instruction* (pp. 503–524). Charlotte, NC: Information Age.

Shute, V. J., Rieber, L., & Van Eck, R. (2011). Games … and … learning. In R. Reiser & J. Dempsey (Eds.), *Trends and issues in instructional design and technology* (3rd ed., pp. 321–332). Upper Saddle River, NJ: Pearson Education.

Shute, V. J., Ventura, M., Bauer, M. I., & Zapata-Rivera, D. (2009). Melding the power of serious games and embedded assessment to monitor and foster learning: Flow and grow. In U. Ritterfeld, M. Cody, & P. Vorderer (Eds.), *Serious games: Mechanisms and effects* (pp. 295–321). Mahwah, NJ: Routledge, Taylor and Francis.

Squire, K. (2004). *Replaying history: Learning world history through playing Civilization III*. ProQuest Dissertations, Indiana University.

Steinberg, L. S., & Gitomer, D. G. (1996). Intelligent tutoring and assessment built on an understanding of a technical problem-solving task. *Instructional Science, 24*, 223–258.

Suits, B. H. (1978). *The grasshopper: Games, life and utopia*. Toronto, ON: University of Toronto Press.

Sweetser, P., & Wyeth, P. (2005). GameFlow: A model for evaluating player enjoyment in games. *ACM Computers in Entertainment, 3*(3), 1–24.

Torres, R. J. (2009). Using Gamestar Mechanic within a nodal learning ecology to learn systems thinking: A worked example. *International Journal of Learning and Media, 1*(2), 1–11.

Vogel, J. F., Vogel, D. S., Cannon-Bowers, J., Bowers, C. A., Muse, K., & Wright, M. (2006). Computer gaming and interactive simulations for learning: A meta-analysis. *Journal of Educational Computing Research, 34*(3), 229–243.

Vygotsky, L. S. (1978). *Mind in society: The development of higher mental processes.* Cambridge, MA: Harvard University Press.

Vygotsky, L. S. (1987). *The collected works of L. S. Vygotsky.* New York: Plenum.

Wolfe, J. (1997). The effectiveness of business games in strategic management course work. *Simulation & Gaming, 28*(4), 360–376.

Yee, N. (2006). The demographics, motivations, and derived experiences of users of massively multi-user online graphical environments. *Presence: Teleoperators and Virtual Environments, 15*(3), 309–329.

Zimmerman, B. J., & Schunk, D. H. (2001). *Self-regulated learning and academic achievement: Theoretical perspectives.* Mahwah, NJ: Lawrence Erlbaum.

Chapter 5
Three Things Game Designers Need to Know About Assessment

Robert J. Mislevy, John T. Behrens, Kristen E. Dicerbo, Dennis C. Frezzo, and Patti West

> *We believe that (a) learning is at its best when it is active, goal-oriented, contextualized, and interesting and (b) learning environments should thus be interactive, provide ongoing feedback, grab and sustain attention, and have appropriate and adaptive levels of challenge – in others words, the features of good games.*
>
> Shute & Torres, 2012, p. 92

5.1 Introduction

Advances in technology and learning science open the door to a radically new vision of learning and assessment, characterized by the interaction and adaptation that digital environments afford. Learners can tackle the kinds of problems that engineers, urban planners, medical professionals, and foreign language speakers engage in and learn to think, speak, act, and see the world as they do (Gee, 2003; Shaffer, 2006). For individual players or for thousands at once in massively multiplayer

R.J. Mislevy (✉)
Educational Testing Service, Rosedale Road, Mail Stop 12-T, Princeton, NJ 08541, USA
e-mail: rmislevy@ets.org

J.T. Behrens • K.E. Dicerbo
Center for Digital Experience and Analytics, Pearson, 400 Center Ridge Drive, Austin, TX 78753, USA
e-mail: john.behrens@pearson.com; Kristen.DiCerbo@Pearson.com

D.C. Frezzo
Instructional Research and Technology, Cisco Systems, 300 Berry Street #552, San Francisco, CA 94158, USA
e-mail: dfrezzo@cisco.com

P. West
Cisco Networking Academy, 4085 SE 23rd Terrace, Ocala, FL 34480, USA
e-mail: pw1112@aol.com

D. Ifenthaler et al. (eds.), *Assessment in Game-Based Learning: Foundations, Innovations, and Perspectives*, DOI 10.1007/978-1-4614-3546-4_5,
© Springer Science+Business Media New York 2012

online worlds, games can draw students into a kind of focused, highly engaged state of mind, a pleasant and self-motivating condition called "flow" (Csíkszentmihályi, 1975; Pausch, Gold, Skelly, & Thiel, 1994).

Advances in technology and learning science do something else, too. They make it hard to design and analyze assessments. The first difficulty is that designing a game-based assessment requires several kinds of expertise to come together. Each community has their own distinctive ways of talking and thinking and of framing and solving problems, and much of each perspective is foreign to the others. As an example, we will be looking at a game called Aspire, developed for the Cisco Networking Academy to support multiple goals including engaging students, supporting problem-based learning, and providing feedback in the form of formative assessment. The team that developed Aspire included instructors, network engineers, software designers, instructional technologists, cognitive psychologists, game designers, and psychometricians (Behrens, Mislevy, DiCerbo, & Levy, 2012).

The second difficulty is that the practice of educational assessment is largely organized around the discrete and static tasks that comprise most classroom and large-scale tests and measurement models that evolved to address this kind of data. Rather than discrete tasks, for example, we see continuous and interactive streams of activity; the important features of performances might not be simply right/wrong, but how effective, how efficient, or exhibiting which strategy choice (Behrens, Mislevy, Bauer, Williamson, & Levy, 2004). Performance assessments, such as the hands-on tests used in medical training and for licensing pilots, are an exception, and we can draw on this experience. Only recently, though, has the measurement community begun to recognize, make explicit, and create tools that bring the underlying principles to the surface. This work on foundations helps us use familiar assessments more effectively. More to the present point, it helps us design innovative assessments that leverage new technologies and build on our improved understanding of learning.

The primary purpose of this chapter is to tackle the first of these difficulties. This chapter gives game designers a quick start on the most important things to know about assessment when they find themselves on a team to develop a game-based assessment. It also confronts the second difficulty, by making explicit for assessment experts some ways of thinking and talking about assessment that will help them work with their diverse teammates. We build the discussion around three things that we believe game designers should know about educational assessment (and that assessment experts should know that they know themselves!):

• The principles of assessment design are compatible with the principles of game design. It is because they both build on the same principles of learning.
• Assessment is not really about numbers; it is about the structure of reasoning.[1]
• The key constraints of assessment design and game design need to be addressed from the very beginning of the design process.

Along the way, we introduce the assessment design framework known as evidence-centered design, as a means of integrating the principles of game design and

---

[1] Pearl (1988) quoted the statistician Glenn Shafer as having said "Probability isn't really about numbers; it's about the structure of reasoning."

the principles of assessment design. The ideas are illustrated with examples from Aspire and the simulation-based Packet Tracer Skills Assessments that it builds on.

5.2   Assessment Design Is Compatible with Game Design

The principles of human learning and performance revolve around "the intricate complexity of the unique moment in which a person interacts with an unprecedented material, social and cultural setting" (Claxton, 2002, p. 25). We perceive what is important, make sense of a situation, and choose how to act, all in terms of patterns we have built up through a life of previous interactions, all of which have been structured around the patterns of the language, the culture, and the domains that we move in.

Assessment design and game design both build from this foundation. When we design a game or assessment, we are determining the kinds of situations people will encounter and how they can interact with them. The art of *game design* is creating situations, challenges, rules, and affordances that keep players at the leading edge of what they can do. Serious games do this so that what players must learn to do to succeed in the game are important things to know and be able to do in a domain such as genetics, history, network engineering, or land use planning. The art of *assessment design* is creating situations such that students' actions provide information about their learning, whether as feedback to themselves, their teachers or a learning system, or other interested parties such as researchers, school administrators, or prospective employers. Each of these considerations for a game or an assessment imposes constraints on the situations we design and what can happen in them. Game-based assessments need to address them all at the same time. This section says a bit more about learning principles and how game design principles and assessment design principles are layered over them.

5.2.1   Principles of Learning

Humans excel at working with patterns. We can carry on a rapid back-and-forth conversation by processing sounds, grammar, content knowledge, social norms, conversational conventions, interpersonal relationships, and pragmatic moves—simultaneously, in milliseconds. This remarkable activity is made possible through the continual dance between the larger patterns that structure interactions between people, such as language and cultural knowledge, and each person's ever-adapting neural patterns for recognizing, making meaning of, and acting through these patterns (Wertsch, 1998). We become attuned to between-person patterns through experience, participating in activities structured around them, and discerning the regularities by seeing what happens as others act and what happens when we try them ourselves, becoming in the process more flexible and more capable.

Reviewing studies of how people become experts, Salthouse (1991) found that novices faced similar difficulties across a wide variety of domains:

* They do not know what information is relevant.
* They do not know how to integrate pieces of information they have.

- They do not know what to expect.
- They do not know what to do.
- Even when they know what to do, they cannot do it well enough or quickly enough.

People become experts at something by spending time taking part in its activities: learning to work on the problems, to talk with the people, and to act and interact in the situations. They become familiar with the terms, the tools, and the strategies that have developed in the community, and through use making them their own (Ericsson, Charness, Feltovich, & Hoffman, 2006; Lave & Wenger, 1991). Through reflective practice, best with feedback, often starting in simpler situations and usually with support, they build up their capabilities and overcome the pervasive limitations that plague novices. Experts generally do know more than novices, but it is not just a matter of knowledge. It is knowledge that is organized around underlying principles in the domain, enmeshed with possible actions and ways of interacting with people and with situations as they evolve (Chi, Glaser, & Farr, 1988). Every situation is different, but experts recognize the features and possibilities afforded by recurring patterns (Greeno, 1998)—patterns for recognizing what is important in situations, patterns for reasoning about them, and patterns for acting in situations and for creating them. When we talk about assessing knowledge and skill in this chapter, whether for experts in the professions or students in the classroom, these are the kinds of capabilities we have in mind.

Good simulation environments highlight the key features of challenging situations, for practice, for feedback, and for seeing what happens next, what works, and what does not. The first time an airline pilot's engine fails, he will have worked through a similar situation a hundred times in full motion simulators. Cisco's Packet Tracer simulation provides step-by-step animations of exactly what happens in lightning fast exchanges across routers, so students can build up mental models of what is happening and why and use them automatically and intuitively when they work with real networks (Frezzo, 2009). Simulation environments like these highlight the key patterns for thinking and acting in the domains, allow repetition and diverse practice, and provide critical opportunities for feedback. (These are some of the features that Aspire inherits from Packet Tracer, which suit it to conceptual learning in the game context.)

Games add a layer of engagement. By providing goals and challenges, managed to keep players just at the edge of their capabilities, computer games capitalize on deep principles of learning (Gee, 2003). The "Movie Mayhem"[2] game in *Mavis Beacon Teaches Typing* challenges kids to type moving words correctly before they disappear—simple enough on its face but transformed into an immersive experience by tuning time pressure, increasing levels of difficulty, adding the risk of losing, and providing "power-ups" to strategically burn, slow down, suspend, or clear words from the play area. Engagement is important in assessment, as well; research suggests that when students are more motivated, assessment results are a better reflection of their ability (Schmit & Ryan, 1992; Sundre & Wise, 2003).

---

[2] http://www.facebook.com/apps/application.php?id=123204664363385. Downloaded April 15, 2011.

Fig. 5.1 Screenshot from the Aspire game

An important element of engagement in what David Williamson Shaffer (2006) calls "epistemic games" comes from immersing players in the worlds that professionals inhabit. Students playing an epistemic game tackle challenges in simulated environments that reflect the challenges that journalists or network engineers, say, actually confront, and draw on the language, tools, and practices they use. Aspire is an example of an epistemic game.[3] The Cisco Networking Academy designed it to provide students with opportunities to practice computer networking and entrepreneurial skills and get feedback. Players complete "contracts" to provide computer networking services for a variety of clients by using an underlying simulation engine (see Behrens, Mislevy, DiCerbo, & Levy, 2012 for details). Figure 5.1 is a screenshot from one of the problem scenarios. These contracts build on the kind of networking tasks that were developed and studied in Packet Tracer functionality that Aspire builds on, using the assessment design framework discussed in the next section. Similarly, students playing the *Urban Science* game that Shaffer and his colleagues developed work through a renewal problem with stakeholder interviews, project reports, iterative planning diagrams, and a final proposal (Bagley & Shaffer, 2009). They come to see what real planners see and frame it in ways that real planners think. They learn how to work with and talk with other planners and stakeholders. They use the concepts, the procedures, and the values within the sphere of activities that constitute urban planning—in short, the epistemic frame of the discipline.

---

[3] Behrens, Frezzo, Mislevy, Kroopnick, and Wise (2007) analyzed an earlier prototype of Aspire, called Network City, in terms of the structural, functional, and semiotic symmetries between simulation-based games and assessments.

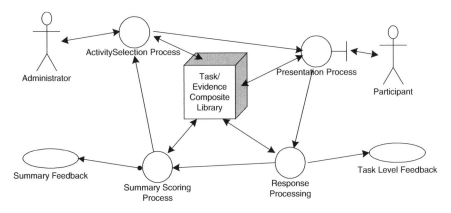

Fig. 5.2 A four-process architecture for assessment delivery systems

5.2.2 Interaction Cycles

Sid Meier, the designer of the influential computer game *Civilization*, described a [good] game as a series of interesting choices (Rollings & Morris, 2000, p. 38). Assessment too is about choices. There are choices of answers to multiple-choice items, of course, but much more interesting choices when the challenge is to solve a complex problem or to carry out an investigation (Schwartz & Arena, 2009). Salthouse's view of expertise helps us understand how to design situations that provoke interesting choices in assessments and games. What kinds of situations evoke choices that are central to a domain, interesting to a student, and informative to an assessor? These are situations that call for knowing what is important, how to integrate information, what actions are available, and what to do next. Their features hold the key to designing situations that help students learn, that get game players engaged, and that provide assessors with clues about what learners know and can do.

Interaction is obviously central to games, and it will have to be in game-based assessments as well. It is less obvious that interaction is central to assessment, especially in the ones we are most familiar with, but seeing assessments in terms of feedback cycles brings out the connection. Figure 5.2 is a schematic of the interacting processes in assessments.[4] Not surprisingly, it looks a lot like the inquiry process in science, the Deming cycle in quality control, and John Boyd's OODA loops (observe-orient-decide-act) in military strategy. A standardized multiple-choice test is once around the loop: *Activity Selection* is when a teacher, an organization, or a student herself determines a test will be taken. In *Presentation*, the student produces the answers the test requires, and the *Response Scoring* and *Summary Scoring*

---

[4] This figure is based on Almond, Steinberg, and Mislevy (2002) four-process architecture for assessment delivery systems. They describe how the processes are structured around the information in student, evidence, and task models discussed later in this chapter. Frezzo, Behrens, and Mislevy (2009) show how it plays out in Cisco's Packet Tracer Skills Assessments.

processes take place after the test is over. The results are used to guide instruction or ground a decision in a final visit back at the *Activity Selection* process.

Computerized adaptive tests (CATs; Wainer et al., 2000) like the GRE® administer items to students based on their previous responses. They cycle through the loop repeatedly:

- The *Activity Selection Process* selects a task for the student. CAT items are pre-packaged situations that provide evidence about the targeted proficiency. Their difficulty is key: Tasks that are most informative for a particular student are those for which she has about 50–50 chances. Not only is the cusp of capabilities optimal for learning and for engagement (a la Vygotsky's (1978) "zone of proximal development"), it provides the best statistical evidence for assessment.
- The *Presentation Process* displays the task, manages the interaction with the student, and captures the work product. In multiple-choice CAT, this is the item response.
- The *Response Scoring Process* identifies essential features of the work or values of observable variables; in this example, each item response is scored just right or wrong.
- The *Summary Scoring Process* updates belief about the student. In CAT, a psychometric model for student proficiency integrates the evidence across items.
- The *Activity Selection Process* makes another decision about what to do next, using this updated belief and other relevant information. If the score is accurate enough, testing ends. If more information is needed, a harder or easier task will be administered, depending on how the student is doing.

Now think about an assessment where every action a student takes within a task provides feedback or changes the situation and different paths and strategies can be evaluated. This is what simulation-based and game-based assessments do. Think about assessment systems where activity selection is not done just by the assessment but by the student herself as well, based on her goals and preferences (Levy, Behrens, & Mislevy, 2006). Now there are loops within loops: tight feedback cycles with fine-grained feedback for moment to moment decisions, larger cycles for marking successes and determining new challenges, and still larger cycles to move students through a space they help determine. This is what games do, too. They use the same principles of adaptation, tuned to optimize the player's experience. There is a sense in which a good game has to be a good assessment, in order to manage the evolving interactions and situations that keep players engaged at the edge of their capabilities (Shaffer & Gee, 2012).

5.2.3 The Bottom Line

Successful games and assessments are grounded on foundational principles of human learning (Gee, 2003). They embody fundamental patterns of thinking and acting in the targeted domain. They construct situations around the features that evoke these patterns, and they tune them to the capabilities of the players or examinees. They provide students with opportunities to make choices and leverage those choices to inform larger purposes, inside the activity or beyond it.

Although both games and assessments are grounded on the same principles, they have distinct constraints to satisfy. Game design is about tuning the challenges, the rules, the situations, and the interactions to optimize learning and engagement, all on top of getting the domain right. Game designers have principles for doing this. They know about narrative structures and game mechanics from experience, from copious user testing, and from a growing research literature on the interplay of psychology and design in computer games (e.g., pioneering investigations by Loftus & Loftus, 1983; Malone, 1981 and more recent work such as Fullerton, Swain, & Hoffman, 2008; Gee, 2003; Salen & Zimmerman, 2004; Shaffer, 2006).

Assessment design is about tuning situations and interactions to optimize evidence about what students know or can do, for some educational purpose. This is generally distinct from the goal of a game. The goal of assessment design is not contradictory to the goal of game design, and they are compatible in that they must both build on learning principles. In a game-based assessment, however, the assessment goal of obtaining and interpreting evidence for an external user imposes design constraints that can trade-off against game design constraints.

5.3   Assessment Is Not Really About Numbers; It Is About the Structure of Reasoning

Familiar tests are collections of items, which students respond to individually, that get scored, and add up to test scores. People who have some formal training in assessment or use it in their jobs know a bit about reliability and validity as they apply to these practices. Psychometricians are applied statisticians who apply measurement models to assessment data. They work with such esoterica as likelihood functions, latent variable analyses, and models for mixed strategies. These methods encompass the machinery for familiar tests but also extend to more complex performances and characterizations of students' capabilities.

Some assessment needs in game-based assessment can be handled with familiar concepts and formulas, but others cannot (Behrens et al., 2004). A network troubleshooting task in Aspire might take half an hour to complete. There are no "items" but rather sequences of actions that lead different students through different situations. What should be "scored"? A student's choices in the game produce the full sequence and time stamps of all actions, the final functioning of the network as a whole, and the final configuration of the network devices individually. After all that thinking and activity, there is surely more information than a simple right/wrong score. Looking through the lens of assessment, we must ask questions about targets of inferences, sources of evidence, and ways of evaluating the activity. How do we determine how to build environments that will give us the right evidence? How do we make sense of the evidence? How do we combine evidence across tasks? How do we characterize the value of the evidence? How do we determine whether what we learn in the assessment holds value beyond the immediate situation, for what a student has learned or can do more generally; in other words, how do we establish whether the student has learned anything more than how to win the game?

The statistical machinery of psychometrics developed to help answer these kinds of questions for familiar assessments like multiple-choice tests and essay exams. The question about the value of evidence plays out as reliability and the broader concept of generalizability. The last question, about what we learn beyond whether the student has succeeded in the game itself, is a facet of validity, at the very heart of assessment. Psychometricians can bring machinery to bear on these fundamental questions in more complicated assessments like games and simulations, partly by using more complicated models when they are needed and partly by helping design the activity to minimize unnecessary complications.

Game designers do not need to become experts in likelihood functions and latent variable models; the psychometricians will do that. But game designers do need to know that the mathematics in the measurement models is simply machinery to manage information in an evidentiary argument: to support inferences from what we see students say or do or make in this handful of particular situations to what they might know or do or ought to do next in other situations. They need to know that their decisions about game features, situations, rules, affordances, and players' actions all impact (1) the nature of the bits of evidence that can be obtained from game play; (2) how hard or easy it will be to identify and make sense of the evidence with models, and (3) the quality of the evidence that results. Game designers need to know about the structure of assessment arguments because it is at this level and through these concepts that game designers, domain specialists, and psychometricians can talk with each other about the nature and quality of evidence, each contributing vital information from their areas of expertise and seeing how their insights fit in with those of the others to the end of designing a good game, about the right stuff, providing useful assessment information.

5.3.1 Evidence-Centered Assessment Design

Messick (1994) succinctly laid out the structure of an assessment argument:

> [We] would begin by asking what complex of knowledge, skills, or other attribute should be assessed, presumably because they are tied to explicit or implicit objectives of instruction or are otherwise valued by society. Next, what behaviors or performances should reveal those constructs, and what tasks or situations should elicit those behaviors? (p. 16)

Psychometricians have been studying ways to move from Messick's guiding questions to more technical structures for assessment task design and analysis; that is, to provide language and tools for explicating the rationale that connects intuitions about students and domains with test construction and psychometric machinery.

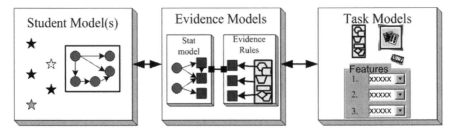

Fig. 5.3 The basic evidence-centered design models

The four-process assessment cycle in the previous section comes from a line of work called evidence-centered assessment design (ECD; Almond et al., 2002; Mislevy, Steinberg, & Almond, 2003; see related work by Conejo et al., 2004; Embretson, 1998; Luecht, 2006). We will use another representation from ECD in this section. We and others have used these tools in a number of applications, including Aspire, and we go into further detail on how they apply to game-based assessment design in Behrens et al. (in press).

Figure 5.3 depicts Messick's quote in terms of schemas for technical pieces that will follow. At the far left end, in the *Student Model*, are stars that represent the claims we would like to be able to make about students' capabilities from their performances. At the far right are *Task Models*, which lay out the key features of the situations that the students act in. The pieces that are between serve to structure our reasoning from what we observe in those situations to claims about students.[5] First, we will walk through them for familiar tests. The rest of the section then explores how they play out in game-based assessments, using illustrations from Aspire in its role as providing formative assessment as it engages students and supports problem-based learning. As mentioned earlier, the assessment design in Aspire builds on the assessment design work in the Packet Tracer simulation environment, which was developed to support problem-based learning and formative assessment. This conceptual level is where game designers and assessment designers can best work together to achieve reliability and validity, rather than at the technical level of the psychometric models through which these principles are made operational.

Ms. Smith wants to see how well her fifth-grade students can apply the fraction subtraction procedures they have been studying this week (claims about what they have learned). She writes a number of tasks that reflect the important features of the unit, using *Task Models* that are probably implicit in her case but can be made explicit as in Mayer (1981). The students solve the problems; their written answers are the work products. The *Evidence Model* is the bridge from tasks to claims. It contains two phases. The rectangle with jumbled shapes in the box called *evidence*

---

[5] These depictions and the narrative discussion of them set the stage for the more technical specifications that experts will need to address, such as measurement models, scoring algorithms, and generative task models. The interested reader is referred to Mislevy et al. (2003) and Mislevy and Riconscente (2006).

rules represents work products, and coming from it are squares that represent the salient features of each student's work—nuggets of evidence called *observable variables*. They would usually be just 1 or 0 for right or wrong for Ms. Smith's test. The *statistical model* accumulates the evidence across tasks, in this case just adding up the number of correct responses. A classical test theory (CTT) model considers the score to be a noisy version of how a student would do on average over many such tests, since his performance would vary due to the differences from one set of items to another and the inherent variation in peoples' performances on different occasions. In CTT, this variation is expressed in a "standard error of measurement." This single score and its standard error provide evidence for a claim about a student's proficiency with these kinds of items (the *Student Model*). The points are that scores should not be taken at face value, some are more trustworthy than others, and a statistical model tells us something about the quality of the information we are marshaling for our argument. We will say more shortly about more complex measurement models that extend these ideas in ways that can prove useful to game-based assessment.

The same conceptual student, evidence, and task models can be used to design more complex interactive activities like Aspire that can serve as a basis for assessment. These models structure the activities and the messages that comprise the assessment cycles we discussed previously. Examples from the process of developing Aspire and other games demonstrate how ECD principles serve to build a chain of reasoning from constructs to behaviors to tasks.

The technical domain covered in Aspire was driven by the Cisco Certified Entry Networking Technician (C-CENT) certification objectives. The tasks in the game were then designed to elicit behavior to provide evidence of these constructs. For example, in the area of troubleshooting, students at the C-CENT level must be able to troubleshoot basic IP addressing. Tasks were then designed to evoke this skill. For example, students are given a contract in which a physician indicates that three of four PCs in her office are not able to connect to the internet. The player enters the office and must diagnose and correct the problem (they should discover that the PCs are incorrectly addressed). Evidence rules were developed to identify features of the players' contracts to be evaluated to create observable variables. In the example above, the addresses of the PCs can be observed and scored, as can whether the PCs can send messages across the network. The currently used statistical model accumulates evidence about students' performance on the constructs mentioned above, namely, aspects of their proficiency with network cabling, configuration, and troubleshooting. These are the variables that constitute the student model—the terms in which the students and their instructors receive feedback in terms of claims about aspects of their capabilities in networking skills.

It is worth pointing out that the contracts inside the Aspire game build on the kinds of stand-alone simulation tasks that the Cisco Networking Academy has developed over the previous 10 years. Essential questions about features of task, simulation capabilities, evidence rules, and connections with instruction were studied in a program of research growing originally from hands-on performance assessments with real equipment, then the NetPASS simulation prototype (Williamson et al., 2004),

Cisco Network Simulator (CNS) tasks, and the Packet Tracer system for designing, scoring, and sharing simulation tasks (Frezzo et al., 2009). This work provided information about the features of situations and processes that lead to sound assessment in simulation-based tasks for computer networking skills, all of which could be capitalized on in the game. We will say more about this in the following discussion of measurement considerations in game-based assessment.

5.3.2   Reliability and Validity

Reliability and validity are core values in assessment. Messick (1994, p. 13) reminds us that "such basic assessment issues as validity, reliability, comparability, and fairness need to be uniformly addressed for all assessments because they are not just measurement principles, they are *social values* that have meaning and force outside of measurement wherever evaluative judgments and decisions are made" (emphasis original). One front of psychometric research is extending the technical machinery of measurement to the context of games, in order to address these criteria in the contexts of game-based assessment (Rupp, Gushta, Mislevy, & Shaffer, 2010).

In assessments like Ms. Smith's fractions test, psychometricians gauge reliability by the extent to which the different items tend to agree with one another in assessing students' overall proficiencies in the full set of items. The same formulas often do not apply to game-based assessments for several reasons. Different students may be acting in different situations, because their actions at one time point influence what they see and do at successive time points. They may be learning as they move through problems. Their actions may need to be modeled in terms of multiple aspects of knowledge and skill. The patterns we are interested in may not be simple overall proficiency—for example, patterns that signal misconceptions or inconsistencies in performance (Moss, 1994).

But we still care about reliability in a more general sense. Just how much support do we have from particular game performances? If the data were just a little different or if a different judge evaluated the performance, would our conclusions change dramatically or would they be pretty much the same? When more complicated measurement models are used to make sense of evidence about various aspects of a student's capability based on a complex performance, the model can provide indications of the strength of evidence in ways that properly reflect the performance and the claims (Mislevy, 2004). These more complicated models address the complexities in data listed in the previous paragraph. Among the models that can be pressed into service in games contexts are item response theory (Lord, 1980), diagnostic classification models (Rupp, Templin, & Henson, 2010), and Bayesian inference networks (Pearl, 1988). In each case, unobservable variables in the student model represent aspects of students' capabilities, and the specific form of the measurement model indicates how their actions depend probabilistically on the student model variables. Models can be assembled in pieces as the game proceeds in accordance with the situations a student encounters and the aspects of knowledge and skill that are called for in those situations. For example, Valerie Shute (2011) uses Bayesian inference networks to carry out continuous, unobtrusive, assessment in games and indicate the strength of evidence, where the data are more complicated patterns of performance. And in applications where no formal model is used and instead simple statistics are accumulated, their accuracy can be gauged using empirical methods based on the effects of repeatedly leaving different pieces of the data out of the calculations (Shao & Tu, 1995).

The exact methods for gauging reliability that can be applied in any given application are not essential for the game designer to know in detail, but having some measure of the value of the various nuggets of evidence is essential. Only with criteria that quantify the quality and the amount of evidence can designers investigate how different challenges, different interfaces, different mechanics, different work products, or different scoring rules will affect the evidence that a game provides.

Validity addresses the broader question of evidence beyond the game performance itself. We may find we have reliable evidence to describe students' capability to custom-design dragons in a game. But can they use the underlying principles to reason about breeding dogs or to explain genetics tests for prospective parents? A student exhibits twenty-first-century skills of communication and problem-solving in World of Warcraft™. Should we expect to see improved communication and problem-solving in science investigations, or on the football field, or in his summer job at the fast-food restaurant?

This question of transfer is a critical aspect of validity in game-based assessment. Part of the answer comes from design: a strong argument about the nature of knowledge and skills that are at issue, how the features of the assessment match key features of targeted real-world situations, and how the challenges and affordances of the assessment match those of the real-world situations. The other part comes from empirical validity studies: Do students for whom the assessment recommended certain instruction actually do better? Does success in the game actually correlate with better decision-making in real situations in the same domain or in different domains? Discussing the kinds of research that are needed, Fletcher and Morrison (2007) point to studies where training for pilots in one simulator produced superior performance in real planes, while training in a superficially similar simulator did not. The difference appeared to be fidelity to cognitive demands rather than physical similarities of actions and situations. Design choices drive validity, in ways that may not be obvious.

Assessment situations, no matter how authentic they seem, are never exactly the same as the real-world situations we ultimately care about. We want to make sure we include in the assessment settings those features that are most critical to eliciting the knowledge and skill we care about. Leaving them out threatens validity; Messick (1994) calls this "construct underrepresentation." We also want to avoid demands for knowledge and skill that are irrelevant to what we ultimately care about. Messick refers to this threat to validity as "construct-irrelevant sources of variance." Every member on the design team for a game-based assessment should read Messick's

(1994) short paper on task design and validity in complex tasks, "The interplay of evidence and consequences in the validation of performance assessments."

5.3.3 Implications of Assessment Principles for Design

The world of a game inevitably differs from the real world. Messick (1994) tells us that what matters is what is left in and what is left out. The features of situations in the domain that are critical for the student to interact with must be *in*. The means for the student to act on the system, or its affordances, for expressing choices must be *in*. And the reactions of the system to the student's actions that reflect the underlying principles of the system must be *in*. When we use a game in assessment, what should be *out* are features that require too much knowledge or skills that are not central for the aspects of performance we care about, or add irrelevant complexity. A balance will thus need to be struck between elements that produce evidence and elements that produce fun; fun must be *in* too, but some techniques in game experts' repertoire for emotional engagement (Koster, 2005) can generate fun without generating evidence.

Designers should consider the skill levels of their targeted audience when thinking about fidelity of the game. A system that faithfully captures the way experts view problems may not be accessible to beginning students (Roschelle, 1996). For assessing beginning students, it may be better to leave some components that are present in the real world out of the simulated world.

Working out ECD task models makes the design space explicit: What features are necessary in situations in order to evoke the targeted knowledge, skills, strategies, etc.? What ranges of variation are appropriate, and what complications and interactions can be moved up or down in demand as students work through challenges? The features and the complexity of the game environments can be tailored to the student using this information. Initial Aspire challenges involve simple networks and standard protocols, but they are designed so students must work through the principles of networking and the strategies of troubleshooting to solve them. Increasingly complex problems add new devices and more complicated configurations, always pushing students' frontiers.

The features of situations that a game can present, its affordances, and the game's responses will structure the Presentation Process and capture work products. To be a good assessment, various work products will need to provide evidence about students recognizing what is important, taking effective actions, and evaluating how well they are faring and then adjusting their actions. In the context of massively multiplayer online games (MMOGs), Nelson, Erlandson, and Denham (2011) discuss kinds of students' actions that can hold clues about their knowledge and skills: movement patterns, interactions with objects, and communications of several types to other real players or non-player characters, in or out of character, or representations they produce such as notes or reports. In game design, choices about placement of objects and game elements are largely based on aesthetics. However, in serious games, when we want to infer meaning from where students go and when, these choices must also be considered in terms of implications for evidentiary arguments. For example, if it is meaningful which area of a virtual environment a player chooses to explore first, the space might be designed so a naïve player would be drawn to a superficially attractive but less critical area. With careful consideration about the importance of such information in the design phase, it can be gathered and evaluated in Response Processing and accumulated in Summary Scoring.

In encapsulated multiple-choice questions, the item writer has built the key features into the situation. In performance tasks, some critical features come about only as a student works through the task. Two students troubleshooting the same network can work themselves into different situations. Games are often designed such that critical features only become available at certain points; for example, a player can only gain access to a sword after they have defeated the monster on level two. When we think about games as assessment, we must ensure that, if we need to observe an activity in order to get evidence about a particular aspect of their capabilities, all potential paths require players to engage in that activity. For example, if we want evidence about a player's capability to interview a stakeholder, then all paths must have this requirement somewhere along the line.

What is required is to be able to recognize essential features of key situations that may be different in their particulars for different students, and evaluate actions at this level of abstraction. Margolis and Clauser (2006) show how the National Board of Medical Examiners (NBME) evaluates unique paths of actions in the Primum® computer-simulated patient management problems. Psychometric research that leverages cognitive psychology to design and analyze encapsulated tasks[6] can be brought to bear on this challenge, as it brings the focus to meaningful features of recurring situations in the domain and recurring features of successful action.

Another way to ensure that needed evidence is gathered is to require some more focused work products. Examples are a summary report of stakeholders' concerns in *Urban Science* and an insurance form detailing interpretations of medical test results in a patient management problem. In a similar vein, some Cisco certification tests present multiple-choice items to answer after the candidate has had a chance to explore a network in an open-ended simulation.

Designers can expect to encounter trade-offs among a desire for fidelity, the goal of maximizing "fun," and an assessment constraint of securing evidence. Both optimal fidelity and the desire for "fun" imply openness in what examinees can do in a virtual environment and uninterrupted flow. Open-ended interaction with a virtual environment can provide rich work products (a log of every action and its time stamp), but more reliable and valid evidence might be obtained by requiring a more focused work product. When a player performs an action in a game environment, it can be difficult to infer whether they have acted through understanding or because of a construct-irrelevant game cue. More direct questioning may be required to be confident about inferences made about examinee knowledge, skills, and abilities.

---

[6] Susan Embretson's (1985) *Test design: Developments in psychology and psychometrics* was a watershed publication on this problem. Leighton and Gierl (2007) provide more recent examples.

5.3.4   The Bottom Line

To be a good assessment, a game-based assessment needs to be valid for the uses it is meant to inform with a level of accuracy those uses require (less for low-stakes and formative purposes, more for high-stakes decisions). Fleshing out student, evidence, and task models helps design teams make explicit their assessment arguments, which are ultimately the source of reliability and validity. The design process is informed by an understanding of the elements that need to be in simulation and game situations and what students must do to provide evidence about their thinking.

5.4   Address Key Assessment Constraints from the Beginning

To help ground the design of a simulation-based certification for architects, Katz (1994) carried out a study comparing expert and novice architects' solutions to a set of site design problems. The results yielded important insights for designing tasks for the new Architectural Registration Examination (ARE). They provide invaluable insights for the design of game-based assessments more broadly.

5.4.1   The Site Design Study

Katz's site design tasks consisted of a client's goal and a list of constraints. One such task asked subjects to design a new fire station, on the site of the old station, with 12 work spaces and ten constraints (e.g., "The Terrace shall be shaded from the noonday summer sun"). Katz found that the design process for these problems was invariably iterative. Experts and novices alike crafted an initial partial solution that met some constraints and modified it repeatedly to accommodate more constraints, always working from the provisional solution they had generated so far. Sometimes, both experts and novices had to scrap some work and back up to accommodate another constraint. The key difference was that the novices' rework was more often substantial and discarded much more previous work. What had happened was that the novices had encountered conflicting and hard-to-meet constraints only when they were further along, whereas the experts identified and addressed, even if provisionally, these challenges early on.

The lesson Katz drew for the ARE was that varying the number of constraints, the difficulty of meeting them, and the degree of conflict among them were cognitively relevant ways to control task difficulty. Systematically varying the numbers and kinds of constraints lets task designers produce easy and hard tasks, focus on targeted aspects of architectural proficiency, and write families of comparable tasks for each new test form (Bejar & Braun, 1999).

5.4.2 Implications for the Design Process

We can draw a more general lesson from Katz's study for designing game-based assessments: To first design a great game, then try to figure out "how to score it," is not a good way to design a game-based assessment. If Messick's guiding questions have not been addressed from the start, the prototype is susceptible to predictable problems:

- If the targeted aspects of knowledge and skill have not been identified explicitly, features of game situations and affordances for interaction may not be in place to effectively evoke them.
- For the same reason, features and affordances may impose demands for irrelevant knowledge and skill to a degree that degrades the relevant information.
- Even when relevant knowledge and skill are evoked, choices and actions may not effectively capture evidence about them. Log data about whatever actions are taken, however voluminous, is not necessarily good evidence about what we care about (Bennett & Bejar, 1998). Data mining iterating with design beats data mining alone.
- Even when work products hold evidentiary value about what we care about, we may not have effective strategies for identifying and evaluating the evidence—that is, the task level scoring process.
- Even when appropriate data are gathered and evidence can be identified, we may not be able to sort through interdependencies and synthesize evidence across performance with available statistical models—that is, the test level scoring process.

These potential problems reveal essential constraints that must be satisfied for any assessment to be reliable and valid. To address them only after many cycles of increasingly detailed tuning of game design constraints risks discarding a great deal of work, because game design requires many cycles of testing and revising, to tune the interactions of interfaces, modeling capabilities, flow of play, and feelings of engagement (Fullerton et al., 2008). Similarly, designing an assessment then trying to add game features will produce a poor assessment and a poor game.

A better approach for a new design is to start from the very beginning taking the key principles of assessment into account as well as those of simulations and games (Chung et al., 2008). Early discussions and paper prototypes need to include a skeletal evidence argument: What kinds of knowledge and skill do we care about and what kinds of things do we need to see students say, do, or make in what kinds of situation? How do we make sure that our game environment and rules provide this kind of environment and the right kinds of affordances?

Development cycles will continue to include interface and user experience testing, as in any game design project. But they should also include think-aloud solutions and small expert-novice studies to make sure that evidence is being captured about the targeted knowledge and skill. Provisional fitting of measurement models, if they are to be used, is explored early on as well. Trade-offs among game and assessment objectives can be anticipated. Certain less-central game choices may be restricted, for example, in order to provide stronger assessment evidence through more essential choices. Checkpoint work products may be introduced to make student rationales explicit, at the cost of slowing game play. And before any high-stakes uses are made, larger-scale pilot tests are carried out to verify that reliability and validity are sufficient for any decisions that are to be made from the results.

We have argued that it is best to design game-based assessments with game constraints and assessment constraints both addressed from the beginning. That said, there will inevitably be projects that start with existing simulations and games, especially simulations and games that have been designed for learning. If they have been designed well, the designers have considered questions of situational features and interactions that help users learn targeted skills. Because of the natural overlap between situations that stimulate learning and situations that provide evidence of learning, such products can provide a jump start toward assessment. It should not be assumed, though, that even if an environment has been optimized for learning, it will make a good assessment with just an overlay of measurement machinery. We should anticipate development cycles that revise situation features, affordances, and interactions, in order to provide informative and interpretable work products, evaluation algorithms, and observable variables. When measurement models are needed, we should expect iteration here too: not just building and testing the measurement models but also insights that feed back to simulation features and work products. Indicators of reliability and validity, defined appropriately to the patterns being modeled and the purposes of the assessment, provide criteria for evaluating these revisions.

5.4.3   The Bottom Line

To succeed, a game-based assessment must satisfy constraints that come from three rather different sources. It must get the principles of learning and acting in the domain right. Students need to be doing the right kinds of things in the right kinds of situations, building around the right kinds of activity patterns with the right kinds of thinking. It must get the game principles right. It must provide situations and challenges that pull the student in, keep her at the edge of her capabilities, and provide feedback and rewards that keep her engaged. And it must get the assessment right. A coherent argument must exist between what the student does in what situations and why that tells us about what they know and can do beyond the immediate game-world situations. An effective design process will address key constraints across these three sources from the start, loosely at first and proceeding iteratively with an eye toward satisfying them all.

5.5 Discussion

Designing assessments and designing games are both challenging endeavors in their own right. Game-based assessments face the combination of constraints across perspectives. What is more, few people are experts in all of the domains whose perspectives and experience must come together. Of course it is hard! What are we to do?

Three interweaving lines of work ease the way. The first is worked-through examples. Some pioneering examples take a long time. The NBME began working with computer simulations for assessing patient management skills more than 30 years before Primum® cases became part of the United States Medical Licensing Examination. Other examples, like the games in *Mavis Beacon Teaches Typing*, are very simple. We can learn from all kinds of examples. Each one helps us think in concrete terms about abstract issues of fidelity and flow, reliability and validity, and competing constraints and multiple objectives. We see what these terms come to mean in each particular project. We learn what mechanisms and strategies the design team used to balance game and assessment perspectives in their unique setting. Recognizing the value of this approach, the MacArthur Foundation has supported the Worked Examples website (http://workedexamples.org/) for interactive learning (Barab, Dodge, & Gee, in press). Several examples there illustrate the interplay of games with assessment.

The second line of work is theory. What we mean by this is discovering and making explicit the concepts and principles that underlie simulation, game, and assessment design, so that understanding can be shared across unique exemplars. Salen and Zimmerman's (2004) *Rules of Play: Game Design Fundamentals* exemplifies this kind of work for games. The ECD framework does so for assessment. Conceptual papers that bridge the fields are particularly needed. Such a perspective helps us recognize profound similarities across instances that differ on the surface, deepening our understanding of the examples and better preparing us for new projects than the examples alone can do. Perhaps most importantly, they begin to provide a language that experts from different fields can use to work with one another. Examples of an ECD approach to the design of simulation-based assessments appear in Behrens et al. (in press), Clarke-Midura and Dede (2010), Mislevy, Steinberg, Breyer, Johnson, and Almond (2002), and Williamson et al. (2004). Examples in game-based assessment appear in Nelson et al. (2011), Shaffer et al. (2009), and Shute (2011).

The third line is producing reusable elements for designing and implementing game-based assessments. Theory helps us think about what we are doing, and examples show us how others have done it. Reusable pieces, both conceptual and mechanical, help us work more efficiently. These are not new ideas. At the conceptual level, Alexander, Ishikawa, and Silverstein (1977) introduced design patterns in architecture to describe recurring problems in a general form, lay out strategies for tackling them, and providing talked-through examples. Gamma, Helm, Johnson, and Vlissides (1994) brought the approach to software engineering. Extending the idea to assessment design, the Principled Assessment Design for Inquiry (PADI) project developed design patterns to help test developers target hard-to-assess aspects of science such as systems thinking (Cheng, Ructtinger, Fujii, & Mislevy, 2010) and model-based reasoning (Mislevy, Riconscente, & Rutstein, 2009) in ways that support game design in these areas.

Many game editing programs are available for various aspects of development to help designers focus their energies on content and interaction rather than low-level programming. Just as game mechanics are available for reuse in environments that may look quite different on the surface, so too are forms of work products and evaluation strategies for assessment (e.g., Scalise & Gifford, 2006) and statistical model building blocks (e.g., Netica[7]) that can be pressed into service when games are used as assessments. Designers who know what styles of interaction support efficient evaluation can use them early on, rather than finding out down the line that the styles they happened to use did not produce good evidence. Design patterns, editing environments, and reusable objects are available and familiar to practitioners in the domains of games and assessments. These tools have lessons from experience and design strategies built into them for tackling constraints in a given domain. The need to deal jointly with constraints across domains will be supported by hybrid approaches, such as Vendlinski, Baker, and Niemi's (2008) (conceptual level) templates and (implementation level) objects for authoring simulation-based problem-solving assessments. Similarly, Mislevy et al. (2002) provided schemas for recurring situations around which task authors could write unique problem-solving cases for dental hygiene students in forms that linked to reusable task-scoring and test-scoring machinery.

The technological and psychological foundations for game-based assessment are now in place (Quellmalz & Pellegrino, 2009). With a variety of examples and the beginnings of theory, we now endeavor to develop practices to apply the ideas efficiently and validly. A shared space of language, principles, and tools that integrate the big ideas across the contributing domains is key to scaling up.

Acknowledgments The work reported here was supported in part by a research contract from Cisco Systems, Inc., to the University of Maryland, College Park, and the Center for Advanced Technology in Schools (CATS), PR/Award Number R305C080015, as administered by the Institute of Education Sciences, U.S. Department of Education. The findings and opinions expressed in this report are those of the authors and do not necessarily reflect the positions or policies of Cisco, the CATS, the National Center for Education Research (NCER), the Institute of Education Sciences (IES), or the U.S. Department of Education.

References

Alexander, C., Ishikawa, S., & Silverstein, M. (1977). *A pattern language: Towns, buildings, construction*. New York: Oxford University Press.
Almond, R. G., Steinberg, L. S., & Mislevy, R. J. (2002). Enhancing the design and delivery of assessment systems: A four-process architecture. *Journal of Technology, Learning, and*

---

[7] http://www.norsys.com. Downloaded May 1, 2011.

Assessment, 1(5). Retrieved May 1, 2011, from http://www.bc.edu/research/intasc/jtla/journal/v1n5.shtml.

Bagley, E., & Shaffer, D. W. (2009). When people get in the way: Promoting civic thinking through epistemic gameplay. *International Journal of Gaming and Computer-mediated Simulations, 1*, 36–52.

Barab, S. A., Dodge, T., & Gee, J. P. (in press). The worked example: Invitational scholarship in service of an emerging field. *Educational Researcher.*

Behrens, J. T., Frezzo, D. C., Mislevy, R. J., Kroopnick, M., & Wise, D. (2007). Structural, functional, and semiotic symmetries in simulation-based games and assessments. In E. L. Baker, J. Dickieson, W. Wulfeck, & H. F. O'Neil (Eds.), *Assessment of problem solving using simulations* (pp. 59–80). New York: Erlbaum.

Behrens, J. T., Mislevy, R. J., Bauer, M., Williamson, D. M., & Levy, R. (2004). Introduction to evidence centered design and lessons learned from its application in a global e-learning program. *International Journal of Testing, 4*, 295–301.

Behrens, J. T., Mislevy, R. J., DiCerbo, K. E., & Levy, R. (2012). An evidence centered design for learning and assessment in the digital world. In M. C. Mayrath, J. Clarke-Midura, & D. Robinson (Eds.), *Technology-based assessments for 21st century skills: Theoretical and practical implications from modern research* (pp. 13–53). Charlotte, NC: Information Age.

Bejar, I. I., & Braun, H. (1999). *Architectural simulations: From research to implementation. Final report to the National Council of Architectural Registration Boards (ETS RM-99-2)*. Princeton, NJ: Educational Testing Service.

Bennett, R. E., & Bejar, I. I. (1998). Validity and automated scoring: It's not only the scoring. *Educational Measurement: Issues and Practice, 17*(4), 9–17.

Cheng, B. H., Ructtinger, L., Fujii, R., & Mislevy, R. (2010). *Assessing systems thinking and complexity in science (Large-Scale Assessment Technical Report 7)*. Menlo Park, CA: SRI International.

Chi, M. T. H., Glaser, R., & Farr, M. J. (Eds.). (1988). *The nature of expertise*. Hillsdale, NJ: Erlbaum.

Chung, G. K. W. K., Baker, E. L., Delacruz, G. C., Bewley, W. L., Elmore, J., & Seely, B. (2008). A computational approach to authoring problem-solving assessments. In E. L. Baker, J. Dickieson, W. Wulfeck, & H. F. O'Neil (Eds.), *Assessment of problem solving using simulations* (pp. 289–307). Mahwah, NJ: Erlbaum.

Clarke-Midura, J., & Dede, C. (2010). Assessment, technology, and change. *Journal of Research on Technology in Education, 42*, 309–328.

Claxton, G. (2002). Education for the learning age: A sociocultural approach to learning to learn. In G. Wells & G. Claxton (Eds.), *Learning for life in the 21st century* (pp. 19–33). Oxford, UK: Blackwell.

Conejo, R., Guzmán, E., Millán, E., Trella, M., Pérez-De-La-Cruz, J. L., & Ríos, A. (2004). A web-based tool for adaptive testing. *International Journal of Artificial Intelligence in Education, 14*, 29–61.

Csíkszentmihályi, M. (1975). *Beyond boredom and anxiety*. San Francisco, CA: Jossey-Bass.

Embretson, S. E. (Ed.). (1985). *Test design: Developments in psychology and psychometrics*. Orlando: Academic.

Embretson, S. E. (1998). A cognitive design system approach to generating valid tests: Application to abstract reasoning. *Psychological Methods, 3*, 380–396.

Ericsson, A. K., Charness, N., Feltovich, P., & Hoffman, R. R. (2006). *Cambridge handbook on expertise and expert performance*. Cambridge, UK: Cambridge University Press.

Fletcher, J. D., & Morrison, J. E. (2007). Representing cognition in games and simulations. In E. Baker, J. Dickieson, W. Wulfeck, & H. O'Neil (Eds.), *Assessment of problem solving using simulations* (pp. 107–137). New York: Lawrence Erlbaum.

Frezzo, D. C. (2009). *Using activity theory to understand the role of a simulation-based interactive learning environment in a computer networking course*. Doctoral dissertation, ProQuest. Retrieved August 29, 2011, from http://gradworks.umi.com/33/74/3374268.html.

Frezzo, D. C., Behrens, J. T., & Mislevy, R. J. (2009). Design patterns for learning and assessment: Facilitating the introduction of a complex simulation-based learning environment into a community of instructors. *The Journal of Science Education and Technology*. Retrieved April 10, 2012, from Springer Open Access http://www.springerlink.com/content/566p6g4307405346/.

Fullerton, T., Swain, C., & Hoffman, S. S. (2008). *Game design workshop: Designing, prototyping, and playtesting games* (2nd ed.). Burlington, MA: Morgan Kaufmann.

Gamma, E., Helm, R., Johnson, R., & Vlissides, J. (1994). *Design patterns*. Reading, MA: Addison-Wesley.

Gee, J. P. (2003). *What video games have to teach us about learning and literacy*. New York: Palgrave/Macmillan.

Greeno, J. G. (1998). The situativity of knowing, learning, and research. *American Psychologist, 53*, 5–26.

Katz, I. R. (1994). Coping with the complexity of design: Avoiding conflicts and prioritizing constraints. In A. Ram, N. Nersessian, & M. Recker (Eds.), *Proceedings of the sixteenth annual meeting of the Cognitive Science Society* (pp. 485–489). Mahwah, NJ: Erlbaum.

Koster, R. (2005). *A theory of fun for game design*. Scottsdale, AZ: Paraglyph.

Lave, J., & Wenger, E. (1991). *Situated learning: Legitimate peripheral participation*. Cambridge: Cambridge University Press.

Leighton, J., & Gierl, M. (Eds.). (2007). *Cognitive diagnostic assessment for education: Theory and applications*. New York, NY: Cambridge University Press.

Levy, R., Behrens, J. T., & Mislevy, R. J. (2006). Variations in adaptive testing and their online leverage points. In D. D. Williams, S. L. Howell, & M. Hricko (Eds.), *Online assessment, measurement, and evaluation* (pp. 180–202). Hershey, PA: Information Science Publishing.

Loftus, E. F., & Loftus, G. R. (1983). *Mind at play: The psychology of video games*. New York: Basic Books.

Lord, F. M. (1980). *Applications of item response theory to practical testing problems*. Mahwah, NJ: Erlbaum.

Luecht, R. M. (2006). *Assessment engineering: An emerging discipline*. Paper presented in the Centre for Research in Applied Measurement and Evaluation, University of Alberta, Edmonton.

Malone, T. W. (1981). What makes computer games fun? *Byte, 6*, 258–277.

Margolis, M. J., & Clauser, B. E. (2006). A regression-based procedure for automated scoring of a complex medical performance assessment. In D. M. Williamson, R. J. Mislevy, & I. I. Bejar (Eds.), *Automated scoring for complex tasks in computer-based testing* (pp. 123–167). Hillsdale, NJ: Lawrence Erlbaum.

Mayer, R. E. (1981). Frequency norms and structural analysis of algebra story problems into families, categories, and templates. *International Science, 10*, 135–175.

Messick, S. (1994). The interplay of evidence and consequences in the validation of performance assessments. *Educational Researcher, 23*(2), 13–23.

Mislevy, R. J. (2004). Can there be reliability without "reliability"? *Journal of Educational and Behavioral Statistics, 29*, 241–244.

Mislevy, R. J., & Riconscente, M. M. (2006). Evidence-centered assessment design: Layers, concepts, and terminology. In S. Downing & T. Haladyna (Eds.), *Handbook of test development* (pp. 61–90). Mahwah, NJ: Erlbaum.

Mislevy, R. J., Riconscente, M. M., & Rutstein, D. W. (2009). *Design patterns for assessing model-based reasoning (Large-Scale Assessment Technical Report 6)*. Menlo Park, CA: SRI International.

Mislevy, R. J., Steinberg, L. S., & Almond, R. A. (2003). On the structure of educational assessments. *Measurement: Interdisciplinary Research and Perspectives, 1*, 3–67.

Mislevy, R. J., Steinberg, L. S., Breyer, F. J., Johnson, L., & Almond, R. A. (2002). Making sense of data from complex assessments. *Applied Measurement in Education, 15*, 363–378.

Moss, P. (1994). Can there be validity without reliability? *Educational Researcher, 23*(2), 5–12.

Nelson, B. C., Erlandson, B., & Denham, A. (2011). Global channels of evidence for learning and assessment in complex game environments. *British Journal of Educational Technology, 42*, 88–100.

Pausch, R., Gold, R., Skelly, T., & Thiel, D. (1994). What HCI designers can learn from video game designers. In *Conference on human factors in computer systems* (pp. 177–178). Boston, MA: ACM.

Pearl, J. (1988). *Probabilistic reasoning in intelligent systems: Networks of plausible inference*. San Mateo, CA: Kaufmann.

Quellmalz, E., & Pellegrino, J. W. (2009). Technology and testing. *Science, 323*, 75–79.
Rollings, A., & Morris, D. (2000). *Game architecture and design*. Scottsdale, AZ: Coriolis.
Roschelle, J. (1996). Designing for cognitive communication: Epistemic fidelity or mediating collaborative inquiry? In D. L. Day & D. K. Kovacs (Eds.), *Computers communication and mental models* (pp. 13–25). Bristol, PA: Taylor and Francis.
Rupp, A., Gushta, M., Mislevy, R. J., & Shaffer, D. W. (2010). Evidence-centered design of epistemic games: Measurement principles for complex learning environments. *Journal of Technology, Learning, and Assessment, 8*(4). Retrieved April 10, 2012, from http://ejournals.bc.edu/ojs/index.php/jtla/article/download/1623/1467.
Rupp, A., Templin, J., & Henson, R. (2010). *Diagnostic measurement: Theory, methods, and applications*. New York, NY: Guilford.
Salen, K., & Zimmerman, E. (2004). *Rules of play: Game design fundamentals*. Cambridge: MIT.
Salthouse, T. A. (1991). Expertise as the circumvention of human processing limitations. In K. A. Ericcson & J. Smith (Eds.), *Toward a general theory of expertise* (pp. 286–300). Cambridge, UK: Cambridge University Press.
Scalise, K., & Gifford, B. (2006). Computer-based assessment in E-learning: A framework for constructing "Intermediate Constraint" questions and tasks for technology platforms. *Journal of Technology, Learning, and Assessment, 4*(6). Retrieved July 17, 2009, from http://ejournals.bc.edu/ojs/index.php/jtla/article/view/1653/1495.
Schmit, M. J., & Ryan, A. (1992). Test-taking dispositions: A missing link? *Journal of Applied Psychology, 77*, 629–637.
Schwartz, D. L., & Arena, D. (2009). *Choice-based assessments for the digital age*. Palo Alto: Stanford University.
Shaffer, D. W. (2006). *How computer games help children learn*. New York: Palgrave/Macmillan.
Shaffer, D. W., & Gee, J. P. (2012). The Right Kind of GATE: Computer games and the future of assessment. In M. Mayrath, J. Clarke-Midura, & D. H. Robinson (Eds.), *Technology-based assessments for 21st century skills: Theoretical and practical implications from modern research* (pp. 211–228). Charlotte: Information Age Publishing.
Shaffer, D. W., Hatfield, D., Svarovsky, G. N., Nash, P., Nulty, A., Bagley, E., et al. (2009). Epistemic network analysis: A prototype for 21st century assessment of learning. *The International Journal of Learning and Media, 1*, 33–53.
Shao, J., & Tu, D. (1995). *The jackknife and bootstrap*. New York: Springer.
Shute, V. J. (2011). Stealth assessment in computer-based games to support learning. In S. Tobias & J. D. Fletcher (Eds.), *Computer games and instruction* (pp. 503–524). Charlotte, NC: Information Age Publishers.
Shute, V. J., & Torres, R. (2012). Where streams converge: Using evidence-centered design to assess Quest to Learn. In M. Mayrath, J. Clarke-Midura, & D. H. Robinson (Eds.), *Technology-based assessments for 21st century skills: Theoretical and practical implications from modern research* (pp. 91–204). Charlotte, NC: Information Age Publishing.
Sundre, D. L., & Wise, S. L. (2003). *'Motivation filtering': An exploration of the impact of low examinee motivation on the psychometric quality of tests*. Paper presented at the annual meeting of the National Council on Measurement in Education, Chicago.
Vendlinski, T. P., Baker, E. L., & Niemi, D. (2008). Templates and objects in authoring problem solving assessments. In E. L. Baker, J. Dickieson, W. Wulfeck, & H. F. O'Neil (Eds.), *Assessment of problem solving using simulations* (pp. 309–333). New York: Erlbaum.
Vygotsky, L. S. (1978). *Mind and society: The development of higher psychological processes*. Cambridge, MA: Harvard University Press.
Wainer, H., Dorans, N. J., Flaugher, R., Green, B. F., Mislevy, R. J., Steinberg, L., et al. (2000). *Computerized adaptive testing: A primer* (2nd ed.). Hillsdale, NJ: Lawrence Erlbaum.
Wertsch, J. (1998). *Mind as action*. New York: Oxford University Press.
Williamson, D. M., Bauer, M., Steinberg, L. S., Mislevy, R. J., Behrens, J. T., & DeMark, S. (2004). Design rationale for a complex performance assessment. *International Journal of Measurement, 4*, 303–332.

Part II
Technological and Methodological Innovations for Assessing Game-Based Learning

Chapter 6
Patterns of Game Playing Behavior as Indicators of Mastery

Klaus P. Jantke

6.1 There Is No Digital Games Science

The present chapter has a rather narrow focus: the discussion of a few basic concepts and the derivation of practical consequences from the proposed conceptualizations and concept revisions, respectively.

In 2005, Costikyan has been bewailing missing terminologies of digital games, game design, and game playing from a practitioner's point of view: "I have no words & I must design" (Costikyan, 2005). Philips (2006) has made explicit the badly missing essentials of any language of discourse about digital games: "It is not only for lack of trying that a good vocabulary for describing game experiences does not exist. It is downright hard to describe video games and experience of playing them" (ibid., p. 22).

Every science needs a certain terminology for describing phenomena, for formulating hypotheses, for agreement and contradiction. For digital games, there is no language of discourse—there is not yet any digital games science.

6.2 The Serious Games Confusion

Writing about game-based learning, in general, and about assessment in game-based learning, in particular, does apparently rely on the assumption that there are games that are suitable for learning—the concept of a serious game arises, a term first introduced by Abt in 1970 (Abt, 1970). Since the early days of game-based learning,

K.P. Jantke (✉)
Children's Media Department, Fraunhofer IDMT, Kindermedienzentrum,
Erich-Kästner-Straße 1a, Erfurt 99094, Germany
e-mail: klaus.jantke@idmt.fraunhofer.de

D. Ifenthaler et al. (eds.), *Assessment in Game-Based Learning: Foundations,*
Innovations, and Perspectives, DOI 10.1007/978-1-4614-3546-4_6,
© Springer Science+Business Media New York 2012

there are authors trying to distinguish those games they are willing to aim at and to call serious games. Definitions vary largely.

Whatever definition is preferred, it should be useful or—at least and a bit less ambitious—it should be usable. Given a particular game, the definition in use should allow to determine whether or not this particular game meets the defining conditions and, thus, is a serious game, at least to some extent.

Ritterfeld, Cody, and Vorderer (2009) characterize serious games as "any form of interactive computer-based game software for one or multiple players to be used on any platform and that has been developed with the intention to be more than entertainment" (ibid., p. 6). Jantke and Gaudl (2010) discuss the problems with such a definition in some detail. Assume you are relying on the perspective of Ritterfeld et al. When you are presented some new game, for deciding whether or not one should consider this as a serious game, there is no need for a closer look at the game, to start the game, or even to play the game. Instead, you need to contact the designers and/or developers to find out their intentions which are the defining characteristics.

In contrast, the author—in accordance with Sawyer and Smith (2009)—agrees that literally every game is a serious game. Even those games that are surely developed without any intention such as education may be used for serious purposes. On the one hand, naturally, every digital game may serve as a basis for studying a variety of aspects of computer science such as data structures, programming, and interface design. On the other hand, games frequently allow for many further specific in-depth investigations seriously.

For illustration, consider the game "Left Behind: Eternal Forces" published by Inspired Media Entertainment (formerly Left Behind Games) in 2006. This is a game propagating particular religious positions in a very fundamentalist way. The game is worth to be considered as learning material in high school courses of ethics, e.g., in this way serving as a serious game.

Let us take "Paraworld" (Deep Silver, 2006) as another illustration. The virtual co-occurrence of humans and dinosaurs is essential to the game play. Thus, one may use the game in school when dealing with ages.

Digital games such as "Deus Ex" (Ion Storm, 2000), "Black & White" (Lionhead Studios, 2001), "Fahrenheit" (Quantic Dream, 2005), and "Fable" (Lionhead, 2004), e.g., may be used to support a variety of educational topics in coaching executive staff using their particular conflicts in game play; see Helm and Theis (2009) for further studies of game-based coaching.

Whatever digital game one takes into account, it may be used for the one or the other serious purpose. The only questions are:

- For which purpose (discipline, problem, etc.) the game shall be employed?
- Which particular audience shall be addresses for game-based learning?
- What are possible scenarios of game-based learning or training?

Every game is a serious game in the appropriate context, as stressed in (Jantke, 2011), where the idea named *the art of context* has been outlined (see also Lampert, Schwinge, and Tolks (2009) for a very specific perspective at context).

6.3 The Art of Context

When learning about the "Super Columbine Massacre Role Playing Game" (Danny Ledonne, 2005), the majority of people are shocked or embarrassed. You can replay the massacre at the Columbine High School in Littleton, CO on April 20, 1999. And you can virtually shoot as many of your virtual school mates as you like. This shall be a game? Never!

When you put this game into an appropriate context, it really becomes a valuable peace of art and it may be used for a variety of serious purposes. Naturally, you need to offer opportunities of reflection and discussion to the human players, especially to the younger and less experienced. Without such a context, one should not make the game accessible to children.

Many games that have been intended to be serious badly failed because the designers, the developers, and the publishers completely missed the key issue—to design the game together with an appropriate context.

Games such as "GENIUS: Unternehmen Physik" (RADON Labs, 2004) and "GENIUS: Task Force Biologie" (RADON Labs, 2005) are designed and developed with no suitable context in mind. In classes, they are not playable. And it remains open how teachers should use them as educational tools. Investigations (Jantke, 2007) have been demonstrating that these games fail.

When digital games are seen and developed in particular contexts, phenomena of relevance to the game effect and impact will frequently reflect certain contextual relations. What is of interest from the serious games perspective does very likely unfold in the conditions of the context.

There have been developed taxonomic concepts (Jantke & Gaudl, 2010) which relate game play to the environment. For illustration, there is the taxonomic dimension of extra game play describing the anticipated necessity to interrupt game playing for particular purposes such as, e.g., gathering information or performing extra game activities.

There are several patterns beyond the limits of conventional game play. The occurrence of (instances of) those patterns correlates with mastering the game mechanics, with pleasure or frustration, respectively, when playing the game.

6.4 Patterns of Experience Exemplified

Before the author's rather formal approach to concepts of patterns in game playing experience is introduced subsequently, some short illustration by means of a successful commercial game is intended to ease the reader's access to the following abstractions and formalizations.

"Gray Matter" (Wizarbox, 2010) is a point & click adventure with a quite appealing story written by Jane Jensen. One of the peculiarities of the game is that the human player acts as an illusionist performing several tricks of the mind magic category (Lemezma, 2003). Those tricks, if they would be performed in

Fig. 6.1 Appearance of (an initial part of) a pattern instance in playing "Gray Matter"

real life, were requiring particular motor skills and related training as well as some convincing style of the magician's performance and a certain charisma to motivate an audience to suspend their mistrust.

When playing the digital game on your computer, instead, you move the mouse cursor, push mouse buttons and, perhaps, hit the one or the other key.

For successfully playing "Gray Matter," you need more than a dozen times to put some of the virtual characters of the game world off the scent. When opportunity knocks, the mouse cursor changes its form to a magic hat as shown in the upper right part of Fig. 6.1. If the player responds with a click, this initiates a certain sequence of (inter-)actions as sketched in the left lower part of Fig. 6.1. It follows a short utterance of your in-game character followed by an opening of a magic book. In Fig. 6.1, the left screenshot depicts a situation in which the cursor changes when moved over a particular person and the right screenshot shows the opened grimoire.

The following game play is rather straightforward, at least, seen on a sufficiently abstract level. It is based on preceding game play during which you learned something particular about the in-game character to be deceived. You need to select the right trick first (let us abbreviate this by the term [st]). For this purpose, you turn pages of the magic book to find some trick ([tp]), the display of which includes a script of subsequent actions to be performed. There is some menu for scheduling the concrete actions you are anticipating. When the right trick has been selected, the menu opens automatically ([mo]). The player has to generate a script of actions—in analogy to the script shown in the magic book—to be executed for outwitting the in-game character ([gs]). A magic wand serves as a button to start the execution of your trick ([mw]). As long as the script is not yet correct, pushing the magic wand

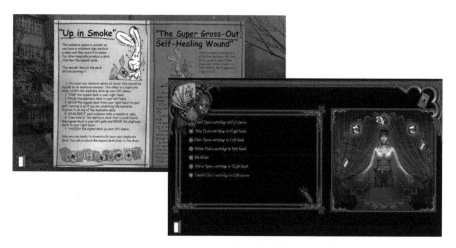

Fig. 6.2 Scripting a trick (on the *right*) according to a grimoire template (on the *left*)

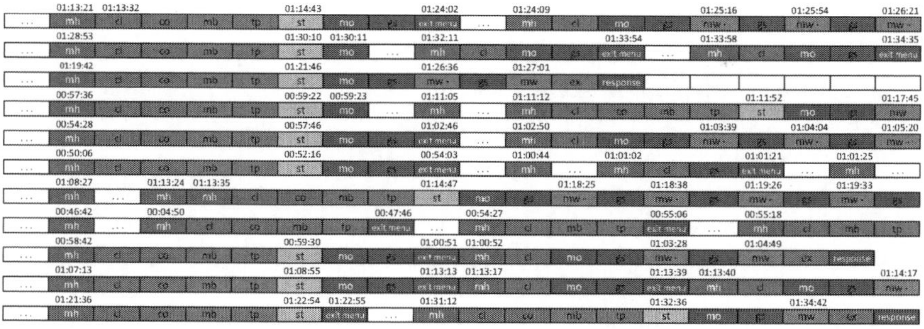

Fig. 6.3 Excerpts from recorded game play of 11 subjects performing some trick

button brings you back to the scripting interface ([mw-], as in Fig. 6.3, the top string, e.g.,). If the trick is finally scripted correctly, performing [mw] by pushing the magic wand results in an execution of the sequence of actions setup ([ex]).

Let us abbreviate the actions illustrated by means of the preceding figure by [mh], [cl], [co], and [mb] for the change of the cursor to the magic hat, for clicking on the corresponding in-game character, the comment which is generated in response, and for the opening of the magic book, respectively.

What happens during optimal game play may be written as some string [mh] [cl] [co] [mb] [tp] [st] [mo] [gs] [mw] [ex]. Different terminologies may lead to varying structures—an issue of layered languages of ludology (Fig. 6.3).

The actions of the script in the magic book (left screenshot in the Fig. 6.2) need to be interpreted in terms of the present situation (right screenshot). Players operate the menu for scripting their trick (as shown on the right) through drag and drop actions. The page of the magic book is not in sight. This makes the writing of a script a bit error-prone and, perhaps, frustrating to those players who depend on trial and error.

The above-described quest type of acting as an illusionist is reflected by the games magazines in different ways. Due to a missing systematic background, most utterances miss the point. Some call the mentioned quest type a *felicitous alternation* (Brehme, 2010) and others quite euphorically name it *the most innovative idea for quests* (Klinge, 2011) in adventure games.

But does it really work? Do players experience to act as an illusionist performing tricks, impressing an audience and fooling others? The author has undertaken some qualitative study—details are beyond the limits of this chapter which, instead, concentrates on the underlying concepts—which reveals that players never experience being a deceiver who deceives, being a trickster who tricks, being an illusionist or a magician. Instead, the players are facing the task of writing some short script according to some template. They understand that the script is listing essential actions of some trick and, at best, they are learning the sequence of actions.

The game play of those who succeed in learning the action sequences of a trick differs in a syntactically recognizable way from other cases in which players poke around in the dark.

In the author's study, human players have been playing "Gray Matter" for about 2:40–2:50 h. After about 45–85 min, everyone has been for the first time experiencing the turn of the mouse cursor into a magic hat. The corresponding game play is represented as a string of actions as shown in Fig. 6.3 where some excerpts from 11 different game plays are on display. Subsequently, the first fully performed trick has been distilled automatically.

Time, in general, is no indicator of anything interesting when studying tricks in "Gray Matter." Some start trick performance earlier, others later. Some need less time, others more. In contrast to time, the structure of action sequences is telling and reflects the human experience of success or failure.

As discussed above, there is an optimal action sequence of length 10. From these 11 subjects investigated, 5 succeeded with 10–12 steps of play. Those reflect clearly that they have learned something about mind magic. All other subjects spent between 18 and 31 steps (average 23.5) with clearly less learning success. Much knowledge is hiding in game playing sequences.

6.5   Patterns of Game Playing Experience

The particular string [mh] [cl] [co] [mb] [tp] [st] [mo] [gs] [mw] [ex] of abstractly described game play investigated in the preceding section is seen as (an instance of) something more general named *a pattern*.

The pattern concept did appear in science with Alexander's work, 1979, characterizing essential structural features in architecture the repeated appearance of which is seen fundamental to the functioning of a building. However instructive and useful, these pattern concepts are still quite vague and leave some space for (mis)interpretations (Alexander, 1979).

Subsequently, pattern concepts have been mostly developed and used for the systematization of design and specification processes ranging from software technology, in general, through interaction design (Borchers, 2001) to digital games design (Björk & Holopainen, 2005), in particular.

Those approaches are basically characterized by the imagination of a human designer who wants to gain control over highly complex processes and, for this purpose, intends to rely on former experience which has been somehow condensed in so-called design patterns.

In contrast, Angluin (1980) asks for regularities that show in processes. She studies the problem of extracting those regularities from observations. Even more ambitiously, she asks for algorithms that perform such a pattern extraction automatically—a case of computational learning (Jain, Osherson, Royer, & Sharma, 1999). This approach does perfectly meet the needs of unobtrusive media studies.

In Jantke (2008) an approach has been developed to the use of patterns in the sense of Angluin (1980) for studies on the impact of playing games. Essentially, you observe game playing and record both the unfolding play and certain aspects of the human response. In particular, the response may be seen on a qualitative level such as face expression, e.g., or may be measured by means of psychophysiological methods (Kivikangas et al., 2010).

The so-called *patterns experience evaluation program* (Jantke, 2009) relies on the assumption that there is something in game playing that may cause effects and that is potentially observable. Without such an assumption, there is no hope for any scientific study into the impact of game playing. Under the assumption of observability, one may set up experiments in which human players are playing games and game play is continuously recorded. The recorded data structures may contain regularities which can be taken as a basis of further investigation. Jantke's previous work on patterns in game playing is still rather preliminary. The present chapter is intended to provide the first thorough introduction of the author's formal patterns approach.

Pattern approaches depend on the level of granularity on which game play shall be represented and investigated (Lenerz, 2009). For every particular study, a particular representational terminology is assumed.

6.6 Fundamentals of a Playing Science

Beyond the limits of examples such as in Sect. 6.4 of the present chapter, there is a need to clarify more thoroughly what patterns are and where their instances may occur.

Whenever we speak about game playing, we need to decide what to speak about and what to ignore. This is at the same time a decision about the level of granularity and about the terminology to describe what happens during game play. When playing the PS2 game "Shadow of the Colossus" (Sony Computer Entertainment, 2005), for instance, it makes a difference to speak about pressing the Δ button on the game pad or mounting a horse. When the human player's motor skills necessary to master games such as "Soul Calibur" (Namco, 1998) are in focus, it is appropriate to describe the game play on the level of buttons pushed. A slightly higher level of combinations of finger movements is adequate, e.g., if so-called clothing destruction in "Soul Calibur IV" (Namco, 2008) is under consideration. As soon as the story experienced by a human player comes into focus, higher levels of description may be more appropriate. There are several layers in between. Think, for illustration, about moments of being frightened when playing "Fahrenheit" (Quantic Dream, 2005). This happened, for sure, for the first time when you saw in your bathroom mirror the face of the man you killed shortly before. Any description of this tiny game playing sequence is above the level of key strokes, but far below story telling.

Very formally speaking, there is always a certain vocabulary of atomic expressions used for describing sequences of game playing. We summarize the actions taken into account by means of some finite set M; the letter shall resemble the term *moves*. From a practical point of view, there is no need to determine M in advance. The elements of M may be accumulated when game playing descriptions are generated. However, from the perspective of conceptualization, M is given. Choosing M means to prefer a certain layer from the so-called *layered languages of ludology* (Lenerz, 2009).

Within the illustration of Sect. 6.4 above, M contains elements such as [cl], [co], [ex], [gs], [mb], [mh], [mo], [mw], [tp], and [st].

Note that M may contain player actions on the chosen level of granularity and actions of the game system as well. There is nothing such as a finest possible level of description, because one might dive into the technicalities of the game engine and, perhaps, into the physics of the computer or of the interface components such as key board, game pad, joy stick, and dance mat. On a much higher level, M may also contain descriptions beyond the human–computer interaction such as, for instance, activities of extra game play as discussed by Jantke and Gaudl (2010). For any of the subsequent discussions, we assume that the alphabet M is temporarily fixed.

6.6.1 Basic Notions and Notations

Game playing is abstractly described as some sequence of elements from M. In mathematics and computer science, it is custom to denote the set of all finite sequence over M by M^*. Given a particular digital game G, the game mechanics determines which sequences of actions over M are possible and which are not. In simple and well-known games such as Chess, e.g., there are conventional alphabets M in use and the well-known game mechanics describes uniquely—up to a few exceptions of tournament rules—which moves may follow one another. Here is an example known as the Blackburne Trap provided for the convenience of those readers who are less familiar with the formalisms of mathematics.

e4 e5 Nf3 Nc6 Bc4 d6 Nc3 Bg4 h3 Bh5 Nxe5 Bxd1 Bxf7+ Ke7 Nd5#

Note that this little Chess game occurs in several variants and under different names and is always characterized by a queen sacrifice as shown. It is said that the key idea has been played for the first time by the French Chess player Legall de Kermeur in Paris in the year 1750. For this reason, this short game is frequently called *Légal Mate*. It occurs as a life role playing game in act two of the operetta *Der Seecadet* by Richard Genée. For this reason, it is named *Seekadettenmatt* in German.

The string above is a finite sequence $\pi \in M^*$ of elements from the set of Chess moves M. The whole sequence π describes some complete game play. Particular symbols such as *e4* and *Bxf7+*, e.g., are elements of M. The move *Nd5#* indicates that the game is over.

In general, when some game G is given and some terminology M has been chosen, $\Pi(G)$ is used to describe the set of all completed game plays according to the game mechanics of G.

When G is a digital game, $\Pi(G)$ may be seen as some formal language (Hopcroft & Ullman, 1979).

It is extremely rare that all potentially playable sequences of $\Pi(G)$ are really played by some human players. For digital games of any reasonably interesting complexity, it applies that large parts of $\Pi(G)$ are never played. This motivates some further conceptualization. $\Psi(G)$ denotes the subset of $\Pi(G)$ which contains exactly all those sequences really played at least once. In contrast to $\Pi(G)$, the set of strings $\Psi(G)$ usually is not a formal language.

These terms are setting the stage for some particular investigation into the problem of intentionally correct digital game implementation. Although this issue is not central to the present chapter, it is included because it allows for an illustration of some practically relevant peculiarities of digital games.

Digital games are software systems and, as such, they share with more conventional software systems the problems of high level specifications, of implementation process models, and of correctness.

6.6.2   *Excurse to Implementation Correctness*

Assume that some human game designers have a certain exceptionally clear imagination of the game they are going to design and to implement. Assume, in particular, that the designers have a clear vision of the human players' forthcoming game playing experiences they are aiming at. Let us assume, furthermore, that there is a way to express what the designers have in mind. Those assumptions are strong. The majority of contemporary approaches to systematic game design, see (Holopainen,

Nummenmaa, & Kuittinen, 2010), e.g., provide very helpful systematizations and explicate design principles, in general, and steps of design, in particular, but never come up with something such as a comprehensive design document describing anticipated player experiences, although Löwgren and Stolterman (2007) name specifications a design goal. For the purpose of this thought experiment, some more precision is assumed. The term $\Phi(G)$ is a formal specification of all the sequences of game playing behavior to be made possible by the particular game G under development. How to characterize the correctness of an implementation of G with respect to the specification?

In conventional computer science, correctness means $\Phi(G) = \Pi(G)$, i.e., the implementation allows for exactly the game playing sequences specified. Interestingly, any game under discussion will meet the designers intentions if only $\Phi(G) = \Psi(G)$ holds, i.e., if all the anticipated experiences become true. Because $\Psi(G) \subset \Pi(G)$ holds for all nontrivial digital games, the correctness of a digital game's implementation is obviously different from the traditional correctness concept in use in computer science.

This simple observation is remarkable, because it may be demonstrated by means of only a very few formal concepts—$\Pi(G)$, $\Psi(G)$, and $\Phi(G)$—and a few elementary arguments. The insight has some far reaching consequences.

In computer science, when some formal specification text $\Phi(G)$ is given, one may think of a more or less automatic transformation of the specification into an executable program G (Bauer, Möller, Partsch, & Pepper, 1989). Furthermore, if $\Phi(G)$ is some formal language as well, it may be used for automatic test generation. A large amount of work has been put into the transformation of very precise specifications into running programs relying on a firm mathematical basis such as universal algebra (Ehrig, Mahr, Claßen, & Orejas, 1992).

In contrast, $\Psi(G)$ is never a formal language. Consequently, there does not exist any formal method for proving the equivalence of $\Phi(G)$ and $\Psi(G)$. Designing a digital game which meets the designers' expectations and which bears the potentials of unfolding anticipated game playing experiences remains an art, by nature.

Dealing with $\Psi(G)$ requires media studies grounded in social sciences, because $\Psi(G)$ cannot be fully determined by means of only formal methods.

6.7   Formal Patterns in Game Playing

In the two Sects. 6.6.1 and 6.6.2, there have been introduced and investigated the sets of sequences $\Pi(G)$, $\Psi(G)$, and $\Phi(G)$. Throughout the remaining part of the chapter, we will confine ourselves to a study of only $\Pi(G)$ and $\Psi(G)$ with respect to any given game G. Usually, it holds $\Psi(G) \subset \Pi(G) \subset M^{*}$.

In dependence on the current focus of investigation and on the related choice of M, game play may reveal the occurrences of certain (instances of) regularities. These regularities will be called patterns subsequently.

Given a particular string $\pi \in \Pi(G)$, a certain pattern instance might occur. Thus, a pattern may be seen as a property of strings and some given string may either have this property or not.

Having scenarios such as the *patterns experience evaluation program* ((Jantke, 2009), see above) in mind, two basic requirements seem essential:

- Patterns are local properties.
- Patterns are decidable properties.

The practical meaning of these two properties is quite obvious. Assume that a human investigator has a certain hypothesis about the relevance of some pattern (instances) to the impact of game playing. When observing human players and recording their game playing, it must be clear whether or not pattern instances occur and when they occur. Only if those occurrences can be localized, they can be related to human responses quantitatively or qualitatively. Abstractly speaking, one may imagine the recorded game play as some sequence $\pi \in \Pi(G)$ and the human response as some parallel stream. Investigating the impact of game playing means, first, to identify an instance of the pattern in π and, second, to extract some related human response.

There are doubts about the existence of universal decision procedures. But looking more closely into these phenomena requires more precise conceptualizations. At least, for a given game G, decidability is required.

Further treatments need a few notations to allow for concise statements. For any two strings $\pi, \pi' \in M^*$, $\pi \leq \pi'$ denotes that π is a (not necessarily proper) substring of π'. The inequality of π, π' is not required. The irreflexive subrelation of $\leq$ is denoted by $\pi < \pi'$. Furthermore, given any two strings, $\pi \cdot \pi'$ means the concatenation of π and π'.

In case some pattern φ holds for some string π, one may ask for some shortest part of π where this pattern holds. Assume π may be decomposed into three substrings such that $\pi_1 \cdot \pi_2 \cdot \pi_3 = \pi$ holds. In case we have $\pi_2 \models \varphi$, but the pattern does not hold for any proper substring $\pi_2' < \pi_2$, this particular string π_2 is said to be an instance of φ.

These formalities shall be illustrated by the following little toy example. Assume $M = \{a,b,c\}$. The pattern under consideration shall be the subsequent occurrence of two letters a separated by exactly one other different letter. Obviously, there are infinitely many strings such as, e.g., *abcabc* and *aabbaa*, in which this pattern does not hold. But it holds, for illustration, in *aaabaaa*. In this particular string, *aba* is the instance of the pattern.

Authors with some mathematical background might appreciate stronger definitions of the crucial properties of locality and decidability, respectively.

Suppose φ to be any logical property of strings over M. φ has the property of *locality* if and only if for any string $\pi \in M^*$ it holds:

$$\pi \models \varphi \rightarrow \forall \pi_1, \pi_2 \in M^* \ (\pi_1 \bullet \pi \bullet \pi_2 \models \varphi)$$

Interesting variants result from a restriction to $\pi \in \Pi(G)$ instead of $\pi \in M^*$.

φ has the property of *decidability* if and only if there is a fully computable predicate δ over $\Pi(G)$ such that it holds:

$$\delta(\pi) = 1 \leftrightarrow \exists\, \pi_1, \pi_2, \pi_3 \in M^* \,(\pi = \pi_1 \bullet \pi_2 \bullet \pi_3 \,\&\, \pi_2 \mid = \varphi)$$

Decidability problems of this type are known to be usually of a very high computational complexity (Angluin, 1980). Even worse, there might be no universal decidability procedure over all potentially occurring digital games.

The present subsection will be completed by the discussion of a certain pattern which is known from conventional games such as Chess where it is named zugzwang (an enforced move, but classical Chess literature uses the original German word). Interestingly, this pattern occurs in playing digital games very frequently, especially in point & click adventures ranging from "The Secret of Monkey Island" (Lucasfilm 1990) to "Gray Matter."

In the Blackburne Trap Chess example above, after playing the sequence $\pi \in M^*$ of moves *e4 e5 Nf3 Nc6 Bc4 d6 Nc3 Bg4 h3 Bh5 Nxe5 Bxd1 Bxf7+* the *Black* player is facing such a situation of an enforced move. According to the game mechanics, the only admissible move in M is *Ke7*.

In other words, after playing $\pi \in M^*$, there does exist a unique move $\mu \in M$ such that in any completed game play π^c according to the rules the sequence π must be followed by μ. A thoroughly formal expression looks as follows:

$$[\chi_1^{zz}] \quad \exists \mu \in M \,\forall\, \pi^c \in \Pi(G)\,(\pi \leq \pi^c \rightarrow \pi \bullet \mu \leq \pi^c)$$

This formula abbreviated by χ_1^{zz} describes the strongest version of an enforced move—zugzwang in Chess—as it appears in the Blackburne Trap. Note that the relationship $\pi_1 \leq \pi_2$ of two strings π_1 and π_2 indicates that the left string is a subsequence (not necessarily of a proper one) of the right string. Later on, the notation $\Pi^{\leq}(G) = \{\pi \mid \exists \pi' \in \Pi(G)\,(\pi \leq \pi')\}$ will be useful. The big advantage of such a formal approach is that it immediately reveals the existence of several nonequivalent variants of this property as follows.

$$[\chi_2^{zz}] \quad \exists \mu \in M \,\forall\, \pi^c \in \Pi(G) \exists \pi' \in M^* \,(\pi \leq \pi^c \rightarrow \pi \bullet \pi' \bullet \mu \leq \pi^c)$$

$$[\chi_3^{zz}] \quad \exists \mu \in M \,\forall\, \pi^c \in \Psi(G)\,(\pi \leq \pi^c \rightarrow \pi \bullet \mu \leq \pi^c)$$

$$[\chi_4^{zz}] \quad \exists \mu \in M \,\forall\, \pi^c \in \Psi(G) \exists \pi' \in M^* \,(\pi \leq \pi^c \rightarrow \pi \bullet \pi' \bullet \mu \leq \pi^c)$$

Each formula χ_i^{zz} contains a unique free variable π, i.e., it represents some proposition about π. By existential quantification, every formula χ_i^{zz} results in some pattern $\varphi_i^{zz} = \exists \pi \in \Pi^{\leq}(G)\,(\chi_i^{zz})$.

6.8 Hierarchies of Patterns

Given any pattern such as φ_1^{zz}, for instance, the pattern may hold in the one completed game play, but does not hold in the other. In case π_{BT} denotes the string *e4 e5 Nf3 Nc6 Bc4 d6 Nc3 Bg4 h3 Bh5 Nxe5 Bxd1 Bxf7+ Ke7 Nd5#* known as the Blackburne Trap, $\pi_{BT} \mid = \varphi_1^{zz}$. The already mentioned initial subsequence *e4 e5 Nf3 Nc6 Bc4 d6 Nc3 Bg4 h3 Bh5 Nxe5 Bxd1 Bxf7+* is an instance of the pattern φ_1^{zz} and, by the way, it is the only one in π_{BT}.

Because φ_1^{zz} does logically imply the other three variants of zugzwang, $\pi_{BT} \mid = \varphi_2^{zz}$, $\pi_{BT} \mid = \varphi_3^{zz}$, and $\pi_{BT} \mid = \varphi_4^{zz}$ hold as well.

It naturally depends on the terminology of M which patterns may be identified in sequences reflecting the human playing of some digital game. Consider, e.g., the point & click adventure "Ankh" (Deck13, 2005). There is some camel wash in "Ankh." For successfully completing game play one needs to send some camel through this bizarre installation. Because of this particular enforced move, if π_{ankh} denotes any completed game play, it holds $\pi_{ankh} \mid = \varphi_2^{zz}$. But it never holds $\pi_{ankh} \mid = \varphi_1^{zz}$. In other terms, $\pi_{ankh} \mid \neq \varphi_1^{zz}$.

Let us consider another illustrative example. To master the conventional point & click adventure "The Secret Files: Tunguska" (Fusionsphere Systems & Animation Arts, 2006), players have to resolve almost a dozen of problems of a similar structure. From a particular point of view and expressed in an appropriate terminology, all these problems are of type φ_2^{zz}. But a closer look reveals a certain internal structure. Informally speaking, the human player is meeting computerized adversaries and has to set a snare to each of them. For this purpose, the human player always needs to solve three subsequent subtasks: first gathering relevant information, second collecting appropriate materials, and third setting a suitable trap. If this Tunguska trap is formally named φ^{tt}, it turns out to be a particular case of φ_2^{zz}. Logically, the formula φ^{tt} implies the formula φ_2^{zz}, but not vice versa.

From an algebraic point of view, for every digital game G the set of potential patterns forms a complete lattice. This, in fact, is a theorem which in a mathematical text would require a prove demonstrating that both logical conjunction and logical disjunction inherit locality and decidability. Due to formal arguments, the lattice is infinite. This exhibits the enormous variety of potentially occurring game playing phenomena.

Although an exploitation of the algebraic perspective goes beyond the limits of the present publication, a certain idea shall be briefly mentioned. Suppose some game G is given and some terminology M has been chosen. Among the patterns valid in every game play, there are minima in the lattice. Those minima characterize the present game. Furthermore, different sets of minima may be used to discriminate and cluster digital games accordingly. Pattern concepts may induce categories of digital games finer than genres.

6.9 Patterns of Experience

Logically formalized patterns are surely not the silver bullet of game studies, but they allow for an unprecedentedly clear characterization of phenomena in human game playing and, furthermore, provide a novel approach to the categorization of digital games according to the strongest versions of patterns—minima in the sub-lattice of occurring patterns—which show in every game playing.

Instances of patterns in recorded game playing abstractly described as some $\pi \in \Pi(G)$ illuminate a variety of characteristic game playing behaviors. Occurring instances of patterns are indicators of varying player experiences such as, e.g., fun or frustration, mastery or failure.

Recall "Gray Matter," the digital game considered in some more detail in Sect. 6.4 above. When scripting a particular trick, human players have the opportunity of pushing the magic wand button and finding out by trial and error whether or not their current script is correct. Pushing the button in case of an incorrectly scripted trick is denoted by $[\text{mw - }] \in M$. In such a situation, the game responds by immediately switching back to the environment of scripting. The action is denoted by $[\text{gs}] \in M$.

The author has checked the recorded game plays (see Fig. 6.3) for the repeated occurrence of the extremely simple instance [mw-] [gs] within the substrings describing the scripting of the first trick. Here are a few results sketched very briefly.

In the game play strings $\pi \in \Pi(G)$ describing the behavior and experience of the best five subjects, the instance [mw-] [gs] occurs less than one time, on the average. For the other six subjects, the average is exactly three. Although this is a purely syntactical property of strings, there is an intuitive interpretation. Subjects who understand what it means to script a trick do not depend on trial and error.

Within the framework of a Ph.D. project of the author's department, there has been developed, deployed, and evaluated a particular game useful for learning about German history (Hawlitschek, 2010). The game is a comic-style point & click adventure named "1961." The historic event dealt with is the erection of the German wall in 1961.

Playing the game completely takes always only a bit more than 1 h. This game can be played in school. It has been designed and developed together with an appropriate context of playing (Jantke, 2011).

Anja Hawlitschek, the game's author, has undertaken an evaluation with about 200 students in schools of two different federal states of Germany. This quantitative analysis has been followed by several qualitative studies. This does result in a database of about 200 recorded complete game plays. In other words, there are about 200 different sequences $\pi \in \Pi(G)$ recorded. Indeed, any two sequences are mutually different. Nevertheless, they show several instances of patterns.

Logfiles of playing the game "1961" are written in HTML to support visual inspection. The symbols of M consist of three components. The first one is a time stamp, the second one indicates the type of action and names, if necessary, the actor, and the third one provides some content information. Furthermore, there is some structuring information inserted for readability.

Hawlitschek has been able to cluster the strings of $\Pi(G)$ according to structural properties. Although evaluations are beyond the limits of the present chapter introducing the concepts for the first time, a few lines shall be dedicated to a sketch of some correlations between structural properties—instances of patterns—and mastering game play including learning successfully.

Several letters, i.e., abstractly described actions of game playing, which occur in some $\pi \in \Pi(G)$, describe the opening of a new scenery of the "1961" game world. Those actions are landmarks in π. The frequency and order of those landmarks in a recorded game play characterize the orientation of the human player in the virtual world of the game.

Failure of mastery and confusion are reflected by high frequencies of a small number of scenery openings in certain parts of the string. In contrast, there are several sequences of scenery openings which highly correlate with stringently traversing the digital world, mastering game play, and—as a side effect—learning.

The crucial point is that those indicators are purely syntactical and can be found automatically.

Other instances of patterns illustrate the difficulties some players have been facing. An extremely simple type of pattern describes the repeated execution of one and the same action. Players doing so apparently lost their orientation. In one of the recorded game plays $\pi \in \Pi(G)$ of the game "1961," there occurs the quite extreme case of 18 times performing the same activity. Pattern instances of this type are clear indicators of loosing game control, and those occurrences correlate negatively with learning success.

Let us complete the investigation of pattern instances as indicators of experience by means of another game. The author has developed "Gorge" more to be a digital media research tool than a digital game (Jantke, 2010). In "Gorge," several human players and/or several computerized agents can play together. Every player has a team of four robots that move through some virtual environment according to very simple rules. There is some goal area where robots can score points for their team. Robots occupy cells on some path way. In case one robot reaches a cell where another robot is staying, it is pushing the robot backward to the next available space. As a result of this simple rule, there is some tendency toward building groups acting in a close neighborhood. This bears the potential of more interaction and fun.

"Gorge" seen as a research tool is mostly deployed for developing some technology competence in the field of Artificial Intelligence (AI). For this purpose, human players can choose computerized adversaries to determine their virtual character by assigning them preferences of behavior. For instance, one may set up one adversary's preference such that it tries to fight with others whenever possible. The author has undertaken a series of qualitative studies with subjects of an age between 13 and 20 from several federal states of Germany. Here, the focus will be on a single quite illustrative example.

The paths along which the robots move have some branching points as indicated in the left screenshot of Fig. 6.4. The branching points allow for setting

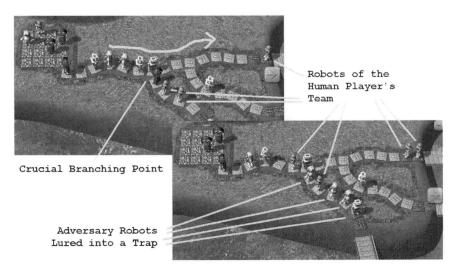

Fig. 6.4 Two screenshots of subsequent situations when playing "Gorge"

traps to adversaries of a certain character. In the particular game discussed here, two of the computerized adversaries are set up to play quite aggressively and to engage in fights with any other player whenever possible. Knowing this, the human player tried to lure those aggressive computerized players into a trap by turning right at the first branching point and waiting shortly after (left screenshot of the figure). Several robots did follow aiming at some battle. The waiting robots of the player have been defeated and pushed backward (right screenshot). As a consequence, the player had been winning the freedom to go another way (arrow in the figure) and to draw advantage from an area almost free of fighting adversaries (Fig. 6.4).

A *pattern of entrapment* may be seen as follows. First, a player's robot turns at some branch into one direction. Second, some adversary robots follow at this branch into this direction. Third, the following adversaries push the player's robot backward to reach a cell before the branching point. Fourth, the player's robot takes the opportunity to move at the branching point into his preferred direction. Players experience the mastery of AI.

6.10 Pattern-Based Assessment Scenarios

Approaches to assessing the impact of playing digital games vary largely. Some researchers rely on measurements taken from players lying in a tube, wearing a helmet, or being somehow differently wired. Other authors rely on questionnaires and some authors such as Drachen, Nacke, Yannakakis, and Pedersen (2010) combine both. Psychophysiological measurements provide a rather objective and sensitive way of getting data about a human body's response to playing a game. However, when the human player's response to the game play is measured, to what does it relate? The author's answer elaborated in the preceding few sections is *to instances of patterns*.

Consider, e.g., the pattern of entrapment discussed at the end of the preceding section. When this pattern did occur in game playing, it turned out in later interviews that all human players did recognize their superiority to the AI adversaries. Furthermore, they did enjoy the game play and found AI a useful technology to make digital games more entertaining.

If in some game play $\pi \in \Pi(G)$ some instance of a stronger variant of the pattern of entrapment (involving two or more of the player's robots as shown in the figure above) does occur, this is a clear indicator of mastery of AI.

When some target patterns are given, the occurrence of instances may be recognized automatically. Thus, if pattern instances tell about game mastery, this effect of game playing may be identified by means of computationally processing the recorded game play.

According to Dana Angluin (1980), there are some even stronger results. When human observers consider certain parts of game playing interesting and see them as potential instances of some unknown (!) pattern, there are algorithmic devices for learning the pattern only from marked instances. This works for a rather large class of patterns, although the ultimate reach of the approach is not yet fully understood. The coming years will witness some investigations into the learnability of more complex logical patterns.

To say this in other words, the present pattern approach does allow for computer support to generate new insights into what it is that affects the human player. This, however, is a research direction still in its infancy.

For fairness and correctness of the presentation, it is necessary to admit that the computational procedures of Angluin (1990) are usually of a high computational complexity. For instance, learning some pattern of maximal detail (maximal length in Angluin's setting) based on instances only is a problem which is NP-hard and, thus, in many cases computationally intractable. Consequently, we refrain from further investigations into the learnability of patterns, at least for the present publication.

In contrast, finding instances of patterns which are indicators of mastery or failure, respectively, is a feasible problem.

A basic scenario is as follows: Find instances of patterns such as those reported from playing "1961" and "Gorge," e.g., and cluster complete sequences $\pi \in \Pi(G)$ accordingly. Next, map the completed game plays to the human players and find out what players of some cluster have in common.

Scenarios not discussed here deal with the investigation of interrupted game playing. Which pattern instances show in game play sequences that are not completed, but do not occur in completed sequences?

An exciting subtask is to find appropriate layers of description M, an issue of layered languages of ludology (Lenerz, 2009).

6.11 Summary

Some authors like Linderoth (2010) find it worth to publish longer articles pondering the phenomenon that playing does not necessarily imply learning. The present chapter, in contrast, is driven by the assumption that the effect of game playing usually depends on a variety of factors such as, for illustration, the human player's conditions and the context of playing a particular game. When game playing unfolds, it is worth to look into the sequence of events for something that bears the potentials of some impact—instances of patterns. Instances of patterns may cause fun or frustration, surprise or thought, frightening or laughing, and in dependence on the context learning as well. Foremost, the chapter aims at introducing the author's pattern concept as a basis for future investigations into assessment. It is intentionally very formal, because missing precision seems to be one of the crucial deficiencies of what once might become a digital games science.

In particular, precise concepts have the advantage to be easier to attack, to correct, to complete, to refine, or even to throw away and to substitute by more elaborate concepts—benefit the emerging games science. In this sense, the author's work may be seen as Popperian (Popper, 1934).

Acknowledgements Particular thanks go to Anja Hawlitschek for her work on the game "1961" and for providing the database of her evaluation and to Christian Woelfert for implementing the touch screen version of the author's little game "Gorge." The present work has been partially supported by the Thuringian Ministry for Education, Science and Culture (TMBWK) within the project iCycle under contract PE-004-2-1.

References

Abt, C. C. (1970). *Serious games*. New York: Viking.

Alexander, C. (1979). *The timeless way of building*. New York: Oxford University Press.

Angluin, D. (1980). Finding patterns common to a set of strings. *Journal of Computer and System Sciences, 21*(1), 46–62.

Bauer, F. L., Möller, B., Partsch, H., & Pepper, P. (1989). Formal program construction by transformations-computer-aided, intuition-guided programming. *IEEE Transactions on Software Engineering, 15*(2), 165–180.

Björk, S., & Holopainen, J. (2005). *Patterns in game design*. Hingham: Charles River Media.

Borchers, J. (2001). *A pattern approach of interaction design*. Chichester: Wiley.

Brehme, M. (2010). Gray Matter. *PC Games, 12/2010*, 112.

Costikyan, G. (2005). I have no words & I must design. In K. Salen & E. Zimmerman (Eds.), *The game design reader: A rules of play anthology* (pp. 192–211). Cambridge: MIT Press.

Drachen, A., Nacke, L. E., Yannakakis, G., & Pedersen, A. L. (2010). Correlation between heart rate, electrodermal activity and player experience in first-person shooter games. In S. N. Spencer (Ed.), *Proc. of the 5th ACM SIGGRAPH Symposium on Video Games, Los Angeles, USA* (pp. 49–54). New York: ACM.

Ehrig, H., Mahr, B., Claßen, I., & Orejas, F. (1992). Introduction to algebraic specification. Part 1 & Part 2. *The Computing Journal, 35*(5), 460–467 & 468–477.

Helm, M., & Theis, F. (2009). Serious Games als Instrument der Führungskräfteentwicklung. In A. Hohenstein & K. Wilbers (Eds.), *Handbuch E-Learning* (pp. 6.10.1–6.10.12). Köln: Deutscher Wirtschaftsdienst.

Holopainen, J., Nummenmaa, T., & Kuittinen, J. (2010). Why gamers don't learn more. An ecological approach to games as learning environments. In P. Lankoski, A. M. Thorhauge, H. Verhagen, & A. Waern (Eds.), *Proc. DIGRA Nordic 2010*.

Hopcroft, J. E., & Ullman, J. D. (1979). *Introduction to automata theory, languages, and computation*. Reading: Addison-Wesley.

Hawlitschek, A. (2010). Ein digitales Lernspiel für den Geschichtsunterricht: Konzeption und Evaluation. In S. Hambach, A. Martens, D. Tavangarian, & B. Urban (Eds.), *Proceedings of the 3rd International eLBa Science Conference, Rostock, Germany, July 2010* (pp. 278–288). Stuttgart: Fraunhofer.

Jain, S., Osherson, D., Royer, J. S., & Sharma, A. (1999). *Systems that learn*. Cambridge: MIT Press.

Jantke, K. P. (2007). Serious games—eine kritische analyse. In P. Klimsa (Ed.), *11. Workshop Multimedia in Bildung und Unternehmen* (pp. 7–14). Ilmenau: Techn. University.

Jantke, K. P. (2008). *Patterns in Digital Game Playing Experience Revisited: Beiträge zum tieferen Verständnis des Begriffs Pattern*. Report DB 33, Ilmenau: TUI, IfMK.

Jantke, K. P. (2009). The pattern experience evaluation program. In A. Ligeza & G. J. Nalepa (Eds.), *DERIS 2009, Intl. Workshop on Design, Evaluation and Refinment of Intelligent Systems* (pp. 70–75). Kraków: AGH University.

Jantke, K. P. (2010). The Gorge approach. Digital game control and play for playfully developing technology competence. In J. Cordeiro, B. Shishlov, A. Verbraeck, & M. Helfert (Eds.), *2nd Intl. Conference on Computer Supported Education, CSEDU* (pp. 411-414). Valencia: INSTICC, Apr 2010.

Jantke, K. P. (2011). Potenziale und Grenzen des spielerischen Lernens. In M. Metz & F. Theis (Eds.), *Digitale lernwelt—serious games* (pp. 77–84). Bielefeld: W. Bertelsmann.

Jantke, K. P., & Gaudl, S. (2010). Taxonomic contributions to digital games science. In P. Lankoski, A. M. Thorhauge, H. Verhagen, & A. Waern (Eds.), *2nd International Games Innovation Conference* (pp. 27–34), Hong Kong, 22–23 Dec 2010.

Kivikangas, J. M., Ekman, I., Chanel, G., Järvelä, S., Cowley, B., Salminen, M., et al. (2010). Review on psychophysiological methods in game research. In *Proceedings of DIGRA Nordic 2010*.

Klinge, H. (2011). Gray matter. *GameStar, 1*(2011), 92–94.

Lampert, C., Schwinge, C., & Tolks, D. (2009). Der gespielte Ernst des Lebens: Bestandsaufnahme und Potenziale von Serious Games (for Health). *Medienpädagogik—Zeitschrift für Theorie und Praxis der Medienbildung*, Themenheft 15/16: Computerspiele und Videogames in formellen und informellen Bildungskontexten.

Lemezma, M. (2003). *Mind magic. Extraordinary tricks to mystify, baffle and entertain*. London: New Holland Publ.

Lenerz, C. (2009). Layered Languages of Ludology—Eine Fallstudie. In A. Beyer & G. Kreuzberger (Eds.), *Digitale Spiele—Herausforderung und Chance* (pp. 35–64). Boitzenburg: Verlag Werner Hülsbusch.

Linderoth, J. (2010). Why gamers don't learn more. An ecological approach to games as learning environments. In P. Lankoski, A. M. Thorhauge, H. Verhagen, & A. Waern (Eds.), *Proceedings of DIGRA Nordic 2010*.

Löwgren, J., & Stolterman, E. (2007). *Thoughtful interaction design: A design perspective on information technology*. Boston: MIT Press.

Philips, B. (2006). Talking about games experience—a view from the trenches. *Interactions, 13*(5), 22–23.

Popper, K. (1934). *Logik der Forschung*. Tübingen, Germany.

Ritterfeld, U., Cody, M., & Vorderer, P. (2009). *Serious games: Mechanisms and effects*. New York: Routledge, Taylor and Francis.

Sawyer, B., & Smith, P. (2009). *Serious games taxonomy*. Retrieved April 14, 2012, from http://www.dmill.com.

Chapter 7
Taking Activity-Goal Alignment into Open-Ended Environments: Assessment and Automation in Game-Based Learning

Brett E. Shelton and Mary Ann Parlin

7.1 Introduction

The creation of interactive simulation systems for education has been increasing in number and complexity in traditional education, military, and corporate contexts (e.g., Barab, Gresalfi, & Arici, 2009; Freeman, Salter, & Hoch, 2004; Kirkley & Kirkley, 2005; Shute, 1993). The premise for this chapter is that the instructional simulation/game simulation—or any other name it goes by—has been designed and executed with the following questions in mind: (1) what is the appropriate model (or real system) the learner should experience, (2) what is the appropriate level of denaturing for this learner? (3) what sequence of problems should the learner solve with respect to this model or real system, (4) what resources should be available as solving takes place, and (5) what instructional functions to augment the learner's own knowledge and skill should accompany solving? (Gibbons & Fairweather, 1998; Gibbons & Sommer, 2007). That is, addressing these questions mandate a foundation from instructional design for assessment that is not dependent on the amount of gamelike features that exist in any given open-ended learning environment (OELE). Therefore, it makes sense to extend our activity-goal alignment theory and create a basis for assessment from constrained, designed educational activities to those that feature open-ended virtual environments as well (see Shelton & Scoresby, 2011).

In recent history, assessing student learning outcomes in open-ended virtual 3D spaces has been of keen interest for instructional technologists and learning scientists (Ketelhut, Nelson, Clarke, & Dede, 2010; Nelson, Erlandson, & Denham, 2010). These researchers are working from evidence-based assessment models (Mislevy,

B.E. Shelton (✉) • M.A. Parlin
Department of Instructional Technology and Learning Sciences,
Utah State University, Box 2830, Logan, UT 84322, USA
e-mail: brett.shelton@usu.edu

D. Ifenthaler et al. (eds.), *Assessment in Game-Based Learning: Foundations, Innovations, and Perspectives*, DOI 10.1007/978-1-4614-3546-4_7,
© Springer Science+Business Media New York 2012

2011; Mislevy, Almond, & Lukas, 2004). We acknowledge the difficulty of creating embedded assessments and issues related to functionally applying current assessment mechanisms into a virtual 3D engine require further study. Key questions include:

1. What design processes and issues arise when creating automated assessments in existing virtual environments?
2. What kinds of instructional strategies will these assessments support, and what features should be built to better support the teacher and learner?

Based on these questions, our team created a prototype embedded assessment tool for analysis within an existing virtual 3D simulation application called FIT (forensic investigation trainer) (Shelton et al., 2010; Stowell, Scoresby, Coates, Capell, & Shelton, 2009). While a number of different approaches could be gleaned from this promising theoretical basis, we propose that *completeness*, *accuracy* of performance, and *timeliness* of the learning task form one way of offering evidentiary support to the learning goals that align well with these emerging assessment strategies.

This chapter is divided into three parts. The first part contains the theoretical basis for operationalizing key assessment points for open-ended learning environments (OELEs), specifically 3D virtual worlds. In the second part, we present an attempt to integrate the points from the theoretical perspective into existing 3D virtual training environments, along with the technical mechanisms that would integrate the assessment strategy (Shelton, Scoresby, Parlin, & Olsen, 2011). In the third part, we offer a validation "test" of the piloted model through a discussion from the standpoint of an entirely new context. The new context presents an interesting backdrop as the model is stretched and modified to conform to different requirements as the new training module is explored.

7.2   Theoretical Perspective

Games and simulations give students opportunities and methods to potentially improve learning, but determining the effectiveness of this medium is contingent on how the learning is assessed within these contexts. As Elton and Laurillard (1979) stated, "the quickest way to change student learning is to change the assessment system" (p. 100). Assessment of student learning within a formal classroom setting may take many forms; learner-centered, teacher-directed, summative and formative assessment including test taking, discussion, and journal writing (Angelo & Cross, 1993). Gee (2008) suggested that "virtual experiences centered on problem solving, recruit learning and mastery as a form of pleasure" (p. 36). This learning as a form of pleasure creates the need for assessments to seamlessly blend into the structure of game play to avoid altering the learning environment. Designers should consider the purpose behind the design of an instructional environment and select the pedagogical learning theory that connects with that purpose (Ketelhut et al., 2010).

If games and simulations can provide new methods of learning, they should also provide new methods of assessment as well. Nelson et al. (2010) are working on three areas of embedded assessments in virtual worlds to discover the essential complexity of learning: content understanding, process understanding, and contextual understanding. In their experiences, efforts in automated assessment typically fall within one of more of these general constructs (see Mislevy, Almond, & Lukas, 2004).

The military developed what is called the debriefing distributed simulation-based exercises (DDSBE). The DDSBE gathers large amounts of data from participants using a simulation and puts that information in a database that can then be used to assess learners' performance such as time on task, training objectives, and overall mission objectives (Freeman et al., 2004). The DDSBE has been used to gather data and assess the work of individual, team, and multi-team performance and on an individual level, as well as completeness, accuracy, timeliness and order (Carolan, Bilazarian, & Nguyen, 2005). Such assessments tend to focus on team and individual process understandings. These systems utilize a scenario-based assessment model (SBAM) (Banuls & Salmeron, 2007). Assessment occurs as alternative scenarios, or a selection of options by the user within the framework, are measured against the forecasted scenario. The College Work Readiness Assessment (CWRA) serves as an example of a SBAM consisting of a single 90-min scenario from which students must respond from a library of online resources (Silva, 2009).

Bridging the gap between simulations within open-ended 3D environments and games is largely one of motivation of the learner extended to the types of activities allowed within the environment, and the structure of in which those activities take place. Several models of learner engagement have been explored in developing learning games, from traditional ARCS models of instructional design (Driscoll, 2000; Keller, 1993) to those more video game centric such as CUPS (Scoresby & Shelton, 2007; Shelton & Wiley, 2006). The CUPS model, modified slightly from ideas researched by Malone and Lepper (1987), helps provide a design metric that should help engage learners during activities in OELEs:

- Challenge—the environment should provide tasks with clear objectives within the activities, enough to produce feelings of accomplishment when achieved, but not difficult enough to make the learner give up.
- Uncertainty—the environment should allow a learner to interact within the space with an amount of control over decisions and sub-actions in order to "own" one's actions and thereby one's accomplishments.
- Proclivity—the activities should be enjoyable or include content that is relevant and interesting to the learner.
- Social—the environment should allow for sharing of information and progress within the activity space enough so that assistance and system-supported feedback is possible.

While a motivated learner is key to leveraging the advantage of game play within game activities for training in OELEs, the activities within the environments should still maintain a close allegiance to the learning objectives set forth by the instructional designer (see Fig. 7.1).

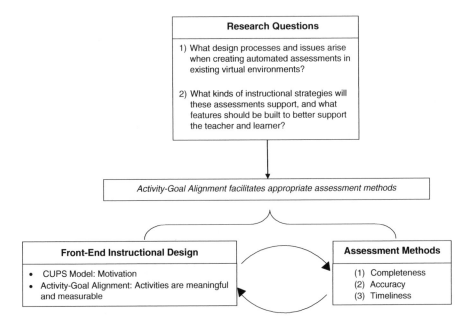

Fig. 7.1 Showing the relationships between research questions and the iterative process of assessment and activity in open-ended virtual 3D spaces

This idea of activity-goal alignment has been explored through various design research projects in creating games for learning (Shelton, 2007; Shelton & Scoresby, 2011) and is the subject of other chapters found within this volume (Belland, 2011). Closely aligning all game-related activity to the instructional objectives should allow for appropriate and designed learning by the player as they complete tasks within the game. The assessment strategy would then be narrowed to include *how* the tasks are performed rather than largely *if* or *how quickly* they were accomplished. Computer-based games that offer narrower user freedoms are more easily constrained in activity-goal alignment design. In taking alignment theory to open-ended spaces where decisions by the learner are more difficult to track, how might this affect the kinds of assessment strategies more commonly associated with completion, accuracy and timeliness?

7.2.1 Techniques

When considering the design of automated assessment functionality within a 3D game engine, an initial consideration is choosing a game engine that supports the desired modifications for embedding required features. The HEAT 3D engine has two embedded features specifically designed to make the engine unique for instructional purposes. These features allow the engine to check and score the actions and decisions for completeness, accuracy, and timeliness. Why? Having undertaken several educationally designed activities in game-based open environments, the analysis of activity and goals can be broadly categorized through these three mechanisms (see Neville & Shelton, 2010; Scoresby & Shelton, 2011). These categorizations have been further substantiated through recommendations by scholars included in this volume (e.g., Mislevy et al., 2004).

The first feature is a decision-making tree. Each choice or decision is stored in a log file in a way that appears seamless to the user during their experience in the 3D environment. The second feature is an automated assessment function designed to score the actions and decisions made by the user during the simulation. This assessment report can also be exported and e-mailed to the instructor with annotations related to the performances. The log files are kept in separate locations and exist as discrete files. These engine features collect data in both real-time and post-performance aspects of the instruction and enable the analysis and distribution of understandable and customized feedback to both the instructor and the learner for both synchronous and asynchronous assessment.

The decision tree algorithms, using the stored data, identify dependent/independent relationships and store information about the simulation activity. Assessment variables include:

1. Completeness, as assessed by using the decision tree logic to determine if all activities in a task are performed.
2. Accuracy, as assessed by recording the order of actions produced and comparing them to an existing "correct" decision tree logic mechanism. This correct model is predetermined by the content expert and the instructional designer.
3. Timeliness, as assessed by measuring actual time on task with time parameters assigned to the activities and point of time between tasks. This time assignment is also related in the decision tree file.

7.3   The Prototype

In this section, we describe the evidence and the design path that informed the prototype development.

7.3.1   Evidence, Objects, and Materials

In developing this automated assessment feature, several design issues emerged. The HEAT 3D engine is designed to create high-fidelity instructional simulations and games. In particular, the engine allows the learner to experience cause-effect elements in the system that is presented. The automated assessment is required to record and analyze these learner movements. The integrity of tasks that are dependent or independent on the completion of another task must be maintained, which presented a

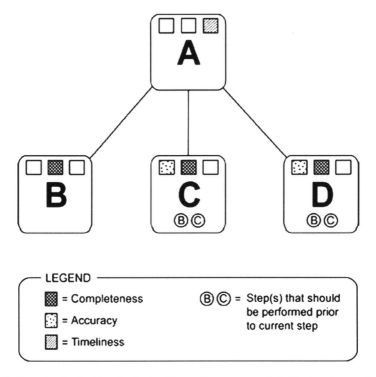

Fig. 7.2 Example of a decision, tracked and logged in an open-ended virtual environment

challenge in scoring. The decision tree, embedded in the engine, is utilized to determine dependencies, and scores are awarded within the decision tree in the engine. For example, (dependent) learner has to do A before B (accuracy, completeness) or (independent) learner can do A or B at any time and still get the completeness points. Figure 7.2 illustrates an example in the operation of a decision tree.

The learner is presented with a problem to solve or a decision to make. For example, in Fig. 7.3, the learner sees a burned area on the wall that indicates further investigative action is required.

When the learner initiates an event (investigation of the wall), an image of the affected area (Fig. 7.3) and a series of options to investigate the burn incident are presented (Fig. 7.4). Depending on the selected options, the information stored in the log window is the order of decisions, the amount of time to make those decisions, and the completion of the tasks scored on completeness, accuracy, and timeliness.

During the prototype development, project researchers also addressed design issues with respect to information delivery to the learner. Information is presented to the learner that is understandable and not distracting from the primary task. The designers chose the "dashboard" presentation method, i.e., colored bars that move to the right as the learner progresses, as a simple and unobtrusive feedback

Fig. 7.3   First-person view within the simulation

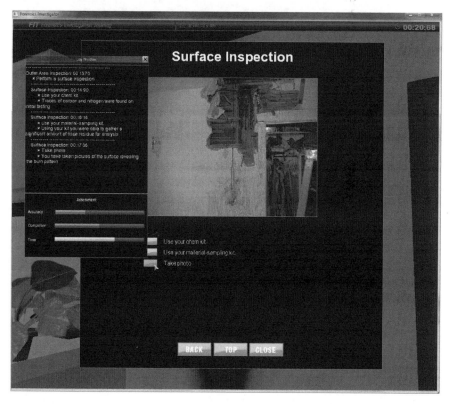

Fig. 7.4   Example of during-simulation assessment with log window displayed, showing real-time assessments to the user

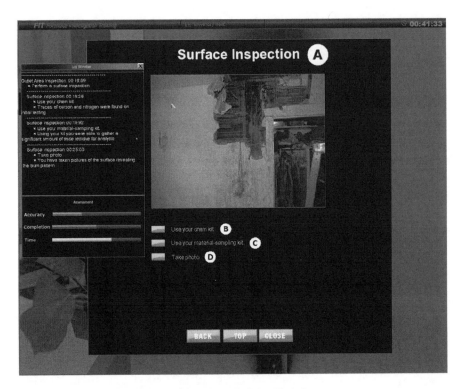

Fig. 7.5 Corresponding display with decision tree nodes labeled

mechanism (Fig. 7.3). Within this dashboard, designers considered providing instant updated feedback on every action. This idea was later rejected because it became clear that this could facilitate and encourage "button clicking" behavior without demonstrating knowledge of learning. To deter this behavior the "dashboard" feedback is only presented after the learner completes the full set of actions within the task. Figure 7.5 represents the corresponding display with related decision tree nodes labeled for clarification.

Another design decision was the amount of information and scaffolding to give the learner. In particular, to what extent does the user need to have all of the information related to the completeness, accuracy, and timeliness provided visually? Project researchers opted to enable instructors and learners to turn this option off (Fig. 7.6) according to the instructional goals, the progress of the learner, the type of practice imposed by the instructor, and whether or not the activity was part of practice or an exam. Figure 7.6 show the "Notes" feature in the Decision Viewer as being turned off or on.

Leveraging the preexisting features of the engine, project designers integrated features of embedded assessment from current models into the user environment so that the user and instructor may determine completeness, accuracy, and timeliness in applying their knowledge within a simulated virtual environment.

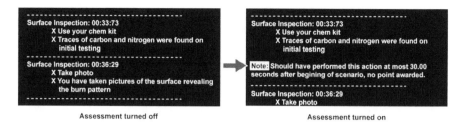

Fig. 7.6 (a) Assessment turned off. (b) Assessment turned on

Within this environment, motivational aspects associated with gaming activities within the OELE were more difficult to implement. Challenge was represented by the searching and discovery of marked areas for interaction within the 3D environment. Uncertainty, fortunately, is a factor native to the first-person shooter environment, allowing freedom of movement and choice within the 3D space. Proclivity here was influenced by a number of extrinsic and intrinsic factors, though it was acknowledged that fire investigation activities may hold little appeal for an average gamer. Finally, the social aspect of the environment was contained within the replay/regen features of the engine itself. Learners expected to have their play reviewed and scrutinized by instructors because all of their movements and actions were stored as files, loaded and replayed in first-person perspective by their teacher. While this example was directed more toward the training simulation side of the games-simulations spectrum, the assessment system itself would work the same regardless of how fantastic the set of actions where. For example, increasing the elements that facilitate challenge, uncertainty, and proclivity within the activity—say, racing to put elements into helpful compounds in the 3D environment—would not have altered the mechanism for assessing the progress.

7.3.2 The Design Path Toward Effective Automated Assessments

The assessment of learning within games and simulations, as illustrated above, tends to focus on the performance of the learners. Carolan et al. (2009) reported that the user is assessed on task completion, if the task is done with accuracy, done within a timely manner and if the preceding actions are done within the correct order. Squire (2003) stated "advances in assessment, such as peer-based assessment or performance-based assessment provide learners multiple sources of feedback based on their performance in authentic contexts" (p. 4). The value of the automated assessment is the instant feedback the user receives during the simulation.

There are several simulation applications that accomplish automated feedback in one form or another. For example, "Virtual Leader" provides feedback to the user in real time and offers a summative report at the end of a level. The overall report is used to determine if the player can move to a different level of play (Aldrich, 2005).

The design of the automated assessment using the HEAT engine delivers information, i.e., accuracy, completion, and timing to both the user and the facilitator, both during instruction and post-instruction. Also, the assessment in the HEAT engine allows for the learner/facilitator to turn the move-by-move dashboard indicator off or hide the post-instruction assessment notes depending on their situation or desire for supporting information. Assessments that offer a high level of adaptability while still assessing time, accuracy, and completion are difficult to produce. This prototype development in a complex 3D virtual environment demonstrates that combining the strategies from other engines, such as data and task tracking, with pedagogical assessment models is one path toward effective embedded assessments.

7.4   The GreenRetrofit Project: A Case in Action

The next logical step in the exploration and design of virtual training system assessment functionalities was to design and develop an applied use for what was created in the prototype. This application is called the GreenRetrofit Project.

There is a national commitment to training professionals from many fields of construction in green retrofitting skills. Green retrofitting skills involve retrofitting existing construction projects with elements that facilitate an increase in energy efficiency. In the GreenRetrofit Project, digital simulations provide opportunity to apply knowledge of energy efficiency management and sustainable energy alternatives in home and commercial retrofitting. The learning environment creates scenarios in which users evaluate and generate recommendations based on building architecture, existing construction and materials, and energy efficiency strategies with possible sustainable energy options. This application utilizes the theoretical research on assessment techniques for digital simulations based on the HEAT prototype to design a training and assessment system.

7.4.1   The Design and Development Objectives of the GreenRetrofit Project

The overall goal of the project is to develop and test a prototype training system for green retrofitting skills that implements the automated assessment principles described in Sect. 3. The purpose of the simulation (game) is to train individuals to assess the energy consumption of buildings and provide solutions to improve efficiency. The simulation exists in a 3D environment meant to provide a realistic virtual experience with immediate feedback. Users learn how to assess the energy efficiency of buildings, diagnose problem areas, and make decisions on how best to improve the efficiency of the building. The purpose of this instruction is to augment and train learners in green retrofitting construction skills.

In order to implement the theoretical underpinnings of automated assessment that were established in the theoretical background, the instructional goals were carefully aligned with the assessment functionalities of completeness, accuracy, and timeliness. The following sections outline key areas of instructional design that assisted in applying the assessment pieces to a virtual world training scenario.

7.4.2   The GreenRetrofit Project Design and Development Approach

The project milestones guiding the evolution of the GreenRetrofit project are summarized below:

- Determine needed functionality components.
- Design software to accomplish the needed functionality.
- Compile scenario information that can be practiced in an instructional scenario.
- Design supplemental instruction including instructional paths and branching, graphic presentation, feedback mechanisms, coaching elements.
- Create databases to contain content and to collect data.
- Integrate content, databases, functionality, and user interface.
- Work with subject-matter experts to test the prototype, with students in green retrofitting skills, which addresses completeness, accuracy, and timeliness.

Audience identification: The subject-matter experts involved in this project train individuals in green retrofitting construction skills. These learners come from a diversified population of occupations and specialty areas:

- Construction workers
- Contractors and subcontractors
- HVAC specialists
- Plumbing firms
- Architects
- Students

Scenario narrative: The user is sent to an older home. The homeowner wants an energy audit to determine if replacing windows will result in a lower energy cost. The simulation goal is to assess the home with respect to energy efficiency, give the home windows an overall energy efficiency grade, and make suggestions to the homeowner to help reduce the bills and increase the energy efficiency.

Game assessment design components: The assessment components are designed at two levels: (1) an *Overall Energy Efficiency Assessment* and (2) a *Specific Solution Implementation Assessment*. Each of these components can be further broken down into sub-assessments related to completeness, accuracy, and timeliness:

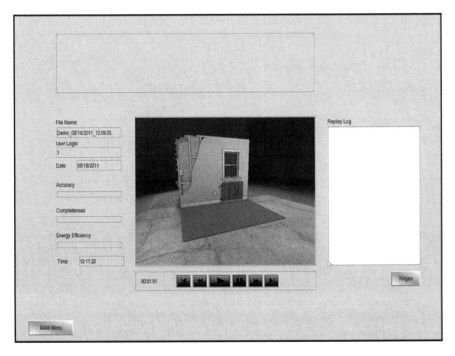

Fig. 7.7 Presentation of the virtual environment

Level 1: Overall energy efficiency assessment—exterior issues

In this stage, the learner is placed in a virtual environment (Fig. 7.7) representing a common building scenario. The learner navigates the environment searching for areas of possible energy loss including windows, doors, heating and cooling appliances, and insulation.

Once a location has been identified by the learner, he or she can navigate closer to it and click on the location. At this point, a window pops up (Fig. 7.8) that provides more specific information about the current energy efficiency of an item. Based on the information given, the learner is prompted to designate the area as "efficient," "needs improvement," or "not efficient."

The learner is presented with choices of priority regarding the area in question (Fig. 7.9).

These specifications are based on training standards. Once the learner has rated the area, she is prompted to move on to find another location and repeat the process. *Timeliness* is not a factor in this component; there are not any time requirements to master or measure. However, *accuracy and completeness* are significant assessment factors in this stage. Once the player scores above a predefined threshold within the components of *completeness* and *accuracy* within this level, they are advanced to level 2.

Fig. 7.8 Closer view of area in question

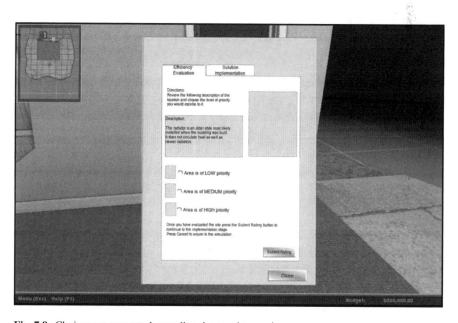

Fig. 7.9 Choices are presented regarding the area in question

Level 2: Overall energy efficiency assessment—interior issues

In this stage, the learner decides, based on the designations given to the efficiency spots in the previous phase and the resources at hand, how to improve the energy efficiency of the building concentrating on specific interior issues that are generally

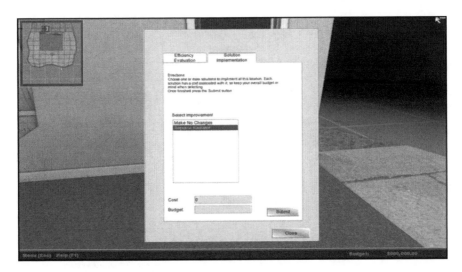

Fig. 7.10 Presentation of options for changes

more detailed and complex than what were addressed in level 1. The learner again navigates the environment to an area she feels needs improvement (Fig. 7.10), relying on the designations made earlier. Once the learner selects an element to improve and clicks on it, a new window appears with options on how to improve this element. After choosing a solution, the learner continues to the next spot that needs improvement. Again, timeliness is not measured for this particular scenario, but accuracy and completeness are measured and scored on a weighted spectrum depending on the instructional designer's assessment strategy.

Level 3: Specific solution implementation assessment

In this stage, the learner enters a more advanced stage of green building retrofitting by integrating aspects of budget analysis and priority in both the interior and exterior of the building. Additional information is offered as to choices the energy auditor can make based upon predefined materials, time-to-implement factors, and overall energy efficiency ratings. These choices are then mapped against the choices that expert auditors choose within the same scenario. Once the player scores above a predefined threshold within the components of *completeness, accuracy,* and *timeliness* within this level, they are considered to have successfully completed the scenario and may be granted access to additional scenarios.

Once the learner makes choices, the "dashboard" reflects the *completeness, accuracy,* and (if relevant, *timeliness*) assessment of the user's movements and choices.

At the end of each session, the learner can view an assessment as to the extent of the completed the goals of the scenario. Learners have the opportunity to reflect on the problems presented to them and investigate the environment to find the best way to implement an energy efficient solution.

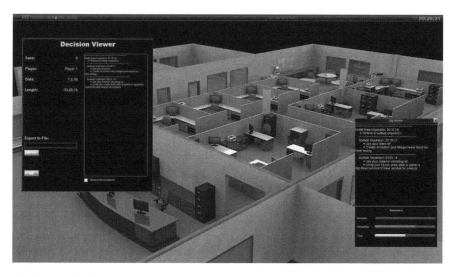

Fig. 7.11 A third-person game based on office politics using the automated assessment feature to track progress

The learner is assessed on whether hotspots are properly identified and rated, as well as the accuracy of the solutions chosen for implementation. The learner is also shown how long it took to evaluate the location. In addition, the building's energy efficiency is indicated on a scale; the low end is what the building was originally rated at, and the high end is the ideal level. Progress bars can be displayed at any time during the simulation. Leveling the play by progressing from simple-to-complex mirrors many traditional game motivational aspects of challenge by offering levels of accomplishment and reflection on one's actions within the environment. Progressing through the entire scenario by completing the tasks at hand through each of the three levels ensures compliance with activity-goal alignment theory and should thereby validate a successful learning experience as well.

7.5 Conclusions

Evaluating success and failures of automated assessment in the design and development of instructional simulations is often a function of who you are (trainer, student, or policy maker), what you are looking for (alignment with instructional goals), and where you look (points of assessment in the simulation). Identifying the array of design decisions and implementing assessment features better informs a strategy of flexibility in meeting the needs of the students and instructor while maintaining system integrity (see Fig. 7.11).

Development work related to building a generalizable and scalable automated assessment system within a complex 3D virtual simulation environment remains an area for further research. The automated assessment should function within the scope of allowing for multiple and complex decision features. In addition, the feedback mechanism needs to provide the user with information regarding the aspects of horizontal, independent choices vs. linear, dependent choices. The system should always provide accurate and pertinent feedback. Creating activities closely aligned with learning objectives is a key in ensuring learning goals will be met. These issues are significant design-side challenges for further automated assessment development within game-based OELEs. We provided descriptions for one case of prototype design and development, along with the transfer of the prototype components into a new application for virtual 3D world assessments. This approach offers at least one design process for automated assessment in simulations and provides an example of the adaptability of this assessment model for general instructional design activities.

Acknowledgments Portions of this chapter were presented at the 2011 American Educational Research Association international conference. The authors wish to acknowledge Chad Coats, Jon Scoresby, Andrew Hayes, and Jeffrey Olsen for their contributions to this work.

References

Aldrich, C. (2005). *Simulations and the future of learning: An innovative (and perhaps revolutionary) approach to e-learning*. San Francisco, CA: Wiley.
Angelo, T. A., & Cross, P. C. (1993). *Classroom assessment techniques* (2nd ed.). San Francisco: Jossey-Bass.
Banuls, V. A., & Salmeron, J. L. (2007). A scenario-based assessment model—SBAM. *Technological Forecasting and Social Change, 74*(1), 750–762.
Barab, S., Gresalfi, M., & Arici, A. (2009). Why educators should care about games. *Educational Leadership, 67*(1), 76–80.
Belland, B. (2011). How to judge if they (are on track to) achieve: The importance of aligning assessment with learning objectives. In D. Ifenthaler, D. Eseryel, & X. Ge (Eds.), *Assessment in game-based learning: Foundations, innovations, and perspectives*. New York: Springer.
Carolan, T. F., Bilazarian, P., & Nguyen, L. (2005). *Automated individual, team, and multi-team performance assessment to support debriefing distributed simulation based exercises (DDSBE)* [online report]. Retrieved from http://www.dtic.mil/cgi-bin/GetTRDoc?AD=ADA460383&Location=U2&doc=GetTRDoc.pdf.
Driscoll, M. P. (2000). *Psychology of learning for instruction* (2nd ed.). Needham Heights, MA: Allyn & Bacon.
Elton, L., & Laurillard, D. (1979). Trends in student learning. *Studies in Higher Education, 4*, 87–102.
Freeman, J., Salter, W. J., & Hoch, S. (2004). *The users and functions of debriefing in distributed, simulation-based team training*. Human factors and ergonomics society 48th annual meeting, New Orleans, LA.
Gee, J. P. (2008). The ecology of games: Connecting youth, games, and learning. In K. Salen (Ed.), *Learning and games* (pp. 21–40). Cambridge, MA: MIT Press.
Gibbons, A. S., & Fairweather, G. B. (1998). *Computer-based instruction: Design and development*. Englewood Cliffs, NJ: Educational Technology Publications.
Gibbons, A. S., & Sommer, S. (2007). Layered design in an instructional simulation. In B. E. Shelton & D. Wiley (Eds.), *The design and use of simulation computer games in education* (pp. 85–102). Rotterdam, The Netherlands: Sense Publishers.

Keller, J. M. (1993). *Motivation by design*. Tallahassee: Florida State University.

Ketelhut, D. J., Nelson, B. C., Clarke, J., & Dede, C. (2010). A multi-user virtual environment for building and assessing higher order inquiry skills in science. *British Journal of Educational Technology, 41*(1), 56–68.

Kirkley, S., & Kirkley, J. (2005). Creating next generation blended learning environments using mixed reality, video games and simulations. *TechTrends, 49*(3), 42–53.

Malone, T. W., & Lepper, M. R. (1987). Making learning fun: A taxonomy of intrinsic motivations for learning. In R. E. Snow & M. J. Farr (Eds.), *Aptitude, learning and instruction, volume 3: Cognitive and affective process analysis*. Englewood Cliffs, NJ: Erlbaum.

Mislevy, R. (2011). Evidence centered design as a framework for understanding games and assessments. In D. Ifenthaler, D. Eseryel, & X. Ge (Eds.), *Assessment in game-based learning: Foundations, innovations, and perspectives*. New York: Springer.

Mislevy, R., Almond, R. G., & Lukas, J. (2004). *A brief introduction to evidence-centered design*. CSE Technical Report 632, The National Center for Research on Evaluation, Standards, Student Testing (CRESST) [online report]. Retrieved from http:// www.cse.ucla.edu/products/reports/r632.pdf.

Nelson, B., Erlandson, B., & Denham, A. (2010). Global channels of evidence for learning and assessment in complex game environments. *British Journal of Educational Technology, 42*(1), 88–100.

Neville, D., & Shelton, B. E. (2010). Literary and historical 3D-DGBL: Design guidelines. *Simulation & Gaming, 41*(4), 607–629.

Scoresby, J., & Shelton, B. E. (2007). *Using videogame motivation analysis during game play activity aligned with learning objectives*. Chicago, IL: American Educational Research Association (AERA).

Scoresby, J., & Shelton, B. E. (2011). Visual perspectives within educational computer games: Effects on presence and flow within virtual learning environments. *Instructional Science, 39*(3), 227–254.

Shelton, B. E. (2007). Designing instructional games for activity-goal alignment. In B. E. Shelton & D. Wiley (Eds.), *The design and use of simulation computer games in education*. Rotterdam, The Netherlands: Sense Publishers.

Shelton, B. E., & Scoresby, J. (2011). Aligning game activity with educational goals: Following a constrained design approach to instructional computer games. *Educational Technology Research & Development, 59*(1), 113–138. Advance online publication. doi: 10.1007/s11423-010-9175-0.

Shelton, B. E., Scoresby, J., Parlin, M. A., & Olsen, J. (2011). *Facing the design and development challenges of implementing embedded automated assessment systems in virtual environments*. New Orleans, LA: American Educational Research Association (AERA).

Shelton, B. E., Stowell, T., Scoresby, J., Alvarez, M., Capell, M., & Coats, K. C. (2010). A Frankenstein approach to open source: The construction of a 3D game engine as meaningful educational process. *IEEE Transactions on Learning Technologies, 3*(2), 85–90. doi:ieeecomputersociety.org/10.1109/TLT.2010.3.

Shelton, B. E., & Wiley, D. (2006). *Instructional designers take all the fun out of games: Rethinking elements of engagement for designing instructional games*. San Francisco, CA: American Educational Research Association (AERA).

Shute, V. J. (1993). A comparison of learning environments: All that glitters. In S. P. Lajoie & S. J. Derry (Eds.), *Computers as cognitive tools* (pp. 47–75). Hillsdale, NJ: Erlbaum.

Silva, E. (2009). Measuring skills for 21st century learning. *Phi Delta Kappan, 90*(9), 630–634.

Squire, K. (2003). Changing the game: What happens when video games enter the classroom? *Innovate, 1*(6) [online report]. Retrieved from http://www.innovateonline.info/index.php?view=article&id=82.

Stowell, T., Scoresby, J., Coats, C., Capell, M., & Shelton, B. E. (2009). Utilizing readily available and open source libraries to create a 3D game engine. *International Journal of Gaming and Computer-Mediated Simulations, 1*(4), 20–49.

Chapter 8
Information Trails: In-Process Assessment of Game-Based Learning

Christian S. Loh

8.1 Introduction

Imagine the following scenario: A large game development company contacted a local high school about the opportunity to beta-test a new digital game pertaining to leadership training (twenty-first century skills) for the seniors. The school administrator, the teachers, and the seniors are all excited about the possibilities offered by the game and are interested to know if game-based learning is indeed as effective as hyped. The seniors were asked to put in about 30 h of game play in order to give the game enough time to "work" its magic. Eager to see game-based learning in action, the teachers and administrator agreed that a third of that time should take place in the school computer lab under the teachers' supervision. The Non-Disclosure Agreement was signed and all went well.

After 3 months or so (10–12 weeks), the project was concluded amidst much fanfare, but many had questions about the outcomes. Besides feeling great, is it possible for the students to evaluate their own success objectively? How can the teachers ascertain if 30 h of game play (as recommended by the game company) is adequate to acquire the skills taught in the game?

Extracurricular activities, such as the Future Business Leaders of America (FBLA) and National Honor Society, have been the venue for student leadership training; how well would the game compare to these traditional approaches? Some teachers were wondering if there is a way to know which of the classes performed better and considered contacting the game company for a breakdown of the records. Should they even bother? Are such records being kept at all? How would the school administrators document the effectiveness of the game in a report for next month's Parent–Teacher Association (PTA) meeting?

C.S. Loh (✉)
Virtual Environment Lab (V-Lab), Department of Curriculum and Instruction, Southern Illinois University Carbondale, 625 Wham Drive, Mailcode 4610, Carbondale, IL 62901, USA
e-mail: csloh@siu.edu

D. Ifenthaler et al. (eds.), *Assessment in Game-Based Learning: Foundations, Innovations, and Perspectives*, DOI 10.1007/978-1-4614-3546-4_8,
© Springer Science+Business Media New York 2012

123

8.1.1 Who Is Asking the Question?

"How do we assess the effectiveness of game-based learning?" is obviously the big question that is begging to be answered. But before we proceed to discuss the implications of that question (as will be dealt with in the rest of the chapter), let us consider first, who is asking the question?

While it is natural to focus on the play-learners (the high school seniors, in our scenario) as the target audience in a discussion about assessments for game-based learning, we need to recognize that these learners are not necessarily the "customers" of the serious games. We counted at least three different user-groups of game-based learning, and each came with their own agenda. In fact, out of the three user-groups, the learners are probably the ones with the least interest about assessment of game-based learning. We will examine who these user-groups are and what added values game-based learning will bring for them:

1. The first user-group consists of the *Learners*, who are the primary target of game-based learning. They are the ones who will have firsthand experience with the game and are supposed to benefit most from its usage. As such, the learners need to have a sense of what goals they have achieved (over time spent) throughout the learning process. Information that is useful to this group of users includes keeping scores on the number of outstanding and completed learning goals, time taken to complete certain levels of learning, total time spent in the learning environment per day/week/semester and bottlenecks (where they may be "stuck" or killed in the game). Such information needs to be made available to the learner in the form of a simple report for self-evaluation purposes.

   While the Learners are indeed the primary "consumers" of game, they are not necessarily the "customers" of game-based learning applications; meaning, the Learners are not the selectors and purchasers of these resources. These learning applications are "often chosen or paid for indirectly by program sponsors, not the participants themselves" (Aldrich, 2009, p. 15). Whereas, in the digital games for entertainment market, the purchasers are the one who tend to be using the games.

2. The second user-group is made up of the *Trainers*. They are the assessors of the game-based learning and have immediate supervisory role over the learners. These are school teachers in our scenario, but could easily be instructors or supervisors in the business training industries, or sergeants in the military. Because of their responsibilities over the learners, they need to keep track of what is happening in the virtual game environments and monitor the learners' activities to ensure the learners are on-task. As assessors, they require a means to easily visualize the learners' data, both individually and en masse.

   Some kind of software-based reporting is necessary for the assessors to monitor the learning progress of the learners, track the number of objectives met, identify mistakes made by the trainees, and allow for appropriate remediation to be prescribed in a timely manner. This means that the report should ideally reflect real-time data and not an "after action report" made available only after the game is completed (3 months later according to our scenario). Data visualization functions are very important to the Trainers group because outlier(s)—i.e., learner(s) who are behaving differently from the expected norm—must be spotted as early as possible. A real-time report would empower the Trainers to take action early enough in the training cycle to alert the learner(s) of their situation, evaluate said action (that is out of the norm), and correct that action via remediation (or not), before the mistakes become entrenched.

3. The *Administrators* made up the third user-group. They may be sponsor(s) of the game-based learning or the reporting officer(s) situated above the Trainers in the organization chart, or both. In very large organizations, there may be more than one level of administrators. In a military context, for example, the administrators could be the commanders of a large-scale joint-exercise. In our scenario, the PTA and district superintendent may also be included in this user-group.

This group of users is usually less interested in individual performance reports about the learners. Instead, as sponsors, they are most concerned with the benefit–cost ratio (BCR) of the game-based learning. In other words, from an investment point of view, the Administrators are the purchasers, and they want to make sure that the game-based learning products actually "deliver." Sometimes, performance data of Trainers may also be of interest to the Administrators. Trainers' data that are associated with Learner achievements can be used to show additional efforts put in by the trainers, and to determine which Learning Center is out-performing others. Let's say a certain school was found to have the best achievement score among others in the same district after a certain multiplayer online game for learning was implemented. The superintendent may be interested to find out if this particular school had used a different approach to raise achievement scores. All this information should be presented in some kind of intelligent online assessment report, capable of highlighting the weaknesses, strengths, accomplishments, potentials for improvement, and may need to be sortable by trainers, learning centers, and other filters.

While all three user-groups, Learners, Trainers and Administrators, benefit from the addition of a powerful assessment reporting system in game-based learning, no such assessment system exists (to the best of the author's knowledge) at the time of the writing. Obviously, as long as the needs of the customers of game-based learning are not being satisfied, the demand for assessment of game-based learning will continue to grow.

8.2 Assessments and Game-Based Learning

In education, assessment is regarded as an important and integral part of the learning process. If learning is likened to a journey, then textbooks, classroom teaching, e-learning, games and simulations are the vehicles that deliver the learners from starting point A to end point B. From an Administrator's point of view, assessment is the quality assurance protocol that ensures the learners have indeed arrived at the correct destination—i.e., achieving the stipulated learning goals based on the benefit/cost negotiated. Learning activities without an assessment component are informal and similar to the endeavors of hobbyists, at best.

Proponents of game-based learning have asserted this to be a highly suitable medium to impart twenty-first century skills to the gamer generation (see Aldrich, 2009; Gee, 2007; Gibson, Aldrich, & Prensky, 2006; van Eck, 2006). This lead some people to perceive game-based learning as a twenty-first century approach to learning brought on by digital technology. However, Botturi and Loh (2008) found many ancient ties between game playing and learning and suggested that game-based learning is just a new approach to revive an ancient tradition. Some parallels between game playing and learning persist even today: e.g., school principals were regarded as "game masters" of the arena by the ancients.

Unfortunately, digital games are not all created equal and are, therefore, not all suitable for learning. As Chen and Michael (2005) noted, the inclusion of assessment components appears to be the main difference distinguishing the more "serious" games from the rest that were created for entertainment. Sans the requirement for learners to demonstrate the "abilities" they have acquired from the course of instruction (Joosten-ten Brinke, Gorissen, & Latour, 2005), there are no means of knowing if the learners have indeed "arrived" at the learning destinations.

Outside education and research communities, game-based learning has also received acclaim from the business industries and training sectors (e.g., Aldrich, 2009; Kapp and O'Driscoll, 2010). However, the appeal of serious games and game-based learning to these industries is not so much in the ability to automate training tasks (as do other computer-based instructions), but to co-locate massive numbers of trainees simultaneously to mitigate the high costs typically associated with training (e.g., Duffy, 1997; Wilson et al., 2008). As the military, large corporations and institutions of higher learning implement large-scale virtual environments for training and e-learning, the demand for formalized assessments with game-based learning is sure to increase.

8.2.1   Two Types of Assessments

Newcomers to the games and simulations research will probably be overwhelmed by the massive body of literature (see Hays, 2005; O'Neil & Robertson, 1992; Tobias & Fletcher, 2007) covering all sorts of issues from design, graphics, mode of delivery, narratives, theories, and philosophies to their potential uses for learning. Although some researchers are currently working to address the need for assessment in game-based learning (e.g., Rupp, Gushta, Mislevy & Shaffer, 2010), more effort is needed to fill the gap.

Educator–researchers refer to two different kinds of assessment: summative (assessment for learning) and formative (assessment of learning). Summative assessment is typically conducted towards the end of a course of instruction because

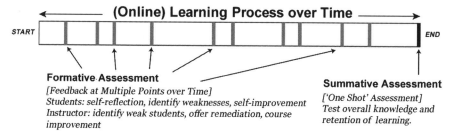

Fig. 8.1 Overview of formative and summative assessments in a learning environment

it is designed to test a person's understanding, retention, or mastery of the subject after a course completion. The after action reports (AAR) used by the military are a prime example of summative assessment. Formative assessment *of* learning, on the other hand, is designed to measure the amount of learning that is still taking place while the course of instruction is ongoing, and that assessment can occur as many times as deemed necessary by the trainer or instructor.

When taken as a conterminous process, assessment of learning is actually more useful to educators than summative assessment because it helps them fine tune the instructional and learning processes. Feedback, often cited in formative assessment research, has been found to be the single most powerful influence in learning improvement (see Black & Wiliam, 1998, 2009; Hattie, 1987). Likewise, in peer- and self-assessment (used as formative assessment) among students of online collaborative learning environments, the feedback received at multiple points over the learning process has been shown to provide students with self-reflection on the learning process, help them identify areas for improvement, and take ownership of their own learning (Lee, 2008). It is clear that an effective formative assessment component would benefit not only the instructors, but also the learners, in an interactive online learning environment such as game-based learning (see Fig. 8.1).

8.2.2   Assessing Game-Based Learning: The Issues

When both instructor and learners are face-to-face, an instructor can directly observe the learners' physical behaviors as evidence of learning and participation (Harrington, Meisels, McMahon, Dichtelmiller, & Jablon, 1997). Traditional assessment metrics such as test scores, classroom participation, and time-on-task were originally crafted to take advantage of the simultaneous presence of both the trainers and trainees at one physical location.

The situation changes dramatically when trainers are no longer able to "see" learners face-to-face. (Some online learning applications attempt to overcome this problem by allowing trainers to "see" the learners using web-cams and video streaming technology.) Until there is a safe way to put probes into the minds of learners to directly measure the amount of learning that occurs, trainers must rely on external measures for assessment. Although some online learning environments allow students to virtually "raise their hands" to ask questions during online lessons, other direct observational measurements of human actions, behaviors, and expressions still prove to be difficult. This means that researchers in the field must create new tools to collect better data. This area of research is obviously still in its infancy as current literature is equivocal about how best to conduct assessment with game-based learning. There also appear to be more problems than available solutions at this juncture. For instance:

1. Without properly designed games, there will be nothing to assess with. Should educators create new games from the ground up with commercial game engines (i.e., the industry model), or modify existing commercial games using development kits (i.e., the "grass root" model)? Current game development models used by the game industry tend to exclude teachers' inputs. Cheaper and easy-to-use game development tools are in order, as are game development models that are suitable for use by educators (see Younis & Loh, 2010).
2. Because many of the known traditional assessment methodologies are not directly useable within virtual environments, researchers may need to search for new, effective, and meaningful ways to conduct assessments with game-based learning. Traditional statistical methods are not as effective compared to educational data mining (EDM) in dealing with massive amounts of data obtainable from online learning environments. New assessment and data analysis methods are both in demand.
3. Based on the criticism that combining assessment with games can severely interrupt "flow" (Csikszentmihalyi, 1990) and render the game "not fun to play" (Prensky, 2001), some researchers have proposed workarounds through "stealth assessment" (e.g., Shute & Spector, 2008; Shute et al., 2010). However, others have reported that the effects appeared negligible (e.g., Reese, 2010). More research is needed in this area.
4. Some researchers see game-based learning as an extension of e-learning and suggest that the assessment component should be integrated into a learning management system (LMS) that is compliant with SCORM (i.e., Sharable Content Object Reference Model) (Moreno-Ger, Burgos, Martínez-Ortiz, Sierra & Fernández-Manjón, 2008). Others see this type of learning to be digital games with instructional intent, and they should therefore, have the feel of "real games" approximating commercial production quality (van Eck, 2006). If so, then the assessment component ought to be integrated into the game engine (e.g., Loh, Anantachai, Byun & Lenox, 2007), and not reside within an LMS. Is there a third, or even a fourth, approach to resolving this issue?
5. Current understanding of game-based learning is built upon summative assessment studies conducted after training has been completed. Researchers need to move out of their comfort zones and begin looking into the development of formative assessments that take place throughout game-based learning (e.g., Loh & Byun, 2009; Reese, 2010).

The list of issues goes on.

8.2.3 Measuring Performance in Virtual Environment

In today's workplace, be it virtual or physical, performance improvement has much to do with waste reduction and output increase. While many work incidents could indeed contribute to "waste" and require reduction, one of the worst types of waste is "habitual man-made mistakes" because it costs the company twice as much to re-train workers to unlearn their mistakes. Moreover, as is the case of a recent study by the National Transportation Safety Board, flaws in flight simulators used to train airline pilots have been linked to more than half of 522 fatalities in US airline accidents since year 2000 (Levin, 2010). Such flaws and mistakes—even when it was not directly the fault of the workers—result in losses for the company, both in terms of legal compensations and reputation. It is important, therefore, for trainers and trainees to strive to recognize human errors in tandem during training and rectify these mistakes before they have a chance to become entrenched and turned into costly errors.

Although physical training games such as basketball, javelin throwing, and sprinting build up real muscles in the body and improve psychomotor skills, training with digital games is more suited for the building up of "brain muscles" and cognitive thinking skills. Hence, advocates are calling for the development of more game-like environments that teach twenty-first century skills, which include leadership, project management, and negotiation skills (Aldrich, 2009; Prensky, 2006). Apparently, "brain muscle" training in game-like environments is not unlike physical (muscle) training, as the core features in many serious games consisted of numerous "trials and errors and repetition of steps" (Saridaki, Mourlas, Gouscos, & Meimaris, 2007). Evidently, both physical and cognitive training games utilize regular practice and just-in-time feedback to "strengthen" relevant muscle groups in the learners as they progress towards the learning goals.

Due to the amount of repetitive training and the number of trainees involved in some multi-user online (training) games, monitoring all the events that are happening would easily lead to trainer fatigue. Since it is deemed more cost-effective to co-locate trainers with trainees in a one-to-many ratio, trainers will necessitate appropriate supports to better monitor trainees' actions en masse; especially if they are expected to detect deviations in the trainees' behaviors that could lead to habitual errors.

Bearing in mind that some game-based training may last as long as 20–40 h (spread over several weeks), unchecked errors have the good possibility of becoming entrenched through reinforcement. The greater the potentials of an online multiplayer training millions of trainees simultaneously, the greater the risk; as even one small error can quickly accelerate to reach critical mass. Therefore, besides presenting appropriately designed contents for learning, a good, game-based training must also support formative assessments that are targeted at both the instructors as well as the trainees, for all the reasons and the learning supports mentioned in earlier sections.

8.3   Gathering Empirical Data

In commercial game development, once a game is completed, it is quickly turned into profit. Very few developers would actually be interested in *in-process* data collection unless it somehow contributed to the usability of their games (which might, in turn, affect overall profits). In this chapter, the term "in-process assessment" is used specifically to refer to an ongoing formative assessment conducted throughout the game-based learning while the game session is ongoing.

Adding an assessment components to serious games (mentioned by Chen & Michael, 2005) would constitute additional work for the programmers, who must be paid. Game developers see assessment components in games as an additional cost overhead that undercut their profit margins. Unless developers knew beforehand about how to recuperate the costs, they would be reluctant to invest in the creation of an assessment component, much less to integrate one into a game engine. This might explain why there have been very few games created with assessment components, despite high interest among the game-based learning community for them. Fortunately, the tide began to turn after Georg Zoeller presented on "developer-facing telemetry for games" at the Game Developer Conference (GDC) 2010. (More information can be found at http://gdc.gulbsoft.org/talk)

8.3.1   Telemetry

The American Heritage Dictionary defines "Telemetry" (n.d.) as "The science and technology of automatic measurement and transmission of data by radio or other means from remote sources to receiving stations for recording and analysis." In simpler terms, telemetry is a technological process that allows remote data collection and information retrieval. Since telemetry's origin in the nineteenth century, it has been used by many industries, including the medical field, law enforcement, wildlife research, space exploration, motor racing, and traffic control. In many cases, the objects of interest were tagged with technological devices that allowed remote tracking and the data collected by these devices were compiled into metrics, which were then remotely sent back to the researcher for recording and analysis. A "developer-facing telemetry" suggested that the results of the analysis were meant for developers' (and not gamers') consumption. Based on our discussions, assessments for game-based learning can be said to be comprised of "learner-," "trainer-," and "administrator-facing" telemetries.

In his presentation, Zoeller (2010), a Lead Technical Designer of Bioware, disclosed how he had made use of a data collection server during the development of Dragon Age: Origins (2009) to track and reward developers' activities and to collect in-process beta testers' data for game balancing and design improvement. (The same telemetry is also employed in *Dragon Age 2* (2011), evidence of this can be found in the config.ini file.) The most difficult part of the telemetry to him was the "data visualization" process: to convert the raw data into a humanly understandable format, to afford him a better understanding of the information, and to use it to steer

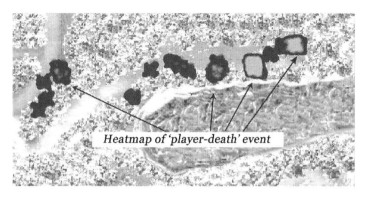

Fig. 8.2 Example of a "heatmap" showing the zones where "player-death" event occurs *most frequently.* (Partial screenshot of *PeTRA*, used with permission)

game improvement. Traditional graphs are not useful for this type of analysis because of the unconventional data collected. New ways of data visualization are required and must be "invented" accordingly on a scenario-by-scenario basis.

Some months later, Pruett (2010), an independent game developer, published an article detailing how he had created a small-scale metrics reporting system for telemetry and used it to improve a mobile phone game he had developed. Once the data were obtained through telemetry, Pruett used the "heatmap" technique (see Fig. 8.2) to help him visualize the "bottlenecks" in his mobile game and subsequently improve its game play via "balancing." Bottlenecks, in this case, meant areas that were too difficult for players (i.e., they died), and "balancing" meant tweaking the game to provide players with better weapons, weaker bosses, more health potions, etc. (to help them overcome the bottlenecks). The overall intent was to provide gamers with a challenging, but enjoyable time instead of making them feel frustrated to the point of giving up.

We should recognize that game developers and academic researchers will both benefit from enhanced game engines, imbued with telemetric capabilities to track and report player and game events remotely. On one hand, the data analysis process provides insights to the game developers on how to improve the usability and design of their games. On the other hand, the game metrics are of value to researchers for the *in-process* assessment of game-based learning. The creation of game development tools integrated with telemetry could throw open the flood gates and help make assessments for game-based learning a reality in the future.

8.3.2   Psychophysiological Measurement

Researchers in the fields of psychology, cognition science, usability testing, and human–computer interface have had a long history in using automatic event loggings to study human (and animal) behaviors within interactive systems (e.g., Skinner, 1938). Since digital games are interactive systems, such psychometric methodologies have also proven useful for researchers in the field of "game play experience" research. In these studies, players' reactions during game play are meticulously recorded and matched to game contents, using a combination of quantitative and qualitative approaches including: video recordings of game play sessions, interviews of attitudes, self-reports, and psychophysiological measurements (which graph emotional responses and states of arousal of players during game play).

Video game "user experience" (UX) researchers believe that the combinations of data are indicative of the levels of "flow" (Csikszentmihalyi, 1990) and engagement in the players. As such, the research findings can reveal how players perceive the game contents (as boring, engaging, fun, etc.). Such information is useful to the game publishers who can then decide to take advantage of the information (or not) to adjust and improve their products. Some of the psychophysiological measurement includes:

1. Measurement of skin electrical conductivity indicative of fear and excitement using galvanic skin response (GSR) and electro-dermal activity (EDA).
2. Measurement of brain wave patterns of players during game play using electro-encephalograms (EEG).
3. Measurement of cardiovascular activities (e.g., heart rate variability, beat per minutes) of players under different levels of excitement and fear using electro-cardiograms (ECG).
4. Measurement of facial muscle activities (e.g., smile, frown, etc.) during game play using electromyography (EMG).
5. Measurement of pupil diameter under different emotional and arousal influence through pupillometry and eye-movement.
6. Measurement and analysis of gaze directions upon the computer screen during game play using electro-oculograms (EOG).

However, as digital games grew in complexity, researchers have begun to voice the need for an integrated logging framework that would afford automatic psychometric data collection and make game play research easier (see Nacke, Lindley, & Stellmach, 2008; Sasse, 2008). As expected, game publishers are slow to comply with the request; none have so far. While the inaction could be due to the additional cost incurred, or the failure to see a quick profit turn-around; it is also possible that the call is once again being perceived as another "academic advice" (as mentioned in the previous section).

Since a person's motivation and engagement level can greatly impact learning, psychophysiological data can indeed be useful for the assessment of players' "affective performance" in game-based learning. At the very least, psychophysiological data should be usable in conjunction with other assessment methods to triangulate research outcomes. In this early stage, only findings with first-person-shooters have been reported (e.g., Nacke, Grimshaw, & Lindley, 2010 Nacke & Lindley, 2010; Nacke et al., 2008). Would the psychophysiological measurement prove to be equally informative for other game genres, including: role playing games, strategy games, and massively multiplayer online games? The large gap in literature indicates that this field has a lot of potential for growth in the future.

8.3.3 The "Black Box" Effect

In order to improve the process of learning and instruction, educators must constantly experiment with new methods of instruction and assess their effectiveness. Pretest–posttest experimentation is a common research method employed by educators in traditional classrooms to ascertain the effectiveness of untested instructional processes. On the first look, the pretest–posttest methodology may appear to be useful for the assessment of game-based learning (e.g., Kebritchi, 2008). Typically, two identical tests are administered, one before (pretest) and one after (posttest) a certain experimental method of instruction (i.e., intervention). Keeping other variables constant, the difference in achievement scores (Δ), i.e., posttest minus pretest (t_2-t_1), may then be attributed to the improvement brought about by the intervention itself.

Even though the pretest–posttest method of inquiry can indeed demonstrate positive effects for game-based learning, it cannot fully explain which chain of events or sequence of actions performed by learners (in the game) actually contributed to those positive effects. In this sense, game-based learning remains an impenetrable "black box" because no one knows for sure how or why the intervention works (even if it does). Unless we educators quarantine learners individually, prevent them from speaking with one another, and restrict access of external learning materials, how can we be sure that the change in achievement scores (Δ) truly reveals the amount of learning gained?

Moreover, the "black box" effect renders the intervention vulnerable to external threats because it is impossible to identify if any external factor has entered the system and has affected the data collected. For example, there is no way to tell if trainees are trying to "game the system"—i.e., exploiting properties of the system to succeed in the environment rather than learning the materials as intended by the system designer (see Baker, Corbett, Roll, & Koedinger, 2008). Naturally, the Administrator group could not allow the existence of a loophole as big as this within the system.

From the perspectives of the Trainers, the over-reliance on posttest results is also unsettling. By the time the (overall) effects of game-based learning can be determined via the *posttest*, it may be too late and too costly to re-train the Learners. While this problem is not immediately apparent in "clinical" research studies that subject learners to only 1–2 h of game play, the effect is amplified in commercial off-the-shelf (COTS) games that require much longer (20–40 h) to complete. The inclusion of telemetry into serious games would be the first step in the right direction towards true assessments for game-based learning.

This does not mean that researchers should not use other methods to assess the effectiveness of game-based learning. For instance, qualitative analysis remains an important research methodology when we are looking for rich data involving small group of learners, or in case studies. Because the data collection processes for qualitative analysis often require long hours of video-recording, record-keeping, and meticulous audio transcriptions, it is not practical for the assessment of game-based learning involving a large population of learners. For every hour of game play which requires three times that amount of time to analyze, it would take far too long to analyze thousands of learners who have each accrued 20–40 h of game-based learning. (For a longer treatise on this topic, see Loh, 2009.)

8.4   Introducing Information Trails©

The research leading to *Information Trails* began with one supposition: if a person's actions and behaviors are determined by his/her decision-making process, is it possible to break down (or reverse engineer) the decision-making process based on the person's actions and behaviors? The logic behind the supposition is very similar to a crime scene investigation in which a CSI agent tries to determine how a crime was committed based on the evidence found at the crime scene. If decisions are the products of a person's knowledge schema, then it should be possible to express the effects of learners' actions (e.g., speed, accuracy, and strategy) in a learning environment as a function of their understanding of the learning problems vs. their problem solving skills or abilities (Loh, 2006). Go down that road and substitute multi-user virtual environments (MUVE) for "learning environment," and the path will eventually lead to *Information Trails* (Loh, 2006b; Loh et al., 2007). The only obstacle remaining is the "back box" of game-based learning, which can be cracked open using telemetry.

Conceptually, *Information Trails* is a series of event markers deposited within any information ecology at certain intervals over a period of time. The event markers can later be retrieved from the information ecology for storage and data analysis. In practice, streams of user actions are automatically tracked and recorded at intervals, triggered by "event calls" issued from the game engines over the entire course of game-based learning (see Fig. 8.3). The detailed data collected can be used to visualize the most common paths taken by learners to reach certain learning goals, and may be used to compare a learner's problem-solving strategy against that of an expert's. Deviations from the normal route could either mean unusual approaches to reach learning goals or be indicative of misguided decisions leading to man-made errors.

With large amounts of data collected in massively multiplayer environments, hidden patterns of learner behaviors can be uncovered through EDM. It is then up to the trainers to decide what course of action should be taken to remediate or to correct the deviation. The framework has been successfully developed into several working prototypes through a series of funded research. Not surprisingly, the military was the first party to show some interest in the project. This explains why player-movement was the first feature to be investigated (and implemented). Besides military and business training, preliminary data suggest that *Information Trails* can also be used to trace learning within online virtual learning environments (VLE) for medical simulation/training, and virtual worlds.

8.4.1   From Games to Information Trails

Debuted in 2002 and 2006, the commercial off-the-shelf *Neverwinter Nights* (*NWN* and *NWN2*, produced by Bioware, and Obsidian Entertainment, respectively) were part of a series of third-person role-playing games published by Atari. The game has its origin as a pen-and-paper *Dungeons & Dragons* game set in a fictional world

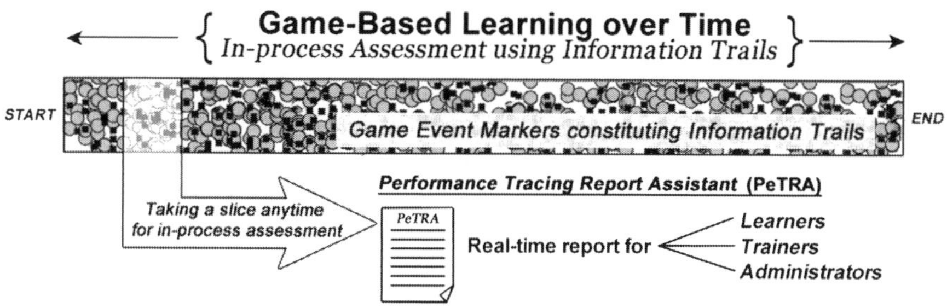

Fig. 8.3 *Information Trails*: In-process assessments for game-based learning

called *Faerun*, where men and other fantastic creatures (e.g., dwarves, elves, dragons, giants) inhabited the land. One unique feature that separates *NWNs* from many other COTS games is the included game development kit (GDK). With the GDK, gamers are given the authoring tool to create their own game modules/stories for sharing. This social game *mod*-ification practice was later named "game modding" by the gamer community.

Although the default language of the game is English, it is fairly easy to modify the game's user interface into other languages, including Chinese. As a role-playing game, *NWNs* have great potential for use in the teaching of a foreign language. Educators who used *SecondLife* (*SL*) to create virtual environments for the teaching of foreign languages will, no doubt, find many similarities between modding in *NWNs* and rezzing in *SL* (Kaplan-Rakowski & Loh, 2010). Despite the medieval settings of the game environment in *NWNs*, it did not deter the US military and NATO from adapting the game for training (Weil et al., 2005) and research (Warren & Sutton, 2008).

Over the years, the modifiable game has steadily garnered a large group of followers; among them are many educators and researchers who have learned to "mod" the game according to their needs. For example, some were created for scientific research (Gorniak & Roy, 2005), while others have been used to teach classroom learning subjects, ranging from journalism (Berger, 2006), to story writing (Robertson & Good, 2005) and mathematics skills (BBC News, 2007). Reader should note that *all* of the "game modules" produced in this manner are standalone games, and are therefore, not directly assessable.

In order to create an *Information Trails* empowered game with assessment capability, *in-process* data collection (while the game session is ongoing) is a necessary step. User-generated data must first be retrieved from the game engine (as the game is being played) and then be stored apart from the game, in order to facilitate retrieval for data analysis (independent of the game). An event listener, *NWNX*, is employed to achieve the "handshake" between the game engine and the remote/external database server (*MySQL*). The *NWNX* was originally created by *NWN* gamers (Stieger, 2008) to transform the standalone *NWN* into a server running online "persistent worlds," which are very early forms of massively multiplayer online games (MMOGs).

Once a communication channel between the game engine and database server is established, it is finally possible to transmit data for telemetry. The final step would be to create the online reporting interface according to the needs of the clients—be it Learners, Trainers, or Administrators. Since it would yield far too much data if we set out to capture every available event in the game, we have chosen to capture only a selected list of game events, using an Objective Hierarchy Map that ranked the events by importance according to game story development, and relevance to learning/training goals.

The game events currently being recorded include: conversations between players, players' death, players' spawn, players entering and exiting the game, items gained or lost, experience points gained by players, enemies killed, and learning goal(s) achieved. Movements of the players (as x-, y-coordinates) were recorded at regular intervals using the "heartbeat script." As the name suggests, a heartbeat script is a script that is auto-fired by the game engine (just like a regular heartbeat).

8.4.2   An Integrated Assessment System for GBL

By leveraging the knowledge base amassed by the community of *NWN* "game modders" (i.e., gamers who modify existing games for personal enjoyment), we were able to create the first working *Information Trails* system and showcased it at the 2008 international conference for Computer Games: AI, Animation, Mobile, Interactive Multimedia, Educational & Serious Games (CGAMES). Since then, we have continued to improve upon the user interface (UI) and the database engine of *Information Trails*, refining the workflow into a viable process for the tracking of user-generated action data in game-based learning using telemetry.

As Zoeller mentioned, the most difficult piece of the telemetry was data visualization. When we first began working on the data visualization of *Information Trails*, we had no idea what it would eventually look like, except that it should show the movement of the player's avatar graphically. After several iterations of product design and development, we believe we have succeeded in creating an online assessment system for game-based learning (Loh & Li, 2010), comprised of a front-end for user-facing data collection (tracking), and a back-end for trainer-facing data analysis (reporting).

As shown in Fig. 8.4, the *Information Trails* system is made up of several integrated components, including:

1. An online game with user authentication (to facilitate tracking of individual learners).
2. An event listener or a trigger for the data collection processes.
3. A database server to facilitate data collection and record keeping.
4. A component to visualize the data as useful information (in this case, *Performance Tracing Report Assistant*, or *PeTRA*).
5. An optional game engine for in-house creation of game-based learning modules. (The making of the game may be outsourced to commercial game development companies.)

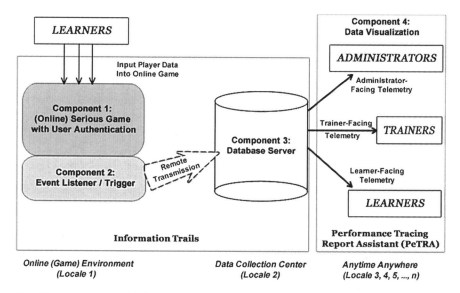

Fig. 8.4 Components of *Information Trails* and their relationships with *Performance Tracing Report Assistant* (*PeTRA*)

8.4.3 Finding New Ways to Visualize Data

After several attempts to visualize the collected user actions data, we finally settled on a bird's eye view of the area map. We used the game map to show positions of the learners within the game world over time as a series of connected dots. In the later versions of the report, we were able to overlay the path traversed on top of the area map, unlike in earlier versions (see Fig. 8.5). The inclusion of the full-color area map was important to the trainers because the visual cues (i.e., the geographical layout) enabled them to understand the decisions behind the learners' actions (movements).

As soon as game-based learning begins, user-generated action data become available through *PeTRA*. An automated data recording, analysis, and visualization process is important to *Information Trails* (and possibly, assessment of game-based learning in general) because not all trainers are versed in handling vast amounts of data, or in interpreting what they mean. Trainers will appreciate not having to deal with the raw data in order to make sense of the information contained therein. The report also allows for the replay of users' actions in a step-by-step fashion for debriefing purposes. Time taken by learners to meet various learning objectives is reported and compared against that of the experts. In this case, as practice time increases, the time taken to complete a particular learning task is expected to decrease as the learners move towards mastery. In addition, since *PeTRA* is fully interactive, performing a "mouse-over" above the dots will reveal the user actions

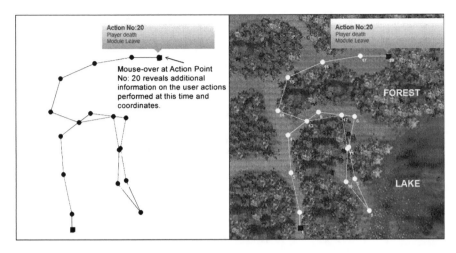

Fig. 8.5 Data visualization of user actions. (*Left*: Early JAVA version without area map, *right*: Later version with area map). (Partial screenshot of *PeTRA*, used with permission)

that took place at that particular time and coordinates. Such real-time interactive features are highly suitable for software-based assessment (as in game-based learning) and are simply not possible with paper-based reports.

At this time, *PeTRA* is used mainly in debriefing, for Trainers to review and evaluate a player's action in a game-based learning session. Future plans for *PeTRA* include creating a customizable interface to suit different user-groups, as well as looking into new ways to visualize the data collected as "useable information." For example, a learner should be able to access *PeTRA* at any time to review individual in-game actions and performance data for self-improvement. A trainer, on the other hand, may need to visualize the performance of multiple Learners who are under their charge. An administrator may only be interested in the performance index or the overall ROI of the game-based learning application.

8.4.4 Current Limitations

In an ideal situation, the telemetry for *Information Trails* should have been integrated into the game engine, with internal function calls available for remote data retrieval and transmission. However, since there was no such game engine available before *Information Trails*, we had to create the telemetry magic through much scripting. As a result, some of the *NWN2* game functions were too simplistic and limited for highly detailed behavior analysis. For example, Bioware's developers used just two functions, namely *item_gained* and *item_lost*, to cover all events involving the adding or removal of items from a player's inventory. For obvious reasons, players could gain items in more than one way:

- Obtained treasure chest
- Bought from merchant
- Stole from a nonplayer character (NPC)
- Looted from a fallen enemy
- Made by combining items (crafting) in the player's inventory
- Created by a special spell
- Given by an NPC, or another player in a persistent world

Since only one event call, *item_gained*, was available, it was impossible to truly tell how the item was "gained" or obtained; a similar problem also existed for the event call, *item_lost*. We rectified the problem through the implementation of an "Add Remark" function to allow us to easily annotate game events when needed.

As mentioned before, the economy for game development is very different from that of academic research. From the point of view of the game developer, all seven possible methods of gaining items (i.e., obtain, bought, stole, looted, crafted, created, given) were mere semantic differences that could easily be represented using one function: *item_gained*. Writing seven functions to represent each semantic possibility is viewed as inefficiency by programmers, regardless of the values they might hold for academic researchers. Game telemetry has the potential to change all that. Since items gained are often connected to the narrative of the story, understanding how players obtained certain items in the game may help improve the story and make a better game. As developers add more detailed user actions to their games, the data obtained by *Information Trails* will also become richer.

8.4.5 Future Development

Even though *PeTRA* is already functional, our intention is to expand it into a full-fledge research system for in-process assessment of game-based learning, by standardizing the framework for users' action data and meta-data collection through game telemetry; that is, a complete learning design system from the development of *Information Trails* powered games to *PeTRA*-powered online assessment reports.

The *Information Trails* assessment system requires the addition of several "missing links" to make *in-process* assessment for game-based learning possible. The interdependent relationships among various components, which include game engine, event listener, external database server, actionable learning and game objectives, and the in-process reporting tool, *PeTRA* are shown in Fig. 8.6. (It should be obvious that without the assessment components, a standalone GBL engine will only produce more games that cannot be assessed.)

Given that *NWN2* is a 6-year-old product, there is a need to expand *Information Trails* to other newer game engines—hopefully, one with integrated telemetry.

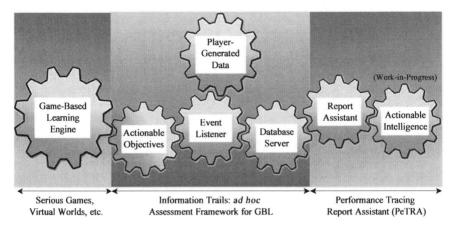

Fig. 8.6 Relationships among various components of GBL with formative assessment capability

As more game engines gain telemetry in the future, we hope to work with researchers around the world to standardize the list of user-generated action data, as well as the database structure to allow for open collaboration across other learning domains.

A standardized open database is also necessary for the development of new report assistants that will benefit user-groups from other industries. The separation of the report assistant from the game-based learning application is a necessity, because administrators and trainers who are not using the serious games can still gain access to the data visualization report, anytime, anywhere.

Future development of *PeTRA* will likely include a mobile or tablet version, which will provide the trainers and administrators access to the report while they are in the field. As cloud computing and ultra-portable mobile devices (such as iPAD2 and Android Tablets) gain popularity in the future, training organizations will begin looking into means to conduct "distributed briefing" with these devices by directly obtaining data from the "clouds." As such, a *Report Assistant* for game-based learning will need to be cloud-friendly and be accessible through a browser from any of these mobile devices.

8.5 Conclusions

Assessment is a very important issue for game-based learning because without it there is no way to know if the learners have indeed achieved the proposed learning goals. Fortunately, the issue has begun to draw the attention of educator-researchers (as evidenced by this book), as well as game developers (in form of usability testing). Telemetry has been used in many areas in our lives although few have connected telemetry with game or assessment until now.

Even though game-based learning has the potential to revolutionize the way people learn, ineffective assessment methodologies will only muddy the waters and result in conflicting reports that will diminish the value of game-based learning. As it is, many technologies have been criticized as "useless," "ineffective," and showing "no significant difference" in improving education (cf. Clark, 2007; Cuban, 2001). It is all the more important for researchers to focus their efforts in creating the right tools and finding the best assessment methodologies for the job.

Designing game-based learning is very different from designing entertainment games because the former requires the designer to take into consideration the many elements of learning assessment (such as learning objectives, instructional activities, etc.) and the latter has no need to do so. Linda G. Roberts, ex-Director of Education Technology for the US Department of Education, once said, "I believed that researchers could improve the design and collection of data. Just as new technology created new opportunities for learning, it created ways to invent new tools for research and evaluation, particularly ways to track and monitor what, how, and when learning occurred" (Robert, 2003, p. viii).

In the next few years, telemetry will gain importance as developers turn towards it to improve the usability and design of their games. As game engines with telemetry capabilities become available, assessment for game-based learning will become a reality. Data visualization will become the most challenging step in the assessment process as researchers and trainers struggle to make sense of the massive amount of data obtained from the online game-based learning environments. Instead of reinventing the assessment wheel at every turn, researchers should work together to solve common problems for the advancement of the field. This book (Ifenthaler, Eseryel, & Ge, 2011) will become the cornerstone of that endeavor.

Acknowledgments The research work in this article is made possible in part through funding from the Defence University Research Instrumentation Program (DURIP) grant from the US Army Research Office (ARO). Screenshots of *PeTRA* (Figs. 8.2 and 8.5) are used with permission from the author.

References

Aldrich, C. (2009). *The complete guide to simulations and serious games* (p. 576). San Francisco, CA: Pfeiffer.

Baker, R. S., Corbett, A. T., Roll, I., & Koedinger, K. R. (2008). Developing a generalizable detector of when students game the system. *User Modeling and User-Adapted Interaction, 18*(3), 287–314.

BBC News. (2007). Computer game to boost key skills. Retrieved Jan 22, 2011 from http://news.bbc.co.uk/2/hi/uk_news/education/6254989.stm.

Berger, A. (2006). "Neverwinter Nights" in the classroom. UMN News. Retrieved Sept 9, 2011 from http://www1.umn.edu/news/features/2006/UR_83484_REGION1.html.

Black, P. J., & Wiliam, D. (1998). Assessment and classroom learning. *Assessment in Education: Principles, Policy and Practice, 5*(1), 1–73.

Black, P. J., & Wiliam, D. (2009). Developing the theory of formative assessment. *Educational Assessment, Evaluation and Accountability, 1*(1), 5–31.

Botturi, L., & Loh, C. S. (2008). Once upon a game: Rediscovering the roots of games in education. In C. T. Miller (Ed.), *Games: Purpose and potential in education* (pp. 1–22). New York, NY: Springer Science.

Chen, S., & Michael, D. (2005). Proof of learning: Assessment in serious games. Gamasutra. Retrieved Jan 12, 2011 from http://www.gamasutra.com/features/20051019/chen_01.shtml.

Clark, R. E. (2007). Learning from serious games? Arguments, evidence and research suggestions. *Educational Technology, 47*, 56–59.

Csikszentmihalyi, M. (1990). *Flow: The Psychology of Optimum Experience*. New York, NY: Harper & Row.

Cuban, L. (2001). *Oversold and underused: Computers in the classroom*. Cambridge, MA: Harvard University Press.

Dragon Age: Origins (2009). [Computer software]. Redwood City, CA: EA Games.

Duffy, J. (1997). *The role of virtual reality simulation in full scale joint military exercises* (p. 17). Newport, RI: Naval War College.

Gee, J. P. (2007). *What video games have to teach us about learning and literacy* (p. 256). New York, NY: Palgrave Macmillan.

Gibson, D., Aldrich, C., & Prensky, M. (Eds.). (2006). *Games and simulations in online learning: Research and development frameworks* (p. 402). Hershey, PA: Information Science.

Gorniak, P., & Roy, D. (2005). Speaking with your sidekick: Understanding situated speech in computer role playing games. In R. M. Young & J. E. Laird (Eds.), *Proceedings of the first artificial intelligence and interactive digital entertainment conference (AIIDE 2005), June 1–5, 2005*. Marina del Rey, CA: AAAI.

Harrington, H. L., Meisels, S. J., McMahon, P., Dichtelmiller, M. L., & Jablon, J. R. (1997). *Observing, documenting and assessing learning*. Ann Arbor, MI: Rebus.

Hays, R. T. (2005). *The effectiveness of instructional games: A literature review and discussion* (p. 63). Orlando, FL: Naval Air Warfare Center.

Hattie, J. (1987). Identifying the salient facets of a model of student learning: A synthesis of meta analyses. *International Journal of Educational Research, 11*(2), 187–212.

Ifenthaler, D., Eseryel, D., & Ge, X. (Eds.). (2012). *Assessment in game-based learning: Foundations, innovations, and perspectives*. New York, NY: Springer Science+Business Media, LLC.

Joosten-ten Brinke, D., Gorissen, P., & Latour, I. (2005). Integrating assessment into e-learning courses. In R. Koper & C. Tattersall (Eds.), *Learning design: A handbook on modelling and delivering networked education and training* (pp. 185–202). Berlin: Springer.

Kaplan-Rakowski, R., & Loh, C. S. (2010). Modding and rezzing in games and virtual environments for education. In Y. K. Baek (Ed.), *Gaming for classroom-based learning: Digital role playing as a motivator of study* (pp. 205–219). Hershey, PA: IGI-Global.

Kapp, K. M., & O'Driscoll, T. (2010). *Learning in 3D: Adding a new dimension to enterprise learning and collaboration* (p. 416). San Francisco, CA: Pfeiffer.

Kebritchi, M. (2008). Effects of a computer game on mathematics achievement and class motivation: An experimental study. PhD Thesis. University of Central Florida, Orlando, Florida.

Lee, H. (2008). *Students' perceptions of peer and self assessment in a higher education online collaborative learning environment*. Unpublished Ph.D. dissertation, Graduate School of the University of Texas at Austin, Austin. Retrieved February 8, 2011 from http://www.lib.utexas.edu/etd/d/2008/leeh55399/leeh55399.pdf.

Levin, A. (2010). Simulator training flaws tied to airline crashes. *USA Today*. Retrieved March 1, 2011 from http://travel.usatoday.com/flights/2010-08-31-1Acockpits31_ST_N.htm.

Loh, C. S. (2006). *Tracking an avatar: Designing data collection into online games*. Paper presented at the Annual Conference of the Association for Educational Communications and Technology (AECT 2006). Dallas, TX.

Loh, C. S. (2006b). Designing online games assessment as "Information Trails". In D. Gibson, C. Aldrich, & M. Prensky (Eds.), *Games and simulation in online learning: Research and development frameworks* (pp. 323–348). Hershey, PA: Idea Group.

Loh, C. S. (2009). Researching and developing serious games as interactive learning instructions. *International Journal of Gaming and Computer Mediated Simulations, 1*(4), 1–19.

Loh, C. S., Anantachai, A., Byun, J. H., & Lenox, J. (2007). Assessing what players learned in serious games: *In situ* data collection, Information Trails, and quantitative analysis. In Q. Mehdi (Ed.), *Proceedings of the computer games: AI, animation, mobile, educational & serious games conference (CGAMES 2007)*. Wolverhampton, UK: University of Wolverhampton.

Loh, C. S., & Byun, J. H. (2009). Modding Neverwinter Nights into serious game. In D. Gibson & Y. K. Baek (Eds.), *Digital Simulations for Improving Education: Learning Through Artificial Teaching Environments* (pp. 408–426). Hershey, PA: IGI-Global.

Loh, C. S., & Li, I. H. (2010, Oct 10–13). Reducing re-training cost through on-demand, *ad hoc* assessment. *Proceedings of the MODSIM world conference and expo 2010—21st century decision-making: the art of modeling & simulation*, Hampton, VA: MODSIM World Conference & Exposition.

Moreno-Ger, P., Burgos, D., Martínez-Ortiz, I., Sierra, J. L., & Fernández-Manjón, B. (2008). Educational game design for online education. *Computers in Human Behavior, 24*, 2530–2540.

Nacke, L., Grimshaw, M., & Lindley, C. (2010). More than a feeling: Measurement of sonic user experience and psychophysiology in a first-person shooter game. *Interacting with Computers, 22*(5), 336–343. doi:10.1016/j.intcom.2010.04.005.

Nacke, L., Lindley, C., & Stellmach, S. (2008). Log who's playing: Psychophysiological game analysis made easy through event logging. In P. Markopoulos et al. (Eds.), *Fun and games 2008, lecture notes of computer science* (Vol. 5294, pp. 150–157). Heidelberg, Germany: Springer.

Nacke, L., & Lindley, C. (2010). Affective ludology, flow and immersion in a first-person shooter: Measurement of player experience. *Loading, 3*(5). Retrieved March 12, 2011 from http://journals.sfu.ca/loading/index.php/loading/article/view/72/71

O'Neil, H. F., & Robertson, M. M. (1992). Simulations: Occupationally oriented. In M. C. Alkin (Ed.), *Encyclopedia of Educational Research* (6th ed., pp. 1216–1222). New York, NY: Macmillan.

Prensky, M. (2001). *Digital game-based learning*. New York, NY: McGraw-Hill.

Prensky, M. (2006). *Don't bother me mom—I'm learning!* St. Paul, MN: Paragon House.

Pruett, C. (2010, Sept). Hot failure: Tuning gameplay with simple player metrics. *Game Developer Magazine. 19*(9). San Francisco, CA: Think Services. Retrieved March 7, 2011 from http://gamasutra.com/view/feature/6155/hot_failure_tuning_gameplay_with_.php.

Reese, D. D. (2010). Introducing flowometer: A CyGaMEs assessment suite tool. In R. van Eck (Ed.), *Gaming and cognition: Theories and practice from the learning sciences* (pp. 227–254). Hershey, PA: IGI-Global.

Robert, L. G. (2003). Forewords. In G. D. Haertel & B. Means (Eds.), *Evaluating educational technology: Effective research designs for improving learning* (p. 290). New York, NY: Teachers College Press.

Robertson, J., & Good, J. (2005). Story creation in virtual game worlds. *Communications of the ACM, 48*(1), 61–65.

Rupp, A. A., Gushta, M., Mislevy, R. J., & Shaffer, D. W. (2010). Evidence-centered design of epistemic games: Measurement principles for complex learning environments. *The Journal of Technology Learning and Assessment, 8*(4), 3–41.

Saridaki, M., Mourlas, C., Gouscos, D., & Meimaris, M. (2007). *Digital games as a learning tool for children with cognitive disabilities: Literature review and some preliminary methodological and experimental results*. Paper presented at the European Conference on Games Based Learning, Scotland

Sasse, D. (2008). *A framework for psychophysiological data acquisition in digital games*. Unpublished Master thesis, Lund University, Lund. Retrieved March 12, 2011 from http://citeseerx.ist.psu.edu/viewdoc/download? doi: 10.1.1.140.5284&rep=rep1&type=pdf.

Shute, V. J., Masduki, I., Donmez, O., Dennen, V. P., Kim, Y.-J., Jeong, A. C., et al. (2010). Modeling, assessing, and supporting key competencies within game environments. In D. Ifenthaler, P. Pirnay-Dummer, & N. M. Seel (Eds.), *Computer-based diagnostics and systematic analysis of knowledge* (Part 4, pp. 281–309). Boston, MA: Springer. Retrieved March 5, 2011, from http://www.springerlink.com/content/t5261055733n18h2/.

Shute, V. J., & Spector, J. M. (2008). *SCORM 2.0 White paper: Stealth assessment in virtual worlds*. Retrieved March 12, 2011, from http://www.adlnet.gov/technologies/evaluation/library/additional resources/letsi white papers/shute - stealth assessment in virtual worlds. pdf.

Skinner, B. F. (1938). *The behavior of organisms: An experimental analysis*. Cambridge, MA: B.F. Skinner Foundation.

Stieger, I. (2008). *Neverwinter Nights eXtender 4 (version 1.09)* [software]. Starnberg, Germany: Stieger Hardware-und Softwareentwicklung. Retrieved April 12, 2012, from http://www.nwnx.org.

Telemetry. (n.d.). *The American Heritage Stedman's Medical Dictionary*. Retrieved March 9, 2011, from http://dictionary.reference.com/browse/telemetry.

Tobias, S., & Fletcher, J. D. (2007). What research has to say about designing computer games for learning. *Educational Technology, 47*(5), 20–29.

van Eck, R. (2006). Digital game-based learning: It's not just the digital natives who are restless…. *Educause Review, 41*(2), 16–30.

Weil, S. A., Hussain, T. S., Brunyé, T. T., Ferguson, W., Sidman, J. G., Spahr, L.S., & Roberts, B. (2005). Assessing the potential of massive multi-player games as tools for military training. *Proceedings of the interservice/industry training, simulation, and education conference, (I/ITSEC 2005)*. Orlando, FL: NTSA.

Warren, R., & Sutton, J. (2008, April). Using a computer game for research on culture and team adaptability: Lessons learned from a NATO experiment. *Proceedings of the NATO Research and Technology Organization (RTO) Human Factors and Medicine Panel HFM, 142 Symposium on Adaptability in Coalition Teamwork*. Copenhagen, Denmark.

Wilson, K. A., Bedwell, W. L., Lazzara, E. H., Salas, E., Burke, C. S., Estock, J. L., et al. (2008). Relationships between game attributes and learning outcomes: Review and research proposals. *Simulation & Gaming, 40*(2), 217–266.

Younis, B., & Loh, C. S. (2010). Integrating serious games in higher education programs. *Proceedings of the academic colloquium 2010: Building partnership in teaching excellence*. Ramallah, Palestine: AMIDEAST.

Zoeller, G. (2010). *Development telemetry in video games projects*. Paper presented at the *Game Developer Conference 2010*. San Francisco, CA. Retrieved March 1, 2011 from http://gdc.gulbsoft.org/talk.

Chapter 9
Timed Report Measures Learning: Game-Based Embedded Assessment

Debbie Denise Reese, Ralph J. Seward, Barbara G. Tabachnick, Ben A. Hitt, Andrew Harrison, and Lisa Mcfarland

9.1 Introduction

Recognizing the power and potential of game-based technologies to enhance achievement and learner-centered education, policy leaders like the National Science Foundation (Borgman et al., 2008), the Department of Education (2010), and the National Research Council (NRC, 2011) set a national agenda for educational research. Such research will discover, validate, and disseminate sound methods for design, development, and implementation of instructional games that enhance and assess learning. The current study investigates the accuracy and sensitivity of an assessment tool built into a videogame world: the Timed Report. This work is part of a research program that applies cognitive science analogical reasoning theory (e.g., Gentner, 1983; Holyoak, Gentner, & Kokinov, 2001; Kurtz, Miao, & Gentner, 2001) to design and develop instructional games that (a) enhance students' preparation for learning targeted concepts and (b) assess growth in the learner's mental model through measures of gameplay behavior. We have designed and developed the instructional game *Selene: A Lunar Construction GaME* and a suite of assessment tools that includes the Timed Report. We set the game within an interstitial, online

D.D. Reese (✉) • R.J. Seward • A. Harrison • L. McFarland
Center for Educational Technologies, Wheeling Jesuit University, 316 Washington Ave.,
Wheeling, WV 26003, USA
e-mail: debbie@cet.edu; rjseward@cet.edu; andrew@cet.edu; lisamc@cet.edu

B.G. Tabachnick
Department of Psychology, California State University, 18111 Nordhoff St.,
Northridge, CA 91330, USA
e-mail: btabachnick@csun.edu

B.A. Hitt
Serenity Hills Informatics LLC, 2217 Haclett Ave., Wheeling, WV 26003, USA
e-mail: ben@serenityhill.info

D. Ifenthaler et al. (eds.), *Assessment in Game-Based Learning: Foundations,
Innovations, and Perspectives*, DOI 10.1007/978-1-4614-3546-4_9,
© Springer Science+Business Media New York 2012

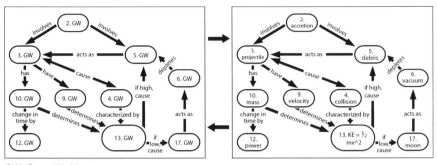

GW=Game World

Fig. 9.1 The cyberlearning through game-based, metaphor enhanced learning objects (CyGaMEs) application of analogical reasoning theory to instructional game design (Copyright 2009 Debbie Denise Reese and Charles A. Wood. Used with permission)

environment that allows us to manipulate conditions and collect gameplay data. We aspire to validate the efficacy of the approach to instructional game design and embedded assessment. Within the current study we sought to replicate and extend earlier findings (Reese & Tabachnick, 2010) that Timed Report is a sensitive measure of learning.

9.1.1 Theoretical Framework: Analogical Reasoning

Cyberlearning through game-based, metaphor enhanced learning objects (CyGaMEs) is an approach to instructional game design (Reese, 2009b) derived from the cognitive process of analogical reasoning (Gentner, 1983; Holyoak et al., 2001). When people analogize (see Fig. 9.1), they map relational structure from a relatively well-known domain (source) to a relatively unfamiliar domain (target). During mapping, an analogizer puts two domains into alignment and projects from the known to unknown. Where new knowledge is incomplete, mapping enables people to make inferences. Analogizers are often unaware they are engaged in mapping (Lakoff & Johnson, 1999). Although domain novices and young thinkers often create superficial analogies mapped according to irrelevant attributes (e.g., color), people prefer deep analogizing (Gentner & Markman, 1997) in which the two domains share richly branched, leveled, and connected domain knowledge. This type of analogizing supports higher order thinking, such as rules and schemas (Hummel & Holyoak, 1997). Mapping is constrained by the analogizer's immediate goal structures (Holyoak & Thagard, 1989; Spellman & Holyoak, 1996). Thus, context dictates the direction and characteristics of mapping. Furthermore, people appear to be hardwired to translate their physical transactions into basic-level metaphors that become the foundation for individuals' cognitive structures (Lakoff & Johnson, 1980, 1999). Because game worlds are relational systems in which game goals guide player discovery and application through virtually embodied transactions, games can be engineered by applying the principles of analogical reasoning.

The CyGaMEs approach specifies a target domain (a process similar to task analysis) and then constrains and designs a game world that is relationally consistent with (isomorphic) the target. To apply structure mapping theory within instructional game design (see Fig. 9.1), the designer maps from right to left: (a) specifies target domain subconcepts and the relationships that connect them and (b) holds the relational structure constant and replaces the subconcepts with game world (GW) objects. The learner maps from left to right, using the game world to make inferences about the target domain.

CyGaMEs' design of instructional games translates what is abstract, invisible, and known inside experts' heads into a game world that is concrete, discovered by learners through embodied transactions, and procedurally visible. Using the CyGaMEs approach (Reese, 2009b), we created *Selene: A Lunar Construction GaME*. *Selene* players discover and apply fundamental geological processes as they form Earth's Moon through accretion and then change it over time through the processes of impact cratering and volcanism. Because the game world is designed as the relational analog of the targeted science concepts and because the game goals were designed to guide the player to gameplay that models those fundamental processes, embedded measure of player progress toward game goals is a learning trajectory for growth in players' mental model of the targeted conceptual domain. We call this assessment tool the Timed Report.

9.1.2 The Timed Report

CyGaMEs videogames' Timed Reports provide a meaningful synopsis of player behavior above the gameplay gesture level. The *Selene* game collects Timed Reports every 10 s of gameplay. The 10-s interval was determined by (a) the time required to initiate and complete a *Selene* gameplay gesture and (b) drain on computer resources. The *Selene* game continually collects raw data measuring player progress toward the game goal(s). Then it applies rules (equations) to determine player progress toward the game goal(s). This study investigated player progress toward a solitary game goal, scoring if the player progressed toward the game goal (+1), made no change in progress (0), or moved away from the game goal (−1). Currently, a Timed Report post contains the raw data and the Timed Report value from −1 to 1. Raw data for each targeted phenomenon—developed as a gameplay goal—includes a numeric value for a target goal and current progress toward that goal.

Specifically designed as a component of instructional game design, development, and implementation, Timed Report embeds assessment as immediate, actionable, formative, and summative information. Timed Report is a complex example of the rule-based methods recognized, recommended, and supported by the NRC Committee on Science Learning (2011). The committee requires that (a) "assessment tasks must be embedded effectively and unobtrusively" and (b) the learning goals must be established at the "outset of game design" to ensure alignment between the game, the assessment, and the learning goal (p. 103). Timed Report is a generic element for instructional game design methods, like CyGaMEs, that derive from alignment between the targeted learning domain and the game world.

In previous work the first author reviewed video of a case study player's gameplay and identified the learning moment, accretionLM. AccretionLM is the aha! moment when a *Selene* player realizes that large kinetic energy collisions fragment, but attenuated collisions adhere (accrete). The author triangulated video data with gameplay velocity and Timed Report data, demonstrating that all three aligned. The author screened two phases of player gameplay data to identify 22 accretionLM exemplars. Statistical analysis within players for pre vs. @&Post accretionLM shows that the Timed Report explained 95% of the variance (Reese & Tabachnick, 2010). The exemplars scored near-zero progress before learning and nearly continuous progress @&Post the learning moment. The current study continues that line of quantitative inquiry. We used the earlier work to develop an algorithm that automates identification of the learning moment (accretionLM). It also identifies players who are Always Progressing toward the goal. We attempted to replicate and elaborate the previous findings across the entire sample of gameplay data. Specifically:

1. Does Timed Report distinguish player progress before learning (pre) from progress @&Post the moment of learning?
2. Is the Pearson's correlation coefficient of a learning trajectory (a cumulative Timed Report regression line segment) a sensitive learning representation for categorizing type and moment of learning?
3. Does Timed Report distinguish between accretionLM players and players who always progress?
4. Is Timed Report progress better when players watch a round of gameplay before playing; that is, is there a higher slope to the learning trajectory?
5. Is there an interaction between type of gameplay (accretionLM vs. Always Progressing) and watch vs. play conditions?
6. Is Timed Report progress better if participants watch gameplay and then watch instruction (video) about targeted content before playing; that is, is there a higher slope to the learning trajectory?

The NRC committee (2011) champions the promise of game-based assessment but recognizes that (a) much game research to date is limited by lack of alignment and rigorous specificity among targeted learning, the game world, and the assessment and (b) game-based assessment is in its infancy. The U.S. Department of Education's National Education Technology Plan (2010, p. xvii) recommends:

> research and development that explores how embedded assessment technologies, such as simulations, collaboration environments, virtual worlds, games, and cognitive tutors, can be used to engage and motivate learners while assessing complex skills. (U.S. Department of Education Office of Educational Technology, 2010, p. xvii)

Integrated within research programs like CyGaMEs, a measure like the Timed Report moves game-based, embedded assessment toward maturity.

9.1.3   Finding the Learning Moment by Velocity

This method for detecting an accretion learning moment is specific to *Selene Classic* scale 1 accretion.[1] It is based upon two separate but related metrics that are derived from a player's velocity data: specifically, the speed at which a player shoots (slingshots) an asteroid at his or her protomoon. The two metrics are running mean and running standard deviation. Both are calculated using a moving "left-aligned" window of 20 data elements.

The learning moment is determined by iterating through a player's velocity data and finding the minimum (or earliest) time wherein:

- Running mean is ≤8.
- Running standard deviation is ≤5.
- Running mean and running standard deviation are both descending (on the "downhill" slope of the graph).

If and when a player's data are all below the two thresholds (running mean of 8 and a running standard deviation of 5), then that player is determined to be "Always Progressing" since the player's data indicate an understanding of the proper methodology from the beginning of game play.

9.1.3.1   Player A: Finding the Learning Moment

Player A experienced an accretion learning moment, i.e., accretionLM (see Fig. 9.2). We use Player A data as an example to illustrate identification of an accretion learning moment.

This subset of the velocity data for Player A, inclusive of the learning moment, runs from time 401 to 782 s. Call this array q^2:

[55.868187, 69.24777, 55.639595, 7.0804834, 55.01195, 16.006914, 16.120817, 3.2676246, 27.223476, 23.208958, 11.813951, 27.782402, 15.910621, 2.807408, 4.397901, 9.0733795, 30.824404, 15.620095, 22.062431, 4.222125, 26.439013, 43.313507, 9.903498, 2.0468307, 28.390434, 22.197634, 30.463423, 40.821922, 45.14512, 1.3485506, 40.268764, 21.807476, 21.086195, 20.6541, 1.0925303, 29.993856, 19.487682, 20.57898, 30.352562, 20.957647, 30.21956, 5.1152263, 67.3791, 50.381554, 9.78752, 39.251865, 82.97805, 31.260138, 1.8033514, 21.869253, 35.038376, 79.83573, 1.6028731, 18.332253, 17.965775, 53.781544, 41.728107, 8.034504, 3.433007, 0.15590267, 0.9266992, 8.019719, 5.01988, 4.5591364, 7.9384265, 2.7186017, 8.108616, 4.702808, 2.6132252, 0.9225479,

---

[1] This algorithm followed an approach developed for CyGaMEs by James Pusteovsky under the direction of Larry V. Hedges.

[2] We plot learning moment graphs using Python MatPlotLib and calculate running means, running standard deviations, slopes, and Pearson's correlation coefficient *r* using the linregress function within the Python 2.6 SciPy stats sublibrary.

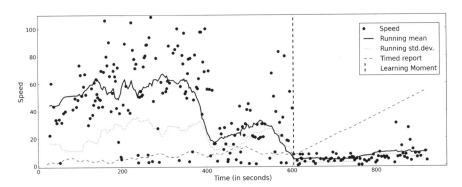

Fig. 9.2 Player A Timed Report trace: velocity, Timed Report, running averages, and learning moment

8.341124, 4.5541077, 3.9929488, 5.042764, 2.6977708, 4.2475567, 4.8065324, 9.335254, 2.9597094, 8.137656, 4.929109, 3.05843, 3.8736098, 4.933989, 5.269574, 8.343284, 5.965714, 5.6828933, 3.3991897, 4.7966566, 0.27719992, 4.480157, 0.42012483, 3.5510721, 2.4610674, 3.575081].

The first window of 20 elements in array q is:

[55.868187, 69.24777, 55.639595, 7.0804834, 55.01195, 16.006914, 16.120817, 3.2676246, 27.223476, 23.208958, 11.813951, 27.782402, 15.910621, 2.807408, 4.397901, 9.0733795, 30.824404, 15.620095, 22.062431, 4.222125].

The mean of this array is 23.659. So this 23.659 would be the left-aligned running mean for this first window and is the first element of our array of running means. Similarly, if we continue to move the window of 20 to the right, we may obtain the following array of running means (let us call it runmean):

[23.659524624999996, 22.188065924999997, 20.891352774999998, 18.604547924999999, 18.35286529, 17.021789489999996, 17.331325490000001, 18.048455789999998, 19.926170660000004, 20.822252860000003, 19.729232490000001, 21.151973140000003, 20.853226839999998, 21.112005539999998, 22.00434014, 21.839071605000004, 22.885095430000003, 22.31825933, 22.56620358, 22.980710129999999, 23.817486229999997, 24.00651358, 22.096599545000004, 24.970379645000001, 27.387115810000005, 26.456970110000004, 27.309681659999995, 29.935413010000001, 29.457323810000002, 27.290235380000002, 28.316270500000002, 28.054751099999997, 30.956163800000002, 29.981997705000005, 29.865905355000006, 30.709567590000006, 31.89895199, 33.010973240000006, 32.383749440000003, 31.03777169, 29.997684473500005, 28.533041433500006, 28.678266068500005, 25.560305068500004, 23.269184188499999, 23.1767295135, 21.3500663485, 17.6065946485, 16.278728148500001, 16.319221838499999, 15.271886583499997, 13.937023983499998, 10.1729428685, 10.292446653500001, 9.6279722035000006, 8.8645719935000002, 6.3878726285000003, 4.5417938984999999, 4.6068313985000007, 4.5831665184999997, 4.9822541850000004,

5.1823746750000002, 4.9343102249999999, 4.8769967149999998, 4.895739345, 4.7622967199999993, 5.0435308349999994, 4.936385735, 4.9853900000000007, 5.0246882250000002, 5.2183936600000003, 4.8151974560000008, 4.8114999210000011, 4.6328587225000009, 4.5582741275000007, 4.5464389575000013, 4.5128151724999999, 4.4973563710526321, 4.2285842805555554, 4.3032239794117642, 4.0635719781250002, 4.0058695100000001, 4.0735437607142853, 4.0889232961538449, 4.0185011541666666, 3.9047672590909084, 3.460915585, 4.2285842805555554, 4.3032239794117642, 4.0635719781250002, 4.0058695100000001, 4.0735437607142853, 4.0889232961538449, 4.0185011541666666, 3.9047672590909084, 3.460915585].

Similarly, with a left-aligned window of 20 we may obtain the following array of values for running standard deviations (let us call it rsd):

[20.095362075391726, 18.63735887574747, 15.890597989019074, 13.777200981700602, 14.042231649872162, 11.396975966851585, 11.451897811042025, 11.815410193740647, 12.316262190955866, 13.472782401599563, 14.139225570390479, 14.720506908674595, 14.639268135674042, 14.59297028452861, 13.946074751270773, 14.183270048700978, 13.961963617314591, 13.852371765632419, 13.770307544068631, 13.878691172060025, 13.174831843242883, 13.241376949838436, 13.06363477021192, 16.18832164456116, 16.19389067345038, 16.660756779030201, 16.866442179272564, 20.971399585223303, 20.818589672827482, 21.348696051430466, 20.513064794778462, 20.385608277170839, 23.361872771369672, 24.186756149334887, 24.239399869831928, 23.466540890581733, 24.024552609210581, 23.934388685934849, 24.436432722140466, 25.28098128803251, 26.13112438904097, 26.926847242703108, 26.801440921542007, 25.665416565743275, 25.376666169365858, 25.431677756015802, 25.528132554402301, 21.12504314987282, 21.056197223243043, 21.027653512538279, 21.257071309357954, 20.783448292090654, 13.896452151951737, 13.828987239957703, 13.741345658372396, 13.677719431253532, 8.6924705138763887, 2.5238876340422127, 2.6330271288064107, 2.646226230414098, 2.5432683382537031, 2.3580812553617987, 2.3042328974446815, 2.316216994019288, 2.3150258532306811, 2.2046985456202584, 2.2874732771530151, 2.184204289078147, 2.1896756041726793, 2.1515830686199506, 1.9253282917234915, 2.0754644224564287, 2.0760198460152259, 2.2925876590721344, 2.3027922186124443, 2.3134411602995288, 2.3228814291123805, 2.3854765912654345, 2.138215705937998, 2.17971725496627, 2.0066037436012572, 2.0632460693713175, 2.1237851172416251, 2.2096940481044731, 2.2926627245497411, 2.3687940687315265, 1.9562259428499709, 2.138215705937998, 2.17971725496627, 2.0066037436012572, 2.0632460693713175, 2.1237851172416251, 2.2096940481044731, 2.2926627245497411, 2.3687940687315265, 1.9562259428499709].

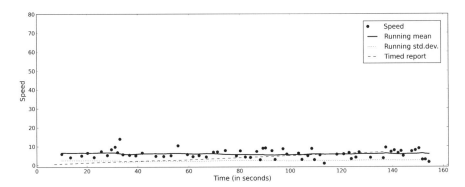

Fig. 9.3 Player B, an Always Progressing player

Now we may iterate through the arrays of running means and running standard deviations and compare each value with the required running mean ≤8 and running standard deviation ≤5. Doing this reveals that the 58th elements of each array satisfy these requirements since runmean[58]=4.54179 and rsd[58]=2.52389. Next, we may observe that the running means and running standard deviations beyond these data points are generally descending and, if graphed, show a downward trend. This, then, is Player A's learning moment. Specifically, accretionLM occurred at 603 s into the game, and we indicate this within Fig. 9.1 as a vertical line.

9.1.3.2 Player B: Always Progressing Gameplay

Player B data illustrate identification of gameplay behavior for a player who always progressed toward the game goal (see Fig. 9.3).

Velocity data for Player B are:

[5.9060163, 4.1072884, 5.0164943, 6.452271, 4.152547, 7.3566284, 5.2569237, 8.457776, 9.716882, 6.821046, 13.95762, 5.620788, 5.32263, 5.05642, 6.5177045, 4.7286086, 4.6543684, 5.031529, 10.419466, 5.6730804, 4.547686, 5.029058, 4.357358, 6.9630795, 7.0907516, 7.7697973, 4.8710523, 7.6062036, 4.2868924, 4.0468373, 7.2268205, 2.7708209, 8.942168, 9.146299, 7.6725473, 2.899134, 8.690738, 5.7698364, 6.272572, 2.8916936, 4.9004855, 8.788435, 2.8066642, 5.3699336, 0.90155417, 5.6566315, 5.8182845, 6.6143613, 3.2509341, 4.028238, 6.8673906, 3.9152768, 3.639079, 9.407682, 7.1331472, 7.914287, 6.491003, 7.537201, 4.9032264, 7.3792524, 7.970784, 8.889764, 2.8291974, 2.890643, 1.5434355].

Using the same method as above, we may obtain an array of running means as:

[6.5113044000000002, 6.4433878850000017, 6.4894763649999998, 6.4565195500000003, 6.4820599750000003, 6.6289702049999999, 6.6496286500000013, 6.63033508, 6.5877564600000014, 6.3162569800000012, 6.1775465450000011, 5.8410065700000002, 5.6985082150000004,

5.8794851149999996, 6.0839790649999994, 6.1417212049999996,
6.0502474749999999, 6.2520659550000008, 6.288981325, 6.0816366249999998,
5.942567285, 5.9602072599999998, 6.1481761099999996, 6.0706414199999994,
5.9909841249999998, 5.6815242534999992, 5.5758659634999983,
5.6232275735000004, 5.5736354584999992, 5.5218375434999993,
5.5209075784999992, 5.502936083499999, 5.5601588784999993,
5.2950044285000004, 5.3080735785000002, 5.2811035734999994,
5.5318612234999991, 5.4218744735, 5.5102427034999995, 5.4417754234999993,
5.6661533634999994, 5.8196682884999991, 5.8247347385000001,
5.8258613984999998, 5.7018968684999995, 5.7339909349999996,
5.7380624842105261, 5.7336057055555552, 5.6817965529411758,
5.8337254562499998, 5.9540912866666664, 5.8888556214285703,
6.040669376923077, 6.2408019083333324, 5.9529037181818181,
5.8348793700000003, 5.7336057055555552, 5.6817965529411758,
5.8337254562499998, 5.9540912866666664, 5.8888556214285703,
6.040669376923077, 6.2408019083333324, 5.9529037181818181,
5.8348793700000003].

And an array of running standard deviations as:

[2.4597648311886471, 2.4958448411090211, 2.4586696574723881,
2.4837429599655705, 2.4863219654211219, 2.4275433095930992,
2.4358055888198389, 2.4489105029976432, 2.4227280258415704,
2.3569708490424253, 2.4068057245103556, 1.5955169412609997,
1.7371973813453949, 1.878748627410713, 2.002925662216227,
2.03251543851936, 2.1378961231053513, 2.1890937162717727,
2.1735984554861139, 1.9445687357262544, 2.0706929488320833,
2.0596580420256885, 2.1401773313767749, 2.2344817009242495,
2.2293839247292415, 2.4837408280697275, 2.4346929274325704,
2.4294682694330683, 2.3967628382794359, 2.4368934427862898,
2.4374894327406222, 2.4255456043680934, 2.3705748554188562,
2.2666843663018921, 2.2906851789174594, 2.2644058510854124,
2.26443240079589, 2.1536375592155772, 2.2043293516786799,
2.2006680491754445, 2.1552853995813361, 2.2066119107530078,
2.213891369001078, 2.212279767983373, 2.3066237169488559,
2.2398150394549461, 2.3011151566320653, 2.3677435802379656,
2.4300746211759372, 2.4249507500159644, 2.4600912896590752,
2.5394577377613574, 2.5761787439175543, 2.583023076433677,
2.499024245289859, 2.6016864112309444, 2.3677435802379656,
2.4300746211759372, 2.4249507500159644, 2.4600912896590752,
2.5394577377613574, 2.5761787439175543, 2.583023076433677,
2.499024245289859, 2.6016864112309444].

As every running mean is below our required running mean ≤8, and every
running standard deviation is below our required running standard deviation ≤5,
we hypothesize that this player "got it" from the start. We, therefore, label this
player as Always Progressing.

Fig. 9.4 The instantiation of
the CyGaMEs adaptation of
Schwartz and Martin's (2004)
double transfer paradigm
experimental design, as used
in the current study (Copyright
2009 Debbie Denise Reese.
Used with permission)

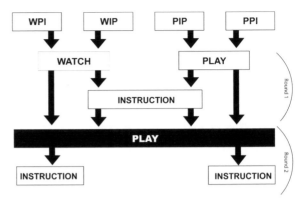

9.1.4 Game Design to Scaffold Learning

CyGaMEs uses instructional games to provide experiences that serve as viable prior knowledge for future learning. The cognitive and learning sciences as well as other educational fields have long known that appropriate prior knowledge scaffolds learning (e.g., Anderson, Reder, & Simon, 1998; Ausubel, 1968; Piaget & Inhelder, 2000). For this reason instructional models evoke or induce viable prior knowledge as preliminary events of instruction (Merrill, 2002; see also Schwartz & Bransford, 1998). Indeed, learning scientists have called for the "development of new instructional methods" that prepare learners for knowledge acquisition and assessments that evaluate that preparation (Schwartz & Martin, 2004, p. 130). Schwartz and Martin introduced the double transfer experimental paradigm for research involving these interventions. Since the cognitive function of analogical reasoning is to prepare the analogizer with viable intuitions about the target domain, instruction often uses analogies to introduce new domains. Unfortunately, many instructional analogies are ad hoc or misspecified and, themselves, foster misconceptions (e.g., Feltovich, Coulson, & Spiro, 1988; Johnstone, 1991). CyGaMEs obviates that issue. It is a formal approach to analogical specification and development (Reese, 2009b) that applies cognitive science structure mapping theory (Gentner, 1983). A CyGaMEs environment is a formally engineered, procedural analog of a targeted, abstract, conceptual domain. CyGaMEs researchers have demonstrated:

- A written narrative and illustrations developed according to the CyGaMEs approach scaffold viable domain inferences (Diehl & Reese, 2010).
- CyGaMEs *Selene* causes participants to make viable inferences about the accretion concept (Reese, Diehl, & Lurquin, 2009).

CyGaMEs research adapts Schwartz and Martin's (2004) double transfer paradigm experimental design, and CyGaMEs' architecture modularizes game and research environment elements to support unlimited manipulation of components within that design. This study uses one instantiation of the CyGaMEs *Selene* double transfer paradigm (see Fig. 9.4). *Selene* participants are sequentially assigned to conditions as they registered to play. Half the players watch round 1 gameplay, and half play the game. Then half of each condition watches about 12 min of video instruction on the targeted concepts. During round 2 all participants play *Selene*. Then all players who have not watched instruction do so. This results in four conditions: WIP=watch & instruct=watch–instruction–play; WPI=watchers=watch–play–instruction; PIP=play–instruction–play; and PPI=play–play–instruction.

9.2 Method

9.2.1 Learning Moment Algorithm

We developed an algorithm based upon exemplar gameplay, using running mean and running standard deviation calculated from a player's velocity data (a player gesture that determines kinetic energy of the collisions) by using a moving left-aligned window of 20 data elements. The learning moment accretionLM is determined by iterating through a player's velocity data and finding the minimum time wherein (a) running mean is ≤ 8, (b) running standard deviation is ≤ 5, and (c) the running mean and running standard deviation at that point for both must be *descending* (on the "downhill" slope of the graph).

If and when all of a player's data are below these two thresholds, a player is determined to be Always Progressing since all of the player's data indicate proper application of the accretionLM concept.

9.2.2 Participants

We applied the accretionLM algorithm to gameplay data from 221 players: primarily white (74%), but with representative proportions of African American=7%, African=1%, Asian=3.9%, mixed=3.5%, and Native American=0.9%; primarily 13–18-year-olds ($\overline{X}$=14.5, min=13, and six individuals>18); Female=40%, Male=59%; $\overline{X}_{school\ level}$=ninth grade; $\overline{X}_{gpa}$=B, mode=A; $\overline{X}_{mother/father's\ level\ of\ education}$=college, with 33.6% of mothers concluding education at high school and 38% of fathers concluding education at high school.

Players were recruited by 61 adult volunteers. Recruitment ranged from 1 to 22 players per recruiter ($\overline{X}$=3.6, median=2, mode=1). Players volunteered to participate and reported they lived in 26 states within the United States as well as outside of the country (n=4). Condition assignment was independent of recruiter.

Previous work with these data using self-organizing maps (Hitt, 2012; Reese & Hitt, 2009) "revealed no clear relationship of demographics to *Selene* gameplay. In other words, player performance … seemed independent of player demographics." Furthermore, this environment is self-contained, so once the game starts they are working independently of recruiter context.

We were interested in the sensitivity of the Timed Report tool to differences in participant learning trajectories before vs. @&Post learning for players during their initial round of gameplay (during discovery and application of the accretion concept). Results pertain to the *Selene* Timed Report and generalize across gameplay by *Selene* players who complete a round of accretion gameplay. Given data characteristics and these parameters, analyses were not corrected for (a) distribution within or outside the United States, (b) nesting within recruiter, and (c) attrition.

9.2.3   The Selene Classic Game Scenario

This analysis concerns scale 1 of the *Selene* accretion module, which has one concept and learning goal:

• Concept: High kinetic energy collisions fragment. Low velocity collisions accrete (stick together).
• Learning goal: Discover the accretion concept. Apply it to accrete particles and form the protomoon. When the moon reaches goal mass, the player progresses to the next scale (game level).

Data for this study were collected using the *Selene Classic* version of the game.[3] When accretion scale 1 begins, a giant impact has hit the early Earth (protoearth), and particles from the impact have coalesced to form a ring, like the ring of Saturn. *Selene* instructs the player (see Fig. 9.5):

> Start gathering materials to build your moon. To throw an asteroid, click on a loose piece, and drag in the opposite direction of where you want it to go. Think of it like a slingshot! Try to get a good sense for how fast you can throw things before they shatter.

Players enter this scale with a Godlike perspective, located inside the ring of debris (see Fig. 9.6). Players select an asteroid (click), give it a velocity through a slingshot gesture (drag, see white line representing velocity in Fig. 9.7), and release it to construct the protomoon.

9.2.4   Measures

Velocity. Velocity is a parameter of the slingshot gameplay gesture (see Fig. 9.8). The player selects a planetesimal by clicking, determines velocity speed and direction by dragging, and releases to throw the planetesimal. The player clicks the particle at

---

[3] CyGaMEs has since developed and released *Selene II*, providing optimized gameplay and performance, enhanced graphics with 3D effects, and new sound effects and animations. A still shot from the *Selene II* Solar System accretion module can be viewed here: http://selene.cet.edu/. A West Virginia Public Broadcasting feature at segment 4:45–5:09 discusses and illustrates the accretion scale 1 module and those leading to it, available here: http://www.youtube.com/watch?v=ZBPq3Hc_g1Y.

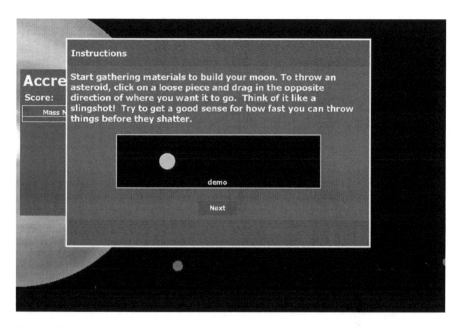

Fig. 9.5 The instruction screen at the start of *Selene Classic* accretion module, scale 1 (Copyright 2011 Debbie Denise Reese. Used with permission)

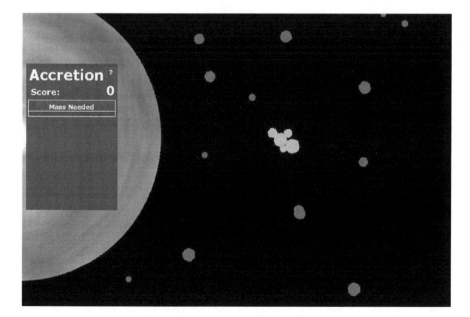

Fig. 9.6 Accretion scale 1 screen: the protoearth (*left*), the ring of debris (*darker dots*), and the initial protomoon (*center* collection of *light-colored dots*) (Copyright 2011 Debbie Denise Reese. Used with permission)

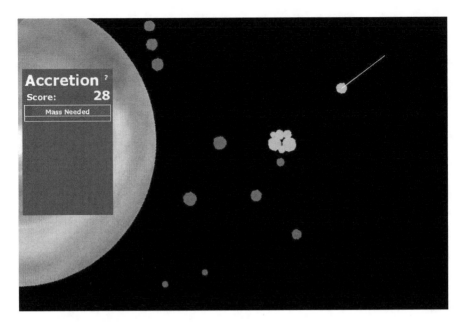

Fig. 9.7 *Selene Classic* accretion scale 1 during a slingshot gesture, after selection (*click*) and velocity (*drag*, see *white line* to the *top right* of selected particle), but prior to release (Copyright 2011 Debbie Denise Reese. Used with permission)

(a) and imparts direction and speed by dragging to (b). In this analysis we use speed but not direction.

Type (of Learning). We used velocity data and the learning moment algorithm to categorize player type as Always Progressing or accretionLM.

Learning Moment (LM) and Stage (Within HLM). The accretionLM algorithm categorized velocity data as pre or @&Post learning moment (LM). We divided Always Progressing players' data into pre or @&Post LM at the median Timed Report. With the hierarchical linear modeling analysis, we used "Stage" to label accretionLM category: Stage 1 = pre and Stage 2 = @&Post LM.

Condition. The *Selene* environment had assigned players to one of four conditions (see Fig. 9.3). This study limits analysis to players' initial round of accretion gameplay to investigate learning trajectory as players discover and apply targeted knowledge. *Selene* activities for the two conditions playing *Selene* accretion round 1 are identical, so we aggregated them for this analysis. Thus, the three experimental conditions are:

- Players (PIP/PPI): Play round 1 ($n = 137$).
- Watchers (WPI): Watch round 1—Play round 2 ($n = 48$).
- Watch & instruct (WIP): Watch round 1—Instruction—Play round 2 ($n = 36$).

Imbalance in sample size is because of round 2 attrition. Again, we generalize only to those players who completed a round of accretion gameplay. Watchers could

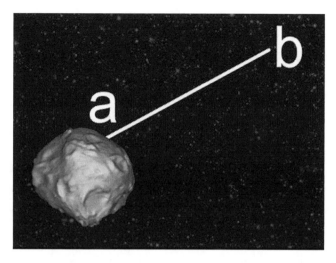

Fig. 9.8 A screen capture of the *Selene II* accretion slingshot gesture (Copyright 2011 Debbie Denise Reese. Used with permission)

only complete gameplay during round 2 of the game. We assumed watching the full demonstration of *Selene* round 1 gameplay would increase participants' ability to successfully play the game. The algorithm allows us to identify type of learning (Type: pre vs. @&Post LM) and statistically model its effect. The primary concern of our study is to ascertain Timed Report's efficacy, and we model Condition and Type. Therefore, we retain all players, regardless of their round 2 attrition status.

We adjust alpha level to correct for unequal sample sizes and other unmet statistical assumptions.

Dependent Variable: Timed Report. CyGaMEs *Selene* calculates the Timed Report measures each 10 s of gameplay by comparing current game state to previous game state to determine whether the player has made progress toward the current game goal (closer = 1, further away = −1, no progress = 0). Within the period under investigation here, scale 1 of the *Selene* accretion module, Timed Report scoring is straightforward. Within scale 1 there is only one goal: to achieve the scale's target mass. The player is evaluated every 10 s for progress toward that goal. That is, for accretion module scale 1 Timed Report, the *Selene* game compares the player's current protomoon mass to the goal protomoon mass and then to the player's previous protomoon mass. Part of the motivation for this work was to see which measures of Timed Report would be sensitive enough to be useful. Here, we report three studies comparing approaches to Timed Report analysis. Each study represented the Timed Report information in a different way.

Dependent Variables: Pearson's Correlation Coefficient r and Slope. Cumulative Timed Report is calculated by adding the value of each new Timed Report post to the sum of those that preceded it. We used the velocity timestamp for accretionLM to divide Cumulative Timed Reports into pre vs. @&Post LM. Then we calculated intercept and Slope of best fit lines for the cumulative Timed Report slopes and the

Pearson's correlation coefficient statistics for postings separately at Stage 1 and Stage 2, that is, pre vs. @&Post LM.

9.3 Results

Three studies were conducted to compare the strength and quality of the Timed Report.

9.3.1 Study 1: Multilevel Modeling of Timed Report Using Raw Timed Report Values

Hierarchical models are those in which data collected at different levels of analysis (e.g., participants, trials) may be studied without violating assumptions of independence in linear multiple regression. For example, the fact that individuals differ from each other implies that responses for each individual are not independent of one another. Multilevel modeling takes account of these dependencies by estimating variance associated with a higher level unit (participant), differences in average response (intercepts), and higher level differences in associations (slopes) between predictors and DVs (e.g., individual differences in the relationship between Timed Report and learning). This is accomplished by declaring intercepts and/or slopes to be random effects.

First-level units of the multilevel model were trials for which raw Timed Report values (-1, 0, 1) were measured, a total of 5,512, with the number of trials varying among participants. Predictors at first level were Stage and all second-level interactions that included Stage as a component as well as sequence within Stage. Second-level units were the 221 participants. Predictors at second level were Learning Type, Condition, and their interaction. Condition was dummy coded into two variables: play (PPI and PIP) vs. watch (WPI and WIP), and instruction (WIP) vs. no instruction (WPI, PPI, and PIP).

A model based on individual differences alone, without predictors, permitted calculation of the variance associated with individual differences. There were significant differences among participants (measured as a random effect), χ^2 $(220) = 1,009.42$, $p < 0.001$, $\rho = 0.09$. Tables 9.1a and 9.1b display the results of the two-level model. Using full maximum likelihood estimation, the full model with all predictors was significantly better than a null model, χ^2 $(12) = 61.44$, $p < 0.001$.

The statistically significant three-way interaction between Learning Type, Stage, and Play Condition is in Fig. 9.9. There is little or no difference between watchers and players among those who always progress, but a large difference between watchers and players for those who have an aha! moment. During Stage 1 players must discover the accretion concept, whereas watchers have the opportunity to apply what they have seen. During Stage 2 all participants are applying the concept.

The interpretation of the statistically significant main effects of Stage and Learning Type and the Stage by Learning interaction is limited by the three-way

Table 9.1a Fixed effects (averaged over participants)[a]

Effect	Parameter est.	Stand. error	t-Ratio	Approx. df	p-Value
For intercept					
Intercept	0.82	0.01	69.88[b]	215	<0.001
Learning Type	−0.30	0.04	−7.36[b]	215	<0.001
Instruction Condition	0.00	0.02	−0.06	215	0.951
Play Condition	0.00	0.01	0.37	215	0.712
Learning Type × Play Condition	0.15	0.02	6.31[b]	215	<0.001
Learning Type × Instruction Condition	0.10	0.06	1.67	215	0.097
For slope					
Stage	0.07	0.02	4.28[b]	5,499	<0.001
Learning Type × Stage	0.20	0.04	4.73[b]	5,499	<0.001
Stage × Play Condition	−0.01	0.01	−0.75	5,499	0.454
Stage × Instruction Condition	0.01	0.02	0.26	5,499	0.799
Learning Type × Stage × Play Condition	−0.15	0.02	−6.13[b]	5,499	<0.001
Learning Type × Stage × Instruction Condition	−0.10	0.06	−1.65	5,499	0.099
Learning moment sequence	0.00	0.00	−3.20[b]	5,499	<0.005

[a]With robust standard errors
[b]$\alpha < 0.05$

Table 9.1b Variance components

Random effect	Variance component	SD	χ^2	df	p-Value
Participant intercepts	0.006	0.076	288.25[a]	215	0.001
Residuals	0.331	0.575			

[a]$\alpha < 0.05$

interaction. The statistically significant fixed intercept indicates that the grand mean of responses is greater than 0, averaged over all subjects and trials.

9.3.2 Study 2: Repeated Measures Analysis Using Slope

The slope measure showed strong negative skewness in all cells of the design. The most effective transformation involved taking the absolute value of the reflected logarithmic transformation of the slopes. The remaining nonnormality was handled by setting $\alpha = 0.025$.

Timed Report accurately profiled both the behavior predicted by theory and by learning due to gameplay. A $3 \times 2 \times 2$ between-between-within ANOVA (Condition by Learning Type by Stage) was performed on transformed slopes. Table 9.2 shows that all of the main effects are statistically significant at $p < 0.025$. However, these are modified by statistically significant two- and three-way interactions (Fig. 9.10).

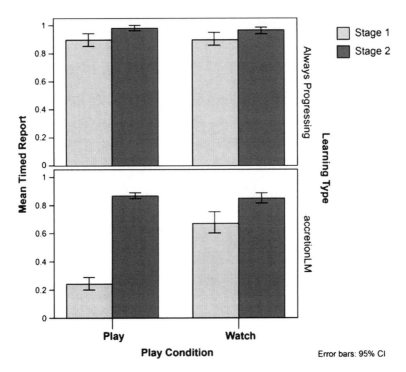

Fig. 9.9 Three-way interaction between Stage, Learning Type, and Play Condition (Copyright 2011 Debbie Denise Reese. Used with permission)

As theory would predict, post hoc Tukey tests reveal that during Stage 1 watchers with instruction (WIP) make the best progress (mean = 1.63) and players the least progress (mean = 1.12). However, player Stage 2 performance equals that of watchers. Thus, players both discover and successfully apply the targeted learning concepts. AccretionLM participants displayed the most dramatic improvement over stages, $F(1, 102) = 139.97$, $p < 0.001$, partial $\eta^2 = 0.58$, with 99% confidence interval from 0.41 to 0.69.

9.3.3 Study 3: Repeated Measures Analysis Using r

We used Pearson's correlation coefficient r statistics as the dependent variable. Five outliers (more than 3.3 standard deviations below cell mean) were adjusted. Outlier values were moved to the lower boundary −0.01 (corrections = +0.01, +0.01, +0.04, +0.02, +0.11). Alpha was set at 0.01 to correct for nonnormality, heterogeneity issues, and unequal sample sizes.

We conducted an omnibus 3 × 2 × 2 mixed ANOVA with Condition (players, watchers, and watch & instruct) and Type (accretionLM vs. Always Progressing) as the between subjects factors and Learning Moment Stage (Stage 1: pre vs. Stage 2:

Table 9.2 Study 2 omnibus source table cumulative Timed Report slope

Source	SS	df	MS	F	p	Partialη^2	97.5% Confidence interval of partial η^2 Lower	Upper
Between-subject								
Condition	1.033	2	0.517	10.34[a]	<0.001	0.09	0.02	0.17
Learning Type	0.624	1	0.624	12.49[a]	<0.001	0.06	0.01	0.13
Condition × Learning Type	0.816	2	0.408	8.16[a]	<0.001	0.07	0.01	0.15
Error	10.75	215	0.05					
Within-subject								
Stage	0.782	1	0.782	16.51[a]	<0.001	0.07	0.01	0.16
Condition × Stage	1.75	2	0.877	18.52[a]	<0.001	0.15	0.06	0.24
Learning Type × Stage	0.032	1	0.32	0.67	0.415	0	0	0.04
Condition × Learning Type × Stage	0.461	2	0.230	4.87[a]	0.009	0.04	0.11	0.11
Within-subject error	10.18	215	0.047					

[a]$\alpha = 0.025$

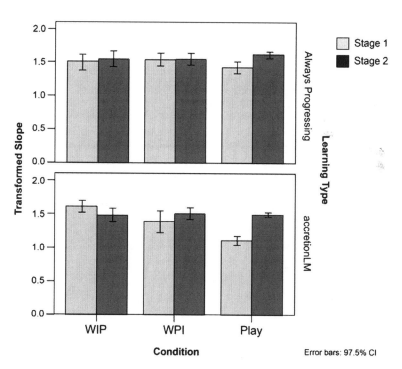

Fig. 9.10 Three-way interaction between Stage, Learning Type, and Play Condition using reflected logarithmic transformation of the slopes as the DV (Copyright 2011 Debbie Denise Reese. Used with permission)

164   D.D. Reese et al.

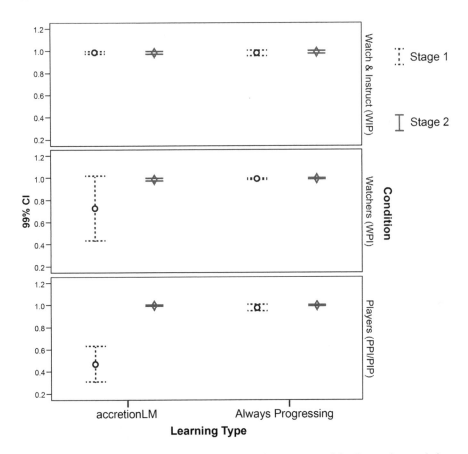

Fig. 9.11 The Condition by Type by Stage interaction as captured by Pearson's correlation coefficient analysis (Copyright 2011 Debbie Denise Reese. Used with permission)

@&Post LM) as the within factor. The Type×Stage interaction, $F(1, 215) = 10.44$, $p < 0.001$, partial $\eta^2 = 0.05$, is the effect of greatest interest. The Timed Report as represented by the Pearson correlation coefficient was sensitive (a) to distinctions between players who continually progress toward the game goal and those whose progress improves after the learning moment and (b) to the improvement in progress @&Post the learning moment. More importantly, the primary post hoc one-way repeated measures ANOVA for Type=accretionLM replicates the original 22 exemplar study, $F(1, 102) = 74.38$, $p < 0.001$, partial $\eta^2 = 0.42$. Timed Report accurately distinguishes pre vs. @&Post LM. As in the 22 exemplar study, this is a strong effect, and attenuation from 95 to 42% is expected when generalized to nonexemplars.

There are modest main effects for Type, $F(1, 215) = 11.41$, $p = 0.001$, partial $\eta^2 = 0.05$, and Stage, $F(1, 215) = 12.42$, $p < 0.001$, partial $\eta^2 = 0.06$. The modest effect is expected due to the characteristics of the Always Progressing data. Effect size is rather weak for the modest, borderline main effect for Condition $F(2, 215) = 4.39$, $p = 0.01$, partial $\eta^2 = 0.04$; the two-way interactions for

Stage × Condition, $F(1, 215) = 4.67$, $p < 0.01$, partial $\eta^2 = 0.04$ and Condition × Type, $F(2, 215) = 4.24$, $p = 0.02$, partial $\eta^2 = 0.04$; and the three-way interaction for Stage × Type × Condition $F(1, 215) = 4.13$, $p < 0.01$, partial $\eta^2 = 0.04$ (see Fig. 9.11). Together, these results support the planned post hoc analysis and warrant additional research.

9.4 Discussion

Studies 1, 2, and 3 replicated and elaborated on previous work, testing the sensitivity of the Timed Report when an algorithm categorized player activity into (a) before a learning moment and (b) @&Post the learning moment. When progress toward the game goal was determined by algorithmically using the viability of the player's slingshot gesture velocity, Timed Report accurately captured the distinction between before and after learning. Methodologically, the three studies supported the same results.

- Timed Report distinguishes player progress before and after learning.
- Timed Report distinguishes between players who are Always Progressing and those who experience a learning moment.
- Participants who played after watching have early success, but those who play without watching make the largest gains in performance, and their after-learning performance (after the aha! moment) equals that of watchers.
- Watching instructional videos aligned with game content (the same targeted concepts) before playing did not enhance performance. Those in the watch & instruct condition did not score higher @&Post LM trajectories.

Thus, the raw Timed Report values and both of the Pearson's correlation coefficients and slopes learning trajectory methods can be used in Timed Report analyses. Among the three analyses, all are effective. Pearson r is the simplest and most straightforward, requiring neither data transformation nor hierarchical modeling. However, other analyses might be more useful in other contexts. These are important results. For example, using a method similar to the accretionLM algorithm, running windows of Timed Report slopes can determine when slope persistently changes and mark learning moments. Degree of pre vs. @&Post learning slopes can be used as measure of learning. They can be applied to compare the effects of experimental interventions. Timed Report can be used with other measures collected by the *Selene* environment, such as the affective states of flow and the seven other dimensions of experience (Reese, 2008, 2009a, 2010), to study the interplay between affect and learning.

Games are an attractive instructional delivery system because they guide learners to discover and apply concepts through procedural and embodied activity. However, controlled research environments and rigorous methods are required to study how best to design these games for learning and how to measure that learning (NRC, 2011). The CyGaMEs *Selene* environment is a modular design that allows researchers to manipulate game modules and randomly assign participants to conditions.

In studies 1–3, modularization allowed us to investigate the effect of passive vs. active learning. Watchers (WPI) viewed an entire round of gameplay before they played *Selene*. Watch & instruct players watched a round of gameplay and then watched about 12 min of instructional video that presented, discussed, and illustrated the concepts translated into *Selene* gameplay. Watchers had the opportunity to learn through observing successful gameplay. Some also had the opportunity to reinforce and elaborate mental models by watching the instructional video. Watchers and watch & instruct players began as passive learners. Players started from scratch. They had to discover the underlying science concepts and then apply them to successfully accrete projectiles to form a protomoon. Players were always active. The Timed Report data demonstrate that passive learning enabled participants in both watcher conditions and gave them an advantage in playing the game. Early on they made the best progress. Players also learned and applied the lunar geology concepts. In the end there was no difference in player achievement. The preparation for future learning paradigm would predict that instruction would enhance performance over the priming effect of watching gameplay. Watching the instruction enhanced watchers' advantage (decreased the variability in scores to near unity) when these learners experienced a learning moment. The deep level of processing and salience required by active discovery suggests that players might learn more deeply and with greater retention than the watchers. On the other hand, Bandura's work (1997) attests to the power of observation learning, especially when an expert (in this case, the expert player in the demonstration game) might serve as role model. The interplay between passive and active discovery and its effect on learning are a topic for future research.

9.4.1 Current and Future Work

9.4.1.1 External Assessments

The CyGaMEs team has subsequently released an elaboration of the environment that contains external assessments. These measures are conceptualized and labeled as "external" because they do not collect during gameplay. They are more traditional measures, such as dragging and dropping onto a timeline and short essay responses. The *Selene* external assessments were designed to assuage critics by warranting the claims that underlie CyGaMEs as a principled approach to instructional game design and embedded assessment:

- Structure mapping theory and principles of instructional design and learning science suggest that *Selene* gameplay learning transfers from game goals to learning goals.
- *Selene* engenders content learning as well as gameplay learning, and Timed Report measures content learning.

External assessment data have shown that players infer a greater number of targeted subconcepts after playing *Selene*, whether or not the players viewed the instructional videos (Reese et al., 2009). *Selene* gameplay increases targeted content knowledge at either the preconceptual or conceptual level.

The external assessments may also help researchers investigate any differential effects of passive vs. active preparation.

In addition, one of these, the mutual alignment external assessment, was derived from work by Dedre Gentner and her colleagues, during which the researchers found that participant activities placing domain analogs in alignment and explaining that alignment act as a "bootstrap" that enhances learning (Kurtz et al., 2001). Schwartz and Bransford (1998) found a similar effect when they asked learners to analyze contrasting cases. We anticipate the mutual alignment assessment will aid players by scaffolding their ability to connect the *Selene* game to targeted content that enhances learning.

9.4.1.2 Limitations of the Current Work

The current work, the three studies reported in this chapter, is limited to scale 1 of the *Selene Classic* accretion module. This is the first level of the game encountered by the *Selene* learner. Scale 1 challenges the player with one learning goal. The unidimensional goal state simplifies Timed Report algorithms and permits data reduction (i.e., −1, 0, and 1). Accretion scale 1 is a good place to begin a research program investigating and developing the Timed Report. It obviates the complexity of ambiguity, competition, or weighting that may occur when multiple goal states are concurrently achievable. *Selene* scale 2 challenges the player with two goal states. Scale 3 has four concurrent goal states. Current success with running windows suggests the method should also apply to game levels that contain multiple, concurrent goal states.

9.4.2 Practical Implications

The NRC Committee on Science Learning: Computer Games, Simulations, and Education extolled the promise of instructional games for teaching, learning, and assessment. However, the committee also lamented the lack of alignment between instructional goals, instructional game design, and embedded measures of assessment (2011):

> Games will not be useful as alternative environments for formative and summative assessment until assessment tasks can be embedded effectively and unobtrusively into them. Three design principles may aid this process. First, it is important to establish learning goals at the outset of game design, to ensure that the game play (sic) supports these goals. Second, the design should include assessment of performance at key points in the game and use the resulting information to move the player to the most appropriate level of the game to support individual learning. Third, the extensive data generated by learner's interaction with

the game should be used for summative as well as formative purposes, to measure the extent to which a student has advanced in the targeted science learning goals because of game play (pp. 103–104).

9.4.2.1 For Instructional Game Developers

CyGaMEs is one approach instructional game developers can apply to address these design principles. The CyGaMEs approach provides developers a way to engineer game-based instructional systems that align learning goals, gameplay, game world, and assessment. Properly applied, alignment ensures gameplay provides more than just copious amount of data. Effective implementation of CyGaMEs alignment of the game system, gameplay, game goals, and assessment produces *information*. The CyGaMEs assessment of learning is the Timed Report. The studies in this chapter provide empirical support that the Timed Report is a sensitive measure of learning for unidimensional goal states.

We have found the running windows method broadly applicable for analysis of Timed Report data. The Timed Report algorithm within the *Selene Classic* game reduced raw data, aggregated at 10-s intervals, to measure of progress (−1, 0, and 1). We first studied the data trends within velocities for players who were exemplars of the accretion learning moment within the *Selene Classic* game. We analyzed those exemplars to derive specific parameters. As described within this chapter, we employed those parameters (a limit for a running mean and running standard deviation) for comparisons between and across running windows to determine a change in behavior as evidence of learning. Subsequently, we have applied the running windows technique to additional algorithms for learning moment detection:

- We developed a procedure with algorithmically determined rather than fixed parameters.
- We developed methods for detecting a learning moment from the Timed Report for a unidimensional goal.

We are currently studying the application of running windows to learning moment detection when *Selene II* game scales contain concurrent, multidimensional goals. We have used running windows to identify learning moments and states (progressing, no progress, failing) through an algorithm using the three calculated Timed Report values (−1, 0, and 1). Today, every *Selene II* Timed Report also posts composite and raw data for each current and concurrent game goal component (a design specification modification suggested in 2009 by Larry V. Hedges and elaborated during *Selene II* design and development). We will apply running windows to those data as well.

Our recommendation to instructional game developers is to carefully study and apply the CyGaMEs approach (Reese, 2009b, 2010) or a method like it. Based upon the speed of gameplay activity, determine a suitable interval for the Timed Report. Use Timed Report data to evaluate the environment. If sections of the Timed Report trace (plot) for an expert and successful test player do not indicate progress, evaluate those components of the environment for alignment:

- Does the game world align with the targeted domain?
- Does the game goal align with the targeted learning goal? That is, does the game goal motivate and reward gameplay analogous to the way target domain relationships interact and support the superordinate concept.
- Does the Timed Report algorithm accurately reflect gameplay progress?

Once the game and Timed Report perform adequately, Timed Reports can be used for research purposes and to provide formative and summative assessments within reporting systems designed for learners, educators, and other stakeholders.

9.4.2.2   For Educators and Learners

The NRC Committee on Science Learning in computer games and simulations projects that effective instructional games will one day provide formative and summative assessment for learners, educators, and other stakeholders. The *Selene* game already provides two layers of formative assessment for learners:

- Immediate feedback in the form of score, points, and short messages (e.g., "great density choice!").
- End-of-module feedback through a results screen. The accretion module results displays a cross-sectional player's moon and the actual Moon, displaying three layers and proportion for crust, mantle, and core. The surface features module results screen plots the Moon's 4.5 billion year history of impact cratering and volcanism activity. Then it plots the player's simulation of that 4.5 billion year evolution, complete with best fit line.

CyGaMEs also provides assessment results for educators. The Timed Report graphs of player progress produced by and for researchers can be produced by and for educators to evaluate player progress. With appropriate approvals and permissions, educators can download individual player datalogs and paste them into Excel files that automate population of Timed Reports and other graphs[4] (measures of affect collected through the CyGaMEs flowometer).

CyGaMEs offers training for educators to help them prepare, read, and interpret CyGaMEs assessment results. Training also includes hands-on activities that enable educators to integrate *Selene* within standards-based curricula. CyGaMEs assessment reports and training meet a priority set by the Department of Education within its 2010 National Education Technology Plan to "build the capacity of educators, educational institutions, and developers to use technology to improve assessment materials and processes for both formative and summative uses" (p. xvii). Capacity building should be accelerated though "knowledge exchange, collaboration, and better alignment between … practitioners and experts."

As future funding permits, we plan the CyGaMEs Learner Feedback Visualization System to show players and their educators (formal, informal, or nonformal) what

---

[4] We appreciate Matthew Petrole's assistance in developing the Excel report template.

players learned. We start with frontend analyses involving youth and their educators to identify how to best translate the learning moments and progress measured by Timed Reports into formative and summative assessment feedback that is useful to learners and their educators.

In the meantime and immediately, educators can turn to CyGaMEs and equivalent programs for training and experience using instructional games with embedded assessment and infusing them within instruction.

9.5 Conclusion

Implementation of cyberlearning environments requires and facilitates embedded assessment. The current study supports the efficacy of the Timed Report. It demonstrates that instructional games combined with the Timed Report and algorithms can be used to cause learning, identify when students learn a new concept, and measure how well they apply that concept after learning. The current work warrants the efficacy of the CyGaMEs approach to embedded assessment. The Timed Report tool for assessing game-based learning is a set of generic specifications that can be incorporated into any interactive environment in which the underlying system is the relational analog for a targeted conceptual domain. Timed Report data analysis is a form of data mining that can be used to measure changes in learner's mental model for targeted content. The processes for design, implementation, analysis, and reporting of Timed Reports advance progress toward effective cyberlearning.

Acknowledgments This material is based upon work supported by the National Science Foundation under Grant DRL-0814512 awarded to Debbie Denise Reese, Charles A. Wood, Ben Hitt, and Beverly Carter and work supported by the National Aeronautics and Space Administration under awards NCC5-451, NNX06AB09G-Basic, NNX06AB09G-Sup-1, NNX06AB09G-Sup-2, NAG-13782, and NNX08AJ71A-Basic to the NASA-sponsored Classroom of the Future. The first author refined the learning moment approach in collaboration with Larry V. Hedges. James Pusteovsky developed the precursor to this learning moment algorithm. *Selene* derived from Charles A. Wood's mental model of lunar and planetary geology, and he is the project's subject matter expert. We are indebted to our colleagues, Janis Worklan and Cassie Lightfritz, and our student researchers, Matthew Petrole and Steven Nowak. Any opinions, findings, and conclusions or recommendations expressed in this material are those of the authors and do not necessarily reflect the views of the National Science Foundation or the National Aeronautics and Space Administration.

References

Anderson, J. R., Reder, L. M., & Simon, H. A. (1998). Radical constructivism and cognitive psychology. In D. Ravitch (Ed.), *Brookings papers on educational policy: 1998* (p. 384). Washington, DC: The Brookings Institution Press.

Ausubel, D. P. (1968). *Educational psychology: A cognitive view*. New York, NY: Holt, Rinehart, and Winston.

Bandura, A. (1997). *Self-efficacy: The exercise of control*. New York, NY: W. H. Freeman.

Borgman, C. L., Abelson, H., Johnson, R., Koedinger, K. R., Linn, M. C., Lynch, C. A., et al. (2008). *Fostering learning in the networked world: The cyberlearning opportunity and challenge. A 21st century agenda for the National Science Foundation*. Arlington, VA: National Science Foundation. Retrieved August 1, 2008, from http://www.nsf.gov/pubs/2008/nsf08204/nsf08204.pdf?govDel=USNSF_124.

Diehl, V., & Reese, D. D. (2010). Elaborated metaphors support viable inferences about difficult science concepts. *Educational Psychology, 30*(7), 771–791.

Feltovich, P. J., Coulson, R. L., & Spiro, R. J. (1988). Learners' (mis)understanding of important and difficult concepts: A challenge to smart machines in education. In K. D. Forbus & P. J. Feltovich (Eds.), *Smart machines in education: The coming revolution in educational technology* (pp. 349–375). Cambridge, MA: MIT Press.

Gentner, D. (1983). Structure mapping: A theoretical framework for analogy. *Cognitive Science, 7*, 155–170.

Gentner, D., & Markman, A. B. (1997). Structure mapping in analogy and similarity. *The American Psychologist, 52*(1), 45–56.

Hitt, B. A., & Reese, D. D. (2012). Knowledge discovery from *Selene* data. In E. Wiebe (Chair), *New measurement paradigms: Psychometric methods for technology-based assessments*: Structured poster session presented at the annual meeting of the American Educational Research Association. Vancouver, BC.

Holyoak, K. J., & Thagard, P. (1989). Analogical mapping with constraint satisfaction. *Cognitive Science, 13*, 295–355.

Holyoak, K. J., Gentner, D., & Kokinov, B. N. (2001). Introduction: The place of analogy in cognition. In D. Gentner, K. J. Holyoak, & B. N. Kokinov (Eds.), *The analogical mind: Perspectives from cognitive science* (pp. 1–20). Cambridge, MA: MIT Press.

National Research Council (2011). *Learning science through computer games and simulations*. Committee on Science Learning: Computer Games, Simulations, and Education. In M.A. Honey and M.L. Hilton (Eds.), Board on Science Education, Division of Behavioral and Social Sciences and Education. Washington, DC: The National Academies Press.

Hummel, J. E., & Holyoak, K. J. (1997). Distributed representations of structure: A theory of analogical access and mapping. *Psychological Review, 104*(3), 427–466.

Johnstone, A. H. (1991). Why is science difficult to learn? Things are seldom what they seem. *Journal of Computer Assisted Learning, 7*(2), 75–83.

Kurtz, K. J., Miao, C.-H., & Gentner, D. (2001). Learning by analogical bootstrapping. *The Journal of the Learning Sciences, 10*(4), 417–446.

Lakoff, G., & Johnson, M. (1980). *Metaphors we live by*. Chicago, IL: The University of Chicago Press.

Lakoff, G., & Johnson, M. (1999). *Philosophy in the flesh: The embodied mind and its challenge to Western thought*. New York, NY: Basic Books.

Merrill, M. D. (2002). First principles of instruction. *Educational Technology Research and Development, 50*(3), 43–59.

Piaget, J., & Inhelder, B. (2000). *The psychology of the child* (H. Weaver, Trans.). New York, NY: Basic Books.

Reese, D. D. (2008, November). *Flowometer: Embedded measurement of learners' flow perceptions within game-based instructional environments*. Paper presented at the 2008 international conference of the Association for Educational Communications and Technology, Orlando, FL.

Reese, D. D. (2009a, October). *Replication supports flowometer: Advancing cyberlearning through game-based assessment technologies*. Paper presented at the 2009 international conference of the Association for Educational Communications and Technology, Louisville, KY.

Reese, D. D. (2009b). Structure mapping theory as a formalism for instructional game design and assessment. In D. Gentner, K. Holyoak, & B. Kokinov (Eds.), *New frontiers in analogy research: Proceedings of the 2nd international conference on analogy (Analogy '09)* (pp. 394–403). Sofia, Bulgaria: New Bulgarian University Press.

Reese, D. D. (2010). Introducing flowometer: A CyGaMEs assessment suite tool. In R. V. Eck (Ed.), *Gaming & cognition: Theories and perspectives from the learning sciences* (pp. 227–254). Hershey, PA: IGI Global.

Reese, D. D., & Hitt, B. A. (2009, June). *Selene knowledge discovery: The interface effect*. Poster presented at Games + Learning + Society 5.0, Madison, WI.

Reese, D. D., & Tabachnick, B. G. (2010). The moment of learning: Quantitative analysis of exemplar gameplay supports CyGaMEs approach to embedded assessment. In J. Earle (Ed.), *Building a knowledge base to inform educational practice in STEM: Examples from the REESE portfolio. Symposium conducted at the annual meeting of the Society for Research on Educational Effectiveness*. Washington, DC. Structured abstract retrieved March 6, 2010, from http://www.sree.org/conferences/2010/program/abstracts/191.pdf.

Reese, D. D., Diehl, V. A., & Lurquin, J. L. (2009, May). *Metaphor enhanced instructional videogame causes conceptual gains in lunar science knowledge*. Poster presented at the annual meeting of the Association for Psychological Science, San Francisco, CA.

Reese, D. D., Diehl, V. A., & Lurquin, J. L. (2009, May). *Metaphor enhanced instructional videogame causes conceptual gains in lunar science knowledge*. Poster presented at the annual meeting of the Association for Psychological Science, San Francisco, CA.

Schwartz, D. L., & Bransford, J. D. (1998). A time for telling. *Cognition and Instruction, 16*(4), 475–522.

Schwartz, D. L., & Martin, T. (2004). Inventing to prepare for future learning: The hidden efficiency of encouraging original student production in statistics instruction. *Cognition and Instruction, 22*(2), 129–184.

Spellman, B. A., & Holyoak, K. J. (1996). Pragmatics in analogical mapping. *Cognitive Psychology, 31*(3), 307–346.

U.S. Department of Education, Office of Educational Technology. (2010). *Transforming American education: Learning powered by technology. National education technology plan 2010*. Washington, DC: U.S. Department of Education, Office of Educational Technology.

Chapter 10
Driving Assessment of Students' Explanations in Game Dialog Using Computer-Adaptive Testing and Hidden Markov Modeling

Douglas B. Clark, Mario M. Martinez-Garza, Gautam Biswas, Richard M. Luecht, and Pratim Sengupta

10.1 Introduction

The three central components of science education in the classroom—learning, teaching, and assessments—have traditionally focused on facts and rote learning. Students in most science classrooms have traditionally memorized equations and names of chemical elements, cloud types, bones, and organs and are usually not provided with meaningful opportunities to develop deep understandings of the relevant phenomena, or use such knowledge to explore natural phenomena. These traditional approaches to learning, teaching, and assessment, however, do not align with current goals for science literacy that focus on students' ability to engage in extended problem solving that involves exploration, explanation, application of integrated conceptual knowledge to rich and realistic contexts (AAAS, 1993; NRC,

D.B. Clark (✉) • M.M. Martinez-Garza
Learning, Environment, and Design Lab, Peabody College, Vanderbilt University,
Box 230 230 Appleton Place, Nashville, TN 37203-5721, USA
e-mail: doug.clark@vanderbilt.edu

G. Biswas
Department of EECS/ISIS, Vanderbilt University, Box 351824,Sta B, Nashville,
TN 37203, USA
e-mail: gautam.biswas@vanderbilt.edu

R.M. Luecht
Educational Research Methodology Department, University of North Carolina
at Greensboro, 240 SOE Building, PO Box 26179, Greensboro, NC 27402-6170, USA
e-mail: rmluecht@uncg.edu

P. Sengupta
Mind, Matter & Media Lab, Peabody College, Vanderbilt University, Box 230,
230 Appleton Place, Nashville, TN 37203-5721, USA
e-mail: pratim.sengupta@vanderbilt.edu

D. Ifenthaler et al. (eds.), *Assessment in Game-Based Learning: Foundations,
Innovations, and Perspectives*, DOI 10.1007/978-1-4614-3546-4_10,
© Springer Science+Business Media New York 2012

173

1996, 2012), and the broader twenty-first century skills recognized as critical for all citizens (NRC, 2010).

Digital games provide an ideal opportunity to support this richer view of science learning (Clark, Nelson, Sengupta, & D'Angelo, 2009; Clark, Nelson, Martinez-Garza & D'Angelo, submitted; Federation of American Scientists, 2006; Honey & Hilton, 2010). This chapter presents a model for operationalizing, supporting, and assessing students' progress and proficiency in alignment with these science proficiency goals. The focus of our approach is on prediction and explanation in game play by integrating computer-adaptive testing (CAT) technologies and hidden Markov modeling techniques to track students' activity and construct models of students' learning within a single-player game (although the approach can be extended to multiplayer games).

10.2   Background and Challenges: Games to Support Science Learning

The idea that games might provide affordances for science learning and inquiry is not idiosyncratic. In 2006, the Federation of American Scientists issued a widely publicized report stating their belief that games offer a powerful new tool to support education (Federation of American Scientists, 2006). The FAS report encourages governmental and private organizational support for expanded research into the application of complex gaming environments for learning. In 2009, a special issue of *Science* (Hines, Jasny, & Merris, 2009) echoed and expanded this call. Many studies have provided evidence for the potential of digital games to support science proficiency in terms of conceptual understanding and process skills to operate on that understanding (e.g., Annetta, Minogue, Holmes, & Cheng, 2009; Barab, Zuiker, et al., 2007; Clark, Nelson, Sengupta, et al., 2009; Coller & Scott, 2009; Dieterle, 2009; Hickey, Ingram-Goble, & Jameson, 2009; Holbert, 2009; Kafai, Quintero, & Feldon, 2010; Ketelhut, Dede, Clarke, & Nelson, 2006; Klopfer, Scheintaub, Huang, Wendal, & Roque, 2009; Moreno & Mayer, 2000, 2004; Nelson, 2007; Nelson, Ketelhut, Clarke, Bowman, & Dede, 2005; Steinkuehler & Duncan, 2008). Studies also show that games can support: (1) students' epistemological understanding of nature and the development of science knowledge (e.g., Barab, Sadler, Heiselt, Hickey, & Zuiker, 2007; Clarke & Dede, 2005; Neulight, Kafai, Kao, Foley, & Galas, 2007; Squire & Jan, 2007; Squire & Klopfer, 2007), and (2) students' attitudes, identity, and habits of mind in terms of their willingness to engage and participate productively in scientific practices and discourse (e.g., Anderson & Barnett, 2011; Annetta et al., 2009; Barab, Arici, & Jackson, 2005; Barab et al., 2009; Dede & Ketelhut, 2003; Galas, 2006; McQuiggan, Rowe, & Lester, 2008). There are, however, challenges involved in using games to support science learning in terms of assessment and in terms of helping players connect intuitive understandings developed through game play with explicit formal understandings. This chapter proposes an explanation dialog model to address these two challenges.

Challenge 1: Assessment. One central challenge for game-based learning involves assessment. Specifically, pre–post multiple-choice tests, while exceptionally common,

Table 10.1 Challenges with standard pre-post approaches to assessment of learning in games

Challenge	Description
Standard pre-post tests cannot track learning processes within a game or activity	While they may, in fact, provide evidence of student learning, standard pre-post tests cannot provide critical information about the conceptual change processes involved (e.g., how students' intuitive concepts guided their answers and their play, what levels of scaffolding were most helpful, and how their emergent understanding guided their game play)
Standard pre-post tests require a large number of items to reliably assess a student's understanding	The span of items administered in the form of decontextualized format of summative assessment often results in test fatigue and disinterest by students, which results in added noise for which most statistical models do not account
Standard pre-post tests are costly in terms of time and opportunity because they are summative rather than purposefully or effectively instructional	Teachers are often not interested in allocating instructional time to the pretest, and if the curriculum/game is short enough, may not be interested in allocating instructional time to an extended post test that doesn't cover an extended span of their curriculum
Standard pre-post tests typically cannot assess extended problem solving	While the new science proficiency standards focus on students' ability to engage in deep extended problem solving involving the application of conceptual knowledge, most pre-post tests do not support or track extended problem solving
Standard pre-post tests often do not capture the connections between intuitive understanding and explicit formal understanding	Most multiple-choice tests focus only on explicit (and rote) representations of ideas. Tests of conceptual physics, such as the FCI, may focus on tacit understanding in their efforts to avoid assessing rote information, and in the process, may not assess students' ability to connect tacit understanding with explicit formal understanding

have many shortcomings in the context of games, such as assessing the richer forms of understanding and performance in science learning that will occur during game play (Clark, Nelson, Sengupta, et al., 2009; Clark et al., submitted). First, pre- and post tests only measure understanding before and after an intervention (i.e., the game)—pre-post tests do not track the processes of knowledge construction within a game or activity. Second, standard pre-post tests require a large number of items to reliably assess a student's understanding. Third, standard pre-post tests are costly in terms of time and opportunity because they are summative rather than being purposefully or effectively formative and, therefore, supportive of the learning process. Fourth, standard pre-post tests typically cannot assess extended problem solving. Fifth, and finally, standard pre-post tests often do not capture the connections between the intuitive understanding that students gain by playing a game and the formal, generalized understanding that students need to develop to become effective problem solvers in the domain of study. Table 10.1 explores these assessment challenges in greater depth. At the same time, other approaches to assessment in games for learning clearly need to be explored (Quellmalz & Pellegrino, 2009).

Challenge II: Connecting intuitive and explicit formal understanding. A second challenge area in games for science learning involves helping students connect the intuitive understandings they develop through game play with the explicit formal representations and concepts of the targeted science disciplines. Research on *Supercharged* (a 3D game in which players utilize and explore the properties of charged particles and field lines to navigate their ship through space), for example, found that students made significant learning gains on the physics post test, but only when the teacher collaborating in the research created activity structures outside of the game to engage students in predicting and explaining what was happening in the game and reflecting on connections of the tacit intuitive knowledge that the students were building through game play to the representations and concepts of the formal discipline (Squire, Barnett, Grant, & Higginbotham, 2004). Masson, Bub, and Lalonde (2011) showed similar outcomes where students appeared to develop intuitive understanding of aspects of the physics involved through the core game-play, but this intuitive understanding did not help students on subsequent assessments that tested explicit formal understanding. Work on SURGE (another conceptually integrated game where students use physics principles to navigate through space to achieve a variety of goals linked to a rescue theme) focused on integrating supports for connections between intuitive understanding and explicit formal physics representations and concepts showed significant gains on test items based on the Force Concept Inventory (FCI), a prominent conceptual test of undergraduate physics understanding about force and motion. Studies with SURGE also showed that further scaffolding is needed to help students build stronger connections between the intuitive understanding developed through game play and the targeted explicit formal concepts. (Clark et al., 2011). Thus the rich integrated conceptual understanding and ability to explain and apply that understanding targeted by the new science proficiency standards requires deeper learning behavior analysis and translating this information into appropriate metacognitive scaffolding within games for learning.

10.3   Framing a Solution to the Challenges

We frame our solution, the explanation dialog model, through two sets of cognitive goals as outlined in this section.

10.3.1   Cognitive Goal 1: Leverage Explanation Within Games to Support Learning and Assessment

If our goals for learning and assessment move beyond transfer and recall of rote information to include the ideas about science proficiency, we need to engage the player actively in processes of thinking that parallel the new science proficiency goals. We propose that engaging students in explanation related to problem solving offers excellent leverage for both the learning and assessment.

Research on self-explanation by Chi and others provides clarity into the value of explanation for learning (e.g., Chi, Bassok, Lewis, Reimann, & Glaser, 1989; Chi & VanLehn, 1991; Roy & Chi, 2005). A recent review of research on students' self-explanation reports that self-explanation results in average learning gains of 22% for learning from text, 44% for learning from diagrams, and 20% in learning from multimedia presentations (Roy & Chi, 2005). Encouragingly, research by Bielaczyc, Pirolli, and Brown (1995) shows that instruction that stresses explanation generation improves performance even after the prompts to explain are discontinued. Mayer and Johnson (2010) have conducted preliminary work in embedding self-explanation in a game-like environment with encouraging results that include gains on transfer tasks.

This emphasis on explanation is mirrored in research on science education. Work by White and Frederiksen (1998, 2000), for example, demonstrated the value of asking students to reflect on their learning during inquiry with physics simulations. This emphasis on explanation is often accompanied with prediction (e.g., Grant, Johnson, & Sanders, 1990; Mazur, 1996 reviewed more generally in Scott, Asoko, & Driver, 1991), promoting metacognition, learning, and reflection (e.g., Champagne, Klopfer, & Gunstone, 1982), enabling conceptual change (Borges, Tecnico, & Gilbert, 1998; Kearney, 2004; Kearney & Treagust, 2000; Liew & Treagust, 1998; Palmer, 1995; Shepardson, Moje, & Kennard-McClelland, 1994; Tao & Gunstone, 1999), while also providing a useful tool for probing and diagnosing students' conceptions of science facts and monitoring conceptual change (Liew & Treagust, 1995, 1998; Searle & Gunstone, 1990; White & Gunstone, 1992).

A growing body of research and scholarship on games and cognition emphasizes cycles of prediction, explanation, and refinement as the core of game-play processes (Games-to-Teach Team, 2003; Salen & Zimmerman, 2003; Wright, 2006). Few games provide coherent structures for externalizing and reflecting on game-play; more often, such articulation and reflection occur outside the game, through discussion among players and participation in online forums (Gee, 2003/2007, 2007; Squire, 2005; Steinkuehler & Duncan, 2008). We propose that supports for this kind of articulation and reflection can be integrated within the game itself.

10.3.2 Cognitive Goal 2: Constraint-Based Thinking Versus Model-Based Thinking

One of the purposes for integrating explanation into a game is to catalyze model-based thinking. Parnafes and diSessa (2004) explored players' thinking in a game-like simulation called *NumberSpeed*. Their research showed that players sometimes engaged in thinking very locally through simple processes of covariation (constraint-based reasoning), and at other times, engaged in deeper thinking about the underlying relationships and components to make more principled or model-based accounts and solutions for the challenge (model-based reasoning). They defined constraint-based reasoning as "using a set of heuristics to meet the problem constraints, usually using simple covariation" (p. 265). Constraint-based thinking involves means-ends strategies focusing on local comparisons and matching, simple motion principles, or pure covariation focusing on a small number of the problem constraints or parameters. Model-based reasoning, as Parnafes and diSessa explain, involves "creating a mental model of the whole scenario of motion, and mentally running the model to reason about the motion situation" (p. 268) to examine plans and modify or develop alternative plans in pursuit of an integrated qualitative solution based on the model.

While constraint-based thinking is fine in so far as it supports the development of model-based thinking, model-based thinking is ultimately needed for deep and integrated understanding. This makes sense from an elemental perspective on conceptual change (e.g., Clark, 2006; Clark, D'Angelo, & Schleigh, 2011; Clark & Linn, 2003; diSessa, 1993, 1996; Hammer, Elby, Scherr, & Redish, 2005; Hunt & Minstrell, 1994; Minstrell, 1982, 1989; Minstrell & Kraus, 2005; Sengupta, 2011; Sengupta & Wilensky, 2009, 2011). According to these perspectives, learning occurs as people sort through and refine their ideas as they build and refine connections between the ideas. If the games only demand constraint-based reasoning of the player, very little substantial reorganization and revision of the player's ideas is required in comparison to games that require model-based thinking. Similarly, from an assessment perspective, if games only elicit constraint-based thinking, we cannot assess what we care most about: students' ability to connect intuitive and explicit formal understandings in a principled manner to solve problems.

10.4   High-Level Model: Integrating and Assessing Explanation in Game Dialog

In addition to the cognitive goals for the explanation dialog outlined above, there are also driving goals from a game design perspective. We cannot just have students write predictions and explanations in a journal, for example, because that would destroy the flow of the game experience. Our intention is to fit explanation generation into the game narrative, in a way that preserves narrative space (Salen & Zimmerman, 2003), allows for identity construction and agency (Gee, 2004; Pelletier, 2008), and respects learners' expectations and aims regarding the essence of play (Caillois, 1961; Huizinga, 1980). All of these are important elements of games and play, which, it is hypothesized, can be disrupted by assessment (Shute, Rieber, & Van Eck, 2011). We propose that explanation generation can be integrated into the dialog of a game by encouraging self-explanation in the dialog between the players and the characters in the game. What might this look like? We outline a general model on how explanation might be enacted in game dialog.

For the purposes of our model, we will assume that there is a "core" game around which a set of "explanation" games will be developed. The core game focuses on a science topic, and the game is structured in a way that the player has to apply science concepts to navigate or work toward the established goals for the game. There are many commercial and educational games types that could provide the basis for a core game (see Fig. 10.1). Many of these are physics games (e.g., Angry Birds, Crayon Physics, Supercharged, SURGE, Switchball, Gravitee), but good examples also exist in chemistry (e.g., SpaceChem) and biology (e.g., SimAnt,

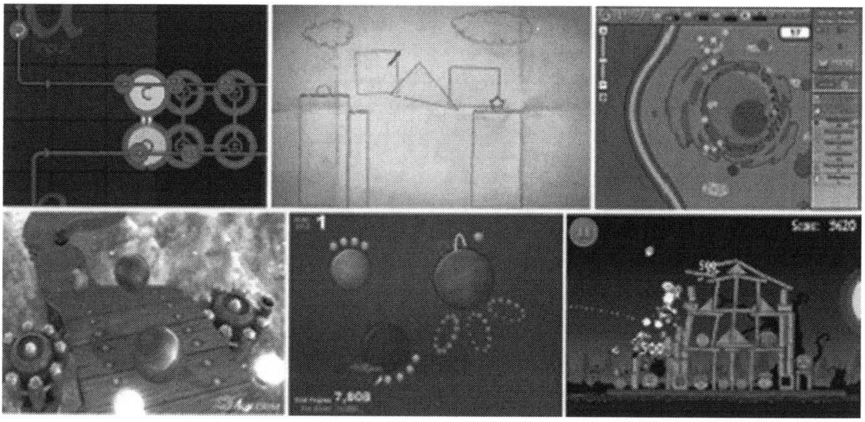

Fig. 10.1 Many recreational and educational games could provide the basis for the core game by engaging the player in applying science concepts to navigate or work toward an established goal. Examples (from *left* to *right*, *top* to *bottom*) include *SpaceChem*, *Crayon Physics*, *CellCraft*, *Switchball*, *Gravitee*, and *Angry Birds*

SimLife, CellCraft). Pedagogical agents and scaffolding might be layered on top of these mechanics to support players in identifying relevant and important ideas in the game play of the core game. One of the primary goals of the core game is to facilitate developing an intuitive understanding of the science concepts through game play (similar to learning by doing). Games, by creating engagement and flow (Csikszentmihalyi, 1991), have traditionally done well in this regard (Clark, Nelson, Sengupta, et al., 2009; Clark et al., submitted).

We then create a parallel explanation game to help students formalize and generalize their models so that they can be applied to a wide range of related problems (i.e., problems that are based on the same set of primary science principles). Levels of the explanation game are interwoven between levels of the core game. We believe that these explanation game levels (or "challenges") can support assessment and also build connections between the intuitive understandings the students develop through playing the core game and explicit targeted formal concepts and representations of the discipline. Essentially, the player first plays the core game "for themselves." Their play in the core game is scaffolded with prompts and suggestions from mentor agents. The player then takes on the role of a mentor in the explanation game. In the explanation game, the player teaches or helps one or more computer-controlled nonplayer characters (NPCs) to solve specific targeted challenges in the game environment. At its core, the explanation game:

1. Engages the student in identifying solutions to specific challenges that highlight and explore one or more core conceptual components from the science domain that were targeted in the core game.
2. Engages the student in developing and explaining this core game solution in a more general form, and at multiple levels of abstraction, with the goal of supporting the student in making the connections between the intuitive ideas developed during the core game play and the explicit formal versions of those ideas.

In this explanation game, players are asked to craft effective explanations that high-light and clarify the formal science ideas (e.g., Newton's Laws and associated key ideas of kinematics) to aid the cause of these characters and thus earn the player additional recognition and in-game rewards. To structure the explanation dynamic in a meaning-ful, appealing, and engaging way, players have the opportunity to explain and justify their strategies and the concepts underlying those strategies to NPCs in order to (a) convince the NPCs to adopt these solutions and (b) help the NPCs successfully over-come similar focused challenges. The challenges faced by the characters will often be presented as contrasting cases tied to common misconceptions (Bransford & Schwartz, 1999; Schwartz & Martin, 2004). Students can get immediate feedback on the quality and correctness of their explanations by observing how well their characters perform when they use the knowledge implied by the explanation to solve their assigned mis-sion tasks. In previous work (e.g., Biswas, Leelawong, Schwartz, Vye, & The Teachable Agents Group at Vanderbilt, 2005; Schwartz, Blair, Biswas, & Leelawong, 2007), we have found that, if properly scaffolded, this motivates the student and helps to direct their attention to mastery as opposed to performance goals (Pintrich, 2000).

Therefore, the explanation game is a manifestation of the hypothesis that, by providing players with multiple meaningful opportunities for explanation embed-ded within the game, as well as appropriate tools and scaffolding for developing and assessing these explanations, the game experience will foster deep learning of com-plex curricular science concepts. This explanation activity is framed in terms of a dialog with characters in the game environment. This game design element is famil-iar to players and also an efficient way to pace and structure the natural flow of information. To make the explanation tasks meaningful and to embed them within the game narrative, the explanation opportunities will be couched in terms of aiding other characters in solving similar puzzles as the ones the student has just solved in the core game. In many ways this taps into the learning by teaching paradigm (Bargh & Schul, 1980; Biswas, Schwartz, Bransford, & The Teachable Agents Group at Vanderbilt (TAG-V), 2001) as well as the self-explanation paradigm (e.g., Chi et al., 1989; Chi & VanLehn, 1991; Roy & Chi, 2005).

In addition to the literature reviewed earlier, we are building on design para-digms focused on adding an explanation task following a feedback event (Mayer & Johnson, 2010). While playing an electronics quiz-based environment that Mayer and Johnson defined as being game-like, students were tasked with answering explanatory questions posed as circuit diagrams. We believe that the results of this study suggest that asking students to perform some activity that connects the gen-eral scientific principles with the task the student just performed (whether they were successful or not) can be very conducive for deep model-based learning in a true game context, particularly if the explanation is integrated within the fabric of the game and, crucially, if the scaffolding surrounding the task is more responsive to students' thinking. That is, we believe that it is through designing scaffolds for sup-porting self-explanations throughout the game that we can foster model-based rea-soning (Parnafes & diSessa, 2004) in students.

We have discussed how the model above might support learning in terms of the dis-cussion of our cognitive goals, but how might we leverage CAT and hidden Markov models (HMMs) to analyze students' explanations and game-play data in real-time to model understanding? More specifically, how could a game developed using this model track and assess a "just-in-time" view of students' understanding within the navigation and explanation components of the game? We propose that game-play data in both components of the game, generated by learners as they play the game, could provide an avenue of assessment that would allow valid inferences about learning behaviors and strategies, and therefore, provide a richer interpretation of learning outcomes (Shute et al., 2011). The goal of the model would be to support formative and summative assessment within the game in terms of the player's understanding of the target formal physics ideas early in the game, how and when that understanding evolves, and the degree of formal understanding the player has developed by the end of the game. These assessment models could then provide diagnostic information to (a) support just-in-time adaptive scaffolding in terms of the actions and suggestions that NPCs in the game make as pedagogical agents to support player learning during the game as well as the order and nature of the levels that the player encounters and (b) provide diagnostic information to researchers and teachers to support inferences about learning and to guide subsequent instruction.

10.5 Structure of the Explanation Game

We now outline a possible structure for the explanation game to explore whether it might be possible to integrate explanation into the dialog in an engaging game-like manner. This example will also facilitate discussion in subsequent sections about the integration of CAT and hidden Markov modeling techniques to assess progress and understanding in real time.

Essentially, a level (or "challenge") in the explanation game involves a multi-tiered challenge that spans a few minutes (maybe 1 min for a player who has a firmer grasp of the concepts underlying the challenge and 3 min for a player who has a less firm grasp of those ideas). The challenge is selected to be (a) a specific difficulty that is adjusted based on the player's previous performance and (b) a challenge the player has not yet encountered.

Each challenge consists of a sequence of roughly four tiers that engage the player in identifying or proposing a solution to a dilemma faced by the computer-controlled NPCs and then justifying or explaining that answer to the NPCs at multiple levels of conceptual abstraction. Advancing in the challenge requires learners to think about physics concepts in a general format using representations that are general and create clear contrasts between different problem types. For example, a challenge might open with one of the NPCs framing an emergency scenario that the player has to solve (e.g., their ship is about to crash). This scenario could be portrayed using the engine from the core game to show what the NPCs are doing in the game and the potential impending problems they face in solving the problem. The player then proposes or identifies a solution and justifies this choice to the NPCs to convince them to adopt the solution. The game engine then models the solution. The player is rewarded appropriately based on the efficacy of the solution for the NPCs' dilemma.

At each tier of the challenge, if the player creates or selects a nonproductive path or strategy, the player receives feedback and support in revising their choices. Thus all players are scaffolded in creating and justifying a functional solution. Scoring is, therefore, based on how efficiently a player moves through the challenge rather than whether or not the player reaches a productive solution (because all players are scaffolded in eventually achieving a productive solution). Each challenge is conceptualized as a learning opportunity that provides formative feedback, rather than simply assessing whether or not a player can solve the challenge.

From a programming perspective, the simplest version of a challenge might employ the standard computer game conventions for dialog. In the standard convention, when a player is asked to respond to an NPC's question in this standard convention, the player is presented a list of choices that are typically text only. This version of explanation is most closely related to the approach pursued by Mayer and Johnson. We also envision more visual and flexible approaches for player input, using combinations of text, images, and diagrams, along with other modes of framing a solution or explanation, either based on causal concept maps (e.g., Leelawong & Biswas, 2008) or discipline-specific representations such as free-body diagrams, flowcharts, or circuit diagrams. Thus, the player then goes through the tiers of the challenge, selecting the appropriate recommendations to help the NPC resolve their perilous situation. When a player chooses or designs a productive approach to a tier, the player moves to the next tier to build and extend on their initial explanation. When players choose a less productive approach to a puzzle, the dialog continues and they get feedback to help them understand the implications of their initial choice and a chance to make a different choice. Thus, a player will ultimately work his or her way through the productive approaches at each puzzle, but may require more or less feedback to do so. This might involve creating a feature in the game where students can unwind (go back a number of steps) and rethink their solution or explanation in light of problems they ran into with their previous solution or explanation.

A player's score in the game is a function of various factors including the number of steps and choices that they use to solve the challenge. This is represented as a counter (or "clock") advancing one step with each choice players make, with extra "time" allotted for achieving a more principled solution to a problem. If the player pursues too many nonproductive approaches, the counter will increase beyond a certain threshold and the game will inform the player that, for instance, their advice will reach the NPCs too late. The player then receives a reward (e.g., a medal) for the challenge depending on their score. A bronze medal, for example, might be awarded for getting to the end with much help and multiple missteps. A silver medal might be awarded for making few missteps in finding and explaining a solution, and gold medal might be awarded when the player can identify and explain the solution perfectly. The flow of the challenges is dynamic; if the player earns a bronze medal, for example, the difficulty of their next challenge might be adjusted slightly downward, a silver medal might keep challenge difficulty roughly the same, and a gold medal might result in adjusting the difficulty of the next challenge slightly higher. To maintain the pace of the game experience, a challenge should take between 1 and 3 min, depending on how much scaffolding the player requires.

Ideally, the game would contain a large library of challenges that have been validated and tested for item difficulty, as well as how they load onto any subscales of

Table 10.2 Possible design principles for structuring an explanation game that functions as an engaging game-like experience, a scaffold for deep learning, and the basis for assessment

1. Each time a player attempts a challenge is considered a trial. A trial involves one session of a player trying to navigate through the dialog forks of one challenge to reach a solution and supporting explanations that will work for that challenge

2. At the beginning of each trial, the game queries the previous trial data for that student to compute the difficulty of the challenge to present and cross-indexes with the catalog of challenges and their difficulties

3. At each fork of a given challenge problem, there is a prompt presented. The player then chooses or specifies a response. These responses can be in open form or presented as a closed set of choices. The response drives which branch of the fork the player moves down

4. An incorrect choice will result in returning to an earlier tier to choose again, with no additional penalty. When a player is returned to a fork where they made an incorrect choice, the incorrect choices are highlighted in some way or are not displayed at all

5. The game engine should be flexible enough to allow other interfaces to be added at given forks to allow the player to create/choose an alternative response (e.g., a concept map or free-body diagram). The general goal is to develop interfaces that have simple enough combinatorial complexity that logical and mathematical operators can be used to map ranges of answers to branches of a fork

   a) For a concept map format, the configuration possibilities for a given tier should be small enough that the combinations could be mapped onto the branches of the fork using logical operators

   b) The free-body diagram interface could use a combination of logical operators as well as computational algorithms, and the resultant composite vector could be mapped onto other branches for appropriate conceptual or procedural feedback

   c) Students could choose sentence fragments from a series of pull-down menus to create an explanation that the software could then assess and act on using a script with formal and mathematical operators and computations that operated on the student's choices to create a score for that explanation (Clark, 2004; Clark, Nelson, D'Angelo, & Menekse, 2009; Clark & Sampson, 2007)

6. The tiers of each challenge should be designed to guide students in crafting principled explanations. A principled explanation is defined as making a choice and providing both abstract reasons in terms of general principles, and specific values for the variables in play

7. We suggest that proper design consideration be given to authoring tools for the creation of challenges, including the use of templates. Ideally, the author can specify the layout for each tier of the challenge in its data file, and the kind of interfaces that may be included, in a straightforward manner. This might involve a separate data file for each challenge and a catalog file that the game engine can reference to identify appropriate challenges in terms of difficulty and focus

interest. A broad range of item difficulties and subscale profiles is a key feature to enable the CAT module. Additionally, several kinds of data would be recorded for each challenge undertaken by a player, so that both assessment and model-based feedback functionalities (see later sections) can be performed. The information stored should be extensive enough to reproduce as much of the player's actions as possible, including not only success/failure and number of trials, but also total time spent on each challenge, time spent on each branch of the challenge. For those interested in additional details, Table 10.2 outlines possible design principles for structuring an explanation game that functions as an engaging game-like experience, a scaffold for deep learning, and the basis for assessment.

10.6   Computer-Adaptive Testing Techniques to Drive
Dialog and Analysis

This approach to supporting the development and use of learners' explanations within dialog lends itself to designing students' interactions and tracking students' progress through computerized adaptive testing techniques. CAT is being increasingly used in educational assessment setting to improve measurement efficiency and accuracy. There are numerous examples of successful, large-scale CAT programs, such as the ACCUPLACER postsecondary placement exams (operated by the College Board), the Graduate Record Exam (Eignor, Way, Stocking, & Steffen, 1993), and the Armed Service Vocational Aptitude Battery (Sands, Waters, & McBride, 1997). As the explanation game progresses, a CAT algorithm could sequentially select and administer challenges matched in difficulty to that student's apparent level of understanding and explanatory skills. Essentially, challenges are the "items" that the CAT functionality administers. For example, as the student performs better along a particular dimension of measurement interest in the game, more difficult challenges are presented. Conversely, worsening performance will cause easier challenges to be administered.

In CAT, the difficulty of every item is directly considered in scoring, since most CATs are based on item response theory (Lord, 1980). IRT has a long history of use in educational settings (e.g., Yen & Fitzpatrick, 2006), especially for scaling and equating end-of-course and end-of-grade tests used by most states. IRT relies on a probabilistic model that related the responses to an underlying proficiency scale, typically referred to as θ (or, the Greek "theta"). A commonly used IRT model is the three-parameter logistic model, $\mathrm{Prob}(u_i = 1 \mid \theta; a_i, b_i) \equiv P_i(\theta) = \{1 + \exp[-a_i(\theta - b_i)]\}^{-1}$. This function generates a probability curve denoting the likelihood that an examinee having a proficiency score, θ, will correctly answer item i, which has a sensitivity or discrimination parameter, a_i, a difficulty parameter, b_i, and a lower asymptote parameter, c_i, where the latter is often conceptually assumed to be related to guessing behaviors on multiple-choice test items by lower proficiency examinees. Different items have different a_i, b_i, and c_i parameters, and these differences are taken into account in scoring. When all of the items are calibrated to a common scale—conceptually similar to calibrating weights or laboratory equipment—we can estimate examinees' proficiency scores, even when they take tests that differ in difficulty. For example, Fig. 10.2 shows the expected number-correct scores for three 25-item tests: an easier test, a moderate difficulty test, and a difficulty (hard) test. A number-correct score of 15 (60% correct) on the easy test maps to a θ score of slightly less than -1.0 (the actual estimate is approximately -1.15). The same number-correct score produces a θ score of about $+0.35$ on the moderate test and a θ score of approximately $+1.15$ on the most difficult test. In other words, the calibrated item statistics automatically adjusts the scoring for the difficulty (and other characteristics) of the test.

Calibrated IRT item statistics are used in CAT to actually target the difficulty of the test form to the apparent proficiency of the examinee. In principle, a CAT test delivery system could produce a unique test form for every examinee. That would

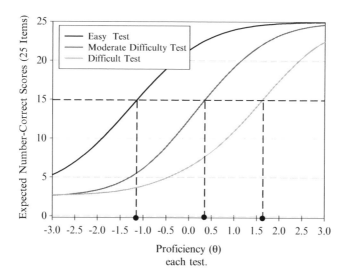

Fig. 10.2 Expected scores for three 25-item tests: easy, moderate, and difficult. Proficiency scores are mapped corresponding to a number-correct score of 15 on each test

imply a unique expected test score curve, similar to the unique expected performance curves in Fig. 10.2, for each examinee. An examinee's actual performance on his or her CAT automatically takes the item difficulty into account. Therefore, getting easier or more difficult items does not penalize the students. Rather, each new, adaptively selected item actually improves the precision of the estimated score profile by systematically reducing measurement errors.

Figure 10.3 shows the proficiency scores for three examinees: one examinee with relatively low proficiency, one with medium proficiency, and one with high proficiency. The item difficulties are shown by a "*" and track fairly closely with the estimated proficiency scores. This is the CAT targeting the item selection to each examinee's proficiency score. The CAT starts near the center for each examinee and then diverges toward the examinee's apparent proficiency. Also, the error bands around each score point continue to shrink in size, demonstrating greater confidence in the accuracy of the score estimates as more items are administered.

Unlike a conventional fixed test form, where every examinee sees the same items, an individually tailored CAT is usually far more precise and takes less testing time than a conventional test form (van der Linden & Glas, 2010). Through enhancements to the CAT item selection algorithm and scoring process involving multidimensional item response theory models (e.g., Luecht, 1996; Segall, 1996; van der Linden & Glas, 2010), it is entirely possible to develop highly informative multidimensional profiles of proficiency that truly are formative and diagnostic in nature. This need for a multidimensional perspective of strengths and weaknesses in formative assessment settings has only recently been demonstrated (e.g., Leighton & Gierl, 2007). Here, that multidimensional perspective can be efficiently applied to simultaneously measuring multiple learning progressions of complex constructs.

Fig. 10.3 Patterns
of estimated θ Scores
for three examinees
(low proficiency, medium
proficiency, and high
proficiency) showing
decreasing errors of
estimate across the 30-item
CAT sequence (*closed
cirle* denotes a correct
response; – indicates an
incorrect response)

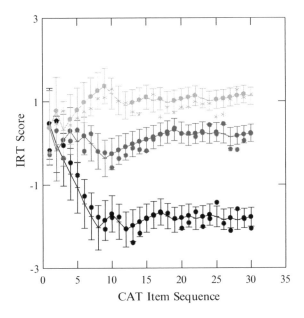

Essentially CAT technology could adjust the difficulty of the challenges that a player encounters within the explanation game. This would allow the game engine to build an ongoing evolving model of the player's current understanding via a multidimensional knowledge and skill profile. As described in the preceding section, challenges within the game would ask the player to explain to other characters in the game why something is happening, why something isn't working, or how to solve a problem systematically using the underlying concepts. These challenges could be developed as general templates so that multiple variants of the challenge could be generated. Variants could be as simple as switching numbers in the question, such as the mass or initial speed of an object, or could involve other variants, such as direction or combination of forces involved. Including multiple variants would allow a student to receive the same challenge (essentially) at a later time as a different variant if they do not answer it correctly in the first encounter and to prevent the sharing of answers in a classroom environment. Thus, integrating this CAT structure to select challenges in the explanation game would allow tracking and rechecking for evolving progress and understanding across game play.

Challenges will be developed, piloted, and ultimately calibrated to each of those multidimensional scales using item response theory, as noted above. Validity of the challenges will also be tied to the cognitively oriented construct maps associated with each of the scales to help ensure that proper interpretations of performance can be made—that is, inferences based on the specific explanations that the players provide. Once an item pool of IRT-calibrated challenges is developed, the explanation software could adaptively select and administer challenges during the game, with provisional scores helping the CAT algorithm to make the best challenge choices insofar as maximizing the precision of a multidimensional proficiency profile (scores and explanations of performance) generated for each player.

10.7   Hidden Markov Modeling to Track Game Play

CAT techniques can track and direct dialog within the explanation game, but another approach is required to track students' learning behaviors and the strategies they employ to develop understanding and problem solutions in the core and explanation games. Individual game play is a reflection of a complex interplay of behavioral, cognitive, and socio-constructivist elements that resist a simple causal construct. This resonates with the theoretical frameworks for game-based learning proposed by Amory (2006), Gunter, Kenny, and Vick (2008), Squire et al. (2004), and others. Hidden Markov modeling techniques provide strong affordances for capturing patterns in this learning as state-based models (Li & Biswas, 2002; Rabiner, 1989). Technically, a HMM describes a probabilistic state machine that describes a phenomena or behavior that evolves over time. The behavior is modeled in a compact form as a set of finite discrete, hidden (not directly observed) states, and probabilistic transitions between these states. The manifestation (or observation) of this behavior are observed symbols or numbers that are defined as the output corresponding to these states. HMMs have been successfully used in speech synthesis and recognition, gesture recognition, and for analyzing protein sequences in bioinformatics (Brand, Oliver, & Pentland, 1997; Juang & Rabiner, 1991; Krogh, Brown, Mian, Sjolander, & Haussler, 1994).

Figure 10.4 shows a hypothetical student's learning behaviors represented as a three-state HMM. While the three states cannot be directly observed, they can be inferred from the students' activity sequences. We can then examine the probabilities of producing each action in a state in order to interpret the meaning of that state. For example, the information-gathering state derives its name and meaning from the activities produced in that state (i.e., the state's output), such as reading resources and taking notes. Similarly, the map building state is associated with activities that include adding, deleting, and modifying concepts and links to create a concept map representation for the topic of study. The monitoring state is defined by actions like asking questions to see if one has understood a concept and taking quizzes provided by an instructor to check how one's performance is on a given topic of study. The transitions in the example model indicate likely sequences of actions a student may take. For example, a student will likely perform a map building action after an information gathering action with a probability of 0.3. But the student may continue with the information-gathering task (with a probability of 0.5), and less likely, a monitoring action to check if their map is correct (with a probability of 0.2).

We have used the HMMs to derive concise representations of student learning strategies and behaviors (Biswas, Jeong, Kinnebrew, Sulcer, & Roscoe, 2010; Jeong & Biswas, 2008). Algorithms for learning an HMM from output sequences are

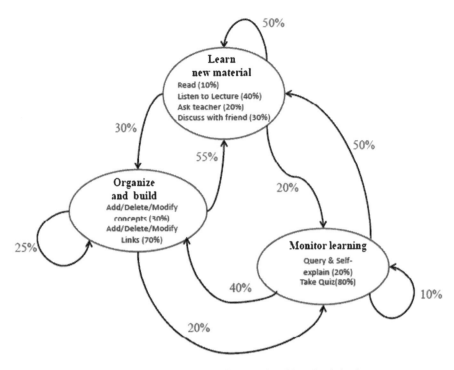

Fig. 10.4 An example of HMM structure describing students' learning behaviors

well-known, but require appropriate configuration/initialization parameters for effective use (Rabiner, 1989). Specifically, HMM learning algorithms require an initial HMM whose parameters are then modified to maximize the likelihood of producing observed output sequences. In particular, the number of states in the HMM and their initial output probabilities are important parameters that influence the structure and interpretation of the learned HMM.

Essentially, HMMs can be learned from observing students' activity sequences during core game play as well as the moves they make in the explanation game. The derived HMMs provide a probabilistic model of students' behavior patterns and their related learning outcomes. The model is derived from sequences of observed activities and the consequent results they produce in the game environment. Such models provide us with a framework for characterizing good vs. suboptimal strategies that students employ in learning and problem solving. A suboptimal strategy may be reflected as a trial and error or a guessing approach to obtaining a problem solution, whereas a good strategy may manifest as deriving a problem solution step by step, checking whether a science principle or concept has been correctly applied for each step and reflecting on intermediate results to check if the expected solution is being generated.

Previously, we have used HMMs to model student learning strategies and their interrelationships in an environment where students learn by teaching a computer agent (Biswas et al., 2010; Jeong & Biswas, 2008). In this work, HMMs have successfully captured underlying structure in sequential data (students' activity sequences and learning outcomes as computed by CAT items) as hidden states with probabilities of producing observable outputs (actions/outcomes), as well as probabilities of transitioning between those states. States represent higher-level cognitive states, such as informed editing of concept maps and using explanation structures to probe the correctness of a causal path structure (for details, see Biswas et al., 2010). Therefore, HMMs learned from student activity sequences can provide an overview of common behaviors/strategies employed by individual students or a set of students during learning, as well as the likelihood of transitioning between strategies while they are working on their learning, explaining, and problem-solving tasks in the game environment.

In more recent work, HMM algorithms have been employed as a bottom-up tool for learning students' behavior sequences from their log activity data (Biswas et al., 2010). This has been combined with top-down modeling approaches, informed by the metacognition and self-regulated learning (SRL) literature (e.g., Azevedo, 2009; Pintrich, 2000; Schraw, Crippen, & Hartley, 2006; Schwartz et al., 2009; Winne & Hadwin, 2008; Zimmerman, 2001) to map observed learning behaviors to (suboptimal and optimal) strategies that students employ for learning and problem solving. The ability to construct and use such models online provides a framework for developing explanatory dialog structures and feedback mechanisms that scaffold and support student learning during their game play activities. Not only can this provide critical diagnostic information to researchers and teachers, but this can also be used to create rich social interactions with the game characters to support conceptual development, metacognition, and engagement/immersion.

In the case of our model, a HMM trained on the moves and choices students make in the game will reveal the (hidden) aggregate state-based model that explains those choice and activity sequences. By monitoring the students' actions and performance associated with the states, the HMM can be used to make inferences, such as recognizing that students are employing "trial and error" methods to determine resultant forces, or a state where students systematically experiment with collisions to study conservation of momentum. Furthermore, since the HMM reports transition probabilities between states, these techniques can track how students combine the use of strategies to solve bigger problems. Longitudinal tracking of students across multiple problems could monitor how states and transitions change over time, providing the basis for inferences about changes in the underlying assumptions that guide students' thinking. Crucially, HMM analyses are performed using time-structured data (not just snapshots of data captured at set moments during the intervention). Hidden Markov modeling is thus well-suited to applications within games for learning, where the dynamic features of students' play and learning evolution can be captured as learners become proficient in the game and the operating principles behind it.

Crucial to all of this is determining the level of abstraction or detail for the input sequences from which the HMM is developed. This could range from individual keystrokes and mouse clicks a student makes (this may be too low-level for our purposes) to more aggregate representations, where small sequences of observed activities are considered to be related and represented as a single activity. HMMs can be developed from any such sequence of activities. The interpretation of the states generated will depend on the level of detail chosen for the activities that make up the sequences. Relevance measures or sequence-mining methods can be used, for example, to define and categorize the primitive actions on which the behavior analysis is based (Biswas et al., 2010; Kinnebrew, Loretz, & Biswas, in press, 2011). Depending on the level of detail chosen for the activity sequences, the hidden states of the HMM or state transitions can be interpreted as behaviors, which can be further mapped onto cognitive and metacognitive strategies that the students apply during their game playing and problem solving. Building more abstract sequence descriptions after the first round of interpretation using sequence mining can provide a framework for generating more aggregate behavior models.

Once interesting patterns and the HMMs have been developed or "learned" with some consistency, they can be used within the game environment to trigger various forms of scaffolding and feedback to support student learning. For example, detection of suboptimal strategies for learning may trigger a suggestion from a peer or mentor agent that guides the student to think of better strategies they may employ for learning and problem solving.

10.8 Connections Between Computer-Adaptive Test Scores and Hidden Markov Model

The combination of computer-adaptive test data and behavior analysis and interpretation can guide the level of feedback provided to the user, and subsequently guide students through learning trajectories (e.g., choice of topics and problems) that help them optimize their learning performance. For example, HMM learning could further analyze the impact of the computer-adaptive test assessments in combination with other game play data. The idea is to extract activity sequences that are linked to scale and subscale assessments and performance. A number of different methods may be applied. For example, one could employ clustering methods to group students by performance in the multidimensional space of computer-adaptive test scores. One could then extract activity sequences by group and derive HMMs for comparative analysis of the behavior structure for each group. The interpretation of the comparative behavior analysis along with the computer-adaptive test profiles by group could provide a rich framework for designing context-relevant argument and dialog structures for providing scaffolds and feedback to support and improve student learning. An alternate approach that could provide much finer-grained analyses of behaviors is sequence mining (Agrawal & Srikant, 1995) in a manner that focuses on fine-grained differential analyses of behavior patterns employed by groups of students (Kinnebrew et al., in press, 2011). These methods could then form the basis for tracking scales and subscales within the game environment.

10.9 Final Thoughts: Does the Proposed Explanation Dialog Model Address the Challenges Outlined for This Chapter?

The proposed explanation dialog model addresses the five concerns raised about standard pre-post approaches to assessment. First, the model tracks learning processes within the game rather than simply before and after. This allows insights into students' learning processes and provides opportunities for real-time scaffolding based on the formative assessment. Second, the explanation dialog does not require a large number of items at the beginning of the game because it integrates initial assessment into the first parts of the game and instead measures progress across the whole game rather than focusing only on static pictures of pre and post performance. The explanation dialog does not require large numbers of items at the end of the game to reliably assess a student's understanding because the embedded assessments have already created a detailed profile of the student's understanding that can be refined through a finite number of additional computer-adaptive summative questions. Third, this model is not costly in terms of time and opportunity because the assessment activities are purposefully formative and instructional, rather than solely summative. Fourth, the explanation dialog could assess extended problem solving rather than isolated decontextualized problems. Fifth, and finally, the explanation dialog provides an approach for capturing and promoting the connections between intuitive understanding and explicit formal understanding.

In terms of the challenge of helping students connect intuitive and explicit formal understandings, the explanation dialog structures the explanation game assessments entirely around specific challenges and common misconceptions. The goal of these challenges involves (a) engaging the student in identifying a solution that highlights a core science concept targeted by the core game and (b) engaging the student in explaining the solution at multiple levels of abstraction, with the goal of supporting the student in making the thinking and connections between the intuitive ideas from the core game and the explicit formal versions of those ideas from the discipline. In doing so, the explanation dialog builds on research on self-explanation and model-based thinking from the psychology, learning sciences, and science education literatures.

We thus claim that the proposed explanation dialog holds the potential to address the challenges to game-based learning outlined at the onset of this chapter. There are, however, limitations and trade-offs. The largest of the current limitations is the simple multiple-choice nature of the standard branching dialog tree (common to games), which does not provide a fully open-ended format. Essentially, writing multiple-choice items that test rote knowledge is simple (as evidenced by the vast proliferation of such items in typical multiple choice tests), but construction of deep conceptual dialog challenges using this format involves the same challenges faced by the multiple-choice format more generally. An interesting challenge for the explanation dialog model involves designing more open-ended interfaces that still support simple and reliable analysis of responses by the underlying software. Essentially, creating open-ended interfaces and formats is relatively easy—the challenge involves designing open-ended interfaces that elicit input that is easily and reliably analyzed to determine feedback, evaluation, and subsequent challenge difficulties. Section 5 of Table 10.2 outlines some of our initial ideas in terms of adapting free-body diagrams and concept maps toward this purpose, but ongoing work will be required to explore this limitation/challenge.

A related challenge involves selecting subject matter domain with multiple conceptually appropriate core ideas that players can leverage as focal "warrants" or explanations for their proposed solutions. In the example game discussed in this chapter, which focuses on mechanics, Newton's laws provide a relatively ideal set of concepts for this purpose. Students can explore and distinguish between the implications of the three laws as they invoke the laws at different times to explain different phenomena. For other domains, however, the underlying warrants for solutions might prove less conceptually rich and/or less well-aligned with the targeted concepts of the formal curriculum. The generalizability of the explanation dialog model therefore requires further exploration across other domains.

In terms of trade-offs and alternatives, at the most proximal level, we might replace IRT or HMM with other approaches within the explanation dialog model. HMM could be replaced, for example, with Sequential Pattern Analysis (Agrawal & Srikant, 1995; Zhou, Xu, Nesbit, & Winne, 2010). Sequential Pattern Analysis would be much less complicated to set up and would be computationally less expensive in terms of processing demands, but Sequential Pattern Analysis only analyzes sequences of events and not actual timings of events. Sequential Pattern Analysis therefore cannot distinguish between two actions taken sequentially vs. two actions separated by time. Therefore, Sequential Pattern Analysis might or might not make sense for specific applications of the explanation dialog model depending on the importance of timing considerations or other factors that one approach handled more or less effectively than the other.

Similarly, the affordances and limitations of the explanation dialog model itself should be compared with other game-based options depending on the characteristics of the underlying game to be assessed. Shute's stealth-based assessment offers another excellent model (Shute & Ke, 2012; Shute & Kim, in press). Stealth-based assessment is more broadly applicable to a larger number of game contexts and is more flexible in terms of what it might track. Training Bayesian nets for each challenge is substantially more complex, however, and connecting player actions to specific reactions or feedback by the game would be less precise. Similarly, SAVE Science's focus on making the core game about engaging in inquiry provides a more detailed assessment of students' ability to engage in inquiry (Nelson, Ketelhut, & Schifter, 2010; Schifter, Ketelhut, & Nelson, 2012), but the save science model is less flexible in terms of the breadth of game contexts to which it applies. As with any assessment choice, therefore, selection of the explanation dialog model, and its constituent components, should be a function of comparing affordances and limitations in light of other options and in light of the characteristics of the game context to which it will be applied.

10.10   Final Thoughts: Can the Explanation Dialog Model Be Fun?

The model for supporting learning games that we propose in this chapter depends on creating an "explanation game" that is central and fun in its own right on equal footing with the "core game." The model we have proposed leverages principles of game design that we believe will be effective at fostering engagement, while feeling familiar and comfortable to all learners. We will do so by generating a seamless flow of game play experience that interweaves levels of the core game with explanatory dialogs for formative assessment.

Engaging in dialog with simulated characters in the game world is a mechanism that has persisted since the earliest days of computer gaming. Since 1967, when Joseph Weizenbaum created *ELIZA*, a computer program designed to emulate interaction between the user and an artificial therapist, designers of interactive entertainment have attempted to incorporate meaningful interactions with virtual characters in order to aid immersion. While other conventions and genres have fallen into disuse, NPCs with branching dialog options remain key features of many game genres (e.g., role-playing and adventure games).

The interaction with the NPC is also important for a deeper reason: this narrative frame allows students to participate in help-giving, which not only provides a layer of meaning to play (cf. Gee, 2004; McGonigal, 2011), but has been demonstrated to be a key behavioral element for learning in small groups (Webb, 1989; Webb, Farivar, & Mastergeorge, 2002). To make the explanation game as similar as possible to the action of giving help to peers in a small group, we believe it is crucial that the dialog with NPCs is flexible, adaptive, and responsive to the learner; it is precisely this adaptive functionality that provides a workable core for an assessment strategy in our proposed model.

In our vision, having an assessment component in a game does not necessarily detract from engagement. We find many possible design choices can be made so that the explanation game and the core game interact in ways that students will find interesting and compelling. For example, by succeeding in the explanation game, students would unlock bonus levels, special one-time boosts for their characters ("power-ups"), customization options for their in-game avatars, etc. Since these awards are represented mainly in the core game, we view these awards as powerful forms of feedback to encourage success in the explanation game. We also envision rewards for outstanding play in the core game that provide smaller, but still significant, boosts that are applicable in the explanation game, such as extra time per challenge stage.

We believe that games for learning will engage students most powerfully if we present engaging, thought-provoking games and avoid the inconsistency of experience caused by interruptions for the purpose of assessment. The goal of our model is that the explanation game and the core game are perceived as two interwoven activities and that by integrating the rewards of one game into the play of the other game, we believe that the experience will be seamless; students will not perceive an interrupt in play and may not even be aware of which part of the game contains the assessment.

References

Agrawal, R., & Srikant, R. (1995). Mining sequential patterns. In *Proceedings of the eleventh IEEE international conference on data engineering (ICDE)* (pp. 3–14). Taipei, Taiwan.

American Association for the Advancement of Science. (1993). *Benchmarks for scientific literacy.* New York: Oxford University Press.

Amory, A. (2006). Game object model version II: A theoretical framework for educational game development. *Educational Technology Research and Development, 55*(1), 51–77.

Anderson, J., & Barnett, G. M. (2011). Using video games to support pre-service elementary teachers learning of basic physics principles. *Journal of Science Education and Technology, 20*(4), 347–362.

Annetta, L. A., Minogue, J., Holmes, S. Y., & Cheng, M.-T. (2009). Investigating the impact of video games on high school students' engagement and learning about genetics. *Computers in Education, 53*(1), 74–85.

Azevedo, R. (2009). Theoretical, conceptual, methodological, and instructional issues in research on metacognition and self-regulated learning: A discussion. *Metacognition and Learning, 4*(1), 87–95.

Barab, S. A., Arici, A., & Jackson, C. (2005). Eat your vegetables and do your homework: A design based investigation of enjoyment and meaning in learning. *Educational Technology, 45*(1), 15–20.

Barab, S. A., Sadler, T., Heiselt, C., Hickey, D., & Zuiker, S. (2007). Relating narrative, inquiry, and inscriptions: A framework for socio-scientific inquiry. *Journal of Science Education and Technology, 16*(1), 59–82.

Barab, S. A., Scott, B., Siyahhan, S., Goldstone, R., Ingram-Goble, A., Zuiker, S., et al. (2009). Transformational play as a curricular scaffold: Using videogames to support science education. *Journal of Science Education and Technology, 18*, 305–320.

Barab, S. A., Zuiker, S., Warren, S., Hickey, D., Ingram-Goble, A., Kwon, E.-J., et al. (2007). Situationally embodied curriculum: Relating formalisms and contexts. *Science Education, 91*(5), 750–782.

Bargh, J. A., & Schul, Y. (1980). On the cognitive benefits of teaching. *Journal of Educational Psychology, 72*(5), 593–604.

Bielaczyc, K., Pirolli, P., & Brown, A. L. (1995). Training in self-explanation and self-regulation strategies: Investigating the effects of knowledge acquisition activities on problem solving. *Cognition and Instruction, 13*(2), 221–252.

Biswas, G., Jeong, H., Kinnebrew, J., Sulcer, B., & Roscoe, R. (2010). Measuring self-regulated learning skills through social interactions in a teachable agent environment. *Research and Practice in Technology Enhanced Learning, 5*(2), 123–152.

Biswas, G., Leelawong, K., Schwartz, D., Vye, N., & The Teachable Agents Group at Vanderbilt. (2005). Learning by teaching: A new agent paradigm for educational software. *Applied Artificial Intelligence, 19*, 363–392.

Biswas, G., Schwartz, D., Bransford, J., & The Teachable Agents Group at Vanderbilt (TAG-V). (2001). Technology support for complex problem solving: From SAD environments to AI. In K. D. Forbus & P. J. Feltovich (Eds.), *Smart machines in education* (pp. 71–98). Menlo Park, CA: AAAI Press.

Borges, A. T., Tecnico, C., & Gilbert, J. K. (1998). Models of magnetism. *International Journal of Science Education, 20*(3), 361.

Brand, M., Oliver, N., & Pentland, A. (1997). Coupled hidden Markov models for complex action recognition. In *IEEE conference on computer vision & pattern recognition (CVPR)* (pp. 994–999). San Juan, Puerto Rico, June 17–19, 1997.

Bransford, J. D., & Schwartz, D. L. (1999). Rethinking transfer: A simple proposal with multiple implications. *Review of Research in Education, 24*, 61–100.

Caillois, R. (1961). *Man, play, and games* (1st U.S. ed.). New York: Free Press of Glencoe.

Champagne, A. B., Klopfer, L. E., & Gunstone, R. F. (1982). Cognitive research and the design of science instruction. *Educational Psychologist, 17*(1), 31.

Chi, M. T. H., Bassok, M., Lewis, M. W., Reimann, P., & Glaser, R. (1989). Self-explanations: How students study and use examples in learning to solve problems. *Cognitive Science, 13*(2), 145–182.

Chi, M. T. H., & VanLehn, K. A. (1991). The content of physics self-explanations. *The Journal of the Learning Sciences, 1*(1), 69–106.

Clark, D. B. (2004). Hands-on investigation in internet environments: Teaching thermal equilibrium. In M. C. Linn, E. A. Davis, & P. Bell (Eds.), *Internet Environments for Science Education* (pp. 175–200). Mahwah, NJ: Lawrence Erlbaum Associates.

Clark, D. B. (2006). Longitudinal conceptual change in students' understanding of thermal equilibrium: An examination of the process of conceptual restructuring. *Cognition and Instruction, 24*(4), 467–563.

Clark, D. B., & Linn, M. C. (2003). Scaffolding knowledge integration through curricular depth. *The Journal of the Learning Sciences, 12*(4), 451–494.

Clark, D. B., & Sampson, V. D. (2007). Personally-seeded discussions to scaffold online argumentation. *International Journal of Science Education, 29*(3), 253–277.

Clark, D. B., D'Angelo, C., & Schleigh, S. (2011). Multinational comparison of students' knowledge structure coherence. *The Journal of the Learning Sciences, 20*(20), 207–261.

Clark, D. B., Nelson, B., Chang, H., D'Angelo, C. M., Slack, K., & Martinez-Garza, M. (2011). Exploring Newtonian mechanics in a conceptually-integrated digital game: Comparison of learning and affective outcomes for students in Taiwan and the United States. *Computers & Education, 57*(3), 2178–2195.

Clark, D. B., Nelson, B., D'Angelo, C. M., & Menekse, M. (2009). Integrating critique to support learning about physics in video games. In *Poster presented as part of a structured session at the National Association of Research in Science Teaching (NARST) 2009 meeting*, Garden Grove, CA.

Clark, D. B., Nelson, B., Martinez-Garza, M., & D'Angelo, C. M. (submitted). Digital games and science learning: Research across the NRC strands of science proficiency.

Clark, D. B., Nelson, B., Sengupta, P., & D'Angelo, C. M. (2009). Rethinking science learning through digital games and simulations: Genres, examples, and evidence. In *Invited topic paper in the proceedings of the national academies board on science education workshop on learning science: Computer games, simulations, and education*, Washington, DC.

Clarke, J., & Dede, C. (2005). Making learning meaningful: An exploratory study of using multi-user environments (MUVEs) in middle school science. In *Paper presented at the American Educational Research Association conference*, Montreal, Canada.

Coller, B., & Scott, M. (2009). Effectiveness of using a video game to teach a course in mechanical engineering. *Computers in Education, 53*(3), 900–912.

Csikszentmihalyi, M. (1991). Flow: The psychology of optimal experience. New York: Harper & Row, Publishers.

Dede, C., & Ketelhut, D. J. (2003). Designing for motivation and usability in a museum-based multi-user virtual environment. In *Paper presented at the American Educational Research Association conference*, Chicago, IL.

Dieterle, E. (2009). Neomillennial learning styles and River City. *Children, Youth and Environments, 19*(1), 245–278.

diSessa, A. A. (1993). Toward an epistemology of physics. *Cognition and Instruction, 10*(2 & 3), 105–225.

diSessa, A. A. (1996). What do "just plain folk" know about physics? In D. R. Olson & N. Torrance (Eds.), *The handbook of education and human development: New models of learning, teaching, and schooling* (pp. 709–730). Oxford, UK: Blackwell Publishers.

Eignor, D. R., Way, W. D., Stocking, M. L., & Steffen, M. (1993). *Case studies in computer adaptive test design through simulation (research report # 93-56)*. Princeton, NJ: Educational Testing Service.

Federation of American Scientists. (2006). *Report: Summit on educational games: Harnessing the power of video games for learning*. Washington, DC: Federation of American Scientists.

Galas, C. (2006). Why Whyville? *Learning and Leading with Technology, 34*(6), 30–33.

Games-to-Teach Team. (2003). Design principles of next-generation digital gaming for education. *Educational Technology, 43*(5), 17–33.

Gee, J. P. (2003/2007). *What video games have to teach us about learning and literacy*. New York: Palgrave Macmillan.

Gee, J. P. (2004). *Situated language and learning: A critique of traditional schooling*. London: Routledge.

Gee, J. P. (2007). *Good video games and good learning: Collected essays on video games, learning and literacy (new literacies and digital epistemologies)*. New York: Peter Lang Publishing Inc.

Grant, P., Johnson, L., & Sanders, Y. (1990). *Better links: Teaching strategies in the science classroom*. Australia: STAV Publication.

Gunter, G., Kenny, R., & Vick, E. (2008). Taking educational games seriously: Using the RETAIN model to design endogenous fantasy into standalone educational games. *Educational Technology Research and Development, 56*(5), 511–537. doi:10.1007/s11423-007-9073-2.

Hammer, D., Elby, A., Scherr, R. E., & Redish, E. F. (2005). Resources, framing, and transfer. In J. P. Mestre (Ed.), *Transfer of learning from a multidisciplinary perspective* (pp. 89–119). Greenwich, CT: Information Age Publishing.

Hickey, D., Ingram-Goble, A., & Jameson, E. (2009). Designing assessments and assessing designs in virtual educational environments. *Journal of Science Education and Technology, 18*(2), 187–208.

Hines, P. J., Jasny, B. R., & Merris, J. (2009). Adding a T to the three R's. *Science, 323*, 53.

Holbert, N. (2009). Learning Newton while crashing cars. In *Poster presented at games, learning and society*, Madison, WI, June 10–12, 2009.

Honey, M. A., & Hilton, M. (Eds.). (2010). *Learning science through computer games and simulations. National Research Council*. Washington, DC: National Academy Press.

Huizinga, J. (1980). *Homo Ludens: A study of the play element in culture*. London: Routledge and Kegan.

Hunt, E., & Minstrell, J. (1994). A cognitive approach to the teaching of physics. In K. McGilly (Ed.), *Classroom lessons: Integrating cognitive theory and classroom practice* (pp. 51–74). Cambridge, MA: MIT Press.

Jeong, H., & Biswas, G. (2008). Mining student behavior models in learning-by-teaching environments. In *Proceedings of the first international conference on educational data mining* (pp. 127–136). Montreal, Canada.

Juang, B. H., & Rabiner, L. R. (1991). Hidden Markov models for speech recognition. *Technometrics, 33*(3), 251–272.

Kafai, Y. B., Quintero, M., & Feldon, D. (2010). Investigating the 'why' in Whypox: Casual and systematic explorations of a virtual epidemic. *Games and Culture, 5*(1), 116–135.

Kearney, M. (2004). Classroom use of multimedia-supported predict–observe–explain tasks in a social constructivist learning environment. *Research in Science Education, 34*(4), 427–453.

Kearney, M., & Treagust, D. (2000). An investigation of the classroom use of prediction-observation-explanation computer tasks designed to elicit and promote discussion of students' conceptions of force and motion. In *Presented at the national association for research in science teaching*, New Orleans, USA.

Ketelhut, D. J., Dede, C., Clarke, J., & Nelson, B. (2006). A multi-user virtual environment for building higher order inquiry skills in science. In *American Educational Research Association conference*, San Francisco, CA.

Kinnebrew, J. S., Loretz, K. M., & Biswas, G. (in press). A contextualized, differential sequence mining method to derive students' learning behavior patterns. *Journal of Educational Data Mining*, 2012.

Kinnebrew, J. S., Loretz, K. M., & Biswas, G. (2011). Modeling and measuring self-regulated learning in teachable agent environments. *Journal of e-Learning and Knowledge Society, 7*(2), 19–35.

Klopfer, E., Scheintaub, H., Huang, W., Wendal, D., & Roque, R. (2009). The simulation cycle: Combining games, simulations, engineering and science using StarLogo TNG. *E-learning, 6*(1), 71–96.

Krogh, A., Brown, M., Mian, S., Sjolander, K., & Haussler, D. (1994). Hidden Markov models in computational biology: Applications to protein modeling. *Journal of Molecular Biology, 235*(5), 1501–1531.

Leelawong, K., & Biswas, G. (2008). Designing learning by teaching agents: The Betty's brain system. *International Journal of Artificial Intelligence in Education, 18*(3), 181–208.

Leighton, J. P., & Gierl, M. J. (2007). Defining and evaluating models of cognition used in educational measurement to make inferences about examinees' thinking processes. *Educational Measurement: Issues and Practice, 26*(2), 3–16.

Li, C., & Biswas, G. (2002). Applying the hidden Markov model methodology for unsupervised learning of temporal data. *International Journal of Knowledge Based Intelligent Engineering Systems, 6*(3), 152–160.

Liew, C. W., & Treagust, D. F. (1995). A predict-observe-explain teaching sequence for learning about students' understanding of heat and expansion liquids. *Australian Science Teachers Journal, 41*(1), 68–71.

Liew, C. W., & Treagust, D. F. (1998). The effectiveness of predict-observe-explain tasks in diagnosing students' understanding of science and in identifying their levels of achievement. In *Presented at the American Educational Research Association*, San Diego, CA.

Lord, F. M. (1980). *Applications of item response theory to practical testing problems*. Mahwah, NJ: Lawrence Erlbaum Associates.

Luecht, R. M. (1996). Multidimensional computerized adaptive testing in a certification or licensure context. *Applied Psychological Measurement, 20*, 389–404.

Masson, M. E. J., Bub, D. N., & Lalonde, C. E. (2011). Video-game training and naive reasoning about object motion. *Applied Cognitive Psychology, 25*(1), 166–173.

Mayer, R. E., & Johnson, C. I. (2010). Adding instructional features that promote learning in a game-like environment. *Journal of Educational Computing Research, 42*(3), 241–265.

Mazur, E. (1996). *Peer instruction: A user's manual (Pap/Dskt)*. San Francisco, CA: Benjamin Cummings.

McGonigal, J. (2011). *Reality is broken: Why games make us better and how they can change the world*. New York: Penguin Press.

McQuiggan, S., Rowe, J., & Lester, J. (2008). The effects of empathetic virtual characters on presence in narrative-centered learning environments. In *Proceedings of the 2008 SIGCHI conference on human factors in computing systems* (pp. 1511–1520), Florence, Italy.

Minstrell, J. (1982). Explaining the "at rest" condition of an object. *The Physics Teacher, 20*, 10–14.

Minstrell, J. (1989). Teaching science for understanding. In L. Resnick & L. Klopfer (Eds.), *Toward the thinking curriculum* (pp. 129–149). Alexandria, VA: Association for Supervision and Curriculum Development.

Minstrell, J., & Kraus, P. (2005). Guided inquiry in the science classroom. In M. S. Donovan & J. D. Bransford (Eds.), *How students learn: History, mathematics, and science in the classroom*. Washington, DC: National Academies Press.

Moreno, R., & Mayer, R. E. (2000). Engaging students in active learning: The case for personalized multimedia messages. *Journal of Educational Psychology, 92*, 724–733.

Moreno, R., & Mayer, R. E. (2004). Personalized messages that promote science learning in virtual environments. *Journal of Educational Psychology, 96*, 165–173.

National Research Council. (1996). *The national science education standards*. Washington, DC: The National Academy Press.

National Research Council. (2010). In M. Hilton (Ed.), *Exploring the intersection of science education and 21st century skills: A workshop summary*. Washington, DC: National Academy Press.

National Research Council. (2012). *Conceptual framework for new science education standards*. Washington, DC: National Academy of Sciences Board on Science Education.

Nelson, B. (2007). Exploring the use of individualized, reflective guidance in an educational multi-user virtual environment. *Journal of Science Education and Technology, 16*(1), 83–97.

Nelson, B., Ketelhut, D., Clarke, J., Bowman, C., & Dede, C. (2005). Design-based research strategies for developing a scientific inquiry curriculum in a multi-user virtual environment. *Educational Technology, 45*(1), 21–34.

Nelson, B., Ketelhut, D. J., & Schifter, C. (2010). Exploring cognitive load in immersive educational games: The SAVE science project. *International Journal for Gaming and Computer Mediated Simulations, 2*(1), 31–39.

Neulight, N., Kafai, Y. B., Kao, L., Foley, B., & Galas, C. (2007). Children's participation in a virtual epidemic in the science classroom: Making connections to natural infectious diseases. *Journal of Science Education and Technology, 16*(1), 47–58.

Palmer, D. (1995). The POE in the primary school: An evaluation. *Research in Science Education, 25*(3), 323–332.

Parnafes, O., & diSessa, A. A. (2004). Relations between types of reasoning and computational representations. *International Journal of Computers for Mathematical Learning, 9*, 251–280.

Pelletier, C. (2008). Gaming in context: How young people construct their gendered identities in playing and making games. In Y. B. Kafai, C. Heeter, J. Denner, & J. Y. Sun (Eds.), *Beyond Barbie and Mortal Kombat: New perspectives on gender and gaming* (pp. 145–158). Cambridge, MA: The MIT Press.

Pintrich, P. R. (2000). The role of goal orientation in self-regulated learning. In M. Boekaerts, P. R. Pintrich, & M. Zeidner (Eds.), *Handbook of self-regulation* (pp. 451–502). San Diego: Academic.

Quellmalz, E. S., & Pellegrino, J. W. (2009). Technology and testing. *Science, 323*(5910), 75–79.

Rabiner, L. R. (1989). A tutorial on hidden Markov models and selected applications in speech recognition. *Proceedings of the IEEE, 77*(2), 257–286.

Roy, M., & Chi, M. T. H. (2005). The self-explanation principle in multimedia learning. In R. E. Mayer (Ed.), *The Cambridge handbook of multimedia learning* (pp. 271–286). New York: Cambridge University Press.

Salen, K., & Zimmerman, E. (2003). *Rules of play: Game design fundamentals (illustrated edition).* Cambridge, MA: The MIT Press.

Sands, W. A., Waters, B. K., & McBride, J. R. (1997). *Computerized adaptive testing: From inquiry to operation.* Washington, DC: American Psychological Association.

Schifter, C. C., Ketelhut, D. J., & Nelson, B. C. (2012). Presence and middle school students' participation in a virtual game environment to assess science inquiry. *Educational Technology & Society, 15*(1), 53–63.

Schraw, G., Crippen, K., & Hartley, K. (2006). Promoting self-regulation in science education: Metacognition as part of a broader perspective on learning. *Research in Science Education, 36*(1), 111–139.

Schwartz, D. L., Blair, K. P., Biswas, G., & Leelawong, K. (2007). Animations of thought: Interactivity in the teachable agent paradigm. In R. Lowe & W. Schnotz (Eds.), *Learning with animation: Research and implications for design* (pp. 114–140). Cambridge, UK: Cambridge University Press.

Schwartz, D. L., Chase, C., Chin, C., Oppezzo, M., Kwong, H., Okita, S., et al. (2009). Interactive metacognition: Monitoring and regulating a teachable agent. In D. J. Hacker, J. Dunlosky, & A. C. Graesser (Eds.), *Handbook of metacognition in education.* New York: Routledge Press.

Schwartz, D. L., & Martin, T. (2004). Inventing to prepare for future learning: The hidden efficiency of encouraging original student production in statistics instruction. *Cognition and Instruction, 22*(2), 129–184.

Scott, P. H., Asoko, H. M., & Driver, R. H. (1991). Teaching for conceptual change: A review of strategies. In R. Duit, F. Goldberg, & H. Niederer (Eds.), *Research in physics learning: Theoretical issues and empirical studies* (pp. 310–329). Kiel, Germany: Schmidt & Klannig.

Searle, P., & Gunstone, R. (1990). Conceptual change and physics instruction: A longitudinal study. In *Presented at the American Educational Research Association*, Boston, MA.

Segall, D. O. (1996). Multidimensional adaptive testing. *Psychometrika, 61*(2), 331–354.

Sengupta, P. (2011). Learning electromagnetism with ElectroHub—A digital game based on participatory simulation. Digital games and science learning. In D. Clark (Org.), *Invited paper session at the Annual Conference of National Association of Research on Science Teaching* (NARST 2011) Orlando, FL.

Sengupta, P., & Wilensky, U. (2009). Agent-based models and learning electricity. In *Paper presented at the annual meeting of the American Educational Research Association (AERA 2009)*, New York, NY.

Sengupta, P., & Wilensky, U. (2011). Lowering the learning threshold: Multi-agent-based models and learning electricity. In M. S. Khine & I. M. Saleh (Eds.), *Dynamic modeling: Cognitive tool for scientific inquiry* (pp. 141–171). New York: Springer.

Shepardson, D. P., Moje, E. B., & Kennard-McClelland, A. M. (1994). The impact of a science demonstration on children's understandings of air pressure. *Journal of Research in Science Teaching, 31*(3), 243–258.

Shute, V. J., & Ke, F. (2012). Games, learning, and assessment. In D. Ifenthaler, D. Eseryel, & X. Ge (Eds.), *Assessment in game-based learning: Foundations, innovations, and perspectives.* New York, NY: Springer.

Shute, V. J., & Kim, Y. J. (in press). Formative and stealth assessment. In J. M. Spector, M. D. Merrill, J. Elen, & M. J. Bishop (Eds.), *Handbook of research on educational communications and technology* (4th ed.). New York, NY: Lawrence Erlbaum Associates, Taylor & Francis Group.

Shute, V. J., Rieber, L., & Van Eck, R. (2011). Games… and… learning. In R. Reiser & J. Dempsey (Eds.), *Trends and issues in instructional design and technology* (3rd ed., pp. 321–332). Upper Saddle River, NJ: Pearson Education, Inc.

Squire, K. (2005). Changing the game: What happens when video games enter the classroom. *Innovate, 1*(6), 25–49.

Squire, K., Barnett, M., Grant, J. M., & Higginbotham, T. (2004). Electromagnetism supercharged!: Learning physics with digital simulation games. In Y. B. Kafai, W. A. Sandoval, N. Enyedy, A. S. Nixon, & F. Herrera (Eds.), *Proceedings of the 6th international conference on learning sciences* (pp. 513–520). Los Angeles: UCLA Press.

Squire, K., & Jan, M. (2007). Mad City Mystery: Developing scientific argumentation skills with a place-based augmented reality game on handheld computers. *Journal of Science Education and Technology, 16*(1), 5–29.

Squire, K., & Klopfer, E. (2007). Augmented reality simulations on handheld computers. *The Journal of the Learning Sciences, 16*(3), 371–413.

Steinkuehler, C., & Duncan, S. (2008). Scientific habits of mind in virtual worlds. *Journal of Science Education and Technology, 17*(6), 530–543.

Tao, P., & Gunstone, R. F. (1999). The process of conceptual change in force and motion during computer-supported physics instruction. *Journal of Research in Science Teaching, 36*(7), 859–882.

Van der Linden, W., & Glas, C. (2010). Statistical tests of conditional independence between responses and/or response times on test items. *Psychometrika, 75*(1), 120–139.

Webb, N. M. (1989). Peer interaction and learning in small groups. *International Journal of Educational Research, 13*(1), 21–39.

Webb, N. M., Farivar, S. H., & Mastergeorge, A. M. (2002). Productive helping in cooperative groups. *Theory into Practice, 41*(1), 13–20.

White, B. C., & Frederiksen, J. R. (1998). Inquiry, modeling, and metacognition: Making science accessible to all students. *Cognition and Instruction, 16*(1), 3–117.

White, B. C., & Frederiksen, J. R. (2000). Technological tools and instructional approaches for making scientific inquiry accessible to all. In M. J. Jacobson & R. B. Kozma (Eds.), *Innovations in science and mathematics education* (pp. 321–359). Mahwah, NJ: Lawrence Erlbaum Associates.

White, R. T., & Gunstone, R. F. (1992). *Probing understanding.* New York: Routledge.

Winne, P., & Hadwin, A. (2008). The weave of motivation and self-regulated learning. In D. Schunk & B. Zimmerman (Eds.), *Motivation and self-regulated learning: Theory, research, and applications* (pp. 297–314). New York: Taylor & Francis.

Wright, W. (2006). Dream machines. *Wired, 14*(4), 110–112.

Yen, W. M., & Fitzpatrick, A. R. (2006). Item response theory. In R. L. Brennan (Ed.), *Educational measurement* (4th ed., pp. 111–153). Washington, DC: American Council on Education/Praeger.

Zhou, M., Xu, Y., Nesbit, J. C., & Winne, P. H. (2010). Sequential pattern analysis of learning logs: Methodology and applications. In C. Romero (Ed.), *Handbook of educational data mining* (p. 107). Boca Raton, FL: CRC Press.

Zimmerman, B. J. (2001). Theories of self-regulated learning and academic achievement: An overview and analysis. In B. Zimmerman & D. Schunk (Eds.), *Self-regulated learning and academic achievement: Theoretical perspectives* (pp. 1–37). Mahwah, NJ: Erlbaum.

Chapter 11
Assessing Learning Games for School Content: The TPACK-PCaRD Framework and Methodology

Aroutis Foster

11.1 Introduction

Game-based learning is varied and so are the assessments and methods used to determine what is learned in games (Caperton, 2010; Shaffer, 2006; Williams, 2005). Disciplinary content, pedagogy, and context play an important role in learning (Gros, 2003; Mishra & Foster, 2007; Squire, 2003, 2006); however, in the discussion of games and learning, all three are usually overlooked. Foster and Mishra (2009) and Mishra and Foster (2007) argue that in order to assess games for learning, researchers should focus on disciplinary content and the role of game genre in contextualizing that content; and game designers should design games with careful attention to disciplinary content and pedagogy. Foster and Mishra (2009) contend that while assessing learning in games especially for school learning, attention should be paid to the role of game genre along with disciplinary content because the genre of a game is an implicit pedagogical stance. In order to focus on the role of genre and content for game-based learning assessment, the technological pedagogical content knowledge (TPACK) framework (Mishra & Koehler, 2006) is repurposed to provide a focus on the content and pedagogy in a game (Foster, Mishra, & Koehler, 2011).

For the assessment of student learning, the analysis of a game using TPACK is insufficient by itself. To assess learning from games without embedded assessments in the games, TPACK should be used as a guide to support the creation of assessments. In addition, the play, curricular activity, reflection, and discussion (PCaRD) model, developed by the author, should be used to guide the game integration process in a classroom and to support student learning in the context of understanding content from digital games in a classroom. A game analysis conducted with TPACK

A. Foster (✉)
Drexel University, School of Education, Learning Technologies,
3141 Chestnut Street, Philadelphia, PA 19104, USA
e-mail: aroutis@drexel.edu

D. Ifenthaler et al. (eds.), *Assessment in Game-Based Learning: Foundations,*
Innovations, and Perspectives, DOI 10.1007/978-1-4614-3546-4_11,
© Springer Science+Business Media New York 2012

aids in providing a focused analysis on content and pedagogy (Foster et al., 2011). TPACK and PCaRD together provide one method for analyzing and focusing on the content and pedagogy in games, creating assessments to support the use of games in formal or informal settings and integrating games for learning.

In this chapter, two studies are used to demonstrate an assessment process for learning in games in two different contexts, one using TPACK and another using TPACK and PCaRD. First, TPACK and how it is used to guide the creation of assessments is described. For a more detailed understanding of TPACK as an analytical lens for games with a focus on pedagogy and content see 1, Foster, Mishra, and Koehler in *Learning to Play: Exploring the Future of Education with Games* (2011). Second, the PCaRD model and its role in integrating games for learning in varying contexts are described. Third, study 1, an after-school study in a computer room with upper-elementary children using a commercial entertainment game is described, followed by study 2 in a high school classroom using a commercial educational game. Finally, the implications of this combination using the TPACK and PCaRD models together to create assessments and to keep the process of game-based learning in classroom focused on contexts, pedagogy, and content are explained. Using both a theoretical and empirical approach, this chapter will show how the TPACK framework and the PCaRD approach facilitated assessment and integration of games for learning.

11.1.1 Technological Pedagogical Content Knowledge

The TPACK framework was designed to describe teacher knowledge for integrating technology in classrooms (see Fig. 11.1). TPACK combines Technological Knowledge, Pedagogical Knowledge, Content Knowledge, Technological Pedagogical Knowledge, Technological Content Knowledge, and Pedagogical Content Knowledge for aiding teachers in integrating technology into their classrooms. Mishra and Koehler (2006) argued that a complete understanding of how to use technology for teaching and learning in classroom is TPACK. In the contexts of games, a form of technology, TPACK has been repurposed in that a complete design of games for learning and teaching should include a focus on content and pedagogy if games are to be used for teaching and learning school content. TPACK has been co-opted for use to aid in designing a framework for studying and creating assessments for learning in digital games (Foster & Mishra, 2009).

Based on a survey of the claims about games for learning, Mishra and Foster (2007) found that the research on games and learning often ignored game genres and their differential potential for learning and treated games as content-neutral. Arguments about learning from games have treated games and their genres as a monolithic entity, leading people to assume that the pedagogical value of one game is the same as that of another. Mixing the strengths and weaknesses across genres of games misrepresents the varied potential that different genres of games can offer. The design of a game, the kinds of choices regarding gameplay, the structure or

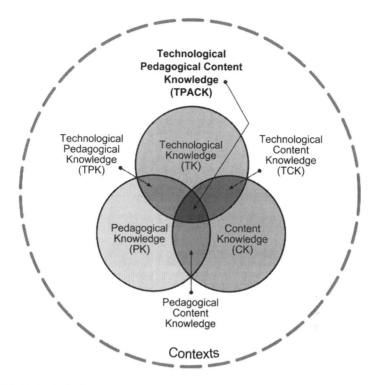

Fig. 11.1 Technological pedagogical content knowledge framework (http://tpack.org/)

rules, the nature of progress through a game, the nature of representation, and so on are all the results of decisions made by game designers. This design stance, from an educational point of view, can be seen as an implicit pedagogical approach—with inherent theories of learning, behavior, and epistemology. *A game genre is an implicit design stance that has pedagogical implications for learning because genres affect interactivity and navigation.* Similar to how action movies tell what to expect in that type movie, a simulation strategy genre tells a player what kind of interactivity and navigation to expect in that type of game. Like the importance of game genre to pedagogy, school content is important if games are to have any significant and meaningful impact on student learning. It is understood that learning is more than constructing content knowledge, but disciplinary or interdisciplinary content knowledge must be focused on in game design or research if students are to value the content or develop personal interest in the content beyond the games for lifelong pursuits (Brophy, 2008, 2009; Gee, 2003).

Based on this research, TPACK was repurposed to analyze games for pedagogy and content (Foster & Mishra, 2009, 2011). This is an important decision in order to know what content and pedagogical approach is in a game and by extension what could be assessed for learning and what to teach. Just like a teacher must know his/her curriculum and content, if games are to be used for learning in classrooms, the content and the pedagogy within a game must be known in order to determine what to assess and what supports students will need in gameplay. For instance, in conducting a study using a real-time strategy genre game about building empires, the researcher should first play the game to analyze what content could be learned to satisfaction. Playing the game also aids in determining the influence of the dominant pedagogical approach on play and how that influences what could be learned. This approach using TPACK allows the researcher or a teacher to treat the game as a curriculum.

For conducting a game analysis, TPACK was repurposed. The game analysis determines what school content or disciplinary knowledge is in a game. It also allows teachers, researchers, and games designers to explore the genre of the game, seeing how it acts as an implicit pedagogical approach in the game. Foster et al. (2011) argue that in using digital games for learning of school content, a game analysis should be conducted with TPACK.

TPACK is crucial to the game analysis because it aids teachers and learners focus on content and pedagogy within a digital game that can be used for learning. TPACK supports a focus on content and pedagogy. It also aids assessment creation and provides a focus on what to teach or learn. Whereas TPACK supports the content and pedagogical focus through game genres, PCaRD aids in the application or integration process of games in classrooms.

11.1.2 Play Curricular Activity Reflection and Discussion Model

PCaRD is a model developed by the author for integrating digital games into classrooms. The model is based on Gros' (2007) approach about games in education for experimentation, reflection, activity, and discussion. PCaRD guides the process of game *play* followed by using novel game-based learning *curricular activities* anchored in cases and culturally congruent instruction. An instructor leads the *curricular activity*. The instructor facilitates the connection between gameplay and the learning goals in teaching using cases and problems that are connected to students' play experiences. After the curricular activities, students engage in *reflection* using secure blogs to express their thoughts and opinions on what they have gained in knowledge from the gameplay and the curricular activity. During the *reflection* activity students are placed in groups or individually for writing posts and told to comment on the posts of peers. In addition, during the reflection session the instructor walks around to support students in groups or one-on-one. After the reflection activity, the instructor scaffolds students' experience in the reflection on what they wrote through a class *discussion*. It is at this time in the *discussion* session, students also ask questions about their posts and support their decisions. The discussion could be seen as a session for presenting findings and supporting those findings. PCaRD also has an additional layer in that all the play, curricular, reflection, and discussion activities include inquiry, construction, communication, and expression (ICCE) through locally situated contexts. ICCE is rooted in Dewey's (1902) work

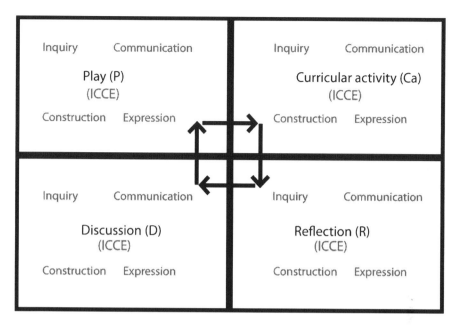

Fig. 11.2 Play, curricular activity, reflection, and discussion (PCaRD) model

that these four components are needed to tap into the natural curiosities of people for learning. Chapter 17 by Katz-Buonincontro and Foster also discusses the role of PCaRD in relation to creativity and cultural identity development using drawings based on a curricular activity about avatar design.

For instance, if students are playing a game to learn the history of Afghanistan, all the activities in PCaRD should include an aspect of inquiry, communication, construction, and expression. That is, the game may or may not contain all four parts of ICCE, but the curricular activity, reflection, and discussion phases should include aspects of ICCE to engage learners and their natural curiosities (see Fig. 11.2). In one case from a classroom study at a high school in Philadelphia, the author used a physics game to support student understanding of the scientific method. The curricular activity for one case was to design a game synopsis using the scientific method. This curricular activity involved inquiry, communication, construction, and expression as the instructor and the students came to an understanding of the process for designing their game synopsis and the connection between the physics game they were playing and the scientific method. In the reflection, students reflected and wrote about their game design, the game they were playing, and how to design a game based on the one they played by incorporating their personal interests and experiences in the process. In the discussion, instructors and students spoke about possible designs to represent the scientific method as a designed game and as a way of thinking to solve problems. Students repeated the design process in the following class until they were able to play the physics game and design a game using the scientific method. The learning goal was for students to understand the scientific method as a way of thinking that can be used outside of science courses. The gameplay helped their content knowledge in physics as well as their interdisciplinary understanding of the scientific method through playing and game designing

The PCaRD model stems from a premise that locally situated experiences (LSEs) are needed to help learners connect personal knowledge to school or pedagogical knowledge through valuing content knowledge and exploring possible selves (identities of what they may or may not want to become) (Foster, 2008; Markus & Nurius, 1986). Thus, the theory building also expands the current notion of situated learning using a theoretical learning approach called LSEs. *LSEs* are local and situated experiences that aid learners in developing or having experiences of possible selves that will eventually lead them to find or define their area of interest or salient identity beyond situational interest.

TPACK provides a lens to analyze digital games for pedagogy and content and PCaRD provides a pedagogical model for integrating games into learning settings in a systematic manner. In the next section, we discuss the first study in which only TPACK was used to aid in the design of assessments.

11.2   After-School Study

In study 1, the after-school game-based learning study, TPACK was used as a framework for developing assessments that facilitated the focus on content, pedagogy, and the game.

The game used was Rollercoaster Tycoon 3: Platinum (RCT3) (Frontier Developments, 2006). RCT3 is a simulation strategy game that provides a third-person gods-eye view perspective of the game world while engaging in gaming. The game has 18 scenarios that provide different theme parks and conditions for each based on managing resources. The purpose of the game is to build, design, and manage theme parks. However, the game also has content relevant for learning basic microeconomics principles and social studies such as opportunity cost and scarcity. Of the 18 scenarios, 6 were used in the study because of the constraints of the 7-weeks duration of the study. The six scenarios used were *Vanilla Hills, Gold Rush, Checkered Flags, Box Office, Fright Night,* and *Go with the Flow.* Each scenario has specific objectives and three levels including Apprentice, Entrepreneur, and Tycoon. The objectives describe the goals players must achieve in order to move on to the next level and eventually, the next scenario. Typical gameplay involves managing time, human, space, and money resources while creating their theme park and this allows players to deal with the microeconomics and social studies content.

The study included 26 participants between ages 9 and 11 who ranged from upper elementary to middle school. The participants had no prior experience in school learning the basic microeconomics principles that were covered in the game. They played games for 2 h per session twice per week for 6–7 weeks for a total of 24 h of gameplay. Participants played the game afterschool in a computer lab equipped with desktops and laptops. Participants were told to play the game as they would at home. They knew they were part of a study and that they would be assessed for what they learned from the game, which included the social setting or context of the study in the room. Participants were told they could do anything in the room including helping each other, communicating, and playing in any way they want in the game. The researcher wanted the study to be as naturalistic as possible to reflect the way players played at home.

11.2.1 Methodology

Prior to the recruitment of participants and before the beginning of the study, the researcher played RCT3 for 6 months and observed peers playing the game using the Playing Research Methodology (Aarseth, 2003; Foster et al., 2011). The researcher played the game in order to know what content could be learned in a meaningful way as well as to discover the genre effect on the pedagogy employed in the game for play. The simulation strategy genre influences the pedagogical approach by way of interactivity and play.

During the assessment creation, the researchers consulted economics experts who had prior experiences with the RCT series of games.

11.2.1.1 Assessment Creation Results

The game analysis described in Foster et al. (2011) using the playing research methodology and TPACK provided the researchers with the following content that could be learned from the game RCT3: Scarcity, ethical and moral decisions, empathy, opportunity cost, pricing, profit, supply and demand, resource management skills, information literacy, technology skills, and basic physics such as momentum. However, the physics content was not assessed in the eventual study because it was beyond the participating students' developmental level of comprehension to be meaningful. The game analysis also showed that the simulation strategy genre had a dominant pedagogical approach of observing actions and then intervening to make corrective measures. The observe and intervene approach is consistent with games using a God's eye view level of interactivity and play and is thus a genre characteristic that influences pedagogy. It was also possible for players who were following the game objectives in gameplay to strategize and plan ahead based on the required objectives to advance in gameplay.

Based on the game analysis for pedagogy and content, the researchers began creating assessments written at a developmental level of comprehension for upper elementary to middle school students. The assessments included the following: (a) Background survey, (b) pre-post knowledge assessment, (c) incremental assessment, (d) log-sheets, and (e) semistructured interview questions. As part of the overall study, there was also a 25-item Likert-scaled modified Intrinsic Motivation Inventory (IMI) (McAuley, Duncan, & Tammen, 1987) with subscales for interest, valuing, perceive competence, and pressure from the context of gameplay and content.

All the assessments were created with the intention that they must address content that could be learned from the game. This allowed for construct validity by not testing for what was missing in the game. *The Background survey* had 20 opened-ended items that examined psychographic and demographic information related to content areas that students could have covered in school, and which would help the researcher know what students knew or did not know about basic microeconomics principles and social studies. The survey also captured students' experiences about the types of games they have played and which ones were their favorites. The background survey aided the researchers in finalizing the creation of test items with content that the students did not already know.

The pre-post knowledge assessment covered the skills and content areas relevant to RCT3 including scarcity, ethical and moral decisions, empathy, opportunity cost, pricing, profit, supply and demand, resource management skills, information literacy, and technology skills. The knowledge test facilitated the process of understanding students' knowledge gain.

The *incremental assessment* included six, 12-item incremental scenario tests. There was one test for every scenario after it was completed. Each scenario test was designed to address the particular scenario that was completed by a participant. For instance, if a student completed the scenario of Vanilla Hills, the incremental assessment for Vanilla Hills was given to the student to assess their knowledge and skills related to that scenario. The knowledge and skills tested were related to the same content areas covered within a specific scenario; however, the incremental assessment provided a step-by-step picture of what students were learning in the game.

After each completed scenario and for each of the six game scenarios, participants' incremental knowledge gain and motivation was assessed. Ten of the twelve questions examined microeconomics and social studies, transfer, and technology and information literacy. The other two questions examined participants' experience in the particular scenario of play and inquired about their interest/enjoyment and if they would recommend that scenario for play to their friends. The incremental scenario assessments provided progressive data on participants' growth in the game in each scenario. In addition, it provided information on participants' development and/or knowledge gain from one level to another.

The log-sheet was a grid-like table with sections for all six scenarios for documenting progress and achievements in gameplay. The sheet logged the game year and month when participants completed each level and, eventually, each scenario. It also logged the awards and achievements earned by participants in each scenario. *RCT3* gameplay is from March to November and tracks progress in years, months, and weeks (e.g., Most Reliable Rides Achievement at Year 1, August, Week 3).

For the semistructured interview, 32 questions were used to document participants' progress, play strategies, content knowledge, and to record their experiences of the study. All sessions were videotaped in order to help the researchers assess participants' navigation strategies, player types, and provide support for knowledge gain. The interviews and the videotaped sessions provided documentation for how the genre influenced navigation and by extension how it affected play and learning. Player styles were taken into consideration based on their preferences in play as determined from the videotaped sessions and interviews.

11.2.2 Results of Study 1

TPACK aided the assessment creation process by providing a theoretical lens, applicable on content and pedagogy when using technology. These approaches made possible the creation of assessments for the known content that could be learned and the dominant pedagogical approach of observing and then intervening, and effectively understand what was learnt in the game. The different types of assessments allowed for triangulation of data through a convergent mixed methods approach using quantitative knowledge and incremental tests and qualitative log-sheets, interviews, and videotaped data. These data sources also facilitated a process of understanding how player styles and navigation affected the pace of advancement and individual knowledge gain by player style.

Foster (2011) discusses the results of this research arguing that students were able to gain statistically significant basic microeconomics and social studies knowledge for what was assessed. In addition, the students were motivated to learn. The results also indicated that there were two main player types of *goal seekers* and *explorers*. *Goal seekers* played to beat the game and/or other students to validate themselves. *Explorers* played with a focus on traversing all facets of the game for a more complete experience and to learn much about it for deeper engagement, even in the face of setbacks.

TPACK played a major role in the creation of assessments for a game-based learning study. However, when a study is part of a regular classroom the creation of assessments becomes part of a larger model of classroom integration and guidance in the integration process. For this approach to assessment, PCaRD is used to guide the process of integration and by extension assessment.

11.3 Classroom Study

In study 2, the classroom study, both the TPACK framework as well as the PCaRD model were used at an urban high school with 21 ninth graders, to support students learning of mathematics school content. As part of an elective course for teaching science, mathematics, and social studies using games, PCaRD was created to guide teachers in a systematic process of using and integrating games in the classroom. The course was designed to be year long with three different sections: Fall focused on Mathematics, Winter on Science, and Spring on Social Studies. Here, the author discusses the Fall assessment and integration process which represents the first time PCaRD was used.

The game used for Mathematics learning was Dimension M (Tabula Digita, 2010). It is a massively multiplayer online game that provides both third and first person options for navigating within a 3D game environment. The game has four missions which are basic mini-games including *Velocity*, *TowerStorm*, *Meltdown*, and *Swarm*. In *Velocity* the aim is to very quickly pick up spheres of different colors that are scattered in the game environment and to race to answer mathematics questions. Players must pickup up to five spheres in a colored order suggested by the game and then run through an energy beam and answer a multiple-choice mathematics question. *Swarm* is best played as a team game. The aim is to build a chain of nodes that connects your nodes to your opponents' nodes. Nodes are designated centers in the game where players may answer questions. By entering a node, players receive pop-up questions and color-displays containing possible answers in a multiple-choice format. If the answer is correct players capture a node. Players must protect the nodes they capture and the first team to build a chain of nodes to their opponents' base wins. In *TowerStorm*, the aim is to race to a fountain and answer multiple-choice questions to collect colored balls. After collecting the colored balls, which may be blue, red, green, or yellow, players run to the Tower and throw the ball. If players answered the question correctly they would score knowledge points (25 points), but if the player also correctly threw their color ball on to right color ring on the tower, the player gained both knowledge and gameplay points (50 points). *Meltdown* is a racing game in which players run, jump, and fly as they try to beat their opponents to the finish line. As the players race, they must answer multiple-choice questions that pop-up on the screen. To win the game a player must stay in their lane and master both gameplay navigation and curriculum.

The four missions provide options for students to cover multiple mathematics topics. The students in this class chose to cover numbers and operations, algebra, and geometry. Examples of numbers and operations problems covered topics such as properties of real numbers and equivalent fractions. Examples of the algebraic problems covered included combinations and permutations and difference of perfect squares. Examples of geometry topics covered included finding sin, cosine, and tangent.

The students played the game for the complete Fall session of the school year, a period of just over 3 months. The class was held in a computer lab with 30 desktop computers. The game was server-based and allowed students to create their own rooms; they played in teams or individually against each other. Each class was 100 min long, but it was broken into two 50-min sessions separated by lunch. Participants were introduced to the game and told to play in an unstructured or free play manner (like in study 1) for 30–40 min in each class. The class was held once per week.

11.3.1   TPACK and PCaRD Assessment Process

Like study 1, study 2 used TPACK to aid in the assessment creation for the classroom. Unlike RCT3, which is a commercial entertainment game, Dimension M is designed specifically to learn mathematics, thus determining the content was easy.

However, the researchers played Dimension M for about a month to decide how the content to be learned was designed, based on the genre of choice, roleplaying game. This has implications for player experience because gameplay and content must be tied to the learning goals for players to learn and value the mathematics content. In addition, the researchers had to decide what specific mathematics content could be assessed based on the multiple-choice questions posed in the game. The questions posed by the game popped up randomly in the multiple-choice format with repeated questions popping up occasionally. Thus, in the class, students were given the following assessments for addressing content learning mathematics: (a) 32-item multiple-choice test that addressed the mathematics topics that could be covered in the game and (b) curricular activities based on problems from students mathematics classes such as connecting inverse variations to supply and demand. As part of the overall study, the researchers also administered (c) a background survey about their media use and school and mathematics attitude, (d) a 28-item Likert-scaled modified IMI with subscales for interest, valuing, perceive competence, and pressure from the context for gameplay and mathematics and, (e) a self-regulation questionnaire for learning with subscales for autonomous and control regulations.

After gameplay students engaged in curricular activities that included problem-based activities such as Avatar design (discussed in Chap. 17 by Katz-Buonincontro and Foster) or teaching problems from the mathematics content they encountered in gameplay. The classroom teacher would go over problems the students encountered in gameplay and ask them similar questions that they would answer in reflections. As students play the game, the game creates a log-file of the mathematics problems they encountered. The log-files were obtained from the computers through the school server. For instance, in gameplay students would encounter problems related to scientific notations or logarithms. The teacher would provide a recap of those problems based on the log-files generated by the game and ask students similar questions to the ones they just had explained to gauge their understanding.

After the curricular activities and after lunch break in the reflection phase students were placed into groups. In the groups, they would think by asking each other questions and answering questions. This process aided their understanding of the problems posed in the curricular activities and the gameplay. Through the reflection process students found ways to connect how the gameplay and mathematics applied to their life.

Such problematizing of mathematics by reflecting and thinking how it connects to their life aids in the transformative nature of learning. It is this type of experience that was possible with PCaRD. Students were introduced to the process of reflecting meaningfully so they could learn from the process through grappling with how abstract mathematics problems would benefit them in the long run.

After reflection, students would ask the teacher questions and engage in discussion about the reflection activity and mathematics. For instance, students would highlight problems about the game such as a disconnection between the gameplay and the mathematics. This impacted their learning because the mathematics content could not be learned through play actions. The mathematics was learned through pop-up screens and was not connected to gameplay. The discussion allowed the students to think about the design of the game; this bolstered their understanding not only about mathematics, but also about the process of design and how it relates to the content they were learning. It also impacted their valuing of and interest in mathematics. The discussion allowed students to communicate and express their frustration about doing mathematics as a pop-up quiz in the game and this negatively impacted their interest in it.

The combination of TPACK and PCaRD provided a good assessment approach for integrating and using games for learning in classrooms. Using TPACK and PCaRD provided a valuable lens in study 2 for a complete design, development, and understanding of learning in games.

11.3.2   Results of Study 2

Using TPACK and PCaRD provided a valuable lens in study 2 for creating assessments and using the game in a classroom. This process led to statistically significant gains for mathematics knowledge for the students, but they were not intrinsically motivated to learn the mathematics or play the game. Nonetheless, through the PCaRD process, students commented that they liked how they found the relevance of mathematics to their lives. At the beginning of course, 19 of students could not see how they would use the mathematics they were learning later in life. Thus, it was a victory to see the students believing mathematics was relevant to their lives after experiencing PCaRD.

The PCaRD process with activities that included inquiry, communication, construction, and expression aided students valuing of mathematics even though they did not like the game. However, without a well-designed game, they did not statistically value the mathematics learning. The fact that students had an aversion to mathematics and low-perceived competence coupled with poor gameplay led to no statistical significant change in their interest even though they could see the global relevance for mathematics. Hence, it was not surprising that there was no statistical significant positive correlation between knowledge gain and motivation, interest, or valuing, or perceived competence.

After months of gameplay, we found from interviews that the students became bored and felt the mathematics questions from the game database was redundant. Even if they did not know how to do the mathematics problem, they could use the process of elimination by asking each other or based on what they had seen before. It appears that the drill and practice method of the game may be the reason for the knowledge gain.

11.4   Conclusions

In this chapter, it is argued that TPACK and PCaRD should be used together in creating assessments, integrating games into classrooms, and analyzing games for learning. In study 1, only TPACK is used, and the process of focusing on content and pedagogy to determine what content to assess is satisfied, but the process of using the game is not clear. Thus, how students learned in terms of what they do and when they do activities is not systematic and clear. In study 2, both TPACK and PCaRD provided a clear understanding of the whole process of using games for learning and understanding systematically what is done and when it is done to aid student learning. This process provides a better way to use games and to support teachers in the process of using games in classrooms.

PCaRD guides teachers in a systematic matter through the steps of the model. The inquiry, communication, construction, and expression activities in each stage of the model allow teacher to be creative and innovative to meet students' needs as described with the scientific method game. In this manner, teachers truly get to include and tap into learners' natural curiosities by inviting them to include their experiences and interests in the learning process. In the mathematics game, the teacher was able to recap problems with students and invite students to reflect and discuss their problems from gameplay. This problem-solving situation and thinking about how the mathematics problems connects to their lives now aided in student valuing the content they did not originally find relevant or interesting.

The cyclical nature of PCaRD each week and activities in each step provides a method to assess students' learning in systematic pedagogical way for learning goals. PCaRD aids in knowledge gain and transfer skills to achieve projective reflection, when students understand a process and grapple with the process to make connections to their lives and beyond the context of games while exploring possible selves.

11.5 Implications of Study 1 and 2

Whereas TPACK provides a lens to analyze digital games for pedagogy and content, PCaRD provides a pedagogical model for integrating games into learning settings and supporting teachers and learners. There are several implications of using TPACK and PCaRD together in game-based learning assessment for designers, researchers, and teachers with respect to game design, game integration into classroom, and student learning and motivation.

Designers should be cognizant about models used in educational technology. TPACK and PCaRD are useful models for designers in thinking how to design games for learning in classrooms. In addition, designers should consider the pedagogical implication of genres for learning content when designing serious or educational games. For assessments, designers should be aware that similar to how games allow for differentiated play for different player types, they should design games to allow for differentiated assessment to account for the knowledge and skills games afford for the different players types, including *goal seekers* and *explorers*.

For researchers, TPACK and PCaRD provide a theoretical framework and an applied model for systematically studying games and learning. The assessment of games for learning is tied to content and pedagogy and how games are used in classrooms. Thus, researchers should know the content, genre implications for pedagogy in the game, and ways in which the game could be integrated in classrooms for students to engage in transformative learning that includes opportunities for inquiry, communication, construction, and expression.

For student learning and motivation, teachers using games should know the content and dominant pedagogical approach in the game to be used. With PCaRD, teachers may strive to accommodate student learning through not only focusing on the content, but also students' motivational valuing and orientation. It is important that in employing PCaRD, teachers include opportunities for inquiry, communication, construction, and expression. This has implications for shaping student's long-term identity and coping mechanisms when they confront information that is novel, difficult, and unfamiliar. PCaRD aids in knowledge gain and transfer skills to achieve projective reflection.

Teachers should be aware that one type of assessment in games for learning would not capture the knowledge and skills of all students. Students of different player types have different motivation and goals in playing games. Thus, teacher assessments for knowledge and skills should address what knowledge and skills could be learned by all player types to get a wider view of learning in games.

Acknowledgments It is with gratitude that the author thanks the School District of Philadelphia and the High School students involved in the class and study for their support in advancing research on games and learning. The author also extends his gratitude to the upper elementary and middle school students in Study 1 for their support. Finally, the author thanks Mamta Shah, Laeeq Khan, and Tae Shin for their feedback on the paper.

References

Aarseth, E. (2003). *Playing research: Methodological approaches to game analysis.* In Paper presented at the digital arts and culture conference, Melbourne, Australia.

Brophy, J. (2008). Developing students' appreciation for what is taught in school. *Educational Psychologist, 43*(3), 132–141.

Brophy, J. (2009). Connecting with the big picture. *Educational Psychologist, 44*(2), 147–157.

Caperton, I. H. (2010). Towards a theory of game-media literacy: Playing and building as reading and writing [Conceptual]. *International Journal of Gaming and Computer-Mediated Simulations, 2*(1), 1–16.

Dewey, J. (1902). *The child and the curriculum.* Chicago: University of Chicago Press.

Foster, A. (2011). The process of learning in a simulation strategy game: Disciplinary knowledge construction. *Journal of Educational Computing Research, 45*(1), 1–27.

Foster, A., & Mishra, P. (2009). Games, claims, genres & learning. In R. E. Ferdig (Ed.), *Handbook of research on effective electronic gaming in education: Information science reference* (pp. 33–50). Hershey, PA: Information Science Reference.

Foster, A. N., & Mishra, P. (2011). Games, Claims, Genres, and Learning. In Information Resources Management Association USA (Ed.), *Gaming and Simulations: Concepts, Methodologies, Tools and Applications* (Vol. 1, pp. 497–513): IGI Global.

Foster, A., Mishra, P., & Koehler, M. (2011). Digital game analysis: Using the Technological Pedagogical Content Knowledge framework to determine the affordances of a game for learning. In M. Khine (Ed.), *Learning to play: Exploring the future of education with video games*. New York: Peter Lang Publications.

Foster, A. N. (2008). Games and motivation to learn science: Personal identity, applicability, relevance and meaningfulness [Conceptual]. *Journal of Interactive Learning Research, 19*(4), 597–614.

Frontier Developments. (2006). *RollerCoaster Tycoon 3: Platinum [Computer game]*. New York: Atari.

Gee, J. P. (2003). *What video games have to teach us about learning and literacy*. New York: Palgrave MacMillan.

Gros, B. (2003). The impact of digital games in education. *First Monday, 8*(7), 6–26.

Gros, B. (2007). Digital games in education: The design of games-based learning environments [Conceptual]. *Journal of Research on Technology in Education, 40*(1), 23–38.

Markus, H., & Nurius, P. (1986). Possible selves [Peer-reviewed]. *American Psychologist, 41*(9), 954–969.

McAuley, E., Duncan, T., & Tammen, V. V. (1987). Psychometric properties of the Intrinsic Motivation Inventory in a competitive sport setting: A confirmatory factor analysis. *Research Quarterly for Exercise and Sport, 60*, 48–58.

Mishra, P., & Foster, A. (2007). The claims of games: A comprehensive review and directions for future research. In C. Crawford, D. A. Willis, R. Carlsen, I. Gibson, K. McFerrin, J. Price, & R. Weber (Eds.), *Society for information technology & teacher education: 2007 18th international conference* (Vol. 2007, pp. 2227–2232). San Antonio, TX: Association for the Advancement of Computing in Education (AACE).

Mishra, P., & Koehler, M. J. (2006). Technological pedagogical content knowledge: A framework for teacher knowledge [Empirical conceptual]. *Teachers College Record, 108*(6), 1017–1054.

Shaffer, D. W. (2006). Epistemic frames for epistemic games [Research]. *Computers in Education, 46*(3), 223–234.

Squire, K. (2003). Video games in education. *International Journal of Intelligent Simulations and Gaming, 2*(1), 49–62.

Squire, K. (2006). From content to context: Videogames as designed experience. *Educational Researcher, 35*(8), 19–29. doi:10.3102/0013189x035008019.

Tabula Digita. (2010). *Dimension M*. New York: Tabula Digita.

Williams, D. C. (2005). Bridging the methodological divide in game research [Conceptual]. *Simulation & Gaming, 36*(4), 447–463.

Chapter 12
Implementing Game-Based Learning: The MAPLET Framework as a Guide to Learner-Centred Design and Assessment

Maree Gosper and Margot McNeill

12.1 Introduction

There is mounting evidence of the success of game-based learning for providing learning experiences which enable students to develop and demonstrate the achievement of learning outcomes from lower order foundational knowledge and skills through to complex concepts and higher order metacognitive and creative skills. Based on a review of the literature on game-based learning, Kirriemuir and McFarlane (2004) found that playing games can support valuable skill development, such as strategic thinking, planning, communication, application of numbers, negotiating skills, group decision-making, and data handling. Other studies have concluded that game-based learning has enabled a merging of play and learning which can lead to imaginative thinking and the development of disposition, demeanour, and outlook of players (Thomas & Brown, 2007); conceptual development (de Freitas & Oliver, 2006); staged learning opportunities that replicate real life (Macy, Squires, & Barton, 2009) and bridge the theory to practice divide (Johnson & Huang, 2008; Van Eck, 2006); and the transfer of knowledge learned from one situation to another (Dede, 2009). Although not exhaustive, this snapshot of findings highlights the potential of games as a tool to facilitate learning. The challenge however, for those wishing to integrate game-based learning into teaching and learning, is in turning this potential into positive learning experiences with measurable learning outcomes.

Assessing game-based learning cannot be achieved in isolation of the wider environment in which the learning is to take place. In doing so the interrelationships between the knowledge and skills to be developed, the characteristics of learners, and the assessment strategies for providing feedback and measuring achievement

M. Gosper(✉) • M. McNeill
Learning and Teaching Centre, Macquarie University, Sydney 2109, Australia
e-mail: Maree.Gosper@mq.edu.au; margot.mcneill@mq.edu.au

D. Ifenthaler et al. (eds.), *Assessment in Game-Based Learning: Foundations, Innovations, and Perspectives*, DOI 10.1007/978-1-4614-3546-4_12,
© Springer Science+Business Media New York 2012

218 M. Gosper and M. McNeill

need to be considered (Bransford, Brown, & Cocking, 2000). As de Freitas and Oliver (2006) point out:

> Having established that it is possible to learn from games, there is still the question of how such resources can form part of curricula. It is not learning from games per se that needs to be considered here; instead it is how learning can be designed for in a way that recognizes particular contexts (e.g., schooling) and the value systems (e.g., assessment frameworks, intended learning outcomes) that shape them (p. 252).

The principle of constructive alignment (Biggs & Tang, 2007) is a well-recognized approach to curriculum design which emphasizes the alignment of learning outcomes with appropriate learning activities and assessment strategies. We know that different types of knowledge and skills require different teaching and learning activities (McKeague & Di Vesta, 1996). In the gaming context, card games, for example, can promote the ability to match concepts, manipulate numbers, and recognize patterns. Jeopardy-style games can promote the learning of verbal information (facts, labels, and propositions) and concrete concepts (Oblinger, 2006). Adventure games in narrative-driven, open-ended learning environments are more appropriate for promoting hypothesis testing and problem solving (Van Eck, 2006).

Not all games, however, are designed with specific learning outcomes in mind and in reality many can be used to support multiple aspects of learning. Hence, if games are to be effective in supporting learning, it is essential that we understand not just how games work, but how they are aligned with taxonomies of learning (Van Eck, 2006) for this will help determine the most appropriate assessment strategies.

When devising assessment, not only is it necessary to consider assessment in its summative role for grading purposes, consideration also needs to be given to its formative role for providing feedback to guide future learning (Bransford et al., 2000). This duality is evident in game-based learning, particularly in ludic games where participants play to win or achieve a particular goal (Ang, Avni, & Zaphiris, 2008). Success in itself can serve a summative function and at the same time the performance-based feedback given to players in the form of advice on correct–incorrect moves, time on task, the number of successful attempts, or consequences of actions serves as a formative, self-assessment tool; thus, assisting students to monitor their progress and set targets for improvement. Game shows, flash cards, mnemonics, and action/sports games designed to support the repeated practice which leads to the recognition and recall of key concepts and skills (Prensky, 2001) can provide the immediate and informative feedback identified as being effective for the development of lower order knowledge and skills (Mory, 2004; Shute, 2008). Moreover, puzzles, simulations, strategy, and role play games (Prensky, 2001) which can illustrate cause-and-effect relationships and expose the consequences of tactical actions have been shown to assist with the development of higher order outcomes associated with understanding complex concepts and problem-solving skills (Mory, 2004; Shute, 2008). It may transpire that the value of such games as formative self-assessment tools far outweighs their worth as a summative assessment tool. Hence, in designing assessment strategies it is important to clearly articulate the intent of the game right from the outset in order that the balance between formative and summative assessment can be achieved.

It is not uncommon for games to be embedded in wider group activity or sets of activities as part of the curriculum, in which case, the achievement of learning outcomes associated with play can be measured through assessment tasks external to the game. *Global Conflicts (*http://www.globalconflicts.edu), for example, is an educational game designed to help teach concepts in citizenship, geography, and media which has detailed lesson plans and assignments for students that serve to integrate the game into the wider program of activities. Another example is *Live Long and Prosper* (http://education.mit.edu/pda/igenetics.htm) which is one of a series of games developed as part of the Participatory Simulations project at MIT. Played on handheld personal devices, the game aims to develop a deep basic understanding of genetics concepts as well as solid understanding of experimental methodology. As learners develop their understanding of genetics, the nature of the gaming activity can progress from exploring basic concepts to participating in more inquiry-based activities which are supported by activity sheets and guided questions. Consequently a range of assessment strategies can be called upon to ascertain the learning that has taken place. These may range from quizzes to test the achievement of lower order outcomes such as recognition and recall through to individual or group assignments, reflective essays, and problem-solving tasks to test higher order outcomes.

Ultimately, the nature of assessment, whether formative or summative, and the design of strategies is context specific; the alignment of aims and outcomes with gaming activity and assessment strategies is of paramount importance in defining the context. Effective learning environments also take heed of learners and the prior knowledge and experiences they bring to the learning context (Bransford et al., 2000). This is pertinent in the gaming environment where success in facilitating learning owes itself, in part, to active participation and interaction being at the centre of the experience (Johnson, Levine, & Smith, 2009).

A range of factors have been identified in digital games that engage the player and encourage learning (Bober, 2010; Gee, 2008). One of these is the intellectual maturation of the learner. From a cognitive perspective, Van Eck (2006) identified the link between intellectual maturation of the learner and their propensity to engage with a game. He proposed that games embody a process of cognitive disequilibrium and resolution; a process which is key to Piaget's cycle of assimilation and accommodation that occurs over an individual's lifespan as they mature. The extent to which games frustrate expectations (create cognitive disequilibrium) without exceeding the capacity of the player to succeed largely determines the extent to which they engage in a game. Further to this, Van Eck (2006) maintains that games that are too easily solved will not be engaging. Games which are successful as teaching tools are those that create a continuous cycle of cognitive disequilibrium and resolution (via assimilation or accommodation) while also allowing the player to be successful.

The link between intellectual maturity, engagement, and learning suggests the need for explicit recognition of the prior knowledge, skills, and capabilities of learners when making decisions about which games are appropriate, for whom and when. Moreover, it also suggests the need for an understanding of the nature of intellectual maturation and the type of activities (including games) that can be utilized to facilitate learning as the learner matures.

Research into the development of expertise can provide insights into the maturation process. As learners develop, they are able to store more domain specific knowledge; organize their knowledge in more accessible ways; perceive domain-related information and patterns faster and more effortlessly; make use of more complex strategies that permit the contemplation of a wide range of alternatives; and make better use of metacognitive skills (Ericsson & Lehmann, 1996; Ericsson & Smith, 1991).

The location of learners along this continuum of maturation can help to identify the optimum time for introducing a gaming experience in order to achieve the necessary stimulation to challenge and engage the learner without exceeding the learner's cognitive capability. For example, a student new to the knowledge domain with limited expertise is likely to find that playing in a rich immersive, exploratory, and open-ended environment requires cognitive strategies and resources beyond their reach. More appropriate would be card or jeopardy-style games or a simulation or role play with a clearly defined narrative and goals.

In summary, realizing assessment in game-based learning calls for a whole of curriculum approach which is inclusive of the learner and their readiness for learning. Van Eck (2006) echoes this with his suggestion that what is needed for the effective integration of games into the curriculum is practical guidance on *how* (when, with whom, and under what conditions) games can be integrated into the learning process to maximize their learning potential.

This chapter proposes an approach to game-based learning that begins to address all these aspects within the one framework. The MAPLET framework combines the fundamental principles of curriculum alignment with a model for intellectual skill development based on the development of expertise. To begin, an overview of the theoretical underpinnings of the framework will be given. This will be followed by a discussion of how the framework can be used as a tool to evaluate the potential of games to facilitate learning and the assessment of the learning that takes place.

12.2   The Maplet Framework

The MAPLET framework (Gosper, 2011) was originally developed to support the integration of technologies into the curriculum by enabling the matching of aims (and outcomes), processes, learner expertise and technologies; hence the term MAPLET. The framework provides a two-dimensional representation of the curriculum space whereby the horizontal dimension represents the principles of alignment and the vertical represents the intellectual maturation of the learner.

The intellectual maturation of the learner is underpinned by a three-phase model of intellectual skill development in which the development of problem-solving skills is the context for learning (VanLehn, 1996). More detail will be provided in the following section, but in summary, the first or early phase of acquisition is signified by the development of an understanding of the scope of the knowledge domain and the establishment of foundational knowledge upon which further knowledge can be developed.

The introduction of the learner to specific facts, rules, terminology or conventions, definitions, simple concepts, and principles falls within this phase. The second or intermediate phase is entered when, having established some understanding of the relevant domain, the learner is in a position to apply and use this knowledge in meaningful ways, for example, to solve problems. Domain knowledge is manipulated so that it is directly embodied in procedures required to perform a particular task or problem and in the process the knowledge base is expanded and refined. In the third or late phase, the knowledge domain is secure and the aim is to improve speed, accuracy, and transferability to novel contexts.

The three phase model of skill acquisition represents the vertical dimension of the framework. When this is combined with the horizontal dimension which is depicted by the process of curriculum alignment, a two-dimensional matrix is formed—as presented in Table 12.1.

Moving across the rows represents alignment at each of the three phases. If the curriculum is aligned then the intellectual maturation of the learner is matched with the teaching aims and learning outcomes, which in turn are linked to appropriate learning processes, activities, and assessment strategies.

Moving down the columns represents the increasing intellectual maturity of the learner and the increasing complexity of the different elements of the curriculum as the learner progresses through the three phases.

In relation to outcomes and processes, parallels can be drawn between the increasing complexity of aims and outcomes associated with each phase and established taxonomies of learning outcomes (e.g., Anderson and Krathwohl (2001); Jonassen & Tessmer, 1997; Glaser, Lesgold, & Lajoie, 1985). Taking Anderson and Krathwohl (2001) Taxonomy for Learning, Teaching and Assessing as an example, six categories of learning objectives/outcomes and associated cognitive processes have been identified. The broad relationship between these and the phases of acquisition is presented in Table 12.2. The early phase can be related to outcomes and processes associated with *remember, understand,* and *apply.* The intermediate phase can be associated with *apply, analyse, evaluate,* and *create.* The final phase encompasses more advanced forms of creative endeavours involving unfamiliar contexts.

It should be noted that learning, by nature, is not a sequential process, therefore the pathway for development may move backwards and forwards between phases (VanLehn, 1996)—hence the circular arrow in Tables 12.1 and 12.2. For example, a student working on a problem in the intermediate phase may need to review or acquire new knowledge located in the early phase to complete the task. Because of this, there is some overlap between Anderson and Krathwohl (2001) outcomes and the phases of acquisition.

In relation to gaming, Prensky (2001) developed a classification of games presented in Table 12.3 that identifies the content for development, the activity taking place, and the games that can support the identified activity. The content for development can be matched with the outcomes and processes described in Anderson and Krathwohl (2001) framework.

Table 12.1 The MAPLET framework: aligning phases of acquisition with the elements of the curriculum

Phases of acquisition	The learner	Aims outcomes	Processes	Activities	Assessment
Early—understanding cope of domain and establishing building blocks					
Intermediate—extending the knowledge base through solving problems					
Late—fine tuning and transfer to novel contexts					

Table 12.2 The relationship between the phases of acquisition and Anderson and Krathwohl (2001) taxonomy for learning, teaching, and assessing

Phases of acquisition	Learner	Aims outcomes	Processes	Activity	Assessment
Early		Remember	Recognizing, recalling		
		Understand	Interpreting, exemplifying, classifying, summarizing		
Intermediate		Apply	Inferring, comparing, executing, implementing		
		Analyse	Explaining, differentiating, organizing, attributing		
Late		Evaluate	Checking, critiquing		
		Create	Generating, planning, producing		

Table 12.3 Classification of games by Prensky (2001)

Content	Activities	Games
Facts	Questions, memorization, association, drill	Game shows, flash cards, mnemonics, action/sports games
Skills	Imitation, feedback, coaching, continuous practice, increasing challenge	Persistent state games, role play, adventure and detective games
Judgments	Reviewing cases, asking questions, making choices (practice), feedback coaching	Role play, adventure games, detective games, multiplayer interaction games, strategy games
Behaviours	Imitation, feedback, coaching, and practice	Role-playing games
Theories	Logic, experimentation, questioning	Open-ended simulations, building and constructing games, reality testing games
Reasoning	Problems, examples	Puzzles
Process	System analysis and deconstruction, practice	Strategy and adventure games
Procedures	Imitation, practice	Timed games, reflex games
Creativity	Play	Puzzles, invention games
Language	Imitation, continuous practice, immersion	Role play, reflex games, flashcard games
Systems	Understanding principles, graduated tasks, playing in microworlds	Simulation games
Observation	Observing, feedback	Concentration and adventure games
Communication	Imitation, practice	Role-playing games, reflex games

As a design tool, the MAPLET framework has particular relevance and application to the context of game-based learning. By relating the knowledge and skills for development to the three phases of acquisition, a developmental pathway can be mapped out that is reflective of the progression of the learner towards expertise in a particular knowledge domain. Games can then be integrated into the pathway based on their capacity to facilitate the development of specified knowledge and skills.

Further, the framework enables a matching of the maturity of the learner with aims (and outcomes), learning processes, gaming activity, and assessment strategies.

12.3   The MAPLET Framework and Game-Based Learning

The existing literature and research can be called upon to populate the cells in the framework by providing examples of gaming activities and assessment and assessment strategies for each of the three phases of acquisition.

12.3.1   The Early Phase

In the early phase of acquisition, aims and outcomes are centred around the acquisition of basic facts, skills and concepts, learning is usually focused on activities involving extended practice. These activities are typically associated with the development of lower order knowledge and skills associated with remembering and understanding (Anderson and Krathwohl 2001). Activities that have been shown to be appropriate for this purpose exhibit clear outcomes, sequenced exercises, and immediate feedback (Fletcher-Flinn & Gravatt, 1995; Kulik & Kulik, 1991).

Researchers have found that games can effectively support outcomes that involve a direct transfer of knowledge (Thomas & Brown, 2007) and skill-based developments such as literacy and numeracy (de Freitas, 2004). For example, Kantaro (1993), a Japanese language program featuring memory games and mnemonics for teaching Kanji is one of the many examples of language tutors that are available. Tetris, an off-the-shelf commercial game where participants stack two-dimensional objects, can be used to develop spatial awareness skills.

Simulations, often associated with higher order learning, can also in certain cases, be used for teaching facts and knowledge. Their characteristic simplification of real-world systems can help students solve problems, learn procedures, understand phenomena, and practice skills safely and efficiently (Johnson & Huang, 2008). The games suggested by Prensky (Table 12.3) to support the acquisition of facts, skills, and procedures also fall within this category.

Assessment of the learning that occurs in this early phase is quite straightforward compared to the other two phases as it focuses on lower order outcomes, related to remembering and understanding. In-built automated feedback functions in games can contribute towards assessment in both a formative and a summative sense. The game metrics can automatically deliver scores in a variety of formats, for example, tallies of correct or incorrect responses, time on task, and number of attempts. As discussed earlier, students can also use this feedback as a form of self-assessment to monitor their progress and adjust their learning.

Table 12.4 Alignment within the early phase of intellectual skill acquisition

	Outcomes	Processes	Possible games	Assessment
Early phase	Acquisition of basic facts, skills, and concepts	Memorization, association, familiarization	Card and jeopardy-style games, simulations	Self-assessment using game metrics. Quizzes and tests for understanding or performance of skills
Intermediate phase	Applying knowledge to the development of solutions to structured problems	Establishing complex interrelationships within the body of knowledge	Simulations, multiplayer games, role play, adventure games, detective games, strategy games	Self-assessment—monitoring cause-and-effect relationships, or consequences of decisions. Self-reflection
		Refining, testing, challenging, understanding, correcting flaws	Open-ended simulations, building and constructing games, reality testing games	Peer assessment—group reflection Problems involving near transfer
Late phase	Automation of skill and concepts	Proceduralization	Card or jeopardy-style games, simulations with extended and varied practice	Game metrics, quizzes, tests
	Transfer to novel contexts	Analogical reasoning, metacognitive processing	Open-ended, multiplayer games, role play, adventure games, strategy games	Self- and peer assessment through reflection Peer assessment
			Open-ended simulations, building and constructing games, reality testing games	Ill-structured problems requiring far transfer

There is little difficulty in devising assessment tasks external to the game in this early phase. Multiple choice quizzes, short answer questions, and competency-based tasks are examples of possible tasks. A summary of the alignment between outcomes, learning processes, games, and assessment at the early phase and subsequent phases is given in Table 12.4.

12.3.2 The Intermediate Phase

The intermediate phase of acquisition involves the expansion of the knowledge base and its application to the solution of problems. During this phase, solving problems and working through targeted activities leads the learner through the processes of refining, testing, challenging, understanding, correcting flaws, and establishing complex interrelationships within the body of knowledge and between wider bodies of knowledge. This ultimately leads to a comprehensive understanding of the structure and organization of the knowledge domain (VanLehn, 1996).

A great variety of aims and outcomes are accommodated within this phase: the development of complex conceptual models; the establishment of the robust interconnected knowledge networks that form problem-solving schemas with embedded principles, procedures, and heuristics; and the development of metacognitive skills are all indicative of the scope of possibilities.

The underlying focus on problem solving within this phase opens a number of opportunities for games to support different aspects of learning. Problem solving involves a constant cycle of hypothesis formulation, testing, and revision. These processes can happen rapidly and often while a game is being played, thus modelling the metacognitive processes so important to the problem-solving process (Van Eck, 2006). More specifically, adventure games in narrative-driven learning environments can promote hypothesis testing and problem solving (Van Eck, 2006). Puzzle games which demand a high level of logical thinking can invoke reflection on the problem and planning for a strategy or solution (Ang et al., 2008). Simulations designed to allow the user to interact with, respond to, and manipulate an underlying model are valuable as heuristic devices to help students understand theoretical relationships in complex domains as well as to test and demonstrate applicability to real-world situation (de Jong, 1998; Johnson & Huang, 2008).

Gee (2008) maintains that solving problems is more than a mental exercise involving the mind and it calls in another of other context-specific dimensions—affective dimensions involving emotions, technological dimensions involving tools and technologies, interactive dimensions involving participation with others, and sociocultural dimensions involving the workings of social and cultural identities and groups. Immersive gaming environments such as MORPGs (multiple online role play games) making use of media-rich integrated tools and applications can potentially bring all these dimensions together to provide a rich problem and experience-based context for learning. Dede (2009) suggests that immersion in a digital environment can enhance learning by enabling multiple perspectives, situated learning, and transfer. These environments enable digital simulations of authentic problem-solving communities and learners can interact with other virtual entities—both participants and computer-based agents. Research on River City reported by Dede (2009) shows that a broader range of students gain substantial knowledge and skills in scientific inquiry through immersive simulation than through conventional instruction or equivalent learning experiences delivered via a board game.

More generally, the games that can be called upon to support this phase are those of the narrative, simulation, and multiplayer variety, specifically those that support judgment, behaviours, theories, reasoning, process, procedures, creativity, language, systems, observation, and communication (refer to Table 12.3).

From an assessment perspective, simulations and other gaming applications, which work towards a defined goal requiring an understanding of complex rules or relationships, can have inbuilt assessment mechanism which facilitate a process of ongoing self-assessment. The actions arising from decisions made by the player as they manipulate characters and observe the consequences that follow or manipulate variables and observe cause-and-effect relationships act as formative feedback, which can be used to inform future actions.

More challenging is the assessment of gaming environments that are open ended, exploratory, and experiential in nature. Where there are no clearly defined goals to determine the endpoint of the game and hence the criteria for winning, there is no straightforward way to assess the learning that has taken place (de Freitas & Neumann, 2009; Dede, 2009). These games are typically aligned with Anderson and Krathwohl (2001) higher order learning categories of evaluate and create (refer to Table 12.2) which have been shown to be difficult to assess. In a recent study by McNeill, Gosper, and Hedberg (2010) of 180 academic staff on the alignment between intended learning outcomes and assessment strategies, it was found that the assessment of higher order outcomes was challenging and assessment criteria often defaulted to lower order quantitative measures such as time on task or interactions, rather than addressing the quality of these interactions.

Where gaming environments are open and explorative, de Freitas (2006) suggests the need for new approaches to assessment including those that incorporate a range of strategies including self and group or peer assessment. Where higher order learning is involved, reflection is central to the learning process, hence tasks which involve solitary consideration, broader discussion, general feedback, and group discussion (de Freitas & Neumann, 2009) are suitable for consideration. It follows, therefore, that assessment for summative purposes can take the form of:

- Self-assessment through tasks (journals or written assignments) that require critical reflection of one's learning and the relevance of the experiences encountered to other contexts, whether they be personal, work based, or more academic.
- Peer assessment in the form of individual or group critiques of the actions and strategies adopted by other players and the consequences of these for the way the game has unfolded.

The assessment artefacts can be at the discretion of teachers and students include portfolios, written reflections, and podcasts. The criteria for assessment need to reflect the complexity and depth of the knowledge acquired. A written reflection, graded using the Solo Taxonomy (Biggs & Collis, 1982), based on five levels of thinking—prestructural, unistructural, multistructural, relational, and extended abstract—is an example of a strategy that could be adopted.

12.3.3   The Late Phase

In the late phase, the knowledge domain is secure and one of the aims of teaching is to improve both speed and accuracy so that procedures can be executed automatically. Underpinning automation is proceduralization. With extensive practice, procedures are fine-tuned to an automated state where they can be executed with a minimum of cognitive effort (Anderson, 1982), thus freeing up valuable resources for more complex endeavours.

Games similar in function to the early phase can be used to provide the extended practice necessary for automation and in this instance the same inbuilt metrics can be used to provide both formative and summative feedback if assessing automated competence is a desired outcome.

Another late phase aim is the transfer of knowledge and skills to novel contexts which is a key outcome associated with higher order learning. Developing transferable skills is an ongoing process that begins within the intermediate phase, with near transfer. Near transfer can be exhibited in defined problem scenarios where solutions involve the application of knowledge learned in similar contexts but with somewhat different surface features (Jonassen, 2000). In contrast, far transfer refers to the application of knowledge and skills to unfamiliar contexts.

Developing situated knowledge attuned to the context in which it is developed will not guarantee far transfer unless it involves varied practice that will allow students to abstract core principles to form generalized rules and approaches (Hesketh, 1997). Immersive environments that are open ended, exploratory, and experiential offer opportunities for participants to explore, construct, or determine their own pathways through different situations. The immersive interfaces can draw on the power of situated learning and enable digital simulations of authentic problem-solving communities in which learners interact with other virtual entities (both participants and computer-based agents) who have varied levels of skills (Dede, 2009), thus providing opportunities for variation in experiences.

Assessment tasks external to the game can be used to ascertain both near and far transfer. Giving students problems to solve that emulate the rules and relationships inherent in the game can test near transfer, whereas ill-structured problems reflecting real-life contexts with multiple solutions (Jonassen, 2000) are more appropriate for far transfer. Reflection is crucial for facilitating higher order cognition and aiding transfer between virtual and lived experiences (de Freitas & Neumann, 2009), hence the reflective activities and assessment strategies suggested for intermediate phase activities are equally applicable in the late phase.

12.3.4 The Framework in Action

Although the concept of alignment may, on the surface appear deceptively simple, in practice alignment can be hard to achieve. An example of the way in which the MAPLET framework can be used to support teachers and designers in clearly articulating the alignment between the intellectual maturity and the different elements of the curriculum is given below. It illustrates how the visual mapping afforded by the framework enables the easy detection of alignment and misalignment. Misalignment can occur when, for instance, gaming activity is not related to specified outcomes; the intellectual maturity of the learner is not matched to the cognitive demands of the game; or related assessment tasks are not appropriate to the outcomes or gaming activity.

PeaceMaker (http://www.peacemakergame.com/game.php) is a strategy role-play game that was developed by a group of university students who were interested in providing serious and engaging and thought-provoking content to teach concepts in diplomacy and foreign relations. It is based on real events in the Israeli-Palestinian conflict with participants taking the role of either the Israeli Prime Minister or Palestinian President with the aim of trying to find peaceful resolutions to conflicts before their term of office expires.

Three levels of difficulty are inbuilt into the game which can cater for differing levels of expertise. Players can draw on a range of authentic historical multimedia information to plan their strategies which can be enacted through negotiation or military action. From a learning perspective, playing the game involves a range of skills including analysing information, interpreting actions, negotiating outcomes, and decision making. The game can be played with students from different locations and early trials were between Carnegie Melon students at the University's Pittsburgh and Qatar campuses. In this context, it was used to prompt thought on complex issues for discussion in the classroom. The assessment of learning for grading purposes was external to the game itself and in the form of an individual reflective essay.

In relation to the framework (presented in Table 12.5), the aims and outcomes associated with the games are placed within the intermediate phase of development. Some understanding of the history of the region, the culture of the people, and background to the conflict have already been established. The processes involved in playing the game are also situated within the intermediate phase.

In playing the game, participants have access to a range of historical, cultural, and geographic data 666666can serve to both consolidate and extend the knowledge base. Being able to access new or previously encountered information reflects the iterative nature of learning whereby students move backwards and forwards between the phases. From a formative learning perspective, the real-time

Table 12.5 The MAPLET framework: a mapping of the use of PeaceMaker showing alignment

	Students expertise	Aims/outcomes	Processes	Activities	Assessment
Early phase			Reviewing historical facts and cultural and geographical information		
Intermediate phase	Prior knowledge of middle east relations is expected	Analysing, evaluating, and participating in situations which involve diplomacy, multiple perspectives and cultural understanding	Analysing information, Interpreting actions, Decision making, Negotiating, Strategizing	Playing Gamemaker, Classroom discussion	Written assignment reflecting on issues and experiences

nature of the game provides the continual feedback necessary to understand intended and unintended implications of actions that can arise within a complex environment. It is the observations of issues and implications arising from the actions incurred when playing the game that are then taken back to the classroom for discussion.

Thus far there is alignment between students' experience, aim/outcomes, processes, and activities. The reflective nature of the essay continues to maintain alignment between the identified outcomes and the gaming process as it is reflective of an intermediate phase task. If, however, the summative assessment was in the form of testing the acquisition of historical or other content encountered throughout the game then there would be misalignment between the assessment task, the intended aims/outcomes, and the skills and processes inherent in achieving the ultimate goal—to negotiate a peaceful outcome.

12.4 Conclusion

Realizing the assessment of game-based learning is not something that can be achieved in isolation of the wider curriculum. For assessment to be effective in both the provision of feedback to inform future learning and in measuring the learning that has taken place, it must form part of an aligned curriculum.

When choosing games we need to be mindful that they are not necessarily tailored to specific learning outcomes, unless they have been developed to do so. The memory games associated with the Japanese language games in Kantaro (Kantaro, 1993), for instance, have been designed explicitly for recognizing and memorizing words and their meaning. However, other types of games can be used in multiple contexts; simulations can be used to simplify the real-world system in order to help the student solve problems, learn procedures, understand phenomena and practice skills safely and efficiently, or even be used for teaching facts and knowledge (Johnson & Huang, 2008). Because of this, it is particularly important that the intention of a game as a learning strategy is clearly defined as this will determine the assessment strategies that are most appropriate for the given context.

The MAPLET framework provides a theoretically based approach to ensuring the alignment of assessment strategies with intended outcomes and gaming activities, as well as with the developing expertise of the learner. It offers a way of guiding decisions on *how* (when, with whom, and under what conditions) games can be integrated into the learning process to maximize their learning potential. One of the limitations of the framework as presented is that the examples of game-based learning that have been used to illustrate the different phases of acquisition and the alignment of outcomes, processes, and assessment strategies have all been drawn from existing research and literature. While this provides a sound conceptual basis for guiding practice, further research and development is needed to populate the framework with empirically based case studies and examples based on existing practice.

References

Anderson, J. R. (1982). Acquisition of cognitive skill. *Psychological Review, 89*(4), 369–406.

Anderson, L. W., & Krathwohl, D. R. (2001). *A taxonomy for learning, teaching, and assessing: A revision of Bloom's Taxonomy of Educational Objectives*. New York: Longman.

Ang, C. S., Avni, E., & Zaphiris, P. (2008). Linking pedagogical theory of computer games to their usability. *International Journal on E-Learning, 7*(3), 533–558.

Biggs, J. B., & Collis, K. F. (1982). *Evaluating the quality of learning—the SOLO taxonomy*. New York: Academic.

Biggs, J., & Tang, C. (2007). *Teaching for quality learning at university* (3rd ed.). London: Open University Press.

Bober, M. (2010). *Games-based experiences for learning*. Bristol: Futurelab.

Bransford, J. D., Brown, A. L., & Cocking, R. R. (Eds.). (2000). *How people learn: Brain, mind, experience and school*. Washington: National Academy Press.

de Freitas, S. (2004). *Learning through Play. Internal report*. London: Learning and Skills Research Centre.

de Freitas, S. (2006). Using games and simulations for supporting learning. *Learning, Media and Technology Special Issue on Gaming., 31*(4), 343–358.

de Freitas, S., & Neumann, T. (2009). The use of 'exploratory learning' for supporting immersive learning in virtual environments. *Computers in Education, 52*, 343–352. doi:10.1016/j.compedu.2008.09.010.

de Freitas, S., & Oliver, M. (2006). How can exploratory learning with games and simulations within the curriculum be most effectively evaluated? *Computers in Education, 46*(3), 249–264.

de Jong, T. (1998). Scientific discovery learning with computer simulations of conceptual domains. *Review of Educational Research, 68*(2), 179–201.

Dede, C. (2009). Immersive interfaces for engagement and learning. *Science, 323*(5910), 66–69. doi:10.1126/science.1167311.

Ericsson, K. C., & Lehmann, A. C. (1996). Expert and exceptional performance: Evidence of maximal adaptation to task constraints. *Annual Review of Psychology, 47*, 273–305.

Ericsson, K. A., & Smith, J. (1991). *Towards a general theory of expertise*. Cambridge: Cambridge University Press.

Fletcher-Flinn, C. M., & Gravatt, B. (1995). The efficacy of computer assisted instruction (CAI): A meta-analysis. *Journal of Computing Research, 12*(3), 219–242.

Gee, J. P. (2008). Video games and embodiment. *Games and Culture, 3*(3–4), 253–263. doi:10.1177/1555412008317309.

Glaser, R., Lesgold, A., & Lajoie, S. (1985). Towards a cognitive theory for the measurement of achievement. In R. R. Ronning, J. Glover, J. C. Conoley, & J. C. Witt (Eds.), *The influence of cognitive psychology on testing and measurement*. Hillsdale: Erlbaum.

Gosper, M. (2011). MAPLET—A framework for matching aims, processes, learner expertise and technologies. In D. Ifenthaler, Kinshuk, P. Isaías, D. G. Sampson, & J. M. Spector (Eds), *Multiple perspectives on problem solving and learning in the digital age* (pp. 23–36). New York: Springer.

Hesketh, B. (1997). Dilemmas in training for transfer and retention. *Applied Psychology: An International Review, 46*(4), 317–339.

Johnson, T. E., & Huang, W. D. (2008). Complex skill development for today's workforce. In D. Ifenthaler, P. Pirnay-Dummer, & J. M. Spector (Eds.), *Understanding models of learning and instruction* (pp. 305–325). New York: Springer.

Johnson, L., Levine, A., & Smith, R. (2009). *The 2009 Horizon Report*. Austin, Texas: The New Media Consortium. Retrieved 16 April 2012 from http://wp.nmc.org/horizon2009/.

Jonassen, D. (2000). Toward a design theory of problem solving. *Educational Technology Research and Development, 48*(4), 63–85.

Jonassen, D., & Tessmer, M. (1997). An outcomes-based taxonomy for instructional systems design, evaluation and research. *Training Research Journal, 2*, 11–46.

Kantaro. (1993). *CD-Rom for Kanji learning*. Australia: Macquarie University.
Kirriemuir, J., & McFarlane, A. (2004). *Literature review in games and learning. Report 8*. Bristol: Nesta Futurelab.
Kulik, C. C., & Kulik, J. (1991). Effectiveness of computer-based instruction: An updated analysis. *Computers in Human Behaviour, 7*, 75–94.
Macy, M., Squires, J., & Barton, E. (2009). Providing optimal opportunities: Structuring practicum experiences in early intervention and early childhood special education preservice programs. *Topics in Early Childhood Special Education, 28*(4), 209–218.
McKeague, C. A., & Di Vesta, F. J. (1996). Strategy orientations, learner control and learning outcomes: Implications for instructional support of learning. *Educational Technology Research and Development, 44*(2), 29–42.
McNeill, M., Gosper, M., & Hedberg, J. (2010). Technologies to transform assessment: A study of learning outcomes, assessment and technology use in an Australian university. In C. H. Steel, M. J. Keppell, P. Gerbic, & S. Housego (Eds.), *Proceedings of ascilite 2010: Curriculum, technology & transformation for an unknown future*. Sydney (pp. 630–640). Retrieved from http://ascilite.org.au/conferences/sydney10/procs/Mcneill-full.pdf.
Mory, E. (2004). Feedback research revisited. In D. H. Jonassen (Ed.), *Handbook of research for educational communications and technology* (2nd ed., pp. 745–784). Mahwah: Lawrence Erlbaum.
Oblinger, D. (2006). Simulations, games, and learning. *Educase Learning Initiative*. Retrieved 16 April 2012 from http://net.educause.edu/ir/library/pdf/ELI3004.pdf.
Prensky, M. (2001). *Digital game-based learning*. New York: McGraw-Hill.
Shute, V. (2008). Focus on formative feedback. *Review of Educational Research, 78*(1), 153–189.
Thomas, D., & Brown, J. (2007). The play of imagination: Extending the literary mind. *Games and Culture, 2*(2), 149–172.
Van Eck, R. (2006). Digital game-based learning, it's not just the digital natives who are restless. *Educause Review, 41*(2), 16–30.
VanLehn, K. (1996). Cognitive skill acquisition. *Annual Review of Psychology, 47*, 513–539.

Chapter 13
Innovative Assessment Technologies in Educational Games Designed for Young Students

Benö Csapó, András Lörincz, and Gyöngyvér Molnár

13.1 Introduction

Feedback is an essential process in regulating complex systems, and it can be found at every level and unit of an efficient educational system, from macrolevels, including entire national education systems, to microlevels of learning processes, including computer games. Therefore, feedback is the overarching concept that helps to explain and interpret the role of assessment in educational games.

Feedback involves collecting and processing information about the actual state of a system represented by some key variables and comparing it to certain predefined standards or normative data. Collecting information may involve a number of means, but for assessing some key target variables of education (e.g., students' knowledge and skills), testing has been considered as the most objective and reliable way. Feedback which is used by the learner is considered the most important, distinctive attribute of formative assessment (Taras, 2005).

For almost a century, paper-and-pencil tests have been used for educational assessment, but since the emergence of the first computers, they have been used for testing students' knowledge as well. Currently, computerized testing, or more generally, technology-based assessment (TBA) is the most rapidly developing area of educational evaluation (Csapó, Ainley, Bennett, Latour, & Law, 2012).

Computerized educational games, on the other hand, focus on teaching, but to maximize their functionality, several assessment mechanisms are embedded in the games to control the learning processes and guide students through the learning

B. Csapó (✉) • G. Molnár
Institute of Education, University of Szeged, Petőfi sgt. 30-34, Szeged 6722, Hungary
e-mail: csapo@edpsy.u-szeged.hu; gymolnar@edpsy.u-szeged.hu

A. Lörincz
Department of Software Technology and Methodology, Eötvös Loránd University,
Pázmány Péter sétány 1/C, Budapest 1117, Hungary
e-mail: andras.lorincz@elte.hu

D. Ifenthaler et al. (eds.), *Assessment in Game-Based Learning: Foundations, Innovations, and Perspectives*, DOI 10.1007/978-1-4614-3546-4_13,
© Springer Science+Business Media New York 2012

tasks. In most serious games, one of the functions of assessment and feedback is to adapt the actual challenge to the cognitive level of the gamer. This procedure, the *dynamic difficulty adjustment* (see, e.g., Westra, Dignum, & Dignum, 2011), is based on monitoring cognitive processes, and matching the complexity of the tasks to the level of gamers ensures optimal learning. The novel feature of the assessment we are experimenting with is monitoring the affective states of the student while playing the game. The feedback gained in this way may be used to optimize the emotional aspects of the gaming process. Due to these similarities, there are areas where TBA and teaching games are converging, and a number of innovations, including detection of emotional states, may be applied in both fields in similar ways.

The project from which this study stems from has been dealing with the form of assessment which is considered very close to the educational games. An *Online Diagnostic Assessment System* (ODAS) is being devised, which, when fully developed, will be able to regularly assess students' cognitive development in three main domains, reading, mathematics, and science, in the first six grades of primary school. The aim of the diagnostic assessment is to identify students' developmental deficiencies and learning difficulties in order to help them to cope with the challenges and overcome difficulties. Diagnostics should be followed by intervention that helps mastering some key concepts, supports understanding, fosters students' skills, and accelerates the development of their abilities. The most obvious method of delivering intervention materials is the utilization of the same online technology which is used in the ODAS.

The main function of diagnostic assessment is to directly support teaching and learning; therefore, it is essentially embedded in instructional processes. The detailed student level feedback information provided by the online assessment can be used to tailor and customize intervention. Therefore, both pedagogical principles and technological conditions suggest the application of teaching games for individualized compensatory instruction.

The first phase of the project has focused on framework development, the establishment of an online platform, and the construction of assessment items. The next phase will aim at devising a number of educational games to compensate for students' learning deficiencies. However, several existing games have been explored, and some new ones have been devised and piloted in the first phase as well. One of such a piloting work is forming the empirical basis of the present study.

In the first part of this chapter, we outline a conceptual framework of assessment in which we describe the parallel functional and technological developments between educational assessment and teaching games. In the second part, we show how innovations are applied in these areas and how they improve the feedback in both systems. We describe the role of contextual information in providing better feedback and introduce the video-based analyses of facial expressions of subjects completing online tests or playing games. In the third part, the piloting work of a game-based training will be presented. This part illustrates how games can be applied for training students for whom ODAS indicates learning deficiencies. Finally, we outline how the elements presented in the first parts of the chapter can be integrated into a complex individualized teaching system in which technology supports both identifying and treating learning problems.

13.1.1 Feedback and Assessment in Education

In the past decades, most impressive developments in education can be attributed to the improved feedback built in several levels of the system. Education, as any other complex system cannot be improved without proper feedback mechanisms. Setting goals, carrying out interventions, assessing the results, and then comparing goals and results are the basic stages of control in any unit of an educational system. The most visible educational feedback systems are the large-scale international projects which assess global outcomes of the entire national educational systems. These international projects, like PISA, TIMSS, and PIRLS, generate feedback information for decision-makers at the national educational policy level.

The unified efforts of large international expert groups advanced educational assessment in a number of fields, such as setting goals (analysis of knowledge to be assessed and framework development); devising assessment instruments; sophisticated methods of data analysis, which include more contextual information (e.g., students' attitudes and their socioeconomic status) for presenting more functional and applicable feedback; and new reporting styles which include visual and innovative presentation of the results (see, e.g., the PISA reports).

There are two developments in international assessments which are closely related to the issues of teaching games:

1. The limitations of paper-based assessment have been reached, and the shift to TBA has been started.
2. New areas of assessment have been explored which include general thinking abilities. For example, problem solving was assessed in PISA 2003 (see OECD, 2004), and dynamic problem solving (Greiff & Funke 2009, 2010) will be assessed in PISA 2012.

International projects draw on the advances of educational measurement in some countries, and later the scientific and technical outcomes of the international projects are utilized in several other areas of assessment; for example, many developed countries introduced a national assessment system. The national assessment systems mostly provide school level feedback which then can be used for institutional improvement and accountability.

The third level of assessment provides feedback at student level and helps directly the teaching and learning processes. This level requires frequent and detailed assessment and rapid feedback. These requirements cannot be satisfied by the traditional paper-based testing.

13.1.2 Technology-Based Assessment

Due to the developments described in the previous section, there is a growing interest in developing TBA systems and making them available for broad everyday use.

Many international[1] and national[2] initiatives aim at developing new assessment systems utilizing the potential of information-communication technology.

There are a number of advantages technology offers for assessment (see Csapó et al., 2012). Traditional domains can be assessed with a greater precision and efficiency. By the means of technology, assessment can be extended to new domains which cannot be assessed by other means. These are domains where technology is essential for the definition of the construct (e.g., ICT literacy, problem solving in technology-rich environment, reading electronic texts, etc.) and domains where technology is instrumental for the assessment (e.g., assessing dynamics, teamwork through network connection; see Tzuriel, 1998).

Technology accelerates data collection, supports real-time automatic scoring, speeds up data processing, and allows immediate feedback. Technology improves the precision of measurements as well. A variety of instruments may be used for data entry and response capture (innovative use of traditional input instruments, touch screen, drawing, microphone with voice recognition, video camera with analysis software, specific interfaces for capturing complex movements), and in this way, large amounts of data can be collected within relatively short periods. Instead of providing single indicators, such as a test score, TBA may produce rich, contextualized, well-structured data sets. Assessment data can easily be stored and analyzed, and this possibility supports the transition from single testing to complex systems of assessments.

Technology revolutionizes the whole process of assessment, including item development (authoring software, automatic item generation). TBA supports item banking, storing of items, and item metadata in large databases. It also vitalizes testing situation, increases motivation, and may improve validity. TBA allows innovative task presentation, including multimedia (sounds, animation, video, simulation).

Technology supports adaptive testing which means that the actual item presented depends on the success of the student in solving the previous item. Therefore, in computerized adaptive testing (CAT), items are scored real time, and a decision about the next step is made depending on the result. In this feature, CAT is similar to the assessment embedded in teaching games.

13.1.3 Assessment for Learning: Integrating Assessment into Teaching

Large-scale assessment projects aim at assessing outcomes of usually at least one, but more frequently several years of learning. Therefore, the actual *summative tests* may cover only a small sample of the entire knowledge to be assessed.

---

[1] See the Assessment and Teaching of 21st Century Skills project, http://atc21s.org.

[2] At present, the US Race to the Top Assessment Program is the largest national initiative.

Student level feedback requires a different approach, and for this purpose, *formative* and *diagnostic* tests are applied (Ainsworth & Viegut, 2006; Black, Harrison, Lee, Marshall, & Wiliam, 2003; Clarke, 2001, 2005; Leighton & Gierl, 2007). As the feedback in this case is used to control learning processes and to adapt the next phase of learning to the actual needs of the student, the test should cover every relevant area of the students' knowledge which is an essential precondition for a later learning task.

There are several consequences of this requirement. First, formative and diagnostic tests should be built on a careful analysis of the domain (see, e.g., Seel, 2010; Spector, 2010; Strasser, 2010). A model of the structure of knowledge is needed to describe how the pieces of knowledge are related to each other (e.g., a hierarchy of skills and component skills). Second, a large number of items have to be constructed to cover the domain in sufficient details. Third, formative and diagnostic tests should be administered to students frequently enough, so that learning problems could be identified early enough, and the necessary interventions could be implemented. Frequent diagnostic assessment may prevent the accumulation of deficiencies.

There are several problems with this ideal model of applying formative tests. First, paper-based testing is expensive, scoring may require a lot of work, and the feedback may be too late for being efficient. Second, learning and assessment may compete for the same instructional time; too much time spent for testing may endanger learning. Third, if we want to administer paper-and-pencil tests matched to the individual needs of students in different phases of development, what is always the case in practice, complex logistics is required. Because of these difficulties, formative and diagnostic assessment may not be systematically implemented in the regular classrooms.

TBA may be a solution for these problems. A testing center serving a large student population may reduce developmental costs per student to a reasonable level. Online delivery reduces costs, and applying a certain level of adaptive testing (CAT or multistage testing) may help to adjust the actual assessment to the needs of individual students. Some of the testing time may be regained if feedback information is accompanied by some brief immediate customized (online) tutoring. Formative assessment which may be efficient in practice does not only provide students with feedback information, but at the same time, it promotes their learning as well.

13.1.4 Learning and Assessment in Educational Games

Teaching games represent the other side of the coin. They are designed to support students' learning (e.g., Meyer & Sorensen, 2009), but at certain points, they assess students' knowledge as well. To optimize the use of instructional time, the increase of the direct impact of the assessment on learning was proposed in the previous section. As far as optimizing the time from the perspective of teaching games, and multiple utilization of time spent playing games are concerned, a similar approach is proposed here. The information gained by the assessment within a teaching game should be made available outside of the game.

From this perspective, serious games and computerized diagnostic assessment systems may be considered as similar instruments. Both may be used for assessment and, although to different extents, for teaching as well. Beyond the assessment of the outcome variables, teaching games may be utilized to gather other types of information about the learner which in turn helps to further optimize the learning process.

Similar functions of serious games and TBA systems promote the convergence of the two systems. Research on serious games and on TBA may mutually fertilize the other fields.

The development of the ODAS and the utilization of teaching games for intervention aim at benefiting from these fertilizing effects. Given that the same infrastructure is utilized for both aims, further integration seems possible. Integrating the two systems may result in further positive effects in other domains as well. As for the affective aspects, games are associated with pleasure and enjoyment, while assessment is linked to stress and anxiety. Gaming is driven by intrinsic motivation, while in case of assessment, extrinsic motivation is dominating. In order to reduce anxiety and improve motivation, teaching games should be utilized more frequently for assessment purposes.

13.2   Innovative Assessment Technologies for Logging and Analyzing Metadata

13.2.1   Recording and Analyzing Contextual Information

As we mentioned earlier, contextual information is playing a growing role at every level of educational assessment. The information gathered this way contributes to understanding the examined phenomenon and helps to explain what influences the actual values of the observed variables. For example, students' socioeconomic status can be used to estimate the "added value" of the school, the proportion of variance that can be attributed to the school, if the results are controlled for students' social background.

Such contextual information may be essential for the type of assessments we discussed earlier: the online diagnostic assessments and the assessments related to educational games. The standard gaming and testing situation in these cases are very similar or identical: the gamer/testee sits in front of a computer which is equipped with several response capture or input instruments. With these instruments, virtually every controlled or unconscious reaction of testee can be recorded and logged and can be analyzed separately or in relationship to the targeted cognitive achievement variables.

There are data entry instruments which are standard equipment for every computer, such as keyboard and mouse. Microphone and webcam are also broadly available, while touch screen displays, including monitors with large touch screen surfaces, may be purchased at reasonable prices. Some other instruments, such as gaze tracking equipment, are already in use in cognitive laboratories. If specific pieces of equipments routinely used in physiology and cognitive neuropsychology research are also considered, the possibilities are really unlimited; heartbeat rate, breathing rate, and brain activity can also be monitored.

In this chapter, we only consider those instruments which are broadly available and can be used in an average school computer laboratory, and present the analyses of data collected by webcam in details.

Logging keystrokes are the most common way of collecting metadata. Recording time between keystrokes allows analysis of students' reasoning speeds and thinking and test-taking strategies. Especially rich datasets can be collected if a testee may scroll up and down between items and may revise the solutions of the items. Guessing, e.g., can be identified this way, and it can be checked if solving one item can prompt the revision of the solution of another item. This logging is allowed by the platform used for ODAS, and the related analyses can be carried out any time.

13.2.2 Using Video for Detecting Head Movement and Facial Expression

Special tools using infrared light have been developed for gaze direction estimation and communication by gaze interaction.[3] They have been applied to assess what is salient (Itti, 2007) and what is relevant visual information under free viewing conditions (Peters, Iyer, Itti, & Koch, 2005) and in task-related behavior (Renninger, Verghese, & Coughlan, 2007) and what drives visual attention (Baluch & Itti, 2010). The cost of the infrared instruments, however, prohibits widespread utilization, e.g., in the classroom or in mobile phone applications. There is an ongoing and quick change that decreases the cost of the tools and will increase the number of participants by orders of magnitudes in the near future.

Advances of computational power and the availability of webcams on computers, e.g., laptops, their utilization in games and in assisting technologies (Hévízi, Gerőfi, Szendrő, & Lőrincz, 2005), and their widespread use in video chats accelerated face-related evaluation technologies, such as facial expression of estimation and gaze direction estimation. Enabling technology components of webcam-based monitoring and automated annotation includes:

1. Efficient open source computer vision libraries in C and C++)[4]
2. An efficient face detector (Viola & Jones, 2001)
3. Two- and three-dimensional face landmark identification algorithms using either active appearance models (Matthews & Baker, 2004) or constrained local models (Cristinacce & Cootes, 2008; Saragih, Lucey, & Cohn, 2011)
4. Gaze direction estimations (Ishikawa, Baker, Matthews, & Kanade, 2004)

---

[3]COGAIN—Communication by Gaze Interaction. http://www.cogain.org/wiki/Main_Page.
[4]Open Source Computer Vision Library: http://en.wikipedia.org/wiki/OpenCV.

Annotated databases on faces and facial expressions are available from Carnegie Mellon University,[5] University of Basel,[6] HUMAINE (HUman-MAchine INteraction Network on Emotion),[7] the database of the Rensselaer Polytechnic Institute,[8] among many others.

High-quality facial expression estimation is in the focus of interest, and the main conferences as well as research networks are measuring progress at each possible occasion on different benchmarks (see, e.g., the CVPR 2011,[9] the ICCV 2011[10] conferences).

High-quality videos, off-line evaluations, and infrared light measuring techniques have shown the potentials on learning special individual facial gestures, predicting performance and attention levels, e.g., from blink rates (Chermahinia & Hommel, 2010) to mention only one example of the many behavioral signs. Interviews, avatars, and multiplayer games have been used to provoke, detect, measure, and evaluate intentional and unintentional facial expressions in social interactions, including intentional deception and subconscious emotions and microexpressions (see, e.g., Biland, Py, Allione, Demarchi, & Abric, 2008; Ekman, 2006; Porter & ten Brinke, 2011). It is expected that low-cost webcams will eventually enable real-time estimations of user intentions and other hidden parameters, including cognitive and emotional profiles through monitoring performance, development, and facial expressions during games, training sessions, and interactions with human partners and avatars in real situations. The main challenges include robust head pose independent facial expression estimation, robustness against light conditions, and subject to occlusions. Partial solutions to these challenges have been worked out in the literature (see, e.g., Gross, Matthews, Cohn, Kanade, & Baker, 2010; Jeni, Hashimoto, & Lörincz, 2011; Saragih, Lucey, & Cohn, 2011).

Keystrokes and mouse movement are already widely used during internet searches to characterize and predict users and their intentions during surfing the internet; if one types "(user monitoring) and (advertisement)" after 2009 into Google's Scholar, then a large number of patents appear as the most important hits.

Our intention is to include such innovative tools into education in order to better characterize the students and to improve personalization of the training materials for them. With regards to personalization, machine learning techniques supporting collaborative filtering and recommender systems have also undergone considerable developments in recent years. In this task, one assumes a large matrix containing scores of users on subject matters, e.g., grading of videos or grade points received at courses. These matrices are partially filled since only a small fraction of videos (courses) are seen (taken) by individuals. The question is what should be the next video or course that gives rise to the best grading or added value.

---

[5]Cohn-KanadeAU-CodedFacialExpressionDatabase: http://vasc.ri.cmu.edu/idb/html/face/facial_expression/.
[6]Basel Face Model: http://faces.cs.unibas.ch/bfm/main.php?nav=1-0&id=basel_face_model.
[7]http://humaine-emotion.net.
[8]RPI ISL FaceDatabase: http://www.ecse.rpi.edu/~cvrl/database/ISL_Face_Database.htm.
[9]http://clopinet.com/isabelle/Projects/CVPR2011/home0.html.
[10]http://fipa.cs.kit.edu/befit/workshop2011/.

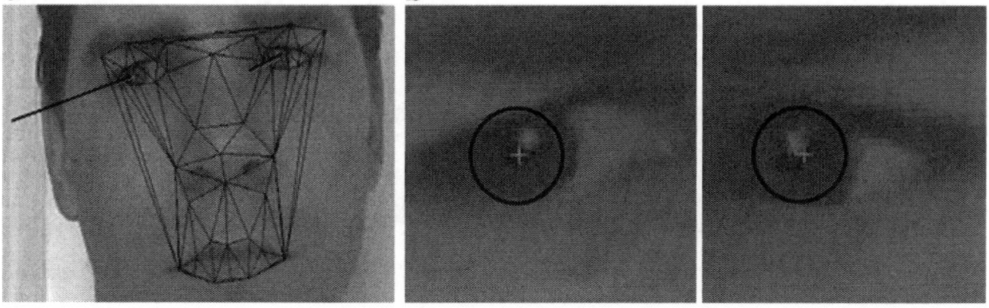

a   b

Fig. 13.1 Estimation of facial landmarks (**a**), iris borderlines (**b**), and center positions of the pupils (**c**). (**a**) Face with markers. Markers are connected with *lines*. Estimated gaze direction is shown by *straight lines*. (**b**) *Right and left* eyes with the iris. Estimated borderlines of the iris are shown by *circles*. *Plus* signs depict the estimated positions of the centers of the pupils

The problem is called matrix completion in mathematics. The problem is feasible if the matrix is of low rank. Recent developments showed that under certain, fairly restrictive, but still rather general conditions, the missing values can be filled in "exactly" (Candès & Recht, 2008; Candès & Tao, 2009; Chen, Xu, Caramanis, & Sanghavi, 2011). The method has been applied to a number of problems. For a fairly comprehensive list on methods and applications, see the Nuit-Blanche blogspot.[11] Recently, group-structured dictionary learning methods (Jenatton, Obozinski, & Bach, 2010) have been introduced to collaborative filtering since these methods search for the low-rank subspace *and* for more sophisticated structures (Szabó, Póczos, & Lőrincz, 2011). The long-term goal is to keep the student in the zone of his/her proximal development as predicted by collected data on students' learning trajectories and teachers' experiences (Tudge, 1992). This problem, i.e., the task to make recommendations for users about subject matters as a function of time, has been approached in the literature recently (Gantner, Rendle, & Schmidt-Thieme, 2010; Thai-Nghe, Drumond, Horváth, Nanopoulos, & Schmidt-Thieme, 2011).

During the spring semester of 2010–2011, we collected video information during the pilot study that we describe in the next chapter. We also collected videos with nonspeaking, severely constrained, but speech understanding children. We are evaluating the collected materials. Using the experiences, we also utilize and develop tools for aiding automated annotations. At present, we can detect in many cases (1) if the student is present, (2) if she/he is engaged with the training material visible on the screen, or not, and (3) if she/he is talking (Fig. 13.1).

However, in other cases, our fits are not sufficiently precise, especially for large pose angles and untypical light conditions. For certain important cases, we develop special face model to improve tracking (Fig. 13.2). Model construction, however, is cumbersome. Collection of massive databases requires further improvement of our software.

---

[11] http://nuit-blanche.blogspot.com/.

Fig. 13.2 Classroom, video recording, and a model of the user. (**a**) Working with the software in the classroom. (**b**) A video frame recorded by the webcam. (**c**) Model of the user (Model constructed with FaceGen Modeller: http://www.facegen.com/modeller.htm)

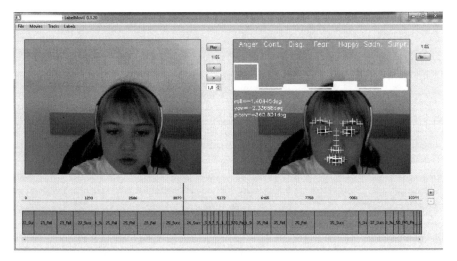

Fig. 13.3 Outputs of the facial expression analysis: *Left hand side* shows the original image. *Right hand side* shows the results of the evaluation. *Crosses*: marker points of the annotation. Roll, yaw, pitch: angle of head pose. Anger, etc.: emotions. *Solid white rectangles*: individual estimations of the different emotion sensors that may be misguided by similarities of the different emotions. *Larger open rectangle*: classification of the emotion

At present, we are evaluating the data and are looking for correlations with the performance measures that we collected. We are in the process of improving our face tracker and emotion estimation algorithms. We need to improve monitoring time since—at present—a relatively large portion of the data cannot be analyzed because of occlusions, e.g., if part of the face is out of the view of the camera or if it is covered by the hand. Similarly, improvements of robustness against light conditions and head pose angles are desired. These works are in progress at the moment.

We show two examples in Fig. 13.3. They exemplify additional research problems that automated annotation is facing and should solve. Notably, facial expressions during active participation (a) might need the analysis of a whole series of images in the context of the task and (b) can be distorted by mouth movements related to the actual choice. Analysis says that the student in Fig. 13.3a is happy. However, she is uncertain about the solution of the problem and is about to take the risk. This can be inferred from the frame series (Fig. 13.3b) and the context of the task on the screen, but not from this single frame.

13.3 Game-Based Training of 6- to 8-Year-Old Students' General Thinking Abilities: A Pilot Study

The purpose of this pilot study is to investigate the opportunities and effectiveness of applying teaching games following the results of online diagnostic tests for compensating students' learning difficulties. As ODAS is still in experimental phase, no real feedback information is available yet at the main assessment domains (reading, mathematics, and science). However, several online assessments have been carried out to measure the achievements on an inductive reasoning test (see Csapó, Molnár, & Tóth, 2009). Therefore, the development of inductive reasoning by a teaching game was piloted, as a model for further similar computer games at other domains.

The training is based on Klauer's theory of inductive reasoning (Klauer, 1989; Klauer & Phye, 2008) and consists of 120 learning tasks integrated into a game, which can be solved through inductive reasoning. To verify the hypothetical assumptions, a 4-week pilot study was implemented. First and second grade students constituted the experimental and control group.

13.3.1 Methods

13.3.1.1 Participants

First and second grade students constituted the experimental group ($n=42$), who were diagnosed with developmental deficiencies and where it seemed essential to enhance the development of students' inductive reasoning skills. The performance of these students proved to be significantly lower than 50%. The control group consisted of students from the same grade in the same elementary school ($n=64$) with similar socioeconomic background (parents' education, number of owned books at home, own computer with internet connection, own room at home, etc.), but their achievement was 50% or above.

13.3.1.2 Instruments

The game-based inductive reasoning training consisted of 120 learning tasks integrated into a game, which can be solved through the application of appropriate inductive reasoning processes. The games are designed for young children, which means that they have to meet several specific requirements compared to some traditional games: (1) the images, objects, and problems were fit into the program according to the interests of today's children and the stories they are familiar with; (2) touch screen computers were used during the study to eliminate the possible effect of mouse usage skills; (3) headsets were used to avoid the influential factor of reading skills by the training; and (4) special attention was paid to the task and help giving to ensure the interactivity of the games. Students perceived the training as playing games, not as learning. For a more detailed structure of the training, see Molnár (2011).

The effectiveness of the training was measured with a computer-based test of inductive reasoning (delivered by the ODAS), developed specifically for young learners. The test consisted of 37 items. When devising the items, special attention was paid to ensure the nonverbal character of the test. The reliability index of the whole test was Cronbach $\alpha=0.87$.

The background questionnaires were filled out by the parents. By means of the paper-based parent questionnaire, we intended to gain information about students' socioeconomic background variables and motivation regarding the game-based training. A five-point Likert scale (1: strongly disagree…5: strongly agree) was used to explore students' attitude and motivation regarding the game-based training.

13.3.1.3 Procedures

In the first phase, the sample was divided in two groups according to students' inductive reasoning skill level. Students with lower skill level belonged to the experimental group, while the remaining part of the sample belonged to the control group. In the evaluation study, students were given the training individually. The time required for the work of development depended on the individual students. It was recommended that each session should last for 40 min and contain 20 tasks at most. This meant that the 120 tasks were divided into six sessions on average, depending on the students' skill level, ability to concentrate, motivation, and level of exhaustion. Every student received permanent feedback during the training after each game. This type of formative assessment, the real-time automatic scoring provided students not only with feedback, but it also supported their learning process directly. They could only get to/access the next game only if they managed to provide right solution/answer for the previous one. In other words, students had to repeat every game as long as they did not get the right solution.

The test-based data collections took place before and immediately after the training process. The interval between the pretest and the posttest was 1 month, the period during which the training was performed. To measure the stability of the training effect, a third data collection was conducted 1 month after the end of the training in the experimental group. All groups took the same reasoning test.

Besides the test-based data collection, innovative assessment technologies are explored by logging and analyzing metadata, such as keystrokes, mouse movement, head movement, and facial expressions. These data were collected by means of web cameras.

Table 13.1 Means and standard deviations of the inductive reasoning test (%)

Group	Pretest		Posttest		Follow-up test	
	M	SD	M	SD	M	SD
Experim. group ($n=42$)	28.3	7.9	43.2	9.9	43.7	12.5
Control group ($n=64$)	70.0	10.5	70.8	9.6	–	–

13.3.2 Results of Training

Significant differences were found between the performance of the experimental and the control group ($t=-21.1$, $p<0.00$) prior to the experiment. On the posttest, the control group still significantly outperformed the experimental group ($t=-13.1$, $p<0.00$); however, the differences were significantly lower (see Table 13.1).

There was no significant change in performance in the control group in this period of time ($t=-0.81$, $p=0.42$), while the experimental group managed to achieve significant development in the experimental period ($t=-9.4$, $p<0.00$). A month after the end of our training program, the follow-up study still indicated a significant ($p<0.001$) improvement in the inductive reasoning skills of the experimental group. The effect of the training proved to be stable over time.

In case of the experimental group, the comparison of the distribution curves for the pre- and posttest indicates that each member of the experimental group attained significant improvement in performance as a result of the training (see Fig. 13.4). However, despite the training, the distribution curve of the experimental group in the posttest still inclined to the left, indicating the need for more training. The control group has normal distribution curves in both of the pre- and posttest.

These results are supported by the two diagrams in Fig. 13.5 that show the changes in experimental and control group performance at student level. The performance levels recorded during the first and second data collection are projected onto each other. The abscissa shows comparative performance from the first data collection stage, and the ordinate displays this from the second. The symbols for students who performed identically in the two cases fall on the line. If a symbol is positioned above the line, it means that the given student showed a development between the two data collection points, while if it is below the line, it represents worse performance on the posttest than on the pretest. The broken lines indicate one standard deviation.

In case of the experimental group (see graph on the left), the symbols are distributed homogeneously around the mean line; i.e., the majority of these students performed better in the posttest than in the pretest. There were no students in the experimental group whose performance dropped significantly from pretest to posttest. Several students improved by more than one standard deviation; moreover, there was one participant who reflected a development of more than 40%. As the effect of the training, several students reached the developmental level of students in the control group, which consisted of students without diagnosed developmental deficiencies. A different tendency is displayed on the right-hand graph, showing the performance of the control group.

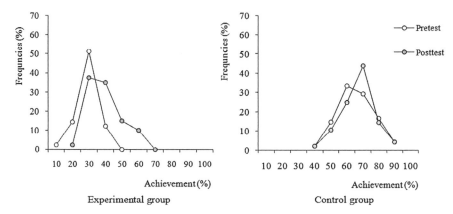

Fig. 13.4 Distribution curves of experimental and control groups in the pre- and posttest

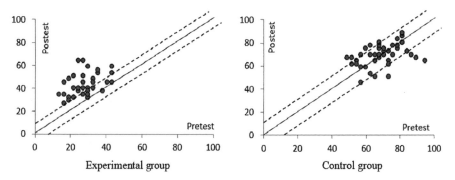

Fig. 13.5 Changes of the achievement of the experimental and control group from pretest to posttest

In case of the control group, the symbols are distributed homogeneously around the mean line; i.e., the majority of these students performed quite similarly in the two data collection phases.

Tables 13.2 and 13.3 show the mean performance of the experimental and control groups, by grade and gender. No differences are realized in the performance of first and second grade students in both the pre- and posttest in case of the experimental group. In the control group, first grade students achieved significantly higher on the pretest than second grade students, while their performance did not differ on the posttest.

No subsamples displayed significant differences in the relative performance of boys and girls in the experimental group, i.e., the training effect is not gender specific. Similarly, no gender-based differences were found in the control group either.

Table 13.2 Means and standard deviations of the inductive reasoning test by grade (%)

Group	Grade	Pretest M	SD	Sign. t	Posttest M	SD	Sign. t
Exp.	1	26.6	7.1	n.s	40.5	8.1	n.s
Exp.	2	30.0	8.4		45.6	10.9	
Contr.	1	75.9	8.3	$t=5.1; p<0.001$	72.2	9.6	n.s
Contr.	2	63.3	8.7		69.5	9.5	

Table 13.3 Means and standard deviations of the inductive reasoning test by gender (%)

Group	Gender	Pretest M	SD	Sign. t	Posttest M	SD	Sign. t
Exp.	Male	26.1	7.3	n.s	41.6	10.9	n.s
Exp.	Female	30.5	8.0		44.7	9.0	
Contr.	Male	66.2	10.5	n.s	68.2	12.8	n.s
Contr.	Female	71.3	10.3		72.1	7.4	

Table 13.4 Student and parental level of motivation and attitude towards game-based fostering

Variable	Experimental group M	SD	Control group M	SD
Students' attitude towards the training	4.93	0.27	–	–
Students' attitude towards computer-based games	–	–	4.44	0.94
Parents' attitude towards game-based training	4.43	0.55	4.13	0.59

The effect size of the training program was $d=1.66$ ($p<0.01$). Using Cohen's (1988) convention for describing the magnitude effect size, it is clearly a large effect.

Table 13.4 presents the mean results regarding motivation and attitude towards game-based fostering. Students' attitude towards the game-based training were absolutely positive, most of them chose the highest response category (5: I liked it very much.) on the Likert scale. This is supported by the low value of the standard deviation (0.27).

Parent's attitude is absolutely positive towards game-based fostering (see Table 13.5). There is no significant difference between the parental opinions of the experimental and control group students. However, 85% of the parents support both kinds of trainings, about 10% of the parents only prefer technology-based training to other kinds of fostering, and about 3.5% of the parents completely reject technology-based fostering. There are no parents in the sample who consider the need for any kind of training unnecessary.

Table 13.5 Parents' opinion about training with or without technology

Question	Parents' of the experimental group (%)	Parents' of the control group (%)
Training using different technology tools	12.5	10.4
Training without using different technology tools	2.5	4.2
Training with or without different technology tools	85.0	85.4
No training is needed	0.0	0.0

13.4 General Conclusions and Directions for Further Research

In this chapter, we placed innovative assessments applied in educational games into a broader theoretical framework. We consider feedback as the most important function of assessment; therefore, we showed how it works at the different levels of the education system. We described recent tendencies of TBA and highlighted the advantages it offers for improving feedback. We pointed out that feedback is most needed in everyday teaching processes where supporting students' learning requires reliable detailed and frequent feedback. This can best be done by diagnostic tests tailored to the actual developmental level and individual characteristics of students. We showed that this cannot be done by means of traditional tests; therefore, this is the context where TBA is most beneficial.

We analyzed the similarities and differences between online diagnostic assessment and educational games. As for functional similarities, the main mission of both diagnostic testing and assessment in educational games is guiding the learners through a series of learning tasks, so that they could always deal with learning tasks which are matched to their actual developmental level. The difference is that diagnostic assessment focuses on feedback and orients students' learning process towards the next learning tasks, while educational games support learning in a more direct way by presenting learning material and developmental stimuli. Educational games may play a complementary role to diagnostic assessment and can be used for compensating deficiencies identified by assessment. On the other hand, feedback cycles within educational games are even smaller; therefore, they should be more frequent than that of the diagnostic assessment. As for the technological aspects, similar or identical methods can be applied both in diagnostic assessment and in educational games. Therefore, innovations may be utilized in both areas in similar ways.

The empirical work presented in this chapter has been carried out in the framework of a project aiming at developing an ODAS. The experiment was designed so that it modeled the integration of educational games into (a renewed, assessment based) teaching process. One of the novel aspects of the study was that gaming took place in a school environment where students were together in the classroom space and at the same time played individually without disturbing each other. This shows how the types of teaching games we are experimenting with can later be embedded into the regular teaching processes. In this experiment, student played with the same game, but in later practical implementations, students may play different games, according to their individual needs (identified by the diagnostic system).

A variety of assessments were carried out in the course of the experiment. Eseryel, Ifenthaler, and Ge (2011) distinguish internal and external assessments in the contexts of game-based learning. Internal assessment is part of the game, "Optimally assessment is part of the action or tasks within the game-based environment" (Eseryel et al., 2011, p. 166.). In our experiment, the real-time automated scoring of students' solutions played this role; it allowed an instant feedback and guided students through a series of games. This is not an original solution but can be applied in novel way in the future, when not only the difficulty level or complexity is taken into account, but, depending on the solutions students find or mistakes they make qualitatively, different types of tasks may be presented in the following steps. This development requires further research, especially on a better mapping of the construct defined in the framework into the gaming activity.

Two types of external assessment were applied. According to Eseryel et al. (2011), external assessment may take place before, during, or after playing the game, and as it is not part of the game, especially if applied during paying the game, it may disturb the player. We applied a pre- and posttest design, as proving the efficiency of the game was also part of the experiment. These assessments took place independently from the gaming sessions; therefore, they have not influenced students when playing the game. On the long run, only games with the proven efficiency will be introduced into the practice, so these assessments may be eliminated. On the other hand, when the games will be integrated into the diagnostic system, the information generated by the system may be utilized to monitor the effects of the games. While the way we have evaluated the effects of the game was not new, utilization of the diagnostic information for this purpose may result in novel solutions.

The most innovative aspect of the assessment we are dealing with is capturing contextual information while students play the game. This is also an external assessment, but it is carried out seamlessly, therefore, if it does not disturb the gaming process. The contextual information we focused on in this paper is related to one of the most rapidly developing areas of ICT, face recognition, and identification of emotional expressions. We have demonstrated that the automatic analysis of video data is accurate enough to provide significant feedback in the given contexts. It is also important to note that the precision of our face tracker—which was trained on databases of adults—is considerably worse on children than on adults. In turn, we need to retrain our system on facial expression databases of children. These works—which are in progress at the moment—further improve the precision of the system.

In the present phase of the research, the components examined here have not been completely integrated yet. However, the first results demonstrated the possibilities in each area. In the next phase of the project, more educational games will be developed: they will be connected to the results of the diagnostic assessments, and during their application, more contextual data will be collected. As for the identification of emotional expressions, the automated real-time evaluation of the affective states and the results of cognitive processes may be connected. These assessments can be used themselves as feedback in the learning processes and can be utilized to improve educational games as well.

Acknowledgments The research reported in this chapter was funded by the European Union and co-funded by the European Social Fund and the European Regional Development Fund. Project ID numbers: TÁMOP 3.1.9.-08/1-2009-0001, TAMOP 4.2.1./B-09/KMR-2010-0003, KMOP-1.1.2-08/1-2008-0002. We are grateful to Brigitta Miksztai-Réthey for her thoughtful assistance during the experiments and in the ongoing evaluations.

References

Ainsworth, L., & Viegut, D. (2006). *Common formative assessments. How to connect standards-based instruction and assessment.* Thousand Oaks, CA: Corwin.

Baluch, F., & Itti, L. (2010). Training top-down attention improves performance on a triple conjunction search task. *PLoS One, 5*, e9127.

Biland, C., Py, J., Allione, J., Demarchi, S., & Abric, J.-C. (2008). The effect of lying on intentional versus unintentional facial expressions. *European Review of Applied Psychology, 58*(2), 65–73.

Black, P., Harrison, C., Lee, C., Marshall, B., & Wiliam, D. (2003). *Assessment for learning. Putting it into practice.* Berkshire: Open University Press.

Candès, E. J., & Recht, B. (2008). Exact matrix completion via convex optimization. *Foundations of Computational Mathematics, 9*, 717–772.

Candés, E. J., & Tao, T. (2009). The power of convex relaxation: Near-optimal matrix completion. *IEEE Transactions on Information Theory, 56*(5), 2053–2080.

Chen, Y., Xu, H., Caramanis, C., & Sanghavi, S. (2011). Robust matrix completion with corrupted columns. arXiv http://arxiv.org/abs/1102.2254.

Chermahinia, S. A., & Hommel, B. (2010). The (b)link between creativity and dopamine: Spontaneous eye blink rates predict and dissociate divergent and convergent thinking. *Cognition, 115*(3), 458–465.

Clarke, S. (2001). *Unlocking formative assessment. Practical strategies for enhancing pupils learning in primary classroom.* London: Hodder Arnold.

Clarke, S. (2005). *Formative assessment in action. Weaving the elements together.* London: Hodder Murray.

Cohen, J. (1988). *Statistical power analysis for the behavioral sciences.* Hillsdale, NJ: Erlbaum.

Cristinacce, D., & Cootes, T. (2008). Automatic feature localisation with constrained local models. *Journal of Pattern Recognition, 41*(10), 3054–3067.

Csapó, B., Ainley, J., Bennett, R., Latour, T., & Law, N. (2012). Technological issues of computer-based assessment of 21st century skills. In B. McGaw & P. Griffin (Eds.), *Assessment and teaching of 21st century skills* (pp. 143–230). New York: Springer.

Csapó, B., Molnár, Gy, & R. Tóth, K. (2009). Comparing paper-and-pencil and online assessment of reasoning skills. A pilot study for introducing electronic testing in large-scale assessment in Hungary. In F. Scheuermann & J. Björnsson (Eds.), *The transition to computer-based assessment. New approaches to skills assessment and implications for large-scale testing* (pp. 113–118). Luxemburg: Office for Official Publications of the European Communities.

Ekman, P. (2006). Darwin, deception, and facial expression. *Annals of the New York Academy of Sciences, 1000*, 205–221.

Eseryel, D., Ifenthaler, D., & Ge, X. (2011). Alternative assessment strategies for complex problem solving in game-based learning environments. In D. Ifenthaler, K. P. Isaias, D. G. Sampson, & J. M. Spector (Eds.), *Multiple perspectives on problem solving and learning in the digital age* (pp. 159–178). New York: Springer.

Gantner, Z., Rendle, S., & Schmidt-Thieme, L. (2010). *Factorization models for context-/time-aware movie recommendations, in challenge on context-aware movie recommendation (CAMRa2010).* Barcelona: ACM.

Greiff, S., & Funke, J. (2009). Measuring complex problem solving: The MicroDYN approach. In F. Scheuermann & J. Björnsson (Eds.), *The transition to computer-based assessment. New approaches to skills assessment and implications for large-scale testing* (pp. 157–163). Luxemburg: Office for Official Publications of the European Communities.

Greiff, S., & Funke, J. (2010). Systematische Erforschung komplexer Problemlösefähigkeit anhand minimal komplexer Systeme. In E. Klieme, D. Leutner, & M. Kenk (Eds.), *Kompetenzmodellierung. Zwischenbilanz des DFG-Schwerpunktprogramms und Perspektiven des Forschungsansatzes* (Beiheft der Zeitschrift für Pädagogik, Vol. 56, pp. 216–227). Weinheim: Beltz.

Gross, R., Matthews, I., Cohn, J., Kanade, T., & Baker, S. (2010). Multi-PIE. Image and Vision. *Computing, 28*(5), 807–813.

Hévízi, G., Gerőfi, B., Szendrő, B., & Lörincz, A. (2005). Assisting robotic personal agent and cooperating alternative input devices for severely disabled children. *Lecture Notes in Artificial Intelligence, 3690,* 591–594.

Ishikawa, T., Baker, S., Matthews, I., & Kanade, T. (2004). Passive driver gaze tracking with active appearance models. In *Proceedings of the 11th world congress on intelligent transportation systems.* Nagoya: Japan.

Itti, L. (2007). Visual salience. *Scholarpedia, 2*(9):3327.

Jenatton, R., Obozinski, G., & Bach, F. (2010). Structured sparse principal component analysis. *JMLR Workshop and Conference Proceedings, 9,* 366–373.

Jeni, L., Hashimoto, H., & Lörincz, A. (2011). *Efficient, pose invariant facial emotion classification using 3D constrained local model and 2D shape information.* In Workshop on Gesture Recognition, Colorado Springs, USA. Retrieved June 20, 2011, from http://clopinet.com/isabelle/Projects/CVPR2011/posters/jeni_hashimoto_lorincz.pdf.

Klauer, K. J. (1989). *Denktraining für Kinder I.* Göttingen: Hogrefe.

Klauer, K. J., & Phye, G. D. (2008). Inductive reasoning. A training approach. *Review of Educational Research, 78,* 85–123.

Leighton, J. P., & Gierl, M. J. (Eds.). (2007). *Cognitive diagnostic assessment for education. Theory and applications.* Cambridge: Cambridge University Press.

Matthews, I., & Baker, S. (2004). Active appearance models revisited. *International Journal of Computer Vision, 60*(2), 135–164.

Meyer, B., & Sorensen, B. H. (2009). Designing serious games for computer assisted language learning—a framework for development and analysis. In M. Kankaaranta & P. Neittaanmaki (Eds.), *Design and use of serious games* (pp. 69–82). New York: Springer.

Molnar, G. (2011). Playful fostering of 6- to 8-year-old students' inductive reasoning. *Thinking Skills and Creativity, 6*(2), 91–99.

OECD. (2004). *Problem solving for tomorrow's world. First measures of cross-curricular competencies from PISA 2003.* Paris: OECD.

Peters, R. J., Iyer, A., Itti, L., & Koch, C. (2005). Components of bottom-up gaze allocation in natural images. *Vision Research, 45*(8), 2397–2416.

Porter, P., & ten Brinke, L. (2011). The truth about lies: What works in detecting high-stakes deception? *Legal and Criminological Psychology, 15*(1), 57–75.

Renninger, L. W., Verghese, P., & Coughlan, J. (2007). Where to look next? Eye movements reduce local uncertainty. *Journal of Vision, 7*(3), 1–17, http://journalofvision.org/7/3/6/, doi:10.1167/7.3.6.

Saragih, J. M., Lucey, S., & Cohn, J. F. (2011). Deformable model fitting by regularized landmark mean-shift. *International Journal of Computer Vision, 91*(2), 200–215.

Seel, N. M. (2010). Essentials of computer based diagnostics of learning and cognition. In D. Infenthaler, P. Pirnay-Dummer, & N. M. Seel (Eds.), *Computer-based diagnostics and systematic analysis of knowledge* (pp. 3–14). New York: Springer.

Spector, J. M. (2010). Mental representations and their analysis: An epistemological perspective. In D. Infenthaler, P. Pirnay-Dummer, & N. M. Seel (Eds.), *Computer-based diagnostics and systematic analysis of knowledge* (pp. 27–40). New York: Springer.

Strasser, A. (2010). A functional view toward mental representations. In D. Infenthaler, P. Pirnay-Dummer, & N. M. Seel (Eds.), *Computer-based diagnostics and systematic analysis of knowledge* (pp. 15–25). New York: Springer.

Szabó, Z., Póczos, B., & Lörincz, A. (2012). *Collaborative filtering via group-structured dictionary learning. Lecture Notes in Computer Science, 7191*, 247–254.

Taras, M. (2005). Assessment—summative and formative—some theoretical reflections. *British Journal of Educational Studies, 53*(4), 466–478.

Thai-Nghe, N., Drumond, L., Horváth, T., Nanopoulos, A., & Schmidt-Thieme, L. (2011). Matrix and tensor factorization for predicting student performance. In *CSEDU 2011—Proceedings of the third international conference on computer supported education* (Vol. I, pp. 69–78). Noordwijkerhout: The Netherlands.

Tudge, J. (1992). Vygotsky and education: Instructional implications and applications of sociohistorical psychology. In L. C. Moll (Ed.), *Vygotsky and education: Instructional implications and applications of sociohistorical psychology* (pp. 155–172). New York, NY: Cambridge University Press.

Tzuriel, D. (1998). Dynamic assessment of preschool children: Characteristics and measures. In J. M. Martínez, J. Lebeer, & R. Garbo (Eds.), *Is intelligence modifiable?* (pp. 95–114). Madrid: Bruño.

Viola, P., & Jones, M. (2001). Rapid object detection using a boosted cascade of simple features. *IEEE Computer Society Conference on Computer Vision and Pattern Recognition (CVPR'01), 1*, 511. doi:ieeecomputersociety.org/10.1109/CVPR.2001.990517.

Westra, J., Dignum, F., & Dignum, V. (2011). Guiding user adaptations in serious games. In F. Didnum (Ed.), *Agents for games and simulations II. Trends in techniques, concepts and design* (pp. 117–131). Berlin: Springer.

Part III
Realizing Assessment
in Game-Based Learning

Chapter 14
Interactivity[3] Design and Assessment Framework for Educational Games to Promote Motivation and Complex Problem-Solving Skills

Deniz Eseryel, Yu Guo, and Victor Law

14.1 Introduction

Digital game-based learning has been receiving increasing attention from educational researchers in recent years (cf. Gee, 2003; Prensky, 2006, 2007; Shaffer, 2006). Among many genres of digital games, massively multiplayer online role-playing games (MMORPGs) are especially touted. MMORPG is a genre of role-playing video games that can be described as a "persistent, networked, interactive, narrative environment in which [large] number of players collaborate, strategize, plan and interact with objects, resources, and other players within a multi-model environment [of a virtual game-world]" (Dickey, 2007, p. 254). These unique affordances of MMORPG make it an ideal candidate to serve as an open-ended learning environment that support contextualizations (Cordova & Lepper, 1996; Parker & Lepper, 1992), situated cognition (Brown, Collins, & Duguid, 1989; Lave & Wenger, 1991), intrinsic motivation (Rieber, 1996), and social communication (Gredler, 2004; Wideman et al., 2007). Hence, the proponents of MMORPGs strongly argue for their potential in promoting students' motivation and complex problem-solving skill development (e.g., Gee, 2007; Greenfield, 2010; van Eck, 2006, 2007; Yanuzzi & Behrenhausen, 2010).

However, little empirical research exists to support these assertions. Based on their review of empirical literature published in the past 20 years, Eseryel, Ifenthaler, and Ge (2010) conclude that the potential of digital game-based learning is unrealized due to lack of empirically validated instructional design frameworks to support

D. Eseryel (✉) • V. Law
Department of Educational Psychology, University of Oklahoma, 820 Van Vleet Oval Rm 323B,
Norman, OK 73019-2041, USA
e-mail: eseryel@ou.edu; vlaw@ou.edu

Y. Guo
Oklahoma State University, 100 Telecommunications Center, Stillwater, OK 74078, USA
e-mail: bryan.guo@okstate.edu

D. Ifenthaler et al. (eds.), *Assessment in Game-Based Learning: Foundations,*   257
Innovations, and Perspectives, DOI 10.1007/978-1-4614-3546-4_14,
© Springer Science+Business Media New York 2012

students' motivation and complex problem-solving skill development. In order to address this gap, for the past few years, we have been engaged in design-based research (DBR) that aim at eliciting educational MMORPG design principles to facilitate students' motivation and complex problem skill development (cf. Eseryel & Ge, 2010).

The goal of this book chapter is to present the Interactivity[3] design and assessment framework that has emerged from this DBR effort. Special attention is paid to bridging three levels of interactivity that were identified in our study as having crucial importance for effective educational game design: (1) interface interactivity, (2) narrative interactivity, and (3) social interactivity.

In the remainder of this chapter, we first introduce the details of our DBR initiative that was launched by carrying out a series of studies in a rural high school in the Midwest United States. Then, we explicate the design model and the accompanying evaluation framework to help guide the development and testing of different levels of interactivity in educational game design. We then present a study that shows the validity of the Interactivity[3] design and assessment framework for MMORPGs. We conclude with the discussion of the findings of the setting an agenda for future research.

14.2   Design-Based Research Framework

In order to arrive at design principles for effective educational MMORPGs to promote students' motivation and complex problem-solving skill development, we investigated with *McLarin's Adventures*, an educational MMORPG that was being developed by the K20 Center at the University of Oklahoma.

McLarin's Adventures is an educational adventure MMORPG, in which middle and high school students collaborate to solve complex problems that call for cross-disciplinary learning (mathematics, literacy, science, and social studies) (see Wilson & Williams, 2010 for details). When students first enter *McLarin's Adventures*, they are presented with a news video reporting on eccentric trillionaire Jonathan McLarin's dream of interplanetary and interstellar travel. His company, McLarin International, has finally produced a vehicle capable of traveling one light year in a single day. In this news video, Mr. McLarin announces the plans to send a team of experts to explore and survey Earth-like planets outside of our solar system. To select a team who will receive this great honor, McLarin International is holding a competition for mathematicians, scientists, and journalists. Each team will have to prove their abilities to survive while meeting the specified goals. Then, McLarin International's Chief Operating Officer appears and invites potential applicants to apply and the game begins.

This background game narrative calls the students to play the role of mathematicians, scientists, and journalists competing to prove their capabilities to McLarin International. The game narrative divides the overall complex problem-solving task into several whole-task problem scenarios including locating water resources, determining the quality of water supplies and purification, settlement planning and

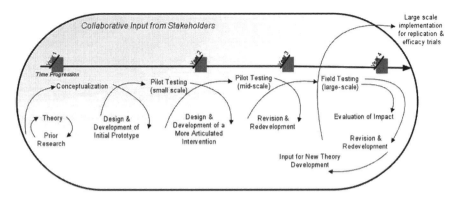

Fig. 14.1 Design-based research framework

building of shelters, locating food sources for colonization, creating an inventory of supplies and requirements for additional supplies, building a sanitation system, and so on. The competencies required to solve these problem scenarios are aligned with the learning standards outlined by the State Department of Education.

In the game environment, whole-task scenarios are presented through a communication kiosk. After student teams complete each task, they submit their reports to McLarin's International through the system, receive automated confirmatory feedback from the system, and proceed to the next kiosk for the next task. In order to assist students during their game play, the game interface includes navigation support tools, in-game applications (journal, spreadsheet, e-mail, etc.), and research instruments (pH meter, thermometer, pedometer, etc.) that allow the students to authentically collect, organize, analyze, and report data while in the game. In addition, a chat client is included to support the interteam communication of the students.

Figure 14.1 depicts the DBR framework that guided our investigation with *McLarin's Adventures* MMOG. The study presented here reports the findings at the end of the third year during the mid-scale pilot testing.

14.3   Interactivity³ Design Model for Educational MMORPG

Crawford (2010), who have been developing commercial games since 1978, summarizes our findings best when he said

> If the entire thrust of my career could be reduced to a bumper sticker, it would read, "It's the interactivity!" Interactivity—not graphics, not animation, not sound—is the essence...
> (p. 334)

Salen and Zimmerman (2004) identified four modes of interactions in commercial games in terms of player's level of engagement: (1) functional interactivity which means the interaction with the material part of the system, such as how sticky the

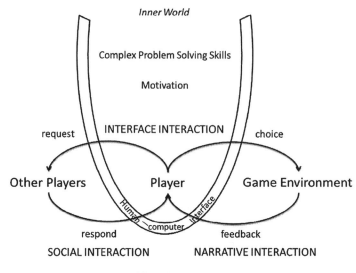

Fig. 14.2 Interactivity[3] game design model

keys feel; (2) explicit interactivity, which refers to the actual play motion, like
clicking and hitting keys; (3) cognitive interactivity, which is "the psychological,
emotional, and intellectual participation between a person and a system" (Salen &
Zimmerman, 2005, p. 70); and (4) cultural participation, which is the participation
beyond the in-gameplaying, and construction of the game culture in the real world.

Salen and Zimmerman's (2004) model provides a good blueprint to describe
interactions in commercial games; however, in order to design an educational game,
we need to pay special attention to the functionality, game play, referentially, social,
and pedagogical issues (Konzack, 2002; Liarokapis, 2006). In educational settings,
especially when we target learners' motivation and complex problem-solving skills,
we take the explicit interaction between players and games as a persistent cycle of
making choices through the game play. Hence, the findings of our DBR effort point
out to three levels of interactivity that are important to the success of the educational
game design to support both learning and motivational outcomes: (1) interface
interactivity; (2) narrative interactivity; (3) social interactivity. Figure 14.2 depicts
the Interactivity[3] game design model, which integrates these three levels of interactivity for designing educational MMORPGs to support student motivation and complex problem-solving skill development.

Interface interactivity is a super category of functional interactivity in Salen and
Zimmerman's (2004) terms, which includes both player's device input and system's
visual output. Because other levels of interaction are conveyed through the interface, the effectiveness the interface design either enhances or impedes all other
levels of interactivity.

Narrative interactivity is a subconcept of what Salen and Zimmerman (2004) refers to as cognitive interaction. Narrative interactivity refers to learner's cognitive interaction with the game's complex storyline. Role-playing games rely heavily on storytelling, where players construct their mental game space and make sense of game play. This is where most of the high-order cognitive activities occur. Therefore, it is the foremost important level to consider when designing educational MMORPGs to support acquisition of complex problem-solving skills. Social interactivity is a salient feature of educational MMORPG that was not addressed by Salen and Zimmerman's (2004) modes of interactivity. Nevertheless, in commercial games, cultural participation occurs spontaneously outside the game environment without game designers' prescription. Therefore, it is not a designed feature of commercial MMORPG. Instead, in educational MMORPG, designers need to pay special attention to social interactivity that occurs among learners during game play. Hence, our game design model emphasizes social interactivity instead of cultural participation. Social interactivity brings dynamic human interactions throughout game play and interacts with the game narrative to provide learners' with ever-changing storyline and endless decision-making possibilities.

The three levels of interaction are also aligned with the evolution of video games in terms of their gradually increasing complexity: Back in the era of Pac-man, the players had hardly anything to learn except for smartly dodging from the ghosts, which focus on the functional interactivity. When role-play games (RPGs) dominated video games 2 decades ago, the players were able to immerse themselves into the story with multiple characters and complex storyline. Hence, narrative interactivity becomes more important, through which players learn complex relationship of time, location, characters, events, and rules in the game. With the advancement of the Internet, MMORPGs emerged by pushing the interactivity requirements to a more complex and advanced level, emphasizing the participation of, and communication among real people behind game avatars.

In the following sections, we further describe these three levels of interactivity and then elaborate on how they influence learners' motivation and acquisition of complex problem-solving skills in educational MMORPGs. This by no means indicates that these three levels are distinct and separated. Instead, it is separated in three levels for the convenience of the designers with different types of expertise. For example, graphical designers and programmers may focus on the level of interface interaction while content experts and storytelling experts can focus on narrative interaction and social interaction.

14.3.1 Interface Interactivity

Interface interactivity refers to the direct interaction between players and game systems. Like in a learning environment, where designers cannot directly design the learning experience but design artifacts and activities to elicit desired learning experience, game designers cannot directly design the interactive experience that the player would have during game play. Rather, through carefully designed interface, designers can manipulate players' game experiences and help them achieve the desired interactivity. Therefore, we focus at the features that facilitate effective and engaging interface interactions such as navigation (Dondlinger & Lunce, 2009), data visualization, and interface metaphor (Fullerton, Swain, & Hoffman, 2004).

Navigation refers to the wayfinding in the game. In real world, people find their ways by recognizing land marks, street signs, asking the way, and so forth. In virtual world, in addition to these elements, game designers also need to provide maps and depth cues, which can help players locate desired objects and places, hence focus on what is important in the game to avoid cognitive load caused by unintuitive navigation. In understanding way-finding affordance, Dondlinger and Lunce (2009) stated: "the challenge for the virtual environment designer is to provide navigational affordances without cluttering the information landscape" (p. 2). We adopted their criteria of successful navigation in an educational MMORPG, which includes audio, maps, landmarks, depth cues, signs or pathways, and avatar perspective. Adjustable avatar perspectives enable player to flexibly explore the game environment and therefore support navigation in the game space and facilitate way finding.

Visualization refers to presenting quantitative data by graphics and charts, which allows players to know the approximation of game-related data at a glance. For example, the health status of avatars in a game is represented by a color-coded bar in the dock of the game interface. When an avatar's health is in good condition, the bar is full and is green. When an avatar is attacked by enemy, the bar dwindles and changes color into red to alert the player to avoid further injury. Good visualization also evolves in ways in which data is organized; the consistency of screen layout and clear data hierarchy are all helpful design elements to help players' quick retrieval of data.

Interface metaphor or the theme of the interface can affect the mental status of the players (Fullerton, Swain, & Hoffman, 2004). For example, in science adventure games, the high-tech look control panel and the dark color scheme create immersive atmosphere for the players to engage into the scientific game play and make them believe that they are scientists or commanders and their decisions matter much. While in some life simulation games, the cozy look control panel and warm color scheme elicit emotions of love and care.

Interface interactivity is a layer through which all other levels of interactions are realized. The design quality of this layer directly affects the overall success of the game in different ways: good design helps to set up the tone of the game play and to optimize clear transmission of information from other levels of interaction; flawed designs impede and block such interactions, which will cause players frustration.

14.3.1.1 Interface Interactivity and Motivation

An interface consists of sensory stimuli including visual, auditory, or tactile stimulation. These elements can create a sensory curiosity as a motivator (Malone, 1980). They are also used to distort players' perception and to create temporary acceptance of an alternate reality (Wilson et al., 2009). Such make-believe traits or physical fidelity (Crawford, 1984) enable video games to present a designed virtual immersive environment and make players feel the environment and the tasks in such environment are authentic. Brown et al. (1989) argued that learning outcomes can be optimized when learners acquire knowledge and skills or solve problems in authentic situated learning environments. Therefore, the ability to represent an authentic environment gives MMORPG the affordance of enhancing learners' immersion, which in turn positively affects learners' motivation.

14.3.1.2 Interface Interactivity and Complex Problem-Solving Skills

People have difficulty with solving complex problems because the factors that affect a complex problem situation can be numerous and a change in each factor may cause a chain of changes in many other factors (Dörner, 1987). Problem solvers often neglect some minor cues, which are actually important factors in problem-solving processes. Blumberg, Roshenthal, and Randall (2008) found that game players relied on different cues in problem-solving during gameplay. The success of the problem solvers depends on the accuracy of the mental model they build to depict the cause-and-effect relationships among the factors affecting the complex problem situation.

An MMORPG is an ideal environment to present complex problems in that designers can naturally incorporate all the factors and their effects naturally in a game environment. Well-designed interface interactivity allows players to access every details of the game environment through different navigation and visualization tools so that they can discover factors that help them discover the causal relationships among problem constituents. In a complex problem situation presented by an MMORPG, players need to have a good interface to lead them to identify the problem, collect necessary and all the resources that they need.

14.3.2   Narrative Interactivity

In a RPG, players are engaged in a higher cognitive level of interaction beyond interface interaction, which is the interaction with the narrative. Narrative is the story that players experience during game play. Game narrative "strings together the events of a game, providing a framework and what can alternately be called a justification, a reason, or an excuse for the gameplay encounters" (Dansky, 2007, p. 5). Game narrative is prescribed by the game designers in order to give players the information to advance the plot. Well-designed narratives can clearly state the goal of the game, naturally define rules of the game, sets the player's role, and provide meaningful choices to the players to proceed for further play.

To design good narratives, we adapted the design principles of Goal-Based Scenarios (Schank, Berman, & Macpherson, 1999). A goal-based scenario "is a

Fig. 14.3 Cycle of choice

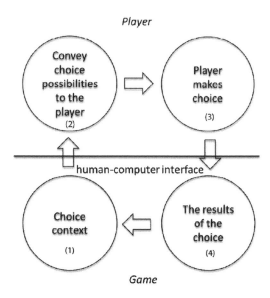

learn-by-doing simulation in which students pursue a goal by practicing target skills by using relevant content knowledge to help them achieve their goal" (Schank et al., 1999, p. 165). Game narrative and goal-based scenarios share important features such as highly goal-oriented tasks, a movie-like plot with settings and protagonists, and the activities that require target skills to be applied to achieve the ultimate goal. The concept of learning by doing also matches well with game-based learning in an MMORPG, where players are given authentic tasks situated in a context of a story that call for complex problem solving.

Well-designed narratives present consistent and fully developed choices to players. In order to assess the quality of the choices provided by the narrative, the following five questions should be asked for each choice point (Salen & Zimmerman, 2005): (1) What happened before the player was given the choice? (2) How is the possibility of choice conveyed to the player? (3) How did the player make the choice? (4) What is the result of the choice? How will it affect future choices? (5) How is the result of the choice conveyed to the player? In order to make meaningful choices, the context of the choices should be clearly perceived by the players. By assessing the situations they are in, as well as hints or guesses they are given during the play, players make choices. We argue that question five can be combined with question four (Fig. 14.3) in that conveying the result of a choice to the player can be the same process of presenting "what happens before the player's *next* choice is given." Moreover, in complex problem-solving situations, some consequences of player's choices may not be immediately available to the player, imitating the time delays seen in real life in those situations. Instead, the consequences of these choices may have some prolonged effects on the overall storyline. This adds to the complexity of the problem that players are attempting to solve since it makes it harder for the problem solver to build the mental model of the complex problem. Therefore, the human–computer interface also separates question (2) and (3), which happen to the player, from questions (4) and (1), which happen inside the game narratives.

14.3.2.1 Narrative Interactivity and Motivation

Narratives can be a significant intrinsic motivator if the storyline incorporates well-designed elements such as fantasy (Malone, 1980), uncertainty, and inevitability (Eifferman, 1974; Kagan, 1978; Malone, 1980; Salen & Zimmerman, 2005). Fantasy is the make-believe setting of the story; uncertainty means the ambiguity of the result or the winning of the game play; inevitability refers to the imminent results such as nonrenewable resource or irreversible processes, which add to emotional tension of players. Dempsey, Haynes, Lucassen, and Casey (2002) found that incorporating challenges, clear goals, and sufficient feedback into narratives are important for players gaming experiences. Ideally, the narrative can bring player into the state of *flow* (Csikszentmihalyi, 1991), in which player completely focus on the task at hand, and forget about self, about others, about the world around themselves. Players also lose track of time, feel happy and in control, and become creative and productive (Csikszentmihalyi). In contrast, if the game narrative is not well designed, the game can at most serve as a brief extrinsic motivator or merely a shell to link discrete tasks together. Under such circumstances, players would soon lose interest in the game because they are not intrinsically motivated. Furthermore, a poorly designed narrative can also confuse, frustrate, and turn players away from a game.

14.3.2.2 Narrative Interactivity and Complex Problem-Solving Skills

The narrative in an MMORPG is a complex and ill-structured problem space that provides players ample opportunities to be engaged in higher order thinking. Players usually do not know how the story develops; therefore, they need to constantly evaluate their current surrounding environment and emerging incidents to define the problem they need to solve. MMOROG usually provide players with small quests, in which players can refine certain areas of their skills and then proceed to more advanced quests. This complies with the processes of solving complex problems: articulating the problem domain and constraints, identifying alternative opinions and perspectives, generating possible solutions, assessing alternative solutions, monitoring problems representations, implementing and monitoring solutions, and adapting the solution approaches (Jonassen, 1997).

As interface interaction provides physical fidelity, which is the make-believe traits at interface level, good narrative interaction provides psychological fidelity, which means players should feel that the story is authentic and real. Studies suggest that students could be benefited from authentic learning environment (e.g. Ge, Thomas, & Greene, 2006). In their meta-analysis of problem-based learning, which allows students to learn in an authentic environment, Dochy, Segers, van den

Bossche, and Gijbels (2003) also found that students exposed to problem-based learning are better in applying their knowledge. Narrative in a game allows authenticity to be emerged through the participation of players (Barab, Squire, & Dueber, 2000), which is a more natural way to engage players in authentic learning.

14.3.3   Social Interactivity

Social interactivity in game-based learning environments refers to the communication and collaboration between human players. Social interactivity is a salient characteristic of MMORPG because players do not only interact with the game environment but they also interact with other players via their self-created avatars (Steinkuehler, 2004). Players in the game world can carry on a text or voice chat when their avatars are physically close to each other. Alternatively, they can use distance communication tools such as in-game emails or pagers to contact their partners. Through social interactions, players learn and solve problems together replicating real-life complex problem-solving situations. In contrast to predesigned narratives, the social interactivity with players is live, dynamic, and may happen spontaneously if the scenarios within a game are designed to promote communication and collaboration. Therefore, social interaction constantly changes the game content and presents players a slightly different game play experience every time they play. Such features give social interaction strong affordance in support of social learning, collaborative learning, and players' engagement in a context-rich virtual world.

Amory (2007) suggested the use of social capital theory as a lens to understand the collaborative behaviors in games. Social capital is defined as "the sum of the actual and potential resources embedded within, available through, and derived from the network of relationships possessed by an individual or social unit" (Nahapiet & Ghoshal, 1998, p. 243). Nahapiet and Ghoshal (1998) applied the theory in organizational settings to suggest social capital can facilitate the creation of intellectual capital, which is a form of learning. In an educational game context, it means players learn from other players.

Drawing from Granovetter's notion of embeddedness (Granovetter, 1985), Nahapiet and Ghoshal (1998) suggested three dimensions in social capital: (1) structural, (2) relational, and (3) cognitive. The first dimension of social capital is the structural dimension which concerns with the network structure as a whole. In an MMORPG, it will be whom a player can contact, and in what ways they can contact with others. In order to have social interaction, a player has to be able to contact other players. However, the presence of ties among players is not enough. The strength of ties, which refers to the frequency of contact among the players, is also important. An effective MMORPG would provide an easy mechanism through which communication among all players is made easy so that a dense communication network can be formed to support social interactivity.

The second dimension of social capital is the relational dimension, which describes the personal relationship among the players (Nahapiet & Ghoshal, 1998).

Relationships among players can be demonstrated by the trust among them, approval among each other, and norms and identification seen in the community. To the contrary, negative relationship elements can be demonstrated by the relational conflict among the players.

The third dimension of social capital is the cognitive dimension, which refers to the shared interpretation of the meaning among the players (Nahapiet & Ghoshal, 1998). The shared languages and narratives among the players provide them common ground to exchange ideas and create new meanings (Nahapiet & Ghoshal).

14.3.3.1 Social Interactivity and Motivation

Social interactivity during gameplay, such as competition and collaboration with others who are also playing the game, plays an important role contributing to learners' motivation. Existing research findings suggest that social interaction fosters learners' motivation. For instance, Chen, Dun, Phuah, and Lam (2006) stated that positive social interaction in an MMORPG, such as pro-social behavior, trading, and collaboration can enhance players' engagement while negative social interaction behaviors, such as begging, politics, scamming, and leeching impede engagement. The studies conducted by Sweetser and Wyeth (2005) and Yee (2006) concur that social interactions that allow players to compete, collaborate, and connect lead to game flow experiences. Therefore, the collaborative tasks and the three dimensions of social interactivity should be carefully designed in educational MMORPG to make the gaming experience more motivating and more authentic.

14.3.3.2 Social Interactivity and Complex Problem-Solving Skills

Good social interactivity in games not only leads to players' engagement but also supports players' complex problem skills development. Cognitive flexibility theory (cf. Feltovich, Spiro, Coulson, & Feltovich, 1996) suggests that multiplicity, such as multiple representations of problems and multiple methods to solve problems, is important in solving complex problems. Through productive discussions and argumentation among each other, well-designed opportunities for social interactions in game-based learning environments allow learners to realize that there are multiple interpretations of the complex problem scenario of the game and there are multiple solution alternatives. Azevedo, Winters, and Moos (2004) examined how students learned environmental science concepts collaboratively. They found that students learned significantly more about ecology after working collaboratively. In another study, Uribe, Klein, and Sullinvan (2003) also found that student pairs outperformed students who worked alone in solving ill-structured problems. Therefore, designing MMORPGs to promote social interaction at all levels is essential for players' complex problem-solving skill development.

14.4 Assessment Framework

Based on the Interactivity[3] MMORPG design model, we developed a framework to assess educational MMORPGs. This framework has three dimensions, which capture different salient aspects of educational games: (1) interface interactivity, (2) narration interactivity, and (3) social interactivity.

Each dimension involves several elements that must be carefully integrated into the overall game design. Each of these elements is assessed on a rubric that measures the level of interactivity design from *level 0* to *level 3*. Level 0 indicates the lowest level of each element, which in general refers to a negative impact on learning goals or learning approaches. For instance, level 0 on *sound* means the audio in the game is confusing to the players and/or it is uninteresting, which makes it harder for the players to understand the context, negatively impacting learner engagement. Level 1 indicates the absence of such interactivity. For the *sound* category, it means audio is absent from the game. Level 2 indicates an adequate level of interactivity. Level 3 indicates a good level of interactivity. For instance, a level 3 of *sound* means that the audio provides clues to the players in a meaningful way. In the following sections, we explicate how we evaluate three types of interactivity in an MMORPG.

14.4.1 Assessing Interface Interactivity

Drawing from Dondlinger and Lunce (2009), there are six elements that can help with navigation: sound, map, landmark, depth cue, signs or pathways, and avatar perspective. The rubric to assess interface interactivity is presented in Table 14.1.

Sound should relate to the environment in the same way it does in the real world. Nevertheless, it does not have to be realistic. Actually, controlling the amount and variety of sound in the game can give players clues without taking up needed cognitive capacity for puzzle solving. Carefully timed and placed audio cues can tell players how close they are to a location or give them useful feedback as to if they are making the right decisions in the game. Conversely, arbitrary use of audio would distract and confuse the players.

A map should be built in the game and include landmarks that visually connect the objects in the 3D space. Referencing the map by the users should minimally affect their flow of the game. In some cases, the issues of flow can be solved by integrating use of the map into the story line and characterizing the map in a way that it belongs to the story. Augmenting a quick reference *bird's eye view* onto the screen can also be a way, in which a map can help users navigate without disrupting game play.

Rendering an object in a 3D program is not the only way to create a 3D experience. In some virtual environments, navigational elements rendered as 2D or 2½D objects can more effectively convey crucial navigational data than 3D objects (Dodlinger & Lunce, 2009; Komerska & Ware, 2003). Other artistic techniques such as color treatments and horizon lines can also contribute to the depth information. Making clever use of depth cues can help the player focus on what's important in the game as well as minimizing the load time for the computer. No matter what

Table 14.1 Rubric for assessing interface interactivity

Categories	Criteria	3 Good	2 Fair	1 Lack	0 Negative
Navigation					
Sound	Sounds are timed to give clues about proximity to a location within the plot of the game. For example, train noises get louder as player gets closer to the train station or the music becomes tenser as player approaches a pivotal moment				
Map	Map is directly related to the space it refers to. Map also integrates into the story, game play, and can be accessed without interrupting the flow of the game				
Landmark	Landmarks are naturally integrated and serve specific purposes within the overall goal of the game				
Depth cue	Depth cues employ a number of illusion techniques in order to serve specific purposes within the overall goal of the game. This may take form of 2½ dimensions and dramatic shading to emphasizing certain objects and subdue others. These tools can be used to simplify and control the user's navigation experience				
Signs or pathways	Signs and pathways are naturally integrated into the story and the environment. They are visually designed in a way that creates curiosity and adventure for the player as he follows them				
Avatar Perspective	Avatar perspective is simple to use and enhances the player's spatial knowledge. Avatar perspective allows player to feel emotionally or physically attached to the events of the game and enhances the mood and goals of the overall game				
Visualization					
Consistency	All data and buttons are always in a consistent location				
Grouping of data	Data is grouped in such a way that related information can be quickly compared and common tasks that require menus can be completed without interrupting the flow of the game				
Interface metaphor					
Interface theme	The metaphor should be consistent with the goal and the player's role throughout the game				

techniques are used they should be done in a way that there is no confusion about where objects are in the game space.

Street signs, sidewalks, and stepping stones are tools that humans are accustomed to making and using. These tools can help game designers direct the players when designed carefully. There are other aspects to include such as avatar perspective. Data visualization category consists of consistency, grouping of data, hierarchy of data, and interface metaphor. Not all tools are necessary for a successful virtual experience. However, allowing players to be successful navigators in different ways is advantageous because each player may have a different personal style of navigation. More importantly, any counterproductive navigation or visualization tools could lead to frustration and rejection of the game by the players.

14.4.2   Assessing Narrative Interactivity

The elements of the assessment of narrative interactivity (Table 14.2) are driven from the design principles of Goal-Based Scenario framework proposed by Schank et al. (1999). It consists of seven essential components: goals, mission, cover story, role, scenario operation, resource, and feedback.

Goals in this scenario are the learning goals that the players are supposed to achieve during gameplay. The mission is the tasks through which they can achieve the goal. The cover story is the background story that expresses the need to go on to the mission and to achieve the goals. The role is the player's identity in such missions. The scenario operations are the sum of activities, including all the choices players make towards the goal. Feedback is the just-in-time information of players' progress during their activities.

The cover story can be revealed at the very beginning of the game or while playing by cut scenes, which are also referred as in-game movies. Cut scenes can take many forms such as video clips, emails that the players receive in the game environment, and so forth. These cut scenes serve as an indication of the accomplished goals, giving information or hints of the mission that the players are about to go through, and push the plot to go forward by setting up new goals. For example, when a player first enters the game environment, the cover story, which may take a form of a video clip, could be played to define the roles of the players and their missions. After the player achieves some goals, in order to advance the plot to a new stage, a cut scene may be presented through a nonplayer character (NPC), who may direct the player to new quests. Well-designed narratives clearly state the goal of the game, define the rules as well as the player's role, set the mood, and motivate the players to move forward in their game play.

Scenario operation needs to ensure that the activities players are given directly contribute to the realization of the goals by utilizing the target knowledge and skills to be learned by the players. The causal connection between players' action and the system's reaction should be clear. The system should also provide rich possibilities for players to make meaningful choices. In addition, the game environment needs to provide carefully organized information resources that players should access in

Table 14.2 Rubric for assessing narrative interactivity

Categories	Criteria	3 Good	2 Fair	1 Lack	0 Negative
Mission					
Goal distinction	Both the overall goal and the subgoals are clearly stated; the goals are in great consistency; the criteria for achieving each goal is clear to students				
Goal motivation	The goals of the game are in accordance with those that the students already have or are appealing to the players so that they are willing to adopt these goals. The goals are intuitively challenging but attainable				
Target skill dependence	The process of achieving goals foster and require both domain specific and generic ability of the players. Players achieve the goals depending on the target skills that they are supposed to acquire in the process of playing				
Situativity	The environment in which the goal is embedded is authentic and appropriate so that it facilitates transfer. Players may freely interact with the environment				
Flexible completion criteria	Players could have multiple paths to accomplish the mission. Each path will ensure the players to experience all the cognitive process that are required to accomplish the goal				
Backstory					
Consistency	The cover story clearly conveys the mission background, the role of the player, and the mission itself to the player. It provides evidences for players to predict the boundaries of and the relationship in the game play. It gives the player plot hooks and uncertainty to motivate the player to go on with the game. It is neither too short nor too long				

(continued)

Table 14.2 (continued)

Categories	Criteria	3 Good	2 Fair	1 Lack	0 Negative
Grouping of data	They appear right in time to provide information such as strategic prompts of upcoming tasks or give hints of navigation; They also reinforce the mood and tune of the game				
Roles	The roles of the players are consistent with the mission. Avatars accumulate experience and skills to enable them to accomplish high-level tasks. The characters of the avatars have both strength and flaws, which changes during the game				
Scenario operations	Tasks and quests should contribute to goals and mission. Provide ample opportunities for player to make choices and should have clear consequences that either have a immediate or long-term impact on the game play				
Resources	Information and tools that are necessary to achieve the mission and the goal must be provided and is well organized for easy access. Should be embedded naturally in the storyline.				
Feedback	Situated in the game play, give player just-in-time feedback and customized information support to help advance the game				

order to successfully achieve their goals. Contextualized and just-in-time feedback is also crucial in scaffolding learners during gameplay (Schank et al., 1999).

14.4.3   Assessing Social Interactivity

To evaluate the social interactivity of a game, we suggest rating the game in four dimensions: (1) the degree of collaborative activities, (2) the structure dimensions of the game, (3) the cognitive dimensions of the game, and (4) the relational dimensions of the game. The rubric is presented in Table 14.3.

Table 14.3 Rubric for assessing social interactivity

Categories	Criteria	3 Good	2 Fair	1 Lack	0 Negative
Collaborative task	Players need to collaborate most of the time to complete the tasks				
Structural dimension	Players can reach all other players and communicate with them easily				
Cognitive dimension	Share representations and meaning, such as shared stories and language, generated from the game can be found in many occasions				
Relational dimension	Relational evidences, such as respect, trust, obligation, identification, and norm, that are generated from the game can be found in many occasions				

In order to have meaningful social interactivity among the players, a game should incorporate meaningful collaborative tasks, which allow them to interact naturally. As a result, each of the players can share their expertise or workload to solve problems together. Therefore, we first evaluate the degree of collaboration in the task, ranging from level 0, which indicates collaborative activities having a negative impact on the goal of the learning exercise, to level 3, which indicates that the game requires (or strongly encourages) learners to collaborate most of the time.

Drawing from social capital theory (Nahapiet & Ghoshal, 1998), we also include in our rubric a structure dimension, a cognitive dimension, and a relational dimension to measure social interactivity in MMORPGs. The structural dimension of social capital refers to the structured embeddedness of a social system (Nahapiet & Ghoshal). It can be measured by the interconnectivity among the players in a game. A highly interconnected game allows any players to connect to other players all the time. In addition, communication among players should be ubiquitous.

Another dimension in social interactivity is the cognitive dimension. This dimension is concerned with shared meaning of the players, which requires shared representation and a common language and knowledge base (Nahapiet & Ghoshal, 1998). A zero score refers to the situation where players do not understand each other to the point that players are confused about each others' meaning. A low score means that the players do not have any shared representation nor a common language. It is possible that players share their understanding and interpretations before they play the game. We still consider that they have shared representations. However, we give higher ratings to educational games only if shared representations are generated and cultivated through game design; in order words, good educational games should be designed to promote shared representations.

Finally, relational evidences are defined as any actions among players, which show trust, approval of each other, and norms and identification seen in the community (Nahapiet & Ghoshal, 1998). A zero score refers to poor relationship among players to the point that they distrust and do not want to work with each other. A low relational score means that the players have not so good relationship, but they may still be able to work with each other. It is possible that players already have had a good relationship before they play the game. We still consider that the game support this dimension. However, we give higher ratings to the educational game only if the relational evidences are generated from the game.

14.5   The Present Study

In this section, we summarize the results of the studies conducted at the end of the second and third cycles of our DBR (Fig. 14.1) to investigate the effect of *McLarin's Adventures* on student motivation (cf. Eseryel, Miller, Ge, Ifenthaler, Law, & Guo, 2010; Miller, Eseryel, & Ge, 2009) and complex problem-solving development (cf. Eseryel, Ge, Ifenthaler, & Law, 2011). We also present the evaluation of the design of *McLarin's Adventures* MMORPG based on the assessment framework described in Sect. 4 to demonstrate the utility of the Interactivity[3] game design model (Fig. 14.2) in guiding the design of educational MMORPGs when coupled with its assessment framework.

14.5.1   Participants and Procedure

A rural high school in the Midwest of the United States was used as a test bed for the experimental studies conducted at the end of the second and third cycles of our DBR (Fig. 14.1) to investigate the effect of *McLarin's Adventures* on motivation and complex problem solving.

Three hundred and forty-nine ninth-grade students participated in the first study conducted at the end of the 2nd year design cycle. These 349 students were randomly assigned to one of the 19 classes; of which ten of them were then randomly assigned to treatment (game group) condition and nine classes were randomly assigned to control (no game group) condition. The data reported here were from 251 students, from whom we received both parental consent and student assent forms. Of these 251 students, 156 were in the experimental group and 95 were in the control group. There were 47% males and 53% females.

The study at the end of the third year design cycle was conducted with the incoming ninth grade students during the following school year at the same high school. Three hundred and forty-three ninth grade students participated. These students were randomly placed into 16 classes. Out of these 16 classes, eight were randomly assigned to treatment (game group) condition and eight were randomly assigned to control (modeling group) condition. The data reported here were from 280 students, from whom we received both parental consent and student assent forms. Out of these 280 students, 137 (48.9%) were in the treatment group and 143 (51.1%) were in the control group.

The data collection procedures in both studies were the same. Following the pretest data collection, students in the experimental group played the *McLarin's Adventures* MMOG 2 days a week for 16 weeks during the 50-min class period. At the same time, the students in the control group participated in a class that was specifically developed to facilitate students' interdisciplinary STEM learning and improving their leadership, management, and decision-making skills. In this sense, both the game-based learning environment and the traditional class curriculum attempted to facilitate, in their own ways, complex problem-solving skill acquisition in an interdisciplinary STEM curriculum. At the end of the 16 weeks students in both groups took the posttest, which was the same as the pretest.

In addition to these studies, at the end of second and third design cycles, a team of game researchers, graduate students who specialize in educational games, and students played with the *McLarin's Adventures* game and evaluated it on the assessment rubric presented in Sect. 4.

14.5.2 Data Analysis Framework

In order to track the changes in students' developments in their *complex problem-solving* skills as a result of gameplay, each student's *structural knowledge* of the complex problem-solving domain was elicited in both pretest and posttest by asking the student to build a causal representation of the problem-solving domain that served as the situated context in the *McLarin's Adventures* MMORPG (Eseryel et al., 2011).

Each student's annotated causal representation was compared with the expert causal representation on six measures as suggested by the Highly Integrated Model Assessment Technology and Tools (HIMATT) (Ifenthaler, 2010; Pirnay-Dummer & Ifenthaler, 2010): (a) *surface matching*, which compares the number of propositions (concept—relation—concept) within two causal representation; (b) *graphical matching*, which compares the diameters of the spanning trees of the causal representation, which is an indicator for the range or complexity of conceptual knowledge; (c) *structural matching*, which compares the complete structures of two causal representations (expert and subject) without regard to their content; (d) *gamma matching*, describes the quotient of terms per concept within a causal representation; (e) *concept matching*, which compares the sets of concepts within a causal representation to determine the use of terms (semantic correctness); and (f) *propositional matching*, which compares only fully semantically identical propositions between two causal representation.

In order to measure student motivation, during pretest and posttest in both studies, all students were provided with a packet of motivation instruments related to self-determination theory (Ryan & Deci, 2000). The instruments were retrieved

from the Basic Needs Satisfaction Survey (http://www.psych.rochester.edu/SDT/
measures/needs.html):

- The Autonomy subscale (seven items)
- The Competence subscale (six items)
- The Relatedness subscale (eight items)

Cronbach alphas for our instruments were: autonomy = 0.57; competence = 0.47;
pretest relatedness = 0.74; and relatedness = 0.82.

14.6   Results

Tables 14.4 and 14.5 present the evaluation of the *McLarin's Adventures* after the
second and third design cycles. After the second design cycle, out of the three interactivity dimensions, *McLarin's Adventures* scored relatively well in the narrative
interactivity dimension with a good storyline and a clear mission, although the
subtasks and feedback were not well designed. The scores on the roles, scenario
operations, resources, and feedback measures were also low. In addition, the game
scored quite poorly in the interface interactivity dimension, where navigation and
visualization have relatively poor scores. The score for social interactivity dimension was also low, where the tasks in the game were not collaborative in nature.
Despite the fact that the backstory announced that each player would be hired in
different roles, the avatars of the students were still the same and did not reflect any
differences in their roles or in appearance. All subtasks during the game still had to
be completed individually by each player. The players could use the chat function
in the game to communicate with each other and share strategies but that distracted
the players from the game and added to their cognitive load.

Upon the improvements in the overall game design on the third design cycle, the
evaluation scores after the third design cycle also improved. In general, interface
and narrative interactivity scores visibly improved. The evaluation results suggested
that *McLarin's Adventures* provided an exciting backstory, a clear mission, clearly
defined roles, and a lot of resources, which provided initial motivation. The interface also fitted nicely with the backstory of a scientific fiction. However, the navigation supports and visualization supports still needed improvement to eliminate
distractions.

Despite the improvement in the social interactivity scores, the score for collaborative task was very low. The backstory of the game called for players to assume
different scientist roles to complete the tasks while playing the game as teams of
four. Each player was able to customize their avatars based on the roles they
assumed. However, the tasks in the game still required to be completed by each
player individually. In addition, it was hard for each team member to locate other
team members in the game. Although a map function was provided, it was not easy
to use. However, some tasks were very difficult to understand and these caused the
players to seek other players to help them figure out the tasks and the functionalities

Table 14.4 Aggregated evaluation results of *McLarin's Adventures* after second design cycle

Elements/rating	Comments
Interface interactivity	
Navigation 1.14 pts	The navigational cues in the game were rather weak. There was some clipping, which might distract the player from taking the game seriously. For example, avatar could walk through objects that should be solid. Also, the environment is a vast space. It is hard for the players to determine which way to go, etc. Some buildings, roads, trees, etc. could be placed appropriately to help situate the player and give them additional navigational cues
Visualization 1 pts	There was a lack of visualization of data in the game. Players had to dig deep in menus to find their health status. Overall, the interface did not invoke a sense of hierarchy, curiosity, not do they emphasize any objects over others
Interface metaphor 2 pts	The interface of the game is appropriate given the context of the game. However, the user interface requires some time for the players to figure out where all the tools are. It can be improved to make it more visible to the students
Narrative interactivity	
Mission 3 pts	The mission of the game was clearly defined
Backstory 3 pts	The backstory set the tone of the game play; it was motivating and allowed the players to naturally enter the game environment
Roles 1 pts	The players took on the role of researchers and needed to conduct a series of experiments on the island to examine the environment for survival. However, in the game environment, all the player avatars were the same and did not help distinguish different roles players assumed
Scenario operations 1 pt	Although the tasks required target skills to be accomplished, the individual tasks did not contribute to the overall goal. The individual tasks also did not have strong casual or logical relationships among themselves that could help the player to build a mental model required to solve the overall complex task (mission) in the game
Resources 1 pts	Formula and charts of mathematical calculations were available in players' backpacks. However, there was no cue to help players relate the problem they encountered in the game to those resources
Feedback 1 pt	The game environment did not provide immediate or long-term feedback to players' operation, which usually confused and frustrated players. The only feedback they could get was at portals when they finished a task. A nonplaying agent appeared and gave a summary and then assigned a new task when players finished a task
Social interactivity	
Collaborative task 0 pts	Although *McLarin's Adventures* is claimed to be an MMORPG, collaborative activities could not be found in the game
Structural dimension 1 pt	Finding other players in *McLarin's Adventures* was not supported. There was chat function for players to communicate but it is not sufficient and distracted players from the game and contributed to added cognitive load
Cognitive dimension 1 pt	During the problem-solving tasks, the players could understand each other easily, but there was no evidence that the shared representation or meaning was generated from the game
Relational dimension 1 pt	The relationships among players were built up unintentionally. The first task was designed poorly, so it took the players a lot of effort to find the answer. As a result of the collaboration, trust and respect were built

Table 14.5 Aggregated evaluation results of *McLarin's Adventures* after third design cycle

Elements/rating	Comments
Interface interactivity	
Navigation: 2 pts	The navigational cues in the game were mostly OK supported by a map. Objects placed in the environment gave a sense of situatedness to the players so they could figure out which direction they should be moving. However, the map function could be improved. It is not easy to read the map to figure out where everything is
Visualization: 2 pts	The game environment provided appropriate visualization tools. However, it was not always easy to figure out where they are. So, the user interface could be improved to make it easier for the players to find visualization tools
Interface metaphor: 3 pts	The interface metaphor fitted nicely with the story. Most of the pages have a consistent high tech science fiction feel
Narrative Interactivity	
Mission: 3 pts	The mission was clearly defined and it was motivating for the players
Backstory: 3 pts	The backstory set the tone of the game play allowing the players to be immersed into the game plot smoothly
Roles: 2 pts	The players took on the role of researchers and needed to conduct a series of experiments on the island to examine the environment for survival. Although the game provided four different avatars for the players to choose from, no avatar possessed distinctive ability than others to fit specific tasks
Scenario operations: 2 pt	Although the tasks required target skills to be accomplished, the individual tasks did not contribute to the overall goal. The individual tasks also did not have strong casual or logical relationships among themselves that could help the player to build a mental model required to solve the overall complex task (mission) in the game
Resources: 2 pts	A detailed resource guide is included in the game. However, it is not apparent to the players when they can consult the resource guide to help with their game play. Automated feedback from the game could prompt players to consult the resource guide when they fail to complete specific activities
Feedback: 1 pt	Although the players were collecting points as a result of their game play, it was not apparent when and how they were collecting these points. Also, the point structure was not tied to their winning or losing the game. It was more of a counter that did not mean much in the context of game play. The game environment did not provide immediate or long-term feedback to players' operation, which usually confused and frustrated players. The only feedback they could get was at portals when they finish a task. A nonplaying agent appeared and gave a summary and then assigned a new task when players finished a task
Social interactivity	
Collaborative task: 1 pt	Each player is expected to complete each task separately even though players play in teams of 4 comprising different scientist roles
Structural dimension: 2 pts	Finding other players in *McLarin's Adventures* was supported by the map but it was not easy to use. Chat and voice chat allow players to communicate seamlessly

(continued)

Table 14.5 (continued)

Elements/rating	Comments
Cognitive dimension: 2 pts	The game tasks were not set up to promote shared representation or meaning to be generated among game players who play in the same team
Relational dimension: 2 pts	The game was not designed to support relationships among players. However, the unclarity surrounding some of the tasks and interface features led to some players communicate to figure them out together. However, this communication happened outside the game, where students sought each other face to face in the classroom. As a result, a sense of community, collaboration, and trust was built among players. It would be great if an external virtual learning community is designed to support players share tips and experiences related to the game

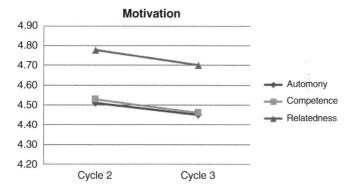

Fig. 14.4 Comparison of student motivation between second and third cycles

within the game. In general, this led players to develop trust and respect during the game. Voice chat function made it easier for players to communicate during game play but players also relied on face-to-face interactions in the class to seek out help from other players in the class during game play.

Figure 14.4 depicts the comparison results of student motivation after the second and third design cycles. Students' motivation was measured with the self-determination constructs: autonomy, competence, and relatedness. Although the results showed a small decrease in motivation, the differences in motivation between cycle 2 and cycle 3 were insignificant ($p > 0.05$).

On the other hand, significant improvement was observed in students' complex problem-solving skills from the second design cycle to the third design cycle ($p < 0.01$; effect size for the gamma dimension is $d > 0.05$; all other dimensions $d > 0.20$). Figure 14.5 depicts the comparison of the results along the six dimensions of the *structural knowledge* variable that measured their conceptualization of the complex problem in which the game was situated. This shows that the improvements made in interface and navigation interactivity were effective in promoting students' complex problem-solving skills despite the lack of major improvements in

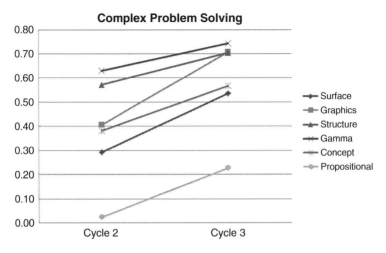

Fig. 14.5 Comparison of student complex problem-solving skills between second and third cycles

the social interactivity dimension. However, further studies (see Eseryel et al., 2011) spoke to the importance of the social interactivity dimension by including tasks in the game narrative that are complex enough to require a teams of players, each of whom possess a different skill set. Dynamic modeling feedback was also identified as having crucial importance in helping player teams to build shared mental models of the complex problem domain in the game narrative by scaffolding teams' cognitive co-regulation (Eseryel et al., 2011).

14.7   Conclusion and Future Directions

In this chapter, we presented the Interactivity[3] model for designing educational MMORPGs in addition to its assessment framework. This design and assessment model resulted from a 4-year DBR study. Interactivity[3] model highlights three levels of interactivity that were found to be crucial for the educational MMORPGs to promote student motivation and complex problem-solving skills: (1) interface interactivity; (2) narrative interactivity; and (3) social interactivity. This design model is not meant to provide exhaustive guidelines in the design processes. Rather, it serves as a heuristic model that is intended, together with its accompanying assessment framework, to support educational game designers to connect the three levels of interactivity and direct their attention to the most important points when designing each level of interaction.

Although commercial game literature emphasized the importance of interactivity in game design it is not highlighted and integrated in educational game design. Drawing from our findings and from the commercial game literature (e.g., Fullerton et al., 2004; Salen & Zimmerman, 2004), we argue that interactivity is one of the most salient characteristics to which educational game designers should attend, especially in the context of educational MMORPGs.

In this chapter, in order to illustrate the utility of the Interactivity³ design and assessment framework, we also presented the findings from the second and third design cycles of our design-based research study that guided the design of an educational MMORPG called *McLarin's Adventures*. The findings of this study confirmed the importance of all three levels of interactivity in promoting student motivation and complex problem-solving skill development. When the interface and narrative interactivity scores were improved during third design cycle, the students' complex problem-solving skills also showed improvements.

However, after the third design cycle, there was still room for improvement, especially in the social interactivity dimension. The detailed findings of the experimental studies after the third design cycle (cf. Eseryel et al., 2011; Eseryel, Miller, et al., 2010; Miller et al., 2009) confirmed that student motivation and complex problem-solving skill development was still not at the desired level when compared with the control group. This highlighted the importance of social interactivity dimension and the need for the interface and narrative interactivity to seamlessly support the social interactivity during game play. Indeed, one of the affordances of MMORPGs that make it more unique when compared with other types of games is its ability to support multiple players to collaborate together in a situated learning environment to solve complex problems situated in the game narrative. In the *McLarin's Adventures* MMORPG, even though the mission of the game constituted a complex problem, it was divided into arbitrary subtasks that represented simpler problems. In addition, the backstory of the game called for players to assume different roles and play as a team of four scientists. However, each player is expected to complete the game individually and received individual scores. This is identified as one of the main reasons contributing to less-than desired improvements in student motivation and complex problem-solving skills. In the fourth design cycle, the improvements in the game design included redesigning subtasks to cultivate social interactivity with interface and narrative interactivity enabling social interactivity ubiquitously.

In commercial MMORPGs, we see that when the social interactivity is intentionally cultivated in the game design, it usually contributes to the popularity of the game (and its market share). *Star Wars Galaxies* is one of these highly popular commercial games. Upon their analysis of *Star Wars Galaxies*, Ducheneaut and Moore (2004) identified three major design instruments that educational game designers can use to encourage or even force social interaction: (1) difficult quests, (2) complex ecology of professions, and (3) exchange of goods or ideas. Difficult quests are small missions that are impossible for one individual player to achieve. Like in the real world, the complex ecology of players' professions provides diversity and the need for collaboration in MMORPG. In Star Wars Galaxies, not all players are warriors. Instead, many of them chose to take professions such as entertainers or healers. The difference of profession determines the difference of the skillset that a player has. Everyone has his or her strength and weakness. Therefore, they have to work together to take advantage of others' strengths and to cover their weaknesses. In the case of an educational MMORPG, players can chose to be a mathematician,

D. Eseryel et al.

a geologist, or a physicist according to their interest in real life. Then, the game design should require for them to team up and bring their individual expertise on the table to solve complex problems collaboratively. The difference of profession results in the differences of resources that the players own. Hence, the exchange of resources is made inevitable, which provides players valuable opportunities to communicate and to socialize. Designated places such as a bazaar or a market where players can meet, talk, and trade would be helpful devices in enhancing social interaction. In an educational MMORPG, in addition to trading goods, players can also exchange information such as the data collected by scientists from different disciplines. Places that can host such communications can be a lab or even a tent in the wild.

This leads to another requirement for game designers: To extend their game design by designing and cultivating online learning communities, in which players could come together and share their experiences. In successful commercial games, such as *World of Warcraft*, we see the power of such virtual learning communities that exist outside the game environment. Educational game designers should consider designing and cultivating such virtual learning communities in addition to the game environment to enhance learners' engagement and complex problem-solving skill development.

Despite the popularity of educational games in today's discourse, its research base is still at its infancy. We do not know how to design effective educational games, especially MMORPGs, so that they can fulfill their unique affordances as situated learning environments to support higher order thinking and problem-solving skill acquisition while maintaining high student motivation. To facilitate the design of educational games, validated assessment models are crucial. However, there are very few game evaluation models available for the educational game designers. Sweetser and Wyeth (2005) focused on enjoyment and developed an evaluation model to evaluate players' enjoyment in games. Nevertheless, in educational games, enjoyment is only part of the picture. We need to ensure learning occur among the players. Drawing from ARCS motivational model, Gagne's events of instruction, and Piaget's ideas of schema, Gunter, Kenny, and Vick (2008) developed a more comprehensive game evaluation model for educational game. Nevertheless, it is a generic game evaluation model, which does not explicitly account for salient features in MMORPGs, such as the narrative of the game and the interactions among the players. The interactivity[3] design and assessment framework presented in this chapter is intended to bridge this gap in the literature. It is our sincere hope that the Interactivity[3] design and assessment framework would be beneficial to educational game designers and that other educational researchers would build on it with further empirical support.

Acknowledgments *McLarin's Adventures* MMOG is developed by the K20 Center at the University of Oklahoma through a Star Schools research grant from the U.S. Department of Education. It is with gratitude that the authors thank the K20 Center game development team for allowing our research team to use the game, hence, contributing advancement of research on games and learning.

References

Amory, A. (2007). Game object model version II: A theoretical framework for educational game development. *Educational Technology Research and Development, 55*(1), 51–77.

Azevedo, R., Winters, F. I., & Moos, D. C. (2004). Can students collaboratively use hypermedia to learn about science? The dynamics of self- and other-regulatory processes in an ecology classroom. *Journal of Educational Computing Research, 31*(3), 215–245.

Barab, S., Squire, K., & Dueber, W. (2000). A co-evolutional model for supporting the emergence of authenticity. *Educational Technology Research and Development, 48*(2), 37–62.

Blumberg, F. C., Rosenthal, S. F., & Randall, J. D. (2008). Impasse-driven learning in the context of video games. *Computers in Human Behavior, 24*(4), 1530–1541.

Brown, J., Collins, A., & Duguid, P. (1989). Situated cognition and the culture of learning. *Educational Researcher, 18*(1), 32–42.

Chen, H., Dun, H. B. L., Phuah, P. S. K., & Lam, D. Z. Y. (2006). Enjoyment or engagement? Role of social interaction in playing massively multiplayer online role-playing games (MMORPGS). In R. Harper, M. Rauterberg, M. Combetto (Eds.), *Entertainment computing—ICEC 2006: 5th international conference* (pp. 262–267). Cambridge, UK.

Cordova, D. I., & Lepper, M. R. (1996). Intrinsic motivation and the process of learning: Beneficial effects of contextualization, personalization, and choice. *Journal of Educational Psychology, 88*(4), 715–730.

Crawford, C. (1984). *The art of computer game design*. Berkley, CA: McGraw–Hill.

Crawford, C. (2010). Interactivity, process, and algorithm. In R. van Eck (Ed.), *Interdisciplinary models and tools for serious games: Emerging concepts and future directions* (pp. 333–346). Hershey, PA: IGI Global.

Csikszentmihalyi, M. (1991). *Flow: The psychology of optimal experience*. New York, NY: Harper Perennial.

Dansky, R. (2007). Introduction to game narrative. In C. Bateman (Ed.), *Game writing: Narrative sills for videogames*. Boston, MA: Charles River Media.

Dempsey, J. V., Haynes, L. L., Lucassen, B. A., & Casey, M. S. (2002). Forty simple computer games and what they could mean to educators. *Simulation & Gaming, 33*(2), 157–168.

Dickey, M. (2007). Game design and learning: A conjectural analysis of how massively multiple online role-playing games (MMORPGs) foster intrinsic motivation. *Educational Technology Research and Development, 55*(3), 253–273.

Dochy, F., Segers, M., Van den Bossche, P., & Gijbels, D. (2003). Effects of problem-based learning: A meta-analysis. *Learning and Instruction, 13*(5), 533–568.

Dondlinger, M. J., & Lunce, L. M. (2009). Wayfinding affordances are essential for effective use of virtual environment for instructional applications. *MERLOT Journal of Online Learning and Teaching, 5*(3), Retrieved February 19, 2011, from http://jolt.merlot.org/vol5no3/lunce_0909.htm

Dörner, D. (1987). On the difficulties people have in dealing with complexity. In K. Duncan, J. Rasmussen, & L. Leplat (Eds.), *New technology and human error* (pp. 97–109). Chichester, NY: Wiley.

Ducheneaut, N., & Moore, R. J. (2004). The social side of gaming: A study of interaction patterns in a massively multiplayer online game. In J. Herbsleb & G. Olson (Eds.), *Proceedings of the 2004 ACM conference on computer supported cooperative work* (pp. 360–369). New York: The Association for Computer Machinery.

Eifferman, R. R. (1974). It's child's play. In L. M. Shears & E. M. Bower (Eds.), *Games in education and development* (pp. 75–102). Springfield, IL: Charles C. Thomas.

Eseryel, D., & Ge, X. (2010). *Designing effective game-based learning environments: Implications for design research*. Paper presented at "Educational Design Research: Local Change, Global Impact": A Special Conference to Honor Professor Thomas C. Reeves Upon his Retirement from the University of Georgia, March 26–27, 2010.

Eseryel, D., Ge, X., Ifenthaler, D., & Law, V. (2011). Dynamic modeling as a cognitive regulation scaffold for complex problem solving skill acquisition in an educational massively multiplayer online game environment. *Journal of Educational Computing Research, 45*(3), 265–287.

Eseryel, D., Ifenthaler, D., & Ge, X. (2010). Alternative assessment strategies for game-based learning environments. In D. Ifenthaler, K. PIsaias, D. G. Sampson, & J. M. Spector (Eds.), *Multiple perspectives on problem solving and learning in the digital age* (pp. 159–178). New York, NY: Springer.

Eseryel, D., Miller, R. B., Ge, X., Ifenthaler, D., Law, V., & Guo, Y. (2010). *A longitudinal study on the impact of digital game-based learning on complex problem solving skill acquisition and student motivation.* Paper presented at the 2010 Annual Convention of Association for Educational Communications and Technology, Anaheim, CA, October 26–30, 2010.

Feltovich, P. J., Spiro, R. J., Coulson, R. L., & Feltovich, J. (1996). Collaboration within and among minds: Mastering complexity, individually and in groups. In T. D. Koschmann (Ed.), *CSCL: Theory and practice of an emerging paradigm* (pp. 25–44). New York, NY: Lawrence Erlbaum.

Fullerton, T., Swain, C., & Hoffman, S. (2004). *Game design workshop: Designing, prototyping, and playtesting games.* San Francisco, CA: CMP Books.

Ge, X., Thomas, M., & Greene, B. (2006). Technology-rich ethnography for examining the transition to authentic problem-solving in a high school computer programming class. *Journal of Educational Computing Research, 34*(4), 319–352.

Gee, J. P. (2003). *What video games have to teach us about learning and literacy.* New York: Palgrave-Macmillan.

Gee, J. P. (2007). Games and learning: Issues, perils, and potentials. In J. P. Gee (Ed.), *Good video games and good learning: Collected essays on video games, learning, and literacy* (pp. 129–174). New York: Palgrave/MacMillan.

Granovetter, M. (1985). Economic action and social structure: The problem of embeddedness. *The American Journal of Sociology, 91*(3), 481.

Gredler, M. E. (2004). Games and simulations and their relationship to learning. In D. Jonassen (Ed.), *The handbook of research on educational communications and technology* (2nd ed., pp. 571–581). Bloomington, IN: AECT.

Greenfield, P. M. (2010). Video games. In R. van Eck (Ed.), *Gaming and cognition: Theories and practice from the learning sciences* (pp. 1–21). Hershey, PA: IGI Global.

Gunter, G. A., Kenny, R. F., & Vick, E. H. (2008). Taking educational games seriously: Using the retain model to design endogenous fantasy into standalone educational games. *Educational Technology Research and Development, 56*(5), 619–641.

Ifenthaler, D. (2010). Relational, structural, and semantic analysis of graphical representations and concept maps. *Educational Technology Research and Development, 58*(1), 81–97.

Jonassen, D. H. (1997). Instructional design models for well-structured and III-structured problem-solving learning outcomes. *Educational Technology Research and Development, 45*(1), 65–94.

Kagan, J. (1978). *The growth of the child.* New York, NY: Norton.

Komerska, R., & Ware, C. (2003). Haptic-geozui3D: Exploring the use of haptics in auv path planning. *Proceedings 13th international symposium on unmanned Untethered Submersible Technology UUST'03*, Durham, NH.

Konzack, L. (2002). Computer game criticism: A method for computer game analysis. In F. Mayra (Ed.), *CGDC conference proceedings* (pp. 89–100). Tampere, Finland: Tampere University Press.

Lave, J., & Wenger, E. (1991). *Situated learning: Legitimate peripheral participation.* Cambridge, UK: Cambridge University Press.

Liarokapis, F. (2006). An exploration from virtual to augmented reality gaming. *Simulation & Gaming, 37*(4), 507–533. Mahwah, NJ: Lawrence Erlbaum.

Malone, T. W. (1980). *What makes things fun to learn? A study of intrinsically motivating computer games* (Cognitive and Instructional Sciences Series CIS-7 (SSL-80-11)). Palo Alto, CA: XEROX Palo Alto Research Center.

Miller, R. B., Eseryel, D., & Ge, X. (2009) *Surviving in Space: The effects of a massively multiplayer online game (MMOG) on students' motivation.* Paper presented at the Annual Meeting of the American Educational Research Association, San Diego, April 13–17, 2009.

Nahapiet, J., & Ghoshal, S. (1998). Social capital, intellectual capital, and the organizational advantage. *Academy of Management Review, 23*(2), 242–266.

Parker, L., & Lepper, M. (1992). Effects of fantasy contexts on children's learning and motivation: Making learning more fun. *Journal of Personality and Social Psychology, 62*(4), 625–633.

Pirnay-Dummer, P., & Ifenthaler, D. (2010). Automated knowledge visualization and assessment. In D. Ifenthaler, P. Pirnay-Dummer, & N. M. Seel (Eds.), *Computer-based diagnostics and systematic analysis of knowledge* (pp. 77–115). New York: Springer.

Prensky, M. (2006). *Don't bother me mom–I'm learning.* St. Paul, MN: Paragon House.

Prensky, M. (2007). *Digital game-based learning.* St. Paul, MN: Paragon House.

Rieber, L. (1996). Seriously considering play: Designing interactive learning environments based on the blending of microworlds, simulations, and games. *Educational Technology Research and Development, 44*(2), 43–58.

Ryan, R., & Deci, E. (2000). Self-determination theory and the facilitation of intrinsic motivation, social development, and well-being. *American Psychologist, 55*(1), 68–78.

Salen, K., & Zimmerman, E. (2004). *Rules of play.* Cambridge, MA: MIT.

Salen, K., & Zimmerman, E. (2005). Game design and meaningful play. In J. Raessens & J. H. Goldstein (Eds.), *Handbook of computer game studies.* Cambridge, MA: MIT.

Schank, R. C., Berman, T. R., & Macpherson, K. A. (1999). Learning by doing. In C. M. Reigeluth (Ed.), *Instructional-design theories and models: A new paradigm of instructional theory* (Vol. II, pp. 161–181). Mahwah: Lawrence Erlbaum.

Shaffer, D. W. (2006). *How computer games help children learn?* New York: Palgrave Macmillan.

Steinkuehler, C. A. (2004). Learning in massively multiplayer online games. In Y. B. Kafai, W. A. Sandoval, & N. Enyedy (Eds.), *Proceedings of the 6th international conference on learning sciences* (pp. 521–528).

Sweetser, P., & Wyeth, P. (2005). GameFlow: A model for evaluating player enjoyment in games. *ACM Computers in Entertainment, 3*(3), 1–24.

Uribe, D., Klein, J., & Sullivan, H. (2003). The effect of computer-mediated collaborative learning on solving Ill-defined problems. *Educational Technology Research and Development, 51*(1), 5–19.

van Eck, R. (2006). Building intelligent learning games. In D. Gibson, C. Aldrich, & M. Prensky (Eds.), *Games and simulations in online learning: Research and development frameworks.* Hershey, PA: Idea Group.

van Eck, R. (2007). Six ideas in search of a discipline. In B. Shelton & D. Wiley (Eds.), *The educational design and use of computer simulation games.* Boston, MA: Sense.

Wideman, H., Owston, R., Brown, C., Kushniruk, A., Ho, F., & Pitts, K. (2007). Unpacking the potential of educational gaming: A new tool for gaming research. *Simulation & Gaming, 38*(1), 10.

Wilson, K., Bedwell, W., Lazzara, E., Salas, E., Burke, C., Estock, J., & Conkey, C. (2009). Relationships between game attributes and learning outcomes. *Simulation & Gaming, 40*(2), 217–266.

Wilson, S., & Williams, L. (2010). Serious games for the classroom: A case study of designing and developing a massive multiplayer online game. In R. van Eck (Ed.), *Interdisciplinary models and tools for serious games: Emerging concepts and future directions* (pp. 264–287). Hershey, PA: IGI Global.

Yanuzzi, T. J., & Behrenshausen, B. G. (2010). Serious games for transformative learning: A communication perspective on the radical binarisation of everyday life. In R. van Eck (Ed.), *Interdisciplinary models and tools for serious games: Emerging concepts and future directions* (pp. 74–102). Hershey, PA: IGI Global.

Yee, N. (2006). Motivations for play in online games. *Cyberpsychology & Behavior, 9*(6), 772–775.

Chapter 15
Measurement Principles for Gaming

Kathleen Scalise and Mark Wilson

15.1 Introduction: The Psychometrics of Games

Game developers know how to make great games. Over the last few decades, gaming has become one of the main forms of entertainment media worldwide, comparable in some aspects to the film and music industries (Kirriemuir, 2002). Recent market research reports total consumer spending on game content just in the USA alone exceeded $15.4 billion annually (The NPD Group, 2010). But what makes a game great, and in particular, what makes a successful gamer?

Here we explore the psychometrics of games and begin to consider how we can know what gamers accomplish in their gaming efforts. Especially of interest for education may be the psychometrics of "serious games" or games constructed for complex problem-solving processes, situated cognition, and collaborative learning in a digital environment (Gee, 2003; Squire, 2006). Numerous researchers have linked game strategies with successful learning in such settings (Lieberman, 2006; Shute, Ventura, Bauer, & Zapata-Rivera, 2009). Given the high interest in games generally, whether online or console-based, educators for some time have anticipated that serious games, virtual simulations, and other interactive computer activities can also supply credible assessment evidence to inform teaching and learning (de Freitas, 2006; Gredler, 1996; Stenhouse, 1986).

However, realizing high-quality assessment in game-based learning can be a challenge both for game developers and for those trying to use the results of serious games to make inferences about learners. Researchers have described the lack of information on assessments in gaming, both in theoretical understanding and in

K. Scalise (✉)
Educational Methodology, Policy and Leadership, University of Oregon,
4716 Bennett Valley Road, Santa Rosa, CA 95404, USA
e-mail: kscalise@uoregon.edu

M. Wilson
Mark Wilson, Professor, University of California, Berkeley

D. Ifenthaler et al. (eds.), *Assessment in Game-Based Learning: Foundations,*
Innovations, and Perspectives, DOI 10.1007/978-1-4614-3546-4_15,
© Springer Science+Business Media New York 2012

research studies (de Freitas & Oliver, 2006; Vogel et al., 2006). In this chapter we explore how game developers can embed strong evidentiary practices into games through robust measurement principles, using the UC Berkeley Evaluation and Assessment Research (BEAR) Assessment System, abbreviated as BAS (Wilson, 2005; Wilson & Sloane, 2000), which describes techniques used in the construction of high-quality assessments generally across many venues, but applied here in gaming.

As in other assessment contexts, the basics of good measurement practices can help to make inferences more accurate and useful. To illustrate, here, we briefly consider four examples of gaming products. The products are examined for the soundness of their assessment strategies according to the BAS framework, which describes four principles and offers four "building blocks" to design good assessments and engage in formal measurement practices.

We begin with a description of the four principles and then consider each game example in light of one of the principles. Each was selected as an exemplary model illustrating aspects of one principle (Scalise et al., 2007). Developers of gaming software can use this information to consider assessment approaches in light of good measurement practice, to better understand the range of decision-making approaches available to technology platforms, and to optimize some of these strategies in regard to drawing inferences about what students know and can do. Also, those involved in the selection of educational gaming products for use in teaching and learning can employ examples such as these to help evaluate the quality of assessment data that is produced from different gaming products and how that data is used, either within the product or subsequently by teachers and students.

15.1.1 Principles of Assessment

An "embedded assessment" system designed and used in assessment development at the University of California, Berkeley, called the BEAR Assessment System or BAS (Wilson, 2005), is described in the following section. It is based on four principles and consists of easy-to-use tools for generating solid diagnostic information and feedback. Approaches can be embedded into many online formats, including serious games. The system was named for its origin at the BEAR Center and is a comprehensive, integrated system for assessing, interpreting, monitoring, and responding to student performance. It provides a set of tools for instructors and students to:

• Reliably assess performance on central concepts and skills
• Set standards of performance
• Validly track progress over the year on central concepts
• Provide mechanisms for feedback and follow-up

The term *embedded assessment* means just what it says: Activities are "embedded," or become part of, learning activities. Instructors do embedded assessment all the time: a homework assignment, a laboratory procedure, a classroom discussion, an essay. Any of these and many more can be considered embedded assessment activities if a student produces something that can be rated, or observed and assessed in some manner. The difference between these examples and what we discuss here as more formal embedded assessment is that the latter calls for attention to task design and formal "calibration" of assessment tasks in relationship to a framework that describes the learning to take place. The framework is used to generate interpretable, valid, and reliable diagnostic information.

Embedded assessment is desirable because when a task is also a learning activity, it does not take time away from instruction, *and* the number of tasks can be increased to improve measurement, diagnostics, and accountability (Linn & Baker, 1996).

The potential usefulness of embedded assessments can be greatly enhanced when the framework on which they are based is consistent with that for the more formal assessments used in accountability assessments, such as campus, school district, or state assessments. This potentially enhances the value of formal assessments (for a discussion of this point, under the topic of "assessment nets," see Wilson & Adams, 1995).

Three broad elements on which every assessment should rest are described by the U.S. National Research Council Committee on the Foundations of Assessment and published in their report, *Knowing What Students Know* (National Research Council, 2001). According to the NRC report, an effective assessment design in any mode or media always requires an "Assessment Triangle" of interacting components:

- A model of student cognition and learning in the field of study
- Well-designed and tested assessment questions and tasks, from which observations can be made
- Ways to make inferences about student competence for the particular context of use, based on the observations and mapping back to the model of student cognition and learning

The Assessment Triangle is a model of the essential connections in a coherent and useful assessment system. In this triangle, assessment activities (the observation vertex) must be aligned with the knowledge and cognitive processes (the cognition vertex) through the instructional process, and the scoring and interpretation of student work (the interpretation vertex) must reflect measures of the same knowledge and cognitive processes. Meaningful connections among the three vertices—cognition, observation, and interpretation—are deemed essential for assessment to have an optimal impact on learning.

These elements are of course inextricably linked and reflect similar concerns as addressed in the conception of constructive alignment (Biggs, 1999), regarding the desirability of achieving goodness of fit among learning outcomes, instructional approach, and assessment.

Models of student learning should specify the most important aspects of student achievement to assess, and they provide clues about the types of tasks that will elicit evidence and the types of inferences that can relate observations back to learning models and ideas of cognition. To serve as quality evidence, questions and tasks themselves need to be systematically developed with both the learning model and subsequent inferences in mind, and they need to be tried out and the results of the trials systematically examined. Finally, the inferences provide the "why" of it all—if we don't know what we want to do with the assessment information, then we can't figure out what the student model or the items should be. Of course, context determines many specifics of the assessment.

The four BAS principles relate directly to the Assessment Triangle. The BAS is based on the idea that good assessment addresses the Assessment Triangle through four principles: (1) developmental perspective, (2) a match between instruction and assessment, (3) the generating of quality evidence, and (4) management by instructors to allow appropriate feedback, feed forward, and follow-up.

Whether for gaming or for other purposes, the four BAS principles (Wilson, 2005) that any assessment system arguably must address to be useful in learning settings and to provide diagnostic information are summarized here:

1. Assessments should be based on a developmental perspective of student learning.
2. Assessments should be clearly aligned with the goals of instruction.
3. Assessments must produce valid and reliable evidence of what learners know and can do.
4. Assessment data should provide information that is useful to teachers and students to improve learning outcomes.

Principle 1, a developmental perspective of student learning, means assessing the development of student understanding of particular concepts and skills over time, as opposed to, for instance, making a single measurement at some final or supposedly significant time point. A developmental perspective requires clear definitions of what students are expected to learn and a theoretical framework of how that learning is expected to unfold as the student progresses through the instructional material. Traditional classroom assessment strongly supports a developmental perspective. Here we affirm what is perhaps the obvious: For diagnostic information to be diagnostic, it must be collected in relationship to some set of goals about what is to be learned.

Principle 2, establishing a good match between what is taught and what is assessed, means that the goals of learning and the measurements and inferences made regarding learning should be related. Reports abound of teachers interrupting their regular curricular materials in order to "teach the material" students will encounter on state, national, or other tests. As some researchers have argued (Resnick & Resnick, 1992), "Assessments must be designed so that when teachers do the natural thing—that is, prepare their students to perform well—they will exercise the kinds of abilities and develop the kinds of skill and knowledge that are the real goals of educational reform." Diagnostic assessment approaches that do not match the goals of instruction fail this test.

Principle 3, high-quality evidence, addresses issues of technical quality in assessments. By making inferences about students that are reliable, valid, and supported by evidence, gaming assessment procedures are beginning to gain "currency" in the educational community. Reliability concerns the reproducibility of results, while validity relates to whether an assessment measures what it is intended to measure. To ensure comparability of results across time and context, these issues must be addressed in any serious attempt at developmental assessment systems in gaming products.

Principle 4, the value of assessment data to teachers and students, is also key: Gaming assessment systems that are intended to be diagnostic should provide information and approaches that are useful for improving learning outcomes. Teachers must have the tools and knowledge to use systems efficiently and to explain resulting data effectively and appropriately. Students should also be able to participate in the assessment process, and they should be encouraged to develop essential metacognitive skills that will further the learning process. If teachers and students are to benefit from information on performance, they need a good understanding of what students are expected to learn and of what counts as adequate evidence of student learning. Teachers are then in a better position, and a more central and responsible position, for presenting, explaining, analyzing, and defending their students' performances and outcomes of their instruction. Students are better able to develop their own metacognitive skills and to bring them to bear in the learning process. In addition, even in gaming, assessment procedures should be accessible to teachers to avoid a climate of "black-box" assessment, in which the logic of the assessments and the inferences made are known only to the software developers or others outside the student environment.

A number of other frameworks, such as Evidence-Centered Design (Mislevy, Almond, & Lukas, 2003) and Intelligent Assessment (Bennett, 1990), also employ formal principles of assessment similar to those described here. Such frameworks suggest that generalized assessment principles can be applied across numerous contexts, including games and simulations.

15.1.2 Types of Games

Author Margot McNeil in this volume describes how games, virtual worlds, and other similar technologies that have strong potential for assessment of higher-order thinking and processes seem underutilized. We have made similar findings in the use of simulations, where an extensive literature survey found many technology products that effectively employ interactive simulation formats in the learning materials default to more rote assessment practices (Scalise, Timms, Clark, & Moorjani, 2009). One reason for this may be that developers do not have frameworks that allow them to easily embed strong assessments directly into game structures (Shute, Masduki, & Donmez, 2010; Wilson et al., 2010b). Principles and systems of development therefore are important to provide, in order to realize the potential of assessment in game-based environments.

For the purposes of these examples, a game will be defined according to the Clark, Nelson, Sengupta, and D'Angelo (2009) description: Digital games are "digital models that allow users to make choices that affect the states of those models" having "an overarching set of explicit goals with accompanying systems for measuring progress" and including "subjective opportunities for play and engagement."

Types of games are numerous, of course, but the leading online game category is the high-end massively multiplayer online games (MMOs) or MMOGs (Hariri,

Shirmohammadi, & Reza Pakravan, 2008). These have been suggested as strong candidates for assessment of complex problem-solving, situated cognition, and collaboration in gaming environments (Steinkuehler, 2008; Young, Schrader, & Zheng, 2006). From a technology perspective, researchers have described game traffic for MMOs (Hariri et al., 2008) as:

> Massively multiplayer online role-playing games (MMORPG) such as World of Warcraft are online games in which a large number of players interact with one another in a virtual world. First-person shooters (FPS) games such as "quake" are those MMOs [massively multiplayer online games] that provide large-scale, sometimes team-based combat in real time virtual environment. Real time strategy (RTS) games, [such] as "age of empire" typically combine real-time strategy with a large number of simultaneous army commanders in resource competition. Turn based strategy games (SG) such as Panzer General 3D are games that focus on socialization instead of objective-based game play. In such games two or more participants make their moves sequentially in turns. Massively multiplayer online racing are online versions of racing games, and simulators such as Grand Prix simulate certain aspects of the real world.

Games can also be described more formally, such as in digital game taxonomies (Jantke & Gaudl, 2010), where innovations of interface, artificial intelligence, and so forth are described in a game-specific discourse language. We will not use the detail of such taxonomies here for these examples, but as assessment in gaming matures, taxonomies should be extended as necessary to incorporate principles of assessment. This will be necessary to align learning and assessment.

15.2 Gaming Examples: Principles into Practice

Through four examples, we next take up two questions: How do we know students have learned in educational games? And what do we assess, and how do we assess, students' learning outcomes in a game-based learning environment?

The BAS four principles described above are associated with four measurement "building blocks" or assessment components for game developers to incorporate into their development process. The components help to bring about good practice through the principles and can readily be implemented in games and other technology formats to bring the principles into practice.

Four gaming products will be considered as examples mapped to the principles. This chapter is a first effort to illustrate well-supported practices of each principle within at least a single one gaming context. Multiple examples or examples that show both alignment and misalignment with the principles could also be helpful. Future work could examine a more fully comprehensive review. However this chapter is intended to give game developers interested in practices of strong assessment evidence a way to examine their products. The examples are intended to show how a match can be made between principles and practice within the serious gaming format. Of course, the instances described illustrate only a few ways in which such principles might be well satisfied. The key for developers is to consider what the principles are and *how* they might be addressed with good utility within their gaming practices:

- Case 1: Epistemic Games' *Urban Science*, a game modeled on the professional practices of urban planners intended to inform understanding of ecology and to build self-confidence and presentation skills. It was selected to illustrate the first principle because the expert-novice framework shows one way in which a developmental perspective can be structured. The approach helps to more clearly specify what types of behaviors indicate a beginning, emergent, and more mastery learner in ways that can be reflected throughout the assessment construct.
- Case 2: Cisco's adult-learning game *Aspire*, which teaches computer networking, business, and entrepreneurship skills through a single-user gaming approach, utilizing interactions with the computer. Aspire was selected to illustrate creating a strong match between assessment and instruction. It was created through extensive job task analysis that informed both the assessment game and the associated instructional materials, to establish fit that the important goals of instruction are also what is measured in the serious gaming assessment.
- Case 3: *EverQuest® II* (EQ2), a popular MMORPG from Sony, which will be considered here applied as a social networking assessment. It is an innovative example of using formal measurement models to examine the quality of data collected and to explore the potential utility of drawing on it for inferences about gamers.
- Case 4: Harvard's *River City*, a multi-user virtual environment (MUVE) accessed through a gaming interface, established for middle school scientific inquiry and twenty-first-century skills. It is an example of creating assessments through serious gaming that are designed to be useful for teachers and instructors. Tools and supports for the classroom are part of the design considerations and the research studies related to River City.

15.2.1 Principle 1: Developmental Perspective in Game Assessment. Case: Epistemic Games

Different games attempt to assess different things. Problem-solving and collaboration may be the "construct" or goals of interest to measure (Gee, 2003). Collaboration or assessment in a group setting is also often of interest in games (Wilson et al., 2010a, 2010b). Other goals of measurement may be more discrete, such as using a specific disciplinary tool in context in Quest Atlantis, improving an aspect of evidence discourse in Taiga for a fifth-grade classroom, or comparing two examples of student creativity through their novel work with Spore.

This example considers what could be done with developmental progressions in a serious game such as Epistemic Games' Urban Science (http://epistemicgames. org/eg/category/games/urban-planning/). Epistemic games are so named because

they are intended to help players learn ways of thinking or, in other words, epistemologies. The Urban Science game helps late elementary, middle, and high school
students learn ecological thinking by role-playing as members of an urban planning
firm (Shaffer & Graesser, 2010). The learning environment is modeled on the
professional practices of urban planners. Gamers redesign the city of Madison,
Wisconsin, a northern city in the USA, to learn about ecology. The game developers
hope players begin to view the world through the eyes of a problem-solving urban
planner. They describe how once players finish Urban Science, they don't look at
streets or neighborhoods the same way (Epistemic Games, 2011):

> Players engage in the professional practices of urban planning and learn how to become
> ecological thinkers in the process. They work together to tackle the urban issues that face
> their city, using iPlan, a Geographic Information System (GIS) tool that helps them develop
> a comprehensive plan for their community.

Urban Science has been extended with Land Science, in which players become
interns at a fictitious planning firm. They weigh land use decisions and trade-offs in
ecologically sensitive regions. In the process, they interact with virtual stakeholders.

Epistemic game researchers specifically advocate a developmental framework
for their assessments (Gee & Shaffer, 2010). They describe how learning in any
domain is a complex phenomenon, especially for authentic assessments as in the
goal of their games. They track how a student's decisions and actions are related to
his or her overall development. Thus, the researchers say, assessment "needs to
clearly explain its theory of how the domain being learned works, and how learning
and instruction works best" (p. 8).

Since decisions and actions unfold over time in the games, measurements need
to "show what students can do over time and tell us about the course of their development and how it can be improved…. [They] should tell us about the different paths
that students can take to mastering a domain, and also tell us where any student is
on one of those paths" (p. 8).

Although urban planning is traditionally taught at the university level only, work
in the area can address portions of the educational standards in the USA that involve
understanding systems, order, and organization; considering evolution and equilibrium; and interacting with form and function in natural systems. Epistemic game
developing begins with considering how professional practice is carried on in these
areas and then describes a student model related to an expert-novice approach to
problem-solving in the area. The student model records the student's knowledge
and progress on covering expected material and may also include emotional states
and other learner characteristics.

Epistemic network analysis (ENA) is used to assess how well students can think
and act like professionals during epistemic game play (Shaffer & Graesser, 2010).
ENA is described as built on two key concepts (p. 5):

> (a) that thinking in an ill-formed domain can be characterized by the application of an
> epistemic frame composed of the linkages between skills, knowledge, identity, values, and
> epistemology; and (b) that the development of thinking in an ill-formed domain can be
> quantified, analyzed, and visualized with a dynamic network model of the developing
> epistemic frame. In this sense, ENA provides a computational model of a player's (or a
> mentor's) participation in the culture of a profession—the extent to which a player has

adopted the ways of knowing, being, talking, and acting that characterize a particular community of practice.

This brief example is intended simply to illustrate the principle of having a developmental progression in mind when engaging in assessment for gaming, so we will stop here rather than delving into the more extensive aspects and claims of ENA. Another chapter in this book includes more extensive information on ENA, including how discourse and actions from the epistemic game is coded for the presence of frame elements from the target profession. A standard technique here may involve estimating for any two frame elements A and B the strength of their association computed based on the frequency of their co-occurrence in discourse. In this sense, rule-based methods from expert analysis are combined with statistical techniques.

To summarize the point we are making here, however, the developmental perspective in Urban Science game is a "model of the extent to which an individual has the ways of thinking, talking, and acting that are characteristic of a particular community of practice" (p. 5). In this way, learning goals are defined and assessments are based on a design approach. The relationships identified are designed to serve student needs as they progress through a series of increasingly complex performance levels, lending support to the idea of developing proficiency over time. It makes inferences about a wide range of student knowledge, skills, and abilities in the targeted domain, but does so with a clear idea in mind of the relationships and progressions expected to be seen. This Urban Science game is able to provide a rich, interactive, and personalized learning environment for its students because it is based on a systematic approach to learning and assessment. The conception of students' knowledge, skills, and abilities in the ENA student model can be considered to be one type of developmental trajectory, describing a progression of student learning.

Other approaches to establishing clear developmental progressions in gaming assessment are also available and include Player Modeling and Planning (Drachen, Canossa, & Yannakakis, 2009) and Pedagogical Design Patterns (Weisburgh, 2004).

In each example, the systematic engineering of the assessments is built upon a strong theoretical foundation that clarifies many specifics of what student learning patterns are expected. The products can more clearly say, "What are we looking for?" and "How will we know it when we see it?"

Thus measures are not simply a laundry list of data to be collected, but can be mapped back to relationships expected. These theoretical relationships can then be investigated to show how well the empirical data and patterns in the game support the theoretical beliefs, as will be discussed in the next examples. This sort of assessment engineering, where results can be validated, can greatly strengthen the claims for high-quality assessment evidence and therefore the purposes to which inferences about learning may be put.

15.2.2 Principle 2: Matching Instructional Goals with Assessment in Gaming. Case: Cisco's Aspire

Matching instructional goals with assessment using observations from gaming presents some unique challenges—and some unique opportunities. Part of what the assessment question and task design needs to specifically accomplish is to allow the engagement of the gaming interaction to proceed unimpeded. Games have been linked extensively with strong affective or attitudinal motivation by students—in other words, games have the capacity to engage learners. If assessment information is collected at the same time, much could be gained regarding evidence, assuming that the assessment design does not impede the game design (Klabbers, 2006; Lieberman, Fisk, & Biely, 2009; Wilson et al., 2010b).

Promising approaches in game task design have been identified for a variety of ages including young children (Lieberman et al., 2009; Thai, Lowenstein, Ching, & Rejeski, 2009) and in informal learning as well as in schools (Williamson, 2009). Here we will take up an example of gaming assessment used in adult learning, the Aspire game, by Cisco Networking Academy. It teaches computer networking, business, and entrepreneurship skills through a single-user gaming approach, utilizing interactions with the computer.

Aspire is a game available to students enrolled in the Cisco Networking Academy, which has more than 900,000 students worldwide. The Academy programs teach students how to design, build, troubleshoot, and secure computer networks. Cisco Networking instructors activate materials in the Cisco online "Passport21 for Entrepreneurship" in order to make the Aspire game available to their students. As described in the name, the Passport21 activities are intended to expose students to entrepreneurship opportunities for future networking and broadband careers.

Newly developed Aspire has quickly gained a remarkable reputation online. Facebook postings extol the quality of the task design, and gamers vie for the limited opportunity to play. "Hey guys don't you agree with me?" one Facebooker asked recently. "Cisco should have changed [the name] not to say Aspire *game*. I don't like calling it a game, on such [an] awesome learning tool."

The game has a quasi-3D look and feel. Gamers receive contract offers from characters such as "Maria," who makes virtual contact through interfaces that you can "answer" or "ignore" in a smart phone-like approach. Inside the network equipment store, gamers can purchase the required devices and equipment to complete contracts, and they may also "purchase" so-called premium content that teaches lessons on various topics. A Bank interface gives players access to view their transaction history, make a payment, or take a loan. And if players find they have some spare credit, they can even furnish their virtual "home offices" with personal items, honors, and awards such as earned badges.

"It's beautiful, isn't it?" one gamer says and posts a thumbs-up LIKE for the task design. "It is good," another responds, "but the scenario is too short. I finished quickly. We need more scenarios!"

The match between assessment and instruction has many aspects on Aspire, which was released in March 2011 and was extensively modeled on job task analysis, to align instructional and assessment goals. An intentional decision by the developers specified that Passport21 would be a suite of innovative offerings to supplement the curriculum—but not replace it. Passport21 was intended to be *optional* learning material exposing students to attitudes, mindsets, and skills they will encounter in the global workplace.

To provide students with the right amount of help, the system uses a variety of forms of student scaffolding. These include also scaffolding to increase the difficulty of tasks, such as rapid-fire e-mails from simulated "clients" that are intended to quickly overwhelm the game player. How gamers manage work overflow then becomes part of the assessment.

Critical concepts are reinforced through a series of business case studies and an innovative tool, Cisco Packet Tracer, which supplies a key element of the assessment design. Cisco Networking Academy researchers have been working on how a simulation game with a Packet Tracer platform fits into the Networking Academy. Packet Tracer (PT) is a simulation environment that has been used by Cisco for some time (Frezzo, Behrens, & Mislevy, 2010):

> PT is a comprehensive simulation, visualization, collaboration, and micro-world authoring tool for teaching networking concepts. Packet Tracer can be thought of as providing instructional and assessment services at a number of levels…. At the most obvious level, PT provides a comprehensive Cisco Internetwork Operating System (IOS) and PC network simulation. The behavior of a range of protocols is simulated, allowing for a wide range of practice and exploration. In addition, a number of packet visualization interfaces are provided to help learners visualize difficult to understand concepts. At a second layer of the hierarchy, PT provides a graphical interface that allows the designing and building of networks by simple drag-and-drop functions combined with the underlying simulation layer. At a third layer, authoring features are available to add stories, task requirements, and/or feedback for games or assessments.

PT constitutes an interesting example of the high levels of sophistication that can be achieved in the creation of gaming environments for instructional tasks as well as the possibilities that these kinds of environments offer to the integration of instruction and assessment (Wilson et al., 2010b).

A few other issues related to task design for matching instruction will be mentioned here. The Universal Design for Learning framework attempts to provide a blueprint for creating instructional materials, including assessments, that can work for everyone, including students with diverse learning needs. How game-based assessments can best address UDL is an area of active research (Center for Applied Special Technology, 2009).

Matching instruction with assessment using games also has some other practical aspects for use in classrooms, including the availability of devices, and what is needed in the classroom to make games run effectively (add reference to (Hu, 2011) article). While this is true for all technology applications, high-performance games can offer some unique challenges. For instance, Microsoft's Kodu Game Lab is a wonderful free product that many educators have expressed interest in using in the classroom, but the graphic cards and processor speeds needed to allow the product to function are rarely available even in well-equipped classrooms, much less where technology is older or sparse.

Another challenge for game design that matches instruction and pedagogically situated learning theory comes from an entirely different direction. A body of research has begun to emerge about how students perceive themselves as game-based learners. Some tendencies such as to adopt a "raceless identity" or to avoid gender identification in role-playing or avatar-based games align with instructional design more generally (Hemmings, 1998). An important body of sociocultural research work may be needed to help inform culture models for game-based design, matching instructional practices with assessment (Harris & Marsh, 2010).

15.2.3 Principle 3: Obtaining Quality Evidence. Case: Everquest II (EQ2)

So far this chapter has considered generating a developmental perspective and arriving at a good match between instruction and assessment. Issues of studying and reporting technical qualities of assessment evidence in game-based systems are illustrated in our third example, on *EverQuest® II* (EQ2), a popular massively multiplayer online role-playing game or MMORPG.

It is important to note that Everquest itself is *not* the focus of this example. Rather, it is the use of *statistically modeling the assessment evidence gathered from it* to make formal estimates of assessment characteristics such as *confidence* about the quality of the evidence. Here, a small example of such modeling is evidenced through standard error estimates. This is not to say that this example *fully* models all formal characteristics of the data that might be desirable. However, it is at least an example of *some* formal investigation of the quality of the evidence from the gaming context.

Created by Sony, EQ2 includes an extensive online world where friends and fellow gamers gather for adventure and community. The interface has a high degree of graphical realism. Players immerse themselves in the game's mysterious lands and follow a variety of storylines.

The example will describe an assessment of social networking and associated learning outcomes in EQ2. However, first, a few caveats should be mentioned regarding Principle 3 in this context. Understanding the technical quality of measurement data gathered from such new generation gaming contexts is very much a frontier area of educational assessment, only just beginning to be explored. Often measurement models are applied in a variety of ways to evaluate technical evidence in assessments. Ironically, measurement models in gaming have been used more extensively to investigate technical characteristics of usability, such as online gaming traffic patterns, or for marketing, such as in adaptive recommender systems, than to examine learning outcomes.

Measurement models and other analytic techniques can be used as a way to successfully aggregate data from games and simulations, and generate estimates of proficiencies or diagnostic profiles in a variety of ways (Behrens, Frezzo, Mislevy, Kroopnick, & Wise, 2008; Scalise, in press; Shute, Maskduki, Donmez, Kim, et al., 2010). Here, EQ2 will be shown in a form of social network analysis (SNA). SNA tools are used to estimate and display the social relationships among participants based on patterns of behavior (Wilson et al., 2010b). With SNA, questions can be addressed such as who read or referenced the materials of others, or commented or provided an emoticon in response to another.

Researchers on the project described that the sheer popularity of these games merited interest. Assessments of "complex social behaviors including collaborating on difficult tasks, trading and participating in an in-game economy, and leading teams through the completion of a variety of quests, dungeons and raids" were among the goals of the assessment (Huffaker et al., 2009, p. 1).

The researchers defined expertise as "high, outstanding, and exceptional performance which is domain-specific, stable over time, and related to experience and practice" (p. 1). They examined other studies indicating that experts in actual organizations cooperate more, communicate more to and from their peers or subordinates, and are generally more socially skilled. Being social skilled allowed experts to spread knowledge, capture information more efficiently, and direct the tasks of the group to improve overall performance. In the game (p. 1):

> The primary objective is to complete quests and defeat monsters, which award adventurers with experience points and treasure. Characters gain levels through their accumulation of experience, which typically involves a level cap (level 70 in this case). These levels are visible to all other players. The levels that characters attain can be represented in terms of achievement. However, it represents a crude type of "meta-expertise" [4] equivalent to knowing a person's current job position or status without understanding the way they attained it. In other words, the "process" of achieving expertise is equally important.

In the EQ2 assessments, the program Statnet was applied to aggregate information and generate model-based proficiency estimates, by which the quality of the assessment evidence was considered. Parameter estimation employed Markov Chain Monte Carlo (MCMC) for maximum likelihood estimation of a latent state model. MCMC algorithms can be used to compute MLEs and their standard errors in latent class models, providing also information for diagnostic goodness-of-fit estimates. Model fit estimates were based in part on whether the characteristics of the simulation could be reproduced in multiple trials, and the quality of the evidence was found to be acceptable by the researchers, for the purposes of examining expert behavior in the game (Huffaker et al., 2009). It should be noted that while this is not intended to describe a complete body of technical evidence desirable for assessments, it begins to illustrate some of what can be done within gaming contexts. This can be combined with some of the other chapters in this book to consider emerging ideas of technical quality in game-based assessments.

To collect the data processed by the models in this example, the chat networks of approximately 1,500 players in EQ2 were collected over a 5-day period. Assessment questions of interest to be addressed by SNA through the gaming data included characteristics of what makes a good gamer. For instance, are achievement and performance experts in EQ2, defined as those achieving higher levels in the game or climbing through levels more quickly than others, likely to communicate in distinctive patterns in the game differently from less-skilled players? Could characteristic patterns be seen in the collaborations that predicted those likely to attain high EQ2 game status? Do people seek experts in these games, and if so, how do experts respond?

Findings showed that achievement experts and performance experts did exhibit different collaboration behaviors within the game, with high achievers more likely to initiate and receive chat messages. Players across levels recognized experts in the game based on their achievement and performance, and looked to the experts for guidance and leadership. But also the top gamers tended to initiate more social interaction, seek information, and exhibit leadership. They were described through the assessments as providing a type of "transactive memory" to the community of gamers.

15.2.4 Principle 4: Making Gaming Assessment Evidence Useful in Classroom Practice. Case: River City

The fourth BAS assessment principle focuses on the usability of information generated by game-based assessments. A challenge for gaming can be providing insight into what the results of the assessment mean in instructional terms. Here we will consider approaches in the River City MUVE.

A number of characteristics of River City make the assessment evidence potentially more useful to teachers and instructors than in many gaming designs. These are described below and include collaborative space and tools designed for students to be useful in the classroom (Galas & Ketelhut, 2006; Ketelhut, Dede, Clarke, Nelson, & Bowman, 2007), opportunities for automated scoring and feedback to assist teachers in collecting and using the assessment data, and reporting mechanisms that include a clear map for teachers between educational standards and the assessments within the game.

Before considering MUVEs, a few aspects of making assessment information useful to teachers and students will be considered. First, the inclusion of at least some automatic scoring and the management of system responses can greatly reduce the practical problem for teachers of having voluminous student work products to review and on which to provide feedback. Games and other online systems can reduce the time it takes instructors to provide at least some of the feedback useful to students, given appropriate contexts and tools. So-called multi-agent scoring systems, often embedded in modern games, are typical systems that are best externalized instead of being embedded into the task and which may be able to offer considerable power in the classroom (Wilson et al., 2010b).

River City is designed to be standards-based. This means that learning objectives for the game have been assigned to educational standards they are intended to address. The game was created to support scientific inquiry. Students should learn about science content including how diseases spread and affect health. But the game players also design and carry out investigations, analyze data, and make conclusions based on evidence. River City focuses on an important trait of games that Shute and others describe (Shute, Rieber, & Van Eck, 2010), integrating learning theory with the strengths of game interfaces.

Other chapters in this book have considered a variety of ways game interaction can become evidence of learning. The scoring or "outcome space" can log sequences of interactions such as keystrokes, mouse movement and use, haptics such as movements of the user, and biometrics such as facial expressions captured by web camera. Assessment data can be collected in this way for cognitive, attitudinal, affective, behavioral, and other constructs. However, whatever data is collected, the interpretation and use should be clear. It is important to have a clear trail of inference, by which the assessment developers in gaming can clearly describe and support with evidence the claims being made about student learning. River City helps teachers and students understand what is being assessed with a clear mapping back to educational standards. This fosters a conversation about the quality of the evidence and how meaningful it is for learning gains. Virtual reality such as in River City can be used for learning with or without gaming attributes (Vogel et al., 2006). River City employs virtual reality through gaming to bring the standards alive for teachers and students.

Planning of the outcome space is often made transparent in various ways to assessment respondents, such as through examples in advance and through reports post-assessment. However, games often may employ stealth assessment (Shute et al., 2009; Wilson et al., 2010b), where assessments are woven into content such that it is not apparent to the respondent what is being assessed or when. Kafai (2006) describes games with stealth assessment as excellent learning environments for twenty-first-century skills. However, here, we remind readers that from an assessment perspective, this technique can be controversial because the hidden nature of the information collected causes lack of transparency for both those being assessed and those using the assessments. We sometimes describe stealth assessment by another term as "unobtrusive, ubiquitous assessment" to better explain its dual purposes of avoiding the interruption of the content experience (unobtrusive) and collecting a dense stream of assessment data with frequent data points (ubiquitous).

15.3 Conclusion

In this chapter, we present four examples of gaming products that include assessments. The products are examined for the soundness of their assessment strategies according to the BAS (Wilson, 2005; Wilson & Sloane, 2000) principles, which describe techniques used in the construction of high-quality assessments generally across many venues, but applied here in gaming. The principles involve a developmental perspective of learning, a match between instructional goals and assessment, the generation of quality evidence, and providing information to teachers and students that is useful to improve learning outcomes.

Principle 1, a developmental perspective of student learning, means assessing the development of student understanding of particular concepts and skills over time, as opposed to, for instance, making a single measurement at some final or supposedly significant time point. A developmental perspective requires clear definitions of what students are expected to learn and a theoretical framework of how that learning is expected to unfold as the student progresses through the instructional materials.

In the first example, we examined the Urban Science game and its approach to establishing a developmental perspective. Theoretical learning trajectories and evidence for their validity are established through a systematic approach involving epistemic learning.

Principle 2, establishing a good match between what is taught and what is assessed, is illustrated in the second example. Reports abound of teachers interrupting their regular curricular materials in order to "teach the material" that students will encounter on district- or statewide tests. Gaming products can avoid this problem if they are matched closely enough to the goals of instruction that they do not become a source of teachers teaching to a test in which there is limited alignment between the assessment and the goals of instruction. The Cisco Aspire example illustrates attention to high-quality observations that closely match assessment and instruction.

Principle 3 involves the issue of technical quality when making inferences about students that can be supported by evidence. Technical studies are important in designing quality assessments and also help game-based assessment procedures to gain "currency" in the educational community. In the third example, we study an interesting example of an attempt to employ technical studies within the context of one large-scale enterprise game. Here, MCMC algorithms are used for computing MLEs and their standard errors in latent state models, and some conclusions are drawn regarding how well the models fit and what their findings may suggest regarding the domain investigated. It is not Everquest itself that is the focus of this example, but the use of modeling the assessment evidence gathered from it to make formal estimates of *confidence* about the quality of the evidence.

Finally, Principle 4 is also critical: Gaming products, if they are to be used for educational assessment, must provide information that is interpretable by teachers and students. Teachers must have the tools to use the system efficiently and to explain resulting data effectively and appropriately. Students should also be able to participate in the assessment process, and they should be encouraged to develop essential metacognitive skills that will further the learning process. The final example considers River City, where the designers took great care to map the products to educational standards, invoke strong practices of learning theory in the product, and communicate the information to teachers and students.

As investments are increasingly made in gaming design and use in formal and informal learning settings for assessment, measurement principles and sound practices are important to consider. Robust assessment practices would help fulfill the promise of the emerging field and might bring to fruition some new tools through gaming that could substantially help instructors and students in the teaching and learning process.

References

Behrens, J. T., Frezzo, D. C., Mislevy, R. J., Kroopnick, M., & Wise, D. (2008). Structural, functional, and semiotic symmetries in simulation-based games and assessments. In E. L. Baker, J. Dickieson, W. Wulfeck, & H. F. O'Neil (Eds.), *Assessment of problem solving using simulations* (pp. 59–80). New York: Erlbaum.

Bennett, R. E. (1990). *Toward intelligent assessment: An integration of constructed response testing, artificial intelligence, and model-based measurement.* Princeton, NJ: Educational Testing Service.

Biggs, J. (1999). *Teaching for Quality Learning at University.* Buckingham: SRHE and Open University Press.

Center for Applied Special Technology. (2009). UDL guidelines 1.0. Retrieved June 20, 2009, from http://www.cast.org/publications/index.html.

Clark, D., Nelson, B., Sengupta, P., & D'Angelo, C. (2009). *Rethinking science learning through digital games and simulations: Genres, examples, and evidence.* An NAS commissioned paper. Nov. 11, 2011. http://www7.nationalacademies.org/bose/Clark_Gaming_CommissionedPaper.pdf.

de Freitas, S. (2006). Using games and simulations for supporting learning. *Learning, Media and Technology, 31*(4), 343–358.

de Freitas, S., & Oliver, M. (2006). How can exploratory learning with games and simulations within the curriculum be most effectively evaluated? *Computers in Education, 46,* 249–264.

Drachen, A., Canossa, A., & Yannakakis, G. N. (2009). *Player modeling using self-organization in tomb raider: Underworld.* In Paper presented at the CIG—IEEE symposium on computational intelligence and games, Milano, Italy.

Epistemic Games. (2011). *What are epistemic games?* (1). Retrieved from May 29, 2011 http://epistemicgames.org/eg/?cat=5.

Frezzo, D. C., Behrens, J. T., & Mislevy, R. M. (2010). Design patterns for learning and assessment: Facilitating the introduction of a complex simulation-based learning environment into a community of instructors. *Journal of Science Education and Technology, 19,* 105–114.

Galas, C., & Ketelhut, D. J. (2006). River City, the MUVE. *Learning and Leading with Technology, 33*(7), 31–32.

Gee, J. P. (2003). High score education. *Wired Magazine, 11*(5), 1–2.

Gee, J. P., & Shaffer, D. W. (2010). *Looking where the light is bad: Video games and the future of assessment, epistemic games group working paper 2010-02.* Madison: University of Wisconsin-Madison.

Gredler, M. E. (1996). Educational games and simulations: A technology in search of a research paradigm. In D. H. Jonassen (Ed.), *Handbook of research for educational communications and technology* (pp. 521–539). New York: MacMillan.

Hariri, B., Shirmohammadi, S., & Reza Pakravan, M. (2008). *A hierarchical HMM model for online gaming traffic patterns.* In Paper presented at the IEEE: I²MTC 2008—IEEE international instrumentation and measurement technology conference. Victoria, Vancouver Island, Canada.

Harris, A. L., & Marsh, K. (2010). Is a raceless identity an effective strategy for academic success among blacks. *Social Science Quarterly, 91,* 1242–1263.

Hemmings, A. (1998). The self transformations of African-American achievers. *Youth and Society, 29*(2), 330–368.

Hu, W. (2011, January 4). Math That Moves: Schools Embrace the iPad, New York Times. Retrieved from http://www.nytimes.com/2011/01/05/education/05tablets.html?_r=1&pagewanted=1&ref=education).

Huffaker, D., Wang, J., Treem, J., Ahmad, M., Fullerton, L., Williams, D., et al. (2009). *The social behaviors of experts in massive multiplayer online role-playing games.* In Paper presented at the 2009 IEEE Social Computing (SocialCom-09). Symposium on Social Intelligence and Networking (SIN-09), Vancouver, Canada.

Jantke, K. P., & Gaudl, S. (2010). *Taxonomic contributions to digital games science.* In Paper presented at the games innovations conference (ICE-GIC). Hong Kong

Kafai, Y. B. (2006). Playing and making games for learning: Instructionist and constructionist perspectives for game studies. *Games and Culture, 1*(1), 34–40.

Ketelhut, D. J., Dede, C., Clarke, J., Nelson, B., & Bowman, C. (2007). Studying situated learning in a multi-user virtual environment. In E. Baker, J. Dickieson, W. Wulfeck, & H. O'Neil (Eds.), *Assessment of problem solving using simulations* (pp. 37–58). Mahwah, NJ: Erlbaum Associates.

Kirriemuir, J. (2002). Video gaming, education and digital learning technologies: Relevance and opportunities. *D-Lib Magazine, 8*(2), 1–14.

Klabbers, J. H. G. (2006). *The magic circle: Principles of gaming & simulation.* Rotterdam: Sense Publishers.

Lieberman, D. A. (2006). What can we learn from playing interactive games? In P. Vorderer & J. Bryant (Eds.), *Playing video games: Motives, responses, and consequences* (pp. 379–397). Mahwah, NJ: Erlbaum Associates.

Lieberman, D. A., Fisk, M. C., & Biely, E. (2009). Digital games for young children ages three to six: From research to design. *Computers in the Schools, 26*(4), 299–313.

Linn, R. L. & Baker, E. L. (1996). "Can performance-based student assessments be psychometrically sound?" In J. B. Baron & D. P. Wolf (Eds.), Performance-based student assessment: Challenges and possibilities. Ninety-fifth Yearbook of the National Society for the Study of Education, Part In (pp. 84–103). Chicago: University of Chicago Press.

Linn, R.L. & Baker, E.L. (1996). "Can performance-based student assessments be psychometrically sound?" In J.B. Baron & D.P. Wolf (Eds.), Performance-based student assessment: Challenges and possibilities. Ninety-fifth Yearbook of the National Society for the Study of Education, Part In (pp. 84-103). Chicago: University of Chicago Press.

Mislevy, R. J., Almond, R. G., & Lukas, J. F. (2003). *A brief introduction to evidence-centered design.* Los Angeles, CA: CRESST.

National Research Council. (2001). *Knowing what students know: The science and design of educational assessment.* Washington, DC: National Academy Press.

Resnick, L. B., & Resnick, D. P. (1992). Assessing the thinking curriculum: New tools for educational reform. In B. R. Gifford & M. C. O'Connor (Eds.), *Changing assessments: Alternative views of aptitude, achievement and instruction* (pp. 37–76). Boston, MA: Kluwer Academic.

Scalise, K. (2011). Creating innovative assessment items and test forms including through simulations and gaming. In R. W. Lissitz & H. Jiao (Eds.), *Computers and Their Impact on State Assessment: Recent History and Predictions for the Future.* Charlotte: Information Age Publishing.

Scalise, K., Bernbaum, D. J., Timms, M. J., Veeragoudar Harrell, S., Burmester, K., Kennedy, C. A., et al. (2007). Adaptive technology for e-learning: Principles and case studies of an emerging field. *Journal of the American Society for Information Science and Technology, 58*(14), 1–15.

Scalise, K., Timms, M., Clark, L., & Moorjani, A. (2009). *Student learning in science simulations: What makes a difference.* In Paper presented at the conversation, argumentation, and engagement and science learning, American Educational Research Association, San Diego, CA.

Shaffer, D. W., & Graesser, A. (2010). *Using a quantitative model of participation in a community of practice to direct automated mentoring in an ill-formed domain.* In Paper presented at the Intelligent Tutoring Systems (ITS). May 29, 2011. Retrieved from http://epistemicgames.org/eg/wp-content/uploads/ITS-workshop-shaffer-graesser-041510.pdf.

Shute, V., Masduki, I., & Donmez, O. (2010). Conceptual framework for modeling, assessing, and supporting competencies within game environments. *Technology, Instruction, Cognition and Learning, 8*(2), 137–161.

Shute, V., Maskduki, I., Donmez, O., Kim, Y. J., Dennen, V. P., Jeong, A. C., et al. (2010). Chapter 15. Modeling, assessing, and supporting key competencies within game environments. In D. Ifenthaler, P. Pirnay-Dummer, & N. M. Seel (Eds.), *Computer-based diagnostics and systematic analysis of knowledge* (pp. 281–309). New York, NY: Springer.

Shute, V., Rieber, L., & Van Eck, R. (2010). Games…and…learning. In R. A. Reiser & J. V. Dempsey (Eds.), *Trends and issues in instructional design and technology* (3rd ed., pp. 321–332). Boston, MA: Pearson Education.

Shute, V., Ventura, M., Bauer, M., & Zapata-Rivera, D. (2009). Chapter 18. Melding the power of serious games and embedded assessment to monitor and foster learning: Flow and grow. In U. Ritterfeld, M. Cody, & P. Vorderer (Eds.), *Serious games: Mechanisms and effects* (pp. 297–321). London: Routledge.

Squire, K. D. (2006). From content to context: Videogames as designed experience. *Educational Researcher, 35*(8), 19–29.

Steinkuehler, C. (2008). Massively multiplayer online games as an educational technology: An outline for research. *Educational Technology, 48*(1), 10–21.

Stenhouse, D. (1986). Conceptual change in science education: Paradigms and language-games. *Science Education, 70*(4), 413–425.

Thai, A., Lowenstein, D., Ching, D., & Rejeski, D. (2009). *Game changer: Investing in digital play to advance children's learning and health.* New York, NY: The Joan Ganz Cooney Center at Sesame Workshop.

The NPD Group. (2010). *2010 Total consumer spend on all games content in the U.S. estimated between $15.4 to $15.6 bBillion.* Inc, Port Washington, NY.

Vogel, J. F., Vogel, D. S., Cannon-Bowers, J. A., Bowers, C. A., Muse, K., & Wright, M. (2006). Computer gaming and interactive simulations for learning: A meta-analysis. *Journal of Educational Computing Research, 34*(3), 229–243.

Weisburgh, M. (2004). *Documenting good education and training practices through design patterns, international forum of educational technology & society.* Retrieved May 28, 2011, from http://ifets.ieee.org/discussions/discuss_june2004.html.

Williamson, B. (2009). *Computer games, schools, and young people.* Bristol: FutureLab Series.

Wilson, M., & Adams, R. J. (1995). Rasch Models for Item Bundles. Psychometrika, 60(2), 181–198.

Wilson, M. (2005). *Constructing measures: An item response modeling approach.* Mahwah, NJ: Lawrence Erlbaum Associates.

Wilson, M., Bejar, I., Scalise, K., Templin, J., Wiliam, D., & Torres Irribarra, D. (2010a). *21st-century measurement for 21st-century skills.* In Paper presented at the American educational research association annual meeting, Denver, CO.

Wilson, M., Bejar, I., Scalise, K., Templin, J., Wiliam, D., & Torres Irribarra, D. (2010b). *Assessment and teaching of 21st century skills: Perspectives on methodological issues.* In White paper presented at the Learning and Technology World Forum 2010, London.

Wilson, M., & Sloane, K. (2000). From principles to practice: An embedded assessment system. *Applied Measurement in Education, 13*(2), 181–208.

Young, M. F., Schrader, P. G., & Zheng, D. (2006). MMOGs as learning environments: An ecological journey into Quest Atlantis and Sims Online. *Innovate: Journal of Online Education, 2*(4). Retrieved April 1, 2011, from http://www.innovateonline.info/index.php?view=article&id=66.

Chapter 16
Using Institutional Data to Evaluate Game-Based Instructional Designs: Challenges and Recommendations

Scott J. Warren and Chris Bigenho

16.1 Introduction

As games move further into mainstream education, the challenge of providing findings supporting the value of learning games continues to arise. Some stem from the complexity of the games themselves, as each generates confounding variables that make claims about their effectiveness at influencing achievement, student satisfaction, or other important constructs untenable. Which particular element in the game was most responsible for the statistical improvement? Which was least? What can we change to improve the game? These questions are challenging for any learning game designer.

16.1.1 A Nascent Game Approach: Anytown

To give the space game-like complexity in the Anytown game that was designed to support elementary student literacy practices (e.g., writing, reading, etc.), the sheer number of design elements created to support learning was massive and created a confounding variable that were difficult to measure (Warren, Stein, Dondlinger, & Barab, 2009). Such variables included multiple visual cues ranging from 3D structures representing some small town America to textual components as in-game characters communicated with students. In addition, clicking on objects launched interactive elements to provide students with feedback from fictional characters or

S.J. Warren (✉) • C. Bigenho
Department of Learning Technologies, University of North Texas,
3940 North Elm, Suite G150, Denton, TX 76207, USA
e-mail: scott.warren@unt.edu; cbigenho.unt@gmail.com

D. Ifenthaler et al. (eds.), *Assessment in Game-Based Learning: Foundations,
Innovations, and Perspectives*, DOI 10.1007/978-1-4614-3546-4_16,
© Springer Science+Business Media New York 2012

the teacher. By the end of the research study, statistically significant differences were measured including reduced teacher time spent in answering procedural questions, improvement in standardized student writing achievement, and increases in student voluntary writing (Warren, Barab, & Dondlinger, 2008). However, afterward, the researchers were left wondering which of the Anytown design elements were responsible for the detected changes. Interviews and computer-mediated discourse provided only small clues to what had been successful and what had not (Warren, Dondlinger, Stein, & Barab, 2009). Further, with this research, we were responsible for collecting all data and constructing necessary instruments, which was time consuming and difficult.

16.1.2   Institutional Course Redesign: The Door and Beyond

As Anytown was left behind and attention shifted to designing game structures supporting undergraduate computer literacy, new opportunities were available to leverage the institutional resources of an emerging research university to support our data collection. Seeking to improve undergraduate experience in a course with high drop, failure, and withdrawal rates, game elements, as suggested by Salen and Zimmerman (2004), were integrated into the course. These included interactivity, narrative, win scenarios, a rule set governing play, and conflicts for students to over-come. This resulted in several iterative designs beginning with *The Door* alternate reality game (AltRG). AltRGs are those that "distribute game challenges, tasks, and rewards across a variety of media, both digital and real" (Warren, Dondlinger, Jones, & Whitworth, 2010, p. 42).

In response to evaluation of *The Door* design, we engaged in a complete redesign of the course. As we sought to address identified weaknesses in the original design, *Broken Window* was constructed and included both AltRG and instructional design practice components. Figure 16.1 presents relationships among game, AltRG, and instructional design components.

Since that time, two additional designs responsive to evaluation *of Broken Window* have been implemented. The first was a largely decontextualized, computer-based instruction (CBI) version that guided students into one of three versions of the course depending on entering pretest scores. Lack of student response to this version resulted in *The 2015 Project*, a course that included direct instruction to improve self-regulated learning and an AltRG modeled on McGonigal's *World Without Oil* and centered on United Nations Millennium Development Goals that were part of Dondlinger's *Global Village Playground* (Dondlinger & Warren, 2009). Each iteration was revised based on evaluative feedback in the form of course evaluations, student web log (blog) reflections, and interviews with students and instructors.

Guiding most designs were the institution's major goals for the course which were to improve:

• Student satisfaction as measured by course evaluations
• Number of students dropping the course in the first 11 days

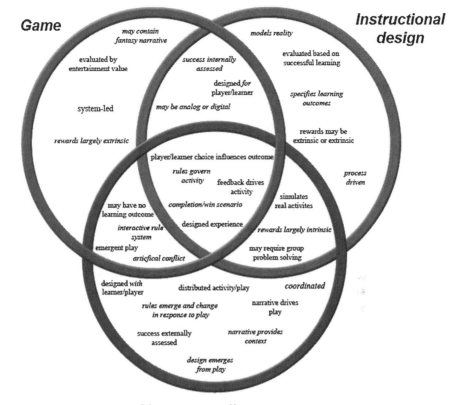

Fig. 16.1 Relationships among game, instructional, and alternate reality game

- Number of students failing the course
- Number of students withdrawing from the course during the semester
- Improve student achievement in the course

However, the designer-researchers were largely reliant on institutional data from the university to inform design and pedagogy decisions. Since the inception of this project, it was discovered that much of this data did not meet normal validity or reliability rigor. Further, often because of insufficient participants completing course evaluations meet, the outcomes do not statistical validity requirements. Additionally, institutional data commonly lacked any context explaining student drops and withdrawals, and there was no control to reduce overrepresentation of failing students in the evaluation sample. This made decisions about what to change in our games prior to each semester difficult, because the data was often negatively skewed.

The goal of this chapter is to discuss the role of institutional data in evaluating the educational game effectiveness. Further, we identify challenges in the availability and quality of institutional data for assessing learning. Finally, we provide approaches used to collect data necessary to assess and evaluate educational game designs.

16.2 Literature Review

16.2.1 Introduction to Literature Review

This review explores the literature for assessment and evaluation of game-based learning environments from several perspectives. Starting with a look at the literature related to game evaluation through play testing and iterative design approaches. Since the games we are using in our work involve alternate reality, narrative-based approaches, these generally involve strong elements of problem-based learning (PBL), so it is appropriate to examine evaluation from that perspective as well. Additionally, both PBL and AltRGs usually involve strong social elements through group or teamwork. Therefore, the effectiveness of the social aspect of these learning environments is also explored. Finally, we look at the literature surrounding the use of institutional data for course evaluation, as this constitutes the official evaluation and includes data important to determining the success of the game as a learning environment. It is also this institutional data that has presented problems that are addressed later in the chapter.

16.2.2 Game Evaluation

Games can be fun to play but how do you know if the game will work or that it will have the right level of challenge and scaffolds to keep the player engaged and maintain the fun? This is where evaluation of the game is critical. Our work employed two interwoven approaches to testing: usability testing associated with play testing and iterative designs.

Usability testing examines components and processes that effect the ability of a player to complete tasks intended by the designer of the software or game environment (Warren, Jones, & Lin, 2010). This was accomplished through the teaching of the course or "play testing" with each successive version of the course.

Play-testing for game evaluation and development is a form of iterative play with changes between each play-testing session (Salen & Zimmerman, 2004). The game is played mentally multiple times by the designer then is realized in a prototype. A play-testing group then plays this prototype where specific elements are tested. The feedback from each session informs changes in the game and the process is repeated. The process of play testing helps to determine game flow and problem points. Additionally, it is important to play-test with multiple groups allowing for different approaches to strategy, and style of play (Salen & Zimmerman, 2004).

One element critical to successful game design is personal engagement. The trick in games for learning is to make the game both personally engaging and educational (Klopfer, 2008). Successful games provide rewards in what Csikszentmihalyi calls Flow "an optimal state of immersed concentration in which attention is centered, distractions are minimized, and the person attains an enjoyable give-and-take with his or her activity" (Whalen, 1999).

Our use of an AltRG for learning provided a unique set of data for each iteration of the course. Students in the course would generate data through "game play" by posting to forums, blog entries, and e-mail to "clients" in the game. This content provided thick records that were analyzed and informed changes for the next version of the course (Warren & Dondlinger, 2009). As of the date of this writing, the course has been through 18 iterations with each design informed by the "play" from the previous version. Additionally, we have leveraged student and instructor interviews providing additional feedback on game elements, learning experiences, and outcomes (Warren, Dondlinger, McLeod, & Bigenho, 2011).

16.2.3   Problem-Based Learning

The designers for the course under study leveraged PBL as a way to provide authentic context for learning (Bonk, Kirkley, Hara, & Denned, 2001). These environments utilized the ill-structured problem characterized by the following traits: unstated goals, multiple or no solution, multiple evaluation criteria, uncertainty, no general rules for predicting outcomes, and learner makes and defends their judgments (Jonassen, 1999). A key element in the development of PBL environments is the use of scaffolding to provide temporary supports for learning beyond the student's current capacities (Jonassen, 1999). Our designs provided multiple supports both at the instructor and design levels. The effectiveness of these scaffolds could be evaluated through an analysis of student blogs, questions posted through forums and e-mail, and instructor interviews (Warren et al., 2011).

Collaborative problem solving and group work are common to both PBL and game environments (Nelson, 1999; Salen & Zimmerman, 2004; Savery & Duffy, 1995). Students provide insight into their group dynamics and group work through their blog and forum posts and occasionally e-mail. Additionally, semistructured interviews provide additional data related to this collaborative work (Warren et al., 2011). While collaborative work is a fundamental part of PBL designs, a recent empirical study looking at the role of collaboration in PBL found that it was not one of the essential components of learning through PBL (Wirkala & Kuhn, 2011). In a study looking at a comparison of three groups comprised of a traditional lecture approach, PBL-individual and PBL-team, Wirkala and Kuhn found PBL to be far superior in long-term learning than the lecture mode but that there was no difference between the PBL-individual and PBL-team. However, we find that group work is very common in today's society (Nelson, 1999) and is a fundamental part of game play in narrative-based AltRGs (Klopfer, 2008).

Using the above methods for game evaluation, we still had issues correlating game experiences with the learning aspects of the design and the overall effectiveness of the course related to student demographics, life experiences, and other student-related characteristics. This led us to look to institutional data related to course and teaching effectiveness. However, this was wrought with challenges that are discussed briefly in the next section.

16.2.4 A Brief Overview of Institutional Course Assessment

Institutional assessment of courses through Student Evaluation Instruments (SEIs) has been examined extensively resulting in a large literature that reaches far beyond the scope of this chapter. The extent of work completed in this arena is evident in the number of publications resulting from studies exploring SEIs. One study completed in 2007 found over 2,980 articles related to SEIs published between 1990 and 2005 (Al-Issa & Sulieman, 2007). With all of this prior work, it may seem strange to continue to add to this canon. Yet, a quick examination illustrates the existing conflicts and deficiencies that still exist pointing toward a need for further work in this area. We have found this to be the case when attempting to use institutional data collected through SEIs to systematically examine the effectiveness of our game-based course designs.

Studies exploring the validity of SEI are not in agreement about how effective students are in evaluating their professors or their course. Some studies argued that students were not able to effectively serve as evaluators of teaching and learning spaces (Driscoll & Cadden, 2010). This ineffectiveness may stem from bias related to student gender (Tatro, 1995), instructor gender (Smith & Anderson, 2005), faculty tenure (Marsh & Dunkin, 1992), learning environment (Mintu-Wimsatt, Ingram, Milward, & Russ, 2006), and expected grade in class (Brown, 2008), method of delivery (Mintu-Wimsatt, 2001; Mintu-Wimsatt et al., 2006).

16.2.5 Gender

Female students tended to rank their professors higher than male students in the class (Denson, Loveday, & Dalton, 2010; Tatro, 1995). In regards to the instructors, female professors tended to receive higher evaluations than the male teachers when significant differences appeared between genders (Feldman, 1993). Additionally, an interaction effect was reported between student and faculty gender with female students ranking female instructors higher than male teachers on measures related to caring and interaction (Bachen, McLoughlin, & Garcia, 1999).

16.2.6 Instructor

In addition to the interaction effects between student and instructor, teachers of higher rank or tenure received more favorable ratings than those with lower ranks and or less experience (Marsh & Dunkin, 1992). How students rank their teachers on SEIs also appear to be influenced by the personality and behavior of their teachers. Teachers who have pleasant likable personalities rank higher than those less favorable (Cardy & Dobbins, 1986). Additionally, teachers who brought food to class or were perceived to have lenient grading policies also ranked higher (Simpson & Siguaw, 2000).

16.2.7 Student Grades and Maturity

A link has also been made between grades and how students rank their professors. Some studies indicate that students who believed they were getting a low grade in the class may rank their professors lower on the SEI (Braskamp & Ory, 1994; Crumbley, Henry, & Kratchman, 2001; Marsh & Roche, 1997). One study indicated that this might even be a bias stemming from students who are attempting to punish their teachers for the grade they earned (Crumbley et al., 2001). Student's maturity and level was also reported as a factor influencing rankings on SEIs. Younger, less mature students tend to rank their professors lower than those who are in their final year as an undergraduate (Frey, Leonard, & Beatty, 1975).

16.2.8 Course Type

Several studies examined links between class size, required vs. elective courses, discipline—Arts, Humanities, Mathematics, Physical Sciences, etc., scheduling, inside and outside of major and other factors. In general, professors teaching larger course sections ranked lower on their SEIs than those teaching smaller sections (Koh & Tan, 1997). Courses that are required but outside of a student's major tended to receive the lowest rankings while elective courses ranked higher than nonelective courses (Denson et al., 2010; Marsh, 1987; Ponder, 2007). Ponder (2007) goes on to indicate that courses that are perceived as harder tend to receive lower rankings that those than are believed to be easier. Significant differences in student evaluations of courses also were found between courses from different disciplines (Driscoll & Cadden, 2010). Courses from the Arts and Humanities frequently ranked higher on SEIs than those from the Physical Sciences, Business, and Economics (Cashin, 1990). Driscoll and Cadden (2010) go on to recommend that "consideration should be given to the use of department measures in evaluations rather than a universal measure" (p. 26). Finally, the time of day that a class is offered also appears to be linked to the level at which the course is ranked on SEIs (Husbands & Fosh, 1993).

16.2.9   Remaining Problems

Faced with difficulties in dealing with limited data available to us through institutional course evaluations, the uniqueness of our instructional methods, and a lack of context between student responses on official course evaluations and unique elements of the course, we have embarked on a new approach leveraging embedded course evaluations focused on both course design and teaching effectiveness. This allowed us to gather contextual information that was lacking in the institutional data collected through official course evaluations and forms the basis for the work presented below.

16.3   Methods

The focus of this study was on the role of institutional data for use in the study of educational games designed to support computer literacy. As such, we examined three undergraduate courses that leveraged game curricula to support learning. Further, each course sought to use institutional data as a means of answering research questions related to each design. During the time these designs were implemented, more than 1,000 students completed the course; however, data for only a small percentage was available.

However, this study does not focus on whether or not students learned the course material. Instead, the focus is on whether and how we were able to leverage institutional data to engage in research related to the complex course game designs. Some questions sought to examine each game design's efficacy as a learning tool, ability to improve learner satisfaction, and to increase student persistence and course completion, among other goals we had for the different game iterations. The research questions were:

1. Is the institutional data provided by the university sufficient to draw statistically supported research conclusions about the effectiveness of the intervention?
2. If the data provided is not sufficient, what is needed?
3. If data is not available, what approaches can be taken in order to collect this data through other means?

16.3.1   Design-Based Research

In order to examine the usefulness of institutional data as a means of answering research questions related to the effectiveness of our learning games, we drew data from the longitudinal design-based research (DBR) study that has accompanied the many iterations of the LTEC 1100 game designs. Barab states that (t)he goal of DBR is to use the close study of a single learning environment, usually as it passes through multiple iterations and as it occurs in naturalistic contexts to develop new theories, artifacts, and practices...(thus), the design-based researcher must demonstrate local impact, at the same time making a case that this local impact can be accounted for in terms of the particular theory being advanced (Barab, 2006, pp. 153–154).

Separately, this iterative research process focus on the systematic design and redesign process for the game has followed Shavelson, Phillips, Towne, and Feuer's (2003) idea that we must examine significant questions, link research to theory, make explicit our reasoning from one report to the next, provide data and methods for external critique, and use inquiry methods deemed credible by the larger community of researchers. It is from the artifacts of this DBR process that our findings are drawn regarding the benefits and challenges to using institutional data to research learning games.

16.3.2 Data Collection

Our DBR process involved monthly instructor, designer, and researcher meetings (both face-to-face and online) to discuss challenges with the design of a game iteration, to suggest improvements that would streamline processes of grading, supporting learners, and collection of data from noninstitutional sources that would later be merged with institutional evaluations. Instructors engaged in active critique of design elements towards a goal of improving the game, instructor workload, and student experience. During these sessions, members of the team took notes and e-mails among team members regarding each game were retained. These served as guides for future game design revisions.

16.3.3 Data Analysis

Those paper and digital documents directly relevant to the question of using institutional data to evaluate the learning games were drawn from the larger body of artifacts from these discussions. We performed content analysis according to methods described by Robson (2002), which included:

1. Start with a research question
2. Sample your documents from the general population
3. Choose a recording unit
4. Construct categories for analysis
5. Test coding on samples of text and assess reliability
6. Carry out the analysis
7. Check for errors
8. Compare findings

We included three reviewers to enact steps 3–8. Each member of the analysis team is a current or former designer or instructor for one or more of the game iterations.

16.3.3.1 Institutional Data Collection

The data we received from the university came in the form of student responses to course evaluations and drop, failure and withdrawal rates. These evaluations were constructed either by the university or the college in which the department was housed. Due to changes in our location and choices made by the institution, these instruments changed three times during the first 5 years during which the LTEC 1100 course redesigns were implemented. The original course evaluations included four questions in which students rated faculty on a Likert scale ranging from 1 to 5. The following were those questions:

- How would you rate the quality of this course?
- Did you feel your instructor was knowledgeable about the subject area?
- Did you feel your instructor was prepared for classes?
- Would you take this course again?

Table 16.1 University Student Evaluation of Teacher Effectiveness (SETE)

Organization and explanation of materials
My instructor explains difficult material clearly
My instructor communicates at a level that I can understand
My instructor makes requirements clear
My instructor identified relationships between and among topics
Learning environment
My instructor establishes a climate of respect
My instructor is available to me on matters pertaining to the course
My instructor respects diverse talents
My instructor creates and atmosphere in which ideas can be exchanged freely
Self-regulated learning
My instructor gives assignments that are stimulating to me
My instructor encourages me to develop new viewpoints
My instructor arouses my curiosity
My instructor stimulates my creativity
Overall opinions
I like this instructor
I am interested in this subject
I think the classroom was appropriate for this class
I would recommend a course taught by this instructor
This class is: (a) required (b) elective (c) not sure
What grade do you expect to earn in this course: A, B, C, D, F

Changes to the course evaluations were implemented in a 2007 pilot stemming from a college initiative to improve the quality of the course evaluations. The original four questions were retained, but an additional 16 questions were added in order to better contextualize student responses on the first four items. However, only the first four questions counted toward instructor's overall ratings of the quality of their teaching.

In 2009, the university changed the entire course evaluation process to the new Student Evaluation of Teacher Effectiveness (SETE), which included variations on the original four questions, but with additional discriminating terms used in the questions, for a total of 16 questions related to the instructor and an additional two questions for context about the student. Table 16.1 includes the university SETE questions with student choices on a Likert scale being *strongly disagree, disagree, agree, and strongly agree.*

It was from these instruments that our institutional data was drawn. Further, it spurred the recursive data analysis process that was at the heart of our data-informed redesigns.

16.4 Designed Game Contexts and Results

During the last 4 years, both the instructional designs of the course and the research methods have changed substantially in response to the responses of the students and the needs of the instructors. Some of the results of the early designs have been reported elsewhere (Warren et al., 2011; Warren, Dondlinger, et al., 2010). However, the goal of this chapter is to focus on the role of institutional data used across all iterations of the game for assessing student learning and evaluating the effectiveness of the course designs, not to report achievement or research outcomes for design iterations.

This study took place at a midsized emerging research university in the southwestern United States with a student population of approximately 35,000. The courses were delivered either completely online or in a hybrid format. The latter format required students to attend face-to-face class meetings every other week.

There were four major design iterations of the LTEC 1100 course. This began with *The Door*, which lasted for 2 years. *Broken Window*, an iteration that overlapped with some sections teaching The Door curriculum, lasted an additional 2 years. During one semester, we also created an iteration, which relied on CBI and Broken Window, but allowed students to self-select a version of the course most appropriate to them based on pretest scores. The current iteration is *The 2015 Project* and has been implemented for 1 year. Each course-game curriculum is described in more detail below along with challenges faced by the designer-researchers in terms of institutional data and expectations.

Table 16.2 Savery and Duffy's framework for problem construction

Anchor all learning activities to a larger task or problem

Support the learner in developing ownership for the overall problem or task

Design an authentic task

Design the task and the learning environment to reflect the complexity of the environment they
  should be able to function in at the end of learning

Give the learner ownership of the process used to develop a solution

Design the learning environment to support and challenge the learner's thinking

Encourage testing ideas against alternative views and alternative contexts

Provide opportunity for and support reflection on both the content learned and the learning
  process

16.4.1   Iteration 1: The Door

This AltRG-based course was designed to allow students to learn basic and more
advanced computer literacy skills by engaging with ill-structured problems using
the very tools they are expected to learn. In a hybrid course format (50% online/50%
face-to-face), students were required to work in small groups of two or three called
Design Teams to engage with problems set up in accordance with Savery and
Duffy's (1995) specifications presented in Table 16.2.

Design Teams coordinated their problem-solving activities using self-selected
productivity and communication tools including the Microsoft Office, e-mail, text
messaging, or anything they felt was appropriate. The game component included a
two-tiered narrative structure used to contextualize course activities.

The first tier required students to work with fictional clients who "hired" student
teams to complete tasks that would be authentic to future work settings outside of
the university. The second allowed students to seek answers to who the clients were
as they successfully completed their tasks and received clues to the identities of the
clients. These came in the form of puzzles, codes, and ciphers embedded in blogs,
web sites, podcasts, and videos. Figure 16.2 is the version of the Walter's blog that
students saw when they first arrived.

The site embedded multiple clues and changed once students received a pass-
word for completing a learning task. Each challenge had to be solved, in order to
complete the game. In addition, students received bonus learning scaffolds from
"winning" certain game components that could help their teams. Figure 16.3 is
Walt's blog upon solving a game task.

Instructors acted as learning facilitators, engaging students in the narrative elements by role-playing characters and a puppet master called the Arbiter. The Door
ran from spring 2007 to fall of 2009 and was scaled from a single section to seven
and all used the 38-page job aid and online resources to guide instruction. A fuller
description of the design and its research findings may be found in Warren and
Dondlinger (2009), Warren, Dondlinger, et al. (2010), and Warren et al. (2011).

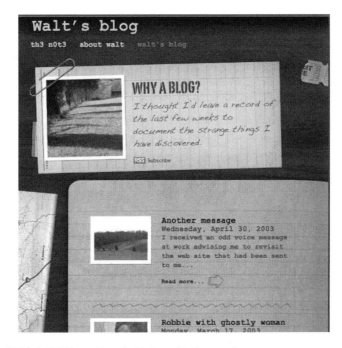

Fig. 16.2 Walt's initial blog with embedded graphical game clues

Fig. 16.3 Walt's changed blog after puzzle solution

16.4.1.1   Institutional Data Challenge

As this iteration went forward, there was a requirement that the designers evaluate the game's effectiveness for addressing three major areas:

- Student satisfaction
- Student retention
- Student achievement

Student satisfaction was to be measured through course evaluations that consisted of only four questions. The small number of questions makes any attempt at explaining why student satisfaction increased or decreased as a function of the game invalid as they are insufficient and ask no questions about the game itself. Further, the comparison of two different sections with different instructional methods (CBI vs. game-based learning) and different instructors as mandated by the study. The differences between the instructors themselves alone may have been responsible for a statistically significant difference in satisfaction rather than the game.

In terms of retention, 32 students were in each of the course sections. As a result, one student dropping the course due to a factor unrelated to the game design could easily have been misattributed to the game. In the first iteration of The Door, a student dropped the course after 2 weeks because he had a death in the family, a fact we did not learn until a year later when he took the course again. However, because of the research design and reliance on the institutional data, we attributed his lack of persistence to our game design, as did the university.

Student achievement was measured using a pretest–posttest design to determine whether there were statistically significant differences in learning between the classes from beginning to end. While The Door was correlated with learning improvements vs. the CBI version, it was unclear whether student game participation was responsible or the increased time-on-task that the game-based course required instead. Later, student interviews indicated it was likely *not* the game design alone, but instead the time-on-task from one tier of the game, while students failed to engage in the second, fantasy tier. Had we relied on decontextualized institutional data, we would likely have drawn improper conclusions about the efficacy of our game treatment and failed to make changes to the design as we moved forward with our DBR process.

16.4.2   Iteration Two: Broken Window

Broken Window diverged from The Door design in order to provide students with a larger, project-based component on which they could practice their computer literacy skills. The format of this course, while also a hybrid, involved students engaging in the Broken Window AltRG for only the first 6 weeks of the semester. The major computer literacy goals of engaging students with the AltRG at the beginning of the semester was to teach them the basics of the Internet, dealing with ethical

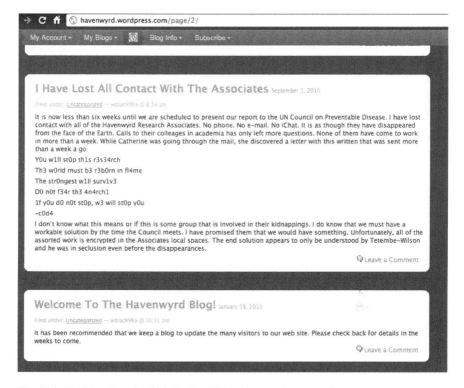

Fig. 16.4   The blog through which Broken Window's narrative emerged

issues, and being safe and secure online. In addition, we sought to have learners come to understand what an AltRG for learning is and provide them with both the cognitive and affective experiences that go along with playing such a construct. This AltRG used the same blending of game and PBL elements that were present in The Door, but had additional narrative tying student actions to understanding how their narrow actions could tie to much larger challenges such as those present in the United Nations Millennium Development Goals such as ensuring maternal and child health, the beginning plot as depicted in Fig. 16.4.

In the remaining 9 weeks, students engaged in two different components. The first was the use of direct instruction using SAM 2007 computer-aided instruction, a version of which had been used prior to the implementation of The Door. This was to address learner and instructor concerns in interviews and blog reflections that the students needed additional scaffolding in the terms of more traditional instruction for them to be successful outside of the course. Beyond the direct instruction, students were also required to work in Design Teams of two or three students to construct their own AltRG for learning tied to one of the UN Millennium Development Goals. They were provided with weekly instruction and materials explaining each step of the ADDIE model of instructional design, which was deemed simple enough for students to follow as they constructed their own games. At the end of the semester, students had peer groups play their games and provide feedback in the form of survey and interviews used to evaluate the success of their designs. This version of the course overlapped with The Door for two semesters and began in the summer of 2008 and ran through the fall of 2010.

16.4.2.1 Institutional Data Challenge

As with The Door, the institutional data we were able to gather was incomplete or limited in such a way that any conclusions drawn from it were likely to be incorrect. Further, as our department moved from one college to another, we had a semester in which no institutional data was gathered related to our drop, failures, and withdrawals. The following semester, a course-evaluation instrument from the new college was mandated that did not match the previous one used for The Door. However, this instrument was as limited in the number of items in much the same fashion as the one we had used in the previous college, thought the questions were different. At the end of Broken Window's use, still another instrument was employed across the university that had a completely different set of questions and numerical scale to evaluate courses and instructors.

At this time, we sought to answer additional questions about different components of the game to determine their success or failure with different demographic groups. When asked for information regarding age, gender, class year, and other characteristics necessary to conduct factor analysis, it was unavailable from the university. Without this data, factor analysis was not possible, limiting findings that could be used to improve the game.

16.4.3   Iteration 3: Multioption Student Choice Version

In the fall of 2009 and spring of 2010, we experimented with a different format that had either no game component (versions 1 and 2) or a variation on the Broken Window AltRG for version 3. Version 1 was created for students that scored low (>65) on the pretest while version 2 was available to students that scored between 70 and 85%. Version 3 was available to students scoring between 85 and 100% and any student scoring over 90% was required to engage in version 3. Students in the margins between the version 1 and 2 or versions 2 and 3 were allowed to choose which version they felt was most appropriate. Students received information about each version of the course before making their decision, but only after they had completed the pretest. In addition, students were required to complete with 100% success a series quizzes over each option to ensure that they understood the differences among them so we could be sure they made an informed choice. Figure 16.5 presents this process.

Versions 1 and 2 of the course provided students with direct instruction using SAM 2007 followed by either one PBL task derived from The Door or three tasks derived from The Door. The tasks stripped away all The Door AltRG game context

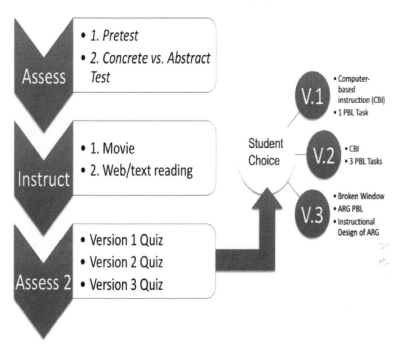

Fig. 16.5   Week one induction process for new students

and only required students to work in small groups to complete them over the course of 1 or 3 weeks. This was intended to assess students' ability to apply skills learned in the course to alternate contexts. This would also indicate that students could use the computer literacy information to solve ill-structured problems. While the least innovative in terms of embedding game or leveraging social constructivist frameworks, it provided students with the broadest choices regarding how they would learn among all game iterations.

16.4.3.1   Institutional Data Challenge

By this time, student satisfaction, persistence, and achievement questions were dropped from our research agenda. Instead, we sought to understand student's preparation for college related to their self-regulated learning abilities, class year, age, and other factors. Again, this data was unavailable from the university, requiring us to create our own demographic survey that would be embedded in the learning management system (Blackboard Vista). Further, the university allows students that fail the course game to complete the course evaluation after refusing to take part in any learning activities, making the statistical outcomes.

16.4.4   Iteration 4: The 2015 Project

In the spring of 2010, interviews and blogs revealed continued student and instructor concerns that even with the major revisions from The Door to Broken Window and then with the direct instruction, multiversion model there were still problems. These included that no version was felt by students to not contain enough direct instruction and that the SAM 2007 had too many problems as a program. Further, the instructors believed that students lacked sufficient self-regulation skills (i.e., time management, self-monitoring, communication skills) to be successful and that all three previous versions were too much work in terms of managing the game vs. traditional instruction. In the course evaluations and blog reflections, students were tracked by the version of the course they took and were asked to explain their choice of version in their blog.

Thus, a new design was undertaken that would

1. Directly teach the self-regulation skills that students were perceived by instructors to lack
2. Construct the new course in Blackboard with which students and instructors were more comfortable
3. More clearly support and engage students with individual components of the UN Millennium development goals modeled on Jane McGonigal's World Without Oil AltRG design
4. Reduce the amount of work for instructors in terms of grading
5. Introduce a new computer-aided instruction product called MyITLab along with a custom textbook created by the instructors

In the first 5 weeks of the semester, the course now engages students with the first nine chapters of the textbook to learn the basics of computer literacy along with specific self-regulated learning skills taken from Zimmerman (1990) including time management, self-evaluation, transformation (breaking up) of tasks, self-consequentiation, and others. These skills were deemed by instructors to be prerequisite to working independently online for the rest of the semester. In addition during this time, students set up e-mail accounts, calendars, and blogs that they would use for the rest of the semester and were expected to support communication, self-management, and metacognitive reflection within and among students.

Starting in week 6, students engaged in The 2015 project (http://start2015.think-tanktwo.info) game using their newfound computer literacy skills. The game takes part in an alternate reality United States in which the massive problems of poor maternal health, HIV/AIDS, and other challenges are now taking place in major cities in America rather than in impoverished locations across the globe. Each week additional story is revealed as the problems become larger and more untenable and

Fig. 16.6 The 2015 Project content management system layout for fall 2011

the solutions put forth by politicians become more radical. The goal is to contextualize the problems locally as a means of students understanding and proposing solutions to the large, ill-structured problems of the world such as combating HIV/AIDS, Improving Maternal and Child Health, increasing access to education, and others identified by the United Nations.

The game was largely constructed using the Joomla content management system (CMS) in order to reduce design and development time, because many of the components we needed to facilitate communication were readily and freely available including chat tools, forums, RSS feedback, and video support. A screen shot of the CMS used to construct several game components (i.e., forum, news items, etc.) is shown in Fig. 16.6.

Beyond a new role for students, the instructor role changed from one of puppet master to one of Champion for one of the UN Millennium Development Goals. Each both monitored and helped drive student discussion as they provided feedback on student suggestions.

At the same time, students began their direct instruction using Pearson's MyITLab to learn the basics of Microsoft Office™, which they used to provide their solutions and recommendations as part of the narrative game. Each of these was expected to be professional and addressed to real people working in the particular goal at an international level. This was expected to connect student's course work to what they can do in the future with the tools they learned. Further, they were engaged in the kinds of ill-structured problems they are likely to face in their future world of work.

16.4.4.1 Institutional Data Challenge

Today, we continue to have many of the same problems that were present in the first game iteration. The university provides no demographic data that can be used for factor analysis related to our research questions. We have no validity or reliability statistics for the questions asked on the new course evaluation and our review of the questions indicates little face validity and problems with the wording that may lead students to particular answers, negating its value. Students continue to drop and repeat the course some students have reported that they only took the course to maintain their financial aid from the university. This makes the validity of university and state-captured persistence rates highly unreliable as measures of the effectiveness of course, game, or instructor.

16.5 Findings

From a research standpoint, there were a number of problems both with missing data and the validity of the data that was collected by the institution. From a design evaluation perspective, there were even more challenges. Lastly, data we expected to have backed up by the department to support longitudinal data was lost due to established policy or lack of foresight on the part of the researchers.

16.5.1 Validity and Reliability Issue: Instruments and Samples

From the standpoint of establishing the data collection instruments as both valid and reliable, there were challenges. The first being that the instruments, especially those consisting of only four questions, have not had either validity or reliability estimations conducted. Simply viewing such instruments from a test construction perspective, it is not possible to achieve sufficient discrimination among the questions to validly draw conclusions about the quality of the instructor or instruction. On the longer, SETE instrument, there are far more questions, but reliability and validity estimates have not been provided to the instructors, nor are they available through the institution's research office. That office constructed the SETE instrument with minimal feedback from the faculty senate, which is charged with evaluating faculty at the university.

A second problem is the sample sizes that were represented in our course evaluation collection. Except in one case, no instructor received more than seven student evaluations for a class of 24 or more students and the majority received between 3 and 5 evaluations. From a research perspective, this level of response is insufficient to establish the course evaluation findings as either valid or reliable.

From a game design evaluation standpoint, this is problematic. Without valid or reliable data regarding student perceptions of the course, it is not possible to draw conclusions about the quality of the game design. As such, except in two instances, this made the institutional data we received unusable as we sought to make improvements to the course. Further, the questions tended to focus on how students felt about the instructor rather than about course content, instruction, approach, or any particular aspect of the course tied to the game. However, these were not the only problems with the data collected.

16.5.2   Lack of Detailed Data

The data that was collected from 2007 to 2009 consisted mainly of the four established questions. Slightly more helpful was a box in which students could write comments about the course. What was missing was context about the students who filled out the evaluations.

16.5.2.1   Demographic Data

The data provided to instructors by the institution lacked any information about the students, which would have been useful for factor analysis. Prior studies indicated that there were biases issues with gender (Denson et al., 2010; Feldman, 1993; Tatro, 1995) and student maturity (Frey et al., 1975). When we sought to discriminate student evaluations to detect issues like gender bias for or against the design, cultural biases, factors indicating higher levels of success (i.e., whether seniors perform significantly higher than freshmen), and whether or not the student would be classified as a nontraditional student, this information was unavailable and not collected. Without such data, it was not possible to make improvements to the game, because we were unable to reflect about factors in the construction that were likely to have impacted student experience.

16.5.2.2   Student History with the Course

Many students in LTEC 1100 repeat the course due to dropping in the first 2 weeks, withdrawing before the middle of the semester, or outright fail the course due to lack of participation. Some students register, start strong for 2 or 3 weeks, then completely disappear until week 14 when they send an e-mail to the instructor asking if they can still pass the class after it is far too late to withdraw. They then register again the following semester. Some repeat this process of drop, failure, or withdrawal several times.

One challenge for instructors and designers is to evaluate the quality of feedback we receive from students, especially when that feedback comes only through a narrow course evaluation with minimal comments. Because the feedback is blind, we do not know whether the student is one that failed and seeks to punish the instructor? Is feedback predominantly positive because only those that enjoyed the class most completed the evaluation? If the student passed, what grade did they receive in the course (Braskamp & Ory, 1994; Crumbley et al., 2001; Marsh & Roche, 1997)? Can we correlate their grades with their attitudes toward the game and course construction (Driscoll & Cadden, 2010; Mintu-Wimsatt, 2001; Mintu-Wimsatt et al., 2006)? What was the balance between the numbers of students passing vs. those failing that filled out the evaluation? Without this contextual information, it is difficult to judge the success or failure or the game design and even more difficult to make changes to improve the game experience for the future.

16.6   Implications

There are two approaches we propose for rectifying the problems of collecting game evaluation data using institutional data. The first is to work with a willing institutional research office to improve the quality of the data collected in validated course evaluations with established reliability estimates. Further, it will be important to ensure that those evaluations are sufficiently contextualized with student demographic data to allow for factor analysis to guide revisions to the instructional design of the game or course.

The second approach is the one we have now taken. This is to gather this data by constructing course evaluation instruments that have established validity and reliability. In addition, we employ qualitative means using student written reflections, interviews with students and instructors, forum postings, and student assignments.

16.6.1   Proposal 1: Collect Your Own Demographic Data

In terms of the quantitative data collection, we begin by establishing a valid and reliable means of assessing student learning in relationship to the computer literacy course content. However, a valid assessment instrument is not enough to address what factors impact student success or failure in the course. We have identified additional items are necessary to generate valid course game evaluations. Specific demographic questions we have posed are presented in Table 16.3.

Table 16.3 Demographics information requested from students for research

Age
Gender
Major
   Follow-up: Is this course required for their major?
Class year (Freshman, sophomore, junior, senior, other)
Ethnicity/Cultural identity
Is this the first time they have taken the course?
   Follow-up: If they have taken the course before, how many times?
   Follow-up: Did they drop, fail, or withdraw the last time?
   Follow-up: Who was their instructor last time?
How many hours are they taking this semester?
Do they have children?
Are they a full-time student?
Do they work?
   Follow-up: If so, is it part-time or full-time and how many hours per week worked?
   Have they played video games in the past?
   Do they like playing video games?

16.6.2   Proposal 2: Collect Your Own Factor Analysis Data

We gathered 5 years of institutional data along with our games. When we met to conduct longitudinal analysis, we learned that it violated basic standards of validity and reliability. Then, seeking to conduct factor analysis, but having no comparative valid evaluation data, we recommend asking your own questions. For example, we generated a series of questions related to student perceptions of the instructor. These included:

- Did they like the instructor?
- Did they feel supported by the instructor?
- Did they feel that the instructor was knowledgeable?
- Did they feel the instructor helped them be successful with the game?
- Did they like the manner in which the instructor taught?

In order to better understand how student learning preferences may have impacted their experience in the course, we also asked questions related to whether or not the game and course construction agreed with or conflicted with their ideas of what teaching and learning are supposed to be.

- How do you like to learn?
- How well did the game activities match with your learning preferences?
- How well do you feel you know basic computer literacy concepts?
- Would you take a course that included game like this again?

An additional set of data we have found quite valuable is student workload related to the course and related game. Often there are disconnects among institution, instructor, and student perceptions of what is a fair college workload for a three credit course. Therefore, we added the following questions.

- How many hours a week did you work on the course?
- How much work does the student feel is appropriate in a course?
- How much work did the student spend in their other courses?
- How many hours a week did you play the game?
- Was this more or less work/play than you expected?

Finally, we asked specific questions about how successful they felt at the conclusion of the game.

- Did you feel successful at the conclusion of the game?
- Did you feel successful at the conclusion of the course?
- What grade do you expect to earn in the course?
- How much of that success do you attribute to your own work?
- How much of that is the instructor?
- How much do you feel the game contributed to your learning?

As researchers and evaluators of the game component these questions have been valuable for determining the success of failure of the game, and, in the case of our AltRGs, the course. Answers to these questions have allowed us to conduct factor analysis leading to more valid conclusions regarding possible biases and external factors that we must be concerned with as we revise the design. This allows us to improve student game experience and learning outcomes.

16.6.3   Proposal 3: Be Prepared for Collection Challenges

Two major issues we have faced with collecting quantitative data are:

1. Students who fail the course can complete the course evaluation, which skews the data.
2. Students are encouraged to fill out evaluations, but not required by the institution to do so.

At other institutions, students cannot receive their grades until they fill out the course evaluation, but that is not the case everywhere. Therefore, we have required that students complete our unofficial, but extensive, course evaluation prior to being allowed to take the final exam becoming available in the learning management system. This provides valuable, detailed, and demographically contextualized data needed to evaluate the course game.

16.6.4   Proposal 4: Collect Contextual Qualitative Data

Our university does not collect qualitative data as part of their institutional research practices. Therefore, it fell to the research team to collect this data. This was a useful exercise because it allowed us to gather confirmatory and background data in the form of learning artifacts (i.e., written assignments), student forum postings, student and instructor reflections, and interviews may be used to contextualize survey answers. By using this data were able to examine the effectiveness of specific game and academic elements including the narrative, PBL tasks, their perceptions of the value of group work, engagement with characters, and whether the outcomes they achieved in the course matched what we had set forth for them. In order to overcome limited institutional data collection, we suggest that researchers either embed activities in their games that allow them to gather qualitative data or ensure that they speak with instructors to set up interviews with students outside of class time or ask individual students to keep reflective or evaluative reflections each time they complete game tasks. These can be guided or not, depending on whether there are questions about game elements that the researchers are particularly concerned about and want to assess their effectiveness at supporting student learning, affect, or other necessary research construct. Additional quantitative measures such as usability and play-testing surveys are also important means of evaluating the quality of the game that can bolster qualitative findings. Usability and play testing for educational games are discussed in detail by Warren, Jones, et al. (2010).

16.7   Conclusion

Upon completion of the Anytown research and moving into an academic position, it was assumed that institutional data would be shared freely and would be based on validated instruments that would make completing learning game research easier. However, such data is not always collected or made available, because universities do not always understand the value of their institutional data to researchers, narrowing their gaze to reserving it for their own ends. Thus, researchers evaluating constructs as complex as games for learning should take care to ensure that they have access to the data they need and make friends with institutional researchers.

Evaluating the effectiveness of an educational game or simulation is imperative to determine whether players have met educational goals set forth by the designers. The number of variables and instructional design components present in any educational game make assessing either the effectiveness of the game or evaluating the contributions of individual game elements towards student learning challenging at best. Collecting the amount of data necessary to clarify components that were effective and those that were not becomes daunting for educational game designers and researchers. Because the data needed in order to make this assessment is also of value to the educational institutions in which the experimental game methods are used, they are expected to be readily available. As such, leveraging institutional data is a valuable, though not trouble-free, avenue for improving the process of understanding the effectiveness of one's learning game.

In our experience, the data that most contextualizes findings and allows factor analysis is not available and sometimes not collected, whether it is demographic data such as the age and gender of participants in the course. Further, course evaluation data that is usually captured often violates basic parameters of positivist research paradigms, such as sufficient sample size or valid and reliable questions. After years of data collection, we had insufficient demographic data to run simple factor analyses.

Our lesson was learned. Prior to implementing an educational game, it is imperative that instructional designers find a way to gather necessary data. This may either be conducted alone or with the aid of their institution, though one should not expect their cooperation. One can work with institutional researchers to ensure necessary data is available at the onset of the study. If this is not feasible or available, it then falls to the researchers to supply their own instruments data available to adequately evaluate the effectiveness of an educational game.

Acknowledgments We would like to thank the University of North Texas for the Quality Enhancement Plan grant that funded the development of The Door version of this course. We would also like to thank Mary Jo Dondlinger, Julie McLeod, Tip Robertson, and Cliff Whitworth who helped with the development and initial research on that course iteration.

References

Al-Issa, A., & Sulieman, H. (2007). Student evaluations of teaching: Perceptions and biasing factors. *Quality Assurance in Education, 15*(3), 302–317.
Bachen, C., McLoughlin, M., & Garcia, S. (1999). Assessing the role of gender in college students evaluations of faculty. *Communication Education, 48*(3), 193–210.
Barab, S. (2006). Design-based research: A methodological toolkit for the learning scientist. In R. K. Sawyer (Ed.), The Cambridge Handbook of the Learning Sciences (pp. 153–169). New York: Cambridge University Press.
Bonk, C., Kirkley, J., Hara, N., & Denned, V. (Eds.). (2001). *Finding the instructor in post-secondary online learning: Pedagogical, social, managerial and technological locations.* London: Kogan Page.
Braskamp, L., & Ory, J. (1994). *Assessing faculty work: Enhancing individual and institutional performance.* San Francisco, CA: Jossey-Bass.
Brown, M. J. (2008). Student perceptions of teaching evaluations. *Journal of Instructional Psychology, 35*(2), 177–181.
Cardy, R. L., & Dobbins, G. H. (1986). Affect and appraisal accuracy: Liking as an integral dimension in evaluating performance. *Journal of Applied Psychology, 71*(4), 672–678.
Cashin, W. (1990). Students do rate different academic fields differently. *New Directions for Teaching and Learning, 43*, 113–121.
Crumbley, L., Henry, B., & Kratchman, S. (2001). Students perceptions of the evaluation of college teaching. *Quality Assurance in Education, 9*(4), 197–207.
Denson, N., Loveday, T., & Dalton, H. (2010). Student evaluation of courses: What predicts satisfaction? *Higher Education Research and Development, 29*(4), 339–356.
Dondlinger, M. J., & Warren, S. J. (2009). Alternate reality games as simulations to support capstone learning experiences. In D. Gibson & Y. K. Baek (Eds.), *Digital simulations for improving education: Learning through artificial teaching environments.* Hershey, PA: IGI Global.
Driscoll, J., & Cadden, D. (2010). Student evaluation instruments: The interactive impact of course requirement, student level, department and anticipated grade. *American Journal of Business Education, 3*(5), 21–30.

Feldman, K. A. (1993). College students views of male and female college teachers: Part II—Evidence from students evaluations of their classroom teachers. *Research in Higher Education, 34*(2), 151–211.

Frey, P., Leonard, D., & Beatty, W. (1975). Student ratings of instruction: Validation research. *American Educational Research Journal, 12*(4), 435–447.

Husbands, C., & Fosh, P. (1993). Students evaluation of teaching in higher education: Experiences from four European countries and some implications of the practice. *Assessment & Evaluation in Higher Education, 18*(2), 95–114.

Jonassen, D. (Ed.). (1999). *Designing constructivist learning environments* (Vol. 2). Mahwah, NJ: Lawrence Erlbaum.

Klopfer, E. (2008). *Augmented learning: Research and design of mobile educational games.* Cambridge, MA: MIT.

Koh, C., & Tan, T. (1997). Empirical investigation of the factors affecting SET results. *International Journal of Educational Management, 11*(4), 170–178.

Marsh, H. (1987). Students evaluations of university teaching: Research findings, methodological issues, and directions for future research. *International Journal of Educational Research, 11*(3).

Marsh, H., & Dunkin, M. (Eds.). (1992). *Students evaluations of university teaching: A multidimensional perspective* (Vol. 8). New York, NY: Agathon Press.

Marsh, H., & Roche, L. A. (1997). Making students evaluations of teaching effectiveness effective: The critical issues of validity, bias, and utility. *American Psychologist, 52,* 1187–1197.

Mintu-Wimsatt, A. (2001). Traditional vs. technology-mediated learning: A comparison of students course evaluations. *Marketing Education Review, 11,* 65–75.

Mintu-Wimsatt, A., Ingram, K., Milward, M., & Russ, C. (2006). On different teaching delivery methods: What happens to instructor courses evaluations? *Marketing Education Review, 16*(3), 49–57.

Nelson, L. M. (1999). Collaborative problem solving. In C. Reigeluth (Ed.), *Instructional-design theories and models: A new paradigm of instructional theory* (Vol. 2, pp. 241–267). Mahwah, NJ: Lawrence Erlbaum.

Ponder, J. (2007). Is student evaluation of teaching worthwhile? An analytical framework for answering the question. *Quality Assurance in Education, 15*(2), 178–191.

Robson, C. (2002). *Real world research.* Malden, MA: Blackwell.

Salen, K., & Zimmerman, E. (2004). *Rules of play: Game design fundamentals.* Cambridge, MA: MIT.

Savery, J. R., & Duffy, T. M. (1995). Problem-based learning: An instructional model and its constructivist framework. In B. Wilson (Ed.), *Constructivist learning environments: Case studies in instructional design.* Englewood Cliffs, NJ: Educational Technology Publications.

Shavelson, R., Phillips, D., Towne, L., & Feuer, M. (2003). On the science of educational design studies. *Educational Researcher, 32*(1), 25–28.

Simpson, P. M., & Siguaw, J. A. (2000). Student evaluations of teaching: An exploratory study of the faculty response. *Journal of Marketing Education, 22*(3), 199–213.

Smith, B. P., & Anderson, K. J. (2005). Students ratings of professors: The teaching style contingency for Latino professors. *Journal of Latinos and Education, 4*(2), 115–136.

Tatro, C. (1995). Gender effects on student evaluations of faculty. *Journal of Research and Development in Education, 28*(3), 169–173.

Warren, S. J., Barab, S., & Dondlinger, M. (2008). A MUVE towards PBL writing: Effects of a digital learning environment designed to improve elementary student writing. *Journal of Research on Technology in Education, 41*(1), 113–140.

Warren, S. J., Dondlinger, M., Jones, J., & Whitworth, C. (2010). Leveraging PBL and game to redesign and introductory course [Research]. *i-manager's Journal of Educational Technology, 7*(1), 40–51.

Warren, S. J., Dondlinger, M., McLeod, J., & Bigenho, C. (2011). Opening the door: An evaluation of the efficacy of a problem-based learning game [Research]. *Computers & Education, 58,* 1–15.

Warren, S. J., Dondlinger, M., Stein, R., & Barab, S. (2009). Educational game as supplemental learning tool: Benefits, challenges, and tensions arising from use in an elementary school classroom. *Journal of Interactive Learning Research, 20*(4), 487–505.

Warren, S. J., Jones, G., & Lin, L. (2010). Usability and play testing: The often missed assessment. In L. Annetta & S. Bronack (Eds.), *Serious educational game assessment: Practical methods and models for educational games, simulations and virtual worlds* (pp. 131–146). Rotterdam: Sense Publishers.

Warren, S. J., & Dondlinger, M. J. (2009). *Examining four games for learning: Research-based lessons learned from five years of learning game designs and development.* Paper presented at the Association for Educational Communications and Technology. Louisville, KY, USA

Warren, S. J., Stein, R., Dondlinger, M. J., & Barab, S. (2009). A look inside a design process: Blending instructional design and game principles to target writing skills. *Journal of Educational Computing Research, 40*(3), 295–301.

Whalen, S. P. (1999). Finding flow at school and at home: A conversation with Mihaly Csikszentmihalyi. *Journal of Secondary Gifted Education, 10*(4), 161–166.

Wirkala, C., & Kuhn, D. (2011). Problem-based learning in K-12 education: Is it effective and how does it achieve its effects? *American Educational Research Journal, 48*(5), 1157–1186.

Zimmerman, B. J. (1990). Self-regulated learning and academic achievement: An overview. *Educational Psychologist, 25*, 3–17.

Chapter 17
Examining Students' Cultural Identity and Player Styles Through Avatar Drawings in a Game-Based Classroom

Jen Katz-Buonincontro and Aroutis Foster

17.1 Introduction

Game-based assessment models do not sufficiently address the critical area of students' cultural identification and creativity in the context of learning subject matter content. This chapter expands these models by describing an innovative way to promote students' critical and creative thinking about their identity and learning goals using drawings—visual art media—with 3D digital game-based media. We explain the need and process of carefully integrating these seemingly incongruous types of media with ninth-grade students in a charter school located in a large Northeastern USA city.

First, we situate the chapter in student identity and game-based learning assessment literature. Next, the avatar-drawing project is described within the context of the overall game-based learning research project as well as the school setting. The methodology of arts-based educational research and the qualitative approach is described as well as emergent themes generated from four data sources: students' drawings, observations of students' drawing and alternately engaged in "gameplay," and small and whole-class group discussions from September to December 2010. The avatar drawings, discussions, and videotaped observations of gameplay fit into either a "race-less" or "race-based/cultural" model of student identity when learning mathematics content through the digital game *Dimension M*.

J. Katz-Buonincontro(✉) • A. Foster
School of Education, Drexel University, 3141 Chestnut Street,
Philadelphia, PA 19104, USA
e-mail: jkb@drexel.edu; aroutis@drexel.edu

D. Ifenthaler et al. (eds.), *Assessment in Game-Based Learning: Foundations,*   335
Innovations, and Perspectives, DOI 10.1007/978-1-4614-3546-4_17,
© Springer Science+Business Media New York 2012

17.2 Theoretical Perspectives

Our theoretical framework spans two areas: student identity and an assessment approach to game-based learning and game-playing styles. Using games in classrooms is not new (Charsky & Mims, 2008). People have been using digital games for learning in formal environments since the 1960s (Rabin, 2005). However, there is a paucity of empirical, game-based learning models for use in classrooms (National Research Council, 2011) that promote creativity. For the learner, creativity means perceiving characteristics of the self in learning, curriculum, and instruction. Many games may be designed well, but are incompatible with school curricula. Squire (2003) and Egenfeldt-Nielsen (2005) showed that integrating games into classroom takes considerable effort for teachers and students. Therefore, few game-based educational models provide transformative learning experiences. We contend that students can learn sufficient knowledge and skills and become reflective, creative thinkers in game-based learning environments that are carefully constructed and revised based on research.

17.2.1 Student Identity

Shaffer's (2004) theory of pedagogical praxis argues that students should develop epistemic frames, the basic knowledge and skills required to participate in developing the identities of a core professional area or career in epistemic games. Epistemic games (Shaffer, 2006) are designed to engage students in learning what it means to be a professional in a career. In classrooms, experiences similar to what epistemic games provide for developing professional identities aid students in exploring possible selves, which may lead to identity formation for academic learning (Foster, 2008; Markus & Nurius, 1986). Gee (2003, 2004, 2005) characterized student exploration of identities as projective identities in which learners project their real identity on to a virtual character, and a transactional relationship shapes the learners possible selves.

As symbols of human identity, avatars allow students to engage in the process of identity exploration by way of possible selves—selves that they may or may not want to be. Bailenson and Bell (2006) suggest that avatars' appearances and behaviors are plastic. But, as researchers immersed in urban educational research projects, we also perceived a need to explore the significance of race and gender in avatar development. In the present study, we did not go into the classroom with the goal of raising or enhancing student awareness about their racial identities. Rather, the students brought up the issue of race voluntarily. Students discussed how avatars used in the digital game were Anglo-American and that they did not like that feature of the game. This instigated a new study focus on how students articulated their racial identity in their avatar drawings, conversations, and large-group discussions. Data pointed towards a lack of racial identity in the avatars that influenced student motivation and interest in the mathematics game and by extension transformational learning.

Linking students' identity in the classroom with sociocultural factors of how they perceive themselves as gameplayers can help students who have an oppositional stance to mainstream learning culture (Fordham & Ogbu, 1986; Ladson-Billings & Tate, 1995). For example, Fordham and Ogbu (1986) argue that minority students must adopt a "race-less identity" to overcome oppositional views of cultural framing for achievement and motivation. On the other hand, Harris and Marsh (2010) and Hemmings (1998) argue that minority students who have stronger connections to their culture achieve more. Thus a theoretical framework for generating sufficient opportunities for students to learn core academic skills while exploring identities related to academic achievement whether it is a *race-less identity* or a *race-based identity* perspective is important. In particular, this study focuses on students' identity in the context of avatar design and construction through the act of drawing.

17.2.1.1 Descriptions of Students' Gameplay and Personalities

Player styles and motivation orientation can provide insight about students' cultural identity affiliation and learning. "Race-less" or "race-based" identification when associated with player types and motivation may have long-term implications for student learning and attitude. Player styles have been shown to reflect student achievement goal orientation (Foster, 2011; Heeter, 2009). Achievement goal theory research has shown that there are generally two types of motivational orientations for learning, including mastery (approach and avoidance) and performance (approach and avoidance) (Elliot & Church, 1997). Performance goal orientation is defined or characterized as students focusing on external goals such as scores and grades, to validate their success (Ames, 1992; Grant & Dweck, 2003). These students tend to cope less when placed in difficult situations. Students in this category need external factors to motivate them. For mastery motivation orientation, students' sense of satisfaction comes from the detailed understanding of the work and is not influenced by extrinsic factors such as scores or grades (Ames, 1992; Grant & Dweck, 2003).

Foster (2009, 2011) has shown that learners usually adopt two general player types: (1) *goal seekers* who play to beat a game and other students to validate themselves and (2) *explorers* who are focused on traversing all facets of a game for a more complete experience to learn much about it for deeper engagement even in the face of setbacks. *Explorers* are not concerned with beating other players. *Explorers* display the characteristics of what defines mastery goal orientation, which is more beneficial for long-term learning, valuing, and developing identities for areas that are valued. Foster (2009, 2011) argues that both player styles were able to gain statistically significant knowledge, but *explorers* valued or develop personal interest in the content and *goal seekers* did not. Player styles are adopted and can be shaped through careful game-based learning activities to enhance personal interest or epistemic curiosity in content.

Goal seekers are competitors who rely on external factors for motivation. On the other hand, an *explorer's* motivation derives from their internal drive for success—not from others. This has implications for student identity development: It pinpoints factors involving coping and developing personal interest or epistemic curiosity related long-term academic achievement. Whether students have a "race-less" or "race/cultural-based" identification with avatars, game-based learning models in classrooms that have carefully design activities to address achievement goal orientation for developing personal interest or epistemic curiosity can impact student transformational learning. By extension, the game-based learning activities can shape student interest in mathematics regardless of cultural identification.

17.2.2 Assessment Approach to Game-Based Learning

Play, Curricular activity, Reflection and Discussion (PCaRD) is one such empirically model that has been developed to address transformational learning. The PCaRD model integrates digital games into classrooms to guide skills and knowledge construction, motivational valuing, and identity formation through possible selves. "Possible selves" are identities students explore that they may or may not want to be. PCaRD was conceptualized and developed based on the work of Gros' (2007) four-part approach for providing a rich game-based learning experience based on experimentation, reflection, activity, and discussion activities. PCaRD extends this work to guide the process of using games in classrooms through opportunities for inquiry, communication, construction, and expression experiences in game *play*, followed by *curricular activity* that is led by a teacher who connects gameplay to learning goals. This is followed by *reflection* using blogs or wikis in which students write about their gameplay and connect it to the learning goals that were explored in the curricular activity. Finally, in *discussion*, the teacher solicits questions from students and scaffolds students' experience by providing feedback to students based on their written blogs or questions.

PCaRD creates opportunities for inquiry, communication, construction, and expression experiences, known as "ICCE" (Dewey, 1902). In turn, this aids students' learning including identity development and motivation. For instance, if students are playing a game to learn mathematics, all the activities in PCaRD should include an aspect of inquiry, communication, construction, and expression. That is, the game may contain all or some of the four parts of ICCE by design, but the curricular activity, reflection, and discussion phases should include ICCE to engage learners and their natural curiosities.

Thus, PCaRD aids student learning which includes developing student identity for particular content areas or epistemic frames, knowledge construction, and motivational valuing.

17.3 Qualitative Methodology

To examine student identity issues, the avatar-drawing project was constructed as part of a larger mixed methods study on developing ninth-graders' mathematics skills in a game-based learning environment. In order to initiate the study, we worked with teachers to examine extant student test scores, audiotaped discussions, and videotaped interactions to assess student learning, their valuing of the content, and the experience. An inductive approach resonant with principles of grounded theory methodology (Charmaz, 2006; Glaser & Strauss, 1967; Strauss & Corbin, 1990) was used to guide the data collection, management, and analysis phases.

The avatar-drawing project was not initially planned, but grew out of the need to address students' concern about the lack of racial identity represented in the game's avatars. Thus, we sought to better engage students at the beginning of the project as well as the desire to increase student involvement and participation in the actual gaming process. Grounded theory was selected as a suitable approach because of its inductive emphasis: We did not plan to address racial identity at the onset of the project. Secondly, we were not able to unearth research that used drawings in combination with interviews, discussions, and observations in game-based learning settings. The research questions were, "What issues of identity emerged during the drawing process through student comments, and small and large group discussions?" Secondly, "How did drawing affect (e.g., help, hinder, or otherwise change) student engagement in the game-based learning process?"

17.3.1 Sample

We began with a convenient and naturalistic sample of 25 ninth-grade students that enrolled in the game-based learning course about interactive digital environments for learning mathematics and science (Creswell & Clark, 2007; Tashakkori & Teddie, 2003).We recruited all the students to participate in the study as part of the class. Once students shifted classes or transferred at the beginning of the school year, approximately 21 students actually participated in the study; their parents signed consent forms indicating permission for their participation. All student identifiers were removed, and the data remains confidential and anonymous through the use of ID #s and pseudonyms. Of the 21 participants, 12 were female and 9 were male between the ages of 14 and 15. The class had 16 African-American, 1 White, 2 Latino, 1 Asian, and 1 student who describes herself as "other." The school has 97.9% African-American enrollment, 0.7% White, 0.7% Asian, 0.3 Latino, and 0.3 "other" students.

17.3.2 Data Sources

17.3.2.1 Avatar Drawings

At the outset of the game-based research project, students indicated that they did not like how the math-based video game provided avatars with Anglicized physiological features such as white skin and straight hair. Therefore, within the PCaRD application, the researchers devised a curricular activity that included a drawing project designed to give students an opportunity to create and personalize their own avatars. The aim was to enhance students' ability to connect with the mathematics game and develop mathematical identity by designing an avatar they could relate to so that they could integrate their avatar into the mathematics game.

We quickly learned that Dimension M did not offer opportunities for students to engage in inquiry, communication, or expression in the game world, which are pivotal to PCaRD. Thus, the avatar design activity was created as part of the curricular activity and later reflection and discussion to supplement playing the game with ICCE. To reiterate, the PCaRD model aims to scaffold and support student learning, motivation, and identity exploration.

Students were given pencils Crayola Multicultural Broad Line Washable Markers (2011), "multicultural" markers with an "ethnic-sensitive color palette" of pink, tan, brown, and black markers, pencils, erasable colored pencils, and $18' \times 24'$ white drawing-grade paper. In preparation for the art activity, one of the researchers drew a round outline of a head and shoulders with a banner for an avatar name. This basic outline jumpstarted students' drawings so that they could focus on exploring and developing their own individual identities, rather than focus on producing 3D portrait drawings, which are a more conventional and time-consuming drawing assignment. This approach provided a catalyst for launching students' attention on details like skin color, gender, and relevant embellishments. The avatar drawings were photographed and cataloged, and the drawing process was videotaped.

17.3.2.2 Interviews and Observations

In addition to the photographs of avatar drawings, the researchers audiotaped and videotaped conversations with individual students as they drew their avatars, and posed spontaneous questions in the classroom atmosphere to generate discussions and evoke deep thinking in students regarding their identity. Conversations arose from an unstructured interview protocol rooted in the following instructions and questions: "Draw your own avatar that represents you now in the game and give it a unique name. It should represent something special about who you are now and who you wish to be." Other questions we asked were:

- What special powers, skills, and abilities does your avatar have that you aspire to?
- What would your avatar be able to do in order to protect you in real life if that could be done?
- What aspects of your real self have you integrated into your avatar?
- How does the avatar project help you think about mathematics and your life?

When students gave brief responses to the questions, seemed reticent to participate in class activities, or expressed doubt in their ability to draw, researchers used several prompts to help students elaborate on their thoughts, feelings, and perceptions:

"Say more." "I am interested in what you have to say." "What does this mean in your *own* opinion?" "Cool." "I like that."

17.3.2.3 Short Questionnaires

The fourth data source was a short questionnaire created by the researcher and completed by students about their avatars based on the following three questions: "What is the color of your avatar and why?" "What ethnicity/race are your mother and father?" The purpose of the questionnaire was to understand students' reasoning behind their drawing choices—to see how they identified their race and ethnicity, and if they chose colors in their avatar drawings that were either consistent or inconsistent with their race and ethnicity.

17.3.3 Data Analysis

The student questionnaires, comments, and responses to researchers' prompts and questions provided sources of evidence of students' tacit perceptions of their racial identity. These perceptions were triangulated or compared to the students' drawings to either disconfirm or confirm the researchers' inferences of the symbols present in each drawing. Both researchers facilitated the drawing activity, individual interviews, and group "debriefs." The first author drew an example avatar drawing as a model for the students. We encouraged both the math and science teachers to create drawings too, which helped students engage in the drawings. Because the students did not have an arts class, it was important for them to be encouraged to try drawing. During the drawing activity, students revealed deeply personal thoughts and feelings regarding their racial identity as students. For many students, this was one of the first times they had the opportunity to discuss their beliefs about their racial and cultural identity as it related to being a student.

Data analysis centered on the identification of emergent codes that centered on race-based/cultural identity. While gender issues arose during open coding, the main axial codes were race and ethnicity. This included the actual skin color chosen by student artists. In addition, ethnic identity discussed by student artist, for example, "Jamaican," "Hispanic," or "African-American" or "White." This was very important because student demographic data does not capture the nuances in ethnic identity. The second theme was a race-less/cultural-less identity. This was indicated by a lack of reference to skin color, identification with being black, and the symbolism of each students' avatar name. These were names that reflected student aspirations or conversely a lack of academic aspiration. In addition to racial and ethnic identity, gender was also a focus of student artists, which included bodily adornment, for example, earrings and accentuated facial features, for example, red lips/lipstick; large, curled eyelashes. In addition to aspects of racial identity, tacit perceptions of schooling emerged and names that reflect gendered aspirations, for example, "Prissy."

17.4 Results

17.4.1 Student Perceptions of Their Racial and Cultural Identity and Schooling Experience in Avatar Drawings

In this section, we first give brief descriptions of the overarching themes and then discuss two students who represent the opposites in the continuum of race-based vs. race-less identity and their player types and motivation orientation expressed in the avatar drawings, interviews, debriefs, short questionnaires, and observations. Figure 17.1 gives an example of two avatar drawings and how they symbolize each student's cultural identity.

In the next section, we highlight two students, Shakil and Mitchell, who displayed characteristics consistent with what we are calling either a "race-based" or a "race-less" African-American cultural identity. Pseudonyms are used in the reporting of the data analysis. We describe these two students in terms of their game-play styles and their motivation as it relates to performance and mastery motivated orientations.

17.4.2 "Race-Based/Cultural" Avatar Drawings

For the race-based/cultural identity category, Shakil displayed the strongest affiliation. The following quote is a brief excerpt that illustrates his belief and identification with African-American culture as a source of power:

> My avatar is basically like Barak Obama…I want my avatar to symbolize something like Barack Obama to help people out. In the game, instead of scoring points, I'm looking to help people or just to have fun. I want…a power that can lead. I want to help people.

This quote shows how Shakil consciously modeled his avatar drawing after his own role model, President Barack Obama. Shakil extracted the values that Obama embodies to him for key attributes of his avatar drawing. Shakil's attempt to showcase his identity as a young African-American male was evident in his avatar drawing. This was linked to his affinity with President Barack Obama as a political leader and African-American role model. In keeping with the patriotic theme in his avatar, Shakil responded on the short questionnaire, "The color of my Avatar is Red, White, Blue because it is symbolic to American, and a symbol of honor." Although this appeared to be a "race-less" response, Shakil later discussed his avatar in a large-group discussion as reflecting his own skin color. He also described how it was important to keep his own facial features as well as his desire to emulate the qualities of Barack Obama as the "first Black president." The extensive dialog that transpired over several weeks in the research project was useful for revealing students' tacit perceptions of their own racial and student identity.

Shakil was one of the first students to become interested in starting and completing his avatar drawing. Compared to some other students, he did not doubt his drawing

Race-based Avatar Drawing: "Obama-56" *Drawn by Shakil*	Raceless Avatar Drawing: "Bored-1" *Drawn by Mitchell*
	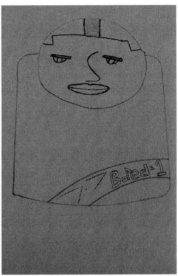
This avatar drawing indicates Shakil's attempt to showcase his identity as a young African-American male, which is linked to his affinity with President Barack Obama as a political leader and African-American role model. Prominent features of this drawing include skin color that reflects the students' skin color; a mustache that is very similar to his own mustache. The helmet with visor symbolizes his desire to transform into a confident warrior. The stars reflect his American identity and his chosen avatar name.	In contrast to the avatar drawing on the left, 'Bored-1' exemplifies Mitchell's lack of engagement with school as indicated in the quoted passage above. Additionally, Mitchell uses minimal lines and no color to express his identity. He reported that the stripe on top of the head was a Mohawk hairstyle to symbolize his desire for greater novelty and challenge in his academics.

Fig. 17.1 Race-based vs. race-less avatar drawings

abilities and freely experimented with the art supplies. He was able to concentrate for long stretches of time while other students worked on their drawings (in groups of 4 at a time) and continued to play the mathematics video game.

For Shakil, generating unique, highly individualized attributes of his avatar seemed to come easily. Therefore, it can be deduced that his creativity level seemed fairly high in this particular project. Prominent features of this drawing include skin color that reflects the students' skin color—a mustache that is very similar to his mustache (see Fig. 17.1). The helmet with visor symbolizes his desire to transform into a confident warrior. The stars reflect his American identity and his chosen avatar name. Overall, he did not struggle to produce a creative drawing that represented an especially evolved racial/cultural identity.

17.4.3   Player Types, Motivation Orientation, and Cultural Identity by Personal Affiliation

At the outset of the yearlong research study, Shakil's orientation towards gameplay seemed very generous. As mentioned in the quote above, his main goal was to help others score points. He commented that in middle school, he was considered a leader in the classroom and regarded by others as someone who helps his peers to benefit the group.

Shakil's gameplay was characterized as being very helpful to peers and less focused on doing well in the game to gain mathematics knowledge. Shakil seemed more focus on self-validation for helping peers and knowing how to play chess and by extension being able to do mathematics. However, he described himself as loathing mathematics. In gameplay, he competed in a team that included some of the best gameplayers in the class and commends himself on being able to help them. However, Shakil was always scoring the lowest points in the game for mathematics knowledge. This seemed inconsistent with his creativity and seeming desire to help other learners in the classroom, as indicated in the above section. In addition, he had only a one-point gain from pretest (13) to posttest (14) on a 32-item Mathematics Knowledge assessment. Thus, Shakil's attitude in helping other students may have been a result of his attitude or his inability to do well in mathematics and play the game. He indicated that he did not like mathematics, but his valuing of the activity increased from pretest to posttest. This is likely not due to playing the game to learn mathematics, but results of the PCaRD model to engage students and allow Shakil help other and see the connects of mathematics in the avatar activity to possibilities of what he may want to be.

Six months after the phase 1 of the yearlong game-based learning course, meetings with school principal, teachers, and experiences with two other games, it was observed that Shakil started being truant in school. Over time, he had become dissatisfied with his school experiences. Shakil believed that he is smart and intelligent and can perform well, but his scores on the assessments in the game-based learning course and meetings with teachers say otherwise. He told the researchers that he came to school on some Thursdays only to be in the game-based learning course.

Shakil exhibited behavior consistent with being a *goal seeker* with self-validation and motives based primarily on external factors. He sought to help others not because he truly wanted to help but because he did not want to do the mathematics. His helping of other students to avoid doing mathematics was sabotaging his own chances of constructing mathematics knowledge and identity; though at the outset of forming teams, he sought to be on the strongest teams to compete against his classmates to win.

17.4.4 *"Race-Less" Avatar Drawings*

In addition to drawings that fell into the race-based/cultural category, drawings that did not feature colors, symbols, and names reflective of students' racial and ethnic identity were created. Mitchell displayed strong characteristics of "race-less" African-American cultural identity. For Mitchell, his lack of desire to accentuate his race, gender, and culture seemed to be related to his lack of engagement as an academic learner. In the following discussion between Mitchell and the first author, the student discusses why he named his avatar "Bored 1" (see Fig. 17.1).

> *Researcher [R]*: In the game [that you are creating], do you get to decide how you dress and act too?
> *Mitchell [M]*: Ahuh.
> *R*: Is this name of the avatar [being drawn] part of the game too?
> *M*: No, it's just my personality.
> *M*: I'm bored.
> *R*: Tell me what you're bored with.
> *M:* I guess, school.
> *R*: This is your first year at this school, right?
> *M*: Ahum.
> *R*: Is it more boring than last year at your other school?
> *M*: It's a little less boring here, but…
> *R*: What makes it boring to you?
> *M*: Schoolwork is kinda easy.
> *R*: That's because you already know the kinda stuff they're trying to teach you?
> *M*: I catch on so quickly, that it's not that…
> *R*: Yah, it's not that challenging? What's one power your avatar could have to improve and change that situation?

After this exchange, Mitchell discussed the desire for others to be lazy and to do away with homework. But these solutions still didn't address his interest in being challenged in school. After several prompts from the first author, he finally said that he wanted his avatar to have a symbol of novelty, which he represented with a Mohawk style haircut. Although Mitchell could not directly address the issue of being disengaged or suggest why he was not more motivated to participate in class activities, Mitchell did incorporate his desire for novelty into his drawing (see Fig. 17.1).

For Mitchell, deriving new ideas about his avatar was challenging. His creativity seemed stifled which paralleled his lack of engagement and interest as a learner in the classroom.

In contrast to Shakil's avatar drawing named "Obama-56," the avatar drawing "Bored-1" exemplifies Mitchell's lack of engagement with school as indicated in the quoted passage above. Mitchell uses minimal line in bold, black marker and no skin color to express his identity. He lingered over, drawing only the outlines of essential features such as his eyes, eyebrows, mouth, and nose. Notably, Mitchell did not choose to embellish his "Bored-1" with regard to his clothing or other symbols. "Bored-1" has little expression and a flat affect—his eyes seem to glower at the viewer. Mitchell reported that the stripe on top of the head was a Mohawk hairstyle to symbolize his desire for greater novelty and challenge in his academics.

17.4.4.1   Player Types, Motivation Orientation, and Cultural Identity by Personal Affiliation

In addition, in the discussion activity focused on the avatar drawing and race/cultural identity, Mitchell did not identify his character as having African-American features nor did he describe it as having academic prowess in mathematics. However, his avatar displayed novel attributes and along with his personal ability of playing the mathematics game very well. Mitchell was one of the best players at the game; however, he did not focus on mathematics learning.

Unlike Shakil, Mitchell did not offer much help to others unless asked. His gameplay was focused on doing well at the game, though he had no interest in or enjoyed mathematics. Shakil and Mitchell were teammates and often had clashes about who was doing the most work to support the team. Mitchell would also have arguments with another team Mike who competed with him for best players in the class in terms of gameplay. Mitchell's attitude to do well in the game was not because of an interest in mathematics. Of all the students in the class, only female students like or had interest in mathematics. Nonetheless, he had a six-point gain from pretest (17) to posttest (23) on a 32-item Mathematics Knowledge assessment. Like Shakil, Mitchell also valued the gaming and the activities to engage in mathematics learning, even though he had no initial interest in mathematics.

Mitchell displayed a goal seeker play style and a mastery orientation motivation approach to learning. Six months after the mathematics game, he displayed the same gameplay characteristics from the mathematics game for a physics game and a social studies game. He did not offer to help others unless the researchers asked him to support others, and he is always the first player to do well at the game. His focused was always to do well at the game even if it meant he had to learn the school content. He did not seek to self-validate, but to work purely in isolation to challenge himself.

17.5   Discussion of Student Identity

In this section, we compare and contrast the results of this study with literature on student identity and arts-based research. As symbols of human identity, the avatar-drawing project allowed students to explore, discuss, and interrogate a "possible self," that is, who they may or may not want to be (Foster, 2008; Markus & Nurius, 1986). Building on the notion that avatars' appearances and behaviors are plastic

(Bailenson & Bell, 2006) and that working in digital media is fluid and thus fosters constructability (Brown & Sorensen, 2010), we contend that student identity—based on the analysis of their avatar drawings, interviews, and observations—reveals significant portraits of students' racial and academic identity.

And yet the way the students portrayed themselves in the avatar drawings remains complex and, in some ways, contradicts extant literature. This study links students' identity in the classroom with sociocultural factors of how they perceive themselves, as gameplayers can help students who have an oppositional stance to mainstream learning culture (Fordham & Ogbu, 1986; Ladson-Billings & Tate, 1995). Fordham and Ogbu (1986) argue that minority students must adopt a "race-less identity" to overcome oppositional views of cultural framing for achievement and motivation. Mitchel did not have an oppositional stance, but rather, an indifference stance. He did not have a positive attitude to mathematics, but achieved well in mathematics and learned to value mathematics through the gaming activities of PCaRD. Mitchell adopted a race-less stance and displayed a mastery approach to gameplay. He was interested in doing well at the game and but not interested in mathematics content. He said he was bored because he was not being challenged. Boredom might have been the reason why Mitchell played the game so diligently, even though he had no interest in mathematics and had a statistically significant increase in Mathematics Knowledge.

On the other hand, Harris and Marsh (2010) and Hemmings (1998) argue that minority students who have stronger connections to their culture achieve more. However, Shakil displayed characteristics, which are counterintuitive to this argument. He displayed a performance-avoidance orientation motivation and *goal seeker* player styles, which indicates a negative approach to learning and motivation to learn. He did not have statistically significant difference in mathematics knowledge, but he valued the activity of doing mathematics in game after the experience.

With regard to arts-based research methods, this study expands the way drawing is used as a 2D form of media in combination with game-based media. In this chapter, we systematically examined how students' symbols and color choices reflected their views of "self" and how the act of drawing was a "medium of expression" (Eisner, 1997, 2009).

As a medium of expression, students talked more easily and fluidly about school when drawing. This became a significant part of their engagement in two ways: First, the avatar-drawing project helped to catapult their engagement in the mathematics learning process. When prompted, students articulated their goals for being more successful math problem solvers. As we discussed in the PCaRD model-based on inquiry, communication, construction, and expression, the drawing activity helped to foster student creativity. As a stand-alone commercial game, Dimension M would not have developed student creativity. However, because we created a curricular activity (Ca) involving avatar design that tied to students locally situated experiences for cultural/racial identification and continuously prompted the students to reflect and discuss their values, they developed new thoughts on their academic and future goals, as well as their racial and cultural identity. The PCaRD model facilitated students' interests and aided valuing of mathematics even if they had no initial interest in the activity. The model provided opportunities for these African-American students to value mathematics in the gaming activity regardless of their racial/cultural identification.

Secondly, the act of drawing avatars allowed students to imagine themselves more easily as gameplayers. Because students became so immersed in playing the games, we were able to observe what type of game-playing style they exhibited. Thus, the drawing afforded us an understanding of their goal seeking vs. exploring style. Students play style and motivational orientation allowed us to get better understanding of them as learners.

In keeping with McNiff (1998), the drawings collectively provided a window of insight into students' subconscious thoughts, feelings, and perspectives about engagement and disengagement in schooling, race-based vs. race-less identity, and academic goals. Prior to the avatar-drawing activities, students struggled to concentrate, and interpersonal conflict was not uncommon when we asked them to work in teams to play the game and solve math problems. The avatar drawing helped increase their ability to concentrate, argue and talk less about social gossip, and use nonverbal communication expressed in visual symbols.

The visual symbols used in the drawings (Siegesmund & Cahnmann-Taylor, 2008) were complex, not simplistic. The drawings represent the students' efforts to express what they KNOW with how they literally SEE themselves (Berger, 1972 in Weber, 2008). This allowed us, as researchers, to more closely examine the phenomenon of student racial and academic identity in a more subtle, complex, and ultimately holistic manner. Students became engrossed in the drawing process, which leads to an increase in their participation in the gaming process and learning about algebraic concepts. To elaborate on the study's findings, we now turn towards implications.

17.6   Integrating Academic, Possible, and Virtual Selves: Towards a Grounded Theory of Student Identity in Game-Based Learning

While grounded theory might utilize more data across multiple sites, this approach best fit our novel use of drawings in combination with more typically utilized data sources, for example, interviews, as well as the novel, under-researched aspect of our research topic. We thus advise the reader to consider the resulting propositions in light of the fact that additional research may be needed to revise this grounded theory. Based on the analysis of students' avatar drawings, interviews, surveys, and group discussions presented in this chapter, we propose a grounded theory of student identity in game-based learning that synthesizes three aspects of student identity oft treated as separate facets in research: academic, possible, *and* virtual selves.

17.6.1 Academic Selves

In order to see themselves reflected in curriculum and instruction, students must truly see race (and other cultural facets of identity) addressed in an open-ended, unproscriptive manner. Prior research indicates that students remain disengaged from curriculum when they do not see themselves represented in the curriculum.

Racially neutral or racially biased games and curriculum ignore student needs, motivation, and input. Engaging students in large urban school districts means reconsidering how we present information. For some students, like Shakil, for example, who is a social learner, he was excited to be a role model like Barack Obama and share his expertise. While this did not reflect nor predict an immediate increase in his mathematics test scores, his motivation and interest in school and mathematics might increase and manifest itself in other ways. This would require following up with Shakil's academic progress using historical, longitudinal research.

Academic self-competence is related, theoretically, to student creativity. We assert that because Shakil's own social nature was enhanced, that his confidence in articulating and expressing ideas was also fostered. Thus, his creative capacities seemed to increase through the act of drawing, discussing his drawing, and helping his peers in the game. Conversely, for Mitchell, who seemed disengaged in school, his creativity did not seem to be enhanced. Although Mitchell did well at math, he preferred to work alone. Thus, to enhance Mitchell's creativity, other curricular means would need to be explored and tailored to his academic competence.

In Fig. 17.1, we envision a student exploring and reifying aspects of himself or herself as an academic learner. In this case, the student practices solving mathematics problems in the game and discussing strategies aloud with peers and with teachers (while computing mathematics problems and participating in other mathematics activities in a separate mathematics class).

17.6.2 Possible Selves

The second component of this grounded theory centers on how students envision themselves in the future. We contend that a student starts to build a desire to solve mathematics problems through embodying an avatar through playing a commercial game. In order for students to develop the future selves they want, they must develop personal interest or epistemic curiosity for the content they may loathe.

Epistemic curiosity or personal interest can be developed in domains that learners see as sufficiently new, complex, or uncertain. This condition is needed in order for learners to want to explore and sufficiently comprehend in a coherent manner, as well as feel confident that they will be able to understand or cope successfully (Brophy, 2008). It is in game-based learning spaces with carefully design activities to scaffold ICCE experiences that students' possible selves are explored for developing epistemic frames or academic identity.

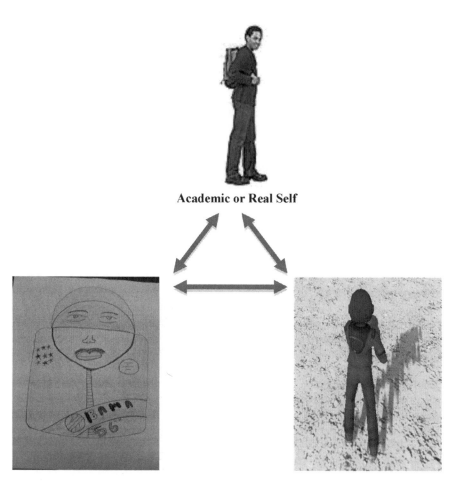

Academic or Real Self

Fig. 17.2 Three elements of student identity based on avatar research project

For learners to develop the epistemic frames necessary for future careers or professions, novel models in virtual spaces are needed to support gameplay and enhance future or possible selves that are not connected to student current self-concept. Exploring possible selves with thoughts removed from current self-concept aids student engagement with possibilities that motivate them to learn as well as shape their identity for achievement (Daisey & José-Kampfner, 2002).

17.6.3 Virtual Selves

The third, final component of the grounded theory focuses on how a student develops an affinity with a specialized set of skills and sense of positive self by representing himself or herself as a unique avatar (see Fig. 17.2) that either incorporates or eschews aspects of his or her own racial/cultural identity.

Students' identity emerges as results of their academic or real self that includes their play styles and motivation orientation, which influences their belief and attitude as learners. Students' virtual self/game avatar reflects their mathematical identity and character with knowledge and skills that the real self does not possess. Finally, the designed avatar is combination of the game avatar and the real self for what students want to project in terms of their cultural identity and possible self. This model reflect the complexity involve in describing students emerging cultural as well as academic self, and that process is dynamic, but can be influenced through game-based learning. Gee (2003, 2004) characterized student exploration of identities as projective identities in which learners project their real identity on to a virtual character, and a transactional relationship shapes the learners possible selves.

While games may aid in the development of situational interest for content such as mathematics (Malone & Lepper, 1987), long-term achievement may depend on the student development of identities that aid the development of epistemic frames. This is possible through game-based learning activities that aid the development of player styles. The promotion of player styles that facilitate the development achievement goal orientations for long-term epistemic curiosity can shape student identities for learning.

Acknowledgment   We wish to acknowledge the ninth grade students' hard work and effort in this research project.

References

Ames, C. (1992). Classrooms: Goals, structures, and student motivation. [Peer Reviewed Empirical]. *Journal of Educational Psychology, 84*(3), 261–271.

Bailenson, J. N., & Bell, A. C. (2006). Transformed social interaction: Exploring the digital plasticity of avatars. In R. Schroeder & A. S. Axelsson (Eds.), *Avatars at work and play: Collaboration and interaction in shared virtual environments* (pp. 1–16). Netherlands: Springer.

Berger, J. (1972). Ways of seeing. London: Penguin.

Brophy, J. (2008). Scaffolding appreciation for school learning: An update. In M. L. Maehr, S. A. Karabenick, & T. C. Urdan (Eds.), *Advances in motivation and achievement* (Vol. 15, pp. 1–48). Bingley, UK: Emerald.

Brown, A., & Sorensen, A. (2010). Integrating creative practice and research in the digital media arts. In H. Smith & R. T. Dean (Eds.), *Practice-led research, research-led practice in the creative arts* (pp. 153–165). Edinburgh, Scotland: Edinburgh University Press.

Creswell, J. W., & Clark, V. L. P. (2007). Designing and conducting mixed methods research. Thousand Oaks, CA: Sage Publications, Inc.

Charsky, D., & Mims, C. (2008). Integrating commercial off-the-shelf video games into school curriculums. *TechTrends, 52*(5), 38–44.

Charmaz, K. (2006). *Constructing grounded theory: A practical guide through qualitative analysis*. Thousand Oaks, CA: Sage.

Crayola Multicultural Broad Line Washable Markers. (2011). Retrieved from http://www.crayola.com/products/list.cfm?categories=MARKERS.

Daisey, P., & José-Kampfner, C. (2002). The power of story to expand possible selves for Latina middle school students. *Journal of Adolescent and Adult Literacy, 45*, 578–587.

Dewey, J. (1902). *The child and the curriculum*. Chicago, IL: University of Chicago Press.

Eisner, E. (1997). The promise and perils of alternative forms of data representation. *Educational Researcher, 26*(6), 4–10.

Eisner, E. (2009). Art and knowledge. In J. G. Knowles & A. L. Cole (Eds.), *Handbook of the arts in qualitative research* (pp. 3–12). Thousand Oaks, CA: Sage.

Elliot, A. J., & Church, M. A. (1997). A hierarchical model of approach and avoidance achievement motivation. *Journal of Personality and Social Psychology, 72*(1), 218–232.

Egenfeldt-Nielsen, S. (2005). Beyond edutainment: Exploring the educational potential of computer games. Dissertation, IT-University of Copenhagen, Copenhagen, Denmark. Retrieved from http://www.itu.dk/people/sen/egenfeldt.pdf.

Fordham, S., & Ogbu, J. (1986). Black student school success: Coping with the burden of 'acting white'. *The Urban Review, 18*, 1–31.

Foster, A. (2011). The process of learning in a simulation strategy game: Disciplinary knowledge construction. *Journal of Educational Computing Research, 45*(1), 1–27.

Foster, A. N. (2008). Games and motivation to learn science: Personal identity, applicability, relevance and meaningfulness [Conceptual]. *Journal of Interactive Learning Research, 19*(4), 597–614.

Foster, A. N. (2009). Gaming their way: Learning in simulation strategy video games. Unpublished dissertation. Michigan State University, East Lansing, MI.

Gee, J. P. (2003). *What video games have to teach us about learning and literacy.* New York, NY: Palgrave MacMillan.

Gee, J. P. (2004). *Situated language and learning: A critique of traditional schooling.* New York, NY: Routledge.

Gee, J. P. (2005). *Why video games are good for your soul: Pleasure and learning.* Melbourne, Australia: Common Ground Publishing.

Glaser, B. G., & Strauss, A. L. (1967). *The discovery of grounded theory: Strategies for qualitative research.* Chicago, IL: Aldine.

Gros, B. (2007). Digital games in education: The design of games-based learning environments [Conceptual]. *Journal of Research on Technology in Education, 40*(1), 23–38.

Grant, H., & Dweck, C. S. (2003). Clarifying achievement goals and their impact. [peer reviewed empirical]. *Journal of Personality and Social Psychology, 85*(3), 541–553.

Harris, A. L., & Marsh, K. (2010). Is a raceless identity an effective strategy for academic success among blacks? *Social Science Quarterly, 91*(5), 1242–1263.

Hemmings, A. (1998). The self transformations of African-American achievers. *Youth & Society, 29*, 330–368.

Heeter, C. (2009). Play styles and learning. In R. Ferdig (Ed.), Handbook of Research on Effective Electronic Gaming in Education (Vol. 2, pp. 826-846). Hershey, PA: Information Science Reference.

Ladson-Billings, G., & Tate, W. F., IV. (1995). Toward a critical race theory of education. *Teachers College Record, 97*(1), 47–68.

Malone, T. W., & Lepper, M. R. (1987). Making learning fun: A taxonomy of intrinsic motivations for learning. In R. E. Snow & M. J. Farr (Eds.), *Aptitude, learning and instruction* (Cognitive and affective processed analysis, Vol. 3). Mahwah, NJ: Lawrence Erlbaum.

Markus, H., & Nurius, P. (1986). Possible selves [peer-reviewed]. *American Psychologist, 41*(9), 954–969.

McNiff, S. (1998). *Art-based research.* Philadelphia, PA: Jessica Kingsley.

National Research Council. (2011). Learning Science Through Computer Games and Simulations. In S. Committee on Science Learning: Computer Games, and Education , M. A. Honey & M. Hilton (Eds.). Washington, DC: Board on Science Education, Division of Behavioral and Social Sciences and Education.

Rabin, S. (Ed.). (2005). Introduction to game development. Hingham, Massachusetts: Charles River Media, Inc.

Squire, K. (2003). Video games in education. *International Journal of Intelligent Simulations and Gaming, 2*(1), 49–62.

Shaffer, D. W. (2004). Pedagogical praxis: The professions as models for postindustrialization [Theoretical]. *Teachers College Record, 106*(7), 1401.

Shaffer, D. W. (2006). *How computer games help children learn.* NY: PALGRAVE MACMILLAN.

Siegesmund, R., & Cahnmann-Taylor, M. (2008). The tensions of arts-based research in education reconsidered: The promise for practice. In R. Siegesmund & M. Cahnmann-Taylor (Eds.), *Arts-based research in education: Foundations for practice* (pp. 231–246). New York, NY: Routledge.

Strauss, A., & Corbin, J. (1990). *Basics of qualitative research: Grounded theory procedures and techniques*. London: Sage.

Tashakkori, A., & Teddie, C. (Eds.). (2003). Handbook of mixed methods in social and behavioral research (1 ed.). Thousand Oaks, CA: Sage Publications.

Weber, S. (2008). Visual images in research. In J. G. Knowles & A. L. Cole (Eds.), *Handbook of the arts in qualitative research* (pp. 41–54). Thousand Oaks, CA: Sage.

Chapter 18
Measurement and Analysis of Learner's Motivation in Game-Based E-Learning

Ioana Ghergulescu and Cristina Hava Muntean

18.1 Introduction

Nowadays, the learners have changed. They belong to a Digital Wisdom generation, and they use and manipulate technology easily. At the same time, significant progress was made in the areas of entertainment games and e-learning. Player's gesture, emotion, motivation and affect are captured and used by the entertainment games. The e-learning systems personalise the educational content and the learning process based on the learner's knowledge, goals and preferences to better suit their needs.

E-learning has started to integrate games in the learning process due to its affordances to support higher-order learning outcome, due to ability to engage the new generation of learners and to bridge the gap between their expectations and the traditional teaching and learning practices. Educational games and game-based e-learning have emerged in this context, and they proved to be effective learning environments.

Prensky has introduced the term "digital game-based learning" as a new learning paradigm—"learning via play". He conceptualised the term digital game-based learning as "any marriage of educational content and computer games" (Prensky, 2001, p. 145).

The term game-based learning covers "learning approach derived from the use of computer games that possess educational value", "software applications that use games for learning and educational purposes" and "the use of non-digital games (e.g. card and board games) as activity to engage learners" (Tang, Hanneghan, & El Rhalibi, 2009, p. 3). Connolly and Stansfield (2006, 2011, p. 1766) defined game-based e-learning as representing "the use of computer games to deliver, support, and enhance teaching, learning, assessment and evaluation". Electronic games for the learning purpose were defined under different terms such as educational games (Tang et al., 2009), digital educational games (Koidl, Mehm, Hampson, Conlan, &

I. Ghergulescu (✉) • C.H. Muntean
School of Computing, National College of Ireland, Mayor Street, IFSC, Dublin 1, Ireland
e-mail: ioana.ghergulescu@student.ncirl.ie; cmuntean@ncirl.ie

D. Ifenthaler et al. (eds.), *Assessment in Game-Based Learning: Foundations,*
Innovations, and Perspectives, DOI 10.1007/978-1-4614-3546-4_18,
© Springer Science+Business Media New York 2012

Göbel, 2010) or eGames (Burgos et al., 2008). Related terminology for the usage of games in education is serious games. However, serious games' term includes games for education such as games for health, training, etc., and may not include game-play elements. Relationships between similar concepts on game-based learning were discussed by Breuer and Bente (2010) and Tang et al. (2009).

Educational games proved to be effective learning tools, presenting a number of benefits such as:

- Improve student's knowledge (Kebritchi, Hirumi, & Bai, 2010; Miller, Chang, Wang, Beier, & Klisch, 2011; Papastergiou, 2009; Tüzün, YIlmaz-Soylu, Karakus, Inal, & KIzIlkaya, 2009)
- Support learner to acquire new skills (Connolly, Stansfield, & Hainey, 2011; Moreno-Ger et al., 2010)
- Increase learner's motivation (Liu & Chu, 2010; Miller et al., 2011; Papastergiou, 2009; Sancho & Fernandez-Manjon, 2010; Tüzün et al., 2009)
- Increase learner's satisfaction (Miller et al., 2011; Moreno-Ger et al., 2010)

At the same time, educational games make knowledge acquisition and knowledge assessment a transparent process, a low cost and risk-free environment.

Games not only are good "learning engines", but they are also good "assessment engines" (Gee & Shaffer, 2010, p. 24). This is because games can track many different types of information about the player over time. Games can also embed assessment into the learning process without disrupting the game flow. However, the implementation of assessment features into game-based e-learning environments is only in the early stages (Ifenthaler, Eseryel, & Ge, 2011).

Most of today's game-based e-learning environments are not adaptive, learners receiving "one size fits all" educational games beside the fact that they have different familiarity with the game, knowledge, motivation, etc. Since learners can easily become demotivated, game adaptation strategies are needed in order to keep learners motivated during the game play.

However, in order to make motivation-based adaptation possible, different kinds of information about learners should be analysed. Assessing player's motivation in real time is a challenging process since learner's speaking tone and behaviour cues cannot be analysed as in traditional learning that involves direct contact with the learner.

Although significant research was conducted for measuring and assessing learner motivation in e-learning, little is known about how to assess the learner motivation and to predict the learner motivation trend, in game-based e-learning.

This chapter presents current trends in the assessment of game-based learning environments focusing on the assessment of learner/player's motivation in particular. Motivation assessment strategies in e-learning and game-based e-learning are presented. Methods for gathering information on learners, used in the assessment process, are discussed. Metrics that use the gathered information for measuring learner's motivation are presented. Despite the multitude of metrics that have been proposed, most of metrics are difficult to be mapped into game-based e-learning as they are learning environment dependent or learning material dependent. To overcome this problem, this chapter proposes four generic metrics for measuring learner's motivation in game-based e-learning. The four metrics are *TimeOnTask*, *NumRepeatTask*, *NumHelpRequest* and *SelfEfficacy*.

The remaining of the chapter is structured as followed. Next section provides a general overview of the current assessment trends in game-based e-learning. This is followed by the presentation of the methods for motivation measurement depending on how the information is gathered, as well as the four generic metrics proposed for measuring and assessing player's motivation in game-based e-learning. The last section concludes the chapter.

18.2 Assessment in Game-Based E-Learning

In an educational context, assessment refers to the process of analysing and interpreting various information in order to diagnose and/or assign a value to learner's knowledge, beliefs, skills and/or affective states. Measurement represents the process of collecting the information needed for assessment.

Various approaches that classify the assessment in game-based e-learning have been proposed in the literature such as assessment based on its purpose (Shute, 2009) or based on the methods the information is collected and assessed (Ifenthaler et al., 2011).

Depending on its purpose, assessment can be categorised in summative assessment and formative assessment. Summative assessment is performed at the end of a major learning event with the goal to evaluate the learning process and gives evidence about the achievement of the learning goals (assessment of learning). Formative assessment is a progressive/continuous assessment with the purpose/goal to diagnose and further improve the learning process (assessment for learning) (Shute, 2009). When the formative assessment is embedded into the learning environment in a way that is invisible to the learners, it is called stealth assessment (Shute).

Depending on the methods the information is collected and assessed, two types of assessments can be identified: external and internal assessments. External assessment is not part of the game environment, while internal assessment is (Ifenthaler et al., 2011).

This chapter proposes to classify assessment in game-centred assessment and player-/learner-centred assessment. Game-centred assessment refers to the assessment of the game environment in terms of different aspects such as game's educational values, enjoyment, usability, quality of experience with the game, etc. Player-/learner-centred assessment refers to learner's assessment in terms of knowledge, skills, emotions, motivation, etc. Research work done on the two approaches is presented next.

18.2.1 Game-Centred Assessment

The assessment of the game environment is done in terms of different aspects such as game's educational values, enjoyment, usability, quality of experience with the game, etc.

Various evaluation frameworks were proposed in order to facilitate the assessment of the game's educational values (Aleven, Myers, Easterday, & Ogan, 2010; de Freitas & Oliver, 2006; Hong, Cheng, Hwang, Lee, & Chang, 2009). Hong et al. (2009) have proposed a framework that examines the educational values of a game based on seven categories: mentality change (promotion of adventure, evaluation of trade-offs, awareness of efficiency), emotional fulfilment (sense of belonging, social interaction, concentration, collaborative relationship, fairness and justice), knowledge enhancement (acquisition of knowledge, reinforcement of knowledge), thinking skills (strategic thinking, memory enhancement, observation and perception, flexible thinking), interpersonal skills (negative emotion management, mutual support), spatial ability (developing the students' spatial ability) and bodily coordination (hand–eye coordination, quick reaction). The framework was applied for the assessment of an online vocabulary game, Super Word Searching Contest. The assessment was made by scholars and game designers. The results showed that the vocabulary game helped the players to develop flexible thinking skills, to improve interpersonal skills and to broaden vocabulary. Aleven et al. (2010) proposed a framework for designing and evaluating educational games. The educational value of the game is evaluated through the Learning Objective Component (prior knowledge, learning and retention, potential transfer). Other proposed evaluation frameworks also included the evaluation of the pedagogic perspective of the learning activities (e.g. pedagogic models, learning activities, proposed learning outcome of the game, etc.) (de Freitas & Oliver, 2006, de Freitas, Rebolledo-Mendez, Liarokapis, Magoulas, & Poulovassilis, 2010).

The *enjoyment* offered by a game-based e-learning environment is also assessed. An example of an enjoyment scale is EGameFlow (Fu, Su, & Yu, 2009). EGameFlow measures the enjoyment offered by the game-based e-learning environment from the learner's point of view. The scale consists of eight dimensions: immersion, social interaction, challenge, goal clarity, feedback, concentration, control and knowledge improvement. Four learning games were used as instruments for the scale validation.

Usability of a game-based e-learning environment is also assessed using traditional usability standards (Diah, Ismail, Ahmad, & Dahari, 2010) or a framework (Yue & Zin, 2009). Diah et al. (2010) have used the ISO 9241-11 standard that defines usability assessment over three components: effectiveness, efficiency and satisfaction. The framework proposed by Yue and Zin (2009) includes six components to be assessed: interface, mechanics, game play, playability, feedback and immersion. The framework was used for the evaluation of an educational game for teaching history (HMIEG, History Multimedia Interactive Educational Game).

Assessment approaches that are used in entertainment games may also be used for game-based e-learning. Various entertainment game-centred assessment approaches are presented next. Takatalo, Hakkinen, Kaistinen, and Nyman (2007, 2010, 2011) have presented two models for measuring user experience on digital gaming. The two measurement models are *Adaptation* and *Flow and Quality*. The Adaptation model measures user adaptation into the digital environment. The theoretical basics were the concepts of involvement and presence. The Adaptation model takes into consideration the following components: role engagement, attention, interest, importance, co-presence, interaction and arousal. The *Flow and Quality* model includes challenge, competence, playfulness, control, valence, impressiveness and enjoyment.

Quality of experience (*QoE*) in games represents the user's perceived quality of the game. Parameters that affect QoE include the visual quality of game, the network delivery conditions and the ambience (Kuipers, Kooij, De Vleeschauwer, & Brunnström, 2010). Player's QoE was mainly assessed in entertainment games (e.g. in First Person Shooter games, multiplayer role-playing games, online strategy games). Various measures were used to express the player's QoE, such as the mean opinion score (MOS) that is represented on a five-level scale (Lin, Wang, & Wei, 2010) or paired comparison-different opinions are compared in order to make judgments (Chang, Chen, Wu, Ho, & Lei, 2010).

18.2.2 Player-/Learner-Centred Assessment

Player/learner assessment is made in terms of knowledge, skills, emotions, motivation, etc.

Learner's *knowledge* (cognitive learning outcome) or gained knowledge through the game is assessed by various game-based learning environments (Garris, Ahlers, & Driskell, 2002; Wilson et al., 2009). Various types of learning knowledge are measured and assessed such as declarative knowledge (knowledge about "what"), procedural knowledge (knowledge about "how") and strategic knowledge (knowledge about "which, when and why") (Garris et al., 2002; Wilson et al., 2009). Learner knowledge is measured and assessed using different approaches such as pre- and post-tests (Miller et al., 2011; Tüzün et al., 2009), in game embedded assessment (Burgos et al., 2008), control/experimental group with pre- and post-tests (Kebritchi et al., 2010), open-ended questions (Tüzün et al., 2009), etc.

Various learner's *skill* types are also measured and assessed in game-based e-learning. For example, Shute, Masduki, and Donmez (2010) assessed system thinking skills using an in game embedded assessment. System thinking refers to one's ability to understand the relationship between elements in a given environment. Conlan, Hampson, Peirce, and Kickmeier-Rust (2009) defined knowledge skills in the game for each task. Learner knowledge skills are assessed using a probabilistic embedded assessment. Other skills that are assessed in game-based e-learning are problem-solving skills (Shih, Shih, Shih, Su, & Chuang, 2010), creative problem-solving (Shute, Ventura, Bauer, & Zapata-Rivera, 2009) medical practice skills (Moreno-Ger et al., 2010), game-based literacy skills (Steinkuehler & King, 2009), etc.

Recently, learner emotions and motivation have been subjects of increasing attention.

Learner *emotions* such as joy or distress towards the game, admiration or reproach towards a helping agent were assessed using a probabilistic method using learner interaction with the game and questionnaire in Conati and Maclaren (2009).

Learner's emotions (i.e. learner achievement emotions) were detected using a probabilistic model (Muñoz, Kevitt, Lunney, Noguez, & Neri, 2011). The achievement emotions that were detected include anticipatory joy, hope, anxiety, anticipatory relief and hopelessness. Transitions between learner's affective states such as frustration, flow, confusion, delight, boredom, anxiety, excitement, anger, sadness and fear were assessed from the dialog game Crystal Island (McQuiggan, Robison, & Lester, 2010).

Learner *motivation* to play as well as to learn is very important in the game-play process as well as in the learning process. Since motivation can easily change during game play, learner motivation should be assessed during the entire game play. Although recently learner motivation in game-based e-learning has started to gain researchers' attention, so far significantly less research was done on measuring and assessing learning motivation in game-based e-learning than in e-learning. The main methods for gathering information needed for assessing learner's motivation as well as the four generic metrics proposed by us for measuring motivation are presented in the following section.

18.3   Motivation Measurement and Analysis

This section presents methods for gathering information in game-based e-learning starting with a discussion on subjective and objective measurement approaches. Significantly less research was conducted on measuring learner motivation in game-based e-learning, as compared to measuring learner motivation in e-learning in general. Therefore, this section proposes four generic metrics for measuring and analysing learner motivation in game-based e-learning starting from metrics used in e-learning. For each proposed metric, the definition, related metrics used in e-learning as well as its usage and interpretation in game-based e-learning are presented.

18.3.1   Methods for Gathering Information

There are two main approaches for measuring learner/player motivation: subjective assessment and objective assessment. Subjective assessment involves the human subjects to provide information on their motivational state and belief. As opposed, the objective assessment involves collecting data about the subject's motivational state without human subjects having to provide it themselves.

Subjective-based assessment methods are considerably better defined, for which reason they are the most used ones. Several general instruments for measuring motivation were defined, and instructions on how these can be used were provided. Examples include the Instructional Materials Motivational Survey (IMMS) (Keller, 1987) based on the ARCS model (Keller, 1987), the Intrinsic Motivation Inventory (IMI) (2008) based in the self-determination theory (Ryan & Deci, 2000) and the self-efficacy scale (Bandura, 2006). The existing motivation measurement instruments were also adapted to be used in game-based e-learning. Additional new instruments for game-based e-learning were created (Chen & Chan, 2008; Miller et al., 2011; Tüzün et al., 2009). The data collected during subjective assessment provides direct means of the learner/player motivation, beliefs and opinion and can be easily interpreted. The subjective data is usually gathered using self-report, questionnaire and interviews where the subjects are asked to rate, specify or describe their motivation and belief.

However, subjective methods present a number of limitations when used for measuring player/learner motivation in game-based e-learning environments. The need for human subjects to provide supplementary information makes the approach time and resource expensive. Furthermore, it is difficult to use these methods for monitoring learner/player motivation in real time. For example, if the assessment is made at the end for all game levels, the player/learner beliefs of the first levels may be influenced by what happened during the following levels. On another side, using them more frequently during the game interrupts the game-play flow.

Due to the limitations presented by the subjective methods, various studies have researched alternative, objective solutions for assessing learner motivation. In their case, the data is automatically collected from the learner/player behaviour and/or psychological reactions. Objective methods are in general non-invasive as in most of the cases learners/players are not aware of the tracking mechanism that is incorporated in the game-based e-learning environment. The main advantage of the objective methods is that they can be used for real-time motivation monitoring and further on motivation-based adaptation of the game. However, objective methods cannot provide concrete subjective meaning for all learners' beliefs and their motivational state.

There are three main methods for gathering information about the learner motivation in game-based e-learning environment:

1. *Through dialog-based interaction* (e.g. questionnaire, interviews), which represents a subjective assessment
2. *Through game-play-based interaction* (e.g. learner actions, player behaviour in game), which represents an objective assessment
3. *Through additional equipment* (e.g. eye tracker, heart monitor), which represents an objective assessment

The pros and cons for each method will be discussed next.

18.3.1.1   Gathering Information Through Dialog-Based Interaction

The dialog-based interaction method is a subjective-based assessment method. The method is mainly used for collecting information about the player/learner beliefs and thoughts (e.g. confidence, importance of the course). This method consists of presenting different questions to the learner and asking for a response, a rating or a self-report. The questions are usually presented using a questionnaire or dialog interaction embedded in the game. Gathering information through direct interaction can give subjective meaning, and using this method is easier to interpret the results. Most of the studies made on assessing player/learner motivation in game-based e-learning assessed learner motivation at the end of playing the educational game (Liu & Chu, 2010; Miller et al., 2011; Sancho & Fernandez-Manjon, 2010; Tüzün et al., 2009) or both at the beginning and at the end of playing the game (Kebritchi et al., 2010; Vos, van der Meijden, & Denessen, 2011). Examples of self-report-based motivation measurement instruments are presented and discussed next.

Instructional Materials Motivational Survey

Instructional Materials Motivational Survey (IMMS) measures motivation on four dimensions: attention (A), relevance (R), confidence (C) and satisfaction (S). For each of these dimensions, the subjects have to answer to a number of self-report questionnaire items by marking the response on a Likert scale. Huang, Huang, and Tschopp (2010) used IMMS to measure motivation for playing a game after 264 participants played an online economical educational game. The authors analysed how the attention, relevance and confidence dimensions could predict the satisfaction dimension. Liu and Chu (2010) examined learner/player motivation to learn English in a given environment that integrated educational games using a variation of IMMS.

Intrinsic Motivation Inventory

Intrinsic Motivation Inventory (IMI) represents a motivation multidimensional instrument based on self-determination theory (Ryan & Deci, 2000). The instrument contains several dimensions: interest/enjoyment, perceived competence, effort, value/usefulness, felt pressure and tension and perceived choice while performing an activity. It was used in several studies involving measuring participants' intrinsic motivation. It can be changed to fit different tasks and activities by modifying the instrument. For example, the same motivation instrument was adapted to measure different types of motivation—e.g. general intrinsic motivation (through all school experience) and learner motivation during the specific lesson (where the participants played the game or made the game).

Vos et al. (2011) analysed student motivation using IMI. The participants ($N = 107$) were divided into two groups: the participants in one group learned by playing a game and the participants in the other group had to learn by making a game. The motivation was measured using 14 items from the IMI. Three subscales were selected—interest, perceived competence and effort. A questionnaire before playing/making a game and a questionnaire after playing/making a game were used to measure participant's motivation. The questionnaire given before playing/making measured general intrinsic motivation (through all school experience). The questionnaire given after playing/making the game measured learner motivation during the specific lesson (where they played the game/made the game). The items in the questionnaire were also reformulated to assess to what extent students were motivated while playing or constructing a game. There were no differences between girls and boys in student motivation on the three subscales (interest, effort and competence). Students who constructed the game felt more motivated than those who played the game. Students were less motivated during the game than during school lesson. When observing the students in the play conditions, it was noticed by the authors that students got bored when playing the game several times.

Self-Efficacy Scale

Scale instruments were used for measuring participants' self-efficacy. Self-efficacy represents the person's belief, self-perception of their capabilities of executing the task at a certain level of performance. It influences people's actions and beliefs (Bandura, 1994). Recommendation on how to construct self-efficacy scale was given (Bandura, 2006). Bandura (2006) suggested the response scale to be a 100-point scale, ranging in 10 units from 0 ("Cannot do at all") through 50 ("Moderately certain can do") to 100 ("Highly certain can do"). A simpler scale can be used (e.g. 1–10, 1–7) with the condition to retain the same structure (from "Cannot do at all" to "Highly certain can do"). McQuiggan, Mott, and Lester (2008) measured learner/player self-efficacy while learned by playing in a game-based e-learning environment and solving genetics problems. Learner self-efficacy was measured at the beginning, during and at the end of the experiment. Based from the participants' self-reports and psychological reaction, McQuiggan et al. (2008) made a self-efficacy prediction model from the psychological reactions.

Other Scales

Other motivation self-report scales were developed. A new motivation measuring scale was proposed by Tüzün et al. (2009). Tüzün et al. (2009) analysed player motivation of 24 students participated in their study and learning geography using an educational computer game. Two versions of the motivation scale were administrated: at the beginning representing the school version of motivation scale and at the end representing the game version of motivation scale. Two subscales on the 5-point Likert scale were used (extrinsic and intrinsic motivation).

Miller et al. (2011) developed an instrument on four dimensions: satisfaction, role-playing experience, usability and motivation to pursue a career in science. The motivation to learn by playing a science education al games was measured as the satisfaction with the game. The authors used the scale in an experiment ($N = 734$) using a science game-based e-learning environment. The results have shown "that satisfaction with the game, the role-playing experience and usability as a hole counted for significant amount of variance in science career motivation but only satisfaction and the role playing experience showed significant predictive power".

Chen and Chan (2008) developed a motivation measuring instrument on four dimensions: attention, relevance, enjoyment and challenge. The instrument was used to measure player motivation to play the game. In their study with 56 participants, two versions of a game to learn Chinese idioms were used . The participants were divided in two groups: a control group—where the participants played the game without full functionality and an experiment group—where the participants played full version of the game. The full version of the game had an increased level of competition. The results have shown significant difference between the two groups. The experimental group had higher relevance and challenge.

Bernard and Cannon (2011) used an emoticon-based instrument to measure motivation. The emoticon-based instrument consisted of a 5-item emoticon-anchored scale ranging from highly unmotivated to highly motivated. The scale was used to measure student motivation in a study ($N = 114$). A management retail simulation game was used in the classroom during the study. The participants indicated their level of motivation at the beginning and at the end of each class period student. Differences were observed between motivation at the beginning of the course and at the end. The motivation patterns were not driven by differences of classroom activities. However, measuring motivation at the end of the activity for motivation at the beginning and at the ending of the class may be biased the study, and the usage of emoticons may be too simplistic for the purpose.

However, learner motivation is a fragile state, and fluctuations in learner motivation do occur. Therefore, motivation should be measured and assessed more often. Gathering information about the player/learner motivation using questionnaires more often may disturb the learner and interrupt the game-play process.

In game-based e-learning, the measurement must be done without interrupting the game-play process. Moreover, measurement must be non-invasive when it is made for monitoring and/or further adaptation of the game. Presenting questions through a questionnaire or asking for a self-report could disturb the game-play process. In game-based e-learning, subjective information about the player/learner can be gathered through direct interaction with the player/leaner in a non-invasive mode by embedding questionnaire items into the dialog between a non-player character and the player, and recording the player answer (Ghergulescu & Muntean, 2010). The cost of using this method consists of embedding additional dialog between player and non-player characters.

However, the method of gathering information through dialog-based interaction with the player/learner cannot give a real-time characterisation of the motivational level without disturbing the learner, as this will imply asking learners to answer questionnaires more often during the game play.

18.3.1.2 Gathering Information Through Game-Play-Based Interaction

Gathering information through game-play interaction methods is an objective assessment. The method uses information gathered through game-play-based interaction (learner behaviour in the game) that gives insides about player interaction with the learning system. The information about the player/learner interaction with the e-learning system can be automatically recorded by the e-learning system in log files, or tracking mechanisms can be embedded in the game. Different types of data can be recorded, such as learner actions, task durations, etc. Measuring learner interaction with the game represents an objective measurement method of learner behaviour. The method is a non-invasive one and does not interrupt the game-play process or does not disturb the player, furthermore being a low-cost solution of measuring various types of data. However, the types of data that will be recorded need to be defined in advance. Because a large amount of numerical data can be recorded, the necessary data for analysis need to be carefully selected.

Significantly less research was made for using this method in game-based e-learning than in e-learning. Researchers started to use the method for gathering information about player motivation (Ghergulescu & Muntean, 2010; Mattheiss, Kickmeier-Rust, Steiner, & Albert, 2010). However, more research is needed in order to propose general models for subjective assessments of learner motivation in the game-based e-learning.

During the new trend in gaming equipment (Wii, Xbox), player movements could be used in detecting player motivation in real time. Research started to be made for joining player motivation and player moves. Levac et al. (2010) measured motivation to succeed using quantity and quality of movements in a Wii Fit game. The objective was to "determine if quantity and quality of the motion outcome for the novice and experienced player were influenced by the motivation to succeed the game" on a Wii Fit games. However, the motivation was measured using a single item and not a general motivation measurement instrument. In their preliminary study, motivation to succeed did not affect the quantity and the quality of the motion outcome.

18.3.1.3 Gathering Information Through Additional Equipment

The method on gathering information *through additional equipment* (e.g. eye tracker, heart monitor) provides information about learner psychological reaction and behaviour cues (e.g. electrophysiological (EEG) data, heart rate, galvanic skin response). The method is an objective-based assessment method. For example, EEG data and skin conductance was used to predict learner motivation (Derbali & Frasson, 2010), while heart rate and skin conductance was used for real-time assessment of player self-efficacy (McQuiggan et al., 2008).

Derbali and Frasson (2010) studied how electrophysiological measurements provide objective indicators predicting the player motivation. Player motivation was assessed during different parts of a game using a shorter version of the IMMS questionnaire. The questionnaire was used several times during the game play. Skin conductance was measured by attaching a galvanic skin response electrode on player's finger. The heart rate was measured using a blood volume pulse sensor that was attached to player's finger. The players had to wear an EEG electrode cap. The results have shown that skin conductance, theta wave in the frontal region and high beta wave in the in the central region provide significant predictors of player motivation. No significant correlation between player's motivation and their heart rate responses was found. Furthermore, the player attention was detected (a distinction between attentive and inattentive) using the alpha–beta and theta–beta ratio (Derbali, Chalfoun, & Frasson, 2011). Player attention was also examined using a portable EEG and self-report (Rebolledo-Mendez, de Freitas, Rojano-Caceres, & Gaona-Garcia, 2010). The proposed assessment model is still under development.

McQuiggan et al. (2008) induced models of predicting self-efficacy from galvanic skin response and blood volume pulse using data from 42 participants while learning in a game-based e-learning environment. Learner self-efficacy was assessed at the beginning of the experiment using Bandura's self-efficacy scale (Bandura, 2006), at the end of the experiment and during the experiment. Training sessions for the model were also performed. During the training sessions, the participants had to solve genetics problems and rate their self-efficacy in solving the given problems. The blood pulse was measured using one sensor on the right finger, and galvanic skin response was measured using two sensors on the right middle and little fingers. Self-efficacy was predicted using naive Bayes and decision tree classifier. The self-efficacy models were produced at different granularity—e.g. two-level model (low, high), three-level model (low, medium, high), four-level model (very low, low, high, very high) and five-level model (very low, low, medium, high, very high).

Work on using eye tracking to detect player engagement was conducted (Renshaw, Stevens, & Denton, 2009). However, the work represented a pilot study and the data analysed was limited. The participants articulate their felling using verbal in play words suggesting their feeling. No relationship was found between the mean fixation duration and verbal probing on the participants' feeling.

The method gathers information in a non-invasive mode without disturbing the game play. However, the additional equipment is costly most of the time and difficult to be incorporated with everyday game-based e-learning scenarios.

Combinations of the three methods can also be used. However, combining different methods will take benefits and/or drawbacks from each one depending on what and how the methods are used.

18.3.1.4   Methods for Analysing the Gathered Data

The methods for analysing motivation can be classified in two main categories: direct computation and data mining. Figure 18.1 presents a representation in time of learner behaviour and motivation analysis methods. Direct computation characterises the motivation as a function or provides rules for characterising the motivation (from beginning through the moment of computation), while data mining involves predicting the motivation. Data mining methods include statistical methods (e.g. factor analysis, logistic regression, latent variables), clustering and the nearest neighbour prediction (dynamic) Bayesian networks, decision tree, etc.

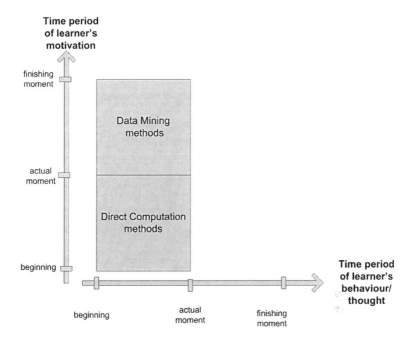

Fig. 18.1   Methods for analysis of motivation in relation with time

18.3.2   *Proposed Generic Metrics for Measuring Motivation*

Various types of information can be used for measuring and assessing learner motivation. Information such as learner thoughts and beliefs (e.g. self-efficacy, confidence, importance of the task), learner interaction with the e-learning system (login, timing, learner's requests), learner behaviour cues (e.g. facial expression, seat posture) and psychological reactions (heart rate, galvanic skin response, etc.) can be collected during the measurement process.

Information about learner interaction with the e-learning system, learner thoughts and beliefs are the most used. This is because collecting information about learner behaviour cues and psychological reaction needs additional equipment unavailable in an everyday e-learning scenario.

The information gathered for assessing learner motivation represents a collection of numerical data. An important question in the measurement regards data that have to be collected (e.g. "what data should be collected?"). The numerical data is labelled as metrics.

With regard to data that is gathered through game-play-based interaction, little research was made in game-based e-learning for presenting the type of data that has to be collected. Mattheiss et al. (2010) have proposed to take in consideration metrics such as feedback reaction time, number of errors, number of hit demands for

Fig. 18.2 Word cloud of metrics for measuring learner motivation

diagnosing learner attention and confidence. Generic metrics for assessing motivation that can be incorporated in several different educational games are needed.

To assess learner motivation level, various metrics were proposed in the literature, such as number of read pages, time spent on reading pages, number of tasks/quizzes taken, time spent on solving a task/quiz, time moving cursor, time spent on solving an exercise, number of attempts, number of mistakes, number of hint/help requests, time between hint requests, confidence, etc. A word cloud of the metrics used for measuring motivation is presented in Fig. 18.2. The font size represents the number of times the word from the metric was used in the proposed metrics.

A direct mapping of motivation metrics used in e-learning to game-based e-learning is difficult to be made. This is not only because of the large number of metrics that have emerged but also because the majority of the motivational metrics used in e-learning are learning environment dependent, or learning material dependent. For example, the metric *time spent on reading a page* on a learning concept may be influenced by various factors such as the difficulty of the learning martial to be read in a page. Different pages may contain different learning concepts that may be more or less difficult to be understood; thus a learner may spend different times to read different pages. Moreover, different learners may need a different time to read a particular page, as the content may be easier to be understood by some learners than others. In this way, individual metrics may not accurately reflect the learner motivation. Furthermore, a number of metrics used for assessing learners' motivation in e-learning may not be applicable at all in game-based e-learning, since games contain different types of interactions. For example, metrics such as *time spent reading a page*, *time spent solving an exercise* and *time spent taking a quiz* may not be sufficient and/or not possible to be measured in game-based e-learning, as the game may not contain quizzes to be taken and pages to be read.

To overcome these issues and help with applying learner motivation assessment metrics from e-learning in game-based e-learning, this section classifies the existing metrics in four groups. Furthermore, a more generic metric is proposed for each of the four groups. The four general metrics are *TimeOnTask*, *NumRepeatTask*, *NumHelpRequest* and *SelfEfficacy*. Metrics' definition and interpretation as well as related metrics used in e-learning are presented next.

18.3.2.1 TimeOnTask

TimeOnTask represents the period of time during which a learner performs a specific task or activity.

In e-learning, TimeOnTask was used as:

- Time spent reading (Cocea & Weibelzahl, 2009, 2011; Costagliola, De Rosa, Fuccella, Capuano, & Ritrovato, 2010; Khan, Graf, Weippl, & Tjoa, 2009, 2010; Khan, Weippl, & Tjoa, 2009; Qu, Wang, & Johnson, 2005)
- Time spent solving a problem/exercise (Arroyo et al., 2007; Khan, Graf, et al., 2009; Khan et al., 2010; Khan, Weippl, et al., 2009)
- Time spent on tests/quizzes (Cocea & Weibelzahl, 2009, 2011; Kim, Cha, Cho, Yoon, & Lee, 2007; McQuiggan et al., 2008)
- Time performing a specific task in the learning environment (Hershkovitz & Nachmias, 2008; Kim et al., 2007; Qu et al., 2005; de Vicente, 2003; de Vicente & Pain, 2002)
- Time spent in the learning environment (McQuiggan et al., 2008; Munoz-Organero, Munoz-Merino, & Kloos, 2010; Qu et al., 2005; de Vicente, 2003; de Vicente & Pain, 2002)
- Related time on task metrics (e.g. time taken to decide to perform a task, first response time, time spent moving cursor, clicking time, time between hint requests, time spent per session, time spent performing an action, average of duration between session, time on task percentage)

TimeOnTask was expressed as the nominal duration needed to perform a task, as the average time to perform a task or as percentage of the total time spent playing.

Further, *TimeOnTask* was used in data mining techniques for the assessment of learner motivation and/or direct computation. Since, most of the time, the metric interpretation was learning material or learning system dependent, a general interpretation of the metric is not provided.

An approach for providing a more general interpretation would be to establish limits for the *TimeOnTask* metric and classify the learner motivational state. For example, experts may examine the log files and established the level of engagement, an indicator of motivation (Cocea & Weibelzahl, 2009, 2011). It was suggested that the necessary time for reading a page can vary from 30 s to maximum 4–5 min; the necessary time for a test varied from a few seconds to a maximum 3–4 min. However, these limits were established given the characteristics of the learning system used—HTML tutor. The learner motivational state could then be classified in engaged—if the learner spends reasonable time on pages, disengaged if the learner spends too much time on pages or she/he moves too fast through pages, and neutral which is a more difficult case to identify (hard to decide).

Johns and Woolf (2006) also defined limits for time solving a geometry problem. They classified the learner motivation state in "motivated", "unmotivated-hint" (unmotivated and exhausting the hints that give the answers) and unmotivated-guess (e.g. if the learner responded to a problem in a time $t < T_{min}$).

Arroyo et al. (2007) defined an estimated time, ETi, to solve a problem and with the standard deviation across other students, SDTi, diagnosed the learner effort, an indicator of motivation using several diagnosing rules. For example, if the learner spends a time less than the difference between the ETi estimated time, and the standard deviation, SDTi, the learner has a low motivation. Limits for time to solve an exercise were also established by Bica, Verdin, and Vicari (2006).

In educational games, different tasks (e.g. finding the right route, reading a book) with different granularity and difficulty can be identified. Therefore, following the same approach, threshold limits can be defined for the *TimeOnTask* metric, and the learner/player motivation state can be diagnosed based on these thresholds. Two thresholds, T_{min} and T_{max}, are defined and used to categorise the learners as demotivated if they spent less than T_{min} or more than T_{max} time on that task and motivated otherwise.

18.3.2.2 NumRepeatTask

NumRepeatTask represents the number of times the learner performed a specific task/activity.

In e-learning, the number of times a learner performs a task/activity may be represented by:

- Number of times reading a page (Cocea & Weibelzahl, 2009, 2011; Hershkovitz & Nachmias, 2008)
- Number of times doing an exercise (Arroyo et al., 2007; Khan, Graf, et al., 2009; Khan et al., 2010; Khan, Weippl, et al., 2009)
- Number of times or a test/pre-test (Cocea & Weibelzahl, 2009, 2011; Hershkovitz & Nachmias, 2008)
- Number of times watching a video (Kim et al., 2007)
- Number of times listening an audio (Kim et al., 2007)
- Number of times taking a survey (Cocea & Weibelzahl, 2009, 2011)

Other learning systems specific tasks/activities on which the *NumRepeatTask* was measured include:

- Accessing various types of information available in that particular system (e.g. hyperlink, manual, help, glossary, communication, search, remarks, statistics, feedback) (Cocea & Weibelzahl, 2009, 2011)
- Forums (Munoz-Organero et al., 2010)
- Updating the learner profile by uploading photos (Munoz-Organero et al., 2010)

Different approaches for measuring the *NumRepeatTask* metric exist, such as measuring the number of times a learner performed a specific task, measuring the average number of times the learner performed related tasks, or measuring the number of times a learner performed a specific task/activity expressed as a percentage from the total number of times the learner performed all the tasks/actions.

Depending of the specific task, *NumRepeatTask* may reflect the number of mistakes/attempts (e.g. when a task consists of solving a specific exercise). The *NumRepeatTask* metric was used in both analysis methods: data mining and direct computation.

The same approach for providing a more interpretation by establishing limits for metric and classifying the learner motivational state afterwards emerged from the literature.

Similarly to the *TimeOnTask* metric, a general interpretation of the *NumRepeatTask* metric can be provided by defining thresholds to be used for classifying the learner motivation. However, these thresholds are task dependent and have to be defined for each particular task in part.

For example, Cocea and Weibelzahl (2009) have established a threshold for the minimum number of pages read in order to classify if a learner is disengaged or not. As opposed, Arroyo et al. (2007) defined an estimated number of repeating times to solve a problem, E_i, and with the standard deviation across other students, SDi, diagnoses the learner effort, an indicator of motivation using several diagnosing rules.

Further, depending on the task type, *NumRepeatTask* may suggest the learner motivation type (e.g. intrinsic motivated, extrinsic motivated). Students who frequently tend to take self-exams are intrinsically motivated.

Following a similar approach, threshold limits can be defined for *NumRepeatTask* metric in game-based e-learning in order to assess the learner/player motivation state. Defining a threshold NRT_{min} for the minimum number of repeats for a task, learners/players can be classified as demotivated if they repeat a task less than NRT_{min} and motivated otherwise.

18.3.2.3 NumHelpRequests

NumHelpRequest represents the number of help requests or hint requests made by the learner. For measuring this metric, the e-learning systems must provide help/hint request functionalities. Various studies have considered the number of help/hint requests in their motivation assessment (Cocea & Weibelzahl, 2009, 2011; Johns & Woolf, 2006; Khan, Graf, et al., 2009; Khan et al., 2010; Khan, Weippl, et al., 2009; Kim et al., 2007; Woolf et al., 2010).

The metric was used for the assessment of learner motivation using direct computation or data mining.

The *NumHelpRequest* metric usually takes small values and may show the learner motivation in achieving the goal of knowledge acquisition. However, when it jumps to higher values, it may show the learner intent of "gaming the system" or as being unmotivated and exhausting the hints that give the answers.

"Gaming the system" is a behaviour aimed at performing well and tricking the system, systematically taking advantages of regularities in the system (e.g. help abuse, spending time in the system and not actually reading/learning). "Gaming the system" detection was made at different granularity. It ranged from only labelling a learner behaviour as gaming the system or not, to labelling the learner behaviour as gaming on subsequence, to detecting how much a learner games the system, to differentiating between different types of gaming behaviour (Baker, Mitrović, & Mathews, 2010).

For example, Johns and Woolf (2006) use *NumHelpRequest* for diagnosing the type of an unmotivated learner. The authors distinguished two types of unmotivated students: "unmotivated-hint" (unmotivated and exhausting the hints that give the answers) and "unmotivated-guess" (unmotivated and quickly guessing answers to find the correct answer). The authors diagnosed a learner as being "unmotivated-hint" if the number of hints seen before responding correctly is higher than a maximum threshold H_{max}.

NumHelpRequest can be used also in game-based e-learning for measuring player/learner motivation. However, the games most have the feature of help/hint request. In games, help or hint can be requested through a non-player character, through a "secret answer book", etc.

By defining a maximum threshold for the number of help/hints for each hint/help that the player can require, NHR_{max}, learners/players can be classified as demotivated if they request a number higher than NHR_{max} and motivated otherwise.

18.3.2.4 SelfEfficacy

SelfEfficacy (Bandura, 1994) represents the person's belief, self-perception of their capabilities of executing that task at a certain level of performance. Self-efficacy is used to retrieve information about the learner belief and self-perception. It was also used as an indicator or a metric for confidence (Kim et al., 2007; Woolf et al., 2010). It was measured using questionnaire items in questionnaire, question item embedded in dialog or self-report. In game-based e-learning, it was proposed to be used as dialog item in an interaction between non-player character and player (Ghergulescu & Muntean, 2010).

For assessing *SelfEfficacy* metric, Bandura's scale recommendation (2006) can be followed. Learner self-efficacy can be represented on a five-level scale, a seven-level scale or a ten-level scale. According to Bandura's recommendations, the learner self-efficacy should be measured on a specific task in terms of "Can do" rather than "Will do", on a scale that should range from "Cannot do at all", through "Moderate can do" to "Certain can do".

In game-based e-learning, *SelfEfficacy* metric can be measured at the important tasks that were identified by integrating questionnaire item in the dialog between a non-player character and the learner following Bandura's recommendations. If a player chooses from "Moderate can do" to "Certain can do", she/he can be categorised as motivated and demotivated otherwise.

18.4   Discussions

Motivation represents the energy, the persistence and the direction of a person for taking and continuing an activity (self-determination theory), and their beliefs and self-perception of their capabilities to execute a task (self-efficacy theory). Three main methods for motivation measurement can be distinguished depending on how the data is collected: through dialog-based interaction, through game-play interaction or through additional equipment. The collected data can be further used in the motivation assessment. The first method is a subjective method, while the other two are objective assessment. Depending on the scope of the measurement, one or another method may be more suitable.

Gathering information through dialog-based interaction may not be suitable to assess player motivation during the game play as this interrupts the game flow. However, if the motivation measurement is made after the game play with the aim to assess the effect of the activity taken (i.e. playing the game), gathering information through dialog-based interaction may be more suitable because it is better defined and easier to interpret as compared to the other methods. In such situations, learner motivation may also need to be measured before the game play in order to have a reference for comparison purposes. Dialog-based interaction can be used as well for measuring the learner motivation before starting to play.

However, in game-based e-learning, we are not only interested in labelling a participant as motivated or not, or labelling the game as motivating or not. We are also interested in taking real-time applicable interventions in order to increase learner's motivation when they are demotivated or are becoming demotivated. When the learner did not reach the end of the game (e.g. drop out) or the game did not motivate enough the player, finding the learner motivation at the end might be too late for taking any intervention. By measuring learner motivation in real time, motivation-based adaptation of the game can be made. Gathering information through game-play interaction and through additional equipment methods are more suitable for measuring learner motivation while playing, since the information collection is done transparently, without interrupting the game flow. Information gathered through additional equipment is difficult to be used in a day-to-day scenario because of the cost of the additional equipment needed. Real-time assessment of the learner motivation has many potential benefits. However, further work is needed to better define objective methods for real-time motivation assessment.

When the aim of the motivation assessment is to measure the effect of the game, a distinction between the motivation to play and the motivation to learn can be made. This is possible because motivation assessment is made before and after the activity of learning through playing. In this case, the motivation to learn represents the energy, the persistence and the direction of the participants to learn, to gain knowledge (independently of the method the educational material is delivered) as well as their beliefs, self-perception of their capabilities to learn. The motivation to play relates to the motivation of executing the task of playing.

However, when the aim is to assess learner motivation to learn in a particular game-based learning environment, the activity of learning is related to that particular environment. Furthermore, when motivation is assessed in real time during the game play or on a particular task in the game, it is difficult to make a clear distinction between the motivation to play and the motivation to learn, because the learner performs the activity of learning while playing. Therefore, in such situations, learner motivation is more of a joint state: motivation to learn while playing.

18.5 Conclusions

This chapter has proved an overview of the main trends in the area of game-based e-learning assessment. The assessment of the game environment is made in terms of different aspects such as of game educational value, enjoyment, usability, player perceived quality, etc. Learner assessment is made in terms of knowledge, skills, emotion and motivation, etc.

The chapter presented and discussed the two approaches in motivation assessment: subjective and objective assessments. The main methods for measuring motivation depending on how information about learner motivation is gathered have been presented and discussed. Information about learner motivation can be gathered through dialog-based interaction, through game-play-based interaction and/or through additional equipment. Each method comes with its pros and cons. A combination of the three methods can be used. Learner motivation assessment is crucial in order to be able to take adaptive actions for motivating the learners and help them achieve the learning outcome. For further motivation-based adaptation, the learner motivation assessment should be made in a non-invasive mode. However, motivation assessment in game-based e-learning is in its early stages.

This chapter builds on top of the significant research work addressing learner motivation assessment in e-learning and proposes four general metrics for assessing learner's motivation in game-based e-learning. A direct mapping of motivation measurement metrics used in e-learning was difficult to be made because most of the metrics were learning environment dependent or learning material dependent. Moreover, because the game scenario is different between different educational games, generic metrics for measuring learner motivation are needed.

Each metric is presented along with other related metrics from e-learning, and its usage and interpretation in gaming-based e-learning are discussed. While individually the metrics may indicate only if a player is motivated or not, it is difficult to rely only on one metric interpretation.

The proposed metrics can be further used for real-time embedded assessment of players/learners' motivation in game-based e-learning. Future work will address evaluation of the proposed generic metrics and how the metrics can be combined in a motivation assessment model.

Acknowledgement This research work is supported by IRCSET Embark Postgraduate Scholarship Scheme, Ireland.

References

Aleven, V., Myers, E., Easterday, M., & Ogan, A. (2010). Toward a framework for the analysis and design of educational games. In *Proceeding of IEEE third international conference on digital game and intelligent toy enhanced learning* (pp. 69–76), Los Alamitos, CA.

Arroyo, I., Ferguson, K., Johns, J., Dragon, T., Meheranian, H., Fisher, D., et al. (2007). Repairing disengagement with non-invasive interventions. In R. Luckin, K. R. Koedinger, & J. Greer (Eds.), *Proceeding of the 2007 conference on artificial intelligence in education: Building technology rich learning contexts that work* (pp. 195–202). Amsterdam, The Netherlands: IOS.

Baker, R. S. J. D., Mitrović, A., & Mathews, M. (2010). Detecting gaming the system in constraint-based tutors. In P. de Bra, A. Kobsa, & D. Chin (Eds.), *User modeling, adaptation, and personalization, Proceedings of the 18th international conference, UMAP 2010.* Notes in computer science, 6075/2010 (pp. 267–278). Berlin, Germany: Springer.

Bandura, A. (1994). Self-efficacy. In V. S. Ramachaudran (Ed.), *Encyclopedia of human behaviour* (pp. 71–81). New York, NY: Academic.

Bandura, A. (2006). Guide for constructing self-efficacy scales. In T. Urdan & F. Pojares (Eds.), *Self-efficacy beliefs of adolescents* (Vol. 5, pp. 307–337). Charlotte: Information Age Publishing.

Bernard, R. R. S., & Cannon, H. M. (2011). Exploring motivation: Using emoticons to map student motivation in a business game exercise. *Developments in Business Simulation and Experiential Learning, 38,* 229–240.

Bica, F., Verdin, R., & Vicari, R. M. (2006). *Towards cognitive modeling of students' self-efficacy.* In Proceedings of 6th international conference on advanced learning technologies, ICALT2006 (pp. 1017–1021). Washington, DC: IEEE Computer Society.

Breuer, J. S., & Bente, G. (2010). Why so serious? On the relation of serious games and learning. *Eludamos. Journal for Computer Game Culture, 4*(1), 7–24.

Burgos, D., Moreno-Ger, P., Sierra, J. L., Fernández-Manjón, B., Specht, M., & Koper, R. (2008). Building adaptive game-based learning resources: The integration of IMS learning design and. *Simulation & Gaming, 39*(3), 414–431.

Chang, Y.-C., Chen, K.-T., Wu, C.-C., Ho, C.-J., & Lei, C.-L. (2010). *Online game QoE evaluation using paired comparisons.* Presented at the 2010 IEEE international workshop technical committee on communications quality and reliability (CQR 2010) (p. 6), Vancouver, BC.

Chen, Z.-H., & Chan, T.-W. (2008). Learning by substitutive competition: Nurturing my-pet for game competition based on open learner model. In *Proceedings of the second IEEE international conference on digital games and intelligent* (pp. 124–131), Big Island, HI.

Cocea, M., & Weibelzahl, S. (2009). Log file analysis for disengagement detection in e-learning environments. *User Modelling and User-Adapted Interaction, 19*(4), 341–385.

Cocea, M., & Weibelzahl, S. (2011). Disengagement detection in on-line learning: Validation studies and perspectives. *IEEE Transactions on Learning Technologies, 4*(2), 114–124.

Conati, C., & Maclaren, H. (2009). Modeling user affect from causes and effects. In G.-J. Houben, G. McCalla, F. Pianesi, & M. Zancanaro (Eds.), *Proceedings of the 17th international conference on user modeling, adaptation, and personalization.* Lectures notes in computer science (Vol. 5535, pp. 4–15). Berlin, Germany: Springer.

Conlan, O., Hampson, C., Peirce, N., & Kickmeier-Rust, M. (2009). Realtime knowledge space skill assessment for personalized digital educational games. In *Proceedings of 2009 ninth IEEE international conference on advanced learning technologies* (pp. 538–542), Riga, Latvia.

Connolly, T. M., & Stanfield, M. (2006). Using games-based eLearning technologies in overcoming difficulties in teaching information systems. *Journal of Information Technology Education, 5,* 459–476.

Connolly, T. M., & Stansfield, M. (2011). From E-learning to games-based E-learning. In Information Resources Management Association, USA (Ed.), *Gaming and simulations: Concepts, methodologies, tools and applications* (pp. 1763–1773). Hershey, PA: IGI Global.

Connolly, T. M., Stansfield, M., & Hainey, T. (2011). An alternate reality game for language learning: ARGuing for multimodal motivation. *Computers & Education, 57*(1), 1389–1415.

Costagliola, G., De Rosa, M., Fuccella, V., Capuano, N., & Ritrovato. P. (2010). A novel approach for attention management in e-learning systems. In proceedings of distributed multimedia systems (DMS) (pp. 222–227). Skokie, Illinois, USA: Knowledge Systems Institute, ISBN/ ISSN: 1-891706-28-4.

de Freitas, S., & Oliver, M. (2006). How can exploratory learning with games and simulations within the curriculum be most effectively evaluated? *Computers and Education, 46*(3), 249–264.

de Freitas, S., Rebolledo-Mendez, G., Liarokapis, F., Magoulas, G., & Poulovassilis, A. (2010). Learning as immersive experiences: Using the four-dimensional framework for designing and evaluating immersive learning experiences in a virtual world. *British Journal of Educational Technology, 4*(1), 69–85.

de Vicente, A. (2003). Towards tutoring systems that detect students' motivation: An investigation. Ph.D. thesis, University of Edinburg, Edinburg.

de Vicente, A., & Pain, H. (2002). Informing the detection of the students' motivational state: An empirical study. In S. A. Cerri, G. Gouarderes, & F. Paraguacu (Eds.), *Proceedings of the 6th international conference on intelligent tutoring systems* (pp. 79–86). London: Springer.

Derbali, L., Chalfoun, P., & Frasson, C. (2011). A theoretical and empirical approach in assessing motivational factors: From serious games to an ITS. In R. C. Murray & P. M. McCarthy (Eds.), *Proceedings of the twenty-fourth international Florida artificial intelligence research society conference 2011* (pp. 513–518). Palm Beach, FL: AAAI.

Derbali, L., & Frasson, C. (2010). Prediction of players motivational states using electrophysiological measures during serious game play. In *Proceedings of 2010 IEEE 10th international conference on advanced learning technologies (ICALT)* (pp. 498–502), Sousse, Tunisia.

Diah, N. M., Ismail, M., Ahmad, S., & Dahari, M. K. M. (2010). Usability testing for educational computer game using observation method. In *2010 international conference on information retrieval & knowledge management (CAMP)* (pp. 157–161), Shah Alam, Selangor.

Fu, F.-L., Su, R.-C., & Yu, S.-C. (2009). EGameFlow: A scale to measure learners' enjoyment of e-learning games. *Computers & Education, 52*(1), 101–112.

Garris, R., Ahlers, R., & Driskell, J. E. (2002). Games, motivation, and learning: A research and practice model. *Simulation & Gaming, 33*(4), 441–467.

Gee, J. P., & Shaffer, D. W. (2010). Looking where the light is bad: Video games and the future of assessment. *EDge: The Latest Information for the Education Practitioner, 6*(1), 1–27.

Ghergulescu, I., & Muntean, C. H. (2010). Assessment of motivation in games based e-learning. In *Proceeding of IADIS international conference cognition and exploratory learning in digital age* (pp. 71–78), Timisoara, Romania.

Hershkovitz, A., & Nachmias, R. (2008). Developing a log-based motivation measuring tool. *Educational Data Mining, 2008*(5), 226–233.

Hong, J.-C., Cheng, C.-L., Hwang, M.-Y., Lee, C.-K., & Chang, H.-Y. (2009). Assessing the educational values of digital games. *Journal of Computer Assisted Learning, 25*(5), 423–437.

Huang, W.-H., Huang, W.-Y., & Tschopp, J. (2010). Sustaining iterative game playing processes in DGBL: The relationship between motivational processing and outcome processing. *Computers & Education, 55*, 789–797.

Ifenthaler, D., Eseryel, D., & Ge, X. (2011). Origins of game-based assessment. In D. Ifenthaler, D. Eseryel, & X. Ge (Eds.), *Assessment in game-based learning: Foundations, innovations, and perspectives*. New York: Springer.

IMI. (2008). Retrieved Sept 15 2011, from http://www.psych.rochester.edu/SDT/measures/IMI_description.php.

Johns, J., & Woolf, B. (2006). A dynamic mixture model to detect student motivation and proficiency. In A. Cohn (Ed.), *Proceeding of AAAI'06 21st national conference on artificial intelligence* (pp. 163–168). Menlo Park, CA: AAAI Press.

Kebritchi, M., Hirumi, A., & Bai, H. (2010). The effects of modern mathematics computer games on mathematics achievement and class motivation. *Computers & Education, 55*(2), 427–443.

Keller, J. M. (1987). Development and use of the ARCS model of motivational design. *Instructional Development, 10*, 2–10.

Khan, F. A., Graf, S., Weippl, E. R., & Tjoa, A. M. (2009). An approach for identifying affective states through behavioral patterns in web-based learning management systems. In *Proceedings of the 11th international conference on information integration and web-based applications & services, iiWAS'09* (pp. 431–435), Kuala Lumpur.

Khan, F. A., Graf, S., Weippl, E. R., & Tjoa, A. M. (2010). Implementation of affective states and learning styles tactics in web-based learning management systems. In *Proceedings of the 2010 10th IEEE international conference on advanced learning technologies* (pp. 734–735), Sousse, Tunisia.

Khan, F. A., Weippl, E. R., & Tjoa, A. M. (2009). Integrated approach for the detection of learning styles and affective states. In *World conference on educational multimedia, hypermedia and telecommunications* (Vol. 1, pp. 753–761) Chesapeake, VA: AACE.

Kim, Y. S., Cha, H. J., Cho, Y. R., Yoon, T. B., & Lee, J.-H. (2007). An intelligent tutoring system with motivation diagnosis and planning. In *15th international conference on computers in education, Hiroshima*. Retrieved April 20, 2011, from http://credits.skku.edu/credits/publications/ICCE2007_Poster.pdf

Koidl, K., Mehm, F., Hampson, C., Conlan, O., & Göbel, S. (2010). Dynamically adjusting digital educational games towards learning objectives. In B. Meyer (Ed.), *Proceedings 4th European conference on games based learning, Copenhagen, Denmark* (pp. 177–185). Reading: Academic.

Kuipers, F., Kooij, R., De Vleeschauwer, D., & Brunnström, K. (2010). Techniques for measuring quality of experience. In *Wired/wireless internet communications*. Lecture notes in computer science (Vol. 6074, pp. 216–227). Berlin: Springer.

Levac, D., Pierrynowski, M. R., Canestraro, M., Gurr, L., Leonard, L., & Neeley, C. (2010). Exploring children's movement characteristics during virtual reality video game play. *Human Movement Science, 29*(6), 1023–1038.

Lin, H.-H., Wang, C.-Y., & Wei, H.-Y. (2010). *Improving online game performance over IEEE 802.11n networks*. Presented at the 2010 9th annual workshop on network and systems support for games (NetGames) (p. 2), Taipei, Taiwan.

Liu, T.-Y., & Chu, Y.-L. (2010). Using ubiquitous games in an English listening and speaking course: Impact on learning outcomes and motivation. *Computers & Education, 55*(2), 630–643.

Mattheiss, E., Kickmeier-Rust, M. D., Steiner, C. M., & Albert, D. (2010). Approaches to detect discouraged learners: Assessment of motivation in educational computer games. In S. Hambach, A. Martens, D. Tavangarian, & B. Urban (Eds.), *Proceedings of eLearning Baltics (eLBa)* (p. 10). Rostock: Fraunhofer.

McQuiggan, S. W., Mott, B. W., & Lester, J. C. (2008). Modeling self-efficacy in intelligent tutoring systems: An inductive approach. *User Modeling and User-Adapted Interaction, 18*(1–2), 81–123.

McQuiggan, S. W., Robison, J. L., & Lester, J. C. (2010). Affective transitions in narrative-centered learning environments. *Educational Technology & Society, 13*(1), 40–53.

Miller, L. M., Chang, C.-I., Wang, S., Beier, M. E., & Klisch, Y. (2011). Learning and motivational impacts of a multimedia science game. *Computers & Education, 57*(1), 1425–1433.

Moreno-Ger, P., Torrente, J., Bustamante, J., Fernández-Galaz, C., Fernández-Manjón, B., & Comas-Rengifo, M. D. (2010). Application of a low-cost web-based simulation to improve students' practical skills in medical education. *International Journal of Medical Informatics, 79*(6), 459–467.

Muñoz, K., Kevitt, P. M., Lunney, T., Noguez, J., & Neri, L. (2011). An emotional student model for game-play adaptation. *Entertainment Computing, 2*(2), 133–141.

Munoz-Organero, M., Munoz-Merino, P. J., & Kloos, C. D. (2010). Student behavior and interaction patterns with an LMS as motivation predictors in E-learning settings. *IEEE Transactions on Education, 53*(3), 463–470.

Papastergiou, M. (2009). Exploring the potential of computer and video games for health and physical education: A literature review. *Computers & Education, 53*, 603–622.

Prensky, M. (2001). The digital game-based learning revolution. In M. Prensky (Ed.), *Digital game-based learning* (1st ed.). New York: McGraw-Hill.

Qu, L., Wang, N., & Johnson, W. L. (2005). Using learner focus of attention to detect learner motivation factors. In L. Ardissono, P. Brna, A. Mitrovic (Eds.), *Proceedings of the 10th interna-*

tional conference, user modelling 2005, Edinburgh, Scotland. Lectures notes in computer science (Vol. 3538, pp. 70–73). Berlin, Germany: Springer.

Rebolledo-Mendez, G., de Freitas, S., Rojano-Caceres, R., & Gaona-Garcia, A. R. (2010). An empirical examination of the relation between attention and motivation in computer-based education: A modeling approach. In H. W. Guesgen & R. C. Murray (Eds.), *Proceedings of the twenty-third international Florida artificial intelligence research society conference 2010, Daytona Beach, FL, USA* (pp. 74–79). Menlo Park, CA: AAAI.

Renshaw, T., Stevens, R., & Denton, P. (2009). Towards understanding engagement in games: An eye-tracking study. *On the Horizon, 17*(4), 408–420.

Ryan, R., & Deci, E. L. (2000). Self-determination theory and the facilitation of intrinsic motivation, social development, and well-being. *American psychologist, 55*(1), 68–78.

Sancho, P., & Fernandez-Manjon, B. (2010). Experiences in using a MUVE for enhancing motivation in engineering education. In *Proceedings of IEEE EDUCON 2010 conference* (pp. 775–782), Madrid, Spain.

Shih, J.-L., Shih, B.-J., Shih, C.-C., Su, H.-Y., & Chuang, C.-W. (2010). The influence of collaboration styles to children's cognitive performance in digital problem-solving game "William Adventure": A comparative case study. *Computers & Education, 55*(3), 982–993.

Shute, V. J. (2009). Simply assessment. *International Journal of Learning and Media, 1*(2), 1–11.

Shute, V. J., Masduki, I., & Donmez, O. (2010). Conceptual framework for modeling, assessing, and supporting competencies within game environments. *Technology, Instruction, Cognition, and Learning, 8*(2), 137–161.

Shute, V. J., Ventura, M., Bauer, M., & Zapata-Rivera, D. (2009). Melding the power of serious games and embedded assessment to monitor and foster learning: Flow and grow. In U. Ritterfeld, M. J. Cody, & P. Vorderer (Eds.), *Serious games: Mechanisms and effects* (pp. 295–321). Mahwah, NJ: Routledge.

Steinkuehler, C., & King, E. (2009). Digital literacies for the disengaged: Creating after school contexts to support boys' game-based literacy skills. *On the Horizon, 17*(1), 47–59.

Takatalo, J., Hakkinen, J., Kaistinen, J., & Nyman, G. (2007). Measuring user experience in digital gaming: Theoretical and methodological issues. In L. C. Cui & Y. Miyake (Eds.), *Proceedings of SPIE: Image quality and system performance IV* (Vol. 6494, pp. 1–13). San Jose, CA: SPIE.

Takatalo, J., Häkkinen, J., Kaistinen, J., & Nyman, G. (2010). Presence, involvement, and flow in digital games. In R. Bernhaupt (Ed.), *Evaluating user experience in games* (pp. 23–46). London: Springer.

Takatalo, J., Häkkinen, J., Kaistinen, J., & Nyman, G. (2011). User experience in digital games: Differences between laboratory and home. *Simulation & Gaming, 42*, 656–673.

Tang, S., Hanneghan, M., & El Rhalibi, A. (2009). Introduction to games-based learning. In T. Connolly, M. Stansfield, & L. Boyle (Eds.), *Games-based learning advancements for multisensory human computer interfaces* (pp. 1–17). Hershey, PA: IGI Global.

Tüzün, H., Yllmaz-Soylu, M., Karakus, T., Inal, Y., & KIzIlkaya, G. (2009). The effects of computer games on primary school students' achievement and motivation in geography learning. *Computers & Education, 52*(1), 68–77.

Vos, N., van der Meijden, H., & Denessen, E. (2011). Effects of constructing versus playing an educational game on student motivation and deep learning strategy use. *Computers & Education, 56*(1), 127–137.

Wilson, K. A., Bedwell, W. L., Lazzara, E. H., Salas, E., Burke, C. S., Estock, J. L., et al. (2009). Relationships between game attributes and learning outcomes. *Simulation & Gaming, 40*(2), 217–266.

Woolf, B. P., Arroyo, I., Muldner, K., Burleson, W., Cooper, D. G., Dolan, R., et al. (2010). The effect of motivational learning companions on low achieving students and students with disabilities. In V. Aleven, J. Kay, & J. Mostow (Eds.), *Proceeding of intelligent tutoring systems* (pp. 327–337). Berlin: Springer.

Yue, W. S., & Zin, N. A. M. (2009). Usability evaluation for history educational games. In *Proceedings of the 2nd international conference on interaction sciences: Information technology, culture and human*, ICIS'09, Busan, Korea (pp. 1019–1025). New York, NY: ACM.

Chapter 19
Assessment of Student's Emotions in Game-Based Learning

Elena Novak and Tristan E. Johnson

19.1 Introduction

In recent years, researchers from various disciplines including psychology, human–computer interactions, computer vision, physiology, education, behavioral science, ergonomics and human factor engineering turned their attention to the role of emotions in human-computer dialogue. Traditionally, cognition and emotions were viewed as two separable mental process (Boehner, DePaula, Dourish, & Sengers, 2007; Chaffar, Derbali, & Frasson, 2009). However, recent research in neuroscience, psychology, and cognitive sciences has demonstrated the interdependence between emotions and cognition (Canamero, 1997; Damasio, 1995; Scherer, 2005). Moreover, researchers have shown that emotions play a critical role in rational, functional, and intelligent behaviors (Myers, 2002; Picard, Vyzas, & Healey, 2001).

Adding emotion recognition and assessment aspect to computing would allow computers to mirror human interactions and positively affect human performance (Scheirer, Fernandez, Klein, & Picard, 2002). Picard (1997) describes affective computing as "computing that relates to, arises from, or deliberately influences emotions" (p. 3). A more recent description of affective computing states that "affective computing is trying to assign computers the human-like capabilities of observation, interpretation and generation of affect features" (Tao, Tan, & Picard, 2005, p. 981). The key element of assessing user emotions in computer-assisted activities is "computer's capability to recognize the user's emotional states during

E. Novak (✉)
Educational Psychology and Learning Systems, Florida State University,
University Center C4600,Tallahassee, FL 32306, USA
e-mail: enovak@fsu.edu

Tristan E. Johnson
Graduate School of Engineering, Northeastern University, 130 Snell Engineering Center,
360 Huntington Avenue, Boston, MA
e-mail: tejohnson@coe.neu.edu

D. Ifenthaler et al. (eds.), *Assessment in Game-Based Learning: Foundations,*
Innovations, and Perspectives, DOI 10.1007/978-1-4614-3546-4_19,
© Springer Science+Business Media New York 2012

379

the interaction, which requires a model of the user's affect" (Conati & Maclaren, 2009, p. 268). The research focusing on assessment of user affective states argues that in addition to recognizing user's emotions, it is important to understand the reasons why people experience these emotions (Conati & Maclaren, 2009; Mandryk & Atkins, 2007).

Most of the research focusing on assessing user emotions has been rooted in the fields of human–computer interactions and cognitive sciences. Although vast majority of the literature on assessment of user affect is not focusing on instructional games, research findings in this domain are directly applicable to the field of instructional gaming. In educational games, adding an affective-sensitive intelligent tutoring system (ITS) may improve students' performance and attitudes toward instructional tasks. "An affect-sensitive ITS would incorporate assessments of the students' cognitive and affective states into its pedagogical and motivational strategies in order to keep students engaged, boost self-confidence, heighten interest, and presumably maximize learning" (D'Mello et al., 2010, pp. 245–246). For example, Conati and Maclaren (2009) argue that one of the reasons why research in the field of instructional games does not provide hard evidence regarding the effectiveness of games as educational tools is because most of the existing games do not respond to specific needs of individual students. The solution that the authors propose is to embed emotionally intelligent pedagogical agents that would provide interventions based on student affective and cognitive states aimed at both facilitating learning and maintaining high level of engagement.

ITSs have been used in computer-assisted learning to implement various tutoring strategies such as providing a timely and corrective feedback, assessing student performance, and having that data guide tutoring, building coherent explanations (Aleven & Koedinger, 2002; Koedinger, Anderson, Hadley, & Mark, 1997; Woolf, 2009). However, in addition to providing tutoring based on students' cognitive assessment, ITSs can be affective processors as well (Issroff & del Soldato, 1995; Picard, 1997).

It is common that the student will experience a range of emotions during a learning process—such as joy, frustration, anxiety, or boredom. Emotions experienced during a learning process provide clues not only to the effectiveness of a learning activity but also to the process of learning. Kort, Reilly, and Picard (2001) identified the following pairs of positive and negative emotions that are commonly present in learning: anxiety–confidence, boredom–fascination, frustration–euphoria, dispirited–encouraged, and terror–enchantment.

Many educational researchers have shown that emotions and cognition are located within the same information-processing frame and directly affect human performance (Boehner et al., 2007; Chaffar et al., 2009; Chen & Wang, 2011). Karaseitanidis et al. (2006) argue that emotions directly affect cognitive load and thereby learning and performance, since emotions maintain balance between task complexity and learner's characteristics (e.g., skills, knowledge, experience, etc.).

Emotions affect various learning outcomes. Researchers have found that positive emotions facilitate long-term memory and retrieval and working memory processes and thereby can potentially improve motivation, creativity, and problem-solving skills (Chen & Wang, 2011; Erez & Isen, 2002). Negative emotions, such as depression, anger, or anxiety, can inhibit learning (Goleman, 1995). However, positive emotions can inhibit learning as well if they create task-irrelevant processing that negatively impacts reasoning and performance (Oaksford, Morris, Grainger, & Williams, 1996). Researches distinguish between outcome emotions and emotions directly related to academic activities and contents (Pekrun, 2006; Pekrun & Stephens, 2011). Outcome emotions are emotions induced by achievement outcomes, such as pride and hope pertaining to success, or shame and anger pertaining to failure. Activity emotions are emotions experienced during academic activities, such as boredom experienced during a monotonic lecture, or surprise about finding a correct solution to a problem. Although vast majority of research on academic emotions has focused on achievement outcome emotions, such as test anxiety (Zeidner, 2007) and emotions following success and failure (e.g., Weiner, 1985), activity-related emotions are equally important and relevant for learning and performance (Pekrun & Stephens, 2011). In a series of interview and questionnaire studies, researchers have found that students experience with equal frequency both positive (e.g., enjoyment, satisfaction, hope, pride, and relief) and negative emotions (e.g., anger, anxiety, shame, and boredom) in academic settings (e.g., Spangler, Pekrun, Kramer, & Hofmann, 2002). These findings suggest that both achievement outcome and activity-related emotions play an important role in human performance and assessing students' emotions can provide clues on how emotions affect learning. Employing affective computing to explore various emotions experienced in computer-assisted learning and the effects of emotions on students' performance, engagement, and motivation can definitely help in promoting academic emotions research.

Another benefit of assessing students' emotions in various computer-based learning settings pertains to the manner in which expert teachers communicate with students. Well-experienced teachers can establish an effective communication with students and even improve students' learning by paying attention to students' emotional states and responding in an appropriate manner (D'Mello et al., 2010; Kort et al., 2001). Moreover, researchers have found that teachers who help students in developing emotions facilitate students' cognitive development and positive learning experiences (Coles, 1998; Reilly & Kort, 2004).

According to many researchers, there is a growing need for measuring the emotional load in human-computer environments and computer-based training environments such as simulations, games, and virtual reality systems in particular. Karaseitanidis et al. (2006) argue that there is significant evidence that emotions play an important role in business and organizations. Emotions can affect the overall acceptance of a workplace and contribute to employee well-being and staff turnover. Negative emotions inhibit human performance as they are strongly related to activation, effort, and energy mobilization processes (Gaillard & Kramer, 2000). Liao, Zhang, Zhu, Ji, and Gray (2006) suggest that affective considerations should be included in the design of human-computer interaction systems, particularly critical, typically high-stress applications such as emergency vehicle dispatchers, air traffic control, pilots, and other military operational contexts. Considering user affective states can reduce the frequency of accidents and incidents of operating such systems. Negative states such as stress, fatigue, anxiety, or frustration are often the main reason for "human error" in a variety of settings, since the adverse emotions negatively affect decision-making and learning.

In fact, the idea of considering students' affective states in designing multimedia instructional materials has been supported by many researchers. Conati (2002), in addition to assessing student's emotions, used an animated pedagogical agent in game-based environment to help the student regulate his/her emotions. Such agents can generate interventions aimed at facilitating the learning process. Some researchers even argue that there is a correlation between learner emotions and different types of multimedia instructional materials, e.g., static text, pictures, animations, and video (Chen & Wang, 2011). Thus in addition to improving human performance, assessing learner emotions can provide valuable insights about (1) the affective process students experience during learning, (2) how students respond to different instructional tasks, learning materials, and system features, and (3) what learning factors cause these affective processes. This information would be extremely beneficial to educators, psychologists, programmers, and graphic- and game-designers.

Although there is limited empirical research showing that considerations about learner emotions in human-computer interaction systems can significantly improve learning and performance, there have been a few successful initial attempts in this area. D'Mello et al. (2010) found that affect-sensitive tutor responding to boredom, frustration, and confusion affective states significantly improved learning for low-domain knowledge students in comparison to nonaffective tutor that did not respond to student's emotional state. Zakharov, Mitrovic, and Johnston (2008) compared the effects of affect-aware agent that tailors its responses to the valence of the student affective state (positive vs. negative) and affect-unaware agent does not tailor its responses to the valence of student emotions on students' learning and attitudes toward the pedagogical agent. Due to the short interaction session with the pedagogical agent, no significant differences in learning between the two treatments were found. However, when ranking the appropriateness of the agents' behavior and its usefulness, affect-aware agent scored much higher than the affect-unaware one. Furthermore, the agents' presence increased students' trust in the tutoring system's ability to guide the students and provide hints.

The goal of this chapter is to present an up-to-date review of emotion assessment methods in computer-based systems and recent research on how these methods have been used in games. The primary focus of this chapter is on emotion assessment in educational games. However, since to date research on affective educational games is quite limited, we discuss emotion assessment methods employed in entertainment games as well and transferability of these methods to educational context. The rest of this chapter is organized as follows. We first describe three emotion-recognition approaches used in affective computing, including detailed description of various emotion assessment methods used within each approach, their strengths and limitations. Next, we discuss recent empirical research on emotions assessment in entertainment and educational games, followed by summary and discussion section addressing challenges in assessing emotions and development of user affect recognition computer-based systems. Finally, we conclude by suggestions for future research on assessment of emotions in educational games.

19.2 Emotion Recognition Issues

One of the recent trends in the gaming field is to design a model that will detect learner's multiple (concurrent) emotions and thus allow an intelligent interactive agent to use this information to tailor its responses to the user's needs. Detecting learner's emotions during game playing can help game developers to assess learner's emotional and motivational states in each particular stage of a game and thus adjust game difficulty and challenge to the learner's needs and/or provide him/her with immediate feedback. Thus, regulating the difficulty of educational game's tasks may allow sustaining learner's motivation at an optimal level during the educational activity.

The biggest challenge in creating such models is hidden in an uncertainty in modeling affect. How is it possible to predict what particular causes lead to certain emotional states? Moreover, how accurate is interpreting game player's emotions? Most of the researchers agree that assessing user emotions is an extremely challenging and difficult task (Bentley, Johnston, & von Braggo, 2005; Isbister, Höök, Laaksolahti, & Sharp, 2007; Mandryk & Atkins, 2007).

Liao et al. (2006) classify emotion recognition and prediction methods as predictive inference (top–down), diagnostic inference (bottom–up), and a hybrid that combines both predictive and diagnostic methods. A predictive approach tries to predict affect based on factors that might influence or cause affect. A predictive inference is usually grounded in established psychological theories, e.g., OCC model developed by Ortony, Clore, and Collins (1988). In contrast to a predictive approach, diagnostic approach makes inferences about affect using physiological or behavioral measurements of the user. These measures may use user's eyebrow movement and body posture, eye region biometrics (eyebrow, pupil, iris, upper/lower fold, and eyelid), physical appearance features, physiological measures (heart rate, blood pressure, skin conductance, color, and temperature), speech symptoms (sentence fragments and articulation rate), face expressions, and voice.

A hybrid approach combines both predictive and diagnostic approaches and thus improves affect recognition accuracy. For example, student characteristics, instructional strategies, or instructional tasks can be combined with physiological and behavioral measures. Most of the probabilistic approaches described later in this chapter are hybrid ones.

19.2.1 Predictive Inference Approach

Predictive inference approach usually employs postinteraction tests or subjective questionnaires or interviews. This approach is useful for results generalization and understanding student attitudes but not emotions, because participants usually have a problem reporting their behaviors and emotions in game situation (Pagulayan, Keeker, Wixon, Romero, & Fuller, 2002). Moreover, these techniques are not suitable to be implemented during the game play, since they interrupt and disrupt game experience. The following research study of de Vicente and Pain (2002) displays the use of predictive inference approach for student's motivation assessment.

De Vicente and Pain (2002) developed tutoring system that assessed and tried to enhance student motivation, a variable closely related to affective states. The researchers relied on single operational measure, i.e., self-report, when inferring a learner's emotion, and trained the system on judgments by expert coders (Baker, D'Mello, Rodrigo, & Graesser, 2010; D'Mello, Craig, Witherspoon, McDaniel, & Graesser, 2008).

Student motivation was assessed by comparing how the tutorial interaction related to the four variables that can influence motivation. These variables included (1) degree of control that the student would like to have over the learning situation, (2) degree of challenge that the student would like to experience, (3) degree of independence during the interaction, and (4) degree of fantasy-based situations to be included in the instructional game. The authors developed a system that could replay the actions of a previous student's interaction with an instructional system. While interacting with this system, the participant was presented first with information about the four variables, i.e., (1) degree of control, (2) degree of challenge, (3) degree of independence, and (4) degree of fantasy-based situations. Then she watched by replay of her interaction with an instructional system. Finally, throughout the interaction, the student was asked to provide verbal comments (which were recorded for analysis) on her motivational states and their possible causes.

This study allowed the authors to generate 61 rules related to recognition of student's motivation. The following example is one of the generated rules: "If the student tries to perform most of the exercises in this lesson and he does not give up, then we can infer that his effort is high."

In their further study, de Vicente and Pain (2003) performed rules validation, where 973 participants answered an on-line questionnaire about the value of the motivational factors. The findings of the evaluation study helped to reduce the original set of 61 rules to 41. According to authors, the validated 41 rules related to automated recognition of student's motivation could be readily embedded into an ITS.

19.2.2 Diagnostic Inference Approach

Diagnostic inference methods such as physiological and behavioral measures have been extensively used in affect evaluation research. In computer-based applications, affect can be measured either by humans or automatically detected by computers (Baker et al., 2010). There are several ways, in which physiological and behavioral affect data may be obtained including biometric sensors, pressure-sensitive chairs, and eye-trackers, videotaping, think aloud protocols, etc. Although technological development and research have substantially improved accuracy rates of automated detection methods over the last decade, reliability of these methods is not yet sufficient to be used in real-world environments (Baker et al., 2010; Conati & Maclaren, 2009). Moreover, there are several practical obstacles associated with using automated methods such as availability of affective sensors and devices in sufficient quantities and skillful personal to operate the equipment. Thus, the majority of affect research is still carried out by humans using various methodologies (Baker et al., 2010).

19.2.2.1 Physiological Measures

Although emotions often visibly affect a person's behavior and expressions, assessing emotional states based on the visual expressions is highly subjective. Biometric measures such as heart rate, blood pressure, skin conductance, color, and temperature (Picard, 1997) can provide a better assessment of emotions. A person usually has little control over these covert biometric measures, and therefore, they could provide a more reliable source of information on a person's affect.

However, information on a single biometric measure is usually not sufficient to recognize a specific emotion. For example, skin conductivity provides a very good indication of general level of arousal, but a poor indicator of the valence of the emotion that caused the arousal (Picard, 1997). On the other hand, heart rate is a good indicator of the valence of the emotion but provides little information about specific emotions (Ekman, Levenson, & Friesen, 1983). Emotions with negative valence tend to increase heart rate more than emotions with positive valence (Cacioppo, Berntson, Larsen, Poehlmann, & Ito, 2000).

Skin temperature changes can indicate stress situation. Stress response causes blood to flow away from the extremities such as hands resulting in a decrease in skin temperature, thus colder hands.

Respiration amplitude and frequency are good indicators of anxiety. Respiration automatically increases because of physical exercise or an emotional reaction, namely fear and sadness.

Galvanic skin response (GSR) is a measure reflecting the electrical resistance of the skin. A high GSR signal is often correlated with high stress level. GSR has a direct link with arousal and is often used to reflect emotional reactions as well as cognitive activities. Electroencephalograph (EEG) signals are a representation of the neural electrical activity present in the brain, called brain waves.

Those physiological signals are good source for affective data collection, since assessing physiological signals can be performed in quasi real-time without affecting the dynamic of the learning session. Furthermore, it is resistant to cultural and personal traits differences (Blanchard, Chalfoun, & Frasson, 2007). Nevertheless, physiological techniques should be used together with other evaluation methods such as questionnaires, interviews, and video analysis, because it is impossible to interpret the valence of the emotion using biosensor data only (Isbister et al., 2007; Mandryk & Atkins, 2007). For example, there is no way to differentiate between joy and anger (Bentley et al., 2005, p. 4). Another drawback of physiological sensors is that it involves obtrusive intervention, which may not be implemented in certain settings or with certain participants since the sensors may distract students and interfere with instructional tasks (D'Mello et al., 2008).

19.2.2.2 Videotaping

Videotaping students' facial expressions, gestures, and body postures is a nonintrusive affect detection method that can be used while students interact with computer. Although videotaping provides rich data, analyzing videotapes might require between 5 and 100 analysis hours for every hour of video (Mandryk & Atkins, 2007). Furthermore, reliability of affect evaluation using videotaping poses a number of challenges as well, since affect evaluation is done based on events (user is frowning now) and not on cues continuity (degree of smile at every point of time). Therefore, videotaping provides only limited insights into the process of play.

Recently, there has been an attempt to design automated video analysis algorithms aiming to recognize user emotions from video analysis of body movements and gesture dynamics (Castellano, Villalba, & Camurri, 2007). The proposed approach allows analysis of human affective states in nonlaboratory settings in nonintrusive way, but still requires further calibrations to reach acceptable levels of accuracy.

19.2.2.3 Think Aloud Protocols

Think aloud protocols is another nonintrusive method that was used to collect information about student emotions during game play. Among the drawbacks of this method are disturbance to the student, impact on the condition, observer expectancy, social conformity effects, and avoidance to share emotional information (Bentley et al., 2005; Mandryk, Inkpen, & Calvert, 2006). In addition, parts of affective processing are occurring in the brain areas that are not readily accessible to language (Isbister et al., 2007; LeDoux, 1996).

19.2.2.4 Speech Emotion Recognition

When using speech emotion recognition technique, human speech is captured using microphones. Emotion recognition is performed based on acoustic-prosodic vocal speech features through modeling emotional cues in speech. Various speech emotion recognition models can evaluate acoustic-prosodic vocal features and dynamics of both acted and spontaneous speech (Wagner, Vogt, & Andr, 2007). Speech emotion recognition is a relatively easy to use nonintrusive method that can be used in real-world settings; therefore many researchers argue to use this technique (D'Mello et al., 2008; Kaklauskas et al., 2010; Mandryk & Atkins, 2007).

19.2.2.5 Keystroke and Linguistic Features Stress Detection

In recent years, there have been initial attempts to interpret user emotions by analyzing keyboard interactions. Vizer, Zhou, and Sears (2009) developed a model that detects cognitive and physical stress by analyzing keystroke and linguistic features of spontaneously generated text. The model is able to distinguish between cognitive-affective stress and nonstress conditions based on user keyboard interactions. The model's accuracy rate is consistent with other affective computing methods. Although this technique is capable of detecting only one affective state, i.e., stress, this method could be attractive in concert with other affect assessment methods. Keystroke and linguistic features stress detection model is nonintrusive and does not require any additional hardware. Moreover, it is adaptive for individual users.

19.2.2.6   Eye-Tracking

Research has shown that human eyelid movement, pupil movement, facial expression, and head movement have a systematic meaningful structure that can be mapped into affective states (Liao et al., 2006). Human eyes movements can be used to evaluate student's attention. According to Prendinger, Ma, and Ishizuka (2007), eye-tracking system can gather quantitative data related to student's attention without distracting from the task. In addition to providing information about student's attention, eye-tracking technique allows a continuous assessment of the student's areas of interest on the screen. Eye-trackers usually use two narrow-angle cameras directed toward the user's left and right eye to measure simultaneously the movements of both eyes. Some eye-trackers use an additional camera to capture the user's screen.

19.2.3   Hybrid Approach

A hybrid approach for emotion assessment combines both predictive and diagnostic approaches. Researchers argue that in order to conduct a research that would yield truly generalizable findings, different methods and data collection techniques should be used to address the same research question (Baker et al., 2010; D'Mello et al., 2010). Particularly in the emotion recognition domain, leveraging any information that can provide evidence about learner's emotions is crucial, since different affect assessment methods often provide ambiguous results and their reliability depends on both the learner and human-computer interaction (Conati & Maclaren, 2009). Karaseitanidis et al. (2006) suggest that combining psycho physiological measures and psychological subjective reports can result in valuable emotion recognition tool. As an evidence to the power of the hybrid approach, the majority of the found studies focusing on affect assessment employed more than one affect assessment data collection method (Conati, Chabbal, & Maclaren, 2003; D'Mello et al., 2010; Mandryk & Atkins, 2007). Very often, student characteristics were combined with several physiological and behavioral measures, e.g., eye-tracking and biometric sensors.

The following section presents several studies focusing on assessment of user emotional states in game-based environment. Most of the studies have utilized a hybrid approach. The studies show different methods for emotion assessment along with associated methodological and measurement issues.

19.3   Assessment of Emotions in Game-Based Environment

This section discusses examples of research studies focusing on assessment of user emotional states in game-based environment, both entertainment and educational. The selected examples illustrate how various philosophical perspectives affect emotion assessment methods and models. In addition, we discuss whether affect assessment methods used in entertainment games can be successfully implemented in educational games.

19.3.1   Entertainment Games

Mandryk, Atkins, and Inkpen (2006) conducted an experimental study to inform the design of a continuous model of emotion based on users' physiological responses. The designed model of emotions would assess user emotional states when interacting with an entertainment game to present a clear and continuous picture of how user felt during the game play. Particularly, the model focused on five emotions: fun, excitement, frustration, boredom, and challenge.

Twenty-four male participants played a sports game in three conditions: against a friend, against a stranger, and against the computer. Each participant participated in each of the three conditions. The focus of the study was not to examine differences between the conditions, since existing research confirmed that there were significant differences between these three play conditions. Rather, Mandryk, Atkins, et al. (2006) were interested to create a model of emotion that would detect differences between the conditions.

The authors used a hybrid approach for emotion assessment. During the game play, participants' emotions were assessed using objective diagnostic methods of (1) videotaping both of the players, their facial expressions, and their use of the game controller, (2) audio of the participants' comments and audio output from the game, and (3) physiological signals. The physiological signals included GSR, electrocardiography (EKG), and electromyography of the face (EMGsmiling and EMGfrowning).

In addition to diagnostic methods, the authors used predictive subjective data collection methods as well. After each game condition, game players filled out a five-point Likert scale questionnaire rating the game condition on the five assessed emotions. In addition, participants completed a postexperimental questionnaire to rate retrospectively which condition was most fun, exciting, challenging, boring, or frustrating.

The model of emotion was built based on the collected physiological data. To analyze the effectiveness of the model, modeled (objective) emotions that were detected during the game play using the physiological signals were compared with reported (subjective) emotions that were gathered through the postcondition and postexperimental questionnaires. The results showed that the modeled emotions significantly correlated with the subjective emotions for fun and excitement. No significant correlations were found for boredom or frustration, although similar trends appeared for these two emotions as compared to the reported ones. An inverse significant correlation was observed for challenge due to modeling challenges and an assumption related to the correlation between a player's arousal and challenge.

Post-hoc analysis showed that (1) it was considerably more fun and exciting to play against a fiend than against a stranger, and (2) it was considerably more fun to play against a stranger than against the computer. Marginal differences in excitement were revealed between stranger and computer conditions.

In summary, Mandryk, Atkins, et al. (2006) presented a powerful method for modeling user emotional states during game play based on objective physiological data. The modeled emotions showed the same trends as the reported emotions for fun, boredom, and excitement. The model of emotion succeeded to detect differences between the game conditions, but failed to reach significance in resembling game players' reported emotional states.

The above-described emotion assessment method is grounded in a premise that emotions are biological constituted facts that can be objectively measured. Some researchers believe that this approach considerably limits and even distorts our understanding of human emotions. According to Boehner et al. (2007), affect is "an aspect of collectively enacted social settings" (p. 280), and therefore emotion assessment methods should take into account social, cultural, and interactional aspects of affect as well. The following example stands in contrast to Mandryk et al.'s (2006) model of emotion. It has been also developed to assess real-time user emotion during game play, but drawing on an interactive perspective trying to take into account user cultural differences as well.

Isbister et al. (2007) have developed the Sensual Evaluation Instrument (SEI) using a hybrid approach to assess user emotional involvement during entertainment game play. The SEI is nonverbal, cross-cultural measurement instrument that consists of hand-size sensual and biomorphic shapes that can be broadly classified into sharp and more rounded, symmetrical and asymmetrical groups. The instrument draws on an interaction perspective. During the game play, gamers were asked to choose and gesture with the objects that would express their emotions. The objects were not coded into specific emotions; rather the researchers asked the participants after the game session why they picked up specific objects and what emotions they tried to communicate.

The authors conducted the experiment with participants from two countries (the USA and Sweden) to test the SEI across cultures. The game players indicated that there were several benefits of assessing user emotions with the SEI. Using the SEI was fun and engaging and it allowed for flexibility in response. Analysis of use patterns and verbal comments indicated that the SEI (1) allowed a feasible way to give immediate in-process feedback without too much disruption, and (2) could be developed into "reasonably consistent instrument" capable of detecting positive and negative emotion valence. However, major cross-cultural differences were observed between Swedes and US participants. Another drawback of the SEI related to the use of the instrument during real-time high-stress situations, since users did have neither the time nor the attention to using the instrument objects. Nor, the SEI was able to provide fine-grained continuous emotion assessment. Additionally, the examination of the SEI suffered from several methodological issues. First, because of small participant pool, no inferential statistical tests were conducted and the reported results indicated only trends. Second, the participants were not rigorously selected.

In summary, after this initial SEI examination, Isbister et al. (2007) suggested that the SEI does not require much user time and attention and is suitable for a low-stress informal dialog between game-designers and users.

19.3.2 Educational Games

Is it possible to transfer emotion assessment methods developed for entertainment games to educational games? This question has not been quite explored in the existing literature. Although some technical issues associated with emotion recognition in entertainment games appear to be similar to those in educational settings, additional considerations should be taken into account as well.

To begin with, some emotion assessment methods can distract or require an additional student's time or attention. In educational games, it is important to keep the process of emotion recognition transparent for a student in order to avoid distraction and extraneous cognitive load. For example, it would be very challenging to implement the SEI methods (Isbister et al., 2007) in educational settings, since it interrupts a learning process and draws student's attention away. Moreover, user emotions in educational games might appear in different rates of occurrence and persistence in comparison to entertainment games. Since entertainment technology pursues different from educational technology goals, the emotion spectrums experienced in entertainment and educational games would not be the same. According to Conati and Maclaren (2009), educational games tend to arouse different emotions in different players. In addition, impact of cognitive-affective states on learning should be considered as well (Baker et al., 2010).

Conati and Maclaren (2009) argued that even technical issues associated with emotion recognition in educational games are not quite the same as in general affect modeling research. The authors discussed the principles underlying emotion assessment in existing literature focusing on modeling user affect and why these principles are not applicable in educational games.

Conati and Maclaren (2009) developed a probabilistic model of user affect to be used by an intelligent agent. The model was developed using a hybrid approach and aimed at achieving several goals. First, it identified multiple user affective states during the educational game play. Second, it allowed an intelligent pedagogical agent to maintain student engagement in the game through various interventions. Finally, the authors tried to improve student's trust and confidence in the system by creating a model that will allow an intelligent pedagogical agent to explain to the students a rationale behind the interventions. The model used Dynamic Bayesian Network in order to evaluate both the causes and effects of emotional reactions.

Predicting emotions from possible causes is not an easy task. Although there are psychological theories that define the mapping between causes and emotional states, in practice information on possible causes does not always provide unequivocal indication on the actual affective reaction.

The authors relied on the cognitive theory of emotions developed by Ortony et al. (1988), known as the OCC model, in order to map between user emotions and sensorial evidence. This theory defines emotions as valenced (positive or negative) reactions to situations consisting of events, actors, and objects. The valence of one's emotional reaction depends upon the desirability of the situation for oneself, which in turn is defined by one's goals and preferences. The OCC theory clearly defines 21 emotions as the result of situation appraisal, thus making it quite straightforward to predict a person's emotions if the person's goals and perception of relevant events are known. The problem is that this information is not always easily available when assessing user's emotions.

The above factors make emotion recognition a task permeated with uncertainty. Most of the existing research on modeling user affect has tried to reduce this uncertainty either (1) by considering tasks that allow monitoring the presence or absence of a specific emotion (Healy, 2000; Hudlicka & McNeese, 2002 as cited in Conati et al., 2003) or (2) by focusing on monitoring lower level measures of emotional reaction, such as the intensity and valence of emotional arousal (Ball & Breeze, 1999 as cited in Conati et al., 2003).

In educational games, neither of these approaches is appropriate, for two main reasons. First, educational games do tend to arouse different emotions in different players. For instance, the exploratory nature of a game can be very exciting for students that mainly want to have fun, while it may cause frustration or anxiety in students that want to learn from the game but tend to prefer more structured pedagogical activities. Second, detecting the student's specific emotions is important for an agent to decide how to correct possibly negative emotional states or leverage the positive ones. For example, if the agent realizes that the student is ashamed because she keeps making mistakes during the game, it can try to take actions that make the student feel better about her performance. Alternatively, if the agent realizes that the student enjoys its character but is distressed with the game, at a particular point in time, it can initiate an interaction with the student with the sole purpose of entertaining her.

Conati and Maclaren (2009) represented learner's emotional state during interacting with a game by six emotions that relate to the appraisal of the direct consequences of an event for oneself. These emotions include joy and distress toward the event that is appraised by the user, reproach and admiration toward the entity that caused the event, and pride and shame toward the entity that caused the event when the entity is oneself. To model detailed user emotions, the authors used an educational game, Prime Climb, developed by the EGEMS group at the University of British Columbia (UBC) to help sixth and seventh grade students learn number factorization.

The evaluation of the model on the included emotions showed that the model achieves a good accuracy (between 46% and 70%) of mutually exclusive emotions toward the game, e.g., joy and distress.

In contrast to Conati and Maclaren (2009) that examined six emotions in relation to learning events or entity that caused the events (i.e., joy and distress toward the event that is appraised by the user, reproach and admiration toward the entity that caused the event, and pride and shame toward the entity that caused the event when the entity is oneself), Baker et al. (2010) focused on assessing six cognitive-affective states during interaction with educational technology.

Baker et al. (2010) examined the affective profiles and persistence of cognitive–affective states during learners' use of educational software across three studies. Six cognitive-affective states (and neutral) were examined across the three studies: frustration, confusion, engaged concentration, delight, surprise, boredom, and neutral (no apparent emotion or feeling).

The authors varied students' cultural background (the USA and the Philippines), age (university and high school), learning environments (dialogue tutor, traditional workbook-style tutor, and a simulation game), different settings (laboratory and classroom), and study domains (Computer Literacy, Algebra, Concrete Logic Puzzles) across the three experiments. By varying various experiment conditions, Baker et al. (2010) tried to study the generalizability of their findings. Although this approach posed many challenges in interpreting differences among environments, it enabled to make stronger judgments regarding the generality of the results that the environments had in common. For example, if a particular result was the same in three different studies, it was reasonable to assume its robustness.

In the first study, 28 undergraduate college students from the USA used AutoTutor system to study topics in computer literacy. AutoTutor is a fully automated computer tutor that communicates with students in natural language (Graesser, Person, Harter, & Group, 2001). First, the students completed pretest, then used the AutoTutor system for 32 min, and finally completed a 36-item posttest on the taught topics. During the tutoring session, students' facial expressions and posture patterns were videotaped along with the content of their computer screen.

In order to assess students' cognitive-affective states, video streams of both the computer screen and the student's face were synchronized. After completing the experiment, each student was asked to review the video records taken during her tutoring session and indicate what cognitive-affective state, i.e., frustration, confusion, engaged concentration, delight, surprise, boredom, and neutral, she had been experiencing at every 20-s interval. Posture data were not displayed to students.

In the second study, 36 high school students from the Philippines used a simulation game to complete a series of logical puzzles for 10 min in laboratory settings. During the interaction with the simulation, each student was observed by several trained observers to gather behavior data indicating an evidence of a cognitive-affective state. The observes judged a student's state based on the student's work context, actions, utterances, facial expressions, body language, and interactions with teachers or peers. The cognitive-affective states were similar to the AutoTutor study. The authors used an observation method that was found highly successful and accurate for assessing student behavior and proved to have a good inter-rater reliability (Baker et al., 2006; Baker, Corbett, Koedinger, & Wagner, 2004).

The observers worked in pairs. Each pair of observers assessed three students per observation period and alternated among them. Each observation lasted 20 seconds and each student was observed once per minute. The observers used peripheral vision, when observers stood diagonally behind or in front of the student not looking at the students directly, in order that the student would not realize when exactly an observation occurred. The observers coded students' cognitive-affective states using a coding scheme developed by (Baker et al., 2004). Inter-rater reliability from coding was acceptably high.

In the third study, 140 high school students from the Philippines used an ITS for learning mathematics for 45 min. The students were observed while interacting with the system using a method identical to the seconds study method.

The authors analyzed the prevalence and persistence of six cognitive-affective states (and neutral) in the three learning environments. In addition, the authors examined the relationships between the cognitive-affective states and the choice to "game the system," a behavior associated with poorer learning (Baker et al., 2004). The results showed that engaged concentration (at least over short periods of the learning process) and confusion were the most common states in computerized learning environments. Confusion is usually experienced when a student is in the state of cognitive disequilibrium, elevated physiological arousal, and more intense thought. Experiences of delight and surprise were rare, while boredom was very persistent. Once a student got bored, it was very difficult to transition her out of boredom. Furthermore, boredom was the major reason for "gaming the system," a behavior known to affect negatively learning. Yet, research has shown that boredom significantly inhibits learning (Graesser, Rus, D'Mello, & Jackson, 2008). The authors argue that interactive learning environments should primarily focus on boredom and aim to prevent it or at least quickly respond to it. This opinion is quite different from the main stream of researchers arguing that frustration is the primary cognitive-affective state that needs immediate remediation (e.g., Hone, 2006). However, according to the results of Baker's et al. (2010) study, boredom should receive greater research attention than frustration. Furthermore, according to Mentis (2007), frustration among interactive technology users should be only of concern if it is associated with events such as a program bug, poor interface design, etc. Gee (2004) has even proposed that frustration can even improve the computer game experience.

When comparing the two emotion assessment methods utilized in Baker's et al. (2010) research, i.e., self-reports that were employed in the first study and observations that were used in the second and third studies, Baker et al. (2010) mention that it is likely that students' self-reports provide more accurate measures, since some students' cognitive-affective states may be unnoticed by trained observes. However, according to Graesser et al. (2006), both methods are comparable, except differences in proportion of confusion and frustration cognitive-affective states. There is still no clear evidence on what assessment method is the best—the trained observers or students' self-reports,—but both methods suffer from actor-observer biases. As such, Baker et al. (2010) suggest that using both forms of assessment would be the preferable method.

19.4 Summary and Discussion

The domain of assessing user emotions is not well articulated and explored, because emotions are extremely difficult to measure (Isbister et al., 2007). Researchers use a broad range of emotion assessment methods grounded in various emotion theories and conceptualizations. Researchers distinguish between subjective and objective affective measures. Objective measures can be obtained without the user's assistance or intervention. Subjective measures are based in part on self-reports (Boehner et al., 2007). Many researchers use mixed methods combining both objective and subjective methods to increase emotion assessment reliability or receive desirable measures (e.g., Mandryk, Atkins, et al., 2006).

Another set of differences between emotion assessment methods is in whether emotions are viewed as a pure biological phenomenon or are constituted of social, cultural, and interactional aspects. Researchers who believe that emotions are objective, biological, context-independent measures tend to use objective methods such as physiological signals. Those who view emotions mainly constructed through social and cultural interactions and interpretations argue that interactional approaches of emotion recognition should be utilized. According to an interactional approach, emotions are context-dependent and a substantial effort should be put into interpretation of human affect (Boehner et al., 2007).

Emotion assessment methods have been also categorized as predictive, diagnostic, and hybrid (Liao et al., 2006). A predictive approach strives to identify factors that might influence or cause affect, while a diagnostic approach categorizes affect based on physiological or behavioral measurements of the user. A hybrid approach combines both predictive and diagnostic approaches. In addition, emotion assessment methods have been classified based on other factors including mathematical tools they use, conceptualization of affect as information or interaction, etc. However, the discussion about other classifications of emotion assessment methods is beyond the scope of this chapter.

Despite extensive investigations in the domain of user affective states in psychology, computer vision, psychology, behavioral science, ergonomics, and human factor engineering, the idea of emotions and how to measure them is still not well understood (Liao et al., 2006; Mandryk, Inkpen, et al., 2006). Furthermore, current emotion recognition methods do not have yet sufficient accuracy and reliability rates to be used in nonlaboratory learning environments. Thus, the majority of affect research still involves human assistance and judgment in assessing students' affective states (Baker et al., 2010).

Liao et al. (2006) have indicated six issues pertaining to the development of user affect recognition computer-based systems. First, different people express emotions in different ways. Sometimes affect expression varies based on time and context even for the same person. Thereupon, measuring emotions presents a very challenging task for researchers. Second, in spite of technological advancements over the last decade, physiological (objective) assessment methods provide often ambiguous, uncertain, and incomplete measures yet. Third, human emotions are very dynamic in their nature and evolve over time and therefore emotion recognition requires real-time assessment methods. Unlike human performance that is not particularly dynamic and of time, emotions are not suitable for delayed measurement. Fourth, since emotions cannot be preserved over the time, affect recognition must be accomplished in real-time. Moreover, to obtain reliable measures, user assistance might be required as well, thus increasing the difficulty of emotion assessment process. Finally, those who consider the nature of emotions being ambiguous or beyond the reach of categorization would argue that people might experience multiple emotions at once or being unclear about the experienced emotion. Since there is no clear criterion or process that allows determining the reliability of the experienced emotion, it is very difficult to validate affect recognition approaches in computer-based applications.

The greatest research challenge in emotion assessment domain is what emotions to measure, and how to measure them (Mandryk, Inkpen, et al., 2006). The research studies presented in this chapter illustrate the variety of (1) assessment methods used to assess affect and (2) affective states proposed to play an important role in human–computer interactions. It is still unclear what emotions should be assessed and how they influence learning, attitudes, and behavior in computer-based games.

Advancing research in emotion recognition domain can particularly benefit research in instructional gaming, since the success of computer-based instructional games heavily depends on the system ability to tailor gaming characteristics such as feedback, challenge, storyline to student's cognitive-affective states. Embedding affective processors into ITSs can address the connections between emotions and cognition and thus facilitate learning (e.g., Chaffar et al., 2009; D'Mello et al., 2010).

19.5 Future Research

Currently, most of the studies exploring emotion recognition and their effect on human performance in computer-based environments are focusing on the accuracy of measurements of learner's affective states. Affect assessment researchers strive to develop systems that would accurately detect user emotions and provide interventions based on the detected cognitive-affective states. Resolving technical and methodological problems associated with emotions assessment will open a new horizon of instructional design issues associated with assessing learner's emotions in educational games. It is important to examine how each particular emotion or a set of multiple emotions affect learning. Furthermore, which cognitive-affective state requires primary motivational and instructional interventions? Instructional games are known for their ability to motivate and engage students in learning process. Harnessing games ability to assess student's motivation in every phase of the learning process and respond in appropriate manner to maintain the optimal engagement and motivation levels will boost learning. Furthermore, what would be the best instructional or motivational strategy to regulate learner's motivation given learner's emotional state? Future research would be needed to develop mapping system between learner's emotional states and motivational techniques that can improve human performance. Probably, motivation theories, such as Keller's ARCS model (1984) and Weiner's Attribution theory (Weiner, 1992), would be good candidates for developing such mapping.

Additionally, knowledge about effects of human emotions on learning would inform gaming design research. More empirical research should be done to link instructional gaming characteristics (design elements of instructional games) with student's cognitive-affective states. Regulating gaming characteristics such as storyline, rules, challenge, or feedback in real-time based on student's emotional state would address individual needs and preferences of an individual student and allow designing more engaging and effective instructional games.

References

Aleven, V., & Koedinger, K. (2002). An effective metacognitive strategy: Learning by doing and explaining with a computer-based cognitive tutor. *Cognitive Science, 26*(2), 147–179.

Ball, G., & Breese, J. (1999). *Modeling the emotional state of computer users.* Paper presented at the UM '99, in workshop on 'Attitude, personality and emotions in user-adapted interaction', Banff, Canada.

Baker, R. S., Corbett, A. T., Koedinger, K. R., Evenson, S. E., Roll, I., Wagner, A. Z., et al. (2006). *Adapting to when students game an intelligent tutoring system.* Paper presented at the Eighth International Conference on Intelligent Tutoring Systems. Jhongli, Taiwan

Baker, R. S., Corbett, A. T., Koedinger, K. R., & Wagner, A. Z. (2004). *Off-task behavior in the cognitive tutor classroom: When students "Game the System".* Paper presented at the Proceedings of ACM CHI 2004: Computer–Human. Interaction Vienna, Austria.

Baker, R. S., D'Mello, S. K., Rodrigo, M. M. T., & Graesser, A. C. (2010). Better to be frustrated than bored: The incidence, persistence, and impact of learners' cognitive-affective states during interactions with three different computer-based learning environments. *International Journal of Human Computer Studies, 68*(4), 223–241.

Bentley, T., Johnston, L., & von Braggo, K. (2005). *Evaluation using cued-recall debrief to elicit information about a user's affective experiences.* Paper presented at the OZCHI, Canberra, Australia.

Blanchard, E., Chalfoun, P., & Frasson, C. (2007). *Towards advanced learner modeling: Discussions on quasi real-time adaptation with physiological data.* Paper presented at the 7th IEEE International Conference on Advanced Learning Technologies (ICALT 2007), Niigata, Japan.

Boehner, K., DePaula, R., Dourish, P., & Sengers, P. (2007). How emotion is made and measured. *International Journal of Human Computer Studies, 65*(4), 275–291.

Cacioppo, J. T., Berntson, G. G., Larsen, J. T., Poehlmann, K. M., & Ito, T. A. (2000). The psychophysiology of emotion. In M. Lewis & J. M. Haviland-Jones (Eds.), *Handbook of Emotions* (pp. 173–191). New York: The Guilford Press.

Canamero, D. (1997). *Modeling motivations and emotions as a basis for intelligent behavior.* Paper presented at the First International Conference on Autonomous Agents. Marina del Rey, CA.

Castellano, G., Villalba, S. D., & Camurri, A. (2007). Recognizing human emotions from body movement and gesture dynamics. In A. Paiva, R. Prada, & R. W. Picard (Eds.), *Affective computing and intelligent interaction* (pp. 71–82). Berlin: Springer.

Chaffar, S., Derbali, L., & Frasson, C. (2009). *Towards emotional regulation in intelligent tutoring systems.* Paper presented at the AACE World Conference on E-learning in Corporate, Government, Healthcare, & Higher Education: E-LEARN 2009, Vancouver, Canada.

Chen, C.-M., & Wang, H.-P. (2011). Using emotion recognition technology to assess the effects of different multimedia materials on learning emotion and performance. *Library and Information Science Research, 33*(3), 244–255.

Coles, G. (1998). *Reading lessons: The debate over literacy.* New York: Hill & Wang.

Conati, C. (2002). Probabilistic assessment of user's emotions in educational games. *Applied Artificial Intelligence, 16*(7), 555–575.

Conati, C., Chabbal, R., & Maclaren, H. (2003). *A study on using biometric sensors for monitoring user emotions in educational games.* Paper presented at the Workshop "Assessing and Adapting to User Attitude and Affects: Why, When and How?" In conjunction with UM'03, 9th International Conference on User Modeling, Pittsburgh, PA.

Conati, C., & Maclaren, H. (2009). Empirically building and evaluating a probabilistic model of user affect. *User Modeling and User-Adapted Interaction, 19*(3), 267–303.

D'Mello, S. K., Craig, S. D., Witherspoon, A., McDaniel, B., & Graesser, A. C. (2008). Automatic detection of learner's affect from conversational cues. *User Modeling and User-Adapted Interaction, 18*(1–2), 45–80.

D'Mello, S., Lehman, B., Sullins, J., Daigle, R., Combs, R., Vogt, K., et al. (2010). A time for emoting: When affect-sensitivity is and isn't effective at promoting deep learning. In J. Kay & V. Aleven (Eds.), *Proceedings of 10th International Conference on Intelligent Tutoring Systems* (Vol. 6094, pp. 245–254). Pittsburgh, PA: Springer Berlin / Heidelberg.

Damasio, A. (1995). *Descartes' error: Emotion, reason and the human brain.* New York: Quill.

de Vicente, A., & Pain, H. (2002). *Informing the detection of the students' motivational state: An empirical study.* Paper presented at the ITS2002, Biarritz, France and San Sebastian, Spain.

de Vicente, A., & Pain, H. (2003). *Validating the detection of a student's motivational state.* Paper presented at the Second International Conference on Multimedia Information & Communication Technologies in Education (m-ICTE2003). Badajoz, Spain

Ekman, P., Levenson, R. V., & Friesen, V. W. (1983). Autonomic nervous system activity distinguishes among emotions. Science 221, 1208–1210.

Erez, A., & Isen, A. M. (2002). The influence of positive affect on the components of expectancy motivation. *The Journal of Applied Psychology, 87*(6), 1055–1067.

Gaillard, A. W., & Kramer, A. F. (2000). Theoretical and methodical issues in psycho physiological research. In R. W. Backs & W. Boucsein (Eds.), *Engineering psychophysiology.* London: Lawrence Erlbaum Associates.

Gee, J. P. (Ed.). (2004). *Situated language and learning: A critique of traditional schooling.* London: Routledge, Taylor & Francis.

Goleman, D. (1995). *Emotional intelligence.* New York: Bantam Books.

Graesser, A. C., Person, N., Harter, D., & Group, T. R. (2001). Teaching tactics and dialogue in AutoTutor. *International Journal of Artificial Intelligence in Education, 12,* 257–279.

Graesser, A. C., Rus, V., D'Mello, S., & Jackson, G. T. (2008). AutoTutor: Learning through natural language dialogue that adapts to the cognitive and affective states of the learner. In D. H. Robinson & G. Schraw (Eds.), *Current perspectives on cognition, learning and instruction: Recent innovations in educational technology that facilitate student learning* (pp. 95–125). Greenwich: Information Age Publishing.

Graesser, A. C., Witherspoon, A., McDaniel, B., D'Mello, S., Chipman, P., & Gholson, B. (2006). *Detection of emotions during learning with AutoTutor.* Paper presented at the 28th Annual Meeting of the Cognitive Science Society. Vancouver, BC, Canada

Healey, J. (2000). *Wearable and automotive systems for affect recognition from physiology.* PhD, MIT, Cambridge, MA.

Hone, K. (2006). Empathic agents to reduce user frustration: The effects of varying agent characteristics. *Interacting with Computers, 18,* 227–245.

Hudlicka, E., & McNeese, M. (2002). Assessment of user affective and belief states for interface adaptation: Application to an Air Force pilot task. *User Modeling and User Adapted Interaction, 12*(1), 1–47.

Isbister, K., Höök, K., Laaksolahti, J., & Sharp, M. (2007). The sensual evaluation instrument: Developing a trans-cultural self-report measure of affect. *International Journal of Human Computer Studies, 65*(4), 315–328.

Issroff, K., & del Soldato, T. (1995). *Incorporating motivation into computer-supported collaborative learning*. Paper presented at the European Conference on Artificial Intelligence in Education, Lisbon.

Kaklauskas, A., Zavadskas, E. K., Pruskus, V., Vlasenko, A., Seniut, M., Kaklauskas, G., et al. (2010). Biometric and intelligent self-assessment of student progress system. *Computers in Education, 55*(2), 821–833.

Karaseitanidis, I., Amditis, A., Patel, H., Sharples, S., Bekiaris, E., Bullinger, A., et al. (2006). Evaluation of virtual reality products and applications from individual, organizational and societal perspectives—The "VIEW" case study. *International Journal of Human Computer Studies, 64*, 251–266.

Keller, J. M. (1984). Use of the ARCS model of motivation in teacher training. In K. E. Shaw (Ed.), *Aspect of educational technology XVII: Staff development and career updating*. New York: Nichols.

Koedinger, K., Anderson, J., Hadley, W., & Mark, M. (1997). Intelligent tutoring goes to school in the big city. *International Journal of Artificial Intelligence in Education, 8*, 30–43.

Kort, B., Reilly, R., & Picard, R. W. (2001). *An affective model of interplay between emotions and learning: Reengineering educational pedagogy-building a learning companion*. Paper presented at the IEEE International Conference on Advanced Learning Technologies, Madison, USA.

LeDoux, J. E. (1996). *The emotional brain*. New York: Simon and Schuster.

Liao, W., Zhang, W., Zhu, Z., Ji, Q., & Gray, W. D. (2006). Toward a decision-theoretic framework for affect recognition and user assistance. *International Journal of Human Computer Studies, 64*(9), 847–873.

Mandryk, R. L., & Atkins, M. S. (2007). A fuzzy physiological approach for continuously modeling emotion during interaction with play environments. *International Journal of Human Computer Studies, 6*(4), 329–347.

Mandryk, R. L., Atkins, M. S., & Inkpen, K. M. (2006). *A continuous and objective evaluation of emotional experience with interactive play environments*. Paper presented at the Conference on Human Factors in Computing Systems (CHI 2006), Montreal, Canada.

Mandryk, R. L., Inkpen, K. M., & Calvert, T. W. (2006). Using psychophysiological techniques to measure user experience with entertainment technologies. *Behaviour and Information Technology (Special Issue on User Experience), 25*(2), 141–158.

Mentis, H. M. (2007). Memory of frustrating experiences. In D. Nahl & D. Bilal (Eds.), *Information and emotion* (pp. 197–210). Medford: Information Today.

Myers, D. G. (2002). *Intuition: Its powers and perils*. New Haven: Yale University Press.

Oaksford, M., Morris, F., Grainger, B., & Williams, J. M. G. (1996). Mood, reasoning, and central executive process. *Journal of Experimental Psychology. Learning, Memory, and Cognition, 22*, 477–493.

Ortony, A., Clore, G. L., & Collins, A. (1988). *The cognitive structure of emotions*. Cambridge: Cambridge University Press.

Pagulayan, R. J., Keeker, K., Wixon, D., Romero, R., & Fuller, T. (2002). User-centered design in games. In J. Jacko & A. Sears (Eds.), *Handbook for human–computer interaction in interactive systems* (pp. 883–906). Mahwah: Lawrence Erlbaum Associates, Inc.

Pekrun, R. (2006). The control-value theory of achievement emotions: Assumptions, corollaries, and implications for educational research and practice. *Educational Psychology Review, 18*, 315–341.

Pekrun, R., & Stephens, E. J. (2011). Academic emotions. In K. R. Harris, S. Graham, & T. Urdan (Eds.), *APA educational psychology handbook* (Vol. 2). Washington: American Psychological Association.

Picard, R. W. (1997). *Affective computing*. Cambridge: MIT Press.

Picard, R. W., Vyzas, E., & Healey, J. (2001). Toward machine emotional intelligence: Analysis of affective physiological state. *IEEE Transactions on Patter Analysis and Machine Intelligence, 23*(10), 1175–1191.

Prendinger, H., Ma, C., & Ishizuka, M. (2007). Eye movements as indices for the utility of life-like interface agents: A pilot study. *Interacting with Computers, 19*(2), 281–292.

Reilly, R., & Kort, B. (2004). *The science behind the art of teaching science: Emotional state and learning.* Paper presented at the Conference on Society for Information Technology and Teacher Education, Atlanta, GA, USA.

Scheirer, J., Fernandez, R., Klein, J., & Picard, R. W. (2002). Frustrating the user on purpose: A step toward building an affective computer. *Interacting with Computers, 14*(2), 93–118.

Scherer, K. (2005). What are emotions? And how can they be measured? *Social Science Information, 44*(4), 695–729.

Spangler, G., Pekrun, R., Kramer, K., & Hofmann, H. (2002). Students' emotions, psychological reactions, and coping in academic exams. *Anxiety, Stress, and Coping, 15*, 413–432.

Tao, J., & Tan, T. (2005). Affective computing: A review. In J. Tao, T. Tan & R. W. Picard (Eds.), *Proceedings of Affective Computing and Intelligent Interaction* (ACCII 2005) (Vol. 3784, pp. 981-995). Beijing, China: Springer-Verlag Berlin Heidelberg.

Vizer, L. M., Zhou, L., & Sears, A. (2009). Automated stress detection using key stroke and linguistic features: An exploratory study. *International Journal of Human Computer Studies, 67*, 870–886.

Wagner, J., Vogt, T., & Andr, E. (2007). *A systematic comparison of different HMM designs for emotion recognition from acted and spontaneous speech.* Paper presented at the Proceedings of the 2nd international conference on Affective Computing and Intelligent Interaction, Lisbon, Portugal.

Weiner, B. (1985). An attributional theory of achievement motivation and emotion. *Psychological Review, 92*, 548–573.

Weiner, B. (1992). *Human motivation: Metaphors, theories and research.* Newbury Park, CA: Sage Publications.

Woolf, B. (2009). *Building intelligent interactive tutors.* Burlington: Morgan Kaufmann Publishers.

Zakharov, K., Mitrovic, A., & Johnston, L. (2008). *Towards emotionally-intelligent pedagogical agents.* Paper presented at the Intelligent Tutoring Systems (ITS), 9th International Conference, Montreal, Canada.

Zeidner, M. (2007). Test anxiety in educational context: What I have learned so far. In P. A. Schultz & R. Pekrun (Eds.), *Emotion in education* (pp. 165–184). San-Diego: Academic.

Chapter 20
Designing for Participation in Educational Video Games

Daniel T. Hickey and Ellen Jameson

20.1 Introduction

Most youth now play video games. And they play them often. Of course, most commercial video games are unrelated to school learning. While many laypeople do not recognize video gameplay as "learning," playing and succeeding in such complex environments certainly requires players to master new knowledge. Arguably, the amount of learning supported by the latest generation of immersive multiplayer video games is unprecedented for designed learning environments. So, it makes sense that educational researchers and game designers continue to search for ways to exploit the educational potential of video games.

This chapter considers some of the tensions that emerge when using video games for educational purposes. It then introduces a framework called *Designing for Participation* (DFP) that addresses these tensions. DFP emerged across iterative cycles of refinement of the *Taiga* educational video game in the *Quest Atlantis* environment. Quest Atlantis is an educational 3D MMOG (massively multiplayer online game) in which students take on professional roles in various content disciplines to work together to solve problems and make progress in the game environment. In Taiga, students become apprentice environmental scientists and collect water quality data to identify the causes of fish decline in an economically significant river. The refinements used design-based research methods and situative approaches to learning assessment to enhance participation, understanding, and achievement while still trying to maintain the appeal of a good video game. This chapter first discusses

D.T. Hickey (✉)
Indiana University, Eigenmann Hall 502, Bloomington, IN 47401, USA
e-mail: dthickey@indiana.edu

E. Jameson
Indiana University, Eigenmann Hall 524, Bloomington, IN 47401, USA
e-mail: ejameson@indiana.edu

D. Ifenthaler et al. (eds.), *Assessment in Game-Based Learning: Foundations,*
Innovations, and Perspectives, DOI 10.1007/978-1-4614-3546-4_20,
© Springer Science+Business Media New York 2012

some of the tensions that emerge when designing, using, and assessing educational video games. It then presents the five design principles that emerged in the Taiga design study that helped address those tensions.

20.2 Competing Approaches to Educational Video Games

20.2.1 Drill and Practice and Expository Approaches

Traditional British empiricist philosophers like Hume and behaviorist theories of learning associated with Skinner influenced the first wave of educational computer games. Early text-based programs like *PLATO* and popular PC games like *Math Blaster* provide "drill and practice" of specific factual and procedural knowledge. These "expository" approaches expose players to numerous specific associations. More recently, a new generation of games like *Dimension M* embed drill and practice in mathematics into complex immersive games.

Drill and practice games are popular in part because they really can raise achievement scores (e.g., the study of Dimension M by Kebritchi, Hirumi, & Bai, 2010). As long as some of the associations that players learn to recognize are relevant to items in a targeted test, scores are likely to increase (Nolen, Haladyna, & Haas, 1992). Humans can easily memorize numerous isolated associations well enough to recognize them when presented (Dudai, 1997). Modern theories of cognition suggest that such knowledge is unlikely to be *recalled* when needed in more typical learning and performance contexts; it is even less likely to be *applied* in real-world situations (Mehrens & Kaminski, 1989).

Critics point out that in most drill and practice games, the relationship between the game activity and the academic content is arbitrary. While this use of extrinsic rewards simplifies game design, any learning regarding the structure, rules, or story of the game itself does not reinforce or enhance the academic content (Rieber, 2005). And extrinsic rewards have been shown in hundreds of studies to diminish subsequent interest and engagement (Lepper & Hodell, 1989). But such games are easy to play, and continued success can motivate extended engagement. When given a choice, most youngsters would rather play them than do conventional schoolwork.

20.2.2 Constructivist and Constructionist Approaches

After the "cognitive revolution" of the 1970s, another wave of educational video games embraced constructivist theories of learning and intrinsically motivated learning. These approaches reflected the continental rationalist philosophy of Descartes and the schema theories of learning associated with Piaget. Seymour Papert's groundbreaking LOGO software took advantage of very early computer graphics to let young children discover programming and geometry in self-directed play. In the PC era, "critical thinking" games like *Freddy Fish* and *the Logical Adventures of the*

Zoombinis emphasized intrinsically rewarding activities that called on fantasy and curiosity while avoiding lower-level content and extrinsically rewarded activity (Lepper & Malone, 1987). Continuing on into the latest generation of problem solving games like *Spore* and *World of Goo*, proponents assume that such games build critical thinking skills and deep conceptual knowledge (Kafai, 2006).

But constructivist and constructionist innovators have traditionally been hard-pressed to show educational impact (Egenfeldt-Nielsen, 2006). The idiosyncratic nature of learning in this class of games makes it difficult to gather evidence to assure educators, parents, and policy makers that the knowledge gained in these games will transfer to more conventional classroom instruction and accountability practices, to high-stakes achievement, or even to other educational video games in the same domain.

20.2.3 Situative and Participatory Approaches

A third wave of innovation in educational games is more consistent with situative theories of cognition (e.g., Greeno, 1998) that focus on learning as successful interaction with social, technological, and informational resources. While these perspectives have been around for decades (e.g., Lave & Wenger, 1991; Pea & Sheingold, 1987), the obviously distributed nature of learning in newer networked multiplayer games has helped many appreciate their relevance.

Gee (2007) points out that much of the learning that occurs in popular multiuser games like *Halo* is due to the social discourse that emerges among players. Gee has extended his well-known distinction between "small-d" discourse concerning individuals and "big-D" Discourse concerning culture to video games. He distinguishes between "small-g" game on the screen and the "big-G" Game where players discuss, modify, blog, etc. This interactive social learning helps explain the astonishing levels of engagement and learning that newer massively multiplayer games can support.

An intriguing possibility of massively multiplayer games is that they can support specific types of social interaction that leads to broader social learning of academic knowledge, as well as the more salient and readily measured individual knowledge. In practice, this often means embedding academic knowledge within rich narrative contexts, allowing players to participate in an authentic situation where knowledge is used (Barab, Zuiker, et al., 2007). In this way, players can confront formal concepts and abstract principles while solving real problems (Shaffer, Squire, Halverson, & Gee, 2005). This allows learners to directly interact with complex social systems that are otherwise inaccessible to them (Squire, 2003).

These newer approaches to educational games allow researchers to bring entirely new perspectives into the game design process. For example, Barab, Zuiker, et al. (2007) conceptualized learning in virtual environments as *situative embodiment*. Dourish (2001) stated that *situative embodiment* "denotes a participative status, the presence and occurrentness of a phenomenon in the world" (p. 18). In video games, situative embodiment involves inhabiting the roles of virtual characters and being immersed in contexts which are designed to be attuned to the goals of virtual characters. Likewise, Gee (2005) characterized learning and identity development in immersive video games with the notion of *projective stance*. This refers to the melding of the virtual characters' identity and the players' real-world identity. Learning in virtual environments occurs when players project their own desires, intentions, goals, and values onto the character and establish a new projective stance. In this way, educational games promise synergy between advances in cognitive science, computer technology, and educational practice.

20.2.4   Reconciling Different Approaches to Game Design

The three very different views of learning described above present designers of educational games a wealth of options. While the differences in practice may not be as clear as presented above, tensions are likely when systematically documenting or improving academic leaning in video games. This is because the design of instruction and assessments necessarily invokes assumptions about the nature of knowledge. These assumptions support specific assumptions about learning that are consistent with some practices for teaching, motivating, and assessing but inconsistent with others. Because practices often take assumptions for granted, the underlying sources of the tensions are often invisible to designers, users, and evaluators. These tensions are amplified when creating games that are specifically designed to foster learning of academic knowledge currently taught using more conventional methods in schools.

The tensions between expository and constructivist approaches are particularly problematic. They are premised on assumptions about individual learning that are ultimately antithetical (Case, 1996). Strictly speaking, the specific associations (i.e., if–then or stimulus–response relationships) fostered in a more procedural game like *Math Blaster* are largely meaningless from the constructionist perspective embodied in *LOGO*. And vice versa: from the more expository perspective that supports drill and practice games, the higher-order logical skills and understanding of geometry that are the focus of LOGO are really just a hierarchy of more specific associations. As elaborated below, these tensions are particularly acute when attempting to assess learning using games or in games. The fluency with specific associations fostered by Math Blaster transfers readily to multiple-choice achievement tests. But those same associations are unlikely to impact learning on more conceptual or logical assessments of mathematical knowledge. Likewise, the kinds of abstract reasoning practiced when playing LOGO (or Freddy Fish or World of Goo) are unlikely to transfer to multiple-choice tests (or any other typical educational assessment). The tension between expository and constructivist approaches is also apparent when using incentives in educational video games. While extrinsic incentives are common in video games and ubiquitous in expository educational games, they are inconsistent with the theory and practice of constructivist games (Lepper & Malone, 1987).

Situative perspectives introduce new tensions when designing video games. This is in part because they focus the designer's attention more on fostering productive social interaction. Consider, for example, pilot testing a design of a multiplayer educational game. Does it matter more if each player can figure out how to succeed in the game or whether interactive practices emerge across players that help them help each other? Because situative perspectives focus primarily on interactive participation, they treat individual behavior and individual cognition as "secondary" forms of this more social learning. This flies in the face of the assumptions behind both expository and constructivist approaches, which generally characterize social interaction through the lens of individual activity (Greeno, Collins, & Resnick, 1996). A particular challenge for researchers is assessing learning in games designed to support social learning because accepted assessment practices focus exclusively on individual learning.

The argument being advanced in this chapter is that pushing *very* hard on situative perspectives leads to a coherent response to these tensions. This is because situative perspectives treat different kinds of individual learning as "special cases" of socially situated interactive participation. This means that the specific associations learned by playing Math Blaster *and* the conceptual schema constructed by playing LOGO are different versions of the same thing. As a caveat, we acknowledge that an unqualified embrace of this perspective is "a bridge too far" for many readers whose assumptions are rooted in more conventional individual models of learning. Our goal here is not convincing learners to accept this theory of learning. Rather, we want to show how design principles that have emerged from efforts that do embrace these assumptions can foster both social and individual learning and a wider range of individual learning outcomes.

What we are suggesting is that efforts to design, refine, and assess educational games focus *primarily* on social learning via interactive participation and only *secondarily* on individual learning outcomes. Put differently, this means that designing and refining features should focus on helping players and teachers informally assess engaged participation in interactive discourse concerning the to-be-learned knowledge. There is not enough space in this chapter to elaborate at length on our definition of interactive participation. We refer readers to the work of other game design scholars who have influenced our thinking (e.g., Barab, Gresalfi, & Ingram-Goble, 2010; Gee, 2007; Squire, 2011). In summary, Greeno's (1998) notion of *engaged participation* offers a particularly comprehensive theorization of the primary focus we are suggesting. We have found Engle and Conant's (2002) notion of *productive disciplinary engagement* to be a practical characterization of the discourse that defines this learning. Such discourse is *productive* in that it becomes more sophisticated as the game progresses, raises new questions among players, and makes connections with other resources. Such discourse is *disciplinary* because it concerns the disciplinary knowledge that the game was designed to foster. Such discourse is *engaged* because it responds to the contributions and actions of other virtual and actual participants and involves shared meaning making across those participants.

By focusing secondarily on individual learning, we mean that the impacts of that game on more abstract conceptual knowledge and on more specific procedural and factual knowledge are both treated as "residue" of that engaged participation. This takes advantage of the unique potential of the very different measures (i.e., performance assessments vs. achievement tests) while sidestepping the tensions associated with focusing primarily on one or the other. While there are many different ways these ideas can be enacted, for us this has meant first focusing on engaged participation when designing and refining educational games, then indirectly assessing the impact using high-quality performance assessments to further guide refinements, and finally measuring long-term improvement and predicting high-stakes impact using externally developed achievement test items.

20.3   Background of the Designing for Participation Framework

DFP is intended for learning environments that are rich with informational, social, and technological resources. While it is likely not useful for learning environments that are entirely focused on drill and practice of procedural skills, it is intended to help designers incorporate such resources into more interactive learning environments.

20.3.1   Origins of DFP

DFP is rooted in collaborations with the developers of inquiry-oriented multimedia environments for science education. These include studies of the *GenScope* genetics program developed by Paul Horwitz of the Concord Consortium (Hickey, Kindfield, Horwitz, & Christie, 2003) and three programs developed by NASA's *Classroom of the Future Program* (Cross, Taasoobshirazi, Hendricks, & Hickey, 2008; Hickey, Taasoobshirazi, & Cross, in review; Taasoobshirazi, Zuiker, Anderson, & Hickey, 2006). These studies and the DFP model that emerged strongly embrace design-based research methods (Cobb, Confrey, diSessa, Lehrer, & Schauble, 2003; Hoadley, 2004; Kali, 2006). Rather than building fundamental theory in controlled studies or testing the application of those theories, these studies built "local" theories within iterative efforts to refine technology-supported learning environments.

  These prior studies involved both curriculum development and assessment development. Indeed, the prior design studies deliberately blurred the distinction between instruction and assessment. As articulated below, situative theories of assessment assume that all learning involves assessment and embrace a very broad view of learning (Greeno & Gresalfi, 2008). In the language of design-based research, these studies started with very general principles about the situated nature of student learning and then derived general assessment design principles by iteratively designing and refining specific features in particular learning environments.

  The curriculum and assessment design principles that emerged from these prior studies were further refined in three other contexts. These included studies of new media high school language arts curriculum developed by Henry Jenkins and colleagues at Project New Media Literacy (Hickey, Honeyford, Clinton, & McWilliams, 2010), university e-learning contexts using the *Sakai* open source course management system (Hickey, McWilliams, Bishop, & Soylu, 2011), and in one of the games in the Quest Atlantis multiuser environment developed by Sasha Barab at Indiana University (Hickey, Ingram-Goble, & Jameson, 2009). The DFP framework as it is presented here consists of the five general design principles that best convey this approach to a broad audience. Each principle is first introduced at this more general level and then followed by more specific principles and features that were or might be used to enact that principle in educational video gaming contexts.

20.3.2 The Five General Principles of DFP

As of this writing, the five general principles that make up the framework are as follows:

1. *Reframe knowledge*: Transform academic skills and concepts into disciplinary tools used in meaningful contexts to frame learning as the appropriate use of tools in contexts.
2. *Scaffold participation*: Embed feedback and motivation to foster discourse about using tools in contexts to help all learners pick up the tools and start using them.
3. *Assess reflections*: Assess students' reflections on their artifacts as evidence of engagement, rather than grading artifacts directly, to maintain learners' agency (i.e., the sense of control) over learning and minimize demands for corrosively specific examples and feedback that can undermine engaged participation.
4. *Remediate accountability*: Downplay individual assessments and obscure external achievement tests to support engaged participation and deliver valid evidence.
5. *Iteratively refine*: Continually refine activities, reflections, and assessments to iteratively improve participation, understanding, and achievement.

Following is an elaboration of each of these general principles and a description of the more specific design principles that emerged when designing and refining features of one educational video game.

20.4 Designing for Participation in the *Taiga* World of Quest Atlantis

From 2005 to 2010, annual cycles of design research were carried out in Taiga, the first of many "worlds" that now make up *Quest Atlantis*. Taiga is a 15–20-h game involving ecological science and socio-scientific inquiry for grades 4–6, in which students investigate the reasons for declining fish populations in a river. The studies were carried out with two elementary school teachers over 5 years. One teacher taught a single class of academically talented fourth graders from 2005 to 2007. The other teacher taught four classes of sixth graders from 2006 to 2010. The specific game design principles and specific features in Taiga will be described below in the context of each of the five general principles.

20.4.1 Reframe Knowledge: Transform Knowledge into Tools Used in Contexts

Summary: The first step in DFP is reframing targeted concepts and skills as *tools*. This reframed learning as practicing using tools appropriately in particular contexts. In Taiga, this meant first defining a compelling narrative game that required using knowledge of ecology and socio-scientific inquiry to play. This then meant fine-tuning that narrative to require student to use more of that knowledge to succeed.

One of the central tensions in educational game design is the manner in which educational content is presented. The obvious manifestation of this tension is the difference between expository and constructivist games described above. The arbitrary relationship between the game and the educational content in many expository drill and practice games means that some of the learning in the game is necessarily unrelated to educational goals. Ultimately, the most crucial educational game design decisions concern *context*. What is the relationship between educational content and the game context? How closely bound should they be? What is an appropriate context for particular content? When it comes to assessing game-based learning, the validity of the evidence is bound up in the relationship of the game context to the assessment context.

Situative theorists emphasize the value of contextualized experiences. Rather than debating whether abstract knowledge actually exists, they point to the pragmatic value of treating abstractions as residue of socially situated experiences (Greeno, 1997). Rather than using problem contexts to build abstract concepts, contextual knowledge is treated as fundamental knowledge (Gee, 2004). This means that the relationship between educational content and the context in which it is presented is never arbitrary. To the contrary, the context in which content is presented ultimately defines that knowledge.

The initial design of Taiga transformed the knowledge of elementary ecological science into practices and resources that could be used to solve important *socio-scientific* problems (Sadler, 2004). Such problems evade simplistic explanations and require balancing of a host of issues in advancing plausible hypotheses and solutions. In Taiga, players serve as apprentices to Ranger Bartle (Fig. 20.1). In this way, Taiga (and most subsequent QA worlds) incorporated the foundational characterization of situative instruction as "cognitive apprenticeship" (Collins, Brown, & Newman, 1989; Lave, 1977).

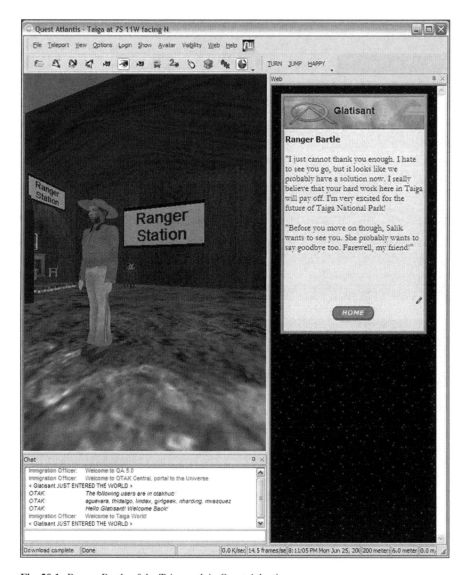

Fig. 20.1 Ranger Bartle of the Taiga park in Quest Atlantis

As elaborated in Barab, Sadler, Heiselt, Hickey, and Zuiker (2007, pp. 61–62), this effort to "narratize" ecological science in Taiga represented the first of three components in an underlying socio-scientific inquiry framework:

- *Narrative* that is "compelling to students and whose solution required using scientific inquiry to use scientific resources in the service of identifying underlying cause(s) of the core problem introduced by the narrative." While such narratives need to connect with prior experiences and values in ways that engage players, they also need to define a trajectory of increasingly productive disciplinary engagement.

• *Inscriptions* that are "objects like graphs, charts, and tables that represent and crystallize knowledge or information and that use a standard convention, thereby requiring specialized understanding to interpret them in meaningful ways."
• *Scientific inquiry* using particular knowledge practices that "can be conceptual or tool-based and can take on many forms, but always involve someone using resources to carry out an activity."

This framework was used to organize activity as players first interview the non-player characters (NPCs) who use the Taiga park for different purposes (i.e., farming, logging, fishing, or hiking) about their competing explanations for the declining fish stock. Thus, scientific processes like erosion and eutrophication and scientific indicators like nitrates and turbidity are all framed as tools that the players must "pick up" and use to participate in the narrative.

The game is organized around five *quests* where players draft and submit reports (Fig. 20.2) for Ranger Bartle. The teacher then "plays" the role of Ranger Bartle in reviewing and accepting the reports. Practically speaking, this means that students are engaged in a great deal of writing. The reports are expected to be 50–100 words long and are structured by detailed prompts. Theoretically speaking, this presented the intriguing potential of having a scripted NPC occasionally played by a teacher. For example, when students are submitting a report to the park ranger character in Taiga, the teacher can role-play as that game character when providing feedback. This, in turn, allows the teacher to engage with the players both as the in-game mentor character and as their classroom teacher.

Taiga was first implemented in 2005 by a fourth grade teacher across 15 periods. At the urging of the US National Science Foundation, substantial effort was invested in developing good assessments and tests from the outset. An open-ended essay on socio-scientific inquiry was used in 2005. As elaborated below, this assessment was strongly "curriculum-oriented" because it was very closely aligned to this particular curriculum. An achievement test was created by identifying two or three released achievement test items aligned to each of ten relevant state science standards; this test was "standards-oriented" in that it was aligned to the standards without regards to the content of the curriculum.

The students in 2005 made tremendous gains in their socio-scientific essays. This made sense because the students really had no experience with these ideas or this kind of scientific inquiry before Taiga. But the scores on the achievement test only went up a little, and the gain was not statistically significant (Fig. 20.3). More importantly, interpretive analyses of the quest submissions showed that many students had failed to even mention the targeted scientific practice or resources in their reports (Barab, Sadler, et al., 2007).

The Taiga design team then added many more opportunities for students to use the conceptual tools in their interactions with the various NPCs. In a process deemed "scientizing the narrative" (Barab, Zuiker, et al., 2007, p. 5), the design team

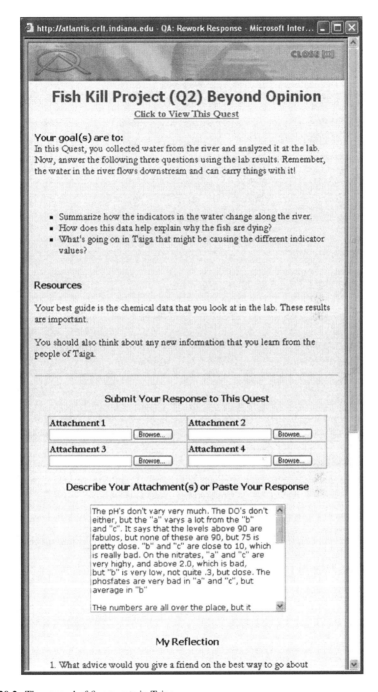

Fig. 20.2   The second of five quests in Taiga

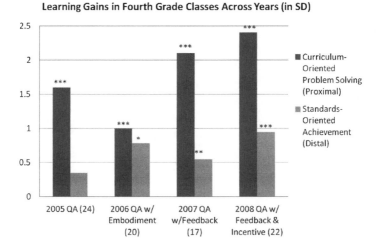

Learning Gains in Fourth Grade Classes Across Years (in SD)

Fig. 20.3 Learning gains in fourth grade class (*p<0.05, **p < 0.01, ***p<0.001)

framed increasingly formal relationships between the targeted scientific formalisms (i.e., tools) and their context of use in Taiga. Their continued refinement of the narrative and the assessments distinguished between formalisms that are *embodied* by, *embedded* in, or *abstracted* from the social and material context of the game:

- A formalism is *embodied* "when it is experienced as part of a concrete situation; that is, the meaning of an embodied formalism is bound up in and dependent on its particular context of use." Rather than introducing scientific formalisms like eutrophication and turbidity as abstractions, students first encounter them as embodied formalisms in their experience of a meaningful narrative social context.
- Formalisms are *embedded* "when a student is engaged in a situation and draws on a formal account that has meaning and is described irrespective of the particular situating context of use." Thus, resources were embedded in the game that students could encounter or access that included more formal and decontextualized representations of the scientific formalisms. Importantly though, these representations were encountered within the broader context of use defined by the narrative.
- A formalism is *abstracted* when it "involves applying and understanding of the formalism originally developed in relation to a particular context to other contexts of use." While some efforts were undertaken to include side narratives in which targeted formalisms were encountered in new contexts, most of the abstracted formalisms in this effort were represented by the assessments and achievement tests described below.

In summary, the entire curriculum was revised to ensure that the activities and dialogues with the virtual characters first illuminated the targeted formalisms; resources were embedded that then allowed students to encounter and use the formalisms more appropriately.

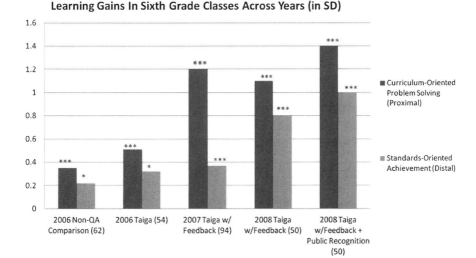

Fig. 20.4 Learning gains in four sixth grade classes ($*p < 0.05$, $***p < 0.001$)

The revised Taiga was implemented in 2006 by the same fourth grade teacher with a new class. The curriculum-oriented assessment was revised to include some knowledge that students might have previously encountered, and the achievement test was revised to include more items for just four of the most relevant state science standards. The revisions were effective in that many more of the students enlisted many more of the domain formalisms in their quest submissions and did so more meaningfully. Specifically, many more of the collected submissions made reference to specific scientific indicators (e.g., turbidity) and processes (e.g., erosion and eutrophication). The gains in understanding on the new curriculum-oriented assessment were smaller but were still statistically significant; the gain in achievement on the standards-oriented test doubled from the previous year and was statistically significant. This provided the first evidence that we knew of for statistically significant gains in "external" achievement with an immersive educational video.

Later in 2006, a sixth grade teacher implemented Taiga for his first time in two of his four sixth grade science classes. As part of a dissertation, Arici (2008) developed a text-based comparison curriculum that covered the same topics for the teacher to use in the other two classes. A comprehensive curriculum-oriented performance assessment of conceptual understanding depicting a complete watershed was developed, but the same standards-oriented test of science achievement was used. As shown in Fig. 20.4, the gains in understanding and achievement were statistically significant for both pairs of classes, but both gains were larger in the Taiga classes (Hickey et al., 2009). Additional analysis of the dissertation data showed many other very positive outcomes in the QA group and showed that the knowledge the students did gain lasted much longer (Barab et al., 2010). However, as we describe next, there was still much room for improvement.

20.4.2   Scaffold Participation: Embed Features to Foster Discourse About Tools in Contexts

Summary: When learning is treated as a product of students' practicing using tools appropriately in particular contexts, learning can be improved by prompting and motivating learners to use those tools (a) initially, (b) more often, and (c) more appropriately. Educational video games can achieve this by providing feedback and incentives that encourage using the feedback to succeed. In Taiga, one way this was done was by improving the feedback that players got when preparing and submitting their reports. This was also done by including incentives to help motivate players to use the feedback and other resources to support their participation.

The nature and amount of player support are crucial design decisions in educational video games (Dondlinger, 2007). Too little support leaves players lost and frustrated; too much support means that players may not end up using and learning targeted knowledge. Other tensions emerge around the support of individual activity vs. more social activity, and vice versa. In short, the way gameplay is supported directly impacts what is learned.

The designers of Quest Atlantis made numerous decisions and refinements concerning student support in every development cycle. This second design principle emerged from a more focused series of refinements around the process of drafting, submitting, and revising the five written quests that organized much of the gameplay. The second quest was a particularly important one because it invited students to synthesize what they had learned about water quality indicators and water quality processes in the previous quests. Analysis of the quests submitted in the sixth-grade classrooms in 2006 confirmed that the teacher had been overwhelmed implementing Taiga his first time with over 50 students in his two classes. The research team consequently helped the teacher review the submissions and provide feedback to players. In an effort to keep the game moving, many incomplete submissions had been accepted, and the feedback on the rejected submissions mostly asked players to write more. Analysis of the content of initial and final reports by the players who were asked to resubmit revealed that the quality of the resubmitted reports did not improve. While the student engagement in the questing processes was very compelling compared to typical writing assignments, the discourse that framed that activity was not very productive, disciplinary, or engaged.

The second author (an ecology graduate student at the time) was invited to join the team in 2007 and improve the performance assessment, quests, and activities leading up to the quests. She created the *Lee River* performance assessment described below and helped create two new information resources to help foster more productive disciplinary engagement around the questing process. Theoretically speaking, both of these resources were intended to help players enlist the targeted formalisms more appropriately in the context of quest submissions. In other words, the earlier round of refinements had succeeded in ensuring that all students initially picked up the targeted formalisms in their interactions with the players and the embedded resources. The quests presented a more formal and more specific context for players to practice using those formalisms appropriately *in this specific context.*

The first new resource was a detailed scoring rubric for the crucial second quest that required the most synthesis of knowledge. Specifically, players had to enlist knowledge of both water quality indicators and water quality processes to advance a hypothesis for the declining fish population. To be coherent, a quest submission needed to use various indicators appropriately relative to the processes and relative to the goal of the quest. In this way, the quest provided a more structured context in which students could practice using this new knowledge appropriately, get feedback on their success in doing so, and then try again. The rubric provided carefully worded examples and feedback that aimed to make this structured discourse more productive and more disciplinary. Examples and descriptions of *incomplete, partial, nearly complete,* and *complete* submissions were included, along with feedback text that could be cut and pasted into the feedback window and then customized as desired for each student. Contingent on each class' progress, the teachers were encouraged to only accept submissions that were complete or nearly complete while asking players to revise and resubmit incomplete or partial reports.

The second new resource consisted of screens of information that were embedded for players to use when revising their reports. Players were told to visit the lab technician (an NPC who had previously helped test water quality samples) when they were ready to revise their submissions. The technician invited them to view up to 30 screens of dense information about what they were working on (Fig. 20.5). One specific design principle that emerged was that lots of new and detailed information could be embedded when these resources were anchored to a problem context that players were quite familiar with. In the language of our nascent situative approach to assessment, we used the notions of embodied and embedded formalisms to make this feedback useful and used in the questing discourse. These experiences were expected to leave the students more prepared to make sense of those formalisms when encountered in their abstract form or when embedded in other contexts.

It seems helpful to consider these new resources in light of the existing research literature on scaffolding and feedback that provided more general inspiration for these refinements (e.g., Quintana et al., 2004; Shute, Hansen, & Almond, 2008). Practically speaking, these resources referenced formalisms that players first encountered in embodied experiences. The existing literature on scaffolding and feedback generally focuses more on helping individuals make sense of abstracted representations of scientific phenomenon. Our concern with many prevailing approaches to scaffolding and feedback is that they generally start with abstracted representations. While these approaches certainly can and do foster productive disciplinary engagement, our concern is that they do so around disembodied

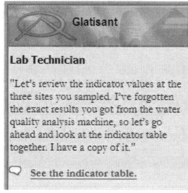

Glatisant

Lab Technician

"Let's review the indicator values at the three sites you sampled. I've forgotten the exact results you got from the water quality analysis machine, so let's go ahead and look at the indicator table together. I have a copy of it."

See the indicator table.

Chemical indicator	Results (A)	Results (B)	Results (C)	Sources and description
pH	6.6	7.0	7.3	A pH of 6.5 to 7.5 is usually very good. Less than 5.5 and greater than 8.5 is usually bad for aquatic life. (Read More)
DO	5.5 ppm	4.5 ppm	4.0 ppm	Dissolved oxygen levels between 5 and 6 parts per million (ppm) are usually needed for are large fish to thrive. Levels below 3 ppm are very stressful to aquatic life.(Read More)
turbidity	6 NTU	2 NTU	22 NTU	Turbidity values of 5 NTU (turbidity units) or less are excellent for many freshwater fish. Values greater than 25 NTU are bad for most fish. (Read More)
nitrates	3.15 ppm	0.96 ppm	2.08 ppm	Nitrate values less than 0.3 ppm are excellent and nitrate values greater than 2.0 ppm are poor. (Read More)
phosphates	3.6 ppm	1.70 ppm	3.08 ppm	Phosphate values less than 0.1 ppm are excellent and phosphate values greater than 3.0 ppm are poor.(Read More)
temperature	17.5 C	22.5 C	22.0 C	If the temperature in a waterway from one location to another changes more than 5 C, aquatic life can become very stressed. (Read More)

Lab Technician

"Please help me to review how the indicators change along Taiga River. Let me know if I am wrong. So in site C near the K-fly Fishing Company, DO, nitrate, turbidity, phosphates are in the unhealthy range for fish. Near the Mulu village,

Fig. 20.5 Lab technician and technical dialogue in formative feedback routine

formalisms rather than the context of use. This matters if you consider context of use to be a fundamental part of domain knowledge:

> The relations between any formalism being learned and a particular context-of-use changes the ontological status of the formalism itself; that is when the focus on learning is first on the context-of-use, rather than on the disembodied formalism, *the very meaning of the formalism changes.* (Barab, Zuiker, et al., 2007, p. 6, emphasis added)

This is why we suggest that formalisms first need to be "picked up initially" before students are expected to use them appropriately. That these resources situated the information they presented in *a* context of use was not particularly important. What seems important and potentially novel is that these resources presented information that referenced a *specific* context of use where the students had previously encountered that information as embodied formalisms.

In 2007, both teachers implemented this revision of Taiga. The submitted reports showed that these refinements led students to use many more of the domain tools appropriately, with the resubmitted reports containing evidence of this much more than the initial reports that students had been asked to revise. As reported in Hickey et al. (2009) and shown in Figs. 20.3 and 20.4, we also observed dramatically larger gains in understanding and larger gains in achievement over 2006. However, feedback usage ranged from players who accessed all 30 screens to players who did not access any of them. Encouragingly, the students who used more feedback made much larger learning gains; discouragingly, just 20% of the students who revised their submissions accessed all of the pages, while 20% of the students did not access any.

These findings led us to wonder about motivation to use feedback. In particular, we wondered about the impact of incentives. Like most commercial video games (but only some educational games), Quest Atlantis offered students various incentives to motivate and reward players. In Taiga starting in 2007, accepted quests were rewarded with backpacks for one's avatar that unlocked special powers and special hats that signified expertise.

After four decades of research, extrinsic incentives in education remain controversial. The behavioral theories of motivation that support expository games (e.g., Cameron & Pierce, 1994) argue that incentives are usually acceptable practice. This is because they motivate players to develop the level of fluency needed for the experience itself to become rewarding. Conversely, modern cognitive theories associated with constructivist approaches (e.g., Kohn, 1996) warn that incentives undermine meaningful inquiry and long-term interest. Situative theories of motivation suggest that we should first look at the impact of incentives on participation in discourse (Hickey, 2003). Furthermore, the arguments about the disempowering potential of incentives in games (Ryan, Rigby, & Przybylski, 2006) overlook the crucial point that most of the incentives in current games (including Quest Atlantis) are associated with the granting of addition power.

In 2008, we removed the incentives in Taiga from two of the classes and emphasized intrinsic reasons for succeeding (like helping the park and helping Ranger Bartle do his job). In the other two classes, we made the incentives more salient and added some additional ones. In addition to the backpacks and hats, accepted quests also resulted in a badge that students could place on their avatar, which corresponded to the quality of the submission as judged by the teacher/ranger (*knowledgeable, expert,* or *wise*; Fig. 20.6). In an effort to further foster the motivational context of commercial games, we also placed a physical "leader board" on the wall in those two classrooms. Students would move a paper version of their avatar across and up the board to display their progress and level.

Observing the conversations and the in-game chat in the incentive conditions confirmed that the different levels of expertise were salient to the students and that they wanted to attain the higher levels. We examined the content of quest submissions to explore whether the incentives impacted the way students took up the domain tools. Simply counting the number of relevant formalisms students included in their focal quest revealed that students in the incentive system referenced more of them. But a systematic scoring of those uses showed that students in the incentive condition also used them more appropriately in the content of the report (Hickey & Filsecker, 2010). For example, many players listed the water quality indicator *turbidity* as a reason for blaming the loggers; that indicator was only used appropriately when referenced in the context of eutrophication.

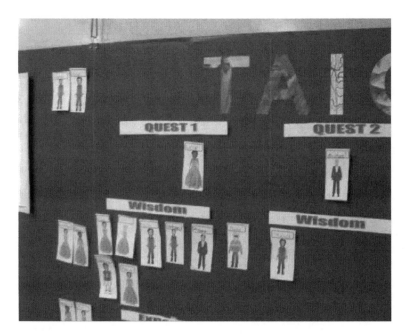

Fig. 20.6 Leader board for avatars

That the incentives led players to enlist formalisms more appropriately suggested that they were *not* taking shortcuts in their submissions to get the incentives. While we were unable to systematically compare feedback use in the two groups, the students in the incentive classes made significantly larger gains in understanding and somewhat larger gains in achievement (see Fig. 20.4). Additionally, they reported slightly higher levels of motivation while completing their reports and slightly larger gains in interest in solving these kinds of problems. Thus, we found no negative consequences of incentives and some positive consequences.

In 2008, we also realized that our enhanced focus on feedback around the quests was overwhelming for the teacher. Because there were five quests, his 100 students submitted 500 initial quests. And because many students resubmitted multiple times (average 3.1), he encountered 1,200 quest submissions during the 3 weeks! In addition, the students were asking for more detailed feedback than he was able to provide efficiently (e.g., "Is THIS what you want!!!!?"). Our response to this in 2009 and 2010 is described below, as the third DFP design principle.

In 2009, we also revised the embedded feedback routines to make them easier to use. The previous feedback screens were a little hard to navigate, and players had to commit to a whole series of them. We changed it, so when students went to the technician for help, he presented them with a list of about 20 questions (essentially FAQs; Fig. 20.7). We also further grounded this feedback in the narrative problem context. While this certainly made the feedback more accessible, gains in understanding in the sixth grade classroom were unchanged. (Gains in achievement dropped substantially in 2009, but issues that emerged concerning

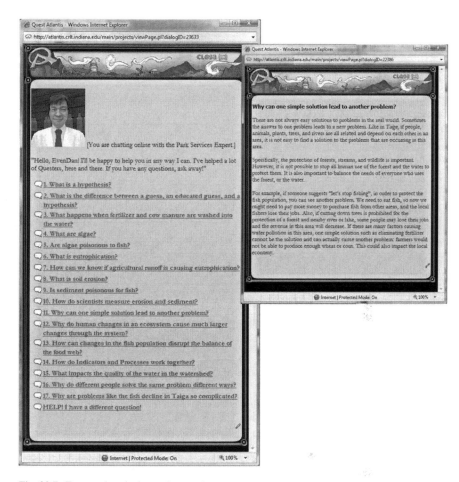

Fig. 20.7 Frequently asked questions and an answer

the test administration and reliability in two of the classes clouded our interpretation of that evidence.)

20.4.3 Assess Reflection: Do Not Grade Student Artifacts Directly

Summary: Detailed scoring and feedback rubrics for student artifacts transfer agency (a sense of control over learning) from the learner to the rubric and the person who interprets the rubric to assign a score. Instead, we recommend that students reflect on their artifacts as evidence of engagement and that these reflections be assessed first. In Taiga, this meant having students include a reflection with their quest submissions in which they reflected on how their reports showed that they had been engaged in the targeted knowledge practices. Their quests were then reviewed primarily according to the reflections; when the content was considered, it was considered in the context of the reflections.

Most educational video games yield some sort of "artifacts" for players. Artifacts are things that have been made meaningful (Lave & Wenger, 1991). The artifacts that students create in project-based learning are more meaningful than worksheets because the personalization possible in a project means that the artifact takes on additional meaning. In some games, these artifacts are virtual items that players have collected or won. In Quest Atlantis, these artifacts include written communications, commentaries, etc. Because of their role in rewarding, acknowledging, and supporting learning, the design and function of artifacts is an important consideration and a potential source of tension in designing educational games.

In Taiga, much of the game is organized around the aforementioned written quests. Taiga's designers worked hard to foster personally meaningful quest submissions, but they had to strike a balance. *Players* needed to feel that the reports they were submitting were unique and their own, but *students* also needed to practice using the domain tools that their teacher was accountable for. The rubric for each quest and the reviewing process had to meet both of these goals without overwhelming the teacher with reviews or exhausting the students with revisions.

Some of the insights for addressing this problem came from prior assessment research. Popham's (1997) prescription against "dysfunctionally detailed" rubrics suggested some refinements to the existing quest guidelines and rubrics to direct attention more towards the domain knowledge. However, this did not help us in enhancing the interaction between players, teacher, and rangers. We needed to find a new way of thinking about "participatory portfolio assessment."

Broad inspiration came from Jenkins' (2009, p. 7) characterization of *participatory culture*: "Not every member must contribute, but all must believe that they are free to contribute when ready and that what they contribute will be appropriately valued." This suggested that we should search for ways of providing feedback on the submissions that would encourage participation without specifically and directly requiring it.

The notion of participatory culture shed new light on the role of *reflection* in portfolio assessment (e.g., Danielson & Abrutyn, 1997). We realized that having students reflect on their artifacts could shift the emphasis away from the actual reports to a broader focus on the meaning of the artifacts relative to the players' engagement. It turned out that QA already included a reflection box at the bottom of the quest submission window. But, the feature had never been used much, and our teachers and students generally ignored it after the first quest.

In 2009, we began experimenting with reflection questions that built upon the subnarrative that Ranger Bartle was a busy mentor. The reflections were framed as requests from Bartle to help him determine whether each report showed evidence that they were fulfilling their responsibility as an apprentice. The reflection questions for the second quest were as follows:

> Remember, you are here as an apprentice. Help me make sure you are becoming a skilled ranger. Explain what it is about your quest that shows you understand the following things about hypotheses:
>
> 1. The things that a hypothesis must include to be scientific.
> 2. That a testable hypothesis must have enough detail for someone else to test it if they want.
> 3. That experts always look for and include other alternative explanations for their hypothesis.
> 4. That experts always consider what they might have overlooked.

We asked the teacher to review the reflections primarily and were pleased with the way that doing so seemed to streamline the reviewing process. Sometimes, when students went to draft the reflection, they would realize that there were things missing from the submission, which they would then go back and complete. We realized that completing the reflections for one quest submission could shape the way that students approached the next submission. The next time, it was expected that students would *start* their submission by considering the reflection while drafting and revising the report; this, in turn, had the potential to shape engagement in the activities leading up to each report. Reviewing the submissions from the second quest in 2009 showed that most (but not all) students took the reflections seriously, and we concluded that reflections were a promising strategy for increasing disciplinary engagement while streamlining the review process.

These ideas did not really come together until the final 2010 study, and several factors precluded systematic study of the reflections. However, we were able to formally implement the reflections on all five quests and asked the teacher to only review the reflections. While gains in understanding and achievement were about the same, we ended up with a more sustainable teacher workload. Compared to 2008, the number of resubmissions declined (from an average of 3.1 to 1.9 per student).

We are still analyzing the massive pool of evidence from these studies to examine the consequences of the incentives and the reflections. We were pleased to see examples of students revising their reports when completing the reflections and reviewing the reflections before beginning their reports. We were also pleased with the way that the teacher was able to refine the practice and use the combination of the reflection and the artifact to help decide where to invest the most time in providing feedback. The nascent design principle here is that the reflections help mentors and teachers (a) more quickly ascertain the level proficiency represented by the artifact while (b) fostering more proficiency when the artifacts are being created and (c) fostering more productive disciplinary engagement around the entire process.

This design principle has been a central focus in subsequent studies in other learning environments. Our studies of e-learning in university contexts show numerous examples of students revising artifacts (Hickey et al., 2011). Further insights have come from Habib and Wittek's (2007) application of *actor–network theory* and sociocultural notions of *internalization, mastery,* and *appropriation* to portfolio assessment. We have drawn specific inspiration from the notion of *consequential and critical engagement* in Gresalfi, Barab, and Siyahhan (2009). Specifically, we are growing confident that conceptual engagement (the usual focus of classroom assessment) can "come along for free" when participants reflect *consequentially* (the consequences of a targeted concept in a particular context) and *critically* (the consequences of the particular context for learning about the particular concept).

20.4.4 Remediate Accountability: Put Assessments and Tests in Their Place

Summary: By treating conventional performance assessments and achievement tests as very specific (and somewhat peculiar) knowledge practices, these resources can serve more broadly useful formative and summative functions. In Taiga, this meant using two educational assessments to fulfill two very different but complementary functions. A curriculum-oriented performance assessment was used to inform refinement of the learning environment (but not to provide individual feedback). An isolated standards-oriented achievement test was used to evaluate improved learning over time and predict impact on high-stakes tests, but not to refine the curriculum.

This design principle responds to one of the central tensions facing educational game designers and a topic of many of the other chapters in this volume. This research is part of a broader exploration of the ways that situative theories of assessment (e.g., Gee, 2004; Greeno & Gresalfi, 2008; Habib & Wittek, 2007; Hickey & Anderson, 2007) can help innovations such as immersive video games enhance and document impact on conventional educational assessments and tests, but without compromising the innovations.

A situative perspective on learning leads to a much broader view of learning assessment. From our perspective, both learning and assessment are taking place when:

- Players assess the impact of their actions on their progress in a game.
- Students assess whether or not they are enacting a curricular routine appropriately.
- Designers assess whether specific game features are being enacted as intended.
- Researchers assess the impact of a game on understanding and achievement of targeted knowledge.
- Policy makers assess whether educational games can help meet existing academic goals.

In our view, all learning involves assessment, which means that the clear distinction between "instruction" and "assessment" disappears (Greeno & Gresalfi, 2008). This view also does away with the sharp distinction between formative and summative assessments. Rather, particular assessment practices are understood in terms of their potential formative and summative functions, along a continuum ranging from informal to formal (Hickey & Pellegrino, 2005). This makes it possible for the same assessment practice to serve both formative and summative functions.

Of course, assessment and testing raise complex issues about the *validity* of the inferences that can be drawn from scores. A situative perspective on assessment argues that one must specify a theory of knowing *and* a theory learning when discussing validity. Achievement tests can provide valid evidence of how much individuals know about broad domains of knowledge that accrue over very long time scales; this means that achievement tests are hard-pressed to provide valid evidence of how much individuals learn from specific learning activities. Conversely, open-ended performance assessments can provide valid evidence of learning from specific experiences, but they are not as useful for comparing how much individuals know about domains (because they are so sensitive to the various contexts in which that knowledge might have been learned).

A situative perspective on assessment raises complex theoretical issues that are beyond the scope of this chapter and are elaborated elsewhere (Hickey & Anderson, 2007). The most important point for this chapter is that situative perspectives suggest careful *alignment* of less formal assessments with more formal assessments. Doing so allows the summative function of the more formal assessment to "protect" the formative function of the less formal assessment. Our open-ended performance assessment let us resist having teachers formally assess whether every student was using every formalism in every quest appropriately. This is a natural tendency and quite consistent with prevailing models of formative assessment. But doing so is terribly problematic. In many cases (including ours), reviewing student artifacts is unsustainable. Reviewing quests at that level also undermines productive disciplinary engagement by turning the "reports" into "assignments" and turning the "game" into "school."

Rather than having teachers formally review the reports, a formal performance assessment was developed and used to evaluate the impact of the overall game on each student's understanding of each of the targeted scientific formalisms. In assessment terms, our performance assessment needed to be "curriculum-oriented" and a "test worth teaching to" (Yeh, 2001). The "Lee River" paper-and-pencil performance assessment that emerged in this work used a somewhat different watershed than Taiga and presented somewhat different problems. In conventional assessment language, each of the items was "somewhat dissimilar" (Mehrens, Popham, & Ryan, 1998, p. 20) from Taiga. This meant that players had to transfer knowledge of underlying formalisms, rather than their knowledge of surface problem features. The Lee River assessment was also sufficiently structured so that the research team could efficiently judge whether or not each student was using the targeted formalisms appropriately in this new context.

Administering a curriculum-oriented assessment before and after Taiga showed how much particular students were learning about the scientific concepts in Taiga and how much students overall were learning about particular concepts. It also showed that some students understood some of the concepts *before* playing. These insights were used to refine the Taiga activities and quests. The increasingly larger gains in understanding showed that these efforts were successful. But, we did not have the teacher who used the Lee River assessment to provide feedback directly to learners. While doing so might have supported more *student* learning, it would have undermined *project* learning about the effectiveness of the curriculum. This is because providing individual feedback would focus the teacher's attention too directly on the abstracted formalisms in the assessment items and would likely prepare students too directly for the posttest throughout the activity.

In other words, asking the teacher to provide formative feedback on the abstracted formalisms represented in the performance assessments might have shifted attention away from the embodied and embedded formalisms in the game and towards the disembodied abstract representations on the performance assessment. While this likely would have increased scores on the performance assessment, it would have made problems in the curriculum more similar to the problems in the performance assessment. At minimum, we would have been unable to differentiate between increased gains over time that resulted from enhancements to the game from increased gains that were the result of the two sets of problems becoming more similar. Over time, this likely would have made the enactment of the game more like conventional schooling; we suspect that it would have also diminished the impact of the game on the more distal achievement test.

But even with our efforts to preserve the validity of the curriculum-oriented performance assessment, the iterative alignment of Taiga to the assessment still introduced an unknown (and essentially unknowable) degree of "construct-irrelevant easiness" (Messick, 1994). This points to a core tension in game-based assessment. These refinements meant that some part of the improvement from one cycle to the next was the result of Taiga better familiarizing players with the problems that would appear on the Lee River. This meant that the Lee River could not yield valid evidence in comparisons with other curriculum or predict impact on external achievement tests. An additional instrument was needed.

A "standards-oriented" achievement test was created by randomly sampling items from pools of items that were aligned to targeted standards, independent of Taiga. Because such items can be answered quickly, it was possible to include a lot of items. As long as an individual has not been directly exposed to the specific associations on the test items, it is possible to efficiently and reliably compare how much individuals know about a domain of knowledge. To reiterate, this same test is a problematic indicator of how much an individual learned from some curriculum. Such tests should not be used to directly shape the way a curriculum is designed or enacted. As argued above, the human mind is remarkably efficient at learning information well enough to use it to recognize specific associations. It is all too easy when designing and/or teaching a curriculum to reference the specific associations that are needed for specific test items.

To reiterate, this design principle suggests that achievement tests only be used for comparing different curricula that target the same standards, estimating impact on mandated standardized achievement tests, and comparing learning in a particular innovation from one refinement to the next. The Taiga tests were developed independent of the curriculum, and the teachers and the curriculum design effort had no idea what items would appear on the test. Thus, the achievement test provided valid evidence that the Taiga students in 2006 learned more than students in classes taught by the same teacher using a conventional text-based curriculum that targeted the same concepts. It also provided valid evidence of the improved alignment of Taiga with the curriculum-oriented assessment across years.

20.4.5 Iteratively Refine: Align Participation, Understanding, and Achievement

Summary: This is the most important principle of all. What makes DFP work is the way that the activities at one "level" are motivated and evaluated by the outcomes at the next. We recommend starting at the closer levels and working out to the more distal levels over time. In Taiga, this meant focusing directly on participation in the game, less directly on understanding, and very indirectly on achievement. In educational game design, this means fostering participation before assessing understanding and fostering understanding before measuring achievement.

As described above, DFP assumes both the method and philosophy of design-based research methods. In key respects, this broader program of research is a synergy between the suggestions of leading design researchers (especially Cobb et al., 2003; Kali, 2006) and emerging situative perspectives on educational assessment. Thus, the primary results from this research are the design principles presented here, along with the additional contextual information that others might need to further refine and use those principles in other contexts to accomplish similar goals.

As introduced in the previous section, the DFP framework is organized around multiple assessment "levels." Learning across levels is increasingly formal and encompasses increasingly broad knowledge. Learning across levels is decreasingly contextualized and occurs over longer and longer timescales (Lemke, 2000). In Taiga, these levels were defined as follows:

- *Immediate-level game activities*: Players informally assess activity with feedback from NPCs, other players, and teacher; designers assess whether players are using tools initially.
- *Close-level questing activity*: Players and teacher/ranger semiformally assess whether students are using domain tools appropriately.
- *Proximal-level performance assessment*: Designers formally assess whether particular players are using particular tools correctly.
- *Distal-level achievement test*: Evaluators measure impact on overall knowledge of the domain.

Rather than presenting different or more difficult problems across levels, students interact with increasingly formal representations of the same domain of knowledge across the levels. The ultimate power of this alignment comes from its potential for coordinating the activities of all of the participants. This includes the students (because activity at one level can be motivated by the desire to succeed at the next level), the designers (by providing a target for activities at each level), the teachers (by providing a goal to shape the enactment of each level), and researchers (by providing project goals and summative evidence of success).

Because the knowledge is transformed from one assessment level to the next, evidence of transfer is obtained. And when increased gains are observed from one cycle to the next, evidence of increased transfer is obtained. By doing so over three or more levels and extending out to the level of the distal achievement test, valid evidence of achievement impact is obtained. However, this evidence is obtained without resorting to directly exposing students to specific associations that might appear on the targeted test.

This alignment of more fleeting and contextualized learning at one level to the more stable and less-contextualized learning at the next level increases the validity of evidence at all levels. This is because the alignment stabilizes the degree of construct-irrelevant variance across two levels while protecting evidential validity of the third level. Practically speaking, this makes the evidence from the proximal-level performance assessment trustworthy for refining the curricular activities and informal assessments; this also makes the evidence from distal-level tests trustworthy for evaluating the impact of those improvements and estimating high-stakes impact.

Thanks to generous support of our project sponsors, we had enough resources to develop and implement the proximal performance assessments and the distal achievement tests from the very start. However, it was a lot of work, and the lack of initial achievement gains was somewhat discouraging. For many educational game designers, we suspect that three cycles of refinement, each aligning just two levels, would be most efficient:

1. *Implementation (immediate and close)*: Work with a few players to refine the features of informal game activities to ensure players pick up domain tools and begin using them; make sure players can then use the tools in a semiformal task or activity in the game.
2. *Experimentation (close and proximal)*: Work with groups of players and experiment with different features (i.e., prompts and feedback) of the semiformal tasks to get more players to use more domain tools more appropriately in that context; make sure players can also do so in a more formal performance assessment outside of the game.
3. *Evaluation (proximal and distal)*: Work with multiple groups of players and formally document the impact of the designed game (and the enacted game) on a formal performance assessment and external achievement tests; compare gains with other students using other curriculum that targets the same content or standards.

A more detailed elaboration of these cycles is outlined in Hickey, Zuiker, Taasoobshirazi, Schafer, and Michael (2006). Forthcoming papers will show how these cycles are being enacted in other innovative educational contexts.

20.5 Summary and Next Steps

This chapter and the design framework it introduces are intended to help address tensions that emerge when designing and using video games to serve educational goals. It argued that these tensions are rooted in fundamentally different theories of knowing and (therefore) learning. To some, we may have overstated these tensions. This may be true, but we agree with Case (1996) and Greeno et al. (1996) that many of the enduring conflicts over instruction, assessment, and reform can be traced back to competing assumptions about knowing learning. We also agree with Olson and Bruner (1996) that many of the stakeholders in the educational process take their assumptions about knowing and learning for granted. This means that when these tensions do emerge, they can be attributed to other factors such as naiveté, faddism, and politics. This is not helpful and can be quite corrosive.

We believe that video games offer tremendous untapped potential for improving formal school and helping youth learn academic knowledge outside of schools. But, we also recognize the tremendous pressure to raise scores on externally developed achievement tests. This pressure is present in many different contexts and at many different levels. This presents the most salient of the many tensions in designing, using, and assessing educational video games. Our evidence with Taiga shows that the design principles presented here will be helpful for addressing this tension. We also believe the examples here showed how other common tensions could be addressed as well.

These same design principles are continuing to be refined in the context of collaborative design studies of university e-learning courses (e.g., Hickey et al., 2011) and high-school language arts curriculum (McWilliams, Hickey, Hines, Conner, & Bishop, 2011). A new collaboration with a commercial educational game designer is getting underway, and additional collaborations are being explored. We are finding that the structure offered by these principles has been helpful for organizing these collaborations and prioritizing efforts going forward. We hope that others will find these principles helpful in a range of innovative contexts and will further refine these ideas and share them with others.

Additional multimedia resources and examples are currently available as "worked examples" at http://www.workedexamples.org and as "working examples" at http://www.workingexamples.org. Additional examples and evidence will be posted as they emerge, along with specific design principles associated with specific learning environments.

Acknowledgments Sasha Barab directed Quest Atlantis project and was the lead developer of the Taiga world and curriculum. Special thanks to James Gee for his support of this research since 2007 via the MacArthur Foundation's *21st Century Assessment Project.* Thanks to Beth Piekarsky and Jacob Summers for helping us implement and refine Taiga and for the students in their classrooms for participating in these studies. Adam Ingram-Goble, Michael Filsecker, Steven Zuiker, Eun Ju Kwon, and Anna Arici were instrumental in the assessment design, curricular revision, implementation support, and analysis in this study and the broader program of inquiry. Anna Arici, Jo Gilbertson, Troy Sadler, and Bronwyn Stuckey contributed to the initial curricular design and continuing refinements.

This research was supported by the US National Science Foundation Grant REC-0092831 to Indiana University and the MacArthur Foundation. The views expressed here do not necessarily represent the views of the National Science Foundation, the MacArthur Foundation, or Indiana University. For more information, contact the first author at dthickey@indiana.edu.

References

Arici, A. B. (2008). *Meeting kids at their own game: A comparison of learning and engagement in traditional and 3D MUVE educational gaming contexts.* Unpublished dissertation, Departments of Learning and Development Science and Cognitive Science, Indiana University, Bloomington, IN.

Barab, S. A., Gresalfi, M., & Ingram-Goble, A. (2010). Transformational play: Using games to position person, content, and context. *Educational Researcher, 39*(7), 525–536.

Barab, S. A., Sadler, T., Heiselt, C., Hickey, D., & Zuiker, S. (2007). Relating narrative, inquiry, and inscriptions: A framework for socio-scientific inquiry. *Journal of Science Education and Technology, 16*(1), 59–82.

Barab, S., Zuiker, S., Warren, S., Hickey, D., Ingram-Goble, A., Kwon, E. J., et al. (2007). Situationally embodied curriculum: Relating formalisms and contexts. *Science Education, 91*(5), 750–782.

Cameron, J., & Pierce, W. D. (1994). Reinforcement, reward, and intrinsic motivation: A meta-analysis. *Review of Educational Research, 64*(3), 363–423.

Case, R. (1996). Changing views of knowledge and their impact on educational research and practice. In D. Olson & P. Torrance (Eds.), *The handbook of education and human development* (pp. 75–99). Cambridge, MA: Blackwell.

Cobb, P., Confrey, J., diSessa, A., Lehrer, R., & Schauble, L. (2003). Design experiments in educational research. *Educational Researcher, 32*(1), 9–13.

Collins, A., Brown, J. S., & Newman, S. E. (1989). Cognitive apprenticeship: Teaching the crafts of reading, writing, and mathematics. In L. B. Resnick (Ed.), *Knowing, learning, and instruction: Essays in honor of Robert Glaser* (pp. 453–494). Hillsdale, NJ: Erlbaum.

Cross, D., Taasoobshirazi, G., Hendricks, S., & Hickey, D. T. (2008). Argumentation: A strategy for improving achievement and revealing scientific identities. *International Journal of Science Education, 30*(6), 837–861.

Danielson, C., & Abrutyn, L. (1997). *An introduction to using portfolios in the classroom.* Washington, DC: Association for Supervision & Curriculum Development.

Dondlinger, M. J. (2007). Educational video game design: A review of the literature. *Journal of Applied Educational Technology, 4*(1), 21–31.

Dourish, P. (2001). Seeking a foundation for context-aware computing. *Human Computer Interaction, 16*(2), 229–241.

Dudai, Y. (1997). How big is human memory, or on being just useful enough. *Learning & Memory, 3*(5), 341–365.

Egenfeldt-Nielsen, S. (2006). Overview of research on the educational use of video games. *Digital Kompetanse, 1*(3), 184–213.

Engle, R. A., & Conant, F. R. (2002). Guiding principles for fostering productive disciplinary engagement: Explaining an emergent argument in a community of learners classroom. *Cognition and Instruction, 20*(4), 399–483.

Gee, J. P. (2004). *Situated language and learning: A critique of traditional schooling.* London: Routledge.

Gee, J. P. (2005). Pleasure, learning, video games, and life: The projective stance. In M. Knobel & C. Lankshear (Eds.), *A new literacies sampler* (pp. 95–113). New York: Peter Lang.

Gee, J. P. (2007). Learning and games. In K. Salen (Ed.), *The ecology of games: Connecting youth, games, and learning* (pp. 21–40). Cambridge, MA: MIT Press.

Greeno, J. G. (1997). On claims that answer the wrong questions. *Educational Researcher, 26*(1), 5–17.

Greeno, J. G. (1998). The situativity of knowing, learning, and research. *The American Psychologist, 53*(1), 5–26.

Greeno, J. G., Collins, A. M., & Resnick, L. B. (1996). Cognition and learning. In D. C. Berliner & R. C. Calfee (Eds.), *Handbook of educational psychology* (pp. 15–46). New York: Macmillan.

Greeno, J. G., & Gresalfi, M. S. (2008). Opportunities to learn in practice and identity. In P. Moss, D. C. Pullin, J. P. Gee, E. H. Haertel, & L. J. Young (Eds.), *Assessment, equity, and opportunity to learn* (pp. 170–199). Cambridge, MA: Cambridge University Press.

Gresalfi, M., Barab, S., & Siyahhan, S. (2009). Virtual worlds, conceptual understanding, and me: Designing for consequential engagement. *On the Horizon, 17*, 21–34.

Habib, L., & Wittek, L. (2007). The portfolio as artifact and actor. *Mind, Culture, and Activity, 14*(4), 266–282.

Hickey, D. T. (2003). Engaged participation versus marginal nonparticipation: A stridently sociocultural approach to achievement motivation. *The Elementary School Journal, 103*(4), 401–429.

Hickey, D. T., & Anderson, K. T. (2007). Situative approaches to student assessment: Contextualizing evidence to transform practice. In P. Moss (Ed.), *Yearbook of the National Society for the Study of Education: Evidence and decision making* (Vol. 106, Pt. 1, pp. 264–287). Malden, MA: Blackwell.

Hickey, D. T., & Filsecker, M. K. (2010). *Participatory examination of incentives and competition on engagement and learning in educational video games.* Paper presented at the annual meeting of the American Educational Research Association, Denver, CO.

Hickey, D. T., Honeyford, M. A., Clinton, K. A., & McWilliams, J. (2010). Participatory assessment of 21st century proficiencies. In V. J. Schute & B. Becker (Eds.), *Innovative assessment in the 21st century: Supporting educational needs* (pp. 107–138). New York: Springer.

Hickey, D. T., Ingram-Goble, A. A., & Jameson, E. M. (2009). Designing assessments and assessing designs in virtual educational environments. *Journal of Science Education and Technology, 18*(2), 187–208.

Hickey, D. T., Kindfield, A. C. H., Horwitz, P., & Christie, M. A. T. (2003). Integrating curriculum, instruction, assessment, and evaluation in a technology-supported genetics learning environment. *American Educational Research Journal, 40*(2), 495–538.

Hickey, D. T., McWilliams, J. C., Bishop, S., & Soylu, F. (2011, April). *Participatory design for engagement, understanding, and achievement in university e-learning contexts.* Paper presented at the annual meeting of the American Educational Research Association, New Orleans, LA.

Hickey, D. T., & Pellegrino, J. W. (2005). Theory, level, and function: Three dimensions for understanding the connections between transfer and student assessment. In J. P. Mestre (Ed.), *Transfer of learning from a modern multidisciplinary perspective* (pp. 251–253). Greenwich, CT: Information Age Publishers.

Hickey, D. T., Taasoobshirazi, G., & Cross, D. (in review). Assessment as learning: Enhancing discourse, understanding, and achievement in innovative science curricula. *Journal of Research in Science Teaching* (version accepted for review December 2011).

Hickey, D. T., Zuiker, S. J., Taasoobshirazi, G., Schafer, N. J., & Michael, M. A. (2006). Balancing varied assessment functions to attain systemic validity: Three is the magic number. *Studies in Educational Evaluation, 32*(3), 180–201.

Hoadley, C. M. (2004). Methodological alignment in design-based research. *Educational Psychologist, 39*(4), 203–212.

Jenkins, H. (2009). *Confronting the challenges of participatory culture: Media education for the 21st century.* Cambridge, MA: MIT Press.

Kafai, Y. B. (2006). Playing and making games for learning. *Games and Culture, 1*(1), 36.

Kali, Y. (2006). Collaborative knowledge building using the Design Principles Database. *International Journal of Computer-Supported Collaborative Learning, 1*(2), 187–201.

Kebritchi, M., Hirumi, A., & Bai, H. (2010). The effects of modern mathematics computer games on mathematics achievement and class motivation. *Computers in Education, 55*(3), 427–443.

Kohn, A. (1996). By all available means: Cameron and Pierce's defense of extrinsic motivators. *Review of Educational Research, 66*(1), 1–4.

Lave, J. (1977). Cognitive consequences of traditional apprenticeship training in West Africa. *Anthropology & Education Quarterly, 8*(3), 177–180.

Lave, J., & Wenger, E. (1991). *Situated learning: Legitimate peripheral participation.* Cambridge, MA: Cambridge University Press.

Lemke, J. L. (2000). Across the scales of time: Artifacts, activities, and meanings in ecosocial systems. *Mind, Culture, and Activity, 7*(4), 273–290.

Lepper, M. R., & Hodell, M. (1989). Intrinsic motivation in the classroom. *Research on Motivation in Education, 3*, 73–105.

Lepper, M. R., & Malone, T. W. (1987). Intrinsic motivation and instructional effectiveness in computer-based education. *Aptitude, Learning, and Instruction, 3*, 255–286.

McWilliams, J., Hickey, D. T., Hines, M. B., Conner, J. M., & Bishop, S. C. (2011). Using collaborative writing tools for literary analysis: Twitter, fan fiction, and *The Crucible* in the secondary English classroom. *The Journal of Media and Literacy Education, 2*(3), 238–245.

Mehrens, W. A., & Kaminski, J. (1989). Methods for improving standardized test scores: Fruitful, fruitless, or fraudulent? *Educational Measurement: Issues and Practice, 8*(1), 14–22.

Mehrens, W. A., Popham, W. J., & Ryan, J. M. (1998). How to prepare students for performance assessments. *Educational Measurement: Issues and Practice, 17*(1), 18–22.

Messick, S. (1994). The interplay of evidence and consequences in the validation of performance assessments. *Educational Researcher, 23*(2), 13–23.

Nolen, S. B., Haladyna, T. M., & Haas, N. S. (1992). Uses and abuses of achievement test scores. *Educational Measurement: Issues and Practice, 11*(2), 9–15.

Olson, D. R., & Bruner, J. S. (1996). Folk psychology and folk pedagogy. In D. R. Olson & N. Torrance (Eds.), *Handbook of education and human development: New models of learning, teaching, and schooling* (pp. 9–27). Oxford: Blackwell.

Pea, R. D., & Sheingold, K. (1987). *Mirrors of minds: Patterns of experience in educational computing*. Norwalk, CT: Ablex.

Popham, W. J. (1997). What's wrong-and what's right-with rubrics. *Educational Leadership, 55*, 72–75.

Quintana, C., Reiser, B. J., Davis, E. A., Krajcik, J., Fretz, E., Duncan, R. G., et al. (2004). A scaffolding design framework for software to support science inquiry. *The Journal of the Learning Sciences, 13*(3), 337–386.

Rieber, L. P. (2005). Multimedia learning in games, simulations, and microworlds. In R. E. Mayer (Ed.), *The Cambridge handbook of multimedia learning* (pp. 549–567). Cambridge, MA: Cambridge University Press.

Ryan, R. M., Rigby, C. S., & Przybylski, A. (2006). The motivational pull of video games: A self-determination theory approach. *Motivation and Emotion, 30*(4), 344–360.

Sadler, T. D. (2004). Informal reasoning regarding socioscientific issues: A critical review of research. *Journal of Research in Science Teaching, 41*(5), 513–536.

Shaffer, D. W., Squire, K. R., Halverson, R., & Gee, J. P. (2005). Video games and the future of learning. *Phi Delta Kappan, 87*(2), 104–111.

Shute, V. J., Hansen, E. G., & Almond, R. G. (2008). You can't fatten a hog by weighing it—or can you? Evaluating an assessment system for learning called ACED. *International Journal of Artificial Intelligence in Education, 18*, 289–316.

Squire, K. (2003). Video games in education. *International Journal of Intelligent Simulations and Gaming, 2*(1), 49–62.

Squire, K. (2011). *Video games and learning: Teaching and participatory culture in the digital age*. New York: Teachers College Press.

Taasoobshirazi, G., Zuiker, S. J., Anderson, K. T., & Hickey, D. T. (2006). Enhancing inquiry, understanding, and achievement in an astronomy multimedia learning environment. *Journal of Science Education and Technology, 15*(5), 383–395.

Yeh, S. S. (2001). Tests worth teaching to: Constructing state-mandated tests that emphasize critical thinking. *Educational Researcher, 30*(9), 12–17.

Chapter 21
Computer Games as Preparation for Future Learning

Rick Chan Frey

21.1 Introduction

After 2 years of working on a design research project looking at the development of student thinking about negative numbers in the context of playing a computer game, I arrived at a critical problem. The game was designed where the principles of working with adding and subtracting positive and negative numbers were integrated into the game play in such a way that students could only achieve best scores across the game levels by utilizing these numeric principles to make decisions during play. In as little as two sessions of 30 min of play, almost all students were able to master the basic principles of working with negative numbers as demonstrated by their success across all four game levels. When it came to measuring learning gains on a traditional pencil and paper posttest, however, students showed significant but limited gains. It was hypothesized that the factor limiting gains in posttest scores was that students' learning had been encoded in such a way as to reflect the purposes, goals, and structure of the game (Gee, 2003, 2007) and that this encoding didn't readily transfer to a traditional worksheet filled with addition and subtraction problems. In order to investigate this hypothesis, a theoretical framework from Schwartz, Bransford, and Sears (2005) was used to see if students' game playing could be conceptualized as a form of "preparation for future learning" (PFL), preparing students to more effectively learn from an instructional activity that bridged between the two contexts. The results give strong support for this conceptualization of transfer in supporting game-based learning and suggest interesting possibilities for bridging game-based learning activities with the reality of more traditional school-based models of assessment.

R.C. Frey (✉)
Department of Education, Graduate School of Education, University of California,
1501 Tolman Hall #1670, Berkeley, CA 94720-1670, USA
e-mail: rickchanfrey@berkeley.edu

D. Ifenthaler et al. (eds.), *Assessment in Game-Based Learning: Foundations,*   431
Innovations, and Perspectives, DOI 10.1007/978-1-4614-3546-4_21,
© Springer Science+Business Media New York 2012

21.2 Background

The research on game-based learning and assessment is a mixed bag that many of the chapters in this volume attempt to clarify and expand. While Gee (2003, 2007) serves as somewhat of a focal point, there is little clarity and focus across the field on the issues, themes, and challenges facing researchers, educators, and game designers. A number of authors have taken on the challenge of creating frameworks for thinking about game design (Egenfeldt-Nielsen, 2007), learning in games (Squire, 2006), or broader themes that affect game-based learning (Mishra & Foster, 2007). Even though the issues of gender gap and violence in games have faded as the "hot topics" of game-based learning research, clarity and focus in terms of a coherent research agenda are still emerging.

21.2.1 Games and Assessment

In a talk at AERA 2010, Gee argued that in a well-designed computer game, the issue of assessment is a nonissue. He asked us to imagine having someone who had completed Halo or who had a level 80 Paladin in World of Warcraft, for example, sit down and take a test to measure their knowledge of game strategies or tactics. Games are designed, he argued, to function as constant assessments. Each encounter, level, and game action is a sort of a test measuring a player's ability to accomplish certain objectives using the game as a tool. Assessment and success are inextricably linked, and the idea of extragame assessment in addition to measures of in-game achievement makes little sense.

Even if we accept this as true for commercial games, the challenge for researchers, educators, and game designers interested in leveraging computer game-based learning in our current educational system is that most commercial games do not teach content that is useful or easily transferable to the needs and demands of traditional educational settings. While games like the Civilization series and Spore are held up as tantalizing approximations of the holy grail of the union of educational and commercial gaming, the reality has not come close to the dream. Exacerbating the divide between game-based learning and public education is the fact that success in public school settings is frequently measured by success on standardized tests. While it is easy to critique standardized testing as a goal or adequate measure of learning, state and federal mandates significantly determine public school practice and will continue to do so in the near future. Thus the issue of student success on more traditional forms of assessment is and will likely continue to be an ongoing concern.

For those interested in bridging the worlds of public schools and computer game-based learning, the question of transfer—the connecting of in-game learning with school-based instruction and assessment—is critical. Solutions to the transfer problem are often conceptualized in one of two ways: by making school more like games or making games more like school. In New York City, Quest to Learn is a charter school built around gaming and game design (Salen, Torres, Wolozin, Rufo-Tepper, & Shapiro, 2011). At the foundation of the school are ten core practices taken directly from Gee's (2003, 2007) and others' analyses of what works in computer game-based learning. Taking on identities, practicing in context, inventing solutions—each of these ideas is a critical element of commercial gaming and forms the basis for the educational design of the Quest to Learn school. While this model of reinventing public education has much to commend it and represents a powerful opportunity for researchers, educators, and game designers, the project is still in its infancy. Not only is there no data by which to judge the success of Quest to Learn, given the nontraditional nature of the project, the means by which students can be assessed are still being developed. And one has to wonder how students raised in such an educational environment will fare on standardized tests (including SAT's, GRE's, etc.) that students from even the most progressive alternative schools will likely take.

The other solution to the transfer problem—making games more like school—has a much longer and more studied history (Egenfeldt-Nielsen, 2007). Early educational games such as Math Blaster or Reader Rabbit, ask the same kinds of questions in the game that students see in the classroom and on traditional tests. In edutainment games, however, questions fly in the air or hide behind rocks and answers need to be shot out of the sky or trapped with a net. When students get correct answers, animated characters dance across the screen or fireworks decorate the display. The main idea of this style of educational game is to support traditional forms of instruction and practice by designing a context that provides extrinsic rewards as motivation. Much of the early research challenging the alleged benefits of computer game-based learning looked at results from students playing these kinds of games (Egenfeldt-Nielsen). While newer versions of educational games have to a certain degree addressed some of these concerns (e.g., introducing nonlinear forms of game play, allowing players to create and embellish avatars that represent them in the gaming environment, attempting to integrate instructional content with story elements), the same structured practice learning model represented in these games, often called "drill and kill," still guides even the newest versions.

21.2.2 Designing a Game for Instruction

The design research project grounding this chapter started from a desire to consider ways in which a computer game could support the development of student thinking in the problematic area of working with negative numbers. Brown (1992) represents the seminal description of the design research methodology, highlighting the challenges of investigating innovative instructional design embedded in the "blooming, buzzing confusion of inner-city classrooms." The design research collective (Design-Based Research Collective, 2003) describes the goal of design research as providing plausible causal accounts of learning and instruction in complex settings which can lead to opportunities for controlled clinical trials. Schwartz, Chang, and

Martin (2008) echo this description of design research by arguing that the true value of design research lies in its ability to create new instruments (both instructional interventions as well as assessments) that reveal aspects of learning or teaching that had previously gone undetected.

Having worked during my college years designing and programming computer games and having spent much of my teaching career using computer games in instructional contexts, I was curious to take and apply this background and experience to more traditional educational concerns. When a colleague presented a design challenge to come up with a game-based instructional activity to support fourth and fifth grade students learning about negative numbers, it seemed like a perfect opportunity. Most mathematics text books use a variety of scaffolds or analogies to conceptually ground instruction about negative numbers—images of elevators going below ground and thermometers showing temperatures below zero abound. While computer games excel at creating supportive representational environments that could have easily fit with this instructional model, my take on the research literature led me in a different direction.

Even with the abundance of literature on the pedagogy related to negative numbers (see Frey, 2009; or Schwarz, Kohn, & Resnick, 1994 for an overview), the topic remains a constant challenge for designing an instructional framework. Studies that address the topic of negative numbers often begin with a look at the history of negative number instruction, describing the age-old quest for a way to make sense of negative numbers intuitively or conceptually, and end the historical review by acknowledging that mathematicians failed in that quest and simply came to accept the role of negative numbers from an axiomatic or rule-based interpretation (Fischbein, 1987; Schwarz et al., 1994). While much of the recent research still outlines frameworks for grounding students' conceptualizations of negative numbers in supportive representational contexts, a few authors offer other alternatives.

Dixon, Deets, and Bangert (2001) and Dixon and Bangert (2005) represent an orthogonal take on the supported representation vs. rule-based argument that runs through the research literature on negative numbers. Starting from a theoretical analysis of how children integrate their early experiences into more general concepts, they propose the idea of principles to describe these general rules that capture the regularities within a range of experience or in a specific domain (Dixon et al., 2001). The principle of direction of effect, knowing that adding makes things bigger and subtracting makes things smaller, is a foundational early mathematical concept—one that is significantly tested by the introduction of negative numbers. Since students rarely if ever encounter negative numbers naturally in their daily lives, my challenge became creating a meaningful, accessible, and enjoyable gaming context to provide students experience with how negative numbers affect this fundamental principle.

In order to solve the challenge, I began imagining of ways of modifying the design and scoring for a simple computer darts game included in a flash programming book I had been working with (Makar & Winiarczyk, 2004). Burgos and Tattersall (2007) and Dempsey, Haynes, Lucassen, and Casey (2002) describe a theoretical rationale and strategies for using and adapting simple, preexisting games for traditional educational purposes. My goal was to embed the mathematical rules of what happens in the adding and subtracting of positive and negative numbers into the scoring system of the game. The students would focus on playing darts, attempting to beat each of the game's levels trying to get the best score possible. The game's design would take those natural inclinations to get a best score and use them to train students' experience and expectations about what happens when positive and negative numbers get added and subtracted from your score. Level 1 introduces game mechanics and the basic scoring system and level 2 introduces alternating turns where points from a dart throw are either added or subtracted from your score. Level 3 makes darts that miss the dartboard worth −15 points and level 4 has players race to get −100 points instead of positive 100 points. There are no math problems, no supportive representations, no pauses in the game while you answer a test question and then see a cute animal dance across the screen—just a chance to play a darts game that requires you to develop strategies for working with positive and negative numbers in order to get best scores (see Appendix 3 for screen shots of the game and further details). The darts game this study is based on is clearly not of the size and scope of a typical "commercial" game—it fits much more closely into the simple web-based game niche or something like a game app for a smart phone or tablet device. But by maintaining the design and feel of a pure game, hopefully the results from this research will shed light on the possible roles games can play in supporting learning.

Through multiple iterations of this design research project, significant game design and redesign, extensive play testing, rounds of data collection, cognitive labs, discussions with colleagues and advisors, and an earlier paper on a previous iteration of the project (Frey, 2009), this chapter focuses on the question of assessment (both in game and on a traditional posttest) and the specific issue of transfer. The critical research question in this chapter is how can students show a mastery of the principles of direction of effect for addition and subtraction of positive and negative numbers in the game context yet not use this to help them answer questions on a posttest? To frame that question more generally in the language of computer game-based learning and assessment, why is it that students can show complete mastery of a concept inside a gaming environment and then fail to access or leverage that knowledge outside the gaming context, in a more traditional educational assessment environment?

21.2.3 Games and Transfer

The question of gaming and transfer is a complicated but critical issue. Transfer is a goal that has challenged and plagued educators and researchers over the last 100 years, even while the basic idea of transfer—the generalizability of learning—is foundational to education. On the gaming front, parents and educators are consistently concerned about the negative effects of computer games while a small group of researchers, popular writers, businesses, professional schools, as well as the US

Army are convinced that games represent the cutting edge of learning technology. While the army has a multimillion-dollar budget to create game-based training environments that match as closely as possible the types of real-world situations soldiers will face, significantly reducing the problems of transfer, most students playing games are fighting monsters, shooting down helicopters, building cities or their sim houses, or playing simple web-based games like Bejeweled or tablet games like Plants vs. Zombies. In these situations, the issue of transfer is fundamental.

There are as many theories about transfer as there are theories about learning and instruction. While the classical transfer theory of mental discipline, the idea that learning a subject like Latin or geometry strengthens one's overall mental faculties, has been mostly abandoned,[1] in its place are a widely varied collection of transfer theories that can be roughly sorted by what they see as the primary agency of transfer. Bereiter (1995), Singley and Anderson (1989), and Sternberg (1982) see the agency of transfer inside individuals, whether as a disposition, mental habit, or trained skill. Socioculturalists such as Greeno, Smith, and Moore (1993), Lave (1988), Engle (2006), and others see the agency of transfer in the context or framing of the activity. To the degree that two contexts are similar or are framed similarly, transfer between the activities is likely to occur. Researchers from an analogical transfer perspective (Gentner, Lowenstein, & Thompson, 2003; Gick & Holyoak, 1980; Reeves & Weisberg, 1994) argue that the primary impetus for transfer comes from the similarity between the target problem and one's prior learning. A last camp of transfer theories (Griffin, Case, & Siegler, 1994; Halpern, 2003; Schwartz, Bransford, & Sears, 2005) argues that transfer is the planned by-product of certain types of carefully designed instructional activities, but the exact mechanism of transfer is undefined.

21.2.4 Transfer as Preparation for Future Learning

From a significant interest in Schwartz, Bransford, and Sears (2005) reconceptualization of transfer, from Schwartz's early involvement with the design research project described in this chapter, and from some months of thinking about the results from the first round of data collection, I began to conceptualize students' time spent playing the darts game as a form of PFL. Schwartz, Bransford, and Sears describe the shortcomings of the traditional pretest, instruction, posttest model of research and instruction by arguing that the effects of some types of instruction do not show up immediately on a typical posttest but can only be seen in students' ability to benefit from future instruction.

In order to demonstrate this effect, Schwartz, Bransford, and Sears (2005) had half of a group of ninth grade students try to invent a formula to solve a descriptive statistics problem while the other half of the group was shown the correct formula

---

[1] Although there's a strong resemblance between the theory that games teach "21st century skills" and the transfer theory that learning a difficult subject makes your generally more capable.

and allowed to practice. On the posttest, half of each group of students were shown a worked example for how to solve a related problem while the other half of each group didn't receive the worked example. On a final transfer test, scores for students who had both done the invention activity and received the worked example nearly doubled scores from all other students. The researchers explained their findings by arguing that the invention activity prepared students to learn from the worked example in a way that the traditional instructional model hadn't. Neither the invention activity alone nor the worked example alone provided any significant benefit over students who received neither—only the combination.

Incorporating Schwartz, Bransford, and Sears (2005) PFL conceptualization of transfer and assessment into my own project reframed each of the elements of the experiment and the game play itself. The pre- and posttests remained the same, but time spent playing the darts game was no longer seen as the primary instructional opportunity—it was now recast as Schwartz, Bransford, and Sears invention/discovery phase, ideally preparing students to learn more effectively from a yet-to-be-designed instructional activity which would hypothetically lead to significant gains on a final posttest. The pretest, game playing, posttest methodology I had used in the previous iteration of this project was amended to include an instructional activity after the second gaming session/assessment, followed by a final assessment. The PFL version of the learning story is that students' gaming sessions gave them an experience of how addition and subtraction with positive and negative numbers worked such that they were uniquely prepared to benefit from a simple learning activity designed to frame that experience in normative mathematical language which would result in significantly higher scores on the final posttest.

21.2.5 *Bridging Between the Game and Assessment*

Given the focus on transfer, the conceptualization and design of the bridging activity are a key piece of this project and a potentially rich research direction for educators, researchers, and game designers interested in computer game-based learning. Based on a variety of embedded assessments designed into the game and the measure of student achievement across the game levels, students had seemingly mastered the in-game content and had accumulated significant experience working with the principles of adding and subtracting negative numbers, which according to Dixon and Bangert (2005) and Schwartz, Bransford, and Sears (2005) could have prepared students for future learning. The question became how best to leverage that preparation. While Schwartz, Bransford, and Sears were able to use a simple worked example and show significant gains with a substantial effect size, our transfer challenge was complicated by differing contexts (game-based learning vs. pencil and paper assessment) as well as a game-based instructional model built around principles and the direction of effect in contrast to a posttest assessment measuring simple operational fluency. Overcoming both of these difficulties presented a significant challenge.

Before deciding on the content of the instructional activity, I had to decide the location—whether to attempt to build the new bridging activity into the game design or include it as an instructional resource outside of the game context. While requesting design changes to existing commercial software might seem a ridiculous idea, the prevalence of modding (end-users programming in minor modifications to a game's design or logic) is becoming more and more common and represents a fascinating avenue for future computer game-based learning research. In this context, as both the researcher and game designer, it was entirely possible to add additional content to the game to help bridge the game-school divide. Adding a fifth level that asked students to solve addition and subtraction problems might have helped with the issue of transfer, but it would have radically transformed the game and turned it into the type of game I was trying to avoid—one where the instructional content is irrelevant to the game context (Dickey, 2005). Those questions had no place in the game, so the location of the support would have to come from outside the game.

As to the question of the content of the instructional activity, if the game play wasn't directly teaching students operational skills with negative numbers but preparing them to learn about them, what type of instructional support would best leverage the experience they had gained from playing the computer game? Schwartz, Martin, and Pfaffman (2005) describes the results from an experiment where students instructed to use mathematical language to describe their actions in solving problems with weights and balance beams significantly outperformed students who weren't given similar instructions. I envisioned an instructional activity that would help students frame or organize their game playing experience with the normative mathematical rules and language regarding adding and subtracting positive and negative numbers. I designed a series of questions that students would use the game to answer that would help them recognize the normative mathematical rules underlying the points system built into the game, develop language with which to understand and interpret these rules (Yackel & Cobb, 1996), and express gradually more abstract statements of these rules (Schwartz, Martin, & Pfaffman, 2005). The first set of questions would ask what happens to your score when you add a negative number on a specific level and a specific type of turn. The second set of questions would ask what happens when you add a negative number in general. The third set of questions was based on Dixon et al. (2001) earlier instructional model and asked students to imagine themselves helping younger students and giving them hints on how to solve problems with negative numbers (see Appendix 1 for a copy of the instructional activity). I envisioned the following learning progression as I designed the instructional activity:

1. Let students use their experience from the game to develop a principled understanding of what happens when adding and subtracting positive and negative numbers.
2. Continuing to use the game's point scoring system as a reference and anchor, simplify the language describing what happens to their score into general mathematical rules.
3. Have participants use the simplified rules to help them solve basic problems adding and subtracting negative numbers.

21.3 Methods

21.3.1 Participants

Five classes of students ($n=114$) from an urban elementary school in California participated in this iteration of the project (two third grade classes, one fourth grade class, a fourth/fifth combo class, and a fifth grade class). Due to logistical difficulties unrelated to the study, only three of the classes ($n=68$) were able to complete all three rounds of play and assessment. Data from all five classes will be used to look at the effects of preliminary testing and game play while data from the three classes that completed the final phase of the study will be used to analyze the overall learning gains. Students ranged in age from 8 to 11 years. The school's ethnic makeup was 40% African American, 28% Caucasian, with small percentages of Asian, Latino, and mixed race students. Twenty-two percent of the students at the school participated in the free and reduced price lunch program. Class sizes ranged from 21 to 24 students.

21.3.2 Procedures

Participants attended a regularly scheduled computer lab session at their school with their entire class where I directed all of the assessment, game play, and instructional components of the study. Students were given 10 min to complete a pencil and paper pretest (see Appendix for copies of assessments) and were then introduced to the computer game. I instructed students on the basics of how to throw a dart; how to navigate the different levels; how to use the menu, restart, and undo buttons; and where to look for the record of their best scores. They played the game for roughly 30 min during their first session. The following week, students came back for a second session of game play (roughly 30 min) followed by an isomorphic posttest. The third, final session took place either the next week during their regularly scheduled computer time or at a specially scheduled additional lab time 4–5 days later. During the final session, students played the game for 5 min and then were given the instructional activity and asked to use the game to help them as needed (see Appendix 1 for copy of instructional activity). Students were given 15 min to complete the activity and then 10 min to complete the final posttest. None of the classes received any instruction related to negative numbers during the 3 weeks of this study.

21.3.3 Description of the Gaming Sessions

The computer lab for the study was comprised of 24 fairly new iMac computers. The game had been installed on each computer and every student was able to play at their own computer with their own mouse and mouse pad (essential elements for high-level dart control). Students were encouraged to talk to each other, to discuss what was happening in the game, and to share strategies, but they were not allowed to touch another student's computer (this was to avoid what happened during a trial run where one student went from computer to computer getting best scores on his friends' computers). The room was highly energetic and most students settled into a fairly natural routine of trial and error, discovery, score comparing, and advancing through game levels. A substantial number of students (10 out of 114 across all 5 classes), however, disengaged from the game. They voiced repeatedly that the game was either too hard or too boring; they mostly got stuck on level 2, clicking the mouse repeatedly, throwing darts alternately adding and subtracting points, not figuring out at all what was possible strategically. This number was significantly higher than in either of the previous rounds of data collection.

21.3.4 Results

In terms of game play, all students (except for the ten previously mentioned) were able to beat all four levels of the game as measured by getting a best score under eight throws. Data collection built into the game showed that students frequently used the restart button, undo button (important strategies for getting a best score), and went back to the menu screen to check their best scores.

Table 21.1 shows all of the available test scores for each of the participating classes. The pretest, midtest, and posttest scores show the average score (measured in number of questions correct out of 23), followed by the standard deviation. Only the fifth grade class made significant gains between the pre- and midtest, a result different from the first experiment (Frey, 2009) where all three classes of fourth and fifth grade students made small but significant gains. Each of the three classes taking the posttest made significant gains from the beginning to end of the project. Effect sizes were substantial, ranging from over half an effect size for the third grade and fourth/fifth grade classes to an effect size of 1.5 for the fifth grade students (see Appendix 2 for a copy of the assessments used in the study).

21.4 Discussion

The primary research question for this study was to see if a PFL methodology framing student game playing as an invention activity (Schwartz, Bransford, & Sears, 2005) and the introduction of an instructional bridging activity would support students transferring their game-based expertise at working with positive and negative numbers to a traditional pencil and paper posttest. While at the most basic level the results seem to strongly support this conclusion, let us consider for a moment some alternate explanations.

Given that only one of the five classes showed a significant gain from the pretest to the midtest, it seems hard to argue that the overall results could be

Table 21.1 Assessment data for all classes and measures

Class	n	df	Pretest (sd)	Midtest (sd)	Posttest (sd)	T-scores and p values			Effect size
						Pretest, midtest	Midtest, posttest	Pretest, posttest	
Third-A	24	23	6.8 (4.2)	7.3 (3.3)	8.6 (2.9)	0.8, 0.4	3.6, $p<0.01$	3.4, $p<0.01$	0.69
Third-B	23	22	8.1 (3.2)	8.0 (3.4)	[a]	0.1, 0.9			
Fourth	23	22	8.6 (3.8)	8.9 (3.6)	[a]	1.3, 0.2			
Fourth/Fifth	21	20	10.3 (4.4)	10.8 (4.3)	12.8 (4.1)	0.9, 0.4	3.0, $p<0.01$	2.8, $p=0.01$	0.62
Fifth	23	22	12.3 (4.3)	14.2 (5.0)	17.0 (4.2)	2.4, 0.02	5.0, $p<0.001$	7.4, $p<0.001$	1.5

[a]Students from both classes were unable to complete the final phase of data collection due to logistical problems unrelated to the study

explained by practice taking the test or time on task. If either of those were the case, it would make much more sense that the gains would progress linearly rather than so abruptly, as is the case with this data. As with any learning activity involving the computer, any gains could easily be attributed to the increased motivation and engagement that typically accompany computer-based learning activities (Squire, 2003) or simply be due to the Hawthorne effect, where the presence of investigators and experimental conditions leads to improved outcomes. If this were the case, once again there should have been some sign of this having had an effect on the midtest. There is little reason to think that the last phase of the study, playing the game for 5 min then using the game to fill out a paper and pencil work sheet, would be significantly more motivating and engaging than playing the game itself.

A final potential critique of this design is that the primary vehicle for student learning could have been the instructional activity itself and that playing the game was incidental. Schwartz, Bransford, and Sears (2005) built into their design a counter to this argument by having half of their participants not do the invention activity in the first phase of the study, having the other half of their participants prepare for the posttest by reading about the correct solution to a statistics problem and practicing worked out problems. On the posttest, their participants were further divided in that half of each group (inventors and noninventors) received additional instruction in the form of a worked example. That way, when it came to the final data analysis, they could show that the group of participants who had not done the invention activity but had received the additional instructional activity didn't perform anywhere nearly as well as the participants who had done the invention activity and received the additional instruction.

While design research studies frequently lack control conditions, there is still strong evidence to suggest that students' time playing the darts game served a critical role in facilitating the gains from the instructional activity. Give the well-documented difficulty students have in learning about negative numbers (Schwarz et al., 1994), it is hard to imagine that 10 min of engagement with a simple worksheet could have produced such significant results on its own. Additionally, the instructional activity was designed such that experience with the game was critical for answering the questions.

Most importantly, however, data from years of mathematics assessments demonstrate that a substantial percentage of students struggle to perform basic operations with negative numbers mainly because the rules governing adding and subtracting negative numbers don't match their intuitions (Schwarz et al., 1994). Adding should always make things bigger and subtracting should make things smaller. Just telling students what the rules are tends to have little instructional effect on their mathematical thinking. It seems much more plausible that an hour's worth of game play—experiencing again and again the effects of adding and subtracting positive and negative numbers in a context where they're naturally attuned to aspects of the game that affect their score—shaped their intuitions such that they were ready to recognize the formal statement of the rules and to see how those rules could help them solve actual problems.

21.4.1 Conclusions

Leaving aside the question of alternate explanations, the results raise two intriguing questions for the issue of computer game-based learning and transfer. First, in the game, students weren't slightly more accurate by the end of their play time on different levels and in different circumstances, they were perfect. They knew exactly how to manipulate adding and subtracting positive and negative numbers to achieve a desired goal. So while this might seem like a ridiculous question, why weren't students perfect on the posttest? The first two problems on each version of the test checked for students' basic mathematical competency. Students across all three grades scored close to perfect on these two questions, so it's not likely that the explanation is a lack of basic math skills. While the data do not suggest an easy answer to this question, there is one repeated finding that occurred in each previous iteration of this study that seems to merit consideration.

In Frey (2009), I discussed a pattern of student errors that I called the set of possible answers. Taking, for example, the posttest problem 2–5 (two take away five), students rarely gave answers like 6 or −4. Their answers almost always consisted of some possible mathematical combination of the two numbers. For 2–5, the set of possible answers is 7, 3, −3, −7. An item response analysis of student answers to varying question types again revealed the prevalence of this pattern and even with the significant gains from the game playing and instructional activity, it showed a mostly even distribution in the errors amongst the three possible wrong answers. What this seems to indicate is that while students did answer more questions correctly, when they made errors, their errors didn't show any pattern of consolidating in the direction of using the principle of direction of effect. In the problem 2–5 it's clear that 5 is bigger than 2, so the answer should be negative. Yet students were just as likely to pick 3 or 7 as they were −7. The continued presence of this error pattern even after game play and instruction highlights the complexity of the topic and the degree to which mastery is multifaceted.

21.4.2 Generalizability of the Results

The second question raised by this study, are these results generalizable, seems by far the most important and culturally relevant question, yet one that is difficult to answer authoritatively. The primary design elements affecting transfer in this study were the nature of the game, the nature of the target instructional content, and the design of the instructional activity supporting transfer. It is entirely reasonable to assume that given a similar game, similar content, and similar care used in designing an instructional activity supporting transfer, results such as these are possible across a wide variety of games and for a wide range of content.

Even though the computer darts game is an incredibly simple undertaking relative to a massively multiplayer game such as World of Warcraft or a major commercial title such as the Sims, the nature of the game play shares a fundamental quality with these other games. In the darts game, there is never any sense in which someone plays the game in order to learn or in order to solve educational problems. The instructional content is entirely subsumed into the nature of the game play such that the learning takes place in a purposeful and strategic manner. It is this quality of purposeful engagement that Schwartz, Bransford, and Sears (2005) designed into their invention activity, having students attempt to solve a problem in which they had been given data that defied easy interpretation. As students struggled to make sense of the data, that experience prepared them to learn from future instruction in a way that students who had only seen the correct answers and been given solved problems were unprepared. In any game that allows players to struggle solving problems, there is learning taking place that could potentially be accessed (Gee, 2003, 2007; Johnson, 2005).

While the darts game was designed with specific instructional content in mind, most games that people find interesting enough to play for any significant amount of time usually represent some type of strategic problem solving and are built on systems of math, physics, logic, biology, statistics, etc. As Johnson (2005) argues, increased gaming expertise almost always means increased learning of the underlying systems. What seems likely is that this model of supporting transfer could work in any gaming environment where players gained significant knowledge, experience, or intuition regarding an underlying area of educational interest. But not every aspect of learning inside computer games is a candidate for thinking about transfer, or at least not from a PFL framework.

One of the great concerns about modern computer games is that much of the content players spend so much time mastering is of little value in the traditional classroom setting. Knowing the full set of statistics for each weapon your World of Warcraft character might carry would not help much in a typical public school classroom, but the mathematics underlying damage/second calculations or armor modifications is extremely useful. While posing a traditional math problem in the garb of computer gaming as a motivational trick is of questionable value (if your paladin earns 20 silver pieces/h grinding and grinds for 5 h, how much money will they have earned?), uncovering, recognizing, and naming the basic principles of rate of change and how that relates to graphing might be a way in which a game player's experience has prepared them for a certain type of instructional activity that can bridge the two contexts (Hutchins, 2005; Yackel & Cobb, 1996).

Some last thoughts on computer games and transfer. While businesses, universities, and professional schools are looking for ways to train students to work together on teams, computer gamers are often experts on a wide range of teamwork-related skills. Gamers solve missions as teams with each player taking on different roles and utilizing different expertise. Game players form into guilds to share expertise and resources, develop new talent, and accomplish larger game-based undertakings than they could accomplish on their own. Gamers publish their insights, strategies, and requests for assistance on web forums and blogs, complete with annotated video and incredibly high level of mathematical and statistical analysis of the problems and solutions, giving and receiving critical feedback and refining ideas towards optimal solutions (Thomas & Brown, 2007). It seems reasonable to assume that the social components of gaming are preparing students for future social learning the same way the cognitive elements of a game are preparing students to learn more traditional content. It would be interesting to design a variant of this study that attempted to assess the PFL effects of social interaction and to design an instructional activity that could leverage that preparation.

21.4.3 Limits of Transfer

Not every type of learning that happens in a game, however, can be easily transferred. Many math professors lament the current tendencies of students to give up on difficult problems after only a minute or two of effort while the same students might spend hours trying to complete a mission or beat a level in their favorite computer game. Students facing these game challenges participate with a set of habits, strategies, and a level of engagement that leads them to observe, experiment, take notes, discover patterns, and evaluate hypotheses. Yet in the classroom, they sit bored during science and math instruction, unwilling to expend the least amount of energy or focus. Strategy games teach players about preparation, taking initiative, and careful monitoring—attitudes that would be exceedingly useful in the classroom—yet these attitudes very rarely transfer to the classroom.

While it is a fascinating to imagine how students could be supported in transferring the set of habits and dispositions they use in solving computer problems to solving classroom tasks, or how we might redesign classroom tasks such that they shared essential components with the game tasks students find so engaging, diSessa and Wagner (2005) argue that the ease of transfer is entirely dependent on the type of knowledge being considered. Learning to use a game-based strategy for solving problems on a related school-based problem is one thing; changing the fundamental way one approaches school is an entirely different matter. It is harder to imagine how attitudes or dispositions to use Bereiter's (1995) term could be accessed, whether through a PFL framework or any other transfer-based framework. In this situation, in order to access this type of learning, it might be a case where traditional school-based activities could benefit from becoming more like computer games.

21.4.4 Summary

This project began as instructional challenge to help fourth and fifth grade students learn about negative numbers. It slowly evolved into a design research project on the nature of instructional support and the role a computer game might play in helping students shape their intuitions and gain experience that could prepare them to learn content that had previously been too difficult. In this phase of the work, the question was simple: are there ways to support the transfer of computer game-based learning to more traditional classroom-based activities and assessments. By adapting the PFL framework, students who had mastered the principles of adding and subtracting positive and negative numbers in the context of a computer game showed significant and substantial gains on a traditional posttest. Given the simplicity of the design, these results suggest that this model could be adapted across a range of gaming environments and educational content and potentially provide a similar benefit.

Appendix 1:   Instructional Activity

Use the game as needed to help you   Name _____
answer the following questions: Class _____

1. Start a new game on level three. Throw a dart and hit the dartboard. Did your score get bigger or smaller when you added a positive number?

2. Your second turn is a take away turn. Throw a dart and hit the dartboard. Did your score get bigger or smaller when you take away a positive number?

3. Your 3rd turn is an add turn again. This time miss the board when you throw the dart. Did your score get bigger or smaller when you add a negative number?

4. This turn will be a take away turn. Throw your dart and miss the board. Did your score get bigger or smaller when you take away a negative number?

Think about these rules for working with numbers:

If you add a positive number, your score goes _____

If you add a negative number, your score goes _____

If you take away a positive number, your score goes _____

If you take away a negative number, your score goes _____

Pretend you see a second grader working on a math test. You don't want to tell them the right answers, but you want to give them a hint. Thinking about how it would work in the darts game, tell them for each problem if the answer is going to be bigger or smaller than the first number:

2 + 1   (bigger or smaller?)   -2 + 1   (bigger or smaller?)

2 - 1   (bigger or smaller?)   -2 - 1   (bigger or smaller?)

2 + -1   (bigger or smaller?)   -2 + -1   (bigger or smaller?)

2 - -1   (bigger or smaller?)   -2 - -1   (bigger or smaller?)

Appendix 2:   Pre-, Mid-, and Posttest
(All Tests Were Isomorphic Versions of This Exam)

Some questions about negative numbers   Name: _____

Class: _____

Try to solve as many of the following problems as you can:

2 + 4 =   7 - 5 =   3 - 8 =   2 + -1 =

4 + -6 =   -2 + 5 =   -1 + -7 =   3 + -4 =

-2 - 4 =   5 - -2 =   -9 - -4 =   5 - -3 =

-3 - -7 =   -2 + -3 =   -7 - 3 =   6 - -2 =

5 + -8 =   -2 - 1 =   -2 - -3 =   -4 + 2 =

1. If you add a negative number to 10, will your answer be bigger or smaller?

2. If you take away a negative number from 10, will your answer be bigger or smaller?

3. Pretend you're playing a game and you have 15 points. There's a question worth 20 points, but you get it wrong and lose the 20 points. How many points do you have now?

Appendix 3:   Screen Shots of the Computer Darts Game

Here are two screen shots of the current version of the game. The shot on the right shows a scene from level 3 where the player has just missed the dart board on their last throw (which at level 3 results in a score of negative 15). The numbers at the bottom update with each throw, and on levels 2–4, the words take away and add alternate on even and odd turns, respectively. The players can see their current best score for this level as well as their current total and their current number of throws. All of these are key pieces of supporting the goal of developing strategies related to the adding and subtracting positive and negative numbers.

Here is the latest version of the Menu screen and the best scores screen. As students play, their best scores are recorded here. I enter the classroom best scores at the end of the day, and the best possible scores are there for the ultimate reference.

References

Bereiter, C. (1995). A dispositional view of transfer. In A. McKeough, J. Lupart, & A. Marini (Eds.), *Teaching for transfer: Fostering generalization in learning* (pp. 21–34). Mahwah, NJ: Lawrence Erlbaum Associates.

Brown, A. (1992). Design experiments: Theoretical and methodological challenges in creating complex interventions in classroom settings. *The Journal of the Learning Sciences, 2*(2), 141–178.

Burgos, D., & Tattersall, R. (2007). Re-purposing existing generic games and simulations for e-learning. *Computers in Human Behavior, 23*, 2656–2667.

Dempsey, J., Haynes, L., Lucassen, B., & Casey, M. (2002). Forty simple computer games and what they could mean to educators. *Simulation & Gaming, 33*(2), 157–168.

Design-Based Research (2003). An Emerging Paradigm for Educational Inquiry by The Design-Based Research Collective. *Educational Researcher, 32*(1), 5–8.

Dickey, M. (2005). Engaging by design: How engagement strategies in popular computer and video games can inform instructional design. *Educational Technology Research and Development, 53*(2), 67–83.

diSessa, A. A., & Wagner, J. F. (2005). What coordination has to say about transfer. In J. Mestre (Ed.), *Transfer of learning from a multidisciplinary perspective* (pp. 121–154). Greenwich, CT: Information Age Publishing.

Dixon, J. A., & Bangert, A. S. (2005). From regularities to concepts: The development of children's understanding of a mathematical relation. *Cognitive Development, 20*, 65–86.

Dixon, J. A., Deets, J. K., & Bangert, A. (2001). The representations of the arithmetic operations include functional relationships. *Memory & Cognition, 29*, 462–477.

Egenfeldt-Nielsen, S. (2007). Third generation educational use of computer games. *Journal of Educational Multimedia and Hypermedia, 16*(3), 263–281.

Engle, R. A. (2006). Framing interactions to foster generative learning: A situative explanation of transfer in a community of learners classroom. *The Journal of the Learning Sciences, 15*(4), 451–498.

Fischbein, E. (1987). *Intuition in science and mathematics: An educational approach.* Hingham, MA: Kluwer Academic.

Frey, R. (2009). *Learning about negative numbers in a computer game.* Paper presented at American Educational Research Association, San Diego, CA.

Gee, J. P. (2003). *What video games have to teach us about learning and literacy.* New York, NY: Palgrave Macmillan.

Gee, J. P. (2007). *What video games have to teach us about learning and literacy* (2nd ed.). New York, NY: Palgrave Macmillan.

Gentner, D., Lowenstein, J., & Thompson, L. (2003). Learning and transfer: A general role for analogical encoding. *Journal of Educational Psychology, 95*(2), 393–408.

Gick, M. L., & Holyoak, K. J. (1980). Analogical problem solving. *Cognitive Psychology, 12*, 306–355.

Greeno, J. G., Smith, D. R., & Moore, J. L. (1993). Transfer of situated learning. In D. K. Detterman & R. J. Sternberg (Eds.), *Transfer on trial: Intelligence, cognition, and instruction* (pp. 1–24). Norwood, NJ: Ablex.

Griffin, S., Case, R., & Siegler, R. (1994). Rightstart: Providing the central conceptual structures for children at risk of school failure. In K. McGilly (Ed.), *Classroom lessons: Integrating cognitive theory and classroom practice* (pp. 25–49). Cambridge, MA: MIT Press.

Halpern, D. F. (2003). Teaching for long term retention and transfer. *Change, 35*, 37–41.

Hutchins, E. (2005). Material anchors for conceptual blends. *Journal of Pragmatics, 37*, 1555–1577.

Johnson, S. (2005). *Everything bad is good for you.* New York, NY: Riverhead Books.

Lave, J. (1988). *Cognition in practice: Mind, mathematics and culture in everyday life.* New York, NY: Cambridge University Press.

Makar, J., & Winiarczyk, B. (2004). *Macromedia Flash MX 2004 game design demystified.* Berkeley, CA: Peachpit Press.

Mishra, P., & Foster, A. N. (2007). The claims of games: A comprehensive review and directions for future research. In R. Carlsen, K. McFerrin, J. Price, R. Weber, & D. A. Willis (Eds.), *Society for Information Technology & Teacher Education: 2007 18th international conference.* San Antonio, TX: Association for the Advancement of Computing in Education (AACE).

Reeves, L. M., & Weisberg, R. W. (1994). The role of content and abstract information in analogical transfer. *Psychological Bulletin, 115*(3), 381–400.

Salen, K., Torres, R., Wolozin, L., Rufo-Tepper, R., & Shapiro, A. (2011). *Quest to learn: Developing the school for digital kids.* Cambridge, MA: MIT Press.

Schwartz, D., Bransford, J., & Sears, D. (2005). Efficiency and innovation in transfer. In J. Mestre (Ed.), *Transfer of learning from a multidisciplinary perspective* (pp. 1–51). Greenwich, CT: Information Age Publishing.

Schwartz, D., Chang, J., & Martin, L. (2008). Instrumentation and innovation in design experiments: Taking the turn to efficiency. In A. E. Kelly, R. Lesh, & J. Y. Baek (Eds.), *Handbook of design research methods in education.* Mahwah, NJ: Erlbaum.

Schwartz, D., Martin, T., & Pfaffman, J. (2005). How mathematics propels development of physical knowledge. *Journal of Cognition and Development, 6*(1), 65–88.

Schwarz, B. B., Kohn, A. S., & Resnick, L. B. (1994). Positives about negatives: A case study of an intermediate model for signed numbers. *The Journal of the Learning Sciences, 3*(1), 37–92.

Singley, K., & Anderson, J. R. (1989). *The transfer of cognitive skill.* Cambridge, MA: Harvard University Press.

Squire, K. (2003). Video games in education. *International Journal of Intelligent Simulations and Gaming, 2*(1), 49–62.

Squire, K. (2006). From content to context: Videogames as designed experience. *Educational Researcher, 35*(8), 19–29.

Sternberg, R. J. (1982). Reasoning, problem-solving, and intelligence. In R. J. Sternberg (Ed.), *Handbook of human intelligence* (pp. 225–307). New York, NY: Cambridge University Press.

Thomas, D., & Brown, J. S. (2007). Play and imagination: Extending the literary mind. *Games and Culture, 2*(2), 149–172.

Yackel, E., & Cobb, P. (1996). Sociomath norms, argumentation, and autonomy in mathematics. *Journal for Research in Mathematics Education, 27*(4), 458–477.

Index

D. Ifenthaler et al. (eds.), *Assessment in Game-Based Learning: Foundations,*
Innovations, and Perspectives, DOI 10.1007/978-1-4614-3546-4,
© Springer Science+Business Media New York 2012

29463180R00274

Made in the USA
Middletown, DE
20 February 2016